To Nora,

Thank you for selecting a career in conservation! I hope you will correct our mistakes!!

Dale
Sept 2023

COMPELLED

From the Yazoo Pumps to Polar Bears and Back

The Evolution of Natural Resource

Conservation and Law

H. Dale Hall

Copyright © 2022 H. Dale Hall

All rights reserved. No part of this publication may be reproduced, distributed, or transmitted in any form or by any means, including photocopying, recording, or other electronic or mechanical methods, without the prior written permission of the publisher, except in the case of brief quotations embodied in critical reviews and certain other noncommercial uses permitted by copyright law. For permission requests, write to the publisher, addressed "Attention: Permissions Coordinator," at the address below.

First printing, July 2022

ISBN: 979-8-9862477-0-0
Library of Congress Control Number: 2022909236

Manuscript Edited by Kate Petrella
Jacket and Book Designed by Barbara Aronica-Buck
Indexed by Sue Klefstad
Cover images: Everglades, istockphoto/THEPALMER; Polar Bear, USFWS/ Lisa Hupp; Northern Spotted Owl, USFWS/John & Karen Hollingsworth; Pallid Sturgeon, USFWS/Katie Steiger-Meister

Published by:
H. Dale Hall, LLC
727 Evans View Lane
Collierville, TN 38017

Distributed by:
Ducks Unlimited, Inc.
1 Waterfowl Way
Memphis, TN 38120
www.ducks.org

Printed in the United States of America
Printed by Seaber Turner Associates

This book is dedicated to Sarah, Erin, Adam and Emily.

Thank you for your love, sacrifices and support throughout the journey.

And to all in conservation who give so much.

CONTENTS

Preface	vii
Introduction	xi
PART 1: WETLANDS AND FISHERIES	1
Chapter 1: Learning about Law and Biology	3
Chapter 2: The Yazoo Basin Project	39
Chapter 3: POWDR Bill and Alaska	66
Chapter 4: The Greatest Story Never Told	87
PART 2: ENDANGERED SPECIES AND WESTERN WATER	103
Chapter 5: Spotted Owl and Western Water	105
Chapter 6: Critical Habitat	129
Chapter 7: Bureau of Land Management Calls For the God Squad	166
Chapter 8: Lujan's Owl Plan	190
Chapter 9: The President's Forest Summit	210
Chapter 10: Central Valley Water	241
PART 3: THE SOUTHEAST AND SOUTHWEST	269
Chapter 11: The Surprise	271
Chapter 12: The Shell Game and the Everglades	286
Chapter 13: The Senior Executive Service and a New President	306
Chapter 14: The Rio Grande and Missouri Rivers	317

Chapter 15: The Lower Colorado River Multi-species
   Conservation Plan   353

PART 4: THE DIRECTOR   373
Chapter 16: The MacDonald Investigation   375
Chapter 17: Arctic Refuge and the Polar Bear   390
Chapter 18: Drafting Endangered Species Act Regulations
   and Opposing the Navy Outlying Landing Field   411
Chapter 19: Finishing the Polar Bear and Killing the Feral Hog   433
Chapter 20: Lunch with the President   469

PART 5: THE CITIZEN CONSERVATIONIST   475
Chapter 21: Ducks Unlimited and Macondo   477
Chapter 22: Johnny Morris and Ducks Unlimited Partnerships   490
Chapter 23: Wetlands America Trust and Justice Scalia   507
Chapter 24: California Floodplains and Finishing Up   521

References   539
Index   547

PREFACE

My journey is not so different from many others. I started from humble beginnings, but in a home filled with love and a place where I was free to explore nature. When I was young and asked my grandparents "What was life like when you were growing up? You were born before the invention of cars or television, and telephones were uncommon," the answer I received was "Oh Honey, we just got by." The culture of Appalachia was to say as little about one's life as possible to anyone outside the family, or family that didn't "need to know." My father and mother were part of the Greatest Generation, and I would never try to dissuade anyone from concurring. But as I was growing up in the hills of Kentucky, the world was beginning to open new horizons in space and technology.

Early in my career, I realized that I wanted to be able to explain more to my children about what growing up in the Baby Boomer generation was like than my grandparents had relayed to me about their early lives. I began keeping copies of nearly all documents associated with both society and my career. By the time I retired, I had accumulated over forty boxes of memoranda, letters, news releases, newspaper articles, court opinions and internal files regarding issues the U.S. Fish and Wildlife Service had faced. In this book, I focus only on those in which I was personally involved in an effort to maintain as much accuracy as possible.

Compelled condenses that information into an evolving story of a young biologist who was blessed to be exposed to some of the greatest environmental law minds of the time, as well as the scientists who were blazing the trail for new chapters in conservation. With each challenging conservation issue, I learned powerful lessons about teamwork and the legal mandates of the executive branch of government that I was able to carry to my next assignment. With each new issue and geographic challenge, the curtain was pulled back ever so slightly to both administer new lessons through failure and reveal new pathways to success. In no case was I the one who obtained success. In all cases, success was achieved by the TEAM. As I wrote this book, I depended on many of those wonderful teammates to keep me true to the facts in relaying the stories.

As the hand of my Creator continued to cut away at my ego and desire to be a "hero for conservation," He charted the course for me to be a member of a team rather than a "combat biologist." I slowly began to understand that a "win" for conservation is short-lived unless it is manifested by a *solution* created through respect for differing opinions, with a compromise that is inside the envelope of the law. I learned that people from all walks of life are conservationists if approached with respect, and that controversy is born when discussions begin with accusations. Those of us in the executive branch of government, whether at the federal or state level, have the responsibility to assist *all* citizens in their quest for life, liberty and the pursuit of happiness, as long as the mandate of the law is satisfied.

During my tenure as director of the agency I love so dearly, our team was able to bring calm analyses and open minds to the challenges we faced. It has been said that there is no failure if knowledge is gained in the effort. If that is true, I certainly had opportunities to gain knowledge. But our real charge in conservation is to find *wisdom*. My sincere hope is that the reader will glean gems of knowledge from these accounts of conservation issues across the spectrum of challenges. Just as data lead to information, and information leads to knowledge, knowledge can lead to *wisdom* if we open ourselves to the humble prospect. The people of the United States deserve a government that strives to administer *wisdom* rather than power. While I make no claim to have achieved it, I was both honored and privileged to be on teams that possessed and shared their wisdom. It is those team members and all who work for conservation and scientific excellence and strive for fairness that this book is intended to honor.

I would like to express my deep gratitude to Mark Madison, Jeff Trandahl, George Dunklin Jr. and Jay McAninch for their guidance and insights while reviewing the drafts of my manuscript. They are both wonderful conservationists and treasured friends. I also wish to thank Ken Will, Sue Klefstad and Kate Petrella for their input and advice, which helped me produce a manuscript that is above my writing capability. The responsibility for any errors, however, rests solely with me.

INTRODUCTION

My early life was spent in the bosom of the Cumberland Plateau of the Appalachian Mountains. Eastern Kentucky is known for its rich coal fields, mountain hollows and moonshine whiskey. Herbert Hall was critically wounded in Papua New Guinea in early 1943, which qualified him as a totally disabled veteran. Unable to do open heart surgery at the time, the military doctors predicted that he had only twenty years left to live. He had grown up in "Bloody Harlan" during the 1930s coal wars of Harlan County, Kentucky, and was determined to make the years he had left as productive as possible.

Ina Frances Colwell grew up in Leslie County, Kentucky, about an hour's drive from Harlan. She lived along the Middle Fork of the Kentucky River just outside the town of Hyden. As a young girl, she contracted polio and was fortunate to be sent to a Lexington hospital, where an operation arrested the harm. While her right calf would be smaller than her left, it was cured and strong. I am convinced I got my love of the outdoors from her father. Rubin Colwell would awake each morning, walk out onto the porch of his mountainside home and give thanks for all of life. I often went out on the porch with him as he stretched his arms high, took a deep breath, then bent over and touched his toes. When he stood back up and exhaled, he would say "Ain't nadur wunnerful!" I never knew anyone who loved to see things grow more than he did.

Herbert and Frances met in Cincinnati, and it was love at first sight. Only ten days after meeting, they were married. Perhaps it was the ominous prediction of twenty years weighing on Herb's mind, or the love Frances had for helping others after her medical ordeal, but the love they shared proved powerful over the years. Their first child, Larry, was born in May 1946. On November 3, 1949, I was born in a three-room house on the outskirts of Harlan. I started first grade after we moved to a house just across the river from the Hight School in Fairview. After my first-grade year, my father was able to buy a home in Loyall, about three miles downstream from Harlan, where I lived until I was a young man.

Loyall was a wonderful place in which to grow up. The headwaters of the Cumberland River flowed by my home on one side, and the railroad tracks that carried coal to the rest of the country sat at the base of the mountain on the other. On our street were families that worked hard and cared for each other. We came to see the river as much a playground as the one at school. We turned over rocks in the riffles and caught "crawdads" and "grampuses" (Dobson fly larvae) for bait as we fished for smallmouth, largemouth and redeye bass, catfish, sunfish, and redhorse suckers. Our boat was a "car top boat"—meaning the top of an old coupe car that had been cut off at the junkyard and flipped over to use as a boat. We all chipped in our lawn mowing or pop bottle return money and got one for about five dollars. The struts that connected the top to the car body were perfect to lean your fishing rod or cane pole against and wait for a bite. A scrap board worked just fine as a paddle.

We walked to Loyall High School, which housed all twelve grades, and received the best education one could have. I accept my bias, but I believe there was a magic in the halls of Kentucky country schools that attracted the best teachers. Wonderful teachers like Mrs. Hill, who taught me not to be afraid to speak in public; Mrs. McFarland, who taught us that hard work accompanied anything worth having; Mr. Smith, who made me learn the poem "Richard Cory" by Edwin Arlington Robinson, so I would understand that appearances of happiness can be nothing more than a mask; and Mrs. Grant, who showered her constant love and affection on us all. From these wonderful mentors I learned that education is tied neither to buildings nor to supplies, but to people who are dedicated and love teaching.

After graduating from high school and attempting to be the first person in my family to achieve a college degree, I received the rude awakening that no longer would there be someone pushing me to fulfill my responsibilities. I had no one to guide me and say "just do your part and go to class, study and learn!" Instead, I enjoyed the freedom of choice, and I chose poorly. After two semesters, the University of Kentucky sent me a very nice letter telling me there was no need for me to return to campus the following fall. Apparently, they didn't think a 1.2 GPA was adequate to remain a student there. But when one door closes, another opens. Our local draft board had no such reservations about my GPA, IQ or any other group of letters and numbers except 1A, no student deferment, report for induction into the Army.

I decided to show the draft board who was in charge and joined the Air Force for four years instead of being inducted into the Army for two! The truth is I didn't know if I had the intellectual foundation to get a college degree. No one in my family had ever achieved one and, after the UK experience, I didn't have the self-confidence. But I knew that the Air Force would spend more time training me, hopefully in a trade I could use when I got out, and I could also get the GI Bill for college or any kind of training I decided to pursue. I bid my mother and father farewell at the Louisville military induction center, boarded the bus for basic training and headed to Lackland Air Force Base, Texas.

I was trained as a Morse code intercept operator and given a top secret codeword clearance for the information I would copy from the enemy and share with both on-the-ground troops in Vietnam and with the president in his daily security briefing. Clark Air Force Base in the Philippines was my first duty station after training, and the issues were real. We knew that our troops on the ground might live or die by the quality of our work, and we took the job seriously. Off duty was another matter, but when we were finding out what Charlie was doing, it was all business. My father had died when I was in Air Force Tech School, and my mother remarried while I was in the Philippines. I was happy for her.

My second tour of duty was in Italy at San Vito dei Normanni Air Station, just outside Brindisi. The huge, circular antenna we used to capture the signals was an FLR-9 omni-directional antenna that was dubbed "the elephant cage." Since everything inside the compound was classified, the traditional answer around the world to questions about its purpose was "that's where we keep the elephants."

Tom Lear, Ken Will and Mike Mesi had been in the Philippines with me and we, along with a hilarious guy who was serving his first overseas assignment, Brad Cooper, decided to rent a villa off base. We needed a name, so we allowed Brad to name it "Huntley Manor" after a high school friend. It soon became the place for everyone to gather. Rich and Linny Wells, Ed and Linda Kostro (we called him Fidel for obvious reasons), Bill DiRosario and his future wife, Kerrie, and others, including Dave Incorvati, Tom Whatley, Bob Locke, Jimmy Hodges, Pete Weeks, Monty Garner and Lynn Keltch, were regulars. This was my new family, and remains so. It is difficult to explain the strength of that bond of love and respect to someone who has never written a blank check to their country, up to and including their lives. Even today, I would give my life for any of my brothers in arms.

As my time in the Air Force ended, I was re-energized with both the confidence and determination necessary to return to college, this time in preparation to be a dentist. Within one month of being honorably discharged from the Air Force, I was enrolled in summer school at Cumberland College, Williamsburg, Kentucky. I was ready and raring to go! Time had been lost, and I wanted to make it up as fast as I could. I took all the class hours the college would allow and completed my bachelor of science degree in biology/chemistry in twenty-seven months. I re-took several of the classes at Cumberland that I had so miserably attempted at the University of Kentucky, but those old UK grades remained on my transcript, and my poor behavior at UK was coming back to haunt me. I was accepted only as an alternate for the UK School of Dentistry because my overall GPA was pulled down by those poor grades. The

UK dental school had just been rated the number two dental school in the nation, and as a result, none of the accepted candidates declined the offer of enrollment. Thus, no one from the alternate list made the class. I realized that I needed to look at different career paths and, with the encouragement from a dentist in Williamsburg and a professor at Eastern Kentucky University, accepted responsibility for my disappointment and enrolled at Eastern Kentucky University graduate school of biology. My study would entail limnology research—limnology being the study of the biological, chemical and physical features of lakes and other bodies of freshwater—on a newly constructed Corps of Engineers lake near Morehead, Kentucky. I was also beginning to feel a strong presence in my life that seemed to be driving me in a different direction from the one I had chosen. I was beginning to understand that I was not in charge.

Dr. John Williams, my major professor at Eastern Kentucky, was a former state police trooper and profoundly dedicated to helping young students grow into professionals. Unfortunately, the head of the department, Dr. Edwin Hess, was not cut from the same cloth. I had completed all my coursework for a master's degree in limnology and only needed to complete data collection on Cave Run Reservoir. I had about four months of field work remaining when I went to get the equipment I needed from the storage room. The photometer, which measures light

Elephant Cage (Courtesy of USAF)

penetration in water, was on the shelf, but had obviously been broken. I could not complete my research without being able to document the entire annual cycle of light penetration in the lake, thus delineating the potential strata of life that would likely form. I was devastated.

I went to Dr. Williams and told him what I had found. No one else was using that equipment in their research, so it was assumed it had accidentally been knocked off the shelf. He went to Dr. Hess, relayed the circumstance, and requested permission to purchase a replacement so I could finish my research. Dr. Hess flatly refused. "What?" exclaimed Dr. Williams. "Are you just going to leave this young man hanging when he did nothing wrong? He has already finished the coursework and needs this piece of equipment, or he has to start over!" "I don't care," Dr. Hess replied. "I'm not spending hundreds of dollars on a piece of equipment that doesn't get used that much. He can just start over." John Williams stormed out of Hess's office and had to go calm down to keep from breaking his "shitty pencil neck!" (Williams 1975)

Dr. Williams got busy trying to find a way to help me out of an impossible situation. His answer came from one of his old classmates, Dr. Fred Bryan, who was now a professor at Louisiana State University. "Send him down right away. I'll give him a position as a graduate assistant if he is willing to work on the early life history of fish." In contrast to Edwin Hess and Eastern Kentucky University, Fred Bryan and LSU accepted a graduate student, sight unseen, based solely on the story that Bryan heard and the recommendation of his friend. I learned the difference between a "school" and an "institution of higher learning that builds lives and careers." Eastern Kentucky had proved to me that it was the former, while LSU stood proud that it was a leader in the latter. The faith and love shown by Dr. Bryan and LSU dramatically changed my life, and I will never forget that.

I met Sarah, my lifetime companion, while at LSU, and then met her wonderful mother, Nell, and father, Herman Reed, as well as her sisters and brother, whom I would come to consider my own. Herman was a farmer in the small town of Bunkie, Louisiana, and he treated everyone he met with kindness and a warm welcome. When I first visited their home with Sarah, Herman met me at the door with his hand out to shake mine and said "Welcome. I'm Herman Reed. Would you like a beer or highball?" Sarah and I were married on May 22, 1976, in Bunkie, and moved into our LSU student housing while I finished up my master's degree.

At that time, if you wanted to work for the federal government, you sent your credentials to the Office of Personnel Management, where you would be rated at a pay grade based on those credentials. I was rated as a GS-5 with 105 points and a GS-7 with 104. One hundred was the maximum, but then I was awarded 5 more points for being a veteran (an applicant who was a disabled veteran would be awarded 5 more points on top of that).

No one was hiring. I sent out over fifty job applications to private, state and federal entities and only received the courtesy of a response from two, both saying they weren't hiring at the time. I saw a job opening on the bulletin board seeking a catfish farm manager in Yazoo City, Mississippi. I needed a job and, even though I had no experience in catfish farming, applied for the position. After an interview, I was hired. Sarah and I moved to Yazoo City, where I worked first for Eden Fisheries and then for Farm Fish, Inc. It was during my time at Farm Fish that I received a call from the U.S. Fish and Wildlife Service asking me if I was interested in a job at the agency's Vicksburg Ecological Services Office. I was about to become a career public servant.

PART 1

Wetlands and Fisheries

CHAPTER 1

Learning about Law and Biology

I received the call from Joe Hardy, field supervisor in the Vicksburg, Mississippi, U.S. Fish and Wildlife Service Ecological Services (FWS ES) Office, in June 1978, and officially reported for duty on September 11. Twenty-three years later, that would become one of those dates that profoundly changed America forever. But this September 11 only changed my life. Yazoo City was about an hour's drive north of Vicksburg, which allowed us to take our time finding a house and making the move. When I arrived at the office in the Merchant's Bank Building, I was welcomed by Joe and the rest of the staff. The other hire Joe made was Mitch King, whose employment originally was not to exceed six months, but Joe wanted to make it permanent. On paper he hired us both at thirty-two hours per week, but from the very first day I was paid for forty hours a week, worked at least fifty, and it was clear that there was ample work for both of us.

The office had a relatively small staff to cover the entire Yazoo Delta in Mississippi, northern Louisiana and all of Arkansas from a wetlands and federal project planning perspective. Steve Forsythe, Robert Barkley and Curtis James were the senior biologists. Mitch and I brought the total to eight staff biologists and two administrative assistants. Charlotte Couch was the senior person and Elaine Smith was a sweet girl straight out of high school who would become like family to my wife, Sarah, and me over the years. Most of the funding for the office came from Corps of Engineers (Corps) transfer funding to fulfill the mandate of the Fish and Wildlife Coordination Act (FWCA). That law requires the Corps to provide an FWS Report that identifies the impacts to fish and wildlife resources as a result of the Corps' proposal with each federal water development project provided to Congress. The report also identifies how much and what kind of mitigation would be necessary to offset the harmful impacts. The FWCA report was required to be attached to the Corps' Environmental Statement and General Design Memorandum provided to Congress for approval through the appropriations process.

In addition, Ecological Services was charged with the FWS responsibility to respond to Clean Water Act (CWA) Section 404 permit requests that were administered by the Corps. The FWS role is to evaluate the proposed wetland development project, either private or governmental, and recommend issuance or denial of the permit. Corps' regulations state that the project must be "water dependent" to qualify, but the Corps paid little attention to that prerequisite. The regulations also state that they would give "great weight" to the comments of the FWS. That received the same attention as water dependency.

The Yazoo Basin encompasses 8 million acres of land with about half of those acres in the hills to the east and the other half in the historical floodplain of the Mississippi River. Prior to construction of the mainline levee system, the floodplain stretched for a hundred miles across Louisiana and Mississippi, creating a tremendously rich and fertile geography. Mitch had been working on Soil Conservation Service (SCS) projects in the hill area for the previous six months, so Joe and Steve Forsythe decided I should split my time between writing FWCA reports and working CWA permits. Joe walked back to my desk and handed me a copy of the 1972 CWA and said "Get up to speed on Section 404. You'll be doing a lot of permit reviews." That was how it began. No training. No "Here's how it works." In those days it was very much sink or swim, and it was up to me to swim. I believe they realized that I was one of the fisheries biologists on staff, if not the only one, who had worked in bottomland hardwood wetlands. Almost all of the biologists had studied wildlife, or specifically waterfowl and their habitats, with little incentive to understand the "naturalist" view of the entire ecosystem. This was common at that time throughout university systems. We all would soon learn about other functional values of bottomland hardwood wetlands in what would seem like a crash PhD course in both floodplain wetlands and the Clean Water Act.

While Joe and I were having our discussions about a potential job in June, Steve Forsythe had been asked by Mike Dawson and Ray Aycock out of the FWS's Jackson Area Office to do a field site visit on a tract of land under consideration for potential acquisition. Located in Avoyelles Parish, about thirty minutes from where Sarah grew up, it had been described as pristine floodplain forests, exactly the kind of land the FWS was trying to acquire. When Steve visited the site, he discovered large-scale land clearing in progress on property owned by Elder Realty, a lumber company that had allowed a developer named Albert Prevot to begin clearing the land for agricultural purposes. Steve reported back to the area office that this was indeed land worth preserving, and action was urgently needed.

The Vicksburg office reported the land-clearing activity to the Corps as a potential violation of the CWA, but had little success in getting their attention. However, other forces were under way. The Avoyelles Sportsman's League had brought a lawsuit against the developer and the Corps for violation of the CWA for clearing and leveling bottomland hardwood wetlands for conversion to agricultural uses without a Corps 404 permit. They were quickly joined by the Environmental Defense Fund (EDF) and the Louisiana Wildlife Federation (LWF). On November 7, 1978, Judge Nauman Scott, federal district judge in Alexandria, Louisiana, granted a temporary restraining order to the plaintiffs prohibiting any further land clearing pending a hearing.

I had barely been on board for two months when Steve and Joe decided that I might be able to bring some expertise regarding fisheries use of bottomland hardwoods into the discussion and should be involved in this effort. While I knew nothing about the law and very little about the impacts of land clearing, Steve allowed me to accompany him to Dallas for a meeting in the offices of Environmental Protection Agency (EPA) Regional Administrator Adlene Harrison to "carry his bags" and give me a chance to learn. Steve Forsythe was a native of Oklahoma and had flown helicopters in Vietnam. He was tall and slender, sandy-haired, and a genuinely good man who had no ego and cared deeply about developing younger biologists. I have no doubt that had he not wanted to give me the chance to be involved in these high-level meetings, my career would have taken a much different path.

One of the undecided issues that needed clarification was what constituted Waters of the United States (WOTUS). This term grew from the old interpretation of the 1899 Rivers and Harbors Act and was historically tied to protection of navigation and commerce. Through the CWA amendments of the Federal Water Pollution Control Act (FWPCA) in 1972, however, the breadth of consideration was expanded to some undefined level to protect both navigable waters *and* other waters of chemical and biological significance. While these terms had not been clearly defined, the Corps' CWA regulations stated that wetlands are

> those areas that are *inundated or saturated by surface or ground water* at a frequency and duration sufficient to support, and that under normal circumstances do support, a prevalence of *vegetation that is typically adapted* for life in *saturated soil conditions.* (Emphasis added.)

When we looked at this definition and consulted with Buck Reed in our FWS National Wetlands Inventory (NWI) center, it became clear that there were three "legal" criteria in the definition: surface or ground water hydrology; vegetation adapted for life in anaerobic conditions (in soil that lacks oxygen) during the growing season; and hydric soils that demonstrated regular and extended periods of saturation. These scientific criteria had been developed by the NWI interagency team of biologists, hydrologists and soils scientists not for regulatory purposes, but for scientific analysis of habitat function. Within the NWI team were Buck Reed (FWS), Rudy Nye (Corps) and Blake Parker (SCS). These scientists were shielded from political/policy interference and were instrumental in helping us develop the basis for a multiple-parameter approach to delineating WOTUS. Using multiple parameters was dramatically different from the single, simplistic vegetative parameter that the Corps had developed. Their list was limited to the wettest of the wet "terrestrial" species of plants: buttonbush, swamp privet, tupelo gum, bald cypress, overcup oak, and bitter pecan (also known as water hickory). (Collins 1979) These species occur at the fringes of cypress/tupelo swamps and are saturated throughout much of the growing season.

The NWI plant database categorized terrestrial plant species that possess adaptations to survive saturation of the root zone for thirty, forty-five, sixty, and more than ninety days during the growing period. The definition of the growing period is from the last killing frost until the first killing frost. This NWI list was significantly more robust than the Corps' list and discussed the physical and chemical adaptations that allowed the plants' survival through this time of stress. It is critical to remember that wetland species are not aquatic species, but rather terrestrial, and changing the rhizosphere (area around the roots) from aerobic to anaerobic through saturation with water is a significant stress. Species found in wetlands are plants that have adapted means to acquire oxygen and nutrients when their root zones are saturated and devoid of oxygen.

Alice Walters, Robert Teskey and Thomas Hinckley (1980) published a series of papers on how bottomland hardwood wetlands function and the types of adaptations that have evolved to give them a competitive edge. Extreme adaptations include cypress "knees" (roots), which grow up out of the water, and mangrove roots that hang down from the tree's branches, but there are others that are more subtle. Lenticels are pores on the trunk of trees that can allow oxygen to enter the tree and waste gases to be expelled. Buttressing, or significant swelling of the base of the tree, allows more stability in wet soils but also increases the surface area for lenticel development. In addition, adventitious roots can sprout above the ground surface on the base of young trees to allow them to have access to oxygen while the sapling is working hard to survive. Some species have the ability to transform natural inorganic compounds that could be harmful into helpful organic compounds. Not all species have these adaptations; thus, species that possess one or more have a competitive advantage for survival in wetlands. Fully aware of these stark differences in what is considered a wetland plant and the number of parameters used in methodology between the FWS and the Corps, Steve and I were prepared for significant disagreement at the Dallas meeting.

We arrived at the offices of the EPA at 1:30 p.m. Regional Administrator Adlene Harrison was gracious, but I immediately sensed that she was not one to suffer fools. Fashionably late, Colonel John Moellering of the Vicksburg District and his entourage, which had flown over on the Corps' airplane (we lowly FWS folks had driven the six-hour trip), arrived shortly afterward. It was clear from the Colonel's expression that he had anticipated being in charge of the meeting and had not expected several of us to be in attendance, especially from the FWS. Steve was there at the request of Justice Department Attorney Fred Disheroon, and ostensibly I was there to take notes and learn. The meeting was to develop the government's position on the question of WOTUS and land clearing in preparation for the November 17 court hearing.

The Corps' scientists were Dr. Donald Rhodes from Louisiana Tech University, Dr. Terry Huffman from the Corps Waterways Experiment Station, Corps hydrologist Phil Combs, and Corps Regulatory Functions Chief Mike Strachn. EPA Permits Branch Chief David Peters accompanied Regional Administrator Harrison. Mr. Disheroon and Ms. Frances Allen, assistant U.S. attorney for the Western District of Louisiana, asked several questions of Rhodes, Huffman, Moellering, Strachn and Combs regarding how they determined the jurisdictional extent of waters of the

U.S., and specifically how they established their jurisdictional findings on the Lake Ophelia tract.

Ms. Allen then asked Peters and Forsythe how the EPA and FWS came to their conclusions of jurisdictional extent on the tract. Colonel Moellering was visibly upset that the Justice Department gave "equal consideration" to CWA jurisdictional questions to the EPA, and especially the FWS. After questioning, it was evident that Mr. Disheroon was sympathetic to the plaintiff's case, supported by the EPA and FWS, and said he was considering asking for a continuance at the November 17 hearing while efforts would be made for an out-of-court settlement. This was not what the Corps expected to hear, and Colonel Moellering was not going to relinquish Corps dominance that easily.

The EDF was represented in the case by James T. B. Tripp. Jim Tripp was a man of slight build, receding hairline, wire-rimmed glasses, and was from New York City. This latter fact alone created angst among the Corps and other defendants. What was a New York lawyer doing in a Louisiana wetlands court case? They would soon find out. As a Yale law school graduate, Tripp had worked for the U.S. Attorney for the Southern District of New York's Criminal Division from 1968 to 1973. Before joining the U.S. Attorney's Office, he had volunteered to litigate in Jackson, Mississippi, on behalf of a young African American whose civil rights had been violated. He was not new to a hostile courtroom. In September 1978, Steve and Don Wilson, attorney for the Avoyelles Sportsman's League, asked Tripp to assist in the case. Steve had become familiar with Tripp during the court case on the Cache River Flood Control Project in Arkansas, another bottomland hardwood drainage project, and was well aware of Tripp's courtroom skills. Wilson quickly agreed to have a national group included as a plaintiff.

The LWF, represented by Michael Osborne out of New Orleans, also joined the lawsuit. The pressure was beginning to mount against the Corps' traditional methods of making jurisdictional determinations, but the final outcome was still unclear. On November 16 Steve and I joined Curtis James in Alexandria in preparations for the court hearing the next day. At the request of Fred Disheroon, Steve would be able to attend the hearing as part of the government. We had breakfast with Jim Tripp, Mike Osborne, Fred Disheroon, Arnold Banner (Vero Beach ES Office) and Don Wilson. My education in policy and law was moving at hypersonic speed, listening to Tripp and Disheroon ponder such questions as what does "de minimus" fill mean? In the regulations, a permit is required for deposition of dredged or fill material into wetlands except for "de minimus" amounts. I was learning fast that each word in law or regulation held significance.

Judge Scott determined that the technicalities of this case revolved around two decisions: what constitutes the extent of Waters of the United States, and what constitutes deposition of dredged or fill material? The attorneys, Steve, and Arnold Banner went to the federal courthouse in Alexandria to meet with lawyers from EPA, the Corps and Mr. Prevot. Buck Reed arrived in Alexandria about 1:30 that afternoon, bringing SCS soils maps that showed hydric soils across the entire tract. We discussed these in conjunction with our scientific arguments while we awaited word on the outcome of the hearing. Science only has relevance insofar as it fits the questions of the law. Fred Disheroon asked for a continuance in hopes of reaching a settlement, which Judge Nauman Scott granted until November 30. Arnold Banner called to tell us that the plaintiff's expectation was that the government would stipulate that the area met the definition of waters of the U.S. and that it was likely the land clearing was deposition of fill material. However, these points would have to be worked out over the next couple of weeks for a consent decree. The Corps, however, was not ready to stipulate these as points of fact.

> I did make the fortunate decision to include the EPA as well as the Corps as a defendant in the complaint. This was appropriate because EPA had the statutorily established role to play in the administration of Section 404. I also thought that EPA

might have a somewhat different view of the issues in the case from that of the Corps of Engineers, as my experience with the EPA Region 6 Administrator Adlene Harrison in Dallas in the Cache River case had made evident. I knew that the inclusion of both federal agencies as defendants meant that the Department of Justice had to represent both and could not simply take the positions that the Corps urged. It was the smartest legal strategic decision that I made in the case. (Tripp 2020)

The Corps had made it clear to the Justice Department that they did not accept either the jurisdictional determination of waters of the U.S. or the determination of deposition of dredged or fill material. At the hearing on November 30, Mr. Disheroon was forced to point out the differing positions of the Corps, EPA and FWS. Though slightly different (EPA determined that about 80 percent was regulated, and the FWS position was that everything but the Lake Long ridge was jurisdictional), both found much more than the 30 percent of the tract that the Corps believed to be wetlands. Judge Scott was having none of this. Lecturing Mr. Disheroon, the judge emphatically stated, "There is only one government and I expect you to come back here in sixty days with one government position of the jurisdiction question!" Judge Scott expected the Department of Justice to do what heretofore had not been done and clear up the question of CWA authority. Tripp's strategy was working perfectly. Conservation history was being written, and we all knew it.

The crux of the conflict lay in the confusion regarding the permit program and who was in charge. Since 1899, the Corps had administered a permit program for docks, piers, ports and structures along navigable waterways under Section 10 of the Rivers and Harbors Act. But this was not the Rivers and Harbors Act; it was the Clean Water Act, and was about pollution of the Waters of the United States, not about navigation. When the CWA amendments to the Federal Water Pollution Control Act of 1972 were passed granting the administrator of the

EPA the authority to oversee the law and veto Corps decisions, the EPA was not ready. The Senate, under the strong leadership of Howard Baker (R-TN), argued that the EPA should have the authority because of significant water pollution issues across the nation. In addition, Edmund Muskie (D-ME) provided significant arguments regarding the protection of wetlands and the values they provided to the people. On the floor of the Senate, he said,

> First, there is the problem of protecting wetlands, that is one of national interest . . . there is no question that the systematic destruction of the nation's wetlands is causing serious ecological damage . . . The wetlands and bays, the estuaries and deltas are the nation's most biologically active areas . . . They are a principal source of food supply.
>
> They are the spawning grounds for much of the fish and shellfish which populate the oceans and they are passages for numerous upland game fish. They also provide nesting areas for a myriad of species of birds and wildlife. (Hall 1985, after Muskie 1977)

There were several amendments offered, *and defeated*, that would have left wetlands out of the law. Thus, this powerful piece of legislative history highlights that Congress did not see this as a law governing "navigation," but one to protect the "chemical, physical and biological integrity of *the nation's waters*." (Emphasis added.) In 1975, *Zabel v. Tabb* brought the extent of navigable waters before the courts and was settled by including in the definition those areas up to the "ordinary high water mark." Navigation, therefore, was discussed and settled in a court case just two years prior to the passage of the Clean Water Act amendments in 1977, where even more direction to protect wetlands was added. This very issue would be front and center nearly fifty years later, when EPA would once again address the Waters of the United States in regulation and attempt to limit jurisdiction to navigable waters and their immediately adjacent wetlands.

The House had been concerned about new approaches that might impact the Corps' ability to continue business as usual for navigation, so the compromise was struck that the Corps would administer the permit program with EPA oversight and *veto authority*. The 1972 amendments passed the Senate by unanimous vote but were vetoed by President Richard M. Nixon. In an unusual move, Congress overrode the veto 52–12 in the Senate and 247–23 in the House, clearly sending the message that both chambers wanted all waters protected from pollution. (Houck 2012) But EPA had minimal field staff, and their main charge had historically been to regulate chemicals and their impacts on people. They had little expertise in wetlands biology or the functional values that bottomland hardwood wetlands provide.

When Steve originally called Dave Peters at EPA and asked that agency to get involved, Peters responded that the FWS had been mapping wetlands as waterfowl habitat for nearly thirty years, and the EPA would defer to our opinion. The FWS, of course, had no legal role in administering the CWA, so the Corps ignored us. They simply added the CWA Section 404 permits to their existing Section 10 Rivers and Harbors Act permit program and continued as if nothing new had happened. It has been said many times and is still true: "In times of indecision, those who act will be in control." The Corps had acted, and the EPA would have to step up and assert itself to wrestle its own authority back.

Fred Disheroon, representing the Department of Justice, found himself having to be the referee between two powerful agencies of government and, more important, to determine what final position the government would take. Justice accepted EPA's final determination and, on March 26, 1979, Disheroon provided the government's position to the court. Judge Scott set a date for a full trial in April on the merits of the case and issued a preliminary injunction against any further land clearing on the tract until the case was decided. Judge Scott had also decided to break the case into two parts: regulated activity and the jurisdictional extent of waters of the U.S. If the activity was not regulated, the WOTUS question would be moot. We all began preparation for possible testimony. Fish use of this tract for spawning and nursery had risen in importance because of the functional values the law was intended to protect. It was almost a certainty that, less than seven months after seeing the CWA for the first time, I would be an expert witness on how it applied to fisheries. Now it was sink or swim among the sharks!

The Corps, through Secretary of the Army Clifford Alexander, requested Attorney General Benjamin Civiletti to rule on two issues: Did the Corps or EPA possess the final authority to determine the extent of waters of the U.S.? Did the Corps or EPA possess the final authority to determine what actions constitute normal agricultural and silvicultural activities under Section 404(f)(1)? The Corps had argued that conversion of forested areas to agricultural production was within the definition of the "normal silvicultural or agricultural activities" identified in Section 404(f)(1), which are exempt from the CWA. They also believed that the determination was within their purview. The National Forest Products Association and the American Paper Institute were blindsided by this approach and wrote a lengthy report defending the 404(f)(1) silvicultural exemptions and stating that conversion of forested lands to agriculture was not a normal silvicultural activity. They in no way wanted their exemptions under the law to be at risk. While the request was being reviewed by AG Civiletti's staff, the first trial was ready to begin.

• • •

Jim Tripp was a city dweller who had never walked in bottomland hardwood wetlands before taking this case. But he loved the natural resources and was doing his best to help all of us save these wetland treasures. The Lake Ophelia tract sat within the pronounced loop of the Red River just north of Marksville, Louisiana, with two major pathways for water to back off the river onto the land during floods. On the north, there were cuts in the natural levee that allowed water to be pushed across what was known as Boone's Farm. The main drainage of the property was through Bayous Jeansonne and Natchitoches, which flowed into the Red River at Marksville. During spring floods, water was pushed out of the river's banks and back onto the property from these two major sources. The sheet flow across this ridge and swale topography, the fingerprints of thousands of years of river course changes, would eventually meet Red River backwater coming from Marksville, and the entire tract, with the exception of the Lake Long Ridge, would be inundated one out of every two to three years. Hans Van Beeke, a geologist who evaluated the site, told us the Lake Long Ridge was a "point bar" and had been formed by the Ohio River thousands of years ago.

Getting a New York attorney ready to represent these historical resources would be no easy task, but the student was chafing at the bit. Since he was suing the government, and we worked for the government, helping him understand the scientific facts of the case took some undercover work. I often picked Jim up at the Jackson airport in the dark of night and headed back west toward Vicksburg and Louisiana. We would stop and pick Steve up as we went through Vicksburg and head straight to Marksville and to one of the cheapest motels we could find. We were allowed a reasonable rate for a hotel, but Jim and EDF had almost no money, so we had to stay where he could afford to do so. Because this would be his first experience in wetlands and he didn't have the proper gear for it, we carried extra hip waders and long-john underwear (he was my size, so I got that assignment) for the trek through the wet woods on cold and damp winter days. Jim was a joy to work with, matter-of-fact in his reasoning and an obvious force to be reckoned with. We were glad he was on our side.

On one such visit we asked Dr. Leigh Frederickson, a well-known expert on waterfowl use of bottomland hardwood wetlands who was with the University of Missouri, to accompany us on a site visit to Lake

Ophelia and give us any advice he might share. Leigh was immediately devastated by the sheer scale of the land clearing and ready to help in any way he could. While I walked through the flooded timber in knee-deep water with Steve, Leigh and Jim, I listened to every conversation with the hope of absorbing some of the knowledge. Then it started to rain, and it was a good Louisiana soaking. We all watched Jim to see how he would respond. If the rain bothered him, he wasn't about to let us see it. All at once Leigh looked straight up at the sky and casually said "It looks like clear-up weather." Jim, in amazement, took the bait and said "Clear up?" to which Leigh said, "Yep. If it doesn't stop raining pretty soon, it's gonna be clear up to our asses!"

Jim probed Leigh and Steve with questions about wildlife and, to my amazement, began asking me about the ways in which fish from the Red River would use this area for spawning and as a nursery. I had evaluated the topography to determine where I thought access points would be and how long the fish would need to stay on-site to be capable of surviving and returning to the river. I leapt at the opportunity to contribute, and soon got questions from Leigh, and from Steve as well—not in a condescending way from a college professor and a seasoned wildlife biologist, but with honest interest in how fish used this type of wetlands. For the first time I didn't feel like just a supporting member of the team; I was made to feel that I was an equal. To a young biologist who knew that he was the least knowledgeable of the group, it was a wonderful feeling. Rain? What rain?

• • •

On April 23, the hearing was convened to determine if the activities of land clearing and ditching required a permit under Section 404 and/or Section 10. Since Judge Scott had broken the case into two parts to logically approach the questions, the first challenge was to establish that land clearing constituted deposition of dredged or fill material and required a permit. If this was not found to be the case, all was lost. We, the FWS, had to be prepared for either outcome and collect whatever biological data we could to support our scientific opinions. We believed the most important information we could provide was to document the biological functions provided by the tract, the diminishment of those values through land clearing, and attempt to tie those values to the purposes of the Act. On April 16, one week before the trial, I borrowed a .5-meter, .505-millimeter mesh conical plankton net from my graduate school classmate Doug Frugé. Doug worked for the Louisiana Department of Wildlife and Fisheries and was prohibited from getting involved in this case. But he quietly loaned me the net. Steve and I went to the Lake Ophelia tract because the March/April backwater flooding was occurring and we hoped to collect larval fishes to prove that the area was used as a fish spawning and nursery area. We rode in a motorboat up Bayou Jeansonne and literally lifted the motor as we crossed over the cattle fence that ran along the bayou. The entire tract was covered to a depth of one to five feet due to the backwater flooding of the Red River.

Using the borrowed net, we made an ichthyoplankton (larval fish) tow over the cleared land of sixty-second duration, then made two thirty-second tows in the flooded hardwoods just south of the cleared area. The shortened tows were necessitated because of the density of the trees and trying to slowly tow the net ten to fifteen feet behind us. The single tow over cleared land yielded five different genera or families (taxa) of fish and a total of 1,084 larval fish. The second two tows in flooded hardwoods yielded eight taxa and 3,695 larval fish (Hall and Forsythe 1979). In both cases, we gathered proof that the area was being used as a nursery ground and, based on the age of the larvae (less than five days since hatching), it was very likely the tract had been used as spawning grounds.

I preserved the larvae in a weak solution of formaldehyde. Formaldehyde is an effective preservative, but also acidic, and the tender larvae would simply dissolve in full-strength solution. Our office was not set up for actual science work, so Steve helped me get permission from

Flooded Wetlands (Courtesy of USFWS)

Dr. Bo Smith at the Corps' Waterways Experiment Station to (quietly) use their dissecting scope and a small room in a trailer to go through the tow samples and identify the taxa. It is ironic that I did the lab work in a Corps of Engineers facility. Larval fish are very difficult to identify to species level due to their primitive development. A larva is still an embryo until the yolk is absorbed several days after hatching. Only after the yolk is absorbed and the developing body parts—especially the gape (mouth)—are functional does the larva begin to look like a juvenile. As a result, taking a specimen to the lowest taxa, or classification level, can often be done only to the family level. Scientific names of animals and plants are broken down by family, genus and species, in order from most general to most specific. For some species one can identify to the genus, but seldom to the species. But for our purposes of demonstrating nursery and probably spawning area use, that was more than adequate.

The vast majority of species that spawn in floodplain wetlands are broadcast spawners, meaning that the male and female come together up in the water column and tilt sideways so their vents, which are the openings for gamete (egg and sperm) movement, are next to each other. Then the female "sprays" her eggs and the male "sprays" his milt (semen) in a cloud in which the eggs are fertilized. The eggs are soft and sticky at this time, but after fertilization they begin to swell with water, their chorion (outer membrane) begins to harden, and they drift to the bottom, where their sticky surface allows them to adhere to upright vegetation in the water column. The evolution of this tactic takes advantage of the submerged vegetation to keep the eggs off the bottom and away from the silt, while also providing cover to the developing embryos. This process becomes significant when determining negative effects under the law. If spawning success is substantially diminished due to eggs drifting to the bottom and being suffocated in the silt, then the removal of vegetation through land clearing may well be a violation of the CWA. The nearly four-to-one ratio of larval fishes in flooded hardwoods to those in the sparse stubble in cleared fields made a strong case. We hoped the judge would come to the same conclusion.

The trial lasted for three full days, and the judge heard from ten witnesses for the plaintiffs, while the defense called eleven witnesses, including Colonel Moellering's testimony entered in writing. The plaintiffs called Phil Combs, Vicksburg District, as their first witness to testify on the general hydrology of the area. Jim Tripp then called Steve to testify about his witnessing of the land clearing as well as the amount of overflow wetlands remaining in Louisiana. Through his slides, which were entered into photographic evidence, Steve did an excellent job of letting

V-blade (Courtesy of USFWS)

the court actually see what these activities looked like, what they did to the natural resources, and how they were negatively impacting wildlife. Tripp explained his objective in entering these photos into evidence:

> In the first trial in Alexandria in April 1979, the FWS biologists who had witnessed and photographed the land-clearing operations on the ground showed slides that graphically depicted the scorched earth bulldozer and windrow building and burning operations with large amounts of soil, roots, stumps, tree trunks and branches being torn up (that is, dredged), moved and dumped (that is, the discharge of dredged and fill material) into huge piles and windrows. The windrowed material would be burned, and residue often placed into holes dug on the tract. (Tripp 2020)

In cross-examination, the lawyer for Mr. Prevot asked Steve how he could tell the difference between pieces of wood to know that he was looking at roots that had been ripped out of the ground in the land-clearing process instead of above-the-ground parts of the plant. We believed he was trying to get into the record that only the parts of the vegetation above the ground had been removed and that there was no deposition of fill material. Steve, with some bewilderment over being asked a question that only someone living in the city who had never seen land cleared for farming would ask, politely said: "A tree stem, branch or trunk is generally straight and usually still has bark on it after being felled. A root is 'gnarled' and all twisted, doesn't generally have bark on it and is the part attached to the root ball at the bottom of the tree lying on the ground." Judge Scott smiled.

The government's (Corps') witness regarding normal forestry practices was Mr. Sid McKnight, a graduate of the Yale School of Forestry and the Environment, and former head of the U.S. Department of Agriculture's Hardwood Laboratory in Stoneville, Mississippi. He testified that clear-cutting was a normal silvicultural practice and that often row crops were planted on the cleared ground until the new tree sprouts grew tall enough to shade out the crops. He was clearly talking about clear-cutting as an interim management step in the culture of trees for forestry purposes. Jim Tripp zeroed in on this:

> On cross-examination, I asked Mr. McKnight basically one question: If a landowner clears his bottomland hardwood forest with no intent to regenerate the forest in any form—and the landowner defendants clearly had no such intent since the intent was to grow soybeans for the foreseeable future—would the land clearing and land preparation constitute 'normal silviculture'? . . . This question was risky since I didn't know what his answer would be, and we had not taken any depositions. However, although it appeared to me that Mr. McKnight's distaste for federal regulation of bottomland hardwood wetlands exceeded his evident dedication to proper use of and admiration for that resource, I did judge him as a thoroughly honest professional who cared about his reputation and credibility. His

response to my question was a straightforward 'No.' That ended my cross-examination. (Tripp 2020)

•••

The morning of April 24, 1979, was typical for central Louisiana. The sun was bright, and the temperature was steadily climbing. By late afternoon it would be 80 degrees, normal for late April. Floodwaters were still covering the Lake Ophelia tract. I was scheduled to testify on what we observed on the tract, as well as the fish larvae we collected. The first witness called by Jim Tripp and the plaintiffs was Dr. Jim Gosselink, a professor at the LSU Wetlands Center. Dr. Gosselink was a recognized wetland expert, and he testified to the ecological processes that occurred as fallen leaves on the forest floor were inundated by rising floodwaters. He described a process that I wrote down and integrated into almost all documents I wrote dealing with bottomland hardwoods for the rest of my career:

> As the floodwaters rise and cover the leaves on the forest floor, leaching of nutrients immediately begins, and this leaching provides nutrition for the emerging phytoplankton. Simultaneously, bacteria and fungi begin to colonize the leaves and extract nutrients for their growth and reproduction. As the microbes begin to break down the leaves into fragments, invertebrates ingest leaf particles and receive nutrients from the bacteria and fungi, much like peanut butter on crackers. The leaf particle is then extruded as waste and recolonized by bacteria and fungi. The process continues until nature has recycled all of the nutrients in the leaf. (Paraphrased from my notes.)

This analogy was fascinating and made me start thinking of the ecosystem not as compartmentalized components, but more as nature making commonsense use of all her parts. It was the first step in my journey to become a naturalist, rather than a scientist in a single discipline.

The next witness was Mike Materne, SCS agronomist from Marksville. Mike Osborne had Mr. Materne describe how many miles of drainage ditches would have to be constructed on the Lake Ophelia tract to provide enough drainage to allow soybeans or other dry crops to be successful. He stated that it would take miles of ditches, but that "Wetlands can be farmed if drainage can be provided. There is no reason they cannot." Mr. Osborne was pleased to get into the record that this SCS agronomist believed the area to be a wetland and unable to be farmed without extensive drainage ditching, even if Mr. Materne hadn't planned on supporting that view. The next two witnesses were John Maillet and Lyle Gremillion, both from Marksville. Maillet was a local hunter and fisherman who had knowledge of the tract, and Gremillion was a local newspaper reporter. Gremillion was able to provide a photo he took of the "V-blade," also known as a "stinger blade," that the bulldozer used to shear off the trees at ground level in the land-clearing operation. When he had finished with these two witnesses, Tripp called me to the stand.

I was accepted as an expert witness in fisheries biology by the court with no objection from the defense. I testified about the larval fish collected on the Lake Ophelia tract on April 16, 1979. Mr. Tripp asked me to describe a larval fish, since most people only know fish by their adult features. I had carried my briefcase to the stand with me in case I needed to refer to documents, so I reached into the briefcase and pulled out the small vials of more than 4,000 tiny larval fishes I had collected and separated by taxa at whatever level I was able. When I started giving a verbal description of the larvae (5–10 millimeters in length, hatch with no mouth, fins or developed organs) I set the vials in front of the judge. Judge Scott closely examined the small embryos and was clearly interested in these tiny, incipient fish. I was told by Jim Tripp that he had never had a witness bring in the fish or wildlife as evidence in this type of trial. He believed it was highly effective.

When Walter Conrad, attorney for Mr. Prevot, started his cross-examination, he began with "Dr. Hall." I immediately interrupted him and said, "No sir, I'm not a Doctor. Just a Mister." While Conrad gave me a stunned look and mouthed the words "Just a Mister," I looked at the judge to make sure he didn't think I was being flippant and was greeted by a wide grin. I was asked by Elder's attorney if what I had done represented a study, to which I quickly responded "No. My collections proved that larval fish were present on the property on the days I collected them, and the area is being used as a nursery. A full study would encompass much more, but my previous research in the Atchafalaya and Mississippi Rivers were full studies, and I found what that research predicted." I left the stand feeling as though I had been treated with dignity and respect by all parties, and hoped I hadn't embarrassed myself or the FWS.

Following me was Vic Lambou, a well-published fisheries biologist with the EPA, who had also spent many years as a biologist with the Louisiana Department of Wildlife and Fisheries. He testified about the aquatic productivity of the Bayou Natchitoches basin, particularly Spring Bayou. Spring Bayou Wildlife Management Area lies due west of the Lake Ophelia tract but is physically connected to the entire Spring Bayou–Bayou Jeansonne–Bayou Natchitoches ecosystem, and he believed the basin had considerable impact on the health of the Red River downstream.

The remainder of the day had witnesses for soil erosion and sedimentation. Testimony presented by Dr. Walter Peevy (LSU agronomist, retired), Harold Lahay (Louisiana Forestry Commission) and Ray Palermo (Louisiana Department of Wildlife and Fisheries forester) established that the erosion/sedimentation rate on forested land was less than .5 tons per acre per year, while cleared land had at least 5 tons per acre per year, which increased as the land was continually worked, ultimately reaching as much as 15–20 tons per acre per year. They all testified to the fact that windrows of trees were piled fifteen to twenty feet high and forty to fifty feet wide, and up to a half mile long. The trees were then burned. The resulting ash was "fairly deep," and the soils were "baked" by the windrow fires. The plaintiffs then rested their case, and Judge Scott directed the defense to be ready with their witnesses the next day. (Hall and Forsythe 1979)

We all went back to the hotel believing that Tripp, Osborne and Wilson had put on a strong case about the filling of wetlands. Slides provided in Steve's testimony showed the bulldozer blades clearly pushing dirt, and the "root rakes" pulling the massive root crowns out of the ground so the land could be disked and plowed. Because bulldozers are controlled by locking one track and having the other track move the dozer left or right, the tops of ridges were clearly being scraped down by the locked track to fill in the "low spots." I listened to the attorneys talk about what they might need to be ready for with the Corps' witnesses. They didn't seem to be too concerned, but declined to make assumptions about the judge's views.

• • •

April 25, 1979, was another beautiful day in Alexandria. The temperature as we headed to court was a comfortable 67 degrees, with a high of 80 predicted in the afternoon. The sun shone, and there was a light breeze. When we arrived at the courthouse, we were feeling good about the evidence that was presented by the plaintiffs and the lack of argument presented by the defendants. However, no one was assuming that Judge Scott concurred. He had run a strict court with every party receiving equal courtesy, but had rarely shown his views. The final day of the trial began with the private defendants making a motion for "Relief." They stated that there was no discharge. Walter Conrad stated, "The plaintiffs have not submitted any evidence that there is a point source discharge and, therefore, no permit is required under either Section 10 or Section 404." Judge Scott denied the motion in the "most part" but left open one portion under advisement. The defense called its first witness.

Mike Strachn, chief of the regulatory branch for the Vicksburg

District of the Corps, stated that there was significant debate as to whether Bayous Jeansonne and Natchitoches were navigable streams. He testified that the list of navigable streams had not been updated, at least not since he came on board in 1974, and that none of these water bodies had been proposed as navigable. Further, he offered that none had been proposed for a federal navigation project. Judge Scott intervened: "Just because they have not been proposed does not mean they are not navigable." The judge went on to say, "The ordinary high water mark is not pertinent to this case. In this trial, the only question is whether the activity would require a permit." We weren't sure what that last comment might mean. Did Judge Scott see the WOTUS question tied only to navigation? That portion of the trial, should we succeed in showing there was deposition of fill, would need to clearly show that navigation was a secondary issue under the CWA.

The next witness called was the land-clearing operations manager, Herbert Costello, from Oak Grove, Louisiana. He was responsible for the land clearing on Lake Ophelia and had been hired by Prevot. It became evident that his role was to show that various bulldozer blades had different functions, and that the blades used to clear the trees were not dirt-moving blades. "A dirt blade is a rectangular steel blade with no teeth. We never brought any such blade on the property," Costello stated. He went on to say that they had cleared about 8,200 acres before the restraining order and never pulled any stumps from the ground.

> Everything was done by a 'V-blade' and 'raking blade,' neither of which was designed to, and could not, move dirt. I have never heard before that bottomland hardwoods were wetlands, and we've been clearing nothing else since the 1950s. We dug five or six holes that were 50 feet by 6 feet to bury the unburned logs before Dr. Rhodes came to the property and advised us that this was a violation. (Costello 1979)

He admitted on the stand that they dug one ditch into Bayou Jeansonne, but said it was outside the "green area" on the Corps' map that they were to use to avoid wetlands. Upon cross-examination from Tripp and Osborne, he became combative and occasionally contradicted himself. He categorically stated that neither the V nor rake blades could carry dirt. He never said they couldn't move it—in direct contradiction to what he stated earlier.

For those of us who had witnessed such a trial for the first time, three days of debate over sometimes precise issues, such as how much dirt a V-blade can carry, left us drained, worried and dazed by all the information that had been generated. We needed to win the argument that a permit was required, or bottomland hardwoods would be raped all across the Lower Mississippi Valley for conversion to soybeans. The international market had soared, and soybeans were worth several times their normal rate. Bottomland hardwood wetlands were being cleared at the rate of 300,000 acres per year. This was compounded by the fact that crop insurance would pay for twenty bushels of beans when a field was ruined by flooding. Some areas were too wet to get planters in after land clearing, so seeds were applied by airplane so they could document "planting." It was becoming a scam on the government by unscrupulous people who called themselves farmers, but had never farmed in their lives. They simply made the minimal investment and claimed the twenty bushels per acre at nine dollars per bushel. As the primary 404 biologist in our office, I only had time to work permit requests that were 10,000 acres or more! We *had* to win this case. But the answer would not come for more than a month.

• • •

Things were beginning to heat up for Steve and me within the Fish and Wildlife Service. Most leadership in the FWS had come up through the national wildlife refuge or hatchery ranks and had little experience dealing with, or desire to be involved in, regulating private landowners. Part of the mission of the refuge and hatchery systems is to be good neighbors, and that was made more difficult when those neighbors were forced to delay land-clearing activities because of a position the FWS was pushing. Higher-ups started paying more attention to this little office in Vicksburg and these troublemakers who were helping a case against the government. Russ Earnest was the manager of the Jackson Area Office, under which the Vicksburg office resided in the chain of command. Russ was our strongest asset, mainly because he didn't ask for permission to approve our activities; he just approved them. Those in the Atlanta Regional Office and in Washington, D.C., remained quiet to avoid accountability. Mike Spear, associate director for Ecological Services in Washington, did approve and direct Buck Reed at the National Wetlands Inventory to assist us in any way possible in making a wetland determination. Other than that order, and Russ Earnest, we were on our own.

Joe Hardy left to go back into the refuge system and Charles Baxter became our new field supervisor. He was considered an expert in the Corps' water project planning process and brought a great deal of knowledge to that significant part of our work. Charles made it clear that we had his unconditional support to take this as far as we could in protecting these important wetlands. He had come from the Ft. Worth ES Office, where he worked in the Trinity River Basin of Texas and fully understood the importance of bottomland hardwoods.

On June 9, 1979, Judge Nauman Scott released his decision and found in favor of the plaintiffs that a permit was needed for clearing of bottomland hardwoods, other than with a chain saw. It was evident that Judge Scott paid attention to every detail and argument made by both sides and found the defense severely lacking. His opinion began with a factual and all-inclusive description of the area in question and its relevance to the Red River. He described the complaints brought before the court and quickly got to the question of soil movement and fill on page three of his decision, where he also referenced the photos that Steve had provided during his testimony:

> Various photos introduced into evidence showing the burned windrows revealed that soil was piled up during the windrowing process. It is not clear whether the blades themselves or the boom-like action of the trees and brush that they were pushing actually scraped the soil and the overlying leaf litter. In any event the photographic evidence clearly demonstrated that soil and leaf litter was piled up during the windrowing process—this movement filled in low areas and along with the discing which followed, had a levelling effect on the surface of the land. (Scott 1979, p3)

Judge Scott's opinion went through an elaborate, detailed reiteration of the definitions in question, the rules of the Federal Water Pollution Control Act, of which the Clean Water Act is an amendment, and the 404(f)(1) exemptions for normal agricultural and silvicultural practices. However, he also highlighted the Section 404(f)(2) override of those exemptions:

> Any discharge of dredged or fill material into the navigable waters incidental to any activity having as its purpose the bringing an area of the navigable waters into a use to which it was not previously subject, where the flow or circulation of navigable waters may be impaired or the reach of such waters may be reduced, shall be required to have a permit under this section. (Scott p8)

In deciding on each of the questions, he began with whether there were point sources of pollution:

> We determine that defendants' landclearing equipment (bulldozers fitted with V-blades, bulldozers fitted with raking blades,

and the tractor-pulled rakes), ditch excavation equipment (the backhoe used to excavate the three-quarter mile drainage ditch as well as any equipment used to excavate the proposed drainage ditches) and discing equipment, (unless used in connection with 'normal farming'), are point sources of pollution. (Scott p9)

Woohoo! Judge Scott had found that the equipment used in transforming a forested wetland into an upland use discharged point sources of pollution in soil and other material moved by the action of the equipment. Land clearing in wetlands would require a Section 404 permit! He stated that it gathered, collected and transported fill material that would qualify as point source discharge. When he discussed the importance of vegetation when considering the "chemical and physical" health of Waters of the United States, he said:

The above quoted definition makes it clear that wetlands include the vegetation that grows thereon. Such lands in the absence of vegetation can supply hardly any of the purposes of the Act. Consequently, in determining what constitutes dredged material in a wetland area, the inquiry does not end at the surface of the earth or water. Rather, any such inquiry must also consider vegetation, the very thing that defines a wetland. Accordingly, we determine that clearing the land of trees and vegetation, which are parts of the waters of the United States under 33 C.F.R. S323.2(a) and (c), constitutes the discharge of dredged material. (Scott p10)

He went on to say:

We feel that our determination follows the spirit as well as the letter of the law. A basic policy of the FWPCA is the protection of our nation's wetlands and the important functions they serve.

The legislative history of the Clean Water Act amendments of 1977 reflects an abiding congressional concern with the functional importance of Wetlands. (Scott p11)

Clearing of the wetland's vegetation will also seriously impair fish spawning. Fish that inhabit the Red River and its basins spawn in the backwater areas. Many of these fishes are broadcast spawners—they spew their eggs out into the water which attach to vegetation by means of an adhesive material that covers them. The eggs won't have any vegetation on which to attach after clearing and as a result the eggs will fall to the bottom where they will be covered with silt resulting in suffocation of the embryo. Fish nursery grounds will also be adversely affected by the clearing. Many fish larvae use the backwater area as a nursery where they feed on detritus and seek out vegetated areas for protection from predators. This will no longer be possible if the wetlands are cleared. (Scott p13)

The FWPCA would be emasculated insofar as wetlands are concerned were we to conclude that the permanent removal of the wetland's vegetation in the process of converting it to agricultural land was not subject to the S404 permit program. (Scott p14)

This opinion was a landmark decision in the history of U.S. ecological and environmental law. I wasn't surprised that Steve's testimony and photographs were strong evidence and would influence the decision, but I was overwhelmed that my testimony had been clearly heard and used by the judge. We didn't quite know how to deal with this very significant victory in the face of so many repeated losses in the ongoing battle to conserve bottomland hardwood wetlands, but we knew this was powerful.

Jim Tripp wrote in his draft memoirs,

> It was a super opinion that made full use of the trial evidence and our legal arguments. For the first time, agricultural operations converting bottomland hardwood wetlands that led to the demise of 80% of that resource in the Lower Mississippi River Basin were subject to federal Clean Water Act jurisdiction, at least for the time being in the Western District of Louisiana. (Tripp unpublished draft)

The Corps had been placed in a secondary role with the EPA, which was involving us more and more in their regulatory activities. We immediately went back to work preparing for the second phase of the trial: what constitutes the Waters of the United States?

In addition to the wonderful things happening on the professional front, Sarah and I had recently learned we were going to have our first child. I was happy and thankful for the spiritual power in my life that was guiding and watching over me in both areas of my life.

The Corps received another blow on September 5, 1979, when Attorney General Benjamin Civiletti responded to the Corps' March request for clarification of who had final decision-making authority under the Clean Water Act. In his letter to Secretary of the Army Clifford Alexander, Civiletti went through his analysis of the Federal Water Pollution Control Act and the Clean Water Act amendments in determining that the administrator of the EPA was the administrator of the Clean Water Act. He stated:

> I therefore conclude that the structure and intent of the Act support an interpretation of S404 that gives the Administrator the final administrative responsibility for construing the term 'navigable waters.' Your second question is whether the Secretary or the Administrator has the final authority to construe S404(f) of the Act. 33 U.S.C. S1344(f). That subsection exempts certain

activities from regulation under SS404, 301(a), and 402. The Corps of Engineers has argued that the responsibility for interpretation of the subsection insofar as it relates to the issuance of the Corps' S404 permits is vested in the Secretary. For reasons similar to those discussed in connection with your first question, I disagree. It is the Administrator who has general administrative responsibility under the Act, 33 U.S.C. S1361(a). (Civiletti 1979)

September 5, 1979, was not a good day for the Corps, and especially not for the Vicksburg District.

...

Cecil Andrus, who was the secretary of the interior at that time, oversaw the activities of the FWS as we were working on the Lake Ophelia court case. Lynn Greenwalt was the FWS director, a career employee for decades and a "family member" of the agency his entire life. He was both born on and grew up on national wildlife refuges, and was phenomenally equipped to lead the agency. His wife, Judy, also an FWS child, was his companion in all things and understood the FWS better than most employees did. Lynn became director when Richard Nixon was president, and the position was "career competitive" then, meaning it was not political; the incumbent was selected from the ranks based on competition and expertise. During Lynn's tenure, that would change.

Lynn is a tall man, about 6 feet 4 inches, with a slender build and a calm personality. He is very deliberate in his speaking, which allows him to master public dialogue. Every word is distinct and carefully crafted to orchestrate the message he intends. I had met Lynn only briefly on one of my trips to D.C., when I was in the hallway and he emerged from his office. He looked at me, cordially said hello and went on about his business. I was a GS-7 biologist at the time and I thought it was amazing that he stopped to allow me to be introduced. When I asked him about it years later, he was forced to admit that he didn't recall the encounter.

When Lynn entered the job of director in 1972, the FWS was called the Bureau of Sport Fisheries and Wildlife. The sister bureau was the Bureau of Commercial Fisheries, which was placed with the FWS in the Department of the Interior and overseen by the commissioner of Fisheries and Wildlife, a position appointed by the secretary of the interior. Richard Nixon was known to have a temper, and the story of how the Bureau of Commercial Fisheries was moved, and the director of the FWS became a presidential appointment confirmed by the Senate, is directly tied to Nixon's temper.

The story goes that the Bureau of Commercial Fisheries had responsibility for sea otters under the Marine Mammal Protection Act (MMPA), and otters were a significant challenge to commercial fishermen along the California coast. San Clemente was known as "White House West" because Nixon, former governor of California, spent considerable time there. On one of his trips to California, Nixon was apparently briefed by representatives of a commercial fishing group who asked for help in controlling the sea otters. They contended that the otters were eating all *their* abalone and getting caught in their nets, a violation of the MMPA. Nixon is said to have sent word to the secretary of the interior to fix this and help his fishermen. The Bureau of Commercial Fisheries then established "otter free zones," where fishermen could fish, and "otter zones," where fishing was prohibited. Otters, of course, didn't read the rules. They continued to swim and be caught in nets of fishermen in "otter free zones," upon which they would be relocated to an island off the California coast. As expected, as soon as they were released they returned to their known food source.

In his second request for assistance, Nixon is said to have been told there was nothing else the bureau would do, and the fishermen would simply have to live with it. Caught in a catch-22 in which, as president, he could not legally order an agency of government to allow the law to be broken but clearly did not want protection of the otters to interfere with the activities of the fishermen, he turned to his attorneys and asked what authorities he might have to deal with this obstinacy from the bureau. He was told there are none, but he did have authority to determine where a bureau is located within the government. He apparently decided to move the Bureau of Commercial Fisheries to the Department of Commerce, under the National Oceanic and Atmospheric Administration, where he is reported to have said "Now let the bastards compete for their budgets with weather satellites." Whether this rendition of why the bureau was moved to Commerce is true or not, the result was the bureau of Sport Fisheries and Wildlife was left as the only bureau under the commissioner of Fisheries and Wildlife in the Department of the Interior.

Congressman John Dingell was a staunch supporter of Lynn Greenwalt and the bureau he directed:

> Dingell and I, along with Nat Reed [assistant secretary for Fish, Wildlife and Parks] set about to determine the future direction of the bureau. The commissioner was probably the single least qualified person for the job, but he had some 'brother-in-law' type connection and was appointed by the secretary. Dingell was fed up with the lack of fisheries and wildlife management knowledge of the political commissioner, so he did what he always did and drafted a law. Dingell decided he would include changing the name back to the Fish and Wildlife Service and require that the director would have to be a person who was qualified by reason of training and experience to be a biologist heading a biological organization. Then he threw in the nomination by the president and confirmation by the Senate!
>
> That changed my life and it changed the Service materially because this outfit, which had been a bunch of 'sparrow cops,' became the only one in the Interior Department whose director

was nominated by the president and confirmed by the Senate. I didn't pay much attention because I didn't have much experience in the political area, but I began to read up on it and I went 'Wow!' Dingell knew what it meant. He thought an awfully lot of the Fish and Wildlife Service throughout his career, from beginning to end. In renaming the FWS, I thought for a millisecond about calling it the U.S. Wildlife Service, much like the Canadian Wildlife Service. Then I was reminded that Dingell had supported the Sport Fish Restoration Act and that option quickly disappeared.

While I had a wonderful relationship with Dingell, he was still the one with the power and, on occasion, exercised that power. I took my son Mark to a hearing on walruses and the Marine Mammal Protection Act where I was to testify. Dingell gave me a really hard time at the hearing, more about the issue than my involvement. After the hearing, I took Mark down and Dingell shook his hand and invited us to lunch. I had to get Mark back to school, so we respectfully declined. On the way home, Mark said 'I don't understand why he was so angry with you.' I said I didn't enjoy it either, but understood why he did. It was to send the message to others that he was in charge.

My confirmation was not arduous because it was the first one, and I had been the director for two years. Nat Reed introduced me and they gave Nat a much harder time than they gave me. Dingell had already received a commitment from Rogers Morton, Nat Reed and company that I would be nominated, so it was really a done deal. As it turned out, I was the last director of the Bureau of Sport Fisheries and Wildlife and the first director of the reconstituted Fish and Wildlife Service, all in the span of one afternoon.

The difference between being a Senate-confirmed position and one that is not is that the cachet that is carried with it is about two notches above other appointees, and could be many notches. It has with it some traditional imparities. If you are Senate-confirmed, you are always entitled by courtesy to be referred to as 'The Honorable' and possess the confirmed title of 'Director' for life. It made a hell of a difference in the Interior Department, and there was a lot of scrambling to justify doing that for some other folks. They jacked up those other positions so they could pass muster, and it didn't hurt the Interior Department at all. It was a little thing, but very significant. Nobody wanted the commissioner any longer. He was the last one and had come out of Alaska, and Dingell didn't want him having any say over me. He remained for a bit, but was rendered harmless and had no real responsibilities. (Greenwalt 2020)

The building of the Alaska pipeline, which runs from Prudhoe Bay, Alaska, on the North Slope of the Arctic Ocean, to Valdez in the Gulf of Alaska, was one of the most challenging efforts of Greenwalt's tenure as director. He described Dingell's support for the FWS, and for Greenwalt himself, through a meeting on the pipeline.

In the early days of the Alaska pipeline, they were trying to figure out how to run the system so all of the requirements, regulations and environmental concerns that people had expressed about construction of the pipeline could be assured. There were people in the FWS who did nothing but work on the pipeline as inspectors and managers of the environmental confrontations, such as how to cross rivers, where to bury and where to run above ground. They were both male and female employees, which was unusual at the time, who had the authority to stop the project if they didn't like how it was being done. Dingell called me over to his office for a meeting. When I got there, here was the chief of the Corps of Engineers and four or five others, all associated with the pipeline.

Here I am, around forty-three and trying to grow a mustache, and he said 'I want you to know this person because those people who are involved and work for the FWS work for this man. This man knows that if something goes wrong, or he does not get the kind of cooperation he feels he should have, he can come to me and I will make it whole.' It was really something for me. This is the big time, and this guy means it! I wouldn't have crossed him for all the tea in China. I respected him and I would move heaven and earth to help him. (Greenwalt 2020)

CHAPTER 2

The Yazoo Basin Project

I spent most of my time in the Vicksburg Ecological Services (ES) Office working on Clean Water Act (CWA) permits and regulatory wetlands issues, but other duties in the office included evaluating Corps of Engineers projects and activities under the Fish and Wildlife Coordination Act. I was given the assignment to evaluate all the previous Corps projects in the Yazoo Basin and summarize the fish and wildlife resource damages that had occurred as a result of the projects, how much mitigation had been requested by the FWS, and how much mitigation had been provided. When I began to read all the previous reports that had been submitted and the nearly absent mitigation that had been implemented, I was amazed.

Federal flood control works by the Corps began in 1939, with the first authorization for flood control studies given by Congress in 1936. The story I discovered was one I had neither expected nor, frankly, thought about. I found a Corps pamphlet in old FWS files that had in big letters on the front, "GOD CREATES FLOODS. MAN CREATES FLOOD DAMAGE!" The apparent position of the federal government prior to the 1930s was that if you built structures or farmed in the floodplain, it was between you and God. The government did not believe its role should be to provide flood protection. But then a few significant events occurred. The flood of 1927, coupled with the Great Depression and Dust Bowl era of the 1930s, forced a change. President Franklin Roosevelt was struggling to get the American economy back on track. With 25 percent unemployment and no short-term answer, he needed a way to get his New Deal initiative under way. The Civilian Conservation Corps was created to build roads, buildings and other structures on federal land. The CCC, or three Cs as they were called, put a great many men to work. But with the havoc created by the historic flood that covered the entire Lower Mississippi Alluvial Valley in 1927 still in play, the Corps of Engineers was asked to find out if there were opportunities to provide federally backed jobs through flood protection for the 100-mile-wide floodplain of the Lower Mississippi Valley. And so it began.

The report, published under the name of the Vicksburg office, was titled "The Yazoo Basin: An Environmental Overview: A Planning Aid Report by the U.S. Fish and Wildlife Service." It was only a little over thirty pages in length, but for the first time collated all the previous calculations of habitat destruction and requested mitigation as a result of the Corps' flood protection projects. Bottomland hardwood wetlands had been significantly impacted in the Yazoo Basin since work began on the projects in 1939. In a 4-million-acre floodplain area of the Mississippi River in the state of Mississippi, 1,860 miles of channelization and 600 miles of levee construction had been planned, with over 1,300 miles of channelization and 300 miles of levee construction completed. The losses included 315,000 acres of bottomland hardwood wetlands with an additional 36,800 acres of cleared land *lost solely to construction of the projects.* The resultant impacts to the aquatic ecosystem were devastating:

> This ecosystem has declined such that recent studies have found that only 20 percent of the stream miles in the Yazoo Basin are capable of supporting a fishery of any kind, with even fewer miles supporting a sport fishery. (USFWS 1979)

In all the reports that had been provided by the FWS to the Corps identifying these impacts and recommending appropriate mitigation, the FWS had very conservatively recommended the acquisition of 195,000 acres of bottomland hardwood wetlands, construction of more than fifty water control structures, and construction of nine greentree reservoirs:

> To date, the only mitigation authorized has been the Muddy Bayou control structure (completed), which cannot be operated to full potential, 15,383 of the 19,000 acres authorized in the Hillside Floodway (transfer completed), nine water control structures in the Big Sunflower Basin (no construction begun), and six greentree reservoirs and nine slough control structures on the Delta National Forest (under construction). (USFWS 1979)

As bad as these losses were, the elephant in the room was the Yazoo Backwater Pumps project, which would place a massive 25,000-cubic-feet-per-second (cfs) pump—or alternatively, a 17,500 cfs pump—on the levee at Steele Bayou to pump the remaining water out of the basin and drain the final 200,000 acres of wetlands in the "Sump Area." To give a reference, the average flow of the Yazoo River was 5,000 cfs. I was also assigned to a team that was preparing another report on that project, and we wanted to give the Corps a clear indication that we would be in strong opposition to the pumps.

The mindset that carried these projects was not to provide flood protection to homes and farmland that had already been developed, but rather a new and dangerous paradigm of blocking floodwaters from large areas of wetlands so they could be developed in the future. Every landowner in the Lower Mississippi Valley watched the flood protection being provided upriver, and that water then pushed down on them, and they waited their turn to receive flood protection and push the water farther downstream to unfortunate towns like New Orleans and Morgan City, Louisiana. Like a giant squeegee coming down the Ohio, Missouri and Lower Mississippi Rivers, the water was constrained by levees and river flows that were once meandering and shifting but were now being turned into the equivalent of a fire hose. No longer were great stretches of the 100-mile floodplain receiving the rich overflow waters of the river. At the writing of the report, an estimated 80 percent of the historical bottomland hardwood wetlands had been cleared, the ground leveled and converted to agriculture.

> In a news report published June 16, 1979, General R. C. Marshall, president of the Mississippi River Commission, was referenced as saying that the Corps of Engineers flood control works in the Mississippi Valley have led to conversion of some 20 million acres of land for agricultural use. The Delta of the Yazoo Basin has been the site of a considerable portion of this conversion. (USFWS 1979)

What nature had carved and nurtured for thousands of years had taken heavy equipment and dirt levees only a few decades to erase. With only about 4 million of the original 24 million acres of bottomland hardwood wetlands remaining in the Lower Mississippi Valley, time was critical. We needed the second decision from Judge Nauman Scott, which we hoped would recognize that these beautiful resources were indeed Waters of the United States.

• • •

In December 1979, the FWS released a scientific document out of the Office of Biological Services that took all the information housed in the National Wetlands Inventory database and applied it to the different types of wetlands across the U.S. That document, titled "Classification of Wetlands and Deepwater Habitats of the United States," contained a scientific classification of habitats based on duration of flooding, vegetative types, salinity and other habitat characteristics that was created by a group of scientists led by Lewis Cowardin. According to Cowardin and his colleagues, any one of the three factors of soils, vegetation or hydrology would classify an area as a biological wetland. (Cowardin et al. 1979)

This interpretation brought in *all* bottomland hardwood wetlands based on vegetation alone, but they could also be included by the presence of hydrology or hydric soils.

When we looked at the definition of wetlands in the Corps' regulations, however, we saw a more restricted set of criteria. Wetlands as defined in 33 CFR 233.2(c) are:

> Those areas that are *inundated or saturated* by *surface or groundwater* at a frequency and duration sufficient to support, and that under normal circumstances do support, a prevalence of *vegetation typically adapted* for life in *saturated soil* conditions. (Emphasis added)

As we reviewed both the science and law, it became clear that nature can determine that an area is a wetland, but that people decide through law how far they are willing to restrict an individual landowner's rights to use his/her property. Instead of the single criterion approach applied in Cowardin et al., we realized we would have to apply the multiple-parameter approach of soils, vegetation *and* hydrology to identify wetlands that qualified for protection under the law. The FWS team—Steve Forsythe, Buck Reed, Arnold Banner and I—knew we would have to defend the wetland determination provided by EPA on February 13, 1979, in preparation for the original court date, when Judge Scott sent Fred Disheroon back to determine the position of the United States. There were those in the Fish and Wildlife Service and in non-governmental conservation groups who were upset with our restricted interpretation. They thought the law should protect all wetlands. But the greatest mistakes occur when people argue what the law *should* say, versus what it *actually says*. This occurs on both sides of the argument, from those who want the law to do more as well as those who want less regulation. The truth rests in the compromise Congress established. We got busy preparing for the second trial.

Buck Reed, in addition to being an outstanding wildlife and wetlands biologist, had brought significant information from Blake Parker and the Soil Conservation Service (later to become the Natural Resources Conservation Service) about the types of soils that populated the Lake Ophelia site. The Sharkey and Tunica clays represented thousands of years of alluvial deposits that formed in these backwaters when these minute soil particles (less than 10 microns in diameter) found water with no movement, which allowed them to drop out of suspension. These soils are classified as hydric and display the typical mottling and gleying, which is the term for a shiny gray color that appears when aerobic bacteria are dormant and anaerobic bacteria become active for extensive periods in the floodplain. Mottling is what gave them the local name of "buckshot" clay. The alternation between aerobic and anaerobic respiration of the bacteria creates rust-colored spots in the soil profile. Gleying occurs throughout the profile when the soil has been anaerobic (saturated with water) for a long enough period that iron and manganese chemically reduce, creating the gray color. These soils also contain the mineral montmorillonite, which allows them to swell when wet and shrink when dry. This creates the cracks observed when clays dry in summer, and is also why it's called "gumbo clay" when wet, sticky and difficult to walk through.

Dr. Rob Teskey was a significant help to our case. He, Alice Walters and Thomas Hinckley had put together the most extensive series of publications on the various aspects of bottomland hardwood physiology and adaptations to stress available at the time. He visited the Lake Ophelia site on several occasions and was well prepared to testify about the biological functioning of the Lake tract and why the species present were "typically adapted" for life in saturated soil conditions. The hydrology was already in the court record from testimony of the Corps' as well as consulting hydrologists, confirming complete inundation at least every third year. With soils, vegetation and hydrology arguments well in hand, we believed we were prepared.

When it came time for the second trial, Russ Earnest, who was the manager of the Jackson Area Office, received word that Regional Director Ken Black would be out of town and could not sign our approval to testify. Steve had forwarded a request for approval based on a recent change in Department of the Interior policy stating

> an officer or employee of the Department shall not testify in any judicial or administrative proceeding concerning matters related to the business of the Government or the contents of official records without the written permission of the head of the bureau or office, or his designee, or of the Secretary. (USFWS 1979)

With radio silence from above the area office in Jackson, Russ Earnest gave us permission, but said he didn't know if it would be overturned. To ensure we could be made available to testify, Steve and I put alternative plans in place. Sarah's hometown of Bunkie is in Avoyelles Parish, and Alexandria is only about a half-hour drive from her parents' home. Sarah and I decided to go visit them the weekend of February 1, 1980, and it was there that the Civil Subpoena from the United States District Court for the Western District of Louisiana was delivered to me by a United States Marshall. I could not be compelled to testify if I was not in the jurisdiction of the court, so Michael Osborne subpoenaed me in Bunkie. I thought it was quite humorous that the subpoena said "Mr. Dale Hall, Eola Highway, Bunkie, Louisiana." Steve made similar arrangements. Time was critical. Over 100,000 acres of bottomland hardwood wetlands were cleared *after* the June 9 decision. The Corps was resisting doing any enforcement in these "non-wetland" areas.

Jim Tripp also needed to connect with his local clients and have them comfortable that he could skillfully carry their message about the natural resources they loved to a successful completion. He recalled his experimentation with the local cuisine:

With Dale Hall and others from the FWS, I was invited to a dinner at the home of one of the members of the League, Lyle Gremillion. They were folks who liked to hunt and fish in the woods. Squirrels that Lyle had shot were on the menu. I remember Lyle asking me to try out squirrel brains as a local delicacy. I did eat a small sample as a demonstration of my admiration for the local culture and local stalwarts who were willing to stand up to 'economic progress,' but I did not like the texture at all. At the other end of the culinary spectrum, during the second trial when I spent a weekend in Alexandria, Dale Hall, at the time a very new FWS biologist who played an important role in this case, invited me for Sunday lunch with his in-laws, Herman and Nell Reed, who lived near Bunkie. His mother-in-law served, among other things, wild duck gumbo. It was just five-star splendid! I still remember the remarkably distinctive and delectable taste of that wild duck. That was reason enough to do what I could do to help preserve the bottomland hardwood resource that was such critical habitat for ducks in the Mississippi Flyway. South Louisiana cuisine, based on wild game and shellfish, is the most distinctive and memorable cuisine in the USA. (Tripp 2020)

• • •

The position of the United States regarding waters of the U.S. had been established before the land-clearing phase of the trial had begun. While the Corps still maintained that only 30 percent of the tract was jurisdictional, and we provided our determination that the entire tract except for the Lake Long ridge was jurisdictional, the Environmental Protection Agency had the final word. The official wetland determination provided to the court on March 22, 1979, declared that approximately 80 percent of the tract contained jurisdictional wetlands. The trial that was about to begin would require providing enough scientific evidence to prove that the approach used, and the determination made, were scientifically logical and commensurate with the legal definition of wetlands.

The trial began on February 5, 1980, a clear day in Alexandria with temperatures in the low 40s as we went to the courthouse. The trial lasted several days with numerous witnesses testifying in regard to fish and wildlife use of the tract and each of the three requirements: hydrology, vegetation and soils. I was called to testify in this trial because of the direct evidence I had provided in the form of fish collected on the tract. This was not a trial separate from the overall suit, simply the second phase, so all evidence and testimony from the April 1979 trial was included by reference. Jim Tripp and Mike Osborne wanted me to reiterate that I believed the Lake Ophelia tract was a functioning spawning and nursery area for the fishes of the Red River and was directly part of that ecosystem. They wanted this reiterated because one of the objectives of the law is to "protect fish and shellfish spawning and nursery areas." This would also help in the jurisdiction question: how can it not be Waters of the United States if it is used regularly by fish for spawning, nursery and supports a commercial fishery? The main additional testimony I provided dealt with pointing out on the map how I believed fish accessed the site and why I believed the Lake Ophelia tract was part of the river ecosystem. Since I had been cross-examined in the first trial, there were few questions from the defense.

In building their case, Tripp, Osborne and Wilson felt that a significant hammer had been added to the regulations in 1977 when the definition of wetlands had been changed from "vegetation that requires" to "vegetation typically adapted" for life in saturated soil conditions. This was a game changer. One could actually make the argument that there are no wetland plants that *require* saturated soils for survival. Wetland plants are terrestrial, not aquatic, possessing adaptations that allow them to survive these high-stress conditions. While they would likely be outcompeted by upland plants in non-wetland environments, they could survive if competition were controlled.

The plaintiffs were depending heavily on getting the witnesses to say on the stand that these plants were adapted. During the trial, Jim Tripp called Ken LaBorde, a local resident who worked for Louisiana Power and Light (LP&L). We learned that Ken's nickname was "Nookie" and he regularly hunted the area with his cousin Cookie, in and out of season. As a lineman for LP&L, he was able to give a good description of how water covered the property before the land clearing and ditching started. At one point, he became nervous about a question regarding his hunting the year before. When his attorney inserted the words "in season of course," he relaxed and answered the questions.

Nookie's cousin Cookie LaBorde was also called to the stand. Cookie, by all accounts from the people in the area who knew him, was a true Cajun wildlife outlaw. It was said that he could lie in the back of a pickup truck at night at any point on the Elder Realty property, look at the sky, and tell you where he was. Locals said he could do this because he had poached wildlife on the Lake Ophelia tract all his life and knew every place to find his prey. He was called for that reason. If anyone knew the wildlife richness of the Lake Ophelia tract and where floodwaters occurred, it would be Cookie LaBorde.

Walter Conrad, the three-piece-suit lawyer from Houston, asked Cookie to look at the map of the Lake Ophelia tract on a tripod next to the witness stand and point out a particular location on the property. LaBorde said in a low voice "I don't read maps." Mr. Conrad said again, "Mr. LaBorde, please point to the area in question on the map." Again, "I don't read maps." Judge Scott was becoming visibly irritated by Conrad's persistence and failure to understand that LaBorde couldn't read. "Mr. Conrad, the witness has clearly answered that he does not read maps. I suggest you pursue another line of questioning." Conrad wouldn't give up. He kept questioning LaBorde and finally asked how many ducks LaBorde thought had been present on the tract the previous winter. After a very long pause, as much as twenty seconds, he rubbed his chin and said "Plenty duck." Judge Scott smiled. After several arduous hours on the stand, Conrad asked LaBorde if he thought he lived in a wetland. "I guess you could say that," Cookie replied. With that simple statement, Conrad had allowed into the record powerful commonsense information so necessary for the plaintiff's case.

The primary challenge for the plaintiffs was in Dr. Donal Hook, a plant physiologist at Clemson University who had worked with the Corps to determine which species of bottomland hardwoods were "wetland" trees and which were not. The government called him to the stand to say that only the limited species that live almost constantly in water have the adaptations for life in saturated soil conditions. Tripp recounts his cross-examination of Hook:

> At the end of Donal Hook's direct testimony, I had no clear idea what I should do on cross-examination. As I walked from my chair to cross-examine him, it suddenly came to me, as kind of an epiphany. I knew that Dr. Hook could compare all the species found on the tract to the five that he had examined in detail in terms of their 'adaptations.' Asking him to group each of the species of trees identified on the transect (from lowest to highest elevations) with one of the five species, the physiology of which he had studied in detail, was risky since I did not know what his response would be. But I decided to plunge in. I, therefore, asked him first about the adaptation mechanisms of the species that he had studied found in the wettest conditions, namely bald cypress, and he then explained about the nature of those adaptations. In response to my question about which other species identified on the transect had comparable adaptations to those of the bald cypress, his response included water tupelo and one other species. I then asked him about the next wettest adapted species that he had studied and the nature of its adaptations to wet conditions, and then inquired what other species found on the tract and mapped on the transect had comparable

adaptations. He mentioned a few other species. Then I inquired and he talked about the third species that he had studied next in line on his gradient, its adaptations and other species on the tract that had similar adaptations. Questions about the fourth species followed.

The bottom line of this line of questioning, and his responses, was that each of the twenty species on the tract had similar adaptations to wet or saturated soil conditions comparable to one of the species that he had researched in detail. In other words, all of the species found in the tract had adaptations, a key term used to describe wetland plants in the Section 404 regulations, of varying degrees of effectiveness to saturated and flooded soils. As Robert Teskey told me later, Dr. Hook was able and willing to describe the adaptations of these species found on the tract in a way that he and perhaps no one else could do. (Tripp 2020)

Jim Tripp's cross-examination of Dr. Hook, in his opinion, was probably the best cross-examination of his career, and sent the defendants' entire case into a nosedive. In a memorandum to the field supervisor, Ecological Services, Vicksburg, following the trial, I wrote:

> The Government's contention, as well as the Plaintiff's, was that 'life' meant surviving critical growing periods in saturated soil conditions (anaerobic conditions) while maintaining necessary life functions. The critical growing period was established through expert testimony to be the months of March, April, May and June when leaf formation was occurring. Conversely, the private parties in the case (Lake Ophelia tract land owners, Louisiana Land Owners Assn., Louisiana Department of Natural Resources) contended through their experts that 'life' meant the *entire* life of the plant; from seed to germination to

senility. In essence, the private parties were saying that the only wetland species were bald cypress, tupelo gum, and their immediate associates; green ash, black willow, and possibly overcup oak and bitter pecan (water hickory). They contended that the cypress/tupelo association was the only community that could withstand permanent (or nearly permanent) swamp conditions. (Hall 1980)

Rob Teskey had done a masterful job of explaining in scientific detail how species adapted, and contributed to the increasingly strong case being built. The primary driver in plant adaptation to saturated soil conditions was their ability to gain oxygen from sources other than the rhizosphere (area around the roots). When the soil becomes saturated with water, free oxygen is driven out of the spaces between the soil particles, and the area becomes anoxic (devoid of oxygen). Aerobic bacteria go dormant or die and anaerobic bacteria spring to life and begin their metabolic activity. Plants can adapt by having increased numbers of lenticels (pores) around the trunk of the tree above the water line through buttressing and spreading their roots laterally. Plants can form adventitious roots—roots that literally sprout out of the base of saplings above ground to allow access to oxygen from the air. Finally, plants with developed adaptations can chemically alter byproducts of anaerobic stress. In the presence of anaerobic conditions, upland plants produce ethanol, a toxic compound. Conversely, a plant adapted to saturated soil conditions, and the anoxia that occurs, can produce compounds that are friendly to the plant's metabolic needs, usually organic acids such as malic, succinic, lactic or shikimic. Hook's testimony proved to be an endorsement of these adaptations.

In Judge Nauman Scott's final opinion, issued on March 12, 1981, he made it clear that he understood the legal questions, the scientific questions and the purpose of regulatory definitions.

> The plaintiffs in this proceeding are representative of those who have fought historically to expand Section 404 jurisdiction to promote pollution control. Private defendants are representative of those who have fought historically for the right to clear and develop forest lands. Thus, the 'wetlands' definition does not answer a scientific need, it satisfies a practical, a social, a political need, the need to define the scope of Section 404 jurisdiction. (Scott 1981, p18)

In this simple declaration late in the opinion, Judge Scott was tutoring everyone on the compromises that are made when laws are written, and stating that the people decide the extent of their reach into private activities through discussion and debate among their elected officials. Throughout my career, I would be reminded of his wisdom as we found ourselves in constant conflict over what differing groups thought the law "should have said," rather than what was ultimately agreed upon.

As the parade of scientists sat in the witness box and answered questions, the three most compelling summaries of facts were: 1) the hydrology of the tract, both subsurface and surface, clearly met the test of "inundated or saturated" for several months during the growing season; 2) the soils were hydric across the entire tract except for the sandy loams of the Lake Long ridge, and; 3) all of the vegetation on the tract possessed "adaptations" that provided them with a competitive advantage over obligate upland species (plants that cannot tolerate saturation). Even the expert witnesses for the private defendants admitted this was true. Tripp, Osborne and Wilson believed they had covered every base necessary to get the opinion they were seeking, *and* believed that Judge Scott had tipped his hand several times during the trial and in chambers, giving them the impression that he agreed with the plaintiffs. They were correct.

In his "Conclusion of Law" portion of the opinion, Judge Scott quoted the CWA:

(a) The objective of this chapter is to restore and maintain the chemical, physical, and biological integrity of the Nation's waters. In order to achieve this objective it is hereby declared that, consistent with the provisions of this chapter—

1. It is the national goal that the discharge of pollutants into the navigable waters be eliminated by 1985;
2. It is the national goal that wherever attainable, an interim goal of water quality which provides for the protection and propagation of fish, shellfish, and wildlife and provides for recreation in and on the water be achieved, by July 1, 1983.

These lofty ecological goals could not be achieved through the limited jurisdiction (ordinary high water mark) traditionally exercised by the Corps of Engineers (Corps). *Such jurisdiction is inadequate to the purpose.* (Scott 1981, p11) (Emphasis added.)

Another argument that had been proffered by the Corps and private defendants was that the term "navigable" was meant to restrict the reach of the CWA to the traditional Rivers and Harbors Act jurisdiction. Judge Scott, in separating the two laws, stated:

Although 101(a)(1) refers to the discharge of pollutants in the 'navigable waters', it is clear that Congress was not referring to 'navigable waters' in the usual physical sense. In fact the statutory definition mentions no physical characteristics such as width, depth, volume or flow. It mentions none of the characteristics normally associated with navigability such as 'ebb and flow of tide' or 'high water mark' or 'low water mark'. *The CWA defines 'navigable waters' in terms consistent with Congress' stated objective to restore and maintain the chemical, physical and biological integrity of the Nation's waters.* (Scott p12) (Emphasis added.)

The final substantive question had to do with the reach of the commerce clause of the U.S. Constitution. In answering this question, Judge Scott quoted Chief Justice Harlan Fiske Stone from a Supreme Court ruling:

> The power of Congress over interstate commerce is not confined to the regulation of commerce among the states. It extends to those activities intrastate which so affect interstate commerce or the exercise of the power of Congress over it as to make regulation of them appropriate means to the attainment of a legitimate end, the exercise of the granted power of Congress to regulate interstate commerce. *See M'Culloch v. Maryland, 4 Wheat 316, 421, 4 L.Ed. 579, 605.*

Scott opined that Congress had the right to be involved, and the use of the commerce clause in this case was not unconstitutionally vague.

All things had been settled except one. Was the EPA use of the science and law accurate, or was it arbitrary and capricious (in other words, was factual information ignored or a position taken without the support of facts)? In his Conclusion section, Judge Scott stated that the Lake Long tract was not a wetland from approximately mid-June–mid-July to the first of December each year. *But,* the tract was inundated or saturated adequate to satisfy the definition from December 1 to June 15 to a sufficient duration to support vegetation typically adapted for life in saturated soil conditions. When the case was appealed, the appellate court upheld his entire decision except for his error in adopting the FWS determination of wetlands on the tract instead of the EPA's, which he felt was inadequate. In federal court cases, the judge is restricted to making rulings under three questions: 1) Is the action in compliance with the U.S. Constitution?; 2) Were proper procedures followed in allowing prescribed involvement of the public in the government's decision?; and 3) Was the decision arbitrary or capricious?

Judge Scott fully addressed the question of constitutionality. The question of following proper procedures was not relevant because this was not an agency action requiring public review, but rather the implementation of regulations that had gone through the public review process. But he interjected his own wetlands determination into the opinion instead of ruling on whether the EPA's determination was adequate under the law. The Fifth Circuit Court of Appeals ruled on September 26, 1983, that Judge Scott had overstepped the role of the court in developing his own wetland boundaries, and ruled that the EPA determination was proper. With the exception of this single error, Judge Nauman Scott set policy for determining the reach and extent of Waters of the United States for the next thirty years. The confirmation from the Fifth Circuit expanded the decision beyond Louisiana to include Mississippi and Texas. The Corps had to accept that bottomland hardwood wetlands were waters of the U.S. for the Lower Mississippi, Atchafalaya and Sabine Rivers, three of the most significant river basins feeding the Gulf of Mexico.

On March 26, 1984, the Corps issued a regulatory guidance letter to all Corps employees relative to the Fifth Circuit decision to uphold Judge Scott's opinion. In "RGL 84-05, Subject: AGRICULTURAL CONVERSION, Fifth Circuit Decision in Avoyelles VS Marsh," the Corps made this simple opening statement:

> On September 26, 1983, the United States Court of Appeals for the Fifth Circuit issued its decision in Avoyelles Sportsman's League v. Marsh. This decision is explained below and is adopted nationwide.

After decades of wetlands being seen as "useless swamps" or "wastelands," the people of the United States, through the legal process, had declared that these natural treasures were valued and worthy of preservation for the intrinsic services they provide. That decision stood for nearly three decades until the U.S. Supreme Court brought confusion to the question of waters of the U.S. in the Solid Waste Agency of Northern Cook County and John A. Rapanos cases. This small group of parish sportsmen and women had changed conservation history. To the plaintiffs and those who supported increased protections for these incredible natural resources, Judge Scott was a hero. To the defendants and those who supported the unlimited rights of private landowners, Judge Scott was a villain. I, for one, revere his name today as someone who made the law come alive and work for the people of the United States and the natural resources that belong to them.

• • •

Just down the road in Morgan City, Louisiana, Sarah's sister Fernell and a group of determined women were also creating conservation history in their battle against a company that, instead of cleaning the environment, was polluting it. Marine Shale Processors claimed it was decontaminating hazardous waste and disposing of it in an environmentally friendly manner. Fernell and a few of her friends looked into the operations of the company and discovered it was lying to the public. Owner Jack Kent, they believed, was intentionally dumping dangerous wastes into lands and waters around their community instead of properly neutralizing contaminants and disposing of the clean material. The U.S. Department of Justice, EPA and Louisiana Department of Environmental Quality eventually agreed with these assertions and brought legal action against the company. It took over two decades, but these tenacious conservationists were able to see Marine Shale settle the case for $15 million, in addition to Jack Kent agreeing to never engage in the waste management business again and one of Marine Shale's main customers, Southern Wood Piedmont Company, paying $200,000 to put a protective cap over hazardous waste at a processing site. The world was changing in its view of these significant natural resources because local people were learning to make a difference by working together. Louisiana wetlands were woven into the fabric of Herman and Nell's lives. It was a proud time for the Reed clan.

• • •

Russ Earnest was a tall man of slender build, black hair and a dry wit. He was the area manager of the Jackson Area, which included Mississippi, Arkansas, Louisiana and parts of Alabama. Bob Misso was the assistant area manager for environment, making him the area supervisor over our office. Bob never gave us anything but his full support and didn't seem to care whether he had permission. If in his mind it was the right thing to do, full speed ahead. Russ was an old "fish squeezer" who had come up through the hatchery system and had a love for the non-feathery constituents we were there to conserve. On a visit to Greer's Ferry National Fish Hatchery, he came upon a bear of a man down in a raceway cleaning the aftermath of a few thousand fish that had lived there for several months, which is neither nice-smelling nor clean duty. He said hello to the guy in the raceway and got "If you're not going to help, get the hell out of here" in response. Russ loved this kind of no-nonsense approach to the job and appreciated David Charles Frederick and his "Kill 'em all and let God sort 'em out" attitude. He prodded Dave to switch over to Ecological Services from Fisheries because there was more need for a combative attitude dealing with the Corps than with fishes, and Russ was leaving to go to DC to work in Ecological Services with Mike Spear. Dave thought about it and agreed. He decided he didn't have any love for the Corps anyway. Dave joined the Vicksburg office in 1980, and that U.S. marine and I immediately hit it off. Charles agreed that I needed help working the 404 permits in the Yazoo Basin, Arkansas and north Louisiana and assigned Dave to work with me. I, in turn, was to teach Dave about the jurisdictional wetlands turnaround that we had just gone through and, together, we were to stop all the bottomland hardwood wetland losses. No problem.

Dave was about 5 feet 10 inches tall, 220 pounds and broad shoulders. He was a Vietnam marine and was awarded a Purple Heart for wounds he sustained there. He openly admitted he had lingering PTSD and that, based on what I had observed in my father, endeared him even more to me. We became brothers for life, and he was always there for me. His wife, Joyce, was the exact opposite personality. She was sweet, always smiled and was working toward becoming a nurse. Her affectionate way of describing Dave was "grubby, chubby and illiterate." He liked that. But many people over time made the mistake of thinking this direct-speaking bruiser was slow. He was highly intelligent and trapped more than one with his backstreet façade.

Together, we started doing all we could to see that permit requests for clearing of bottomland hardwood wetlands were working and an actual recommendation given. Nonetheless, there were still more requests than we could physically work, so we continued to send "No Action" letters, meaning we were unable to comment on many permits due to staffing constraints. Dave was a fast learner and soon capable of visiting a site on his own and making defensible wetland determinations. For me, Dave was a godsend. I was starting to feel the pressure of all those new permit requests and my inability to handle them. The guilt of a biologist seeing the natural resources lost due to one's workload can really have an impact. Self-blame sets in regardless of the truth that it is beyond your control. Dave helped there, as did training others.

In July 1980, Gary Hickman, the new area manager, received a letter from the Corps of Engineers Waterways Experiment Station asking if I could be borrowed to help teach an interagency course in Alaska on the new jurisdictional wetland methodology. The course would apply the techniques we had submitted to the court in 1979 and defended in 1980, and which methodology the court had accepted. The course would occur 28 July to 5 August 1980 and would include "members of all major Federal agencies, Congressional staffers, State agencies, and the private sector." This was a wonderful opportunity to take what we had built and successfully argued in court and show its applicability from Louisiana wetlands to the North Slope of Alaska. Wetlands are the same all over the world and, even where there is only about 18 inches of soil before hitting 2,000 feet of permafrost, there is still mottling and gleying, willow species only a couple of inches tall, and consistent functions. I had never been to Alaska and was really hoping I would be allowed to assist. Since Dave was there to help cover my absence, Charles allowed me to go.

Flying to Alaska from Vicksburg, Mississippi, was the longest trip I had ever taken as a civilian. Bo Smith and Terry Huffman from the Waterways Experiment Station were my traveling companions, and they made the trip a pleasure. When I made my connection in Portland and flew on to Anchorage, we passed over Mount St. Helens. On May 18, 1980, the previously dormant volcano exploded with tremendous force and created serious threats to human life and all of the surrounding natural resources. As we flew over it in July, smoke was still coming out of the crater, and the devastation was clearly visible. The Mount St. Helens eruption reminded me that there are only four real drivers of habitat creation: water (to include ice), fire, wind and volcanos (a mixture of fire with melted elements). I would return to the area a decade later to work in the Portland Regional Office, and the impacts were still being felt in the towns, streams and forests.

Inside the arctic circle, the depth of true soil was sometimes as little as 12–18 inches, and the plants seldom grew taller than a few inches in the truncated growing season. One of the fascinating things about the tundra is the gradual shifting of the ice and the pressure it exerts. Flying over the North Slope in summer, one can easily see depressions that hold water, and areas around them that don't. As the permafrost

Arctic Polygons (Courtesy of USFWS)

thaws and refreezes each year near the surface, pressure is exerted by the newly forming ice, and polygon-shaped areas are created. These polygons can have high centers as a result of ice being pushed toward the center, or low centers as a result of melting and water loss. This highly specific ecosystem evolved to provide subtle, but different habitats during the summer months for the high energy demands of arctic wildlife. Some species of willow (*Salix* spp.) only reach a height of a few inches, but that vegetation, along with lichens and other food sources, sustain animal life ranging from complete herds of caribou on down to ptarmigans within the food chain for tundra species.

Visiting the North Slope also allowed me to see the expansive efforts by the oil and gas industry to recover fossil energy, particularly from Prudhoe Bay, which sits in the North Slope Borough. The oil and gas operations were built by laying several feet of gravel over an area greater than 213,000 acres. The oil is transported through the Trans-Alaska Pipeline, which runs from Prudhoe Bay to Valdez, Alaska. On March 24, 1989, one of the largest oil spill disasters in American history occurred when the *Exxon Valdez*, an oil tanker headed for Long Beach, California, with crude oil from Prudhoe Bay, went aground on Bligh Reef in Prince

William Sound. The effects of that spill would be debated for decades.

As an instructor, I learned more than I could have possibly imparted. Seeing how all the wetland characteristics are the same no matter where wetlands occur helped me become an even stronger follower of the "naturalist" approach to ecosystem science. Often, scientists find themselves absorbed in a single attribute of the ecosystem and fail to see the connectivity of all things. A naturalist looks for the synergy and interdependence of all life. That lesson proved valuable throughout my career. Perhaps the most valuable gift of being a scientist is the freedom to be a student of nature and God's creations, knowing we can never fully understand all its workings.

...

On November 4, 1980, Ronald Wilson Reagan was elected president of the United States. He named James Watt, an ultra-conservative from Wyoming, to be his secretary of the interior. Watt was a fundamentalist Christian and ardent supporter of the Sagebrush Rebellion, a western U.S. effort to stop the acquisition and growth of federal land holdings, and to convey lands currently owned by the federal government to the states. Reagan went on to nominate Ray Arnett, a man who loved waterfowl hunting and wetlands and was Reagan's director of the California Department of Fish and Game, as assistant secretary for Fish, Wildlife and Parks. About three years later we would find out that the Sagebrush Rebellion secretary of the interior also loved wetlands.

...

The other Corps project to which I was assigned to help evaluate and prepare a Fish and Wildlife Coordination Act (FWCA) report was in response to the Yazoo Area Pump Study. Of all the Corps projects under study, this was the most ludicrous. Wetlands had been systematically drained by Corps projects from the top of the Yazoo Delta all the way down to the bottom, where the Yazoo River flowed into the Mississippi River near Eagle Lake, Mississippi. To stop the Mississippi River from backing up the Yazoo River during flood events, a levee was constructed from the Mississippi mainline levee on the east to the hillside on the west. A one-way flow structure was built on Steele Bayou that would allow water to flow out when the Mississippi was low, but prevent Mississippi water from going into the basin during floods. To add insult to natural resource injury, the Pump Study would place massive pumps on top of the connecting levee so that drainage water from within the basin could be pumped over the levee into the higher Mississippi on the other side. This would essentially drive the last nail in the coffin for the Yazoo Basin and its rich natural resource history, all in the name of allowing bottomland hardwood wetlands to be drained and cleared for increased agriculture.

The ninety-foot elevation was the annual flood level for what was now known as the "Yazoo Sump," the last bastion of flooded bottomland hardwoods in the Yazoo Delta. Charles McCabe was the lead biologist on the evaluation, with help from Robert Barkley and me. Because of my previous excursion into past projects during the preparation of "The Yazoo Basin: An Environmental Overview," I was able to write most of the historical project perspective and reiterate what had happened in the basin. Charlie was a seasoned journeyman biologist and had a fire in his gut to fight the Corps. We got along just fine. He was a man of slight build, about 5 feet 8 inches and 150 pounds. His eyes would glow with fire when he was angry, which thankfully wasn't directed at me very often. Charlie was a true outdoorsman. If a turkey flew across the stream to roost, Charlie would strip naked in the winter, hold his clothes above his head and walk in cold, chest-deep water to get to his prey.

We all knew that a lot was riding on this report. The Backwater Pumps project was authorized for study in 1943, but could never pass muster as being appropriate for either environmental *or* economic reasons. Throughout the years, the Corps would raise the head of this ugly pig to see if it could get beyond the study phase. Because the project would be so devastating for the remaining Yazoo wetlands, it never did go further. I viewed this project as being similar to a feral hog; it is non-native, doesn't belong in this ecosystem and causes horrific damage. The feral hog is one of the most habitat-destroying animals in the south. We didn't want to be the ones that let the pumps slip through the gauntlet and make it to project authorization. The report was released on June 11, 1982, and contained sixty-one pages of text and an equal amount of documentation in the appendices to support the assertions.

The transmittal letter set the tone for the entire document and the heavy ammunition we intended to use. The following are a few paragraphs from the letter:

> The Yazoo Area Pump Study is typical of previous water resource planning in the Yazoo Basin and the Lower Mississippi River Valley. These planning efforts have attempted in a methodical manner (on a project by project basis), to solve one project area's problems simply by pushing identifiable problems downstream. This process of solving one problem by creating another is the very foundation of the Yazoo Area Pump Project.
>
> The proposed project is a response to previous flood control efforts in the Yazoo Basin that have, over a span of forty years, expended an estimated $800 million to create an extensive flood control system which deliberately expedites the drainage of over 4,000 square miles into the extreme lower Yazoo Basin for sump storage. Simply stated, the purpose of the Yazoo pumps is to evacuate, through pumping, the interior drainage that accumulates behind the Yazoo Area levee whenever high stages on the Mississippi River prevent gravity drainage.
>
> Completion of the pumping plant would, however, eliminate this sump storage function and in the process insure a continuum

of upstream and downstream flood control problems. Thus, the problem being addressed in the Yazoo Area Pump Study is very much a result of previous Federal flood control projects, and the proposed solution, a pumping plant, might well dictate a similar conclusion in future Federal planning efforts.

The enabling legislation for the Yazoo Pumps, the Flood Control Acts of 1941 and 1965, authorized substantial and expansive structural flood control features. However, these authorizations were predicated on a realization that 'It cannot be claimed that the Government is under obligation to afford equal consideration to all alluvial valley lands. That is a physical impossibility. No great engineering project is ever carried through to completion without the destruction of some existing or prospective property values for the greater good of the general community.' (House Document 359) Subsequently, extensive structural measures were authorized in the Yazoo Basin to provide flood protection to the lands above 90 feet msl [mean sea level, or the average height of the surface of the sea for all stages of the tide]; and *those lands below 90 feet msl, predominately forested wetlands, were dedicated to flood storage and related benefits.* (USFWS 1982) (Emphasis added.)

The report went on to say:

The issues of the Yazoo Area Pump Project are not those of weighing human health, safety, and welfare against fish and wildlife and related natural resources. A conclusion of this nature avoids the problem by instead concentrating on the symptoms. The issues are whether the remaining natural resources of the Yazoo Area will be forgone to expand flood susceptible land use into a federally dedicated sump for a Federal drainage system that extends over 4,000 square miles. Flood control in the Yazoo Area is a proper Federal role. Complex water resource problems exist. These problems need not, nor should not, however, be addressed in a single purpose fashion so prevalent in the past. The same or comparable level of flood control cannot be provided to the entire 4,000 square mile portion of the Yazoo Basin without in turn delivering these same problems downstream. The 1941 and 1965 Flood Control Acts acknowledged this. *The creation of the Yazoo Area sump was the acknowledgement by Congress that an area must be available to store flood waters.* To do otherwise was contrary to the mainstem flood control objectives. These realities are as true today as they were in 1941. (Emphasis added.)

The report concluded with the final admonishment to the Corps for continuing to try to breathe life into this project, and the threat to elevate to higher authority:

If, as a result of the review process, the mitigation plan is eliminated or substantially altered, the Service would oppose the project and consider it a candidate for referral to the Council on Environmental Quality (CEQ).

The president's Council on Environmental Quality is the White House version of a referee between departments of government when environmental disagreements occur. This would literally mean that the arguments from both sides would be heard by an office that directly represents the president. It would take nearly another thirty years, but that would eventually happen. For the time being, the report was enough to cause the Corps to back away and await yet another day, when their hand might be stronger. However, a project authorized for study never goes away unless it is deauthorized for study by Congress or some other action. That action would not occur until I was in my final year with the FWS.

CHAPTER 3

POWDR Bill and Alaska

James G. Watt became the forty-third secretary of the interior on January 23, 1981, and served in that role until November 8, 1983. A proponent of the Sagebrush Rebellion, he was known for making his brash statements as a regular course of business. Watt was a "born again Christian" and believed all his decisions should be based on those beliefs. He believed the natural resources had been given to man by the Creator and were here for us to use, insofar as time permitted. In testimony before the House Interior Committee on February 5, 1981, he stated:

> That is the delicate balance the Secretary of the Interior must have: to be steward for the natural resources for this generation as well as future generations. I do not know how many future generations we can count on before the Lord returns; whatever it is we have to manage with a skill to leave the resources needed for future generations.

In another famous quote, he said "My responsibility is to follow the Scriptures which call upon us to occupy the land until Jesus returns." In October 1983 he said "I never use the words Democrats and Republicans. It's liberals and Americans." No one ever accused Secretary Watt of being timid. The editorial cartoonists of the time had a field day with his outrageous sentiments, or at least with the way he would say them. One cartoon showed Secretary Watt carrying a sign that read "The end is near" while it lambasted the unprecedented increase in coal leases offered on Interior lands.

One quote he vehemently denied was "God gave us these things to use. After the last tree is felled, Christ will come back." Watt responded to that statement by saying "I never said it. Never believed it. Never even thought it. I know no Christian who believes or preaches such error. The Bible commands conservation—that we as Christians be careful stewards of the land and the resources entrusted to us by the Creator." But perhaps the most astonishing statement he made was in November 1983 when talking to the U.S. Chamber of Commerce in reference to members of the U.S. Commission on Fair Market Value Policy for Federal Coal Leasing: "We have every mixture you can have. I have a black, a woman, two Jews and a cripple. And we have talent."

As an employee of the U.S. Fish and Wildlife Service (FWS) and U.S. Department of the Interior, I was sometimes asked what I thought about the secretary, specifically if his views alarmed me. My response was that I never worry about the one making outrageous public statements, particularly about things they don't have exclusive authority to control. My concern is always about the one who is quiet, working behind the scenes and out of view until the damage is done. While I thought he was often an embarrassment, I didn't see James Watt as the latter and didn't believe he had the ability to deliver on most of his agenda. But one thing I didn't expect was his quiet appreciation of wetlands, especially if they were not in his western U.S.

I had become supervisor of the FWS Clear Lake Ecological Services (ES) Office, and in January 1983 I received a message from Mike Spear that I was to report to Washington for a work assignment. All he knew was that I would be working on a team, and the effort was about wetlands. I asked how long it would last, and he said to count on a few days to a week. When I got to the Interior Building and went to the appointed conference room on the third floor, I saw a few familiar and equally clueless faces. Nevin Holmberg was the branch chief for permits and licenses in Ecological Services in the Washington Office. Felix Smith was from the Sacramento field office and an expert on the public trust doctrine. This doctrine espouses that the natural resources *belong to the people* and are held in trust by the government for all the people. It is this principle that is the foundation for many of the authorities of the FWS for migratory species, water and minerals. Ralph Tiner was a scientist from the Patuxent, Maryland, research unit and an expert on the wetlands and habitat needs of waterfowl. Don Barry, a young attorney I had met only once before, worked for the Office of the Solicitor for the Department of the Interior, and he had impressed me as very capable and committed to conserving natural resources.

Don was the only one who knew why we were there, and he had been told he was not permitted to explain. That, he said, would come through the phone sitting in the middle of the table. At that time, there was a popular TV show called *Mission Impossible*, and each episode began with a tape recorder in the middle of a table giving the assignment, should the leading actor (Peter Graves) decide to accept it. At the end of the message, the recording would say "This tape will self-destruct in ten seconds." As we looked at the phone, we couldn't help but draw the humorous parallel with the TV show and its drama.

After about ten minutes, the phone rang and over the speaker we could hear the voice of Secretary Watt. We found out later he was only a few floors above us but, for his own reasons, decided to give the assignment in this manner. He thanked us for being there and helping to strike a blow for wetlands conservation. We looked at each other in amazement. The rumors had been that he strongly disliked Ecological Services and nearly any form of private lands regulation. He went on to tell us that he wanted to leave a legacy of protection for wetlands through the passage of a law to conserve wetlands for future generations. He said he loved waterfowl, as did Assistant Secretary Ray Arnett, and believed they were critical to future water needs. If we were stunned at first, those last words left us paralyzed. Here was the secretary who was so famously quoted for wanting to mine minerals and harvest timber telling us he wanted a cornerstone of his legacy to be conservation of wetlands!

The name of the law would be the Protect Our Wetlands and Duck Resources Act, or POWDR for short. The POWDR bill we were to draft was to include whatever we believed necessary and prudent to ensure quality waterfowl habitat and healthy wetlands for all the functions they perform. Felix was first to speak: "Mr. Secretary, so you're directing us to write a bill that would include whatever provisions we believe to be necessary and prudent to ensure wetland conservation and health?"

"Yes," came the reply from Watt. "I want you to have a free hand as scientists to tell us administrators what we need to hear. As with any bill, it may go through many changes on the Hill, but it must start with your recommendations." We thanked him genuinely for being willing to support wetlands conservation and allowing us the privilege of providing the draft. Throughout the entire process of the POWDR bill, that support was always obvious:

> A lot of stuff we did led to a lot of frustration. We would work hard to push forward what we believed to be the right thing to do, just to have some uninformed pencil pusher from upstairs mess it up. But working on this bill was one of those rare times that never happened. We were respected and left alone to carry out our assignment from start to finish. (Holmberg 2020)

The division offices of the U.S. Fish and Wildlife Service were scattered across Washington, and research was at the Patuxent Lab in Maryland. There apparently wasn't enough office space available in the Interior Building, so each function was housed in a different location. Ecological Services had their offices at 14th and K Street, NW, an area known for hookers and strip joints. One evening as I was leaving their office headed back to the hotel, a hooker approached me. I smiled and told her thank you, but I wasn't interested. She reached around and grabbed my butt and said, "I just wanted to make sure you weren't a cop," apparently feeling for a gun. I stepped up my pace and went to the hotel. After we got our "Mission Impossible" assignment—which we had chosen to accept—Nevin and I, along with Russ Earnest, who was the division chief for Ecological Services, returned to 14th and K to begin our work on the POWDR bill. This was a new challenge, and we knew we would need to draw on others who had experience in writing legislation.

Nevin was in his early forties and had earned his stripes running the Hawaii ES office and then as field supervisor in Green Bay, Wisconsin, prior to going to DC as the branch chief. He was an expert in Section 404, and I was pleased to have him and his experience on this assignment. Felix was about a decade older and had long argued for the conservation of natural resources as property of the people, not of individuals. I had never met Ralph Tiner, but his reputation as a waterfowl and wetlands scientist was excellent. I felt honored to be included with this talented team.

I always enjoyed my details in D.C. because it gave me a chance to work with Russ again. Russ wanted nothing more than to support his troops in whatever they did. He wasn't much for giving speeches, but his demeanor and dedication reminded me of Lynn Greenwalt. He told us that whatever we needed out of his division was at our disposal for the POWDR bill, but the truth was that we simply got a copy of another law as a guide and started filling in the information for each section as we would like to see protections written. We weren't naïve and knew that our draft would likely look nothing like the finished product, but it was certain that if we didn't write what we believed, it wouldn't have a chance of being included.

We worked like madmen for three days and then went back home to clean up the draft and await the opportunity to brief USFWS Director Bob Jantzen. When Bob came in as President Reagan's nominee, he brought a couple of people with him into positions that up until then had generally been reserved for career FWS people. Don Minnich had been the director of Colorado Parks and Wildlife when Jantzen was director of Arizona Game and Fish, and Bob gave Minnich the senior executive position of regional director in Denver. The senior executive service (SES) had been created by Congress at the behest of President Jimmy Carter as a means to recognize the civilian equivalent of a military general or admiral. The Civil Service Reform Act of 1978 established the General Schedule (GS) grades of 1 through 15, with 16–18 being combined into one SES super grade with tiers equivalent to the four stars of the military. President Carter, as a former U.S. Navy officer, believed that an admiral/general should be capable of assuming command of any activity. Therefore, GS 16–18s should be treated the same as those military ranks and be capable of assignment anywhere in government. The law stated that the SES was formed to "ensure that the executive management of the Government of the United States is responsive to the needs, policies, and goals of the Nation and otherwise is of the highest quality."

The assumption was that these leaders possess well-honed executive skills and share a broad perspective on government and a public service commitment that is grounded in the U.S. Constitution. This view of leadership, however, mistakenly overlooked the experience and background so important in government when carrying out specific activities guided by specific laws. To be an effective leader of civilians, one must know the intricacies of the subject matter and become a teacher as well as commander. Civilians cannot be ordered to respect the leader. While in the military, I heard over and again that I was to respect the uniform even if I didn't respect the person. It doesn't work that way outside the military. To gain the respect of the workforce, one must demonstrate knowledge and experience to be able to teach, as well as command. Bringing in someone from outside the federal government to assume the coveted role of regional director didn't sit well with employees of the FWS.

After we had what we believed to be a clean draft of the POWDR bill, a date and time to brief Director Jantzen and whomever else he felt should be present was set. When we arrived at the director's conference room on the third floor of the Department of the Interior Building, we found that the room was filled with interested attendees. Except for seats reserved for us, it was standing room only. This assignment had come directly from Secretary Watt, and everyone wanted to hear what we were proposing. Several associate directors were in the room, as well as departmental attorneys and Don Minnich, who was apparently in DC on business. We didn't get far into the presentation when Minnich broke in and said "Get rid of all that extra wetlands stuff and stick to ducks. That's our responsibility and that's what this should be about." No one on our team worked for Don nor held back in telling him this was our assignment, not his, and he could talk with the secretary if he felt so inclined.

Felix was livid. Jantzen quickly saw this briefing going the wrong way and calmed everything down by saying all views are respected, but no changes would be made, and that "the secretary's direction was clear." At the end of the briefing, the director said he believed we had stayed true to our assignment. Later, over a beer, a red-faced Felix kept saying "Ducks! Ducks! Fucking Ducks! That's all that dumb son-of-a-bitch thinks wetlands are about! If he doesn't understand wetland functions then he should keep his fucking mouth shut!" "Felix," I said, "tell us how you really feel about it." Nevin said, "I agree with Dale. In the end, the director sided with us. It's now moving forward with our draft as we wrote it." That seemed to help, but after what all of us had been through in trying to get wetlands the protection they deserved, it was hard to swallow that a senior executive would think ducks were the only objective.

When we met with Assistant Secretary Ray Arnett, we found someone who was "terse but supportive." (Holmberg 2020) It was clear that he wanted this to succeed and understood the importance of wetlands for waterfowl, as well as other functions. He asked us to assess the reach of the law if it were passed. In other words, how many acres of wetlands would be covered by this bill if passed? How many ducks would be conserved? Other quantitative measurements? Director Jantzen allowed us to bring in staff from the National Wetlands Inventory to help with this assessment. FWS wetland mapping efforts had been going on since the 1950s and were primarily focused on waterfowl habitat, but there were other ways to correlate the information.

While it would be literally impossible to calculate the exact extent of the coverage, we did our best to provide estimates. As the bill moved through Congress, Secretary Watt's prediction proved correct, and the bill morphed significantly. By 1984, a near-complete makeover had significantly transformed our draft. The bill was now called the Emergency Wetlands Resources Act with the focus on migratory waterfowl and, by the way, *also* wetlands. The Lake Ophelia case and its far-reaching ramifications were now well known, and many in Congress believed that wetlands would be protected through the Clean Water Act. The proposed law did include measures such as extension of the Wetlands Loan Act, funding for refuge operations and the Migratory Bird Conservation Fund, and an increase in the price of the federal duck stamp. The funds generated from the duck stamp are used solely to acquire wetlands and other waterfowl habitat.

The bill was ultimately passed and signed into law in 1986. While the Emergency Wetlands Resources Act looked very different from the POWDR bill we drafted, the system worked and we got a good lesson in legislative sausage making. Another significant lesson I took from the POWDR effort was to not assume what the person across the table from you supports or doesn't support. I had developed an opinion of Secretary Watt that wasn't very complimentary, and for good reason. Because of all the brash statements he had made about the environment, I assumed he would never put environmental concerns ahead of economic development. But he showed me, through his support for wetlands, that strong disagreement can occur when dealing with one subject, yet agreement can be reached when dealing with another. It depends upon the lens through which the various negotiators are looking.

That change in my approach made me begin to ask "Why are they upset?" in order to understand the issue, and see if there could be a way to ease concerns and still reach a positive end through negotiations. Too often we let the emotional delivery of a message push us into a defensive posture rather than looking past the emotion to the real concern. Throughout the entire process, we received neither pushback nor interference. Instead, all our efforts were completely supported all the way to the secretary. No leader's views are all correct, nor are they all incorrect. I still believe Secretary Watt was a poor secretary when it came to the larger set of environmental protections he was charged to administer, but he was a champion for wetlands and waterfowl and deserves recognition for that aspect of conservation.

• • •

The largest Corps of Engineers water development project we had was the Galveston Bay Area Navigation Study, also known as the Houston Ship Channel project. Houston was a forty-foot port, meaning it could handle only cargo ships that could navigate in water forty feet deep or less. The Port of Houston wanted desperately to increase the depth of the channel to fifty feet along the entire length of Galveston Bay. This was no small undertaking, and would move millions of cubic yards of dredged material throughout the bay. We assigned Fred Werner, one of our seasoned biologists, to lead the effort. While Fred was a character and quite the handful, there was no question about his capability to handle the project.

As part of my efforts to be the face of the office, I struck up a relationship with Harold Scarlett, the environmental writer for the *Houston Post*. I learned through the Lake Ophelia effort that biologists were terrible about getting in front of the public and providing them the information they would need to support a given effort. Biologists seemed to think "Just trust me, I'm your representative on science," but real strength in conservation is found in eliminating public ignorance and replacing it with facts and knowledge. We were determined to have the people of Houston understand what these projects meant to them and their quality of life. Through the different issues, Harold Scarlett had learned to trust what we told him because we were clear about what we could prove and what constituted our opinion. There is no greater asset a reporter can have than a source that can be trusted every time. Trust drives all relationships, be they in love, friendship, or business. We believed that the Galveston Bay project would have been disastrous, and Harold helped us educate the public.

I was determined to leave the biologists alone to do their work and accepted the new responsibilities I had as their supervisor. Carlos Mendoza, our lead biologist on Section 404, came to my office one day and relayed a discussion he had with Marcos de la Rosa, chief of the permits branch at the Galveston District of the Corps.

"Marcos asked me today, Who the hell does Dale Hall think he is? He's a GS-13 thinking he is equal to the district engineer, who is a full bird colonel, equal to a GS-15 in civilian rank."

"Carlos, if I allowed Marcos to be seen as my equal because of GS grade, where would that leave you? Do you think the folks at the Corps would give you the time of day? Our agencies are different in where *authority* rests. Marcos can be overruled by someone walking down the hall. My authority can only be overruled in Albuquerque. It isn't about me, but about the position of field supervisor. The Fish and Wildlife Service has decided that the *position* I hold is equal to that of the district engineer. As long as they trust me in this position, I will do all I can to make sure I don't disrespect it in any way, and work to ensure that you and all the other staff receive the respect *you* deserve from other agencies. Marcos knows I have a direct line to the colonel, and he doesn't like it. But that's the way it is."

I always believed I had a clear responsibility to support those staff under my responsibility, and to ensure that other agencies knew they spoke for our entire agency when sitting at their table. It is about neither ego nor the power of command. It is about ensuring respect for everyone on the team.

One of the main issues we had not been equipped to handle in the past, but now could, was that of environmental contaminants. The FWS had created the Environmental Contaminants Program at the urging of, and support from, Congressman Sidney Yates. I was told Congressman Yates's wife had died of cancer that he believed was tied to chemicals dumped into the environment. As chair of the House Appropriations subcommittee that oversaw the FWS and Forest Service, he funded the creation of this new program. Rachel Carson wrote about the potential destruction of the environment by contaminants in her 1962 book *Silent Spring*, but there had been no significant appropriations to allow the FWS to act on that knowledge prior to support from Congressman Yates. Within that program, Clear Lake was one of the first field offices to receive funding for a contaminants specialist. The significance of this new conservation tool cannot be overemphasized. It was truly historic.

Dr. Brian Cain joined our office as the contaminants specialist about the same time I came over from Vicksburg. He had been a professor at Texas A&M and was extremely capable. Through his knowledge of the process by which dangerous chemicals are "sealed" over time into the layers of sediment beneath the bay bottom, we were able to do core samples and identify the exact chemicals that would be released by a dredge cutting ten feet deeper. In addition, bays are where freshwater flows into salt water to create the highly productive estuary, where salinity gradients go from near zero to nearly thirty-five parts per thousand of pure seawater just outside the mouth of the bay. A ship channel creates a direct avenue for the heavier seawater to move up the estuary underneath the lighter, fresher water. This, in turn, gets pushed out into the estuary during storms, significantly disrupting the salinity curves (isohalines) of the bay. Oysters, a prime commercial fishery in Galveston Bay, thrive in salinities less than ten parts per thousand. By digging the Houston Ship Channel ten additional feet in depth, the entire salinity equilibrium of the bay would be in turmoil, and that would be in addition to highly toxic chemicals being released into the water column.

When we gave a presentation to the Texas Parks and Wildlife Commission (TPWD) on these two serious issues, and the dangers they posed to the aquatic resources of the bay, the commissioners immediately broke into private conversations on the dais. One commissioner was an attorney in Houston and knew the issues well. Dick Morrison loved Galveston Bay and became the leader in TPWD's attack on the Corps. He was quite ready to take the Corps to court for ignoring the science of a project that could have a devastating effect on the bay and the fisheries resources TPWD was charged with managing. One alternative the Corps summarily dismissed, but we advanced, was the Port of Freeport. Corps regulations required the assessment of port needs to be "Regional," not simply port by port. Freeport was significantly closer to the Gulf, offered opportunity for dredged material to be used for bird islands, had railway access and would have less costs. But the Corps was hell-bent on deepening the Houston Ship Channel.

Jim Blackburn, an attorney and law professor at Rice University, joined with the state and our team to fight the project. Following our presentation to the Commission in Austin, Dick Morrison, representing TPWD, scheduled a public meeting in Houston to have the state receive testimony regarding the desires of Texas residents and the future of Galveston Bay. The auditorium at University of Houston, Clear Lake, was full, and TPWD heard an earful from angry fishermen, oystermen and pleasure boaters who were dead-set against this project. That's all Dick and the state needed to hear.

Harold Scarlett did his job and regularly ran articles giving Houstonians factual information about how the Corps didn't seem committed to a proper analysis of either impacts or alternatives. This was truly a paradigm change for the state of Texas and TPWD. Traditionally, they would have never thought of entering the fray on a federal project that was driven by economic growth, especially shipping. The new information about the dangers of environmental contaminants was especially powerful. Conservation risks were changing in the eyes of the public and state agencies, and Texas deserves credit for stepping up when it mattered. This was no small challenge. But the Corps, by law, could not build a project without the approval of the governor, which was no longer guaranteed. The FWS had clearly established a reputation of only challenging issues when there was adequate science. The public trusted us. In just a few short years, that public trust would change, and every government decision would be challenged. But for now, we held their respect and they followed our lead.

Our Fish and Wildlife Coordination Act (FWCA) report to the Corps ended with the notice that, if the obvious deficiencies in their planning process were not corrected, the FWS would elevate the project to the president's Council on Environmental Quality (CEQ) for resolution of issues. The Corps seldom wins when they have to explain to CEQ why they are taking the action they have chosen and, therefore, they tend to make significant adjustments to head off that kind of embarrassment. We were serious and had obtained permission from the Albuquerque and Washington offices to include elevation language in our FWCA report, as well as in our public comments. One of the most serious mistakes that can be made when in a conflict over the environment is to make a statement (threat) without clearly knowing it can be carried out. Obtaining support, in writing, for the elevation language prior to release of our report was a non-negotiable condition.

The fifty-foot channel was never approved, partly because of the professional work done by a dedicated field staff in Clear Lake with state and public partners, and partly because the move toward super tankers subsided, thus reducing the need for a deeper channel. Regardless of the actual reasons, it was our job to make sure that all concerns were honestly and properly addressed *before* the project moved forward to the point of irretrievable impacts. The tool of environmental contaminants analyses had struck a significant blow. Many complain about the slow pace of government decision-making. The Galveston Bay Area Navigation Study proved to be an excellent case study of why irretrievable government actions should not be rushed to judgment.

• • •

Bob Jantzen left the U.S. Fish and Wildlife Service for other pursuits and, in 1986, President Reagan nominated Frank Dunkle to be the director. By all accounts, Frank was a very unusual man who carried anger with him wherever he went. Since a nominee to a Senate-confirmed position cannot engage in the day-to-day operations of the agency or post to which she or he is nominated, Frank was forced to sit in Denver in a non-position until he was confirmed. This didn't improve Frank's disposition, nor did having Bob Gilmore, a career employee, receive consideration for the same position prior to Frank's selection. Dunkle viewed the world as people who were either for him or against him. There was no in-between. Having a sitting regional director as competition for the job he wanted, even though career people weren't seriously considered, placed Gilmore squarely in the "against Frank" column.

Sitting in Denver with no real assignment gave Frank time to read FWS manuals and learn about the existing structure. Jantzen had continued with program management, which meant that the Washington office program leadership (refuges, fisheries, ES, and others) had control of all the monies and could give assignments to the regional directors, who were their peers. Upon confirmation by the Senate, Frank immediately abolished program management and established line management. Line management placed decision-making in the direct chain of command to the field, which meant the assistant directors had responsibility to formulate and build the budget, but the regional directors had all authority in carrying out the budget. The field welcomed this, but Frank seemed intent on delivering it in a way sure to irritate and demean the assistant directors. He also made it one of his first orders of business to personally remove Bob Gilmore as regional director in Alaska and reassign him to DC in a function with an office in a closet, or very close to it. That was Frank Dunkle.

• • •

Any discussion of conservation history in the United States would be incomplete without understanding Alaska and the tremendous natural resources that occur there. Alaska is believed to have been first settled around 14,000 B.C.E., when migrants crossed what was then the Bering land bridge. The United States purchased Alaska from Russia in 1867. It is generally believed that it was Russia's concern that Alaska not fall into British hands, as well as the low trade received from Alaska, that led to its willingness to sell its possessions in North America. The U.S. Senate approved the purchase for $7.2 million, the rough equivalent of $130 million in 2020. Because Secretary of State William Seward was the champion for the acquisition, it became known as "Seward's Folly," or "Andrew Johnson's Bear Garden," and was unpopular until the discovery of gold.

The gold rushes of the 1890s brought an avalanche of mining prospectors looking for the riches they all believed they would find. Alaska was officially granted the status of a United States Territory in 1912, apparently in response to the need to protect U.S. interests. In 1942, Attu and Kiska, two outer Aleutian Islands, were occupied by the Japanese during World War II, making Alaska the only U.S. lands occupied by the Japanese. On January 3, 1959, Alaska became the forty-ninth state of the Union. By virtue of its expansive size, it immediately became the largest state by geography in the U.S., even if population reflected the opposite. This had been no easy path due to the sparse population, distance from the Oregon border, and low economic productivity. But interests changed quickly when the Japanese invaded Alaska and it became clear that Alaska provided a strategic military opportunity with Russia so close by. But the real impetus came in 1957, when oil was discovered at the

Swanson River on the Kenai Peninsula. President Eisenhower signed the Alaska Statehood Act on July 4, 1958, and paved the way for admission to the Union.

A legitimate attempt to describe Alaska's rich and vast natural resources would require volumes. From the marine waters of Bristol Bay to the tundra along the Arctic Ocean, Alaska is covered by beautiful mountains, dense forests, phenomenal fish and wildlife resources and a mixture of cultures that manifests the centuries of Asian and European influence. But equally abundant are the oil and gas reserves found beneath the shallow soils and permafrost. The discovery of oil on the North Slope at Prudhoe Bay in 1968 created a new urgency in deciding ownership of the 663,300-square-mile state, one twice the size of Texas. A pipeline would need to be built to transport the oil from Prudhoe Bay along the Arctic coast to Valdez in the south, where it could be loaded onto tankers and shipped to refineries. Permits would be required and landowners would need to be compensated. It was time to clearly identify who owned what.

The Native Alaskans believed they should have substantial lands returned to them that had been taken by European settlers in the past. Obviously, with the extra incentive of oil revenues, things began to heat up. In 1971, President Richard Nixon signed the Alaska Native Claims Settlement Act (ANCSA) into law, giving 44 million acres of land and a $963 million payment in exchange for all prior Native land claims. The settlement was divided among regional, urban and village "corporations," which managed their funds however they saw fit. Some did well; others didn't. Planning the pipeline was a massive undertaking: plotting a path across the tundra and through the Brooks Mountain Range, miles of unstable bogs, and engineering a design that would allow heated oil to traverse over shallow permafrost without melting the ice and then sinking, creating pipe ruptures.

It took six years to complete, but ultimately the pipeline functioned properly along the 800-mile path. There was significant involvement from the Fish and Wildlife Service throughout construction, and documentation of impacts was attempted but difficult to ascertain beyond the actual footprint. There was no precedent to guide the way. In response to the new revenues, Alaska established the Alaska Permanent Fund, in which one-quarter of all revenues generated from oil and gas would be deposited in a state account with each man, woman and child resident of Alaska receiving an annual royalty. It is the only fund like it in the nation and the clearest manifestation of the trust doctrine, through which the natural resources are owned by the people and held in trust by their government.

By 1980, pressure was growing to designate the remaining Alaska land base as federal, state or private. With fewer than 500,000 residents in the state, the most significant arguments were between the state and federal governments. On November 12, 1980, the Alaska National Interest Lands Conservation Act (ANILCA) was passed by Congress and signed into law by President Jimmy Carter on December 2. ANILCA, unlike ANCSA, not only decided ownership but also extended legal protections to the most significant amount of natural resource treasures to ever be done through one law. Immediately upon signing of the bill, more than 157 million acres received protection as national parks, national wildlife refuges, national monuments, scenic rivers, national forests, national recreation areas and conservation areas. The Arctic National Wildlife Refuge, the largest in the refuge system, received an additional 9.1 million acres through ANILCA, bringing its total to 19.6 million acres. However, Section 1002 of ANILCA placed a caveat on oil and gas exploration in the Arctic refuge and retained for Congress the responsibility to decide at some later date whether the nation needed energy resources sufficiently to intrude into the refuge. The lands identified in Section 1002 encompass approximately 1.5 million acres along the North Slope for possible development, but few proposals over the years ever amounted to more than 50,000 acres of the refuge. Decades later, the 2017 Tax Cuts and Jobs Act included the directive to the secretary of the interior to develop a program of lease offerings in the 1002 area over the following ten-year period. Congress, after years of debate, reached the conclusion that it was important enough to the nation to open these lands to oil and gas development, and directed the executive branch to carry it out.

A significant portion of the non–government agency work at the Clear Lake office, where I was the field supervisor, dealt with oil and gas in Texas and west Louisiana. The same companies that were headquartered in Houston also had a large presence in the Prudhoe Bay oil fields. I received a call one afternoon from Bob Jacobsen, assistant regional director, Ecological Services, in Anchorage. I knew Bob and respected his approach to conservation: find a solution and don't fool around. The field supervisor at Fairbanks, Jerry Stroebele, had left in March so he could dog-sled across the Iditarod Trail to Nome and assume the role of manager at Selawik National Wildlife Refuge. With spring breakup (when the ice melts) coming soon, Bob didn't have time to permanently fill the position before the critical, and short, summer field season.

Bob had talked to Jim Young (my assistant regional director in Albuquerque), and Jim had agreed to let me go on a detail to Fairbanks if I was willing. I asked two questions: 1) From when to when? 2) Will I be able to keep full per diem the entire summer, instead of the normal reductions over several months? The answers were "May to September" and "Yes." I needed both of those because I couldn't afford a house payment in Texas and an apartment in Fairbanks big enough for our family, and I wasn't going if they couldn't come. I had spent too much time away from them in my career and wasn't going to leave them out of this opportunity to see what my children and my wife, who was from Louisiana, had never seen.

In May of 1986, I flew to Alaska for my second time, but this time I only stayed a day in Anchorage to visit with Bob and then flew on to Fairbanks. Tony Booth and Jim Nilke were the two assistant field supervisors in Fairbanks, and I wanted them to be at ease that I wasn't seeking the job. I was there for a detail and needed their help more than they could know. I knew oil and gas but not placer mining and other significant disturbances that were occurring in Alaska.

On the flight to Fairbanks, I couldn't help but be awed by the majestic mountains, the beautiful streams and all the wonders of the Creator's hand. It is truly a natural resource wonderland. The field season had started on the North Slope and I needed to see what our work there entailed.

I had been to the town of Deadhorse and Prudhoe Bay to teach the wetlands class, but paid little attention to the massive gravel pad that had been laid by the energy companies to support the permanent exploration and development activities. The community of Deadhorse was home base for company employees, who worked shifts of twelve-hour days for one or two weeks, then a week back home. There were so many Texas workers flown up to work on the North Slope that the oil companies would charter planes or fill entire commercial flights with their crews, much the way they used helicopters to ferry crews to and from offshore rigs in the Gulf.

I knew it was a long, hard drive, but I asked Tony Booth if he would drive with me up the "Haul Road" from Fairbanks to Deadhorse. It was only open to company and government vehicles at that time, and he agreed. Thirteen hours later we arrived, wishing we could fly the truck and us back when we left! But it was a phenomenal trip crossing the Brooks Range. When we hit the tundra, the majesty of the summer was in full glory. Because of the seasonal thawing and freezing of the surface ice, unique structures called "polygons" are formed. Some polygons have low centers due that hold water in the summer. Others have high centers due to the pressure of the summer melt refreezing. In summer, the low-center polygons provide water and wetland habitat, while the high-center polygons become green with the sprouting of the small vegetative communities that populate them. I could see the significant impacts that had occurred to the tundra from oil and gas activities, but I could also see their relatively small size when compared to the millions of acres of pristine tundra.

One estimate I was given was that the entire Prudhoe Bay oil and gas development, outside the gravel pad, directly impacted 20,000 acres or less. But in an area that takes decades, if not a century, to recover from tire tracks across the tundra, that is no small number. Oil and gas development is generally restricted to winter months, when the tundra is covered with ice, but the temporary roads made of planks still left prints in some areas. Less invasive techniques were constantly being developed, but this was no minor oil field. One of the things that struck me was the relatively harsh lifestyle the native Alaskans lived. There were few to no paved roads; comforts we take for granted such as basic supplies had to be brought in by airplane or boat; and the residents endured extreme winter conditions nine months of the year.

After my time there, I never again argued that they should not be able to develop their communities and have the same luxuries as we. Yes, it is pristine and beautiful. But the people living there deserve the same human services and dignities that we in the Lower 48 take for granted. The condescension we impose without realizing it was burned into my conscience forever. I was reminded of places in Appalachia that were still denied municipal water or had an outhouse for a toilet. It is wrong for we who have life's necessities to espouse opposition to the basic needs of our fellow citizens. I vowed to spend the rest of my career working for *wise use* of our natural resources, rather than denying human necessities in the name of preservation.

It was nearing time for my detail to be over, but there was another conservation issue that was causing a lot of unchecked destruction. Placer mining is an extremely damaging means of mining, wherein high-pressure water hoses are used to blow out the riverbanks and then the broken soil checked for gold. The Corps had said this was not dredged or fill material, but rather waste material, so there was no need for a Section 404 permit. The EPA said the resulting sludge from hydraulic mining was not waste material, so there was no need for a refuse disposal permit. As a person who could make a lot of people angry and then leave, I thought taking on this issue was something I should do. The staff in

Alaska would have received unmitigated hell from politicians if they had written the letters, so I wrote them.

One letter went to the Corps, reporting several specific placer mining operations for deposition of dredged or fill material without a permit. I cited Judge Scott from the Avoyelles case, in which he clearly stated that soil was a fill material. By then, the Corps had made the judge's decision nationwide in scope. I then wrote a letter to the EPA, reporting these same operations as dumping waste into waters of the U.S. without a permit. Finally, I wrote to the U.S. Attorney for Alaska, provided that office with copies of the other two letters, and stated that the Fish and Wildlife Service would be fine with either decision, but that either the Corps or EPA had an obligation to regulate this highly destructive activity.

I signed all letters as the acting field supervisor of the Fairbanks office. About a week later, I flew back to Houston. When word got out that the FWS had sent these letters, Bob Jacobsen called me. "Thanks a lot! I just got a good ass chewing from the congressional delegation!" He told them I had left and gone back to Texas, and there was really nothing he could do about it. He laughed and said, "I'm not sure I would have told you OK had you asked, but it was nice being able to say I didn't know anything about it. Thanks for the help. Let's hope it makes a difference." The Corps and U.S. Attorney reviewed the letters and decided they had no good answer as to why this wasn't dredged and/or fill material, so placer mining became a regulated activity under Section 404.

I will always remember with reverence my time in Alaska and the beauty and majesty of the mountains, tundra and streams. On future visits, I found myself realizing that the awe I first felt had not subsided. But I will also remember the opportunity we have there to allow growth to be done reasonably, rather than the helter-skelter way it was done in the Lower 48. Native Alaskans deserve the same conveniences we have, and there is real opportunity to do it right this time. I was also humbled by the FWS employees who dedicated their lives to saving as much of these irreplaceable creations as possible.

CHAPTER 4

The Greatest Story Never Told

In 1987, I applied for the position of deputy assistant director–fisheries in Washington, D.C., not really believing I would get the position because it was in another U.S Fish and Wildlife (FWS) program. But I wanted to send the message that I was not only willing to come to D.C., but also willing to work in other programs. To my complete surprise, I was selected. Gary Edwards was the assistant director–fisheries, and was the other person Bob Jantzen had brought into the FWS at the SES (senior executive service) level from a state agency. Gary was genuine and understood fisheries from a state perspective, a good asset to have in building partnerships. He admitted to me that the reason I got the job was because none of the assistant regional directors, nor their deputies, were willing to move to D.C. Once again, I benefited by being willing to do what the agency needed me to do, even if it required me to yet again be without my family for a few months and cost me money in the move. And it did.

As I was preparing to leave the Clear Lake Ecological Services Office, *Houston Post* environmental writer Harold Scarlett came to visit me, this time to say good-bye. We were sitting in my office, I at my desk and he across from me, when he surprised me by asking, "What am I going to do now? I have relied on you for factual information for nearly five years. Would you mind if I called you in D.C. from time to time to get your input and advice?"

To this I simply laughed because I thought he was joking. Then I realized he wasn't. "Harold, you have been a good friend and a true professional in trying to get accurate information in front of your readers. The answer to your question is yes, but you won't call." I got up out of my chair and stood beside it. "Your readers don't care what Dale Hall thinks. They care what this chair has to say, whomever is sitting in it. I say that because it will be the next field supervisor that your readers will look to for information from the FWS on Houston environmental issues. I have just been the name that was fortunate to occupy this chair for the past few years."

Harold disagreed with me and said he was certain he would call. I gave him my new contact information, and then we shook hands and wished each other well. My friend Harold Scarlett died about three years later from lung cancer without ever giving me a call. One of the most important things for anyone in a leadership position to understand is that it isn't about you, but the position you are allowed to occupy, and the people you are blessed to lead. Never allow the position to be denigrated by your actions and never allow someone to stay on the team whose intent is to elevate themselves above their peers at the expense of the team.

•••

The Fisheries Program of the Fish and Wildlife Service is the cornerstone of the agency. Spencer Fullerton Baird was appointed by President Ulysses S. Grant to be the first commissioner of fish and fisheries for the U.S. Fish Commission and created an ambitious program to restore, manage and disseminate fish populations across the United States. In the 1880s, the commission embarked on what became known as the "Fish Car Era," during which a moving train traveling across the country literally served as a fish hatchery, with milk jugs used to incubate eggs that had been stripped from various trout species and artificially fertilized. As the train moved across country, stops at predetermined streams were made and young fingerlings were released to help bolster fish populations, even if the streams had not previously supported those species. Thus, the first introductions of non-native species on a large scale in the United States was done by the U.S. government. Over the years, hatcheries were established across the country to grow and stock various species, from trout to striped bass. It wasn't until 1903 that the first national wildlife refuge was established—Pelican Island National Wildlife Refuge, Florida—making the Fisheries Program the original anchor of what would become the Fish and Wildlife Service.

During my career, I often referred to the story of conservation in the U.S. as "the greatest story never told." When the first European settlers came to our shores, their reasons were founded in freedoms they could not enjoy under a king. Religion is most often cited as the driving force, but as stated in the Declaration of Independence several centuries later:

> We hold these truths to be self-evident, that all Men are created equal, that they are endowed by their Creator with certain unalienable Rights, that among these are Life, Liberty, and the Pursuit of Happiness.

Few people today understand that the depth of these words extends to the right to fish, hunt and gather food for sustenance. In England, wild game belonged to the Crown, and "poaching" was a term used to describe the illegal harvest of the Crown's game, not for hunting or fishing out of season. When the settlers to the new continent arrived, their first objective was to survive, and the land offered an abundance of fish and wildlife to provide food and other needs. When the founders of this nation wrote the Constitution and the Federalist Papers that explained it, they were clear that the people, not the government, would own the air, water, fish and wildlife. English common law was accepted when applied to plants, soil and minerals that were permanently attached to the land, but all other natural resources were to be held in trust by the federal and state governments on behalf of the people. This became known as the "trust doctrine" that Felix Smith spent his career advancing, and it still holds true today.

Theodore Roosevelt was one of the first pioneers in conservation, influenced by what he saw in the West as "waste" of bison and other wildlife. It was an established practice of the federal government to move Native Americans off their lands by starving them into submission. One means to accomplish this was by hiring buffalo hunters to kill as many buffalo as they could, while providing some meat to the soldiers and railroad workers. Roosevelt found this to be shameful and took on conservation as a lifelong mission. The story goes that when Roosevelt was president of the United States, James J. Audubon came to his office and asked for help with saving a small island in Florida that was home to snowy egrets and other "plume" birds. Plume hunting was very profitable at the turn of the century as a means of providing feathers for women's "stylish" hats. Roosevelt is said to have turned to his attorneys and asked, "Do I have the authority to declare this a bird sanctuary?"

His attorneys came back later with the answer: "We can find no law that would prohibit you from creating bird sanctuaries." Roosevelt responded, "Then I so declare it!" Thus Pelican Island National Bird Sanctuary became what would be the first national wildlife refuge. When I first read this account of Roosevelt's view that, if the law didn't prohibit it, then it was legal, it caused me to think about laws differently. Laws are not simply meant to regulate. They are also meant to empower innovation in evolving circumstances. Roosevelt did this because, like other conservationists, he believed in "fair chase" when pursuing game, and the slaughter of birds for their feathers apparently did not satisfy that criterion.

The first challenge for nationwide fish and wildlife management was the violation of state wildlife law, with the violators crossing over into another state to avoid prosecution. State law was limited to the particular state's boundaries, and there was no mechanism in federal law governing the interstate movement of fish and wildlife. The sports and conservation community successfully lobbied Congress to pass the first federal law governing wildlife management. In 1900, the Lacey Act was passed to prohibit the illegal trade of animals and plants, making it a federal offense to violate conservation laws in one state and transport the harvest into another state. This provided the essential link for state fish and wildlife agency cooperation.

The next major challenge was the commercial slaughter of migratory waterfowl for hungry patrons in large cities. Train cars filled with ducks and geese were loaded in the Mississippi Delta and hauled to Chicago, New York, Atlanta and other large cities for restaurant table fare. But commercial hunting of waterfowl was proven to be unsustainable. Sport hunters had not only adopted fair chase as a rule of engagement, but also the commitment to take no more than nature can replenish. The use of "punt guns," "battery boats" and other weapons that could kill dozens with one assault was judged unacceptable by the sport hunter. Through negotiations with Canada and Mexico, sport hunters were able to lobby for and succeed in passage of the Migratory Bird Treaty Act (MBTA), which placed significant responsibilities on each nation to manage migratory waterfowl in a fair and sustainable manner.

Sport hunting was seeing increasing support across the nation from people who loved wildlife and wanted to see populations remain healthy. In the late 1920s, a young editorial cartoonist named Jay N. "Ding" Darling, who was working in Des Moines, Iowa, was busy lambasting the U.S. Army Corps of Engineers in editorial cartoons for their drainage and destruction of "useless swamps" across the nation. When the stock market crash of 1929 and the onset of the dust bowl occurred, President Franklin D. Roosevelt asked Darling to come to D.C. and be the head of the U.S. Biological Survey, the forerunner of the U.S. Fish and Wildlife Service. Darling was specifically asked to come up with ways of holding soil on the farms as a means of mitigating the horrific damage occurring across the U.S. The dust bowl was mostly believed to be anchored in the Midwest, but the dust storms traversing the continent were so strong that the Hudson River could not be seen from the streets of Manhattan. The belief that all lands in the Midwest were rich soils for farming had driven the unwise drainage of those "useless swamps." Darling and other conservationists understood that something had to be done, and it had to be done quickly!

Darling reverted to his basic skill set and decided that selling art on a stamp would be a fine way of raising the funds to restore and protect wetlands both for waterfowl and for the health of the land. In the midst of the Depression and the dust bowl, when farms were being abandoned and unemployment was over 25 percent, sport hunters *lobbied Congress to make them pay to go hunting for waterfowl!* The idea that any segment of the public would ask to be taxed in order to pursue an activity that was currently free would be unheard of today, much less in the middle of the worst economic disaster in the history of America. But they believed they were the conservationists, that someone had to pay and they were willing to do so in order to ensure that populations of waterfowl would be around for future generations. In 1934, the first Migratory Bird Hunting and Conservation Stamp, also known as the duck stamp, was sold at the price of one dollar. In the middle of the Depression, one dollar would go far toward feeding a family with flour, salt, beans, fatback and other staples for a week. Nevertheless, determined sportsmen and women convinced Congress to require a stamp that would allow them to hunt migratory birds. Moreover, the money they paid could *only* be used to purchase or restore habitat. Still today, 97 percent of all duck stamp revenues go on the ground for conservation of wetlands and grasslands.

This proved to be highly successful for federal and state implementation of the MBTA, but the private sector continued to discuss what average citizens could do. A small group of duck hunters sitting in a cabin on the Beaverkill River in 1936 decided there was more that could be done. During the 1930s, the way wildlife management was viewed began to change from the European approach of growing birds in captivity and releasing them for the hunt to one of providing habitat in their nesting grounds so they could reproduce and replenish the natural migratory populations. From this meeting, Ducks Unlimited Inc. was formed and brought into existence on January 29, 1937, with the sole purpose of raising funds from large donors for the protection and restoration of nesting grounds in Canada. Once again, the sportsmen and women decided it was *their* responsibility to see that *their* wildlife were conserved.

In addition to the formation of Ducks Unlimited, 1937 was the birth year for further landmark legislation for wildlife conservation. After seeing the success of the duck stamp, other hunters and shooters began to ask if there was more they could do. Some federal taxes were being collected on the sale of arms and ammunition, but they were not being funneled into conservation. The hunters and shooters joined with the arms and ammunition industry to ask Congress that they be taxed on these products, but that the taxes collected be returned to the state fish and wildlife agencies to support their wildlife management efforts. The authors of the Wildlife Restoration Act were Senator Key Pittman and Congressman Absalom Willis Robertson, and their bill, popularly known as the Pittman-Robinson Act, was signed by President Roosevelt on September 2, 1937.

The states had also begun to require hunting and fishing licenses when pursuing these activities within individual state boundaries, with the funding dedicated to management of fish and wildlife resources. This growing formula for the care and conservation of fish and wildlife by the hunter and angler became known as the "North American Model for Wildlife Conservation" and is the envy of the world. When fish, wildlife and plants have active champions, they seldom see significant declines in their populations. One important fact that supports this contention is that there has never been an extinction of a sport-managed species in the United States of America. At a time when common bird populations across the board are in a 30 percent decline, waterfowl populations are seen to be relatively strong.

In the late 1940s, fishing and boating conservationists had witnessed the tremendous benefits gained through the Wildlife Restoration Act and went to work for passage of a similar bill to tax the purchase of the equipment they used. In 1950, the Sport Fish Restoration Act, also known as the Dingell-Johnson Act in recognition of its champions, Congressman John Dingell and Senator Edwin Johnson, was passed to provide for taxes to be placed on fishing and boating equipment. This effort continued the commitment of the hunting and fishing community to put conservation before recreation, and stewardship before harvest. Between these two laws, more than $1 billion a year is currently returned to state fish and wildlife agencies for conservation purposes. The Fisheries Program of the FWS worked hand in hand with the states and citizen conservationists to make this possible. It is an American legacy.

Few Americans understand just how little of their state taxes go to support the activities of their state fish and wildlife agency. For the vast majority of those agencies, less than 5 percent of their operating budget is provided by the state's general fund. The remainder is contributed by the hunters, shooters, anglers and boaters through the purchase of licenses and taxes paid on their sports equipment. When one visits a state wildlife management area, the overwhelming probability is that the area was purchased by the sportsmen and women of the state and nation. I appreciate and respect the right of citizens to oppose hunting, fishing and other wildlife consumptive activities. But they also have the obligation to respect that these treasures would not be here today without those dedicated conservationists.

Following the Great Depression, nearly all wild game was gone. People needed to feed their families and did whatever was required to do so. I stand without judgment of men who saw their children hungry and harvested whatever food they could to feed their families. Following the Depression, however, it was those same sportsmen who lobbied to be taxed and also created privately funded non-governmental organizations such as The National Wild Turkey Federation, Ducks Unlimited, Rocky Mountain Elk Foundation, Pheasants Forever and other species-specific groups dedicated to restocking and nurturing the return of wildlife populations that had disappeared. Today's wildlife legacy is the culmination of federal, state and private hunter and angler conservationists answering the call to help nature heal. I am proud to be a member of the family that built the North American Model for Wildlife Conservation and grateful that those efforts have helped create wonderful memories during the harvest of a few of God's creations for my family to consume.

I am saddened that anti-hunters have succeeded in referring to the animals that are harvested through legal means as "trophies." We who revere the Creator and are humbled with the sunrise, hearing nature awaken and sharing the spiritual moment with family or friends, understand that these are newborn memories that stay with us for a lifetime. The birds and other animals that are preserved and displayed in our homes or lodges manifest a book of memories, not trophies. Each one has a story and inspires us to make sure there will always be these magnificent creatures to share with the generations. Like the workers in the vineyard who take only a few bottles for themselves while sharing the remainder of the bounty with others, hunter and angler conservationists are proud of their contributions to the non-consumptive pleasures of fellow Americans.

• • •

George Herbert Walker Bush was sworn in as the forty-first president of the United States on January 20, 1989, with his vice president, Dan Quayle. Vice President Quayle proved to be a steady source of material for the press to seize upon through his public gaffes. But more important for the Fish and Wildlife Service, Frank Dunkle was replaced by John Turner, a Wyoming biologist and politician who was a welcomed relief from the anxiety that Dunkle took pride in cultivating within the agency. Turner was the opposite. He was easy mannered, open to disagreement, and was loved by everyone in the FWS. When one is nominated by the president to a Senate-confirmed position, s/he is not permitted to either be involved with the agency regarding decisions that must be made prior to being confirmed or discuss such decisions with the press. But they are permitted to visit with agency staff and sit in on briefings for educational purposes. When I first met John, a few of us gathered in the vacant director's office to have him introduce himself and allow us to start briefing him on pressing issues.

When we sat down, he looked at us and said, "I feel like the corpse at an Irish wake. Everyone knows I need to be here, but nobody wants me to say anything." With that simple stroke of humor and humility, we knew he would do well in the FWS. Our people are down to earth, appreciate humor and approach our careers as if they were a calling. We believe we were spiritually compelled to work on behalf of conservation and would be doing it in one form or another, even if we weren't being paid. A fire in our bellies drives us to conserve these treasures. Many weekends for FWS employees entail volunteering to help our fellow staff at refuges, hatcheries or in law enforcement do their work. A common phrase within the conservation community is "It's hard to separate my work life from my personal life. They're both the same." Another common belief is "There's no such thing as 'it's not my job.'" We have no choice. The Fish and Wildlife Service family, and all in conservation, are *compelled* to do what we can for our precious natural resources. We immediately knew that John Turner, a former rafting guide and former president of the Wyoming Senate, both understood and lived by the same creed. It would prove to be a pleasure to follow him.

• • •

Training in the Fish and Wildlife Service had always been either program specific or, as it was in my case, sink or swim. The National Wildlife Refuge Academy was in Blair, Nebraska, and all who were on track to be a refuge manager attended training classes there. Law enforcement staff received their training at the Federal Law Enforcement Training Center in Glynco, Georgia, as they still do today. That facility trains law enforcement throughout government, with special training classes dedicated to specific agencies and the laws governing the various missions. Fisheries staff received their training at the Fisheries Academy in Leetown, West Virginia, and this facility fell under the control of Gary Edwards as the assistant director–fisheries and me as his deputy. I had direct supervisory responsibility over Wendell Ogden, the head of the Academy, and the responsibility to help increase operational funding when necessary. The Fisheries Academy had not received an increase in funds in over two years, and inflation was beginning to take its toll.

Fisheries had two divisions: hatcheries, and fisheries assistance. One of the staff in the fisheries assistance division was Bill Maxon, an attorney who came on board via the Great Lakes Fisheries Commission. Since the department solicitors were the only authorized legal representatives for the entire department, we were not permitted to have Bill in a job where legal work was his assignment. Instead, he had been quietly assigned to lobby Congress to help move Fisheries legislation and budgets. Bill saw little need to function in the 8–5 workday because he spent many evenings with congressional staff over drinks and/or dinner. He also had no hesitation in walking out of the office in the middle of the day and spending a couple of hours in the bar across the street. This was becoming a management problem for Lynn Starnes, the division chief, and she occasionally called me for assistance in pulling him out of the bar. Coincidentally, Lynn's husband was Wayne Starnes, who had done his PhD dissertation on the Tennessee snail darter, the little fish that was at the center of one of the first real battles under the Endangered Species Act.

Given the situation, I called Bill into my office one morning. "Bill, I have a dilemma. I either need to fire you or find something productive you can do for us." Bill's response was predictable. "I much prefer the latter." After some discussion, during which I recognized not only the positive contributions he made for us under the table, but also the negatives that occurred regularly during normal business hours, I gave him a sink-or-swim assignment. First, he was to be assigned to Wendell Ogden at the Fisheries Academy, where he would not have to report to work on a daily basis with the other staff in D.C. He would have to move to West Virginia, and that was non-negotiable. His one single objective was to secure an increase of $200,000 in the next budget cycle for the Academy, or his position would be eliminated. He accepted the challenge and assured me he could get it done.

Senator Robert Byrd was one of the most powerful senators in Congress and regularly provided "earmarks" for projects he wanted to see accomplished in West Virginia. When Bill met with Senator Byrd's chief of staff, Charlie Estes, for dinner and drinks, he did as assigned and convinced Charlie that the additional funding was critical to keeping federal jobs and the Fisheries Academy in West Virginia. Senator Byrd had regularly supported the Academy, and Charlie understood the importance to the FWS. But all did not go as planned. When Estes briefed the senator on the proposal, Mr. Byrd responded with "Why don't we have a much larger training facility in West Virginia and do all of the FWS training there?"

The result was the senator pushing for, and accomplishing, the authorization and funding for a *$200 million* training facility! None of us in the FWS had asked for this to occur. We had no authorization to pursue a consolidated training facility, and the budget was nearly half of all the FWS operational funding at the time. This was a gag factor that was neither intended nor wanted—but it was done. We could honestly tell Director Turner it was Senator Byrd's idea to bring something big to West Virginia, and it was not good in the long term for the FWS to oppose someone as powerful as Robert Byrd when he thought he was trying to help.

This type of power only resulted from the ability to compromise with fellow senators. To get what was wanted in your state, there needed to be support for what someone else wanted in their state. Earmarks became the name of the game for several years, and the FWS benefited, but not without a cost. We would often be given the "gift" of a new national wildlife refuge with no funds to support management. But at least the land was in the system and protected. The FWS was forced to develop the Land Acquisition Priority System (LAPS) to clearly identify which lands were of higher priority from a natural resource standpoint in order to push "gifts" toward those lands believed in most urgent need of protection. It was also a time when there was true collaboration between the White House and Congress.

The story goes that when Ronald Reagan was president and Tip O'Neill was Speaker of the House, the Speaker would quietly make after-hours visits to the White House, where he and the president would sip good whiskey and decide compromise positions on the various issues. Then each would return to his party and gain the support needed to carry out the decisions. This happened because the leaders had power, and neither abused it. The FWS always fared better when the Democrats controlled the Congress and the Republicans controlled the White House. The President's budget would regularly have cuts in the programs important to the FWS, and the Congress would restore those cuts and even add a little to the pot. Both sides understood that this was what had to happen from each party's perspective and both, with a wink and a nod, agreed to the process.

After the initial shock, Director Turner asked Gary and me to come up with someone in Fisheries who could handle the start-to-finish task of building, staffing and operating something of this scale. The person would work with Deputy Director Bruce Blanchard to pull all the parts of the FWS together to build a first-class training facility. Gary had met one of our sharpest hatchery managers when he visited the Leadville Hatchery in Colorado. Rick Lemon was a tall, slender, easygoing man with a brilliant mind and a calm personality. He was perfect for the job. Rick agreed, with some trepidation, to accept the challenge, and went in with his eyes wide open. He knew he would not only have to navigate the submerged hostility of the programs in the FWS that would lose some of their funding for this, as well as other agencies in the department that would have to contribute, but would also have to completely satisfy Senator Byrd. As time would prove, Rick Lemon was more than up to the task. Working through all the tedious details fully occupied his time for over a half decade. And, yes, Bill Maxon accomplished his task of getting the additional $200,000 for the Academy and kept his job.

• • •

In June 1989 we were preparing to go to China in a few months as a U.S. delegation on Fisheries Cooperation, which was intended to develop a protocol between the two countries, when the "Tiananmen Square Incident" occurred. The Chinese military used massive deadly force to break up pro-democracy demonstrations. In the heart of Beijing, the military opened fire on unarmed protesters. Estimates of those killed ranged from hundreds to thousands, with only the Chinese government knowing the exact numbers. One famous photo shows a lone, unarmed man standing at attention in Tiananmen Square in front of a Chinese tank to block its movement, daring the driver to run over him. This photo caught the eye of all peace-loving people around the world and the Chinese eventually stood down, but only after dealing out horrific punishment to people who were only seeking democratic reforms.

Deeply impacted by this event, I asked our interpreter and guide to China, Steve Kohl, "Who is in charge of this delegation?" He replied, "You are the ranking member and the head of the delegation." I asked if I had the authority to cancel the delegation visit. "I don't know. I'll get you the number of the Chinese desk at the State Department and you can call them." I called the Chinese desk and asked the same questions. The lady on the other end said "As head of the delegation, you have final say on whether the delegation goes or doesn't go." "Thank you," I replied. "Please notify the Chinese that we will not be coming as planned. Until the Tiananmen issues have been resolved to the satisfaction of the United States, this delegation is indefinitely postponed." She said she would do as I asked, and we ended the call. My fellow delegation members, Leslie Holland Bartels (my classmate and friend from LSU), Bill Shake, and Bill Knapp, were all in support of the cancellation. None of us wanted to be puppets for the Chinese propaganda machine saying to the world that "All is well. See, the United States is here, and all is good." We eventually rescheduled the visit many months later, after there was a clear signal from the State Department that they believed the issue was no longer active. But we felt that in some small way we had stood with the Chinese people who were simply seeking the same freedoms we enjoy.

Another catastrophic event, this time environmental, occurred when the oil tanker Exxon Valdez went aground and ruptured on March 24, 1989. The tanker, which was owned by the Exxon Shipping Company, was carrying crude oil from Prudhoe Bay toward its destination of Long Beach, California, when it struck Bligh Reef in Prince William Sound 1.5 miles west of Tatitlek, Alaska. The spill released 260,000 barrels of Alaskan crude and is considered one of the worst human-caused environmental disasters in history. With drift and currents, the oil eventually impacted 1,300 miles of pristine shoreline and remained in heavy amounts for years. The lawsuits that followed lasted a decade and resulted in approximately $5 billion in damage awards. No accurate assessment of total impacts to aquatic, marine and bird life has ever been completed due to the compounding effects that ripple into future generations. But it proved to be the catalyst for significant change in laws and regulations guiding transport of toxic substances, including passage of the Oil Pollution Act of 1990.

PART 2

Endangered Species and Western Water

CHAPTER 5

Spotted Owl and Western Water

In January 1991 I accepted my next assignment: assistant regional director of U.S. Fish and Wildlife Service Ecological Services (FWS ES) in Portland, Oregon, working for Regional Director Marv Plenert. When the time came for me to leave Washington, D.C., Director John Turner didn't completely understand why I would want to leave my relatively non-controversial role in Fisheries to dive into what was rapidly becoming a cauldron in the Northwest. After much discussion about the hard financial stress my family was facing and my inability to stay out of the fray for very long, John wished me well and said, "I want to see if you can ride that bull for the full eight seconds." I had no idea that I was about to enter the most challenging and stressful years I had ever known.

I loaded my little red Nissan pickup with all it would hold and started driving to Portland and temporary quarters. Once again, Sarah and our children would have to wait until we could sell our house in Hamilton, just outside Leesburg, Virginia, before they could join me nearly three thousand miles away. I drove away with tears in my eyes as I looked at Sarah, Erin, Adam and our new daughter, Emily. Waving good-bye would become a repeated scene throughout my career. Some have wondered why I have little empathy for people who sit in one spot for decades and then complain when they couldn't compete well for a promotion. Until you have paid the price, and your family has paid the price, for the experience gained in different locations, the value of doing so will never be understood. Tears through separation from family are a high price to pay for knowledge and experience. But my family stood by me at each step of the way, even if they didn't always know what I was facing at work.

The 2,780-mile drive across country took just under three days. When driving alone, it's easy to keep driving until you need to fill up, use the rest room, get something to munch on and keep driving. I drove fifteen to sixteen hours a day and rolled into Portland on the afternoon of the third day. It was my first time driving from coast to coast, and I was reminded how beautiful America is and how rich we are in natural resources. As I drove along the majestic Rocky Mountains and across Wyoming in the blowing snow, the changes in scenery only brought different types of beauty.

I found my way to the Bonneville Power Administration building, where our regional office was located, and after a quick hello and visit with Marv as well as Deputy Regional Director Bill Martin and Jim Teeter (my deputy assistant regional director), I found my way to the extended-stay hotel. The next day was all about meeting regional office staff and, more important, letting them sniff the new dog. One of the priorities was to make plans for an all-employee meeting where everyone in the Pacific Region Ecological Services offices could get together to discuss where we have been, where we are now and where we need to go. I wanted to do this early in my tenure, as much for my benefit as for theirs. I know the anxiety that occurs when a new leader arrives, and I wanted to put everyone at ease with the assurance that I respected them and looked forward to doing all I could to support them.

We decided to meet in Ashland, Oregon, February 25–27. All staff from Oregon, Washington, California, Idaho, Nevada and Hawaii were invited. We held the conference in February to have everyone engaged early in helping decide what issues or workloads were most important and how we would deal with them. I believed strongly in getting input from everyone, but understood that they expected me to make the decisions and set direction.

As the regional employees gathered in Ashland, much of the West was suffering through another drought. I quickly realized that water would be a prominent issue for at least three of our six states. Because I'd lived only in the southern and eastern U.S., where water was something that was evacuated to control flooding, dealing with drought presented an entirely new challenge.

I also learned the hard way that the Endangered Species Act (ESA) commanded a heavy emphasis. At one of the breaks on February 26, Bob Ruesink, chief of the Threatened and Endangered Species Program, came to me and said, "Judge Zilly has released a decision on the owl critical habitat case and has directed that we have a proposal in the Federal Register by May." I said, "That's fine. What's critical habitat?"

Bob would quickly prove to be one of my most significant mentors. I had spent my career gaining expertise in wetlands, the Clean Water Act, and how laws and biology had to be considered in tandem. I had never worked a single day on endangered species issues. In fact, the Ecological Services Program had intentionally kept ESA biologists separate from the traditional wetlands and migratory bird biologists, and had even established separate Endangered Species offices. Species experts were expected to work all aspects of the ESA for their assigned species. Bob was very patient while I listened. He explained that the listing of the spotted owl was not yet complete because we had not addressed critical habitat (CH) designation. We had been sued by an environmental group for failing to address that portion of the law, and the judge had agreed with the plaintiffs. I obviously needed to learn more about this law that was so new to me, and I needed to learn fast.

The Endangered Species Act of 1973 (ESA, Public Law 93-205) was gaining momentum as one of the most powerful pieces of environmental legislation in the U.S. The stated intent of the ESA is found in Section 2(b):

The purposes of this Act are to provide a means whereby the *ecosystems* upon which endangered species and threatened species depend may be conserved, to provide a *program* for the conservation of such endangered species and threatened species, and to take such steps as may be appropriate to achieve the purposes of the treaties and conventions set forth in subsection (a) of this section. (Emphasis added.)

Congress took the unusual measure of providing explicit guidance to the secretaries of the interior and commerce in Section 4 (U.S.C. 1533) regarding the five questions that must be analyzed and answered in determining if a species qualifies for protection under the Act. Normally, Congress instructs the executive branch to formulate procedures and regulations for implementation, but the ESA is different. This series of questions became known as the "five factor analysis" within the FWS, and all were questions of biology and management. The ESA clearly states that all listing decisions must be made using only the best scientific and commercial information available after consultation with federal and state agencies on any measures that might be under way to aid in conserving the species. Those five factors are, per Section 4[a][1]:

- present or threatened destruction, modification, or curtailment of [the species'] habitat range
- overutilization for commercial, recreational, scientific, or educational purposes
- disease or predation
- the inadequacy of existing regulatory mechanisms
- other natural or manmade factors affecting [the species'] continued existence

A positive response for any one or more of these questions would qualify a species to be listed as either endangered or threatened. An endangered species is one that is currently under threat of extinction. A threatened species is likely to become endangered within the "foreseeable future." This distinction was made to allow more proactive efforts for threatened species in order to reverse downward population trends and address the threats in a timely fashion.

The three categories of taxa that may be considered as "listable entities" are species, subspecies, and distinct population segments. A distinct population segment relates to possible genetic differences between populations, geographic isolation, or other questions within a species or subspecies.

After a decision is made that an entity qualifies under the ESA, Section 4(3)(A)(i) directs that an evaluation be made to determine if there is a need to designate habitat critical to ensure the conservation of the species. In other words, the species would not be considered capable of recovery (conserved and removed from the list) if this habitat were lost. The northern spotted owl had been listed as a threatened subspecies, and it is this habitat evaluation that Judge Zilly had ordered and upon which my long and arduous ESA education began.

In the case before Judge Zilly, *Northern Spotted Owl v. Lujan, 758 F. Supp. 621 (W.D. Wash. 1991)*, the plaintiffs argued that the law was clear in requiring the FWS to concurrently designate CH with the listing of the species or, at a minimum, have designation completed within one year after listing. Because the FWS had not proposed designation more than six months after listing, the plaintiffs argued it was clear that a proposal was not in the works. The FWS had done what it almost always had and simply stated that designation was "not determinable" because of the extensive 57-million-acre range of the owl and the millions of acres of remaining old-growth forests, even though they were shrinking quickly. Judge Zilly based his decision on the purposes of the Act to "provide a means whereby the ecosystems upon which endangered and threatened species depend may be conserved." Clearly, Congress understood that habitat loss was the single most prevalent reason for the diminishment of species numbers and survivability but, unfortunately, the FWS had taken the wrong approach from the beginning with the ESA and had focused on individual species.

Prior to the ESA, the FWS environmental staff were advisors to other agencies and the public on the proper management of species and their habitats, and often wrote reports such as those under the Fish and Wildlife Coordination Act on the Corps of Engineers projects. The FWS was much like the Chihuahua yelping and nipping at the heels of the more powerful construction agencies, but had no real power other than providing input that we were told would receive "great weight." The ESA changed that, and this powerful law was placed in FWS hands. FWS was now the pit bull that other agencies dreaded to see coming. The FWS response? Create individual species experts that would have as their sole responsibility a single species, in some cases for their entire career. Apparently, they believed it would be easier to address the species than the habitat issues. Add to that the isolation of Endangered Species biologists from the habitat-centered Ecological Services personnel, and one has a recipe for almost certainly inadequate biological evaluations. Thus, the FWS had always treated the critical habitat requirement in the listing process as "extra work" rather than seeing habitat conservation as the probable solution. The inherent flaws of focusing on single species management rather than habitat conservation would become eminently clear through the conflict over management of northwest forests.

• • •

The evolution of the Endangered Species Act was one driven by circumstances and conflict rather than the luxury of charting potential alternative approaches. The first tests of the ESA came about by way of a small fish in the Little Tennessee River and the whooping crane on the Platte River in Nebraska. The Tennessee Valley Authority (TVA) began planning a reservoir construction project in the late 1960s that would drown up to 16,500 acres of previously dry ground to create the Tellico

Dam and Reservoir. TVA eventually abandoned the pretense that Tellico Dam would provide much-needed rural power and admitted it was an economic development project. The dam faced opposition almost from the beginning. Governor Winfield Dunn petitioned TVA to cancel the project in 1971 because of anticipated destruction of the Little Tennessee River, while Native Americans opposed it based on the destruction of sacred grounds.

Many others joined in for different reasons, such as farmers over the loss of their farms, and fishing guides and hotels over the loss of recreational dollars. But TVA apparently didn't need the concurrence of the governor, as the Corps did for their projects, and Congress continued to fund the study and eventual construction of the dam. In 1975, the FWS was petitioned to emergency-list the snail darter (*Percina tanasi*), a small fish that would likely be pushed to extinction if the dam were constructed. The FWS agreed, and the snail darter was listed as endangered. The dam was approximately 80 percent complete at the time of the listing. Congress ignored the species consequences and continued to support the project. Zygmunt Plater, a law professor with the University of Tennessee and then the University of Michigan, sued TVA on behalf of the coalition opposing the project as a violation of the ESA. The case worked its way to the Supreme Court of the United States, where Chief Justice Warren Burger wrote:

> One would be hard pressed to find a statutory provision whose terms were any plainer than those in Section 7 of the Endangered Species Act. Its very words affirmatively command all federal agencies 'to insure that actions authorized, funded, or carried out by them do not jeopardize the continued existence' of an endangered species or 'result in the destruction or modification of habitat of such species.' This language admits of no exceptions. (U.S. Supreme Court 1978, p174)

He went on to say:

> It may seem curious to some that the survival of a relatively small number of three-inch fish among all the countless millions of species would require the permanent halting of a virtually completed dam for which Congress has expended more than $100 million. The paradox is not minimized by the fact that Congress continued to appropriate large sums of public money for the project, even after ... [it knew about the dam's] ... impact upon the survival of the snail darter. TVA v. Hill 437 U.S. 153 (1978). (U.S. Supreme Court 1978)

In response to this decision, on April 12, 1978, Senator John Culver (D-LA) and Senate Minority Leader Howard Baker (R-TN) introduced a bill that would amend the ESA and create a seven-member cabinet-level committee with the authority to exempt a federal agency from the Section 7 (ESA consultation) requirements and allow a whole species, subspecies or distinct population segment to go extinct. The secretary of the interior was assigned the authority to call the Endangered Species Committee, also known as the "God Squad" because of its power over the life or death of a species, upon request from another cabinet member. The members of the Committee are specified in the law: Administrator of the Environmental Protection Agency; Administrator of the National Oceanic and Atmospheric Administration; Chairman of the Council of Economic Advisers; Secretary of Agriculture; Secretary of the Army; a representative from the state(s) in question, and Secretary of the Interior. This Committee is charged with determining if any or all of the following conditions are met (Section 4[h]):

- There must be no reasonable alternative to the agency's action.
- The benefits of the action must outweigh the benefits of an alternative action where the species is conserved.

- The action is of regional or national importance.
- Neither the federal agency nor the exemption applicant made irreversible commitment to the resources.
- Mitigation efforts must be taken to reduce the negative effects on the endangered species.

The first tests under the amended law occurred when the Tellico Dam project was elevated to the Endangered Species Committee, along with the Grayrocks Oil Refinery for the whooping crane. The Committee dealt Senator Baker and Congress a significant blow when it denied the applications for exemption.

Pat Parenteau, the attorney for the National Wildlife Federation, sued on behalf of the whooping crane and its possible destruction due to loss of habitat on the Platte River in Nebraska. He gave me this account of events:

> I was the attorney that sued Grayrocks, and Zyg [Zygmunt Plater] was the lawyer for Tellico. We were close friends and allies through this whole saga. My case involved challenging a project on the Laramie River in Wyoming, which was part of the Platte River system. John Van der Walker, who was in Denver in Ecological Services with the FWS and came to D.C. when I was with the National Wildlife Federation, gave an old-fashioned slide show and showed us what was happening on the Platte River and helped me see how important the Platte was to the whooping crane. As a Nebraska boy, I knew about the sandhill cranes and how important the Platte was to them, but I had never seen a whooping crane there and didn't know it was important on their migration route. Van der Walker was blowing the whistle and saying 'we're losing this habitat.' The river's value for migratory birds is well known, but his focus was the whooper. He said he was going to be proposing the area as

critical habitat for the whooper, but if we don't figure out how to stop the dewatering upstream, we're going to lose the habitat. I got all excited about starting a campaign to save the Platte. In the end, I did stop the Missouri Basin Power Project, a 1,500-megawatt coal-fired plant using locally sourced coal and taking out 60,000 acre feet of water a year in a river that had already been depleted by 80 percent. I sued under NEPA [National Environmental Policy Act] and the ESA, and I sued the Corps of Engineers for the Section 404 permit for the dam. I also sued the Rural Electric Administration for the nearly interest-free billion-dollar loans to build it. We litigated the case in Lincoln before Judge David Urbom. We had a hell of a trial that went eight days or more. We had hard science about the transformation that had already taken place on the river.

We won our case and EPA didn't have any idea how to proceed. Although my legal victory was solid, we were on shaky political grounds. For one thing, the water needed for the power project had been allocated to Wyoming by a Supreme Court consent decree on the North Platte, so it was 'Wyoming's water,' and we were arguing 'No, that water belongs to Nebraska.' Of course, Nebraska agreed with us and was in the case on our side only because they wanted the water. They didn't give a damn about the whooping crane, but they sure as hell wanted the water to get to Lake McConaughy, a first-class fishery they were concerned about.

Both Tellico and Grayrocks were on the same agenda for the God Squad. I was sitting there with Zyg in the Department of the Interior auditorium when they all filed out onto the stage with Secretary [Cecil] Andrus leading them. Andrus opened the proceedings and then said 'The first matter before us is Tellico Dam, and I will entertain a motion.' Charles Schultze, the chair of the Council of Economic Advisers, said 'I don't know anything about endangered species, but I know a turkey when I see one! This project, even if you take into consideration all the sunk costs, will never earn a nickel. There's no question in my mind it should be denied.' It took thirty seconds—thirty seconds for the Committee to vote unanimously to deny the exemption for Tellico. After all those years of controversy and hoorah, the guy who said 'bullshit' was the economist! It was wonderful.

We had shuttled from Lincoln to Cheyenne ten times or more to work out our deal. The agreement was to drop one of the units of the power plant down to 1,000 megawatts, offset completely the depletion of water by buying irrigation rights to dedicate flows down to Lake McConaughy and create the Platte River Whooping Crane Trust. That was my idea, and it had to be funded at $7.5 million, a large sum of money in 1978. Because we had that settlement, the NOAA [National Oceanic and Atmospheric Administration] administrator, an Omaha boy like me, made the motion to grant exemption for Grayrocks, but conditioned on the settlement agreement that the parties had reached and, should that settlement agreement not be fully implemented to the letter, the exemption would be revoked. It was unanimously approved. (Parenteau 2020)

However, the Congress and politicians were not done with the Tellico Dam. Congress ultimately passed legislation exempting the Tellico Dam project from the ESA, and President Jimmy Carter signed the Energy and Water Development Act of 1979 into law. The dam was completed on November 29, 1979. The population of the snail darter in the Little Tennessee River disappeared, but other snail darters were found in South Chickamauga Creek, Sewee Creek, Sequatchie River and Paint Rock River. The likely cause of their survival was the stocking into non-native streams by TVA during the planning and construction of the project. Unfortunately, it was not an honorable victory for Congress, which had continually funded a project they clearly expected would end in the extinction of a species. Aldo Leopold once wrote "A wise tinkerer saves all the parts." Congress had not distinguished itself for its wisdom.

• • •

The FWS had a lot of work to do in a short period of time. An evaluation had to be made of at least 19 million acres of potential critical habitat in Washington, Oregon and California that had both old-growth and younger stands capable of helping in owl dispersal. The leader of our effort, Barry Mulder, was the scientific pillar I depended on throughout all the issues with the northern spotted owl. Barry was the "spotted owl coordinator," a position created as our representative on the Interagency Scientific Committee (ISC) and all scientific efforts that followed. The ISC was brought together to help guide the Bureau of Land Management (BLM) and Forest Service (FS) out of the quagmire of political interference that had occurred over the previous decades. How did the situation get so out of hand on the legitimate harvest of timber resources? Why had the annual harvest rate been so much in excess of what nature could provide? The answer rests in appropriations bills passed by Congress for which non-foresters gave harvest targets in the absence of an adequate effort to understand the consequences.

Beginning after World War II, there was an increased need for lumber in the U.S. Returning veterans needed homes, the G.I. Bill gave them the loan opportunity to buy, and America needed to build. In addition, a massive economic engine was revving up and needed raw materials to bring America back to better times. Congress began to assign timber harvests on federal lands across the nation to help augment private lumber company activities and allowed private companies to harvest federal lands by paying the government a fee through a bidding process. These "timber sales" became commonplace and the normal tool for federal forest harvests, both for the FS and BLM. Through proposals from the agencies at congressional appropriation hearings, the heads of these agencies assured Congress they could meet their quotas. Congress, in turn, applied significant pressure to increase harvest to bring jobs to their states. It was a significant positive cycle of economics, but a negative one for forest management. Many in the political realm came to see federal forested ecosystems that belonged to all Americans as simply "tree farms" for producing lumber.

While Congress and the agency heads were busy celebrating the fact that several administrations (Nixon, Carter, Reagan and H.W. Bush) were creating jobs and development, the lumber mills of the Northwest were focusing on only one type of stand: old-growth. Just one section of one log of old-growth Douglas fir could be almost more than a log truck could haul. The mills quickly "tooled up" to cut these massive logs, which often restricted their ability to process logs of younger, smaller, but more abundant trees. There was no real incentive for the lumber companies to harvest a higher number of trees two feet in diameter at breast height (dbh) when one old-growth tree would provide the same milled lumber as a dozen smaller ones. Nearly all mills had abandoned smaller-sized saws and equipment to tool up for massive old-growth logs.

But the public was changing. Passage of the National Environmental Policy Act (NEPA), the Clean Water Act and the ESA all contributed to a sea change in public awareness of and involvement in government activities. NEPA (Public Law 91-190) went into effect on January 1, 1970, and required that every federal agency action have accompanying documentation of environmental, economic and social impacts that would occur as a result of that action. Before NEPA, few people in the U.S. even knew that timber harvest occurred on forests owned by the federal government, and hardly any knew the massive quantity. Through these revelations, NEPA established itself as one of the most significant environmental laws ever written.

When the FS and BLM had to begin putting out for public review both their proposed plans for timber harvest and the required environmental impact statement (EIS), the public got a real awakening. Almost overnight, the federal agencies were having to explain why their mandate of forest management was being treated as timber management. Add to this the passage of the National Forest Management Act of 1976 to accompany the ESA, and the curtains were pulled back on how national decisions were made on lands belonging to every citizen of the United States. The EIS that must be written to address the potential impacts is not a decision document. It is a "full disclosure" document that is expected to disclose the impacts, both positive and negative, that are likely to occur to the natural resources and to people. After full public review and commenting, with comments addressed in the final EIS, the agency makes a Record of Decision, which explains why the chosen alternative was selected. Accountability to the full American public, not just Congress, had arrived.

Environmental groups began to lose trust in the federal agencies, and discovered they could win access to decision-making through the courts and have a larger say in the management of public lands. The trust in government we were once given as the qualified representative of the people under the "trust doctrine" was transposing into a lack of trust for *any* decision, and all of us in government were being painted with the same brush, regardless of whether we had any control over the decision. But the most destructive mistake, in my opinion, to holding agencies accountable in natural resource management came with part of the settlement in the Seattle Audubon suit.

In that agreement, plaintiffs in Seattle Audubon were given approval to choose 1.1 billion board feet (bbf) in sales from a list of fiscal year 1989 sales that contained at least 40 acres of suitable spotted owl habitat. A board foot is a milled board 12 inches long by 12 inches wide by 1 inch thick. If agreement was reached, then other sales on the list *not* released by the plaintiffs would not be offered during fiscal year 1990. The appropriations bill for FY89-90 contained the Hatfield-Adams amendment, which legitimized this agreement in Section 318(f).

It was a terrible mistake. This changed the way non-federal interests looked at federal land management forever. Without any accountability to the public that owned the land, a non-government entity was allowed to decide which sales were released and which weren't. We are a country of laws, and there must be an entity accountable to the people. The Constitution of the United States provides for due process by all citizens through redress in the legislative and judicial branches for grievances against the executive branch. The unintended lesson here was well learned through Section 318: that bringing litigation was both profitable (the non-federal plaintiffs were able to recover all attorney fees) *and* it offered the opportunity to make federal decisions without having to answer for them.

I have always fully supported the citizen's right to sue our government. But I believe it ill-advised to allow one segment of society to have a greater voice than the others. Congress and politically appointed leaders had undoubtedly given that unfair advantage to timber interests, and that demanded correction. But having the pendulum simply move to the opposite side only ensured perpetual motion of the pendulum. Lawsuits became the first mode of action for non-government entities, and they often found the federal government either lacking in their responsibilities or willing to settle to avoid the courts. Clearly, a course correction back toward sanity was needed.

• • •

The pressure on the federal agency heads responsible for management of northwest natural resources was steadily increasing, and they knew they needed to gain control of the issue. "In 1989, Dale Robertson [FS], Cy Jamison [BLM], John Turner [FWS] and James Ridenour [National Park Service, NPS] commissioned a team of scientists to formulate a management strategy for the northern spotted owl in old-growth forests in the northwest. It became known as the Interagency Scientific Committee, or ISC." (Zielinski 2020) That team was led by Jack Ward

Thomas (Forest Service), Eric D. Forsman (Forest Service), Joseph B. Lint (Bureau of Land Management), E. Charles Meslow (FWS), Barry R. Noon (FS) and Jared Verner (FS). In addition to the leaders, the team consisted of biologists from all federal agencies and several academic institutions. Other team members, in alphabetical order, were Mary Ann Bishop (FS), Charles R. Bruce (Oregon Department of Fish and Wildlife, ODF), Gordon I. Gould Jr. (California Department of Fish and Game), A. Grant Gunderson (FS), David W. Hays (Washington Department of Wildlife, WDW), Douglas B. Houston (NPS), Larry L. Irwin (Oregon State University), Bruce Marcot (FS), Dennis Daniel Murphy (Stanford University), Barry Stuart Mulder (FWS) and David Samuel Wilcove (The Wilderness Society). The report produced by the ISC chronicled both the history and the known science surrounding the northern spotted owl. The following excerpts from Appendix B of that report unfold the biological and legal story of this small bird of prey and its rise to the throne of controversy.

Historical Perspective on Northern Spotted Owl Management

Spotted Owl Research and Planning Before the Endangered Species Act of 1973

Before the early 1970s, relatively little was known about the northern spotted owl except that it resided in a variety of forest types in western Washington, western Oregon, and northwestern California. It was considered a rare or uncommon resident in most of its range. (Marshall 1969)

Eric Forsman and Richard Reynolds began searching for spotted owls in Oregon during the late 1960s. Their preliminary work revealed that spotted owls were present in several locations, including some areas where Marshall (1942) and Gabrielson and Jewett (1940) had reported owls many years earlier . . .

Oregon Endangered Species Task Force

Publication of a summary reference for compiling the official list of nationally endangered species drew regional and national attention to the spotted owl in 1973, when it was included as a possible candidate for the list. Shortly after that publication was released, John McKean, then Director of the Oregon Game Commission, proposed that a professional interagency task force be formed to address endangered species management in Oregon. This group, the Oregon Endangered Species Task Force, was formed in 1973 . . .

Spotted Owl Research and Planning After the Endangered Species Act of 1973

The Federal Endangered Species Act, which became law late in 1973, had no immediate effect on spotted owl management, but has served ever since as the yardstick for species protection on public lands . . . Research efforts in Oregon and California continued over the next few years. (Forsman 1976, Gould 1974) Passage of the National Forest Management Act in 1976 and regulations issued pursuant to that Act laid the groundwork for maintaining well-distributed, viable populations of all native species on National Forests.

First Oregon Spotted Owl Management Plan

Both the Oregon State Director of the BLM and the FS Regional Forester (R6) agreed in early 1977 to protect spotted owl habitat in accordance with Task Force interim recommendations, except where sales under contract or current fiscal year timber sales existed. In late 1977, the Oregon Spotted Owl Management Plan was submitted to the various agency administrators for review and comment . . . Both the R6 Regional Forester and the Oregon State Director of BLM agreed to implement the management plan recommendations through their ongoing land management planning processes. Final decisions on distribution, number, and location of sites managed for owls were to be made with public involvement through the planning process. The year was 1977, 4 years after the Task Force began work on the plan . . .

Increasing Effort

After 1978, the effort expended on owl surveys increased considerably on many National Forests in Oregon and Washington, and in 1979, a Washington Spotted Owl Working Group was initiated. In 1980, the R6 Regional Forester directed National Forests in Washington to protect spotted owl habitat for all confirmed pairs, in accordance with Oregon Spotted Owl Management Plan criteria . . .

First FWS Status Review

The Portland Regional Office of the FWS undertook a status review of the spotted owl in 1981 because of concerns about the decline of old-growth forest (USDI 1982). Although the species was described as 'vulnerable' in this review, the FWS concluded that the species did not then meet the listing requirements of the Endangered Species Act of 1973.

The Old Growth Wildlife Research and Development Program

The FS, in cooperation with the BLM, initiated the Old Growth Wildlife Research and Development Program in 1982, which addressed species of concern in western Washington and Oregon. (This program was rechartered in 1986 as the Spotted Owl Research, Development, and Application Program and included both the Pacific Northwest and Pacific Southwest Research Stations.) Under the auspices of this program, numerous studies on spotted owls and associated habitats were initiated in Oregon, Washington, and California. These studies are still in progress and have generated numerous progress reports and publications . . .

FS Regional Guide

The FS issued the final Regional Guide (USDA 1984) for the Pacific

Northwest Region in 1984. The Regional Guide directed the National Forests to analyze the effects of protecting at least 375 pairs in Oregon and Washington as they developed Forest plans. Management was to follow the 1981 proposed revision of the Oregon Interagency Spotted Owl Management Plan. Shortly thereafter, the R6 Regional Office provided further direction for spacing requirements needed to maintain a well-distributed population. This increased to 551 the number of spotted owl habitat areas proposed for management under Forest plans in Oregon and Washington.

FS SEIS

Later in 1984, a consortium of conservation groups appealed the R6 Regional Guide on the grounds that the standards and guidelines it contained were inadequate, and that the proposed plan was a major Federal action requiring an environmental impact statement (EIS). The Chief of the Forest Service denied the appeal, but the Deputy Assistant Secretary for Agriculture reversed that decision and directed the FS to prepare a supplemental EIS (SEIS) on spotted owl standards and guidelines. Preparation of the SEIS began in 1985.

FS Standards and Guidelines in California

Several forests had not yet begun by 1984 to implement the Region 5 standards and guidelines that had been issued 2 years earlier because of delays in preparing individual forest land management plans. The CDFG and R5 (FS) agreed that regional standards and guidelines should be implemented promptly before existing owl management options were lost. As a result, a network of spotted owl habitat areas [SOHAs] were established on all western Sierra Nevada and northwestern California National Forests.

National Audubon Advisory Panel

The National Audubon Society formed a 'blue-ribbon' advisory panel in 1985 to review the status of the spotted owl in Washington, Oregon, and northern California. The panel recommended in 1986 that a minimum of 1500 pairs of spotted owls be maintained in the three States, including in the Sierra Nevada of California, and that much larger amounts of habitat be protected for pairs of owls in the range of the northern subspecies (Dawson et al. 1986). A variation of this recommendation was included as 'alternative M' in the spotted owl SEIS being developed at the time by the FS . . .

Private Industry Becomes Involved in Research

Private industry became involved in research efforts on spotted owls in 1986 through the National Council for Air and Stream Improvement in Corvallis, Oregon. Since then, industry research efforts have expanded to all three States on both public and private lands.

BLM Environmental Assessment

In 1986, the BLM initiated a Statewide environmental assessment (EA) on the spotted owl in Oregon to determine if new information required a supplemental EIS on their existing timber management plans. After public review, the BLM decided in 1987 that a supplemental EIS was not warranted.

FWS Petitioned to List

The FWS acknowledged in early 1987 that they had received a petition from GreenWorld to list the spotted owl as an endangered species under the Endangered Species Act of 1973. A new status review was undertaken and, in December 1987, the FWS announced that listing was not warranted. The decision not to list was appealed to the Seattle Federal Court by conservation groups in 1988. The Court determined that the decision not to list was not biologically based and ordered the FWS to re-address the listing decision.

California's Planning Process

In early 1987, CDFG [California Department of Fish and Game] began filing nonconcurrences with CDF [California Department of Forestry and Fire Protection] when reviewing timber harvest plans where the cutting of old-growth stands in north coastal California was proposed. By later in the year, environmental groups had brought suit to stop several sales where nonconcurrences had been filed but CDF had approved the sale. This litigation caused a review of the CDF's harvest planning process and of the Board of Forestry rules relating to how sensitive wildlife species are handled.

In 1989, the State Legislature passed AB 1580, which directed CDF to develop a system to better track how harvest planning decisions are made, and to develop a scientific data base on timberland habitats and wildlife species so that cumulative impacts of timber harvesting can be better analyzed. At the same time, the Board of Forestry asked CDF to develop a habitat conservation plan so that harvest planning and logging could continue if the northern spotted owl was listed as a threatened species by the FWS at some future date.

Spotted Owl Listed by States

The Washington Wildlife Commission listed the spotted owl as 'endangered' throughout the State in 1988. As a result of the listing, WDW began to develop a State recovery plan with participation by agency and private organizations. That process is ongoing. Late in the year, the Oregon Wildlife Commission, under a new State endangered species act, reaffirmed listing the spotted owl as 'threatened' in Oregon. Such a listing requires protection on all State lands but not on private lands. Protection on private forest lands is now being considered by ODF under recent (1987) amendments to the State Forest Practices Act.

In April 1988, the Interagency Spotted Owl Subcommittee proposed new management guidelines for the northern spotted owl that, for the first time, addressed the entire range of the subspecies in Washington,

Oregon, and northern California. The main features of the Spotted Owl Subcommittee recommendations were to maintain larger population centers, protect all remaining habitat in areas of special concern (such as the Oregon Coast Range), regenerate more habitat in problem areas, maintain an interconnecting network of individual SOHAs of one to three pairs per township, retain an amount of habitat per pair that reflected the mean amount of old growth in home ranges of radio-marked pairs, and provide for replacement habitat. Monitoring and coordination were also addressed. These recommendations were not acted on by any of the agencies responsible for managing the owl. Since that time, the subcommittee has become inactive.

FWS Proposes Listing Spotted Owl as Threatened

The FWS initiated another status review in January 1989 to supplement the 1987 review. The status review was completed in April, with the result that the northern spotted owl was deemed to warrant protection as a threatened species under the Endangered Species Act of 1973. As a result of this decision, an FWS listing-review team was established in October 1989 to review this proposal and make a final recommendation on whether to list the owl in June 1990. The proposal to list the northern spotted owl triggered requirements that the FS and BLM confer with the FWS under Section 7 of the Endangered Species Act. Interim guidelines were prepared by the FWS to assist the agencies in evaluating timber sales that would impact spotted owls. These guidelines increased the size of SOHAs in northern California to 2000 acres and designated some interim 'areas of concern' where timber sales were to be deferred for 1990. This conferencing process is ongoing.

The Scientific Committee Begins

A new interagency agreement was signed in August 1988 by the heads of the BLM, FS, FWS, and NPS. In that agreement, the agencies agreed to work toward a common goal of ensuring population viability for the spotted owl throughout its range. The Interagency Agreement served as the umbrella under which the Interagency Spotted Owl Scientific Committee was formed in 1989.

The Final SEIS

In late 1988, the Chief of the FS issued a Record of Decision on the supplemental spotted owl EIS for Oregon and Washington. The selected alternative (F) directed the 13 National Forests with spotted owls to establish a SOHA network. Standards and guidelines differed for physiographic provinces. Amounts of habitat to be provided in SOHAs varied from 1000 acres in southern Oregon to 3000 acres on the Olympic Peninsula. Habitat was to be identified within 1.5 miles of the center area in Oregon and 2.1 miles in Washington; SOHAs containing three or more pairs were to be no more than 12 miles apart, and single-pair SOHAs were to be no more than 6 miles apart. The Record of Decision was shortly appealed by WDW and by timber and environmental groups, but the Assistant Secretary of Agriculture denied the appeals.

The Hatfield-Adams Amendment

Interest groups obtained injunctions prohibiting the sale of old growth on BLM lands near spotted owl sites, and continuous litigation finally resulted in the 'Northwest Compromise' (Hatfield-Adams Amendment) of 1989. This legislation applied to Washington and Oregon, and was attached as a rider (Section 318) to the 1990 fiscal-year appropriations bill. It declared the FS's Spotted Owl SEIS and the BLM's spotted owl management plans adequate for preparing FY90 sales. The compromise expanded FS SOHA sizes by 12 to 25% and established 12 new agreement areas on BLM lands, for a period of 1 year. It also instructed the FS and the BLM to minimize the fragmentation of 'ecologically significant' stands of old growth in Oregon and Washington and provided for establishing citizen advisory boards to assist the FS and BLM in preparing and modifying sales. Implementation of Section 318 is ongoing.

Committee Established

As a result of the uncertainty surrounding the status of the northern spotted owl, the FS recommended the formation of an interagency scientific committee to address the issue. This recommendation was agreed upon by the heads of the BLM, FS, FWS, and NPS, and in October 1989, the Interagency Spotted Owl Scientific Committee was established. The charge to the Committee was to 'develop a scientifically credible conservation strategy for the northern spotted owl.' The task was essentially completed with the publication of this document. (Thomas et al. 1990)

CHAPTER 6

Critical Habitat

Jack Ward Thomas had earned the respect of the Interagency Scientific Committee (ISC) through his general demeanor, professionalism and willingness to give credit to the full team. He often corrected members of Congress or the public when they referred to the report on northern spotted owl management as the "Thomas Report," reminding them it was the ISC report. I first saw Jack in public when I watched his congressional testimony on C-Span while I was still in Virginia. I was impressed with his candor and directness in laying out the findings of the ISC and explaining their recommendations. His reputation as a scientist and leader was at its pinnacle.

The Congressional Research Service put out a report in 1989 that explained the origin of the owl's role.

> The regulations developed under the National Forest Management Act of 1976 (NFMA) require the Forest Service to maintain viable populations of native vertebrate species; regulations allow using indicator species (i.e., 'species selected because their population changes are believed to indicate the effects of management activities' [36 CFR 219.19]) as a relatively easy way of measuring the health of the ecosystems. The Forest Service selected spotted owls as indicators in National Forests where they occur because of their dependence on the old growth ecosystem. (Corn 1989)

The ISC reviewed all past science and identified old-growth forests and their structure as having several attributes, including multi-layered canopy of trees, large-diameter living trees (some with broken tops), and dead, standing and fallen trees in active states of decay. These characteristics represent a continuum of microhabitats within a single stand. Nature wastes nothing, and climax old-growth stands encompass the entire cycle of life. Old-growth forests provide the needs of all vertebrate species as well as the invertebrate species that serve the same purpose in the food chain as they do in flooded bottomland hardwood wetlands. The reckless rush to supply timber was rapidly eliminating entire hillsides of an ecosystem that took centuries to develop. Section 318 of the FY89-90 appropriations bill set targets of 7.7 billion board feet (bbf) on national forests in Washington and Oregon, and 1.9 bbf on the Bureau of Land Management (BLM) districts of Oregon. This could simply not be sustained over the long term in a system that couldn't regenerate a fraction of that amount in the same time period.

The ISC report attempted to address the needs of the northern spotted owl and, by ecological necessity, the food chain that supported the owl and its prey. While it did address other old-growth-dependent species, it was made clear that their directive was the spotted owl:

> Much of the attention directed toward this bird stems from a growing debate over managing old-growth forests on Federal lands, and from a concern about protecting biodiversity. We understand the significance of these larger issues, but we have kept to our mandate to develop a conservation strategy specifically for the northern spotted owl. (Thomas et al. 1990)

The overarching management strategy of the ISC report was stated thus:

We propose a two-part strategy. The first stage prescribes and implements the steps needed to protect habitat in amounts and distribution that will adequately ensure the owl's long-term survival.

The second stage calls for research and monitoring to test the adequacy of the strategy and to seek ways to produce and sustain suitable owl habitat in managed forests. Insights gained in this second stage can be used to alter or replace habitat conservation areas prescribed in the first stage, but only if the modified strategy can be clearly demonstrated to provide adequately for the long-term viability of the owl. Our strategy largely abandons the current and, we believe,

Spotted Owl (Courtesy of USFWS)

flawed system of one- to three-pair spotted owl habitat areas (SOHAs), in favor of protecting larger blocks of habitat—which we term Habitat Conservation Areas, or HCAs.

In identifying HCAs, they understood that owls would have to travel within this network of healthy blocks of habitat and needed both food and cover adequate to protect them in their journey across areas of timber harvest. They recommended that areas outside the HCAs, yet still on federal lands, be maintained with forests of at least 50 percent of the trees with diameter of 11 inches at breast height, and at least a 40 percent canopy closure. This became known as the "50-11-40 rule." They further recommended that state-owned lands, including HCAs, follow these recommendations as much as feasible. The areas outside the HCAs would later become known as the "matrix," and they created increased difficulty for the BLM due to the checkerboard ownership of the Oregon and California Railroad Revested (O&C) lands.

The O&C lands encompass approximately 2.6 million acres in Oregon and California and were originally granted to build a railroad from Portland to San Francisco. The land was reconveyed to the United States to be managed by the BLM in 1916, but eighteen counties where O&C lands are located receive payments from the United States government at a 50 percent share of timber revenue on those lands. Thus, BLM has a strong mandate to provide revenues to the O&C counties through timber sales. Having HCAs where timber harvest was forbidden, at least until new areas matured to replace the old-growth stands, created significant economic concerns regarding the ISC recommendations. The ISC concluded its report with the understanding that economic and social analyses would follow:

> Our assignment was to develop a scientifically credible conservation strategy for the northern spotted owl. We recognize that the impacts of the strategy we propose will be analyzed by

others. The immediate response, we expect, will be to focus almost solely on the short-term economic and social impacts of implementing the strategy as it affects the availability of timber. This assessment is critically important. Adoption of the conservation strategy, however, has significant ramifications for other natural resources, including water quality, fisheries, soils, stream flows, wildlife, biodiversity, and outdoor recreation. All of these aspects must be considered when evaluating the conservation strategy. The issue is more complex than spotted owls and timber supply—it always has been. (Thomas et al. 1990)

...

The northern spotted owl provided two "firsts" for the U.S. Fish and Wildlife Service (FWS). Never before had the FWS been successfully sued over a listing decision, as was done in 1988 over the denial of the GreenWorld petition to list the owl. Then, on February 26, 1991, the FWS was dealt its first loss over a decision to not designate critical habitat. We were in new territory and there was no time to waste. I assembled a team of FWS biologists from the states where owls occurred who had expertise on both the needs of the species and places where old-growth forests occurred. Barry Mulder was the constant advisor to the team, but because of his role as spotted owl coordinator, he had a plateful working with the Forest Service (FS) and BLM on their management strategies. Bob Ruesink oversaw the team with the principal members—Karla Kramer, Randy Tweten, Steve Spangle and Mike Tehan. They all received extensive support from their home offices in each of the affected states.

I was just getting to know the field supervisors, but my old friend Dave Frederick, who had moved to Olympia as the field supervisor while I was in D.C., provided me with a level of comfort as I became acquainted with my new teammates. We established the goal of having a draft proposed rule prepared by March 29 and a final sent to the Federal Register for publication by April 29, which was ambitious by any standard. In two short months, this team would have to review millions of acres of habitat maps and determine the current condition and what role in the life cycle each block of land provided. Was it nesting, resting, foraging or dispersal habitat? Was it necessary for the conservation (recovery) of the species? If it was lost, would the owl be able to survive? This last was a new question introduced in this section of the law. Instead of using biology only, as is required for listing decisions, Section 4(b)(2) states that

> the Secretary [of the Interior] shall designate critical habitat, and make revisions thereto, under subsection (a)(3) on the basis of the best scientific data available *and after taking into consideration the economic impact, the impact on national security, and any other relevant impact, of specifying any particular area as critical habitat.* The Secretary *may exclude* any area from critical habitat if he determines that the benefits of such exclusion outweigh the benefits of specifying such area as part of the critical habitat, unless he determines, based on the best scientific and commercial data available, that the *failure to designate such area as critical habitat will result in the extinction of the species concerned.* (Emphasis added.)

Not only would this analysis be one of the most complicated biological challenges to be undertaken in what amounted to a month's time, but there would have to be economic and social analyses to determine if those costs outweighed the biological benefits. One twist to this inordinate challenge is that the critical habitat burden rests solely with the federal government. Regulatory actions for critical habitat are only required when the federal government is carrying out, permitting or assisting in the carrying out of the project that may affect critical habitat. Non-federal lands are subject to critical habitat (CH) regulation, but only when there is a federal "nexus" or connection to the project. While directly or indirectly harming the species is a universal prohibition, critical habitat is considered the responsibility of the federal government alone. As the analysis ensued, we were embarking on what amounted to new policy interpretations of the Endangered Species Act (ESA) for operational purposes. Unfortunately, we would get no experienced guidance from the Office of the Secretary.

President George H.W. Bush held significant credentials to be the president of the United States. He had been a member of Congress, ambassador to the United Nations, director of the Central Intelligence Agency and vice president under Ronald Reagan. One of his campaign promises had been "Read my lips, no new taxes," only to pass a substantial tax increase in order to help reduce the federal deficit. He had proven to be true to his beliefs for a "kinder, gentler" approach to leading, and everyone seemed to genuinely like him and his matriarchal wife, Barbara. But politics, especially in the face of tax increases, erases intent.

His secretary of the interior, former New Mexico Congressman Manuel Lujan, was a nice person but seemed to be ill-equipped for the complicated stresses of the Department of the Interior (DOI). Few people understand the breadth and reach of the DOI. The secretary of the interior oversees one in every five acres in the United States; all energy development except hydropower and nuclear; all mineral development as well as oil and gas on federal lands and offshore waters; all Native American fiduciary responsibilities; the national parks; national wildlife refuges and BLM lands; and all U.S. Geological Survey research and monitoring, including volcanos and earthquakes. In addition, DOI works with the U.S. territories and freely associated states (FAS) under the Compact of Free Association to provide FAS with economic assistance, defense and other services and benefits. In return, the FAS grants the U.S. certain operating rights and other exclusive considerations. As likable as Secretary Lujan was, few believed he was up to this extremely demanding, and often conflicting, set of responsibilities.

Section 4 of the ESA directs the secretary of the interior to establish recovery teams of qualified scientists to build a plan that would lead to the recovery and removal of the species from ESA protection. Lujan brought into his office a Senate staffer named Don Knowles. Don previously worked on staff for the Senate Appropriations Committee and had Interior as part of his portfolio. He had been a friend to the FWS over the years but possessed no particular strengths in wildlife management that would give him the credentials to oversee any planning activities for the spotted owl. But the secretary assigned Knowles the responsibility of being his representative to the recovery team. Normally, recovery team activities were delegated to the FWS regional director, but Lujan decided to pull the oversight into his office. I had met Don several years earlier and was eager to do whatever I could to assist the recovery team, which had been appointed in February, just before we received the critical habitat ruling from Judge Zilly. The team's first meeting was March 5, and Marv Plenert was given the responsibility of recovery team leader. Dr. Jon Bart, FWS Ohio State University Cooperative Wildlife Research Unit, was appointed as committee chairman. From a technical standpoint, the team was to advise Marv and the secretary through the recovery plan; thus, Dr. Bart was the day-to-day manager of the team. Section 4 of the ESA directs that

> the Secretary shall develop and implement plans (hereinafter in the subsection referred to as 'recovery plans') for the conservation and survival of endangered species and threatened species listed pursuant to this section, unless he finds that such a plan will not promote the conservation of the species. [Section 4(f)(1)]

These plans are meant to be a road map to improving the condition of a threatened or endangered species to the point that it can be removed from the protection of the ESA. The plan is *not* to identify things the FWS should do, but rather actions necessary for recovery to be

Manuel Lujan (right) and author (Courtesy of USDOI)

undertaken by whomever may contribute. The recovery team is appointed by the secretary or designee in the FWS, and is exempted by the Federal Advisory Committee Act (FACA). FACA exempts specific committees from the requirement of public disclosure of discussions and recommendations given to the government in a non-public way. The plan is also *absent the weight of law or regulation* and is only a recommended guide for voluntary compliance. Thus, it is excluded from the "sunshine" provision of many laws. However, the FWS, by its concurrence and publication of the recovery plan, endorses the identified actions deemed necessary for species recovery and relies heavily upon these plans when carrying out its responsibilities under the ESA, both regulatory and advisory.

In addition, it becomes the accepted "best available science" to guide the public in helping to recover species. Jon Bart was a well-seasoned and credentialed wildlife biologist who brought a significant skill set to the team. In addition to Marv, Don and Jon, the following were recovery team members: Robert Anthony (FWS, Oregon), Melvin Berg (BLM, D.C.), John Beuter (deputy assistant secretary USDA), Wayne Elmore (BLM, Oregon and Washington), John Faye (FWS, D.C.), R.J. "Rocky" Gutierrez (Humboldt State University), Theodore Heintz, Jr. (Office of Policy Analysis, DOI), Richard S. "Holt" Holthausen (FS, Utah), Kenneth Lathrop (Bureau of Indian Affairs, Oregon), Kent Mays (FS, Oregon), Richard Nafziger (Governor of Washington representative), Martha Pagel (Governor of Oregon representative), Christine Sproul (Governor of California representative), Edward Starkey (National Park Service, Oregon) and John Tappeiner (Oregon State University).

Jon assigned the lead role for different aspects of the analysis to team members with particular expertise in those disciplines: Holthausen and Gutierrez—Spotted Owl Biology; Tappeiner—Forest Ecology; Heintz—Economics; Anthony—Other Species; Elmore and Nafziger—Planning; and Bart—Executive. Each team member was on one or more of these subcommittees based on their expertise and experience. Most of the team meetings were held in a conference room at the Portland FWS Regional Office, which allowed full access to our staff for support. I came to appreciate Jon's laid-back demeanor and constant smile. He was able to keep the team on point and on schedule. There were no guarantees that the Bush administration would win reelection, so no one assumed the luxury of several years to complete this massive plan. In addition, the dual efforts of designating critical habitat and creating a recovery strategy required constant communication between the two groups.

One would logically think that measures to conserve the species, recover and delist would by necessity be synchronous with identified habitat believed to be essential to species recovery. But the deadline requirements in the law are backward. The recovery plan that would identify habitat essential to the species' recovery is not required until *after* critical habitat designation, and would likely modify the less informed CH determination. Further, the FS and BLM were working diligently on forest management standards and guidelines to satisfy the National

Forest Management Act (NFMA) and the Federal Lands Policy Management Act (FLPMA), respectively. With all the efforts under way, anyone who was bored and looking for something to do could easily be accommodated.

Inside the FWS, it was all hands on deck. Marv Plenert expected me to be in his office every morning at seven to "brief" him. That was how it read on the calendar, but not how it went. Marv blistered me with questions and criticism about every aspect of what was going on. I was taken aback by that at my first few sit-downs with him. My belief had always been that a good supervisor gave an assignment and then allowed the people to work on it without constantly looking over their shoulder. But this was different. John Turner and the staff in D.C. were as deeply involved in briefings with the secretary, other federal agencies and Congress as we were dealing with western offices of each. That included Don Knowles regularly offering memos to John Turner or his assistant, Mike Brennan, with "suggestions" as to things we needed to explore and explain. That meant Marv was getting questions daily on what was going on and, as it trickles down, I got my lashing each morning and lecture on how it should have been done yesterday. Marv didn't like to say "I don't know, I'll get with my staff and get back to you." I believed, and still do, that this is the luxury one finally achieves when you are no longer expected to be the expert. But we were all under a microscope.

• • •

Judge Zilly ordered that a schedule for designating critical habitat be provided to the court. John Turner signed a declaration that stated the FWS planned to have acreage calculations, legal descriptions of proposed critical habitat boundaries, and camera-ready maps of proposed critical habitat areas by March 15. Internal review and approval of a proposed rule and draft analysis of economic and other impacts of a designation would be completed by April 23, and a proposed rule ready for

Denuded Northwest Forest (Courtesy of USFS)

publication by April 29, 1991. It further stated that, in compliance with law, the FWS would have a public review and comment period of at least sixty days from the date of publication in the Federal Register, with a final designation published "as soon as possible under the circumstances after completion of the public comment period on the proposed rule." (Turner 1991)

The draft economic analysis was carried out by John Charbonneau, an economist in the D.C. office. Because the evaluation to list a species was restricted to the five factors of biological health, it was made clear throughout the discussions that the economic impacts were limited to the *added* impacts from designating critical habitat. This clarification is significant because the overwhelming majority of impacts to the socio-economic sector occurs with the listing of a species, where all activities that might result in "take" are prohibited without prior approval under the ESA. Section 7 of that law provides for the consultation between the FWS and other federal agencies on actions they propose. Section 10 of the Act provides for permits to be issued to non-federal entities when their actions may result in take of a listed species. The impacts from critical habitat designation were, therefore, expected to be much less than the public assumed. There was little doubt within the FWS that the April proposal would not satisfy the level of quality necessary for a sound decision. The habitat designation team had barely a month to perform analyses, prepare maps, write the document and get them into the review process. There was certainly no time for a reasonable analysis of economics or of identifying areas that might be excluded. But the deadline set by the court was being met. The proposal published in the Federal Register identified 11,638,195 acres in the states of Washington, Oregon and California as proposed critical habitat.

We immediately began preparing for the next proposal, which would contain much more science, social and economic analysis. Director Turner assigned Dr. Mel Schamberger from the National Ecology Research Center in Ft. Collins, Colorado, as the leader of the economic analysis team. In a memo to key members of his FWS leadership team, assistant and regional directors (the directorate) Turner said:

> Dr. Schamberger's primary duty will be to serve as a liaison for the Team between my office, the Assistant Director for Fish and Wildlife Enhancement, the Regional Director, Region 1, and the Biological Assessment Team Coordinator, Barry Mulder . . . In this capacity, he will (1) be the Team contact for briefing papers, meeting requests, and status reports on the Team activities and progress; (2) be relied upon to make sure the established milestones for the Team are met; (3) coordinate the review of and responses to all comments regarding the economic issues received during the current public comment period on the proposed critical habitat designation; (4) prepare the appropriate input for the re-proposal presently scheduled for publication the week of August 5; and (5) make sure that any new information regarding the economic analysis received during the comment period will be disseminated to the appropriate Team members. (Turner May 1991)

During the week of May 20, we held four public hearings on the published proposal. On Monday, the hearing was in Eureka, California; on Wednesday, Eugene, Oregon; on Thursday, Olympia, Washington; and on Friday, Vancouver, Washington. These hearings were perfunctory to satisfy public demand, but the rule was so hastily put together that we didn't expect to get much quality input. We knew, however, that we were in the process of building the second proposal, and the comments were expected to be heavily weighted toward economics. The hope was that there would be some factual, rather than just emotional, information provided for the record that would help in Mel's effort.

To provide everyone on the team with the same information, I put out a summary report for the files each week on all aspects of the designation process and progress being made. Mel put out similar reports on the workings of the economic analysis team, with both reports reiterating that the two groups were simply two parts of one team. On June 17, I testified before the Washington State Senate Ways and Means Committee to update them on the process and how economics would be employed in the final decision. These briefing requests were a common occurrence, not only with the three state legislatures, but also with the timber industry and environmental community. I took most of them for two reasons: to ensure that the same information was given in the same way to all requestors, and to make sure that the team members were left alone to perform the herculean tasks they had been assigned. Whenever I stopped in to visit with the team, my heart swelled with pride at the dedication and professionalism they constantly displayed in preparation of the second proposal. Ron Swan, regional DOI solicitor in Portland, was a rock star in helping everyone stay calm and on solid legal footing. Work was going on seven days a week into the night, but Ron was always there when we needed legal guidance. There was literally no part of the team that was not giving everything they had. The second proposal would be significantly better.

In peeling back the layers of the onion and looking at the ESA and critical habitat, we needed to have one definition for each aspect of CH designation to ensure consistency. Terms under the law and regulations had to be dissected and re-clarified. An area that caused much discussion, especially through questions from D.C., was how the critical habitat exercise would mesh with the ISC report, which was still often referred to as the "Thomas Report." Mike Brennan, John Turner's assistant, was someone I could always count on to watch our backs. He was an extremely helpful counterbalance for Don Knowles, who was constantly inserting himself into the process as the "Secretary's representative" but was, in my opinion, attempting to elevate his importance. I always strove to make sure that Mike had the latest information and, on one occasion, sent him a note explaining the differences between the ISC report and our efforts on critical habitat so he would be prepared for questions. Part of the explanation was this:

> The goal of the Thomas report was to *maintain* the population above the level of extinction. This would include a reduction in the number of birds alive today, but would preclude extinction of the species. The Critical Habitat (CH) process must, by definition, contribute to the conservation (defined by law as toward recovery) of the species. Therefore, the Thomas report is only a maintenance tool, where CH is a recovery tool. By directive, the Thomas report was limited to federal ownership, particularly BLM and Forest Service lands. The CH process must be blind to ownership . . . Finally, the Thomas report has no weight of law and is intended to be malleable as a management guideline. The CH, once promulgated by rule, has the weight of law and can only be changed by the rulemaking process. In addition, the Thomas report accepted that there would be socio-economic impacts by assuming that a significant amount of timber would be harvested. The CH process first identifies the biological criteria (needs) of the species, what lands contribute

to those criteria, and clearly identifies boundaries on maps that demark those areas.

After that, the economic impacts are superimposed on those areas to determine if any areas have significantly more costs associated than benefits to the species. At that time, modifications can be made accordingly, provided the species receives adequate protection through the overall process.

The first step of the designation process was to accept the previous science that identified nesting, roosting, foraging and dispersal habitats as the "needs" of the spotted owl. In regulation, this equated to the "primary constituent elements." The next step was to examine the landscape and map those areas that provided one or more of these needs. In performing analyses for purposes of Section 7 evaluations, other terms, such as "adversely modify or destroy," move to front and center in the discussion. Oddly enough, regulations allow habitat value, or even the species, to be diminished, but not to the point at which the critical habitat is adversely modified or destroyed. It allows negative impact, just not elimination of the value for which it was designated.

For the species, "take" can occur as long as it doesn't place the species in jeopardy of extinction. This subtle, but extremely important nuance brings to light the real pathway for recovery. Regulation can prevent designated habitat from being destroyed by federal action and can prevent the extinction of a species, but it cannot demand that landowners *improve habitat conditions* for any species. That can only occur through the *voluntary* actions that the landowner is willing to undertake. Creation of new habitat is strictly voluntary, yet is imperative if we are to improve the status of imperiled species. The analyses and legal discussions we were required to undertake resulted in a much better understanding of not only the ESA, but other laws where regulatory tools are available.

On July 1 and 2, we held our first significant meeting of the whole team in Fort Collins at Mel's offices. Fifteen employees from the FWS, one from the Forest Service, one from the Bureau of Mines and one from Colorado State University were in attendance. It was an excellent meeting during which the legal process, biological balancing and economic balancing were discussed at length. From the FWS critical habitat designation team standpoint, it could not have been more helpful. Mel had brought order and process to the economic analysis and, for the first time, I could see the evaluation and potential exclusion of areas working as the law had intended.

The major questions were these: For any given area, how heavy was the additional economic burden from designation of CH? If that area were removed, could the owl recover? How much 50-11-40 habitat did we need to ensure dispersal within the Coast Range? The Cascades? How much was needed to ensure genetic movement between the two ranges? With a starting point of almost 12 million acres, we knew we had built in significant buffer to allow a more reasonable exercise. Not only were timber harvest impacts addressed; mining, recreation and non–forest product impact areas also were individually identified and evaluated. At the end of the two-day meeting, we were well on our way to a new proposal that eliminated a significant amount of habitat that was deemed not necessary for recovery.

On August 5 the FWS published its second, and much refined, proposal to designate approximately 8.3 million acres as spotted owl critical habitat. The proposal was a reduction of 3.3 million acres from the first proposal and included a mixture of old-growth and younger forests that provided adequate areas meeting the 50-11-40 rule. Three million acres of privately owned land were eliminated from the proposal, due mainly to their interlacing with BLM lands in Oregon and California, as well as to the publicly reviewed management plans of the Forest Service and BLM, which were committed to accomplishing nearly all of what would be needed to provide for the recovery of the owl. Over 6 million acres were on Forest Service lands, 1.3 million on BLM, and the remainder on military and state lands. In a press conference held at the Portland

Regional Office, I rolled out the new proposal and fielded questions from the press. The northern spotted owl was a significant news story nationwide, which commanded coverage by all the major news networks for their respective national evening broadcasts.

George Weyerhaeuser was a powerful head of one of the country's largest timber companies and well known for his involvement with elected officials. The press believed he had unfettered access to President Bush, and I was asked whether Mr. Weyerhaeuser had anything to do with the elimination of private lands from the proposal. I had to hold back a smile due to the question's irony. Neither he nor anyone from D.C. ever pushed us to remove private lands from the designation. We did hear, however, that he was lobbying to have more federal lands as well as his lands *included*! He was a private landowner and needed no federal assistance to harvest timber from his properties, which were substantial. Therefore, his operations would not be affected by having his lands designated as critical habitat above the prohibition of "take." There had already been a ban on international export of raw logs harvested on federal lands, and private timber companies had a corner on the market. We were told he was pushing for more designation so he and private industry could be the only game in town not only for exports, but for domestic needs. Holding back my chuckle, I responded, "All decisions on removal of private lands were made by biologists right here in the Northwest."

The first round of public hearings held in the spring brought the expected protests from the logging community, similar protests from the environmental community, but very little biological information regarding the needs of the owl. We did receive, however, some jewels of economic information that proved helpful to Mel's efforts in helping us pare down the original proposal. As we scheduled our next set of public hearings, we had become lulled into a false belief that people would behave properly and show courtesy even in their objections. We were mistaken.

• • •

Our first public hearing was scheduled for Redding, California, on Monday, September 9. I had some meetings and other scheduling conflicts, so I assumed it would be fine for Ron Swan and our solicitor's office to hold the hearing without the need of my presence. David Klinger, Phil Carroll and Patti Hutton attended the hearing and recorded the sounds coming from the audience of loggers, their families, and mill workers who had been bused to the hearing by their employers and paid to make their presence known. What we all had underestimated was that the name on the Federal Register announcement calling for comments was *mine*. Those who were opposed to designation had decided that, since all comments were to be sent to me, I was the one who would make the final decision. When they realized that I was not there to hear their comments in person, they made sure that no one supporting the designation could be heard. They did not physically harm anyone, but in addition to large signs, they had brought bullhorns and gas fog horns and drowned out anyone trying to speak, including the solicitor holding the hearing. Ron Swan was cut short because of the behavior. It was clear that I needed to attend each hearing so they could see me and know that I was truly hearing what they had to say. Even though the material stated that written comments held equal weight to verbal testimony, they wanted to see the person whom they believed was killing their jobs. It was a serious mistake on my part, and one for which I accepted full responsibility.

The next public hearing was in Medford, and I attended. I also asked Dave McMullen, assistant regional director for law enforcement (ARD-LE) in Region 1, to have two or three of his special agents there so people could see that we would not allow any more disruption. Many of the sheriffs refused to allow their officers to assist because the sheriffs were elected, and these were their voters. But having special agents there with their badges displayed was enough.

At one of the hearings, Special Agent Tom Riley found it necessary to have a discussion with one of the loggers after the man entered the room with a large sign. We had placed a prominent notice at the sign-in table stating that no noisemakers or large signs would be permitted in order to assure respect for all speakers. Two loggers ignored the notice and carried signs into the room. According to one of our staff, Tom, who had been a linebacker for the Baltimore Colts and still looked the part two decades later, went over to where the two loggers were sitting, leaned over with a smile and said "Gentlemen, I'd appreciate it if you would respect others and leave your signs outside as requested." One of the men retorted, "And what if I don't?" Tom is said to have replied, "You can carry them through the door that exists, or I'll make a new one in the wall with your body, or what's left of it," while never losing his smile. The two got up and willingly left the signs outside.

At the other end of the special agent scale was Ken Goddard, special agent in charge of the FWS Wildlife Forensics Lab in Ashland, Oregon. Ken is a man of medium build, sharp intellect, and an even sharper wit. He immediately came to me before the hearing in Medford and said, "I'm a scientist, not a real special agent. If shit hits the fan, follow me, because I'm getting the hell out of here!" I knew Ken would have my back, but his humor helped to calm my nerves. The Ashland Lab is so respected by Interpol and others in the field of law enforcement that it is unofficially known as the "Scotland Yard for Wildlife." That reputation is due in large part to Ken's leadership.

At the hearings that followed in Olympia and Portland there were protests outside the building, with log trucks blocking traffic and people in the timber industry being bused in to show opposition to CH designation, but to their credit, once the protestors were inside they were polite and sincere in their behavior and comments. I felt terrible that both sides lost because of my poor judgment in Redding. I was introduced by the solicitor conducting each meeting at the beginning, sat up front directly facing all speakers and took copious notes. Some believed I was just appearing to take notes, but I was committed to giving good people who feared for their livelihoods their honest opportunity to be heard. I still have many of those notes with names and comments made.

Plywood Petition at CH Hearing (Provided by author)

Most of them were asking to please not shut down their mills and eliminate their jobs, but provided no substantive information that could be legitimately used in making an economic analysis. Neither did they provide any additional science that would argue the owl needed less habitat to recover than had been reproposed.

Through this process of six hours at each hearing, three in the afternoon and three in the evening, I had wood products such as toilet paper, plywood with signed petitions to me, and 2-inch by 12-inch by 12-foot boards laid in front of my table with signatures of all the people who had either lost their jobs or would lose them because of the spotted owl closing the mills. Through these hours, during which I made a point to look each speaker in the eye unless I was writing, people began to understand that I was really listening to them, hoping to find jewels of information that could lead to the best solution. I was raised to respect good people willing to work hard to make a living. With each woman telling me how she didn't know how they were going to support their children; with each man asking me to not take his job; with each person who considered me as the person inflicting this harm, and as the one who could remove it, the stress I was already carrying was multiplied.

On breaks, it often happened that a company representative would strike up a conversation and tell me they appreciated the respect I was showing them. I occasionally smiled and quietly asked "Off the record, when was that mill originally scheduled to close because the company didn't want to spend the money to retool for smaller logs?" A few honest ones would look around to make sure no one else could hear before saying "1988," or "1990." To me, the sad part of the information stream was the mill owners telling the workers the mill was closing and they were being laid off because the spotted owl had shut them down when that was not the truth. With only about 40 percent of the original acreage of old growth remaining, and multiple hillsides completely denuded by clear-cuts, it was disappointing that the mill owners wouldn't be honest with their employees and tell them that they were not willing to retool to smaller, yet plentiful, logs in order to save those jobs.

But that's the way it was. I represented that faceless government that supposedly didn't care about people. To say it didn't impact me deeply would be a lie. It tore me apart to know there was little I could do to help. But I had taken an oath to uphold the laws and Constitution of the United States, so help me God. I was committed to carry out my responsibilities under the ESA and to our natural resources. But I would do that with respect and honesty. We carried out our work on the CH designation with the knowledge that we were doing all we could to consistently be honest with the public and professional in the tasks we were given.

After receipt of the comments from the August draft, a repeat of the meeting we had in Ft. Collins was held to assist Mel in preparing his recommendations to Director Turner. The director remained engaged in all aspects of the assignment and let us know he had our backs, but the challenge was still significant. The original proposal was for just over 11.6 million acres, and the adjusted proposal in August had been reduced to 8.3 million. The economic analysis provided by Mel's team demonstrated that significant outstanding economic hardships remained for many of the counties, especially those in the Oregon O&C, and that there were few benefits for designating state lands that seldom had a federal nexus for any of its harvests. John Turner was determined to provide the proper protection for the owl while minimizing unnecessary impacts to communities and families. On January 15, 1992, six days after my daughter Erin's twelfth birthday, the FWS published the final rule designating critical habitat for the northern spotted owl. The acreage covered by the rule was reduced by approximately 865,000 acres of federal lands, over 582,000 acres of state-owned land and 4,000 acres of military lands from the August proposal. The final rule designated 6,887,000 acres as spotted owl critical habitat.

The decision failed to please either side of the issue, which generally means it was balanced. Mark Rey, director of the American Forest Resource Alliance, responded "The plan constitutes a legal lynching of an entire region by an out-of-control federal agency." The environmental community didn't like it either. They accused us of folding to the timber interests. We, of course, believed we had looked at every aspect available in the record to come up with our final designation. Working for all the people of the United States means that every decision made will be disliked by some. The goal is to have been fair, in compliance with the law and displaying as much wisdom as possible.

• • •

In 1991, southern Oregon and California were still in the throes of a drought wreaking havoc on the U.S. Bureau of Reclamation (BOR) and State of California in meeting their responsibilities to deliver water to farms, people and the environment, including national wildlife refuges. Marv and I set up a dinner with Roger Patterson, the new regional director of the BOR, in February 1991 so we could discuss the Klamath Basin and the water challenges there. The Klamath is one of the most beautiful basins I have ever seen. The drainage starts at Mt. Mazama, better known as Crater Lake, and flows down the Wood and Williamson Rivers, through the agricultural basin and on down the Klamath River past Iron Gate Dam. The National Park Service describes the history of the basin:

> Crater Lake has long attracted the wonder and admiration of people all over the world. Its depth of 1,943 feet (592 meters) makes it the deepest lake in the United States, and the seventh deepest in the world. Its fresh water is some of the clearest found anywhere in the world. The interaction of people with this place is traceable at least as far back as the eruption of Mount Mazama. European contact is fairly recent, starting in 1853. A Native American connection with this area has been traced back to before the cataclysmic eruption. Archaeologists have found sandals and other artifacts buried under layers of ash, dust, and pumice from this eruption approximately 7,700 years ago . . . Accounts of the eruption can be found in stories told by the Klamath Indians, who are the descendants of the Makalak people.

Crater Lake (Courtesy of NPS)

The spirit of the mountain was called Chief of the World Below (Llao). The spirit of the sky was called Chief of the Above World (Skell). Sometimes Llao came up from his home inside the earth and stood on top of Mount Mazama, one of the highest mountains in the region. During one of these visits, he saw the Makalak chief's beautiful daughter and fell in love with her. He promised her eternal life if she would return with him to his lodge below the mountain. When she refused, he became angry and declared that he would destroy her people with fire. In his rage, he rushed up through the opening of his mountain and stood on top of it and began to hurl fire down upon them.

The mighty Skell took pity on the people and stood atop Mount Shasta to defend them. From their mountaintops, the two chiefs waged a furious battle. They hurled red hot rocks as large as hills. They made the earth tremble and caused great landslides of fire. The people fled in terror to the waters of Klamath Lake. Two holy men offered to sacrifice themselves by jumping into the pit of fire on top of Llao's mountain. Skell was moved by their bravery and drove Llao back into Mount Mazama. When the sun rose next, the great mountain was gone. It had fallen in on Llao. All that remained was a large hole. Rain fell in torrents, filling the hole with water. This is now called Crater Lake.

Early settlers and explorers did not hear about Crater Lake from the native inhabitants because this place is sacred to most Native Americans of Oregon and northern California. Makalaks (now Klamath Indians) held belief that the place was so holy that looking upon it would lead to death. There are no stories relating to the crystal blue lake that formed after the eruption, indicating that these people became silent on the issue of Mount Mazama, the mountain that was no longer. Even today, some Native Americans choose not to view Crater Lake. Its beauty and mystery form a religious context. (National Park Service 2020)

The Williamson and Sprague Rivers are formed by the annual snowmelt from Mt. Mazama and flow down through lands inhabited by the Klamath Tribe, who were also known as the Marsh People. This name grew from their use of the marshes that were created by the flat expanse of land surrounding the area now known as Klamath Falls in a watershed that encompasses approximately 3,000 square miles. The Williamson and Sprague join the Klamath River north and northeast of Upper Klamath Lake, which flows through Iron Gate Dam on its journey to the Pacific Ocean. Four Native American Tribes (Klamath, Yurok, Hoopa and Karuk) jointly claim their ancestors have occupied the land for time immemorial. European explorers arrived in the basin in the early 1800s.

When trapper Peter Skene Ogden first saw the Upper Klamath River Basin in 1826, he observed that 'the Country as far as the eye can reach [was] one continued Swamp and Lakes.' Following the end of the Modoc War in 1873, settlers began arriving in the region, eager to raise crops and livestock. However, the expanse of lakes, marshes, and wetlands (covering an area that stretches across what is today the Oregon-California state line), kept them from developing much of the land.

The National Reclamation Act, signed by President Theodore Roosevelt in 1902, made extensive agriculture in the Upper Klamath Basin possible by authorizing the reclamation of swamps and lakes to increase farmable acreage. In 1906, the newly established Reclamation Service initiated the Klamath Project to drain lakes and wetlands for cultivation. The Klamath Project included a network of dams, canals, ditches, and other facilities to drain, move, and store Upper Basin water.

Tule Lake became a sump one-quarter of its former size. To carry out this large-scale experiment in hydrological engineering, California and Oregon had to cede their rights and title to Tule Lake, Lower Klamath Lake, and the surrounding land. (Oregon Encyclopedia 2020)

The Klamath Project would evolve into one of the most ironic exercises in U.S. government history. What began as an effort to drain water off the land, and to limit the extent of lake surface area within the basin, ended with a "bucket brigade" to save water a century later. Several hydropower generating dams were built in the Klamath Basin, with Iron Gate at Klamath Falls one of the most significant from the standpoint of water management. Iron Gate was built by Pacific Power and Light to generate electricity for rural Oregon. This created a permanent barrier for the historically significant salmon migration that supported a robust fishery, particularly in the lower basin. The Bureau of Reclamation (BOR) project was authorized in 1905, and the first component to be constructed was "A" Canal. Roger Patterson later said about the Klamath Project:

The land was so flat you could run water in both directions if needed. The average depth of the reservoirs was about five feet. It was authorized under Reclamation to help 'reclaim' the swampland, but irrigation had to be a key component. We found out the invasive algae was the main enemy of the suckers [listed under the ESA] by pulling the oxygen out of the water during storms, night respiration, etc. We found keeping the water at higher elevations actually hurt the fish and helped the algae, but it took us a while to understand that. Then you had the coho salmon issues on the downstream reaches of the Klamath River. There were a lot of competing interests. (Patterson 2020)

Below the dam, the Shasta, Scott, Salmon and Trinity Rivers add their flows to what was historically a rich basin for salmon, steelhead and other fish species. Above Iron Gate Dam, in the impounded waters of Clear Lake, Upper Klamath, Tule and Lower Klamath Lakes, there were two species of fish that were listed under the ESA, the shortnose (*Chasinistes brevirostris*) and Lost River (*Delistes luxatus*) suckers. The Bureau was required to consult with the FWS on their annual water delivery plans for farmers, refuges and downstream fisheries needs.

Patterson had a slender build and strawberry blond hair. I found him to be friendly, open, very savvy about water issues and willing to work with us in any way he could to keep controversy down while fulfilling obligations for both water delivery and ESA responsibilities. I also began to realize what a difficult job he had trying to meet water contract commitments in an arid environment. In addition, the Klamath Project had been built to help *remove water* from the land. While having dinner shortly after I arrived, Roger asked, "Why do you find it necessary in biological opinions to tell us how to manage the water? Why don't you just tell us what you want for spawning habitat and when; for nursery habitat and when; and for growing the fish to adulthood, and then leave it to us to manage the project to achieve what you tell us the fish need?"

I was taken aback by this, and somewhat confused. "Roger, do we tell you how to manage your project in our biological opinions?" I had been in the endangered species business about two months at this point. He chuckled and said, "Yes." He then offered a proposition: "If you tell us what you want it to look like and when, and we don't do that, I'll tell you I was wrong and you can go back to giving us a water management schedule in the opinions and I won't complain." Since we didn't really have the hydrological expertise to tell his professional engineers what they should be doing to accomplish a task, I told Roger we agreed and would approach our consultations as just that, consultation among professionals with different skill sets. Marv was happy to see me taking this off his shoulders, and I was eager to build a strong working relationship with Roger and the BOR.

Henceforth we relayed what we believed the species needed, and relied on the BOR to manage to achieve those objectives. The result was better management of what water we had for fish in a high desert, while also allowing the water experts to make the most efficient use of water for people. This simple agreement was the beginning of one of the strongest trusts I ever had in my career with counterparts in other federal agencies. Roger and I were able to step that down within our staffs to a significant degree. Cooperative working relationships began to improve at all levels as professional honesty and trust started to grow. This trust would prove to be extremely important as we moved on to face new issues in the Klamath and elsewhere.

I was in my office in Portland in the spring of 1992 when I got a call from Mike Ryan, BOR project manager for the Klamath Project. "Dale, we have a problem. This looks to be the worst drought we've ever seen. Our model runs are projecting that the water in the east lobe of Clear Lake will go completely dry from evaporation by August and the other lakes will likely see record lows as well." I asked Mike how sure he was. His reply was, "I wish I was wrong, but unless it rains a hell of a lot, I'm not." I called Gail Kobetich, the supervisor of our Endangered Species office in

Sacramento, and asked him if he was aware of the dire prediction. Gail was one of the seasoned leaders in the Endangered Species Program and was known for his easy manner and understanding of the law. I had a great deal of respect for Gail and was anxious to hear what he thought about the pending drought. He said he had seen the model information and did not disagree with its findings. 1992 looked to be one of the worst droughts on record for the Klamath Project, and the listed fish.

Clear Lake was one of the smaller lakes in the Upper Basin system and was shaped like a horseshoe, with the west lobe slightly deeper than the east lobe, where the water control structure had been built. We had sucker populations throughout the lake and, when the east lobe was under stress, the fish would sometimes move through the narrow connecting canal to the deeper west lobe in search of better conditions. However, that created a stress on the fish that I felt we needed to avoid, if possible. The other aspect of this was water delivery to the farmers. In a drought year, they would face harsh enough conditions without the added pain of simply allowing water to evaporate away. I asked Gail if we shouldn't plug the canal, deliver the east lobe water to the farmers before it evaporated, and collect the fish in that lobe as the water dropped through delivery. Gail was adamant that he would not, under any circumstances, agree to that plan. I asked why, and he said he didn't believe we would be doing our jobs if we didn't hold all possible water for the fish.

After I hung up, I sat at my desk and asked my executive assistant, Pat Mitchell, to allow me some privacy while I gave it some thought. I kept asking myself what value there would be for the fish if, in the blistering August sun when water temperatures were elevated, we were putting them through the stress of capturing and moving them to the west lobe. There did not seem to be any dispute that would happen, so why would we not do it now when the water was cooler, had more oxygen, and there would be less stress? I settled on my decision when I couldn't find a reasonable answer to those questions. Keeping water from the farmers was simply another negative, not a positive. I called Roger Patterson to tell him what I had decided and asked, "Do you have enough sandbags to block off the canal between the lobes?" His response was, "Absolutely. When do you want them?" I replied, "By the time you can get them and be ready to move, I'll have an amended biological opinion for you."

I called Gail and told him I respected him and his opinion on this issue and, as such, would not even consider asking him to write the amendment. I told him I would be writing and delivering it that day and would provide him a copy for his records. Gail once again vehemently objected, but I said I respected his views and simply asked that he respect mine. As a fisheries biologist, I believed I knew as much about how the fish might respond as he did. We ended the call with no harsh words from either of us. I think it is possible that this was the first, and only, time in Gail's career that he was overruled in his biological opinion. His role as the field Endangered Species staff leader was to let me know his opinion. Mine, as the regional Endangered Species leader, was to accept full responsibility for the decision and move forward.

On April 24, 1992, Gail sent me a handwritten letter telling me that he believed my decision was unacceptable under the law. Because of my respect for Gail, I still have that letter to remind me that leaders are charged with lifting the risk off the shoulders of good, dedicated subordinates. The risk and responsibility were mine. Too many supervisors fail in their duties by not being willing to take ownership of and make the decision. Too often, they would rather stay safe and let the field take the conservative route. My conscience wouldn't allow me to do that. In my view, the law didn't tell me I couldn't exercise scientific judgment, so I did.

I wrote the short amendment to the biological opinion as if I were writing to a judge in a lawsuit. I assumed that I was. I laid out the non-disputed complete evaporative loss in the east lobe by August, the better opportunity to capture fish under better conditions and as a planned exercise, and the importance of having the public understand that they were critical to the recovery of these ancient fish. Turning the public against the fish by forcing them to watch the water evaporate in a drought because the fish were there would, in my opinion, seal the fate for any public assistance in recovery of these imperiled species. Of all fish and wildlife habitat in the U.S., over 60 percent is in private ownership. Threatened and endangered species simply cannot be recovered without private landowners voluntarily providing assistance in the form of habitat protection or creation. As promised, the BOR was ready with sandbags, blocked the flow between the two lobes, and assembled boats and crews to gently salvage the fish and move them to the west lobe as the water was delivered to the farmers. By September 5, 1992, the east lobe of Clear Lake was dry, the west lobe withstood the drought with no fish lost, and no fish deaths were detected in the capture and relocation to the west lobe. The lake surface elevation on Upper Klamath had dropped to 4,136.86, the lowest on record since 1905.

The Klamath Basin sustained one of its worst droughts in 1992. The farmers received less than 40 percent of their contract water. But it is the drought no one ever heard about. Why? Word apparently got out that we were moving fish so water could be delivered:

> I think David Solem, with the Klamath Irrigation District, was significant in letting the farmers know what we had done. Solem was a steady hand that helped keep the farmers at the discussion table with us. I don't think we could have built the partnership we had without him. The farmers are saying 'That's the first time the fish have ever taken a hit in a drought with us.' By the FWS and BOR showing we were one government trying to take care of all the needs of the public, we were able to guide them to success rather than regulating them into submission. (Patterson 2020)

Laws are meant to serve the people, not lord over them. I had seen the pain and hardship in forest communities that ensues when "regulating them into submission" is the strategy. While we had little choice in the northwest forests, we did in the Klamath. Gail would probably never forgive me for taking over the biological consultation and, in his opinion, putting the fish at risk. He did what he believed was right. I did as well. Today I still may be criticized for the way I handled the crisis, but I remain convinced that we did the right thing.

Roger summarized the situation in the Klamath well:

> The problem was that there wasn't enough resource there to work with. There was no way you could meet the needs of the irrigators, take care of the suckers and have water left for coho, all at the same time. That's when we started working together to develop the Klamath Project Operations Plan [KPOP]. One of the most significant problems we had was the lack of ESA understanding by the farmers and ranchers in Klamath. My experience is that if you have not dealt with endangered species issues, some things just seem so crazy, so scary that it took a while for the farm community to understand that you didn't have a choice except to work together to figure out a way to meet the needs of the ESA. One of the main problems early on was that they didn't trust that they would be OK and still make this thing work. The farmers knew a little about the spotted owl issue, and all they had heard from the loggers was that the ESA was going to shut down the logging industry because of the owls. These guys were afraid they would be shut down from farming because of these sucker fish. We had to spend a lot of time working with them. (Patterson 2020)

Our opportunity to help teach people in the Klamath about the ESA came in 1994, when the FWS was sued to designate critical habitat for the Klamath suckers. After the fear of their government that I saw in good, hardworking people during the owl public hearings, I decided to see if we could handle this one differently. We had just started discussions on having a Klamath Basin Ecosystem Office in Klamath Falls so people had faces in their communities that they could spend time with and learn to trust. Our refuge staff enjoyed good interactions with the community for a least two reasons. First, they lived there, went to church with their neighbors, and their children went to the same schools. They were part of the community. Second, in 1964 Oregon Senator Thomas Kuchel spearheaded the Wildlife Management, Klamath Project Act, which required the Department of the Interior to lease lands on national wildlife refuges in the KIamath Basin for agriculture. The maximum was set at 25 percent of the lands, but the legislative expectation was clear that agriculture would occur on those refuges. We established the Klamath Ecological Services office, but I knew that our single largest obstacle to having the community work with us was education about the ESA. We took advantage of our requirement to designate critical habitat for the suckers to try to change that situation.

Critical habitat may well be the most misunderstood mandate of the ESA. Word had gotten around the community that the BOR and FWS were working together to try to find solutions. When we announced that the FWS would hold public meetings on the ESA and critical habitat, I had no idea what the reaction might be. I wanted a set of meetings prior to the hearings because, under the law, meeting rules are far more relaxed than hearings. In meetings, I could answer questions, have a dialogue, ask questions of my own and generally share information. In a federal public hearing, none of that can occur. At the spotted owl critical habitat hearings, we had to sit in the front of the room and have speaker after speaker direct questions to me, only to have the hearing officer inform them that I was prohibited by hearing rules from answering questions or offering information for the record. Rulemaking hearings are held to allow the public to submit comments verbally, as well as in writing. But that's it. The sole purpose is to populate the administrative record with the public's views.

We started the public meetings in Klamath Falls and ended up with the fourth one in Yreka, California. At each gathering, I walked around the room to where the questioner was seated, did my best to get within a few feet of her or him, and make sure there was personal interaction. I told them what was true and what was untrue about what they had heard regarding designation of critical habitat. I let them know the *legal questions* we were required to address and, therefore, how *they* could formulate comments to address the questions that would determine the outcome. Most of the public believes that their ability to comment on federal actions is to "plead their case, and have the government not invoke a rule." But the government agencies don't have that leeway.

The executive branch can only carry out the laws as written by Congress. The questions of the law, whether to list, delist or designate critical habitat, are stipulated and only open to scientific or legal fact-finding. I made sure that the advice I provided was in answer to a question, but I even went so far as to give "example" language about the scientific importance of both the ordinary high water mark of the stream banks and the shallow springs in the lakes as areas critical to the suckers, since they spawned over shallow springs and were seldom found in the floodplain. It could just be a coincidence, but that was included in the comments for the record by local citizens and was also included in the final rule for critical habitat. Mike Ryan was the area manager for the BOR at Klamath, and he let Roger and me know he was hearing positive things about our efforts to work with the community. I was hearing the same from Steve Lewis, our new supervisor for the Klamath Office.

Another example of sharing power with those who are regulated occurred when we did a biological opinion with the Klamath Forest on their grazing operation. Rollie White was a new biologist in the Portland field office, and I held significant optimism that he would be one of our leaders in the future. He had written the opinion in the manner he had been taught, prescribing when to move cattle and to where, rather than what the grazed area should look like when the cattle are gone. One of the FS permittees for grazing asked that I meet to discuss the draft opinion the FS had shared with him. Rollie and I met him in the forest and rode in his truck while he explained how he managed his herd. After enjoying time looking at the beautiful resources of the forest, we stopped at a picnic table by a stream.

As we talked, the rancher was asking the same question Roger had when we first met. He, very politely, reminded me he was the cattleman and knew how to manage herds better than the FWS did. I asked him, "If we change the biological opinion to describe what we need the understory plants to look like when you're finished grazing, will you hold yourself accountable and give me your word you'll see that it's done?" He looked at me for a moment, obviously not expecting that question, and said, "Of course. Would you be willing to do that?" I looked at Rollie and asked what he thought about my proposal. After a moment, he said he would much rather the grazer be responsible than have to spend his time monitoring actions in the opinion. Sitting at that picnic table, an honest rancher, Rollie and I modified the opinion.

I never worried about the cattleman doing what he promised. In his world, as in the one in which I was raised, a man's word is his bond. Paper is for lawyers and courthouses. A person's wealth is measured by their integrity and honesty, not their bank account. The lesson I was trying to teach Rollie early in his career was one I have stated many times: *The only real power any of us has is that which we share.* One can be given authority, but respect and leadership must be earned. By sharing the power of the ESA with an honest rancher, we not only gained a partner in conservation but elevated the status of the FWS in the community. I had shown trust. He would have died before he let me down. I found that to be true with nearly everyone with whom I worked. There will always be the exception that betrays the trust, both on the internal team and with the public, but they are the exception and by their own hand remove themselves from future influence.

Through my work with ARD for Law Enforcement (LE) Dave McMullen and his deputy, Tom Riley, I learned how LE officers approach enforcement: *The ultimate objective of law enforcement is voluntary compliance by the citizenry.* Not arrest and conviction, but voluntary compliance. When laws or regulations are confusing, or when the government agents begin to believe their job is to arrest or regulate, we have failed in our duties. The ESA assigns certain responsibilities to the FWS for administration of the Act. It never, anywhere in the law, states that the FWS is to recover species. The FWS is assigned responsibility to identify those species in need of protection of the ESA, determine what factors or threats brought about the stresses on the populations, oversee the development of recovery plans to provide a road map for the conservation (recovery) of the species, and to *work with others to achieve the goals.* No species has been recovered and removed from the list of threatened and endangered species without the support and assistance of the public. The resources belong to the American people, and it is only they who can save a species from extinction. In my career, the only species I believe to be recovered through regulation are the bald eagle and peregrine falcon (both through restricted pesticide use), and the American alligator (regulated harvest). As a biologist with the FWS, I believed my objective in the Klamath Basin was to have the people who lived there refer to the suckers and salmon as "our fish." When the public accepts responsibility as species stewards, those species will be recovered.

CHAPTER 7

Bureau of Land Management Calls For the God Squad

During all the time that we were focusing significant effort on the designation of spotted owl critical habitat (CH), normal work operations had to continue. In addition to helping with biology and habitat information in Oregon for the CH exercise, Russ Peterson and his staff at the U.S. Fish and Wildlife (FWS) Portland field office were in constant communication with the Forest Service (FS) and Bureau of Land Management (BLM) regarding their ongoing and anticipated timber sales program. Teresa Nichols and Gary Miller worked the spotted owl effort for Oregon, just as Jim Michaels did from Washington and Phil Detrich and Steve Spangle from California. They had proven themselves competent throughout the listing and critical habitat process.

Oregon/Washington BLM State Director Dean Bibles was a man who understood politics and the pressures of his responsibilities to the Oregon and California Railroad Revested (O&C) counties, but also realized the power of the recent court decisions and what they portended. His boss was Cy Jamison, director of the BLM and a true politician. Jamison began his career as an employee with the BLM in Billings, Montana, but then took a job on staff with the House of Representatives Interior and Insular Affairs Committee. His role there was much the same as Don Knowles's was on the Senate side, to advise and carry out the wishes of the congressional committees for whom they worked. When Jamison was appointed by President George H.W. Bush and confirmed by the

Senate in 1989, he came in with bold words that he was going to change the BLM to be more than a logging and mining organization. After he was in office, however, he began to see things differently, especially in the Northwest with the northern spotted owl.

The 175 timber sales that were under consultation with Oregon/Washington BLM for 1991 had been in discussion since the beginning of the fiscal year the previous October. The CH activities had interfered somewhat with the Portland field office's ability to quickly work on these proposed sales, but good progress was being made. On June 13, 1991, I signed a transmittal memo to the BLM with our draft biological opinions on the entire set of 175, including draft jeopardy opinions on 52 of those sales. The regional director of the FWS must sign final jeopardy opinions, but I was authorized to transmit the drafts so consultation could continue. There were regular discussions about various activities that needed to be evaluated under Section 7 of the Endangered Species Act, but the FWS and BLM were usually able to work things out. The National Marine Fisheries Service (NMFS), however, was another matter.

> Dealing with NMFS was a huge, huge challenge. They had inexperienced GS-7 and GS-9 biologists with no field experience whatsoever sitting down with our GS-11 and GS-12 experienced biologists attempting to dictate how things would be done. They believed BLM was evil because we allowed timber to be harvested and they were doing the work of God. They expected us to just ignore the other laws we were charged to carry out! (Zielinski 2020)

I called Elaine Zielinski, Dean Bibles's deputy, and let her know we believed we could work as many as 26 of the 52 draft jeopardies into non-jeopardy opinions with some modifications. She told me she appreciated that insight and agreed we would work on them together to resolve issues. But Dean Bibles and Cy Jamison had other ideas.

The same day we transmitted the draft opinions, we got a reply from Dean to Marv Plenert saying they wanted us to immediately finalize the opinion with the 52 jeopardy sales included so they could free up the non-jeopardy and pursue other avenues for the 52 jeopardy sales. On June 17, 1991, Marv signed the final biological opinion on the 175 sales with 52 posing jeopardy to the continued survival of the species. Over the next three months, discussions with BLM removed 8 of the 52 sales by following FWS recommendations. The remaining 44 would not see an easy exit, in spite of our belief that at least another 18 could likely be modified and approved. That didn't appear to be in Lujan's, Jamison's and Bible's plans.

When Elaine reported to Dean what we had discussed,

> [Dean] told me he and Jamison wanted a final opinion immediately. Cy Jamison, our director, announced his strategy to us for coming up with timber sales. I didn't have much to do with developing the strategy except to have our folks provide data. But Dean had very strong negative opinions about how things were going and was eager for a new approach. Most of us knew this was not going to do anything; this was just going to add fuel to the fire. But that's the way they wanted to do it. After that, Dean and Jamison invoked the God Squad [Endangered Species Committee]. (Zielinski 2020)

On September 11, while we were having our CH public hearings in Medford, Jamison transmitted a formal request to Secretary Lujan to convene the Endangered Species Committee, which had been done only twice before. Lujan, as the secretary of the interior and the decider for convening the Committee, had two of his bureaus at odds over implementation of a law that *he* was charged to carry out. Jamison made the announcement on September 12 in concert with Senator Bob Packwood (R-OR), who had proposed a bill to find a "fix" to the northwest forest issues. Secretary Lujan was not about to oppose Senator Packwood, and Cy Jamison was feeling the political strength of his powerful partner. The proper thing for him to do would have been, as secretary over the two bureaus, to simply decide that the ESA had to be followed within the Department of the Interior (DOI), Congress was the appropriate place to address changes to the law, and there would be no God Squad. But that didn't happen.

Roger Nesbit was the attorney within the solicitor's office that handled BLM activities and is regarded as a significant instigator of the entire God Squad episode. Pete Raynor, associate solicitor for FWS activities, recounted it this way:

> Roger Nesbit, in my opinion, was the prime culprit here. I believe he sold these guys (Jamison and Bibles) that he could win this. I place no fault on Tom Sansonetti [solicitor for DOI] except he should have called Nesbit and said 'You didn't give me a chance to review this. Pull it. I don't want it to go forward. You don't have a winning hand.' He didn't do that, and I think Sansonetti was wrong in not doing it. It was flawed from the beginning. It is very seldom that a staff lawyer like Roger Nesbit can sell so many people on such a bad idea. I think Roger's web spun so fast and sucked so many people in that, by the time people realized what was happening, it was too late. (Raynor 2020)

Secretary Lujan sought cover through his legal team and asked Solicitor Sansonetti to prepare a legal analysis of the BLM application. As the solicitor for the Department of the Interior, Sansonetti was also the legal counsel to the Endangered Species Committee. On October 1, a joint memorandum from Sansonetti and John Schrote, assistant secretary of the interior for policy, management and budget, was transmitted to the "Secretary and Chairman of the Committee" with their analysis of questions under the law. The memorandum identified the threshold determinations required of the secretary as follows.

1. Whether any required biological assessment was conducted;
2. To the extent determinable within the time period provided, whether
3. the Federal agency and permit or license applicant, if any, have refrained from making any irreversible or irretrievable commitment of resources; and
4. Whether the Federal agency and permit or license applicant, if any, have carried out consultation responsibilities in good faith and have made a reasonable and responsible effort to develop and fairly consider modifications or reasonable and prudent alternatives to the proposed action which would not violate section 7(a)(2) of the Act.

In the discussion portion of the memorandum, they fully concurred that a biological assessment had been done and that the BLM had made no irreversible or irretrievable commitment of resources. However, in discussion of the "good faith consultation" question, they were more subdued. The memorandum states that

> questions have been raised by our staff, however, about whether the Bureau's request that the draft biological opinion be made final almost immediately after receiving it (the Service finalized them on June 17, 1991, two days after issuance, and amended them on July 3, see Appendix G) could be perceived as demonstrating or may demonstrate an absence of good faith in the consultation process.

This concern would remain throughout the proceedings, but the memorandum concluded with this:

> The acceptance of the Bureau's application does not foreclose future discussion by the Committee as to whether or not there are any reasonable and prudent alternatives to the agency action.

Indeed, one of the requirements of the Committee is that it consider reasonable and prudent alternatives. The staff concludes [that] the Bureau's consultation with the Service, including its review and consideration of the Service's reasonable and prudent alternatives both in draft and final form, satisfies the third threshold criterion, to carry out consultation as required by the statute in good faith . . . Accordingly, we conclude that the Bureau has met the threshold criteria, and that the application should be considered by the Committee. (Sansonetti 1991)

The memorandum was accepted and concurred by Secretary Lujan as chairman, Endangered Species Committee, October 1, 1991. For only the third time in history, the Endangered Species Committee would be convened. In the previous two times, the snail darter and the whooping crane, the Committee declined to vote a species into extinction. But the spotted owl, with all its publicity and affinity to old-growth forests, presented an opportunity to those who thought timber sales more important than the continuation of one of the Creator's gifts to the world.

Cy Jamison stated publicly that the northwest forests should be managed as tree farms, not diverse forests. Our FWS office now had a new assignment: give staff support and fund the work of the Endangered Species Committee. More than $1 million of scarce appropriations would come from our Fish and Wildlife Enhancement Region 1 budget to support this politically motivated hearing. An administrative law judge would be hired, attorneys would be paid, and our team would have new work to do, as if there wasn't enough already. We were beginning to feel like the proverbial rented mule.

• • •

Secretary Lujan selected Harvey C. Sweitzer, an administrative law judge from Utah, to oversee the Endangered Species Committee evidentiary hearings. Unlike a normal trial carried within the judicial branch of government, this would be a hearing to gather all the existing evidence that attorneys for both sides of the issue wished to have in the record for the Committee to review. It would be totally under the responsibility of the executive branch of government because it was a directed activity under the ESA, and not one in which the judge would render an opinion or verdict. Judge Sweitzer's responsibility was to ensure a fair and equitable hearing with witnesses and introduction of evidence. Witnesses were required to provide written testimony prior to the trial, and opposing attorneys had to declare before the hearing if they wished to cross-examine a witness. If those attorneys passed, the written testimony would be entered, but the witness would not be called. Each side was only allotted a certain amount of time for cross-examination during the hearing, so attorneys chose to cross-examine only those witnesses they believed to be the most injurious to their case.

In addition, the secretary of the interior is required to provide a report to the full Committee after the hearing and prior to convening the Committee that contains all the evidence gathered, including information from cross-examination and potential options for the way to view each of the questions in light of the possibility of granting an exemption under the law. Secretary Lujan appointed Tom Sansonetti to be his representative at the hearings, sit next to Judge Sweitzer during the deliberations, and provide advice to the judge on requested rulings. This created more than a little controversy. Having a person represent a voting member of the Committee in the gathering of the information, when all Committee members had vowed to remain neutral until all evidence is heard, didn't make it look very impartial. Further, there was little doubt that Solicitor Sansonetti would guide the secretary's report to the Committee as well as be there to influence how they viewed the information. When publicly accused of driving the process to a predetermined conclusion, Sansonetti's response was that he "didn't care who won. I just want to make sure this proceeding is handled properly." He made it clear to all of us that he believed the work of the Endangered Species Committee was one of the most important assignments of his career, and he wanted it done right. But that is not how it looked.

I had several meetings with Tom and found him to be knowledgeable and courteous. I respected him and believed there was an ethical line he wouldn't cross. But I also believed there was a clear conflict of interest with one person having multiple responsibilities. In the federal government, it is not necessary to actually have a conflict of interest to be in violation of policy; the mere existence of a "perception" of a conflict is in itself a violation. It is disappointing that he allowed himself to be in a position that few believed would grant him impartiality in the deliberations of the Committee. Whether the accusations were true or not, the perception was real.

A formal notice was published in the Federal Register on November 13 announcing the hearings and calling for petitions from interested parties to intervene. On November 26, Judge Sweitzer signed an order numbered ESA 91-1 that laid out the matters for a prehearing conference. He stated that

> the parties and potential intervenors are herewith provided this Order to enable as much advance preparation as possible in the circumstances and to permit any appropriate discussion thereof at the prehearing conference commencing December 3, 1991. In setting this schedule, it has been necessary to heed the fact that the hearing commences January 8, 1992 (per 56 FR 57633, 34).

His order laid out the rules for supplying witness lists, motions, declaration of intent to cross-examine, and so on, that would guide the official prehearing conference on December 3. Following this order, the BLM and their timber industry intervenors provided a list of eighty witnesses they intended to call or provide written testimony. Many were from the communities affected by the loss of revenues that they asserted would occur as a result of these 44 sales.

Pat Parenteau was hired to represent the FWS with the help of Ron Swan and to argue for the correctness of the jeopardy opinions. I asked Parenteau how his hiring occurred:

> Pete Raynor, associate solicitor at DOI, sought me because of my history with the Endangered Species Committee in both Grayrocks and Tellico. Sansonetti and Dan Shillito recognized the unusual nature of having two Interior agencies as adversaries. Lawyer ethics kicked in, and they said 'There's no way that our lawyers can represent both sides of a controversy.' Sansonetti opted to represent BLM, so they needed to figure out how FWS was going to be represented. They went to the Department of Justice, but DOJ refused because it was not in court, stating 'This is a strange adjudicatory beast. It's not in court and we don't have the authority to represent internal conflicts.' Sansonetti then went to Chairman Sidney Yates on the House Natural Resources Committee to ask for a law to allow the solicitor to appoint a special counsel to represent FWS in the Endangered Species Committee hearings. I believe it's the only time in history where Congress had to authorize this unique position to hire me to represent FWS. It was made clear that it was a specific, one-time deal for the FWS to have authority to hire outside counsel. They chose me because I was the lawyer for Grayrocks in that God Squad hearing, and Pete wanted someone who had gone through the God Squad before. (Parenteau 2020)

Victor Sher, attorney for the Portland Audubon Society (PAS) and nine other environmental groups, and Parenteau provided a list of witnesses they intended to proffer. Those witnesses included Dr. Charles Meslow (FWS), Mr. Gary Miller (FWS), Ms. Teresa Nichols (FWS),

Dr. David R. Anderson (FWS, Colorado State University), Dr. Jack Ward Thomas (FS), Dr. Richard Haynes (FS), Dr. Ed Whitelaw (ECO Northwest), Mr. Ronald R. Sadler (Retired BLM employee), Mr. Philip A. Meyer (Meyer Resources, Inc.) and Director John Turner (FWS). Elaine Zielinski recalled how the attorneys within the DOI's Office of the Solicitor (SOL) were divided to represent two Interior bureaus:

> I clearly remember in SOL the attorneys couldn't talk to each other during the God Squad hearings because they were on the FWS side or the BLM side. I thought that was pretty amazing. I think they put up a wall between them in their D.C. office to keep them separated! (Zielinski 2020)

Pat Parenteau said, "The attorneys were even assigned different restrooms, one floor for FWS and another floor for BLM." (Parenteau 2020)

At the prehearing conference, Parenteau and Sher submitted a motion to the judge that asked for immediate dismissal based on two points: (1) the BLM failed to consult with the FWS before adopting the so-called "Jamison strategy," and (2) the BLM failed to prepare an environmental impact statement on the effect of going ahead with the 44 sales. The first point was based on employing a strategy that Jamison had directed the BLM to use. The second question was related to a letter the Environmental Protection Agency (EPA) had sent to the BLM advising that EPA believed BLM had violated the National Environmental Policy Act (NEPA) by not revising previous timber sale environmental impact statements (EISs) to include and consider new information. Judge Sweitzer considered the motions and dismissed both. There was little doubt in our minds that his decision to follow the same logic as the secretary in saying that he believed BLM had acted in good faith, and the Committee could decide otherwise in their deliberations, was influenced by advice from Tom Sansonetti. Tom made it clear internally that he believed it was preferable to proceed than to have a decision overruled later. The hearing would begin as scheduled on January 8, 1992.

The EPA had asked Judge Sweitzer for, and been granted, intervenor status based on the letter they had sent to BLM and the agency's concerns regarding the adequacy of BLM's environmental documentation. Their letter had stated, in part:

> In the absence of comprehensive analysis of potential impacts, the short-term management options selected by BLM could unnecessarily foreclose long-term strategies which would both address local economic needs and enable conservation of the owls and other biological assets associated with the late successional, old-growth ecosystems. (Sanderson 1991)

At the last minute before the hearings were to begin, EPA withdrew their request for intervenor status. The reason given by the EPA for the withdrawal was the belief that they could enter their information and concerns through the normal process of the hearing and didn't need to be an intervenor. It is true that Parenteau and Sher intended to question the BLM witnesses about the information, but the EPA letter would not be entered into the record through the testimony of its author, Richard E. Sanderson, director of EPA's Office of Federal Activities. Parenteau asked Judge Sweitzer to deny EPA's motion to withdraw, saying it was inappropriate for the EPA to walk away after raising issues that could determine the outcome of the process. But the motion was approved, and EPA withdrew. We were never told who applied the pressure, but speculated that someone in Lujan's office called their counterpart at EPA and made the request on behalf of the secretary. Cy Jamison made it clear that he was pleased with EPA's withdrawal, only increasing the perception of political manipulation.

The hearing, and perceived interference with the process, was getting media attention at the national level in both print and on TV. Just when we thought the owl could not get a higher national profile, another questionable decision had been made by the administration. We were convinced that Lujan had already started working on getting the five out of seven votes needed to approve exemption. Our hope was that there would be trepidation by members of the Committee to cast a vote to potentially eliminate a species like the northern spotted owl.

• • •

Joe Lint, one of the biologists from BLM, had been instrumental in bringing attention to the northern spotted owl through both his graduate research and his work on the Interagency Scientific Committee (ISC). Joe was a member of a tight group that had gone through their own hell in putting the ISC report together. Joe, Barry Mulder and Grant Gunderson were the three agency experts for the BLM, FWS and FS, respectively, and believed that their scientific reputation was more important than pleasing political appointees. When Joe testified at the hearing, he was presented as BLM's witness, but it was Parenteau who scored the points for the record on cross-examination. Under questioning from Parenteau, Lint stated that the BLM's failure to follow the ISC plan, and instead follow the "Jamison strategy," could delay recovery of the northern spotted owl. He had also joined other ISC biologists in signing a statement critical of the BLM's efforts to protect the owl. Parenteau tried to get Lint to state that BLM was the "weak link" in the management of the northwest forests, but Lint refused to endorse that statement.

Cy Jamison decided the ISC report was speculation regarding what owl fledglings needed to disperse, establish new territory and survive. He therefore directed the BLM to follow the ISC in protecting Habitat Conservation Areas, but to disregard the 50-11-40 rule (at least 50 percent of the trees with diameter of 11 inches at breast height, and at least a 40 percent canopy closure) for adequate cover in dispersal. It was in the dispersal habitat that all 44 sales resided. The major conflict occurred when the FWS used the ISC recommendations in carrying out its analyses under Section 7, and the BLM used the "Jamison strategy," which basically directed to "Do the best you can." Joe Lint had helped write the ISC report and believed in its recommendations. But he refused to attack the agency that had allowed him to fully participate in the science. While I believed Jamison had made BLM the weak link, I respected that it was not Joe's place, as a scientist, to say so. That should be decided by the Committee.

The roller-coaster pathway for resolving the spotted owl issue was making the government look like no one was in charge. We published the final rule on critical habitat in January, the draft of the recovery plan was scheduled for release in February, the Forest Service planned to release an EIS on management of 17 national forests in the Northwest in February, and in January the God Squad was on the way to determining if the species could be allowed to go extinct! Anyone halfway paying attention was sure to get a headache trying to parse out all the moving parts, and none of them seemed to be considering any of the others. It was not a good time for confidence in the federal government. I am hesitant to place blame on career employees who tried to warn of impending catastrophe. When you have elected officials demanding that political appointees treat forests that belong to all the people of the United States as if they were locally owned, the result is not difficult to predict.

On January 15, Jack Ward Thomas took the stand as a witness for the FWS. Thomas stated that it was a series of wounds inflicted over time that led to the current situation: "These changes in owl habitat have occurred one timber sale at a time, one fire at a time, one agricultural clearing at a time, one city at a time, over a prolonged period." Roger Nesbit represented the BLM and their intervenors. His line of questioning was to try to find a chink in the armor of the ISC report that could lead to undermining the 50-11-40 rule. Parenteau at one point objected and said Nesbit was undertaking a "microscopic, fly-specking analysis" and should stick to the testimony provided and the science behind it. When it came to the "Jamison strategy," Thomas gave an answer for which any scientist would have been proud: "So far as I know, the Jamison plan never has been put forward in a form that could be evaluated by the scientific community. Whether or not the Jamison plan would stand up under intensive evaluation similar to that undergone by the ISC strategy by appropriately credentialed scientists, I don't know."

When attorney Mark Rutzick grilled Thomas about whether he believed allowing the 44 sales to go forward would cause the owl to go extinct, Thomas replied that it was a "low probability—provided there were no more logging in owl habitat for the next one hundred years"!

One of the FWS witnesses who offered some information about discussions within the BLM over the previous ten years was Ronald R. Sadler, who retired from BLM in 1991 after thirty-three years of service. He stated in written testimony that, as early as 1983, BLM staff foresaw the logging of the last Oregon Coast Range old-growth forests and proposed a system of forest reserves to protect northern spotted owls and other wildlife before it was too late. He testified that those plans were vetoed by top BLM officials and Department of the Interior officials in Portland and in D.C. The BLM attorneys declined to cross-examine Sadler, so he was not called to the witness stand. However, his entire testimony was made part of the record forwarded to the Committee. Elaine Zielinski confirmed Mr. Sadler's statement:

> Before the listing of the northern spotted owl, a group of western Oregon BLM district managers [DMs] went to D.C. and told them we couldn't sustain the cuts we were doing; it wasn't just a timber factory. Jim Cason was a political appointee back in D.C. at the time and he just yelled at everyone and said 'Forget it! You're doing the cut and I don't want to hear about this owl stuff! Just deal with it.' But the DMs all agreed we couldn't sustain the more than one billion board feet cuts per year. (Zielinski 2020)

The last significant witness for the FWS was Director John Turner. To us, John had been a pillar of strength through the whole process and did nothing to deflect heat coming his way. John was a kindhearted person who believed strongly in finding balance between the needs of people and our natural resources. But he also stood his ground when the decision had been made, and took full responsibility for it. He did an excellent job of going through his involvement in the economic analysis and exclusion process. John stood by us at every turn in answering questions and said it was a team effort, but the final decision was his. When asked how he felt about depriving people of jobs, he said, "When we whittle away at our options for long-term management, I think we may do a disservice to the region."

The remaining work was for the attorneys on both sides to provide written briefs, which would lay out why the testimony favored the position of their clients. In February 1992, Daniel Shillito, associate solicitor for the Department of the Interior, wrote a directive to Pat Parenteau instructing him to change verbiage in his draft brief that criticized the BLM by asserting that they knowingly failed to consult in good faith. It was Parenteau's job to fight for the FWS and provide arguments he believed were supported by evidence that bolstered the position of his client. Shillito's letter stated:

> After reviewing the post-hearing brief filed by the Fish and Wildlife Service on February 19, 1992, on the Bureau of Land Management's endangered species exemption application, Michael Hayden, the Assistant Secretary for Fish and Wildlife and Parks, and John Turner, the Director of the Fish and Wildlife Service, have informed me that certain changes must be made in section IX.B.1. of the brief, which is located on pages 225 and 226 of the brief. Attached to this letter is a version of section IX.B.1. that shows the changes Mr. Hayden and Mr. Turner want to have made. Accordingly, I direct you to make the changes noted

in the attachment and, so that the least possible time might elapse before the changes are made, to submit corrected pages 225 and 226 to all parties on the service list by close of business on February 24, 1992. (Shillito undated)

In response to Mr. Shillito's letter, Parenteau wrote:

I received your letter regarding the referenced matter by facsimile today. You have directed me to make certain changes in the post-hearing brief filed in this matter which, for reasons I have already explained, I cannot, in good conscience, do. The changes are not, in my judgment, in the best interests of the Fish and Wildlife Service.

I understand this may not be acceptable from an employment standpoint, and I hereby tender my resignation and withdrawal from this matter effective immediately. Notwithstanding this rather unfortunate conclusion, I have been honored to represent the Fish and Wildlife Service in this very important proceeding. I believe the case we put on and the brief we filed will vindicate the position that FWS took in this matter and that the Committee will grant FWS' request to deny the exemption. I have enjoyed working with the outstanding professionals within FWS here in Region 1 and will take fond memories and new friendships with me. (Parenteau 1992)

In an interview with Parenteau, I asked if he felt constrained in any way due to the differences between a normal court proceeding and the God Squad hearing rules.

My contract, with Shillito as my contract officer, said I would be supervised for contract oversight, but not in terms of day-to-day activities in the hearings. The way Shillito and the solicitor

[Sansonetti] saw my role was to present the biological case for the owl and why this habitat was important, but not to get into 'extraneous matters or issues.' I only felt constrained from the standpoint that, if I were litigating in a courtroom, I would use every law and tool I could think of to support my case, whereas in representing the FWS at the God Squad, I was more focused on why this habitat was so important to call jeopardy and to flesh that out for the Committee, and to educate the Committee about what is going on in old-growth forests.

I started making arguments specifically against the Jamison strategy based on NEPA, not the ESA. I was making the same argument Vic Sher was making on behalf of the environmental intervenors, that the timber sales were a violation of NEPA; ergo, there was no irreconcilable conflict. The applicant must submit that it is in compliance with all relevant laws, and I zeroed in on that right off the bat. I made a motion to Judge Sweitzer first thing to dismiss, that this didn't belong here because it was unknown whether there was an irreconcilable conflict absent NEPA. Sweitzer denied it subject to it being reopened. So, I just put a pin in it. At the end, when we had to submit our final brief—it was at that point that Shillito asked to review all documents, including the final brief.

I was duty-bound to supply it to him and there it was, first argument right out of the chute, that there was a violation of NEPA and it should be dismissed. Shillito saw the NEPA arguments and went ballistic! He ordered me to take that out of the brief. I said 'I will not!' He said 'You're fired,' and I said 'No, I'm not fired, I resign.' I had the two lawyers working with me, Ron Swan for the solicitor's office and Mary Wood, now at the University of Oregon, whom I had hired to help with the case. She and Ron were both brilliant. I told them to take this brief to the airport and send it to the Committee. Mike DeLann was

Chair of CEQ [Council on Environmental Quality], which was the administrative arm to the Committee on this, so I had the brief with the NEPA poison pill sent to Committee staff with our NEPA argument. (Parenteau 2020)

Pete Raynor provided me with additional information as to how the misunderstanding between Shillito and Parenteau occurred:

The misunderstanding was really my responsibility because I told Pat to just go win. I should have been more forthright in terms of the clearances we needed with the Department of Justice. There was no political interference at all. It was simply that when the United States is providing a brief in a case, I had to send it over to Justice to have them check it for consistency with their position because you don't want the United States arguing inconsistent positions. The lawyer who reviewed it said 'This position is inconsistent with the one we have or will take in court, and it has to come out.' I negotiated with the guy, a career attorney, to make as few changes as we could to accommodate Justice concerns. I went to Dan Shillito and said, 'We've got a problem here; Pat's not going to like this,' and Pat resigned.

We went to Portland, made the changes and submitted the brief. I think more than anyone, it was my fault because I didn't fully brief Pat on what we would have to do with his briefs before he filed them. He did exactly what I asked him to do and won the case. There was no political interference from Sansonetti or anyone else. When I got the Justice feedback, I said, 'You're right, we've got to pull that.' Pat was very upset, but it wasn't a political thing. If I had it to do all over again, I would sit down with Pat and say, 'These are the limitations on us, and they are going to be limitations on you.' I feel very responsible for the unhappiness, because I should have thought about it, but I didn't. (Raynor 2020)

Secretary Lujan provided his report to the Committee on April 29, 1992. It contained seven chapters, each addressing a major issue:

- Availability of Reasonable and Prudent Alternatives; Nature and Extent of the Benefits and Costs of the 44 Sales
- Benefits and Costs of Alternative Courses of Action Consistent With Conserving the Species or Its Critical Habitat
- A Summary of the Evidence Concerning Whether or Not the 44 Sales Are of National or Regional Significance
- A Summary of the Evidence Concerning Whether or Not the 44 Sales Are in the Public Interest
- Appropriate Reasonable Mitigation and Enhancement Measures Which Might Be Considered By the Committee
- Whether the Bureau of Land Management Refrained From Making Any Irreversible or Irretrievable Commitment of Resources. (Lujan 1992)

We knew that Tom Sansonetti was overseeing the drafting of the report and assumed it would be tilted toward giving an exemption, especially in light of Shillito's handling of the final brief with Parenteau. We believed we had done our best to provide sound science and ethical judgment for the species, and for the people who were impacted. We could not, however, change the cavalier manner in which Cy Jamison had signaled his lack of concern about the survival of a bird of prey. It was now in the hands of people who would have to live forever with their decision. The nation was watching.

The decision of the Endangered Species Committee on the requested exemption by BLM of 44 timber sales in spotted owl critical habitat came on May 15, 1992. In a seven-page decision, the Endangered Species

Committee decided 5–2 to allow 13 of the 44 sales to go forward and denied 31 sales. The rationale given for the 13 was all over the board and reflected just how difficult it was to "split the baby," which is what we believed was the unspoken objective. They did go through each of the sales and gave their reasoning, which often was that the same sales were being offered up in the 1992 batch, but provided no real explanation that would satisfy their decision either way. We sat back in near-amazement. When we transmitted the draft opinion to BLM on the original 52 jeopardy sales, I relayed to Elaine Zielinski that Russ, Gary and Teresa believed we could work as many as 26 of those sales into non-jeopardy opinions. After removal of 8 afterward, that still left 18 sales that we believed we could make work. The Endangered Species Committee allowed 13.

Pat Parenteau said of the decision:

> The record didn't provide any kind of basis to distinguish among the sales and why those 13 were chosen. This was purely political . . . By the time it got to the end, to the Committee, none of the testimony mattered. Sad to say, this whole elaborate process, this formal process of building a record and testing it against cross-examination . . . in the end I'm not sure it carried any weight at all. Then Vic Sher took it to the Ninth Circuit Court of Appeals, which agreed that it appeared to be politically motivated, and opened it up for discovery, which was a dramatic thing that had never been done before. The Circuit said there was some evidence of chicanery here, improper political influence on the Committee decision, and that they were going to allow discovery. When Clinton got elected and Babbitt became secretary, he [Babbitt] withdrew the application for exemption and said 'We're moving on.' Nothing further happened. (Parenteau 2020)

The irony is imbued with sadness. Over a million dollars of the taxpayers' money, six months of hard work by countless staff in each of the agencies, and the result is less than what we would have given them if Cy Jamison had not wanted to grandstand. The administration changed, and the issue was simply dropped. What had started in my career as the public trusting its government, with good reason, had become a time when the government looked like Keystone Kops. I was determined that the rest of my career would be devoted to winning as much of that trust back as I possibly could. The people of the United States deserve no less.

• • •

The best government training I ever received was through the Senior Executive Service Candidate Development Program (SESCDP). I chose the Federal Executive Institute (FEI) in Charlottesville, Virginia, the only executive training sponsored and carried out by the federal government. The course, which was titled "Leadership for a Democratic Society," Program 182, required me to be on-site in Virginia for a month. Throughout my career I attended numerous training sessions about supervision, personnel, and so on. But this was the real deal. Each week we took a different course, all geared to executive-level challenges and decision-making. The one that still stands out for its excellence and impact on me was J. Cudd Brown's class on the U.S. Constitution.

Cudd had been a legal advisor to President Lyndon Johnson and was on staff at the FEI. He spoke with a strong southern accent and literally made the Constitution, the founding fathers and the ethos of America come alive. He instilled in me the importance of being a federal executive and the responsibility to understand the Constitution under which we were charged to *carry out* the laws, *not adjust them to our beliefs*. In one short week, he walked us through the Declaration of Independence and its bold statement that rights did not come from government, but from the Creator. He emphasized that the Constitution was written to grant rights *only* to the new federal government, and that state and individual rights *already existed* and were meant to be protected, not granted, by the Constitution.

This class, more than any I ever attended, gave me the foundation of fairness to all under the law. There were no good guys or bad guys if actions being taken were legal. There were simply people with different views as to what the law said and how it should be carried out. The charge of the executive branch of government is to fairly and equally carry out the mandates of a given law, ensuring that the rights of citizens are guarded and only diminished when there has been a clear directive from Congress that infringement upon those rights is absolutely necessary for the protection of the public's best interest. This helped me see the industries in the Northwest in a different light. They were neither bad nor uncaring people; they were simply taking advantage of the decisions made by the federal government to allow more harvest than was appropriate. Their elected representatives had led them down this path through laws passed and signed by the president.

Cudd emphasized the brilliance of the authors in establishing a free and independent judicial branch to referee and interpret the original intent of the Constitution and laws. He joked, "Even the founding fathers knew lawyers were never going to agree on legal meaning, so they encouraged the debate by creating the judicial in Article III." From that point forward, I always carried a pocket copy of the Declaration of Independence, Constitution and subsequent amendments in my briefcase and read them from cover to cover at least twice a year. I believed it was my responsibility to understand and carry out this wonderful document to the best of my ability as one who is not an attorney, but did have delegated responsibilities in the executive branch.

In addition, I bought a copy of *The Federalist*, essays published in newspapers of the day by James Madison, Alexander Hamilton and John Jay to explain to the people what the Articles of the Constitution allowed the incipient federal government to do, and what it reserved for the states. The people voting to ratify the Constitution had great reservations about what would happen to their state governments under the supremacy of a federal government, and these essays gave clear explanations as to intent. In all, there were eighty-five individual essays written to cover every aspect of the Constitution, and they continue to provide the foundation for decisions handed down by the Supreme Court of the United States. But even with these, there was anxiety that the Constitution did not clearly recognize *individual rights*.

The last Federalist Paper was published in May 1788, and the Constitution of the United States of America was ratified in June 1788. Supporters of the new Constitution, in an effort to gain ratification without having to make amendments during review by the states, are said to have promised that the first Congress of the newly formed government would propose amendments to the Constitution specifically targeting the identification of protected *individual* rights. In the spring of 1789, the first session of the new Congress focused on passage of the first ten amendments to the U.S. Constitution, also known as the Bill of Rights. All ten amendments recognize the preexisting individual rights of religion, assemblage, to bear arms, and to protect private property, among other rights. In 1791, these amendments were ratified and became part of the Constitution under which we live free today. It is important to remember this sequence, as the Federalist Papers *did not* explain the role of the new Constitution regarding individual rights. That can only be found in the legislative history of congressional debate and arguments highlighting the intent of the Bill of Rights. For those who argue that there was vague reference to the Second Amendment to bear arms in one or more of the Federalist Papers, particularly in reference to state militias, I beg to differ.

Their argument is that the individual's right to "bear arms" is limited to home protection and hunting. I suggest we remember that these citizens had just lived through property and livestock being appropriated, homes being used to billet British soldiers without compensation, and with no right of the citizens to defend themselves. No, the people of the new United States of America were not concerned that they have weapons for hunting. They had just fought their own government for freedom and demanded the capability to fight the new one if it turned tyrannical. The Second Amendment is to ensure that citizens are armed to protect themselves against all foes including, if necessary, their own government. There is no question that there can be "reasonable" intrusions on this right, as history has shown with various restrictions on explosives and fully automatic weapons. But it is clear that the Bill of Rights was specifically established to protect the individual citizen *from the new government.*

• • •

Because I was nearly three thousand miles away from Oregon during the SESCDP training, the fax machines at the FEI worked overtime to provide me with my daily stack of documents from Portland and materials to be given to Pat Parenteau for use in the God Squad hearings. I wasn't there for very much of the actual hearings during that time, but I was engaged every day with duties for both the SESCDP and the Endangered Species Committee. By necessity, I was not afforded the luxury of simply stepping away from my home duties. I offer no complaint. Both were critical to conservation and my education. I will forever be indebted to Cindy Barry and Jim Teeter for carrying the Committee hearing load in Portland. They made sure I was kept fully informed and provided Pat Parenteau with any and all information he needed. The leadership and professional work they performed were beyond reproach.

CHAPTER 8

Lujan's Owl Plan

During the God Squad hearings regarding the Bureau of Land Management (BLM) request that the spotted owl be exempted from the mandates of the Endangered Species Act (ESA), the Jamison strategy took a lot of criticism for its blatant disregard for the National Environmental Policy Act (NEPA) and the ESA. Secretary of the Interior Manuel Lujan, Director of the BLM Cy Jamison and Senator Bob Packwood were starting to see the need for a legislative solution that would bypass what they regarded as "unacceptable" ESA requirements. Congress had already passed "sufficiency" language in Section 318 of the appropriations bill, which was upheld in court, stating that following this law was sufficient to meet the other laws. Lujan, Jamison and Packwood knew they could get around meeting long-term needs of the spotted owl if they could put a plan in place that was approved by Congress. This was similar to the strategy used by Congress in approving the Tellico Dam. In addition, on January 28, 1992, President Bush imposed a ninety-day regulatory moratorium to lift the "burden" of regulation on industry and provide more jobs. The Northwest certainly qualified as an area where jobs had been impacted by federal regulation.

When I returned from the Federal Executive Institute (FEI) training at the end of January, I was greeted by a note from Barry Mulder alerting me to new information about the fate of the recovery plan:

> Attached is a memo from [Don] Knowles on potential delays on the recovery plan for the owl. [Jon] Bart apparently has filled

in Marv [Plenert] on this. As far as I know the Department is looking for ways to delay or stop the recovery plan. Among the options they're considering are:

1. Ceasing the project
2. Using the 90-day regulatory moratorium to at least delay public release
3. Convening the God Squad to consider exempting the owl
4. Requesting that Congress convene a new team to write a plan that could be legislated

Apparently, the Department is unhappy that the plan did not reduce the overall cost of the ISC plan (in fact, the costs and acres are about the same). This memo is being faxed to all team members this AM. I'll keep you informed as I learn more. You may want to attend the team meeting on the 18th to hear the discussion on this (unfortunately, I will be on detail at that point).

In the meantime, Bart is trying to get the draft as complete as possible and finished as soon as possible. To help them get it done this week we may want to hold our new set of comments to the team until we know more. (Mulder 1992)

On February 4, Don Knowles wrote a note to the members of the spotted owl recovery team:

I know all of you are wondering what is going on, so here's an update. Nothing complete and definitive has yet happened. However, it appears increasingly likely that the recovery plan will be deemed to meet the criteria of a regulation or program that would be subject to the President's recently announced 90-day moratorium '... which impose needless costs on consumers and substantially impedes economic growth.' While it is reasonable that the further review under the moratorium would look at ways to foster economic growth, I expect that we will be asked to finish the draft recovery plan and be prepared to release it for public review and comment at some point. I hope to have further information later this week, and will fax to each of you a more complete explanation as to what will happen during the 90 days, and what the recovery team may be asked to do, as soon as I have them. This may be a substantial part of the February 18 team meeting. (Knowles 1992)

This turn of events solidified my need to attend the meeting. A significant shift in strategy was taking place within the secretary's office on the way they wanted to provide a "win" for the president on the spotted owl issue. The problem they were facing, however, was that the time for that had passed when their friends in Congress (including Congressman Lujan at the time) had been so reckless in directing unsustainable harvest of old growth to denude whole mountains of timber. On February 14, I received a copy of a memo from one of our staff, Fred Seavey, that he received from Holt Holthausen of the recovery team. Holt relayed a request from Don Knowles:

> Don asked that we produce some new GIS maps that could be used by *his task force*. These would be very similar to maps produced for the review draft. He wants one map at 1:1,000,000 for the entire range and individual maps at 1:500,000 for each of the states . . . Don also is requesting that you (and possibly me too) consider coming to DC for February 25–28 to help them set up the GIS database on PCs in Don's office. His idea is that you would bring discs with data summarized in a form that would allow 'real time' investigation of options. *He is talking about options where entire DCAs [Designated Conservation Areas]*

would be dropped out from the system, so the questions would involve the assessment of acres, owls, etc. with different sets of DCAs. I told Don that you would need clear direction from the FWS in order to begin making specific commitments to this process, so don't be surprised if you get that clear direction. (Holthausen 1992) (Emphasis added.)

Holt was one of those solid scientists that I respected, and he knew well that we would not approve of Knowles sending work requests directly to staff without clearing it with Marv and/or me. I found it inappropriate that Don was beginning to present himself as being "in charge," while he had no line authority and could not give directions to any staff. But Don was beginning to see that he would be able to have "his team" and work on a plan that would likely be discussed with the president. It was less important that it would not ensure the long-term viability of the northern spotted owl.

Marv was out of town on travel and could not be reached. I called Fish and Wildlife Service (FWS) Deputy Director Dick Smith in D.C. and relayed my concerns about Don's inappropriate request. Dick agreed that Don had no authority to give staff directives and said he would relay the message to Director John Turner. Later that day I wrote a memo to Marv detailing our discussions:

I called Dick Smith and relayed my concerns. He was not aware of much of the discussions that had taken place, but referred the message to Director Turner. Later this afternoon, John called me and we discussed these concerns. John agreed and said that Cy Jamison (BLM) had agreed to pay the expenses of this review. We agreed that: 1) we would assist Mr. Knowles in providing maps and helping set up the computers in D.C.; 2) we would keep accurate expenditure records for reimbursement; and 3) we would make no commitment to future assistance, but would receive direction from his (Turner's) office on a case by case basis. (Hall 1992)

The amount of stress that came daily with the job we were doing left no tolerance for a political appointee trying to carve out a job in operations, a place in which he had neither authority nor expertise. When one is a career employee, the chain of command is the Holy Grail. With approximately eighty political appointees in the Department of the Interior (DOI), fifteen or fewer were nominated by the president and confirmed by the Senate. The designation PAS applies to those positions (presidential appointment confirmed by the Senate). Only PASs have the authority to give directions to staff or make policy decisions. The other political appointments are made by the secretary and do not receive Senate confirmation. These are known as Schedule C appointments. For the most part, I found throughout my career that the Schedule C appointees tried very hard to be helpful and contribute to the mission. Only a very few tried to work things around to give themselves more power than authorized by law, but it did happen. Don Knowles was feeling empowered by the secretary to create a document that would bypass the ESA, have no commitment to recovery and become law. We career employees, who believed we had taken an oath to uphold existing laws, wanted no part of this "alternative plan." But we would provide data, as long as the FWS was fully reimbursed by BLM. We were determined that there would be no monies appropriated to the FWS for conservation used in this exercise.

By March, progress was well under way to create the secretary's plan and provide it to Congress for potential endorsement. Senator Slade Gorton stood in the well of the Senate and announced that the administration was crafting an alternative owl management plan that would restore a significant portion of the northwest timber jobs that were expected to be lost as a result of the ESA recovery plan. He was laying the foundation to ask Congress to approve the plan and override the ESA. He said

Secretary Lujan had asked for the plan because he felt that the job losses (potentially as high as 31,000) would be too high.

On May 14, the secretary made good on his promise to Senators Bob Packwood and Slade Gorton when he released a draft of the "Preservation Plan for the Northern Spotted Owl" for consideration by Congress. It was immediately criticized by every biologist asked to review, and most gave the owl no more than a fifty-fifty chance of surviving the hundred-year life of the plan. The majority said the owl would go extinct, especially given the reasonable expectation that more timber would be wanted after that released by that plan had been harvested. The authors were all political appointees, including Assistant Secretary for Fish, Wildlife and Parks Michael Hayden. John Turner refused to have his name associated with it, as did many others whose ethics demanded a line be drawn. None of the names listed as "Professional and Technical Staff Support" were any I recognized as having credentials to discuss the biological needs of the owl. Don Knowles was, of course, listed as "Professional and Technical Support."

Secretary Lujan held a press conference in the Interior Building to announce his plan. He liked to refer to it as his "Owl Conservation Plan," but he spent the entire press conference referring to it as the "Owl *Conversation* Plan." As we sat in my office in Portland and watched it on TV, several staff started laughing at his confusion between "conservation" and "conversation." I was not amused and reminded them that the average person would view all of us in the department in the same manner in which they viewed our leader. Releasing this "alternative," and his poor handling of the press conference, comprised one of the most embarrassing moments in the department's history.

A secretary of the interior who had taken an oath to defend the Constitution and uphold the laws he was charged to administer was openly abdicating his responsibilities in favor of appeasing short-term job losses in one region of the country. The other embarrassing abdication of responsibility would come under a DOI secretary twenty years later at Malheur National Wildlife Refuge in Oregon, when Secretary Sally Jewell abandoned her employees, allowed thugs to take over a refuge belonging to the people and force FWS employees to leave at gunpoint, and then refused to even make a statement to condemn the armed assault on the American people. Lujan's plan died a relatively swift death when Congress refused to endorse it. We were back on track with a legitimate recovery plan, and it was being pushed back to the FWS as the Department of the Interior retreated, licking its wounds.

•••

The meeting of the recovery team on February 18 was indeed worth attending. The beginning of the divorce by the Department of the Interior and Secretary Lujan from the recovery planning process was noticeable. Don Knowles was clearly shifting his focus to the new plan for the secretary and Congress, and the interest from the department in the ongoing recovery planning process was vanishing. The secretary had pulled back the delegation of authority from the FWS at the beginning of the process. Marv was given the role of overseeing the team activities, but Jon Bart was the clear leader, with Don Knowles whispering in his ear about what the secretary hoped to achieve. We and the FWS had played a support role and funded the activities, but were clearly not in charge. With the new effort gaining traction, Knowles and the DOI were now pushing to have FWS retake the lead, and we were more than willing to do so. In the end, it is the regional director who traditionally has authority to sign the final recovery plan, and it should be at that level where the science and recommendations can be compared on equal footing.

A recovery plan for any species does not carry the weight of law or regulation, but rather offers advice on potential actions that could be done to pave the way for the species' recovery and delisting. It is published for comment, but mainly to ensure that all known science has been used and the potential actions are reasonable. Some actions are restrictions on both government and non-government activities, but all must meet the test of having adequate science to support a given restriction. The legitimate role of the executive branch is to infringe on individual or state rights only when there is adequate science and information to support such infringement. The regional director and her/his staff are usually the ones best informed to make those determinations. One of the most egregious government decisions is one based on "We don't know, so let's prohibit until we do know." This is not in keeping with law or the Constitution. The burden of proof in restricting the rights of citizens rests with the government, not the citizen.

We had several meetings leading to the transition, and on April 1 I met with Marv, Bill Martin, Knowles, Jon Bart, Barry Mulder, Phil Carroll, Holt Holthausen and David Klinger (FWS public affairs officer in Portland) to start building our structure for completing the ongoing recovery planning effort. The first draft was scheduled for release that month, and we needed to be prepared for handling the avalanche of comments that would surely come. We had assumed since February that we would be taking things over and were working to put the right people in place to deal with the various questions. The recovery plan is not obligated to make changes based on economics, as was charged in the critical habitat (CH) analysis, but it does have the responsibility of estimating economic impacts to the degree possible. Mel Schamberger (leader of economic analysis for the CH) and his team continued to help with comments that we had not already addressed in the CH economic analysis. Our good field scientists would now transition from CH to the recovery plan process.

If there were any remaining doubts about Cy Jamison's strategy in meeting legal requirements under the ESA, they were put to rest by the Ninth Circuit Court of Appeals in *Lane County Audubon Society et al. v. Cy Jamison, et al.* On March 4, 1992, the court ruled that the Jamison strategy was an agency action under the definitions of the Endangered Species Act. It further ordered the following.

The Bureau of Land Management is enjoined from announcing or awarding or conducting any additional sales pending completion of consultation, in accordance with section 7 of the Endangered Species Act, with respect to the Jamison Strategy or any other spotted owl conservation strategy, including the Timber Management Plans promulgated between 1979 and 1983, intended to establish the criteria under which sites for sales are to be selected. The injunction shall be effective immediately and shall continue in effect until issuance of this court's mandate or further order of this court. (U.S. Ninth Circuit Court of Appeals 1992)

Our meeting on April 1 was productive, and it identified a full plan for public hearings, schedule of comments and reproposal as well as hiring new staff and pushing the secretary for a final publication date. We learned from the CH process the importance of having the actual biologists from the recovery team at the public hearings, and also how to control the process. At the meeting, we decided to allow one representative of specific interests, such as mill worker jobs, to make a presentation on behalf of those who came for that reason. Everyone would be encouraged to submit written comments, but verbal comments would be by elected officials or other industry or environmental spokespersons. These public hearings would hopefully go much better than the arduous CH public hearings. The draft recovery plan for the northern spotted owl was approved for release by the secretary on May 14, 1992. The full plan spanned 662 pages, with a 36-page executive summary. Jon Bart and his team had done a masterful job of covering details and ensuring that there was ample science to support recommendations. As expected, it significantly reduced the amount of timber available for harvest from previous levels on Forest Service (FS) and Bureau of Land Management (BLM) lands. The uproar over northwest timber industry job losses continued, despite the availability of millions of acres of smaller, harvestable trees.

On May 27, Marv sent out a memo to Jon Bart formalizing the process for completing the recovery plan, including content for the Federal Register notice, how to handle public comments, specific items for the team to address, and a format for how the public hearings would be run (Plenert 1992). It was our responsibility now, and we were determined to get a quality plan over the finish line within the next nine to twelve months.

Through the summer the public hearings went well, and the information that was gathered, both in hearings and in written comments, was handled with efficiency thanks to the structure Jon had created. By August we were seeing some light at the end of the tunnel, and I began to have discussions with our staff about "next steps." Those would first and foremost include how we would integrate the final recovery plan into our ongoing operations as well as provide guidance to other agencies and the public.

When Congress passed the ESA and differentiated between endangered species and threatened species, it also separated the restrictions and protections afforded each. Section 9 of the Act lays out the prohibitions against "take" of an endangered species, but says nothing about a threatened species. Protection of threatened species was addressed in Section 4(d) and directed the secretaries to propose protective regulations for threatened species at the time of listing. This was in recognition of the fact that the threatened status was not as critical and allowed latitude for cooperative efforts to stem the species' decline and remove the existing threats to survival. Section 4(d) states:

> PROTECTIVE REGULATIONS.—Whenever any species is listed as a threatened Species pursuant to subsection (c) of this section, the Secretary shall issue such regulations as he deems necessary and advisable to provide for the conservation of such species. The Secretary may by regulation prohibit with respect to any threatened species any act prohibited under section

9(a)(1), in the case of fish or wildlife, or Section 9(a)(2) in the case of plants, with respect to endangered species; except that with respect to the taking of resident species of fish or wildlife, such, (*sic*) regulations shall apply in any State which entered into a cooperative agreement pursuant to section 6(c) of this Act only to the extent that such regulations have also been adopted by such State.

While the congressional language can be confusing, this section left a blank slate for the FWS or National Oceanic and Atmospheric Administration (NOAA) to provide threatened species whatever protections were believed necessary among those provided to endangered species, but that such provision must be done by rule at the time of listing. NOAA has always treated threatened species in this manner, with a protective rule published with each listing. The FWS, however, chose in the 1970s to publish a Section 4(d) rule extending *all* prohibitions afforded an endangered species to species listed as threatened. It was always my opinion that this significantly limited the ability to work early with other agencies and the public to take actions that might result in "take" of the species in the short term but provide much-needed relief in the long term. Because the FWS had not proposed a 4(d) rule for the spotted owl at the time of listing, all prohibitions against take were extended to the threatened owl.

Jon Bart continued to do an excellent job of keeping the team and plan on target, especially in the absence of "help" from our D.C. representative. The plan would be ready for final review and surname by Secretary Lujan by the end of December. We also received good news from the federal courts that our view of "take" under the ESA did indeed include habitat modification. We had been sued by the Sweet Home Chapter of Communities for a Greater Oregon over our interpretation that significant modification of habitat could result in take of the species. We received a memo from Daniel Shillito, associate solicitor in D.C., dated June 4, 1992, that stated:

U.S. District Judge Norma Holloway Johnson has ruled that the Endangered Species Act (ESA) allows the Fish and Wildlife Service to prohibit activities that modify the habitat of endangered or threatened species provided the habitat modification results in actual death or injury to the species. Judge Johnson's ruling also upholds the Service's long-standing practice of automatically imposing the statutory endangered species prohibitions on a threatened species unless the Service acts affirmatively to create a 'special rule' for the species . . . Section 9(a)(1)(B) of the ESA, 16 U.S.C. 1538 (a)(1)(B), makes it illegal to 'take' an endangered species. The ESA defines 'take' to mean: to harass, *harm*, pursue, hunt, shoot, wound, kill, trap, capture, or collect, or to attempt to engage in any such conduct. 16 U.S.C. 1532(18). [Emphasis added.] The ESA does not define 'harm,' but the Service's ESA regulations define the term as follows:

> Harm in the definition of 'take' in the Act means any act which actually kills or injures wildlife. Such act may include significant habitat modification or degradation where it actually kills or injures wildlife by significantly impairing essential behavioral patterns, including breeding, feeding, or sheltering

This was a significant decision due to the legal nexus between destruction of habitat necessary for the species to survive and prohibitions under the ESA. Almost any statement as to the importance of this decision would be lacking. Most of the species listed under the ESA are there because of habitat loss or modification. Had the ruling been against our interpretation, there is little doubt that species would have gone extinct in the United States at an accelerated pace. However, our friends in DOI were apparently not ready to accept this decision. On August 24, Michael Hayden, assistant secretary for fish, wildlife and parks, sent John Turner a memo titled "Interim Policy Regarding Enforcement of Prohibition Against Taking for the Northern Spotted Owl."

> There continues to be concern over how the Fish and Wildlife Service will enforce taking restrictions with respect to the northern spotted owl (*Strix occidentalis caurina*) on non-federal lands within its range. This concern has centered in part on uncertainty regarding the extent to which habitat alterations would be considered take prohibited under Section 9 of the Endangered Species Act (ESA). The Office of the Solicitor has considered the federal government's ability to successfully prosecute habitat alteration cases. Additionally, the Fish and Wildlife Service must consider the most effective use of enforcement resources. In order to concentrate enforcement of the taking prohibition for the owl on areas that are most likely to produce positive results for the species and to deter serious violations of the Endangered Species Act, you should focus attention on suspected violations that:
>
> 1. show evidence of deliberate intent to cause harm or harassment of spotted owls, or
> 2. produce physical evidence that a direct taking of owls or their parts has occurred, or
> 3. involve destruction of habitat in the immediate vicinity of a known activity center (less than a 500-acre circle centered at the activity center).
>
> In implementing this Interim Policy, please be reminded that by memorandum dated October 2, 1991, the Fish and Wildlife Service Region 1 Office withdrew the document referred to as "Procedures Leading to Endangered Species Act Compliance for the Northern Spotted Owl," (USFWS July 1990). By written

brief filed by the Department of Justice on behalf of the Department and the Service in *Sweet Home Chapter of Communities for a Great (sic) Oregon v. Turner (sic)*, the District Court was advised that those procedures (referred to as 'the Incidental Take Guidelines') were rescinded for external use. The standards from that guidance document may no longer be used in a manner inconsistent with these directions. In this regard, you should continue to assess possibilities for instituting conservation mechanisms for this species through Habitat Conservation Plans or special rules that might be more effective than the prohibition against taking. This Interim Policy will remain in effect until such measures are put in place. (Hayden 1992)

Assistant Secretary Hayden was giving a directive using an argument that is somewhat common within the law enforcement community. Law enforcement officers never have enough resources to enforce every law and meet every demand contained in the legislation. It is quite normal to have directives prioritizing where limited resources should be used. It was, however, highly irregular to use the lack of resources argument when a federal court judge had just upheld the appropriateness of that priority. We viewed this as Mr. Hayden's attempt to interfere with legitimate law enforcement, and our officers were instructed to do their job as they saw fit, and that protecting a species meant protecting them against habitat destruction.

In addition, Assistant Secretary Hayden conveniently omitted my affidavit to the court and my public statement to the media regarding our withdrawal of those guidelines. They had been requested by the timber industry before my arrival and reluctantly provided to assist industry in making their own determinations. The FWS at first refused because they didn't want a misperception of rule versus advice. Then, after requesting the guidance, the industry sued the FWS for providing recommendations without going through the rulemaking process.

After I signed the memorandum with a simple one-sentence directive that the guidelines were withdrawn, I made it clear that they were based on science as we knew it and that we would continue to follow them internally in our investigations. Marv Plenert, Bill Martin, Assistant Regional Director for Law Enforcement (ARD-LE) Dave McMullen and I made it clear to our officers that we would accept responsibility when they ignored the memo and pursued habitat cases. Law enforcement officers working on owl cases were funded out of our Fish and Wildlife Enhancement budget, not from LE appropriated dollars. They, therefore, *had* the resources to pursue habitat cases. I suspect Assistant Secretary Hayden had no idea that was the case and that his directive did not apply to spotted owl law enforcement, even though it was the clear target. The memorandum from Assistant Secretary Hayden was given "great weight."

• • •

On August 25, 1992, then-candidate Bill Clinton sent a letter to the United Brotherhood of Carpenters and Joiners of America regarding a letter they had sent to him asking for help in the northwest forests. His response would counteract two years of work and possibly end the recovery planning process for the northern spotted owl.

> Thank you for your recent letter which so clearly outlined the problems facing the forest products industry. I agree with you that a remedy must be found, and soon. This crisis represents yet another example of a White House long on the politics of blame and short on leadership. George Bush has had more than two years to help the parties find a solution. But instead of looking for answers, this administration has made the problem worse by playing political games and frustrating the process.

I believe that all parties to this dispute feel used and manipulated. They seek new and decisive ways to bring about a resolution that protects both jobs and the environment. Let me assure you that under a Clinton Administration the politics of blame will end. I personally want to take a constructive, hands-on role in seeking resolution of the crisis which is hurting so many of our timber families and dividing too many of our citizens in Oregon, Washington, and California. So on a future trip to the Northwest, I plan to continue a dialogue with all affected parties, including a visit with a timber family.

Furthermore, if there is no resolution to this matter during this Congress, early in my administration I will convene a Pacific Northwest Forest Summit to work out a legislative solution. I will work with the Congress and all interested parties to help break the gridlock which has caused so much pain in our Pacific Northwest communities. It is time for us to all come together and seek common ground. (Clinton 1992, emphasis added.)

• • •

My old friend Mike Spear left his position as regional director in Albuquerque to assume the responsibilities of assistant director for Fish and Wildlife Enhancement in D.C. early in the fall. He walked into a powder-keg court suit in which the Fund for Animals was suing the FWS for not acting, in their opinion, in good faith to address over 400 species considered candidates for listing under the ESA. The lawsuit was titled *The Fund for Animals, et al. v. Manuel Lujan, et al., Civ. No. 92-800 (GAG) (Gesell, J.),* filed in the United States District Court, District of Columbia. The primary basis of the claim was "Plaintiffs assert that defendants are unreasonably delaying the listing of species that are classified by the United States Fish and Wildlife Service ("FWS") as Category

1 ("C-1") and Category 2 ("C-2"). C-1 consists of those species that the FWS believes may be threatened or endangered but for which it lacks sufficient information to make a final determination."

Spear, still new in his position and unaware of the distribution of species that were the subject of the litigation, was faced with pressure from the Department of Justice to settle the case. As if we hadn't had enough surprises in 1992, and without calling to seek our input, he instructed the Department of Justice attorneys to proceed with a settlement in the Fund for Animals lawsuit. What he didn't know was that, of the just over 400 species to be evaluated over the next four years, 314 of those species were in one region: *ours*! On top of the already stressful workload, unbelievable political pressures, and numerous lawsuits dealing with the owl and other old-growth species, we were now charged to do full analyses and prepare decision documents to either propose listing or declare the species not in need of the protection of the law on 314 species in four years.

To put things in perspective, the total number of listed species at the time was around 680, with no more than 70 proposed by the FWS on an annual basis *nationwide*. In the Pacific Region, California had 162, Hawaii had 77, Trust Territories 3, Commonwealth of the Northern Marianas 1, Idaho 14, Nevada 11, Oregon 29, and Washington 17. We were stunned. The Pacific Region had just been assigned more than the normal listing load of the agency nationwide. The remaining few species would be handled by the other six regions. I started toying with the idea that our little team had somehow upset the karma of the universe and was receiving punishment. By the end of my career, my signature appeared on the surname route for over 450 species headed for the list of threatened and endangered species. This is not a fact I ever viewed as an accomplishment. Real accomplishments only occur when the listing process is aborted by removal of the threats, or by delisting a species already on the list because it has been recovered.

Congressional authorization for the ESA expired on October 10,

1992, but the law continued operating under the authority of the 1993 Appropriations Act. Congress is generally divided into two segments: the committees that oversee and authorize functions that are deemed priorities for appropriations, and the appropriation committees that propose funding levels. Authorizing committees propose laws to authorize programs or activities and often place a "sunset" clause stating that the law must be reauthorized after five years. This was the case for the ESA, which was first passed in 1973, then reauthorized in 1978, 1983 and 1988.

But this time was different. The recent turmoil over the northern spotted owl had infiltrated Congress and created a new kind of standoff. Those who wanted to weaken the ESA because they thought it was too far-reaching and exerted too much economic pain were reluctant to open the reauthorization debate in fear of it becoming even stronger. Those who believed it was critical to have species protections, even with economic pain, were reluctant to open the debate for the opposite reason; they feared it would be weakened. As a result, 1993 began with an unauthorized ESA except for the time covered under a single-year appropriations act. That fear on both sides is still prevalent today, and the ESA has not been reauthorized except through one-year appropriations since.

• • •

The schedule for the final recovery plan was to have it to Secretary Lujan by December 15, 1992, for his review and approval, and to be signed by Marv Plenert in March 1993, thus fulfilling the legal requirements of the ESA. But that was not to be. William Jefferson Clinton was elected the forty-second president of the United States on November 3, 1992, defeating President George H.W. Bush and Texas billionaire Ross Perot. The holdover of the "Read my lips, no new taxes" failure never left the public's psyche even in the face of a dramatic military victory in Kuwait. Clinton had convinced America he could bring the leadership that he charismatically campaigned was desperately lacking in the Bush administration. One of Secretary Lujan's last instructions came in a January 14, 1993, memo to Don Knowles, still officially the secretary's recovery team representative, and Regional Director Marv Plenert.

> I have completed my review of the proposed final recovery plan for the northern spotted owl. You and the team have done outstanding work. While the peer-reviewed plan meets the Endangered Species Act standards for recovery plans, I remain concerned about the social and economic impact. Further, I do not wish to take an action that might bind the hands of the next Secretary of the Interior. Therefore, I am deferring approval of the plan to the incoming Administration." (Lujan 1993)

President Clinton was sworn in on January 20, 1993, and immediately nominated Bruce Babbitt, former governor of Arizona, to be his secretary of the interior. Babbitt was confirmed by the Senate and sworn in only two days after his boss's inauguration. He wasted no time calling Marv Plenert and directing him to *not* sign the final recovery plan, but to wait for further instructions. After two years of hard work, significant taxpayer funds expended and a recovery plan for the northern spotted owl complete and ready for signature, we were to "await further instructions." A final recovery plan for the northern spotted owl would not be published until 2008, sixteen years later, with revisions in 2011. Critical habitat was revised in 2012 based on the final recovery plan.

• • •

The last disappointment came at the end of 1992. I had the sad occasion to say good-bye and thank you to my dear friend and deputy ARD, Jim Teeter. Jim retired after well over thirty years of service to the people of the United States, dealing with issue after issue in the old River Basins

Studies, then Ecological Services, then Fish and Wildlife Enhancement as the names changed but the challenges didn't. Jim, along with Cindy Barry and Pat Mitchell, were my anchors, and I never had to ask if they had my back. The team would change, but not the dedication of people who are seldom recognized by a public that doesn't understand just what they have in these career professionals. I wished Jim a wonderful retirement, and then, out of necessity, had to get on with finding my next deputy assistant regional director.

CHAPTER 9

The President's Forest Summit

President Clinton held true to his promise and scheduled a Pacific Northwest Forest Summit for April 2, 1993, in Portland. The flurry of activity that preceded the Summit was like elves working frantically on December 23 to get everything ready. Department of the Interior (DOI) Secretary Bruce Babbitt scheduled a full visit for late March to see the landscape, visit with agency employees, bring new administration people out, have Democratic members of Congress accompany him and meet with people in their communities. Babbitt was a true politician who won you over through his genuine love for the job and the challenge it presented. He and Clinton were much alike. In late 1992, Joel Kaplan, from the House Appropriations Committee Staff, came out for a visit. He had been forewarned that the northwest forests would be an administration priority and wanted to understand the issues. I had known Joel for several years and held him in high regard for his direct approach to issues and willingness to listen.

We took Joel and others who were with him on a three-day tour of the Northwest and tried to have him see each of the three states and the kind of timber harvests that had been dictated by members of his committee and the continuum of administrations. Knowing that the Endangered Species Act (ESA) had expired in October and would need reauthorization, he asked me to send him my ideas on "surgical" changes that could be made to make the ESA work better for all concerned—both the government biologists trying to carry out the law and the affected parties, be they federal or non-federal. On January 22, 1993, I sent Joel a memo with my recommendations:

Endangered Species Act Suggestions for Positive Change

The Endangered Species Act (ESA) is a very powerful and positive Act for the protection of ecosystems and the threatened and endangered species that depend upon them. It has done a great deal of good, but has been tremendously misunderstood by many regarding its perceived limitations. The ESA is quite flexible when in the hands of innovative thinkers and people who honestly want to find solutions to complex issues. It is, however, quite burdensome when forced into strict interpretations by the courts, bureaucracies, or those who are focused on strategies rather than solutions.

The Fish and Wildlife Service (FWS) and National Marine Fisheries Service (NMFS) have been given tremendous responsibilities under the ESA, and mandated to list species, designate critical habitat, write and implement recovery plans, and down/delist species as they improve toward stable populations. The FWS has, however, been given these responsibilities without the proper funding and staffing levels to accomplish these mandates. Because of the slow pace of listing species (due to poor budgets and politics), the FWS has been given several court decisions over the past three years to force listing and designation actions, with no regard for the lack of funding. Indeed, many would argue that the FWS has lost its ability to truly evaluate the priorities for species and habitats and instead has entered into a 'numbers game.' The most recent example is the national court settlement to list or otherwise address around 400 category 1 species within the next four years. This will result in listing actions that in four years will increase the accomplishments of the previous twenty years by 50%. The irony of this is that listing is the *least demanding* action called for under the ESA. After listing, the Section 7 consultations, Section 10 permits, recovery plans/actions, and the Administrative Procedures Act requirements that accompany these actions are set into motion. It can, for example, cost as much as $300,000 to designate critical habitat and perform the necessary economic/social analyses required in such actions. This directly drains funds necessary to support the people to carry out the requirements. As a result, the dedicated career employees of the FWS have been given tremendous workloads and they are frankly on a short road to burnout. So how could one maintain the sound principles of the ESA and all the values it provides, while still allowing for some reasonableness in identifying what is really important?

The ESA is scheduled for reauthorization during FY 1993 (it actually expired in FY 1992 but was 'reauthorized by appropriation'). Many organizations and groups will have clear postures to either 'gut' the ESA or provide even stronger prohibitions. Neither of these is the answer. The purpose of the ESA is to protect ecosystems, not stop development. The primary problem over the past 20 years has been the focus on species, instead of the natural systems that support them. Because no one has been willing to take appropriate measures to stem the decline of habitat quality and associated species before they approach the brink of extinction, we have been forced to focus on throwing a safety net around the species as a last resort. The old Fram Oil Filter commercial summed it up best: 'Pay me now, or pay me later.' The American public and a credit card society has always said 'We'll pay you later.' It is now later.

There are a few moderate changes to the ESA that could improve its effectiveness for resource protection and still allow room for new approaches to development and other uses of the ecosystems. Some of the problems and potential solutions are identified below.

Section 4

Section 4 of the ESA is the section requiring listing of species, designation of critical habitat, and development of recovery plans. The FWS has, over the past three years, had little to no opportunity to address listing as it was conceived by Congress. The ESA directs the FWS to list species based on biology alone; a directive that should *not* be abandoned. However, it gave certain criteria for analysis and directed the FWS to list species based on a priority system of immediate threat of extinction. The FWS developed a species priority system (candidate species lists) as a guidepost to identify those species most in threat. However, Section 4(3)(A) provides that when an interested party submits a petition to list a species, and that petition contains 'substantial scientific or commercial information indicating that the petitioned action may be warranted . . . the Secretary shall promptly commence a review of the status of the species concerned.'

The two most significant impediments to following the priority system, in addition to low funding, have been court directives and petitions. When a qualified petition is received, the FWS *must* initiate the status review and within one year must propose the species, find that listing is not warranted, or find that listing is warranted but precluded by higher-priority actions. Unfortunately, to reach this point as much staff work is required as that for addressing a priority species over a year's time. The Pacific Region of the FWS has been unable to address a priority species for more than two years due to court settlements and petitions.

Recommendation

The ESA could be modified to allow the FWS to decide after 90 days, rather than one year, whether the petition presented enough substantial information to preclude actions on recognized high-priority species. This would place more responsibility on the petitioner; an action that is reasonable if higher, known species are delayed in protection.

Another significant problem has been not only in the funding levels, but in *where* the monies are appropriated. For example, in FY 1993 the FWS received the following: Listing—$5.531 million, Consultation—$9.602 million, Recovery—$20.478 million, Delisting—$748K, and Prelisting—$2.135 million. As can be seen, the emphasis was on listing, consultation and recovery, with the least emphasis on delisting and prelisting. This is a significant fact. What these figures illustrate is that only $2.883 million were allocated to head off listings or remove species from lists, while $35.611 million was allocated to put species on the list, or work toward their removal. This simple funding allocation clearly shows not only the minimal funding for the whole program, but more significantly that only about 7.5% of the funding was directed to the most effective actions that can be taken: to keep species from being in need of listing and removing those no longer in need. These two categories require the same measures: quality improvement or stabilization of the ecosystem. Without an overt effort to salvage ecosystems in decline, the pattern of continual listing is inevitable. An effort *must* be made to recognize that prelisting conservation agreements that incorporate actions to stem the decline in ecosystem health present the only real solution. Unfortunately, the ESA has no clause to recognize this essential tool for bringing some level of scientifically credible management control into the listing dilemma. In addition, the time limitation burdens associated with the ESA require that listing decisions be made within one year (proposal) or a maximum of two years (final). These limitations preempt the ability to work with local citizens, governments, and organizations to develop strategies to ensure the ecosystem decline will be halted. A species in peril is simply a symptom of the disease, and efforts specific to the species will only mask the problem until another symptom (species) comes to light. This is truly no reasonable mode of operation.

Recommendation

The ESA could be modified to recognize that the period during pre-listing is the most opportunistic period during the entire process. The time requirements could be expanded to three years total to allow sufficient time to use the first identified species as the symptom, and the ecosystem health as the cure. Funding should be increased for pre-listing to accommodate the costs of bringing the public into the process, not only for their comments, but for their ideas toward solutions. The ESA is seen by the public as a 'black box.' An emphasis on pre-listing with involvement from the public could go far to eliminate this perception. An extra year in the process may save several years in staff effort down the road. Indeed, it might even save the ecosystem.

Another problem with the ESA, as written, is the requirement that recovery plans be done, but no time frame is identified, while critical habitat must be done no later than one year after final listing. Critical habitat is a *tool for recovery*, not vice versa. The northern spotted owl is a prime example of this error. The FWS was sued because critical habitat was not designated along with listing, and the court ruled that critical habitat be proposed within three months of the decision. This was ordered while a recovery team was being formed to write a recovery plan. At the time of final designation of critical habitat, the recovery team was not yet in an informational position to offer suggestions to the FWS as to how much critical habitat would be necessary to accomplish recovery. As a result, the FWS now has gone through rule making and designated critical habitat for the northern spotted owl, and will no doubt be forced to modify the designation after the recovery plan is finalized to mesh with the recommendations of the plan. The recovery plan may consider any and all 'tools' available, to include management scenarios, suggested special rules, critical habitat, or other measures that, in combination, will achieve recovery. Critical habitat, on the other hand, must look only to identifying geographic areas that *may* be important to recovery, and delineating those areas on maps. Additional consultation is required when federal actions are involved in designated areas. For non-federal actions with no federal nexus, critical habitat has little to no value.

Recommendation

Modify the ESA to require recovery plans within three years of listing and critical habitat to be proposed within one year following the final recovery plan. If the listing process continues as is currently planned, significant funding increases will be necessary to accommodate the backlog, as well as the possible 400 species added over the next four years. If pre-listing emphasis can accomplish ecosystem stability, both listing and recovery actions can be greatly reduced.

Section 7

This section deals with the federal consultation process before a federal agency can proceed with an action that 'may affect' a listed or proposed species. It also lays out agency responsibility to take measures 'in furtherance of the purposes of this

Act.' The basic mandates are that once the action agency has provided an adequate biological assessment of their action and its consequences to listed species or critical habitat, the FWS has 90 days to complete the consultation and no more than 135 days to deliver a biological opinion. This section needs no revisions. It is brought up here for comparison to Section 10 requirements that are discussed next.

Section 10

This section of the Act is the only avenue for a non-federal entity or individual to 'take' a listed species incidental to otherwise lawful activities. Comments here will be addressed specifically to Section 10(a)(1)(B). This section of the Act was added through amendments to provide the private sector with equal opportunity to undertake actions that may affect, but not jeopardize, listed species as that afforded federal agencies. Unfortunately, the procedural demands of this section have led to time frames for completion of permit decisions to encompass years rather than months. This section should be modified to be on par with the Section 7 criteria and time frames identified above. The private sector feels that federal agencies have an unequally high opportunity to receive incidental take authority and comply with the National Environmental Policy Act. The perception is that an agency can get a final opinion (authority) within 135 days, while developers must wait as long as three years. There are some equities that are not often recognized by the private sector. For example, while the FWS must provide an opinion within 135 days of receipt of a *complete* biological assessment, the information gathering for that assessment may have taken a year or more of studies prior to submission of the assessment. Nonetheless, this issue should be addressed.

Recommendation

Section 10(a)(1)(B) should be modified to direct the Secretary(s) to promulgate regulatory procedures to satisfy the intent of the ESA. The specific criteria presently identified in the ESA arguably place a higher standard on the non-federal sector than is placed on federal agencies under Section 7. The Secretary(s) should rely on those with field experience in administering this Section to propose pragmatic requirements for permit issuance. One point that must be completely understood is that the ESA addresses only one half of the equation. There are really only two programs for resource management: that program addressing the endangered/threatened species; and that program that encompasses all other tools (contaminants, hydropower, wetlands permits, etc.) that work to keep species and ecosystems from being degraded to the point where protection under the ESA is necessary. Without equally adequate attention and funding for those activities, we will always be faced with how to make an endangered species program or Act work. With them, we may actually reach a point where the ESA is a minor player.

As can be seen, these recommendations are relatively minor changes to the ESA but could provide a much smoother and positive approach to accomplishing the purpose of the ESA: 'to provide a means whereby the ecosystems upon which endangered species and threatened species depend may be conserved, to provide a program for the conservation of such endangered species and threatened species, and to take such steps as may be appropriate to achieve the purposes of the treaties and conventions set forth in subsection (a) of this section.' (Hall 1993)

These suggestions were the culmination of two years of intensive analysis of the Endangered Species Act that I undertook with the sound educational advice of some of the best biologists with whom I ever had the pleasure to work, as well as lessons learned from various court decisions. While the Act was not reauthorized, I would still support these recommendations today. The ESA cannot be successful by pure dependence on regulatory actions. Species will only be recovered if the public believes the species are "theirs" to cherish and conserve. Only the people who share the environment with these species can decide if *they* take responsibility to ensure species survival. Of all the regulatory authorities encoded in legislation under the purview of the director of the FWS, none provides the authority to require any landowner to *improve* a single acre of habitat. Regulation can and does limit the amount of destruction or diminishment of conservation value that can be allowed, but only *volunteer* actions on the part of the landowner accomplishes improvement.

• • •

April 2 wasn't that far away and a lot of planning needed to be done. Secretary Babbitt scheduled a trip to the Northwest for late in March. Don Knowles wasted no time in trying to show the new secretary that he was on the new team. Barry Mulder sent Marv Plenert and me a note saying he had received a phone call from John Faye in our D.C. office and that Don had convened a meeting on February 18 with Secretary Babbitt present, to discuss how to bring all agencies on board to support a single government position, particularly the implementation of a recovery plan. What was not known was whether this meant the recovery plan was ready for a signature at the Forest Summit or one that would come following that event. According to Barry, not even Knowles knew. Barry was asked to provide copies of current and past interagency agreements for possible use. We would simply have to wait and see.

Early indications of how our new secretary saw things came through his interviews with the press and public statements during confirmation. It was clear that endangered species would be at the top of the list and that he believed there needed to be an overhaul of the way species were protected. He emphasized the need to look at entire ecosystems instead of one species at a time. This fit well with our efforts on the northwest forests and spotted owl. He also emphasized his support for "sound science" and "science-based decisions." He believed that the previous administration had ignored science when making decisions, and leaned too heavily on economics. We found no argument with his approaches to conservation.

For those of us in the FWS, and many in the Bureau of Land Management (BLM) and Forest Service (FS), these positions brought cautious optimism that we would have a reasonable ear to hear our thoughts and ideas about managing forest ecosystems and understanding that nature could not continue providing harvests at anywhere near previous levels. I first met Secretary Babbitt when he invited me to join him and a half dozen others for a private dinner. Jack Ward Thomas was among the group. Babbitt had just read *Cadillac Desert* by Marc Reisner, the epic story of the development of water resources in the West. As a native of Arizona, Babbitt was well versed in water issues and would become active in those negotiations on the Colorado River and in California. He was extremely cordial and made us feel welcome. Given the ordeal we had gone through over the past two years, we listened intently to his views. I left the dinner with the clear understanding that this administration was not going to make any decisions until after the Forest Summit, but I was hopeful that at least a significant part of the work already done would be used in crafting the decision.

The Babbitt tour covered at least a half dozen counties, three states, numerous forests and multiple briefings. We developed a three-ring binder full of information for the secretary as we traveled across Washington, Oregon and California. Congressman Bob Smith joined us for part of the tour, and Secretary of Agriculture Mike Espy was also traveling around with Forest Service personnel. It was quite the show, and the Northwest didn't know how to deal with it all. Words like "carnival atmosphere" and "competing air shows" were used by the press to describe the mayhem surrounding the onslaught of dignitaries to the Northwest. Elaine Zielinski said "Even though we all knew the Forest Summit was pretty much a show, we were all impressed that the secretaries were there, and it definitely helped us with funding over the next few years." (Zielinski 2020)

It was a show. And one in which we were required participants, at least for the pre-Summit site visits. Babbitt performed his political role for the masses, but we found an attentive and interested secretary when we were providing information and advice. It was on the field blitz that I got to know and respect Bruce Babbitt. I didn't agree with all of his positions, but then I'd be surprised if that were the case with any secretary of the interior. But Babbitt didn't like to lose, so he wanted the unvarnished truth, and we were expected to give it. He would do the varnishing.

The April 2 date of the Summit was a Friday, and I needed to be in Las Vegas for some meetings earlier in the week. My plan was to fly to Las Vegas on Wednesday, March 31, and return on Friday, leaving my deputy ARD, Gerry Jackson, in charge in the interim. Gerry, a former environmental contaminants specialist, was a top-notch scientist and didn't tolerate obfuscation. He often told the staff "I don't do nuances; just tell me the truth!" He was my kind of leader and believed in the same straightforward discussions I did.

As planned, I flew to Las Vegas on Wednesday. On Thursday I got a frantic call from Gerry, telling me I needed to fly back immediately. They were giving out credentials to attend the conference, and I had to be there in person to get mine . . . that day! I asked Gerry if we had received instructions regarding allowing substitutes to attend the Forest Summit in our place. The phone went quiet. "Are you still there?" I asked. Gerry replied, "Yes, I'm just in shock. You don't want to go to the President's Forest Summit?" While he clearly was surprised by what I'd said, the fact was that I really didn't have a strong desire to sit all day, unable to leave, and listen to all the arguments I had been hearing for the previous two years. I thought it would be very instructive for him to hear them, since he was new to the Northwest, and I was much happier taking care of business with our staff in Las Vegas. He said the instructions left it as my decision, and one with which he was pleased.

The Forest Summit went off as expected, with a lot of listening, photo ops with the president, and a new set of orders. The existing recovery plan apparently gave pause to this new administration when they saw the level of timber harvest reductions that would be necessary. Jack Ward Thomas was gaining more and more personal involvement with the new president and was starting to drift from the hard stance of the Interagency Scientific Committee (ISC). The ISC report had made it clear that the committee considered economic impacts only lightly, if at all, and the plan was one for the long-term recovery of the northern spotted owl. The report stated that economic analyses would come later and were appropriate. In March, Jack and Jared Verner, from the Pacific Southwest Research Station, had presented a paper at the North American Wildlife and Natural Resources Conference on the economic considerations under the ESA:

> Clearly, any call for 'balance' at this point should be recognized for what it is—a call for decreasing socio-economic impacts by increasing the risk to the recovery of a listed species. After considering the four tries by the four teams described earlier, four congressional hearings, the 'God Squad' proceedings, and a court trial (likely with more to come), we contend that no further reductions in socio-economic costs are possible while remaining in compliance with ESA and, in this case, NFMA [National Forest Management Act]. Assuming that the law should and will ultimately be obeyed, *it is highly likely that the 'balance' was already in place when ISC released its report on 1 April 1990.* (Thomas and Verner 1993) (Emphasis added.)

Bruce Babbitt (left) and author (Courtesy of Bob Fields)

That statement would become a significant lapse of memory just a few months later.

President Clinton was impressed with Jack Ward Thomas, as many of us had been. Jack was a natural leader, with a calming personality and a mind predisposed to sound scientific ethics. After the forest conference, Jack was asked to lead a new effort that would bring the information from the conference to be incorporated with previous reports and information, and to do so in a short time frame. The conference identified economic and job impacts along with several possible ideas to address: training and job creation; community concerns, particularly in the Oregon & California lands, with potential solutions; and, in the category of long-term approach to maintaining ecosystems, four major items—ecosystem management, landscape ecology, restoration and "new forestry." Three workgroups were established to address three issues: ecosystem management assessment, labor and community assistance, and agency coordination.

On Friday, May 7, 1993, the White House Office of the Press Secretary issued a "Media Advisory" with the mission statement for Forest Summit working groups. The explanation of the ecosystem management assessment team mission was

> to identify alternative strategies for a scientifically sound, ecologically credible, legally responsible basis for managing the federal forests of the Pacific Northwest and northern California.

The document went on to give in detail the objectives based on the president's mandates and principles, with guidance on the approach that should be taken. The new group adopted the formal name of Federal Ecosystem Management Assessment Team (FEMAT). Many of the same agency scientists who had worked together through the past efforts remained involved, and there were new political appointees assigned to the labor and community assistance and agency coordination working groups. Jim Pipkin, who was new in the Clinton administration, was assigned to lead the Agency Coordination Team, which included Mike Spear and me, while Jack was assigned the lead role for FEMAT to get this ambitious plan over the finish line.

Bill Clinton was known as "the Comeback Kid" because he had learned early in his political career to take actions that were unpopular at the beginning of his term. As governor of Arkansas, he had only two-year terms and was possibly the best at getting tough things done the first year and charming the public in the election year. He understood better than most that the public has a short memory. As a result, he wanted to get the FEMAT plan done and behind him in the first two years of his presidency, preferably in the first year. The FEMAT was given ninety days to come up with the first draft of a new plan, as well as a supplemental environmental impact statement (SEIS) based upon modifications to the recent Forest Service EIS.

The plan covered 24 million acres of federal lands, with advice for non-federal forest management. *Each agency provided every expert we had to assist in analyzing nearly two hundred vertebrate species, with emphasis on those dependent on old-growth forests.* The first draft was completed and submitted to the president in July 1993. The plan had ten alternatives, and the length of the public comment period was three months. The goal of the plan was to provide protection where old-growth forests remained, while allowing as much harvest as possible. The life of the plan was one hundred years, an unusually long period when taken in context of former plans.

The Draft Supplemental EIS broke down the areas into a new category called Late Successional Reserves (LSRs) to replace Habitat Conservation Areas (30 percent of the federal landscape); Adaptive Management Areas (AMAs, 6 percent), Riparian Reserves for aquatic species and Marbled Murrelets (RRs, 11 percent), Administratively Withdrawn Areas (AWAs, not open for harvest, 6 percent), Managed Late Successional Areas (LSAs, 1 percent), and the Matrix (16 percent), which had the most significant portion of Oregon and California Railroad Revested (O&C) lands where harvest was expected and where species movement between forest blocks would occur. Many of the LSRs, however, had large areas where mountainsides had been denuded and would require time for next-generation growth before liberal harvest in the Matrix could occur. The thought process was that as previously clear-cut areas were replanted and new habitat matured, additional harvest could be made in the Matrix and other managed areas. This approach could only be done when looking at forest management on the century timescale.

To have the plan ready for completion before the end of the year, one representative of each agency was assigned the responsibility to be on the Interagency Implementation Team (IIT). The directive from our regional directors to Elaine Zielinski, Nancy Graybeal, Elizabeth Garr and me stated:

Effective immediately, each of you are assigned to the Interagency Implementation Team for the President's Plan. Your current duties will be reassigned while you accomplish this task. Your duties while on assignment are as follows:

1. Coordinate and facilitate interagency implementation decisions, ensuring timely process flow and issue resolution.
2. Prepare implementation action plans.
3. Establish necessary working teams.
4. Set goals, objectives and timeframes for working teams.
5. Make recommendations to Regional and WO Interagency Executive Teams on issues of strategic importance.
6. Take whatever actions are needed to implement policy and decisions flowing from Regional and WO Interagency Executive Teams.

You are asked to assemble the Regional and/or WO Interagency Executive Teams when strategic decisions are needed; when policy changes are needed; or when allocation of resources are being decided. The exact extent of this assignment is unknown, but we do not anticipate it lasting longer than December 31, 1993. (Plenert et al., 1993)

I was given the responsibility to represent the FWS, Elaine Zielinski the BLM, Nancy Graybeal for the FS and Elizabeth Garr for NMFS. We also had occasional interactions with the National Park Service (NPS) and the Bureau of Indian Affairs. Bob Jacobs (deputy regional forester for the North Pacific) was assigned to oversee the formulation and completion of the SEIS. The IIT was directed by each of our regional/state supervisors to work from one of the bank buildings in Portland to isolate us from normal duties and allow everyone to focus on getting this job done. We were given the unique authority to reach out to any field installation, regardless of agency, and give assignments. The field was instructed to honor the request of any member of the IIT. Given the tasks we had all endured over the previous two years, we stopped using the term "near impossible" and simply adopted the motto "Nothing is impossible if you're not the one having to do the work." Elaine Zielinski assessed the historic nature of this effort:

> The Northwest Forest Plan was the most contentious ever undertaken by federal agencies and the first intragovernmental collaboration BLM had ever done based on a comprehensive scientific report. Implementation of the Northwest Forest Plan institutionalized scientific and management relationships. (Zielinski 2020)

A significant problem occurred when we were told that President Clinton thought the reduction in timber harvest by any of the alternatives that would meet National Forest Management Act (NFMA) and ESA standards was too great. We were told that Jack Ward Thomas and Jim Pipkin were assigned the duty of pulling the parts of alternatives that would result in allowing more harvest, then push the rest of us for as much harvest as possible while meeting legal criteria. This would become the Selected Alternative for the Record of Decision in the SEIS. There was nothing illegal about this request. The National Environmental Policy Act (NEPA) allows the "action agency" to blend alternatives based on public comment during the SEIS process. But this was a bombshell given the short time frame.

Without warning, Bob Jacobs was handed an entirely new Option 9, and told to make the SEIS work to support it. This put us all on a new directive. The SEIS Team and IIT were busy trying to gain an understanding of what the forest standards and guidelines would have to do, as well as how the harvest theoretically would occur across the landscape. Jack was also beginning to show signs of what those of us in the field called "political power intoxication." We had seen it before, and it was not easy to avoid when, as in this instance, an elk biologist from Oregon regularly rubbed elbows with the president of the United States, especially when Dale Robertson had stepped down as the chief of the Forest Service and Jack was a prime contender for the job. Invitations to the White House are not something a field biologist gets every day. We tried not to be judgmental about Jack's behavior, because he had run the gauntlet for scientific integrity up to this point. But it was becoming more noticeable.

As the FWS representative for the IIT, I had to make regular trips back to D.C. to meet with either the Department of the Interior staff or, equally as often, with Katie McGinty, the new chair of the president's Council on Environmental Quality (CEQ). Katie was an attractive brunette with a very sharp mind and a tongue as rough as a sailor's. In the regular closed meetings attended by Katie, Jack, Jim Pipkin and me, it was not uncommon for the "F word" to fly out when she was speaking. I'm sure it was a technique to have us relax and get down to business, but it felt a little different for this field biologist sitting in the Old Executive Office Building. But I genuinely liked Katie and her "get to the point" approach to things. The major challenges I faced usually came from Jack.

Jack, and more likely the president, was obviously trying to get the FWS to agree to more harvest as well as how birds might travel across the Matrix between the Cascade and Coast Mountain Ranges. For the latter, we knew it took as little as one influx of new genes into a population per generation to maintain genetic health and gene diversity. Because Jack was an elk biologist, it made perfect sense to him that we could just capture and move owls from the two ranges and allow more harvest in the Matrix. We jokingly called this "Jack's owl in a suitcase plan." I had to repeatedly remind him that we were discussing a hundred-year plan that was expected to satisfy the laws, and that having to regularly capture and move animals would not satisfy either the definition of self-sufficient populations for the ESA nor vertebrate species viability for NMFA.

The other area of argument was over the LSRs. Jack believed that since the LSRs had been identified and "set aside," more harvest in the Matrix should be allowed. My response became "Fine, Jack, when owls can nest, rest and find cover on a hillside covered with tree stumps in your LSRs, I'll agree that it's habitat and you can cut more in the Matrix. But until then, it's not and I can't say you can." I'm sure I wasn't one of Jack's favorites, but there was no way I could face the team of biologists who had worked so tirelessly for a solid plan if I agreed to something I knew wasn't biologically supportable. No one in the room was an owl biologist. It seemed, at least for the time being, that the roles had evolved. Jack was now an advocate for a plan the president would like, and I had become the representative of the biologists, who had significant concerns with that plan. Whether it was comfortable or not, it was my responsibility to protect their science to the best of my ability.

• • •

On September 10 the FWS officially had a new director. Mollie Beattie was with the Vermont Department of Natural Resources and a forester by training. When I first went in to meet with her and see how much she wanted to be involved in the spotted owl discussions, it was obvious she thought the train was out of the station and that it was far too late in the game for her to engage as John Turner had done. I was told to keep doing what I was doing and let her know if I needed anything. She and John Turner were very much alike in their love for the resource and the people who worked so hard to care for the land, but she wasn't interested in diving into the spotted owl circus. Her main area of change was to significantly push the ecosystem approach to conservation at the landscape level. We welcomed both our new director from Vermont and her desire to improve the way we did business, but she did not engage very heavily in our western issues. My instructions from her when working California water were the same: that I should keep her informed and that she trusted me to make the right decisions. There were times when it wasn't very comfortable for this GS-15 in a region to be making decisions for the agency, but none of us had time to think about those kinds of things.

● ● ●

The final meeting I had with Jack, Katie, and Jim Pipkin on the Forest Plan was at Katie's office, and it included several more of the team. Bob Jacobs, Dick (Holt) Holthausen, Barry Mulder and other FEMAT members were there to put the final touches on the plan before we started the Section 7 consultation and finalized the standards and guidelines under which the national forest lands would operate. During the meeting, Jim Pipkin asked Jack, "Since you were the primary author of Option 9, what do you think is the most important thing we could do now to get this plan over the finish line?" Jack responded "You know, I carried this plan from the beginning, personally wrote the modifications and delivered it with a ribbon. It seems to me the Fish and Wildlife Service needs to do their job and tell us what to do about the marbled murrelet."

As I looked around the table, I saw absolute shock on the faces of dedicated biologists who had given their hearts and souls to this effort, and to Jack. I had to control my anger, but I'm not sure how well I did. "Jack, before you throw your shoulder out of socket patting yourself on the back, might I remind you that there were dozens of biologists assigned to help you get the analysis done, including all government murrelet biologists, and *you* decided to kick the can down the road and 'address murrelets later.' It's insulting for you to sit there with Jim and act as if you two were the only ones involved!"

Katie quickly said "OK, let's all take a deep breath and get back on track." Later that evening at Washington National Airport, those of us flying back to Portland sat in a corner of the bar having a beer. Holt was devastated that his "hero" had behaved so arrogantly. He told us he was going to resign from the Forest Service, that he wasn't sure he wanted to be part of this any longer. Bob Jacobs and I had to talk him out of it by reminding him of the way Jack had been fed the power juice and we all knew Jack was a better man than that.

Thankfully for the Forest Service, Holt reconsidered and stayed with the team. Jack became the chief of the FS in December 1993 as the final touches were being placed on the FEMAT plan and Record of Decision. In my opinion, Jack went on to be the chief of the Forest Service we all knew he could be and settled back down to more of the Jack we had known. Elaine Zielinski said "Jack would call Nancy Graybeal and me and ask us how much timber should be harvested for the fiscal year. Whatever we told him is what he accepted." The old Jack had returned, and conservation was the beneficiary.

In order to finish the plan, a Section 7 consultation would have to occur that would cover 24 million acres and last a hundred years. As the FWS representative on the IIT, it fell to me to get the consultation done and, hopefully, with a finding of "no jeopardy." On October 31, I called the biologists together to discuss how we should proceed. The biologists working on the opinion were Barry Mulder, Russ Peterson, Gary Miller and Mike Horton representing the FWS; Barbara Hill and Mike Crouse from the BLM; David Solice, Grant Gunderson and Hugh Black from the FS; and Mike Tehan from the NMFS, all of whom had been involved in this issue and knew as much about the other side's perspective as they did their own. I decided to try an experiment I hoped would get the job done much faster than usual.

I challenged the biologists to make sure timber was harvested at the level predicted by the plan, about 1.2 billion board feet (bbf) per year. They all looked at me as if I had three eyes. I said "Come on, if you stay in your corners you'll just argue to protect your long-standing positions and be less open to good ideas. If you look at things from the other side, I have absolute faith that you are professionals who will find a solid answer. I'm asking you to take the leadership and help find the places that should receive focus from the timber planners." They thought for a moment, then all agreed it was probably the best approach. If the biologists were allowed to guide the sales, they would know best what would avoid jeopardy. They took the challenge and rose to the occasion.

Consultation began on the last day of October, and a "no jeopardy" opinion was completed in January and signed on February 10, 1994, just over three months later. Most people didn't realize that, in a hundred-year plan covering 24 million acres, we were expecting the take of 10,000 owls, more than the total population that existed at the time. But the management strategies being put in place would ensure growth of the populations over time and result in even healthier owl populations. The opinion was a "programmatic opinion," meaning it authorized the plan but did not give specific, site-located take authorization. That would be done on an annual or individual sale basis. As long as the plan was followed, it was expected that there would be no jeopardy to the owl or other listed and candidate species. I could not have been prouder of this group of dedicated biologists, nor more humbled to be part of the Section 7 discussion that made history.

The SEIS was finalized in February 1994. Lawsuits challenging the appropriateness of the plan were quick to follow. On December 21, 1994, Judge William Dwyer, in whose court other owl cases had been heard, ruled in *Seattle Audubon Society v James Lyons, et al.* and granted the order for summary judgment for the government. He found that the plan was legally consistent with government authorities and went on to say,

> The order now entered, if upheld on appeal, will mark the first time in several years that the owl-habitat forests will be managed by the responsible agencies under a plan found lawful by the courts. It will also mark the first time that the Forest Service and BLM have worked together to preserve ecosystems common to their jurisdictions. (Dwyer 1994, p4)

Normally, federal judges are limited to finding of legal consistency, proper treatment of information and constitutionality. But in this case, Judge Dwyer actually endorsed the plan for its scientific integrity and ecosystem analysis. Part of the plaintiff's challenge had been that the ecosystem approach was too broad and ignored the other laws. Relative to this point, the judge said,

> In addition, the ESA requires federal agencies to carry out their administrative programs so as to conserve the listed species and the ecosystems upon which they depend. Given the current condition of the forests, there is no way the agencies could comply with the environmental laws *without* planning on an ecosystem basis. (Dwyer 1994, p32) (Emphasis as written in the opinion.)

...

The work of the Clinton administration to reduce harvest restrictions, however, was not over with the court's concurrence of the Northwest Forest Plan. As a threatened species, the spotted owl was subject to the full Section 9 protections due to the long-standing FWS 4(d) rule that extended all protections provided for endangered species to those listed as threatened. The FWS retained the right, however, to propose individual 4(d) rules at any time for a threatened species when it determined that a rule tailored to that species provided increased opportunity for management or recovery.

Tom Collier was Babbitt's new chief of staff, and George Frampton was our new assistant secretary for Fish, Wildlife and Parks. My old friend Don Barry from the POWDR bill exercise was Frampton's new deputy. Don was given the assignment from within the DOI, and I from the field, to oversee the crafting of a special 4(d) rule for the northern spotted owl. The reasoning given was based on the Forest Plan focus on federal lands and the hope that lifting harvest restrictions on non-federal lands would encourage volunteer actions by private landowners, as well as possible interest in long-term habitat conservation plans (HCP) under the Section 10 permit authority. But that would not be easy.

Every effort that could be made to provide harvest relief was explored, and reexplored, during the recovery plan (the owl's entire range) and FEMAT (federal lands) efforts. Collier and Frampton put a great deal of pressure on Don, who in turn shared that pressure with me, to agree that much less protection of owl nest sites would be adequate on the non-federal lands. In addition, they contended that the Matrix was less important than the owl territories, just as Cy Jamison had done in the previous administration, even though the Forest Plan had made it clear that these lands were critical to long-term survival and recovery. I had become accustomed to being pushed for concessions, and had just adopted the position that "If our biologists won't agree, I won't." John Turner was allowed to stay on as the director until the Clinton administration was able to get Mollie on board. It was a high compliment to John's integrity that an opposing-party administration respected him enough to not ask him to leave immediately. But his ability to intercede was basically eliminated. He was back to the posture of the corpse at an Irish wake.

From August through the end of the year, my assignments were focused on working from the "Pink Palace," as we came to call the bank building where we were temporarily housed, with the IIT and working with Don Barry on the potential 4(d) rule. Most days I felt as though I couldn't seem to please anyone in the administration with fast-enough responses. On one occasion we had yet another new person from the White House political ranks come join us for a meeting. We already had Tom Tuckman and Will Stelle involved in all our activities, and this woman came to tell us the "White House" wanted us to do another analysis that wasn't on the schedule.

Elaine, Nancy and I sat at the table listening in amazement at the lack of understanding of the enormous amount of work that was going on. After she asked when we could have it done, I spoke up and said

"Absolutely, right away." She smiled with pride at her accomplishment of power while Nancy and Elaine stared at me with mouths open in shock. "As soon as you tell us which of the other 'White House' directed assignments we immediately drop." Her smile went away. Nancy and Elaine relaxed and looked back at her waiting for an answer. "We already have every qualified person fully occupied with other assignments. You will have to take full responsibility for whatever is decided doesn't get done." She said "Oh, I'll have to get back to you on that." She left, and we never heard from her again.

Tom Collier was apparently in direct communication with the White House staff about the 4(d) rule on a daily basis. On one of my regular trips to D.C. to discuss "progress" on the rule, I had a meeting in the conference room on the third floor of the Department of the Interior Building, next to the elevators outside the assistant secretary's corridor. Mike Spear was associate director for Fish and Wildlife Enhancement. He and Don Barry were joined by Pete Raynor, associate DOI solicitor for Fish and Wildlife. Pete was an old friend and a clear advocate for the FWS and our mission. Mike and Don were making me feel as if I were wrestling a tag team, but I had no partner. At one point, Mike said "I think we can reduce the owl circles and the birds will be fine." I had a great deal of respect for Mike and his expertise, but it wasn't in biology. Mike was an economist and had served on a submarine in the U.S Navy. "That's fine, Mike, but until you get a degree in biology, your biological opinion doesn't matter." He smiled and said, "OK, you got me."

I believed Don was pushing to have the owl territory circles reduced and allow more harvest on private lands because Tom Collier was pushing him. I finally said "Fine. We can do that." Don said "You will?" "Yes. We'll write it up with reduced nesting territories, and put a cover memo on it that says 'per your instructions, we have modified the rule to reduce owl territories.' I'll sign it and send it to you." Pete Raynor carried a 6- by 9-inch note pad with wire rings at the top for the notes he had been taking. As soon as I finished speaking, Pete threw the note pad straight up toward the ceiling and yelled "Fuck it, I'm out of here!" As the note pad landed on the table and the door slammed with Pete's departure, I just shook my head. I reminded myself that I didn't have a lot of friends in this meat grinder, and I just lost one. We took a break. About fifteen minutes later Pete returned. I said "Pete, I'm sorry. I didn't mean to upset you." He responded, "You didn't upset me! If you can't agree to this, I won't support it."

• • •

The chief of staff of the Department of the Interior can wield a great deal of influence while staying under the radar as a non–Senate-confirmed executive. This position carries significant nuance that the incumbent speaks for the secretary, the person we all reported to in DOI. Marv let us know he had been told by Collier that the White House would need to approve the 4(d) rule. Because of the political influence we were feeling and the fear it would win the day, we charted a plan for making sure the other regions knew about our challenge. At an internal FWS meeting in D.C., we discussed the questions that would need to be answered. Among them were:

> Do we go with biology and take the heat from the administration?
>
> Do we build the rule to accomplish recovery or simply regulate take?
>
> Do we tweak Option 9? (Not within our authority, but may be necessary.)
>
> What is "significant portion of the range" for recovery purposes? How important are state and private lands?

We didn't believe there was any room left in the definition of take and meeting scientific integrity, nor in satisfying the legislative intent of a 4(d) rule. Tom Collier would pass along "suggested" actions to Don, who would then call me. I called Barry Mulder regularly to run them past him to see if he thought it would work, or to have him run it past the team. This went on for some time, with *minimal* concessions from the biologists. In our view, the rule was not ready for prime time. In the final analysis, the question that must be answered is "Will the rule be adequate to allow survival and recovery of the species?" There was a push, presumably by Collier, to reduce the protective zone around owl nest sites from a minimum of 500 acres down to 200 and then even further. When a proposed rule was finally announced, no one from the career ranks participated.

In December, Assistant Secretary for Fish, Wildlife and Parks George Frampton and Katie McGinty provided the explanation for the rule. They told the press the effort was to remove any further restrictions on non-federal timber harvests and fulfill the promise made by the president to "end the gridlock." It didn't work.

The constant requests of our team in Portland to agree to "just a little more," on top of what everyone had already gone through, was like salt in the wound. In response to questions about the rule, we told the truth. Phil Carroll, as our spokesman, told the press: "A 70-acre circle is not enough to allow an owl to survive in a nesting area. The assumption is they'll either move on or die. Seventy acres is not enough to keep them alive."

This did nothing to mend the lack of trust from the conservation public regarding government decisions. As the millions of trees that had been planted over the years grew and needed to be thinned in accordance with the FEMAT plan, the environmental organizations regularly opposed the "commercial thinning" operations at seemingly every turn. They had no faith that the FS and BLM would not regress to significant clear-cutting to appease the timber interests. As a result, by the time I was once again involved in the northwest forest issues in 2005–2009, the primary threats to the spotted owl were no longer overharvest, but catastrophic wildfires from forests too dense with young trees as fuel, and the barred owl, a competitor of the spotted owl that saw a range expansion into spotted owl habitat.

Once again, Mark Rey and I would be discussing how to deal with these threats, as he became undersecretary of the Department of Agriculture, which oversaw the Forest Service. It was ironic that we were in a position to finally agree on reasonable thinning solutions to achieve the objectives of the Forest Plan, yet the lack of trust from the public halted those actions and created catastrophic wildfires at record numbers and frequencies.

Lack of trust is as significant an enemy of sound conservation as is abuse of science. The FS and BLM made historic changes in the way they approached timber harvest on public lands, but many in the public, and some in the regulatory agencies, refused to acknowledge those changes. Where advocacy voices from the public once served a valuable purpose in forcing the federal agencies to properly carry out their management responsibilities, those same voices were now a significant barrier to healthy forests. The Clinton administration's continuation of treating the issue as a political football didn't help. However, in April 1994, we were able to get Mollie Beattie to instruct Marv to conduct a full reassessment of owl conservation assumptions for the 4(d) rule. That assessment, done by the same scientists who had already said there was no more timber to give, was completed several months later and assisted in convincing the administration to abandon the quest to provide additional harvest on state and private lands. Thanks to Mollie's help, the 4(d) rule was never finalized.

One of the most powerful lessons I learned through working spotted owl issues was that there is little difference between political party administrations once they are in office. In the end, the president must work to find middle ground if s/he hopes to be elected for a second term. Every state counts in the electoral college, and every president tries to satisfy as many voters as possible. Clinton was keenly aware of the support he had gained by holding the Forest Summit, but that wasn't enough. Whole mountainsides had been denuded of trees in the insatiable appetite for enormous logs to provide lumber. It would take at least fifty years to create basic surrogate habitat for the wildlife that lived there. But he only had two before he was in a reelection cycle.

Sacrificing a few more owls, and the other 199 species that depended on old-growth forests, were a secondary consideration. While owls didn't know when they were on federal or private lands, voters did. My awakening to these simple political facts aided me considerably through the rest of my time in Portland, and throughout the remainder of my career. I vowed to work even harder to find biologically acceptable solutions before the issue was taken over by political manipulation. The political answer is almost always worse. One should never expect politicians to be ethical scientists, nor should one expect a scientist to have skills in managing people. Politicians rely on emotional response for survival. Scientists are bound by the simple quest for truth.

Another equally important lesson was how much leadership must depend on the dedication of the people who do the work. I believe that working through the northwest forest issues would have been even more difficult if I had not been honest with our team. When we were dumped on with another seemingly impossible assignment or task, I never sugar-coated my discussions or failed to share information. Honesty is critically important within a team, and a leader's honesty is the highest form of respect that can be shown to the team. By being honest about how difficult the task will be, the leader is sharing responsibility for creating a strategy for success. No one has all the answers. I always knew that the answer likely rested with one of the team members, and sometimes the one least expected. All accomplishments in working the spotted owl issues belong to our great team. All mistakes were mine, and I certainly made some. But I felt privileged to play my role.

Tom Collier went on to lead efforts to open one of the largest, and most controversial, mining operations in Alaska's history, the Pebble Mine. Tom Tuckman and Will Stelle were rewarded with career positions running the new Forest Plan Office and as regional director of NMFS in Seattle, respectively. Don Barry was given the job of assistant secretary for Fish, Wildlife and Parks after George Frampton's departure and did an excellent job once everyone was past the expectations for a 4(d) rule. We also saw another good friend, Bill Martin, retire from the FWS on January 4, 1994, after a long and solid career as one of America's public servants. Marv replaced Bill with Tom Dwyer, a proven professional and great manager. While a lot of activity continued on the Forest Plan for the next three years, it was time for me to move the majority of my attention farther south and deal with difficult California water issues our folks were facing in the Central Valley. Oh yes, and those 314 species that had to be analyzed for possible listing under the ESA.

CHAPTER 10

Central Valley Water

The Sacramento River begins its journey to San Francisco Bay at Mount Shasta, where the Upper Sacramento, Pit and McCloud Rivers converge. The Sacramento is the largest river and watershed system in California and second-largest draining into the Pacific Ocean, only surpassed by the Columbia River. The drainage basin covers a large expanse between the Sierra Nevada and Cascade Range in the east to the Coast and Klamath Ranges to the west. As the snowmelt from the mountains flows down the rivers, the interface between ancient seas and freshwater flows meet in the area of the Sacramento–San Joaquin River Delta, where it continues through Suisun Marsh into San Francisco Bay.

The Delta is believed to have been created 10,000 years ago, at the end of the last glacial period. When the spring rains and snowmelt flowed into the relatively flat lands of the Lower Sacramento and San Joaquin Rivers, at less than 300 feet in elevation, 2 million acres of bottomland hardwood wetlands similar to the shallow, meandering floodplains of the Mississippi Delta became inundated with floodwaters to such a degree that it was described as the "inland lake." Characteristic vegetation included cottonwood, willow, box elder, black walnut, valley oak, sycamore and ash (Strahan 1982–2004). It is estimated that Native Americans have lived in the basin for at least 12,000 years and have depended on the rich fish and wildlife resources of the watershed.

Just as the bottomland hardwood wetlands of the Lower Mississippi River had formed, the floodplain wetlands of the Sacramento–San Joaquin Rivers supplied the same rich habitat and food for fish spawning and nursery needs. Salmon spawn in the cobble riffles of the river, and the young historically moved into the floodplains to secure the abundant food needed to prepare for emigration to the sea. Other native fish species also adapted to spawn in the rich shallows of newly inundated habitat. As the water receded, the explosion of life and food drifted back into the river to supply food and instream nutrients.

Chinook salmon spawning runs occur throughout the year and represent the southernmost run of salmon on the Pacific Coast. As time moved on and man began to manage the fisheries resources of the basin, the fact was somehow lost that water is not habitat. Water is simply a medium in which habitat can be created *if* the proper constituent elements for survival are also present. The same requirements that were brought to light in the Lake Ophelia case to allow access for fish to spawn will need to be resurrected in the Sacramento River Basin if, many years after man's intervention, healthy fish populations are to be restored. The fish evolved in a 2-million-acre inland lake of shallow streams and marshes. The key to fisheries conservation in this watershed is to be informed by that fact.

In the nineteenth century, gold was discovered at Sutter's Mill on the South Fork of the American River, and the California gold rush was under way. In 1862, what was called the "great flood" destroyed much of Sacramento, then a city of 10,000 people. The hydraulic gold-mining activities (placer mining) upstream had released millions of tons of soil that were carried in the flood and buried much of the town, raising the beds of the American, Sacramento and Feather rivers by as much as seven feet. As floods repeated and damage to settlements increased, demand for water management grew. The cycle of the river and flood damages continued to clash, forcing the Army Corps of Engineers and the State of California to begin planning for flood control for towns, as well as water delivery to the rapidly expanding agricultural base.

The Sacramento River Flood Control Project, which was authorized in 1917, provided for a series of bypasses to augment the relatively small levee system along the river. For most of the year, the bypasses remained dry or were used to irrigate wet crops such as rice. But in flood times, they served as release valves to reduce the flood elevations around communities. These bypasses have become essential to the overall management of irrigation waters, as well as for flood control. During the Great Depression, the federal government agreed to undertake construction of the Central Valley Project (CVP), which was designed to manage more than 7 million acre-feet of water per year (one acre-foot is equal to one acre of land covered by one foot of depth) and irrigate more than 3 million acres of agriculture, making it one of the largest irrigation projects in the world. Construction of the CVP began in 1935, and the major constituents were completed by 1948. Shasta Dam was constructed to provide water storage and control runoff from over 6,600 square miles in the upper Sacramento River watershed. That project began in 1938 and was completed in 1945. In 1960, California began construction on its State Water Project with the purpose of providing water to Los Angeles and San Francisco. Evaluations of increasing CVP water management through possible new components continue today.

These projects, and several other smaller efforts throughout California, resulted in the loss of 95 percent of native bottomland hardwoods in the Sacramento Basin, and an equal amount of wetlands throughout the remainder of the state due to urban expansion and commercial development. What had once been a treasured destination for millions of migratory waterfowl, raptors and other species dependent on wetlands was now a shadow of the original habitat-laced system. It has been said that "Whiskey is for drinking and water is for fighting over." California became the front line of those battles. As farmers, environmentalists and municipalities escalated the conflicts over an ever-decreasing water supply, loss of the fish and wildlife inhabitants of the basin was a warning signal that the assault could not continue without rules being put in place to bring sound management to the table.

Jim McKevitt was one of the youngest biologists to reach the position of field supervisor in Ecological Services. In 1978, he was promoted from working on Chesapeake Bay issues to head the U.S. Fish and Wildlife Service (FWS) Ecological Services Office in Sacramento. What he encountered was a new culture of "water wars" that had been going on for nearly a century. In 1980, he began a flow study on the Trinity River to determine how much flow was necessary to sustain a healthy salmon migration. The rivers of northern California were home to some of the strongest populations of salmon in the U.S., surpassed only by Alaska. Existing flows on the Trinity River were approximately 120 thousand acre-feet, with remaining flows shunted to the Sacramento River through the Whiskeytown Tunnel for multiple uses there. He prepared a report stating that the Trinity needed *at least 340 thousand acre-feet* to meet the needs of salmon and the tribes, wrote an environmental impact statement (EIS) to accompany the report, and persuaded Secretary of the Interior Cecil Andrus to sign a secretarial order in 1981 to restore the flows to the Trinity. (McKevitt 2020)

By 1982, the Bureau of Reclamation had agreed to fund a Central Valley Management Study on the American, Stanislaus and Merced Rivers as well as the mainstem of the Sacramento River to determine flows needed for fish. The reduction of flows transferred from the Trinity to the Central Valley had forced a complete reevaluation of existing water resources and how they were being used.

> It became obvious that no stream in California had adequate flows below the dams that were on them. Because of all the diversions out of the river for other purposes, the fishery was really suffering. I wrote an issue paper called "California Water Issues" in 1985 and circulated it through the FWS and sent copies to other people as well. (McKevitt 2020)

In 1984, Secretary James Watt came to California for a visit and sat down with employees in the Department of the Interior. He was going around the room asking what he could do to help when he came to McKevitt.

> When I was asked what he could do to help, I told him he had several national wildlife refuges in the Central Valley that didn't have an adequate water supply. Major Central Valley refuges and complexes only had three thousand acre-feet of water to achieve their objectives. Watt had come out to introduce David Houston [How-ston] as the new Bureau of Reclamation Regional Director, and he turned to Houston and said 'See that that gets fixed.' A year later, Houston got some funding and started the refuge water needs investigation. The study was done by FWS with Bureau funding and lasted from 1985 to 1989. At this point, we had identified severe water deficiencies for fish, loss of wetlands in the Central Valley and needs for water in the National Wildlife Refuge System. The State of California indicated they needed water for the State Wildlife Management Areas as well. While all that was brewing, people were getting behind wanting to restore things. In 1986, the California Water Resources Control Board was beginning to hold hearings on the Sacramento–San Joaquin Delta, where all the water flows into San Francisco Bay. People were focusing on the Delta. (McKevitt 2020)

Providing water needs for human health and safety takes the highest priority in determining water allocation and uses. After health and safety are accommodated, the discussions become intense regarding where and how remaining water should be used. The 1980s signaled an awakening within the Central Valley that natural resources were important and deserved to be considered to the maximum extent possible. But lines had been drawn for decades, and tension was still very present in all meetings.

In 1987 the San Francisco Estuary Project, led by EPA, had all the major agencies involved (federal, state and local). I was on the management team when the need for fish flows [adequate water flows to support native fish populations] came up, and it was a major issue. I remember Bob Potter, who was deputy director of the state Department of Water Resources, screaming at me when I told him how much I thought was needed out of the Stanislaus River. Potter said, 'That's draconian, you can't possibly ask for that!' We ended up getting what we wanted later, but it took federal legislation. We identified the flows needed out of the major rivers into the Bay as a major problem. It all started coming together. The San Francisco area conservation groups joined forces with Metropolitan Water District, which was responsible for water delivery to cities, and formed what was known as the California Water Coalition. They got Congressman George Miller and Senator Bill Bradley involved, who had a copy of my "California Water Issues" paper, which laid out what was needed on each tributary in the Sacramento and San Joaquin Valley. It was a tremendous amount of water, but we kept going and completed the refuge water investigation.

Miller and Bradley met with the California Water Coalition and drafted the Central Valley Project Improvement Act (CVPIA). Metropolitan engaged heavily because they knew they wouldn't get more in southern California if they didn't take care of the Central Valley first. All water agencies who controlled the water came on board for restoration of what was needed in the Central Valley. (McKevitt 2020)

The Central Valley Project Improvement Act (CVPIA) was signed into law in 1992 and represented the most significant transformation of water management California had seen since the appropriation of water rights. There were several new components in the law to benefit fish and wildlife resources. Section 3406 directs the Secretary of the Interior to:

- Meet all obligations under state and federal law, including but not limited to the ESA [Endangered Species Act],
- Assist the state of California in pursuing its goal of doubling anadromous fish populations,
- Modify Central Valley Project operations to provide *reasonable* flows of suitable quality, quantity, and timing to protect all life stages of anadromous fish, and
- [Undertake] other conservation actions the Secretary deems appropriate, which would include refuge water supplies.

When I asked Jim if he helped behind the scenes to draft the CVPIA, he replied, "Tom Jenson and Steve Lanich were the two main staff for Bradley and Miller who wrote the bill. The whole discussion probably wouldn't have happened without my water paper being circulated to provide science, but I didn't help write it." Jim may not have helped write it, but the fish and wildlife resources of the Central Valley owe Jim McKevitt a healthy dose of respect and gratitude.

To assist in performing these conservation actions, Section 3406(b)(2) of the CVPIA states that 800,000 acre-feet of project yield shall be dedicated to conservation purposes under the control of the Secretary of the Interior. Upon passage of the CVPIA, the FWS was given the authority to decide how and when to use what became known as "the b(2) water." Marv had given me the responsibility to represent the FWS in working the water issues in California; thus began my education on western water law.

• • •

Sacramento-San Joaquin Delta (Courtesy of California DWR)

Roger Patterson, who in 1992 had come on board as the regional director to replace David Houston, brought an attitude of cooperation and willingness to make significant improvements in the natural resource base of the Central Valley. Things were definitely looking up for positive teamwork with the Bureau of Reclamation (BOR). Wayne White was a seasoned supervisor in the FWS and had spent time in the field, regional office and D.C. He became the state supervisor for California Ecological Services (ES) operations and was instrumental in making our accomplishments in California water issues, and the Bay-Delta Accord in particular, a reality. When talking about the evolution of what was jokingly dubbed "Club Fed" to the Cal-Fed and then on to the Cal-Fed/Bay-Delta efforts, he explained:

> What started the process was when Governor Wilson and Doug Wheeler had to take on responsibility for coming up with water quality standards for the Bay-Delta. After a long process, they came out with a proposal. Everyone commented—FWS, NMFS [National Marine Fisheries Service], EPA. We all had to provide comments, and we all commented relative to our

own responsibilities. I think Wilson really didn't want to come up with standards, so his ploy was to say 'They have opposing comments. I can't help them without their help.' After that, Marv and I attended a closed meeting in San Francisco with the other federal agencies. Each agency was limited to two, so Marv took me. (White 2020)

Roger Patterson had a similar recollection:

In October 1992, the Central Valley Project Improvement Act was passed. Wilson was elected governor. We had winter run salmon listed; we had delta smelt listed; we had CVPIA passed and we had a water quality plan update going on by the state board, basically under the oversight of the EPA. It was easy for the new governor to be critical of the feds because we were creating a bunch of controversy, and he said we were an 'uncoordinated mess.' We went to San Francisco and rented a room, hired a facilitator, and set out to better define our responsibilities as one government. I was there with Dan Fults [deputy RD], Rollie Schmitten from NMFS, Marv Plenert and Wayne White from FWS and Felicia Marcus from EPA. We said 'Let's see if we can just understand what each of us has going on. The governor is clearly wound up on this and he's directing criticism at us, and he's not all wrong in doing that. We need to collectively figure out how to get our shit together. Each of us has a job to do.' We had a real awakening of what all of us together were doing! We came together as 'Club Fed' to show our cohesion in taking ideas to the governor. That name came about when we were kind of slap-happy late at night; there was this high-profile vacation company by the name of Club Med, so we just laughed and said 'We'll be Club Fed!' (Patterson 2020)

Wayne White:

Then Wheeler said we need to get together with them (the state) and that's when we created CAL-FED. Governor Wilson, in trying to get out of doing water quality standards, forced the federal government to do what they should do: good government, how their things interrelate and how they could be moved into a state water quality standards effort. This evolved into the Water Operations Management Team, where the chief from BOR Ops, Cal Fish and Game, NMFS and I met weekly to talk about actual operations that would conform to the needs of the species when we all agreed it was justifiable. It wasn't FWS or NMFS saying 'This is what you'll do,' but rather looking at all operations to find fish-friendly ways to operate. We got the CAL-FED going and realized we needed to bring in the enviros. Their normal approach to life was, if they didn't like something, pull the pin from the grenade and throw it on the table. What they figured out was that when the grenade went off, they got hit, too. They realized they weren't free to toss it in, walk away and let the pieces fall wherever they may. That realization was a true advantage to bringing them in and accepting the fact that 'You are part of the fix. If you want to blow it up, then you get blown up, too.'

The two major things that hindered the process were, first, that the water was truly overallocated. There was the assumption that water left the system, came back in, and you could reallocate it. They did that way too many times. Second, if you could have purchased Ag out of the Delta it would have made it a lot easier. The Delta folks had to have their water quality and, because of Ag, it made it really hard to avoid saltwater intrusion. For the money that was spent, you could have gone in and paid top dollar to set it aside as habitat. But that was not an option. (White 2020)

•••

Starting in May 1994, Director Mollie Beattie's reorganization of the FWS to focus more on ecosystems and landscapes had me in a new position. Instead of just being the assistant regional director (ARD) for Fish and Wildlife Enhancement, I was given the additional assignment of a geographic area of the region and all operations in that geography except law enforcement. As the new Geographic ARD (GARD) for California and Klamath, I now focused all my time there. Sarah and the kids will attest that I spent more nights in California than I did at home, especially with the additional requirements for D.C. briefings and congressional hearings. After Marv's initial meeting in San Francisco, I assumed all responsibilities for FWS operations there. Roger, Dan Fults, Wayne and I became the Department of the Interior team, and everyone knew it.

The old tactics of trying to divide the BOR and FWS because of the seemingly different missions was gone. I made it clear that the FWS would support any decision Roger made, and he let everyone know he would support any decision I made. Those early dinners and openness to finding new pathways paid off. It is important to understand the significance of this. In life, there are no relationships between organizations or entities. The only relationships that exist are between people who learn to trust each other and, therefore, lead their teams to work together. When the trust goes away, so does the partnership and cooperation. Because I valued Roger's trust, I made sure I had his back. Staff in the BOR and FWS all knew what was expected: *one government, one team*. The other highly significant factor that often is lost in the equation is *fun*! When you know you can trust the people you work with, it relieves some of the horrendous pressure of the challenges and makes both working and having a beer together truly enjoyable experiences.

That became evident at a meeting Roger and I held at his office in Sacramento. We invited representatives of all three interests (agricultural, municipal and environmental) to discuss how we could work together to address the challenges of not having enough water to satisfy all the demands. Roger was at one end of a long table, I at the other, with no less than a dozen people sitting around the table with their lawyers. I turned to my left and asked David Behar of the Bay Institute, "How much water do you think we would minimally need to get the fish moved down the system and out into the ocean?" Without hesitation, he said "More." I looked with amazement and said, "No, how many acre-feet"? Again, he said "More." I said "OK" and moved on to the agricultural interests and asked, "How much water can you get by with and make a crop?" Now that the line had been drawn, his answer was "More." I didn't want to waste time repeating the question as I did for Behar, so I turned to Tim Quinn of the Metropolitan Water District and asked, "How much water would it take to minimally meet health and safety needs of the cities?" He looked at me and said, "If they're not committing, we're not."

I shook my head, looked down the table at Roger and said, "OK, you all just lost your opportunity to participate in the ESA biological opinion and decision-making. You have fought each other for so long, you no longer know what you actually need; you just want to hurt each other." David Behar snapped back "Don't lay that on me!" "I just did," I replied. "Thank you all for coming. Roger and I will work with our staffs and come up with what you will have. Be safe on your ride home." It was a sad situation, but after decades of fighting, I don't think they knew how to do anything but protect their own turf. Everyone having their own attorneys at meetings didn't help either. There was no trust.

Trust must also go up the chain of command. Betsy Rieke was the assistant secretary of the interior for water and science. That made her Roger's assistant secretary, and critical to getting the D.C. team on board with what we were trying to accomplish. Betsy was an unassuming woman who had a tremendous amount of skill and intelligence, but could disarm a potential adversary with her honesty and openness. We all had extremely high opinions of Betsy. Roger talked about her in this way:

Clinton had come in and made Betsy Rieke the assistant secretary for water and science. She was smart enough to figure out that we needed to take advantage of this agency coordination out here. She wanted to show the state that we owed it to them, and ourselves, to show that we were coordinated and working together. The state was pretty jacked up at the time and they created a water policy council, which started the meetings and coordination between the state and federal agencies. Betsy was special. She was an attorney who knew water. She had been the Department of Water Resources director in Arizona and was nominated by Clinton because of her background, and she had a strong relationship with Bruce Babbitt. When she was nominated, she said 'Well, I'm going to go back to D.C., so I'd better get a new pair of glasses.' She went to the optometrist and said she was going back to D.C. for an assistant secretary job and needed a new pair of glasses because her eyes had gone down and she needed a new prescription.

The woman who worked at the optometrist's office asked, 'What are you going to be doing in D.C.?' and Betsy said 'Well, I'm going to be an assistant secretary in the Department of the Interior.' The woman asked 'Are there a lot of assistant secretaries?', to which Betsy replied 'About five.' The woman then said 'Wow, they must produce a lot of materials to need that many *assistant secretaries*!' Betsy later told me 'You know, I could have told her I was going back to this important job that was a presidential appointment, but I didn't see the need to do that.' That was Betsy. She just took things in stride. (Patterson 2020)

Betsy was also not one to be trifled with:

Dan Beard was the commissioner [Bureau of Reclamation] at the time. Ed Osan from the National Wildlife Federation had come over as Dan's assistant commissioner in D.C. Dan was a big opponent of the Bureau of Reclamation and here he was as the commissioner. His big bugaboos were Westlands [Water District] and California, so I said I'm going to have a heart-to-heart with Dan. If he's going to be against us instead of helping us, I'm leaving. I'm not going to put up with this. Dan, to his credit, said 'You know way more about this than I do. It looks like you're doing a good job, so I'm going to stay out of your hair.' I found out Osan was talking directly to my staff and doing all sorts of crazy stuff while we were negotiating contracts. I told Dan 'You have to keep Ed out of my business.' He said 'Well, he's just kinda keeping track of this stuff.' I talked to Betsy and said 'I know I'm taking a risk on this, but Osan has to stay out of this.' She dropped a bomb on Osan and I never saw hide nor hair of him after that. She could come across meek and mild, never create a stir, but he just disappeared.

Betsy liked Club Fed and knew we needed to work with the state, so she said she would be willing to participate at her level. She inherited all of us and treated us with respect. She expected us to solve the problems and work with her and with each other to get things done. She would take the point on any issue and make sure the secretary knew what he needed to do and get it done. She was really the lead for Interior on California water issues.

After you left in 1997 and Mike Spear took over your role in working with us, things changed. Whatever Betsy was trying to achieve through coordination, Spear was the opposite. He was difficult to work with, and we looked to Wayne for FWS coverage. Mike was a total pain in the ass. The two of us decided we needed to go back and meet with Leshy, the DOI solicitor, to get an answer on CVPIA. So, the two of us went back to meet with Leshy and Deputy Secretary John Garamendi. We both laid out our cases and said 'We need resolution to this. We're tired of arguing about it. I'm never going to agree with Mike and he's never going to agree with me. We need a department answer.' Leshy said, 'You guys are both really, really smart and you can figure this out. Get the hell out of here!' Mike and I went out in the hall and said 'That wasn't helpful.' It finally went to court and, when I left Sacramento, it was still unresolved. (Patterson 2020)

The unresolved question Roger was referring to was the use of the 800,000 acre-feet of water dedicated to conservation in Section 3406(b)(2) of the CVPIA. When I was there, Roger and I had worked together to make sure the water achieved its purpose. Roger fulfilled every request I made on behalf of the FWS, and then I allowed him to recapture some of the water and manage the system to provide other benefits. On one occasion, our fisheries biologists came to me and asked for 200,000 acre-feet of water to be released from Lake Shasta to move salmon smolt (young salmon moving down the river and out to sea). As smolt move downstream, a process called smoltification takes place whereby the osmoregulatory functions (physiological regulation and control of water and salt in body fluids) of the fish transform from freshwater adaptations to saltwater physiology. This literally transforms the fish from a freshwater species to a saltwater species. The fish evolved over the eons to take advantage of spring melt and ride the increased flows out to sea.

I went to Roger and made the formal request. Roger agreed and gave the order to the Shasta Dam operators. He then asked, "If I can recapture some of that water around Suisun Marsh and move it over to the San Luis reservoir for future irrigation use, will you allow me to do that?" I replied, "As long as the fish are moved out into San Francisco Bay without hindrance, I am good with the BOR making the most use of the resource." This worked perfectly. The fish were moved into the Bay and out to sea, and a portion of the 200,000 acre-feet of water was recaptured for irrigation use. But this was not acceptable to the environmental community, which was adamant that the water must be "removed from yield."

My view was that the water had fully accomplished the fisheries conservation need, and punishing another water user provided no benefit to achieving the goals of managing scarce resources. This partnership approach was how we were able to make sure the public only saw one government. History had allowed water users to pit the BOR against the FWS, and the environmental community to pit the FWS against the BOR. The two factions were somewhat stunned that those efforts failed with Roger, Dan, Wayne and me. Dan Fults retired around 1994 and was replaced by Frank Dimick, another team player Roger had carefully selected because of his open-minded approach to solving issues.

During this time, we were all moving in the same direction and making what I believe to be real progress in calming the rhetoric and bringing everyone to the table. Betsy's big push was the Bay-Delta Accord, an agreement between the agricultural, municipal and environmental stakeholders on a fair process for managing the CVPIA. Betsy had excellent relationships with the environmental community, and she, Felicia Marcus and Wayne White would go off and have private meetings with them to help bring them to agreement instead of perpetuating their continual conflict. Everyone pulling together helped reach full success on December 15, 1994, with the signing of "Principles for Agreement on Bay-Delta Standards Between the State of California and the Federal Government," also known as "the Accord."

The Accord, among other things, endorsed water quality and flow standards for the Sacramento–San Joaquin Bay-Delta to be adopted by the State Water Resources Control Board. The Accord brought relative peace to the water wars for well over a decade and is still the model for collaborative conflict resolution. I would strongly encourage those involved in similar conflicts to use the Bay-Delta Accord as a case study in building partnerships in the face of conflict. It is only through partnership and trust that solutions are born.

When I left and Mike took over as the manager of the newly formed California/Nevada Operations office for the FWS, he viewed things differently regarding the 800,000 acre-feet. Mike loved the fight, and loved winning even more. I believe I know Mike Spear well enough to know that, for him, this was simply a contest with Roger for dominance. I have no doubt that their trip to meet with Leshy and Garamendi was Mike's idea, and that he believed he had more credibility in D.C. than Roger. But he probably didn't know that John Leshy was the regional solicitor in California before he went into D.C., and John Garamendi, also from California, understood the Central Valley Project very well. Both had worked with Roger in the past.

> Now, believe it or not, the 800,000 has essentially gone away in terms of deciding where it will be used. When we did the Bay-Delta Accord, which brought agreement on operation of the project, I pushed really hard that the impact of the new water quality control plan could be credited against the 800,000. That happened at the time of the Accord, and now they count the impacts of the biological opinions, whatever they may be, against the 800,000. The impacts, plus the Accord's water quality control plan, amount to about 1.2 million acre-feet, which is larger than the 800,000. As a result, there's nothing left for the fisheries. You've got the refuge water independent of that, but that's it. It's not helpful, but it is what it is. (Patterson 2020)

Wayne White summarized the current state of affairs:

> The thing we learned as stakeholders was to work together to try to come up with resolutions instead of having the government sit back and come up with all these plans to pass out, just to have them torn to shreds. I look at it today and don't know why they don't go back to the water operations management team to at

least do the operational stuff. We had Roger Guinee, Jim White from Cal Fish and Game, and FWS. NMFS would be there but they would bring their attorneys. Attorneys are not helpful in the formulation of operational decisions. (White 2020)

...

As a politician, Bruce Babbitt knew that the lifespan as secretary would go eight years at most. That meant every decision was viewed through the lenses of historical significance, voter awareness and longevity of credit. Secretary Babbitt and I were once riding around the mountains of Washington looking at the denuded hillsides while I gave an explanation of how we were trying to bring them back, including placing culverts under the roads to reduce overflow erosion. We hit on the subject of multispecies ESA consultations and habitat conservation plans.

"We are working on a consultation with the Forest Service to cover multiple species in the same consultation. We're excited about this because of the time and staff effort it saves over doing them one species at a time."

"That's fantastic," he said. "No one has ever done one of these before, and this will be historic!"

"Well, no sir, not really. We did one in Nevada just last year, and that was the first." He smiled at me and said, "You don't understand. I'm a politician. Nothing ever happened before I got here, and nothing will happen after I leave."

Bruce Babbitt loved being secretary of the interior and almost became a Supreme Court justice. I met the secretary for breakfast in Orange County one morning in 1993 before he was to speak to a large gathering there. I had just heard on the news that President Clinton was considering him to replace retiring Justice Byron White. Orrin Hatch expressed strong opposition, stating he believed that Babbitt's pro-environmental views had enraged a group of Republican senators who might take revenge on Clinton's nominations if he submitted Babbitt, thus encouraging President Clinton to continue his search. Not knowing exactly how to broach the subject, I said, "Sir, there is a rumor that you are being considered for the Supreme Court. I just want you to know that we in the field are pleased to have you as our secretary and, while not wishing you bad luck, would be happy if you stayed with us." He smiled and said "Thank you, I believe I will." He apparently knew that Clinton was moving on in the search. Ruth Bader Ginsburg was ultimately nominated and confirmed.

The second topic of that breakfast discussion was the reason for his visit. The FWS had been working with Orange County on the idea of a county-wide habitat conservation plan (HCP) and Section 10 permit for resident endangered species. We had put together a "Safe Harbor" agreement, which stipulated that if the county undertook identified actions to help listed species, we would hold them "safe" from enforcement actions later if the conditions around the species changed. This was a proactive effort to stem the decline of species and reward landowners for their actions. When a species is in trouble, the first effort is to stop the bleeding. Then, and only then, can efforts to improve the populations have any chance of succeeding. There had been talk in Orange County that we were going to back out of our promise. They had fulfilled their commitments, but were concerned that we wouldn't hold up our end. I told the secretary about their concerns and said, "If you so choose, we would be pleased if you would tell them that a deal is a deal and the FWS will stand by its word." A large grin came across his face and he said "Dale, I so choose." He had come to Orange County to address an audience anxious to hear where he stood on our agreement. When he told the crowd that he and the FWS believe a deal is a deal, the standing ovation was spontaneous.

But we did not care for all of his decisions. An old friend, Dr. Ted LaRoe in our Research Region, who was a co-author of the Biological Sciences document titled "Classification of Wetlands and Deepwater

Habitats of the United States" (Cowardin et al. 1979), had met the secretary some time back and quickly used Babbitt's temporary employment with the U.S. Geological Survey (USGS) in his early career to his own advantage. Ted believed there should be a stand-alone biological research agency similar to the historic U.S. Biological Survey of the 1930s. He and others convinced Babbitt that this was another historic decision that he would be known for long after his departure. Babbitt took the bait and reorganized all biological research functions in the Department of the Interior into one organization but, instead of making it a separate agency, folded it into the USGS as the Biological Resources Division (BRD).

Not only did the FWS, National Park Service (NPS) and Bureau of Land Management (BLM) lose the ability to direct research to the agency's areas of critical management needs; the first thing Congress did was gut the budget. The FWS's Research Region under Dick Smith had a budget of over $80 million. Between NPS and BLM there was at least another $50 million. When Congress passed the first BRD budget, it appropriated less than $60 million. Biological research within the Department of the Interior has never fully recovered. Of all the good decisions Babbitt made, this was the millstone around his neck that he will never escape. Without the support of the agencies for research in their budget, BRD must elbow its way to the USGS table.

Secretary Babbitt's desire to make positive, historic change did occur in an agreement with the state of California under the ESA. California had its own Endangered Species Act, thus increasing the regulatory process for anyone wanting a permit to develop where species listed under either the federal or state laws were found. A Section 10 permit under the federal ESA required there to be an environmental impact statement (EIS) concurred by the FWS prior to issuance of a permit to take a listed species. Federal permitting agencies do not have staff to write extensive environmental documents on development proposals by private citizens. This is accomplished by the applicant either writing their own draft document or hiring a consulting firm to prepare the document for federal agency review and, hopefully, acceptance. California also has a state equivalent to the National Environmental Policy Act (NEPA), and requires that a document similar to the federal EIS be prepared before the state will approve a project. It is not surprising that one of the most common complaints we heard from homebuilders and other development companies in California was that they "had to run the gauntlet twice to satisfy both the feds and the state for the same species."

The California legislature passed a state law called the Natural Community Conservation Planning Act of 1991 (NCCP) to establish a broad-based framework for conserving ecosystems.

> NCCP identifies and provides for the regional protection of plants, animals, and their habitats, while allowing compatible and appropriate economic activity. Working with landowners, environmental organizations, and other interested parties, a local agency oversees the numerous activities that compose the development of an NCCP. (CDFW 2020)

One of the species that was receiving a lot of attention at the time was the California gnatcatcher, a bird that inhabited coastal sage/scrub ecosystems. These open areas in southern California were viewed by developers as prime real estate for homes, shopping centers and other community growth essentials. We viewed this overlap as an excellent opportunity to find common ground and try new approaches that would yield better coordination and more sound permit decisions. Wayne White described the evolution of discussions:

> When the state passed their law and there was a great parallel with the HCP process, along with Babbitt's desire to do all of those regional plans down in southern California, a tremendous opportunity opened up to blend conservation planning into local planning. In California, all planning is done locally, and

we were not bringing conservation planning to that level. This was that opportunity. It had great benefit. It's challenging bringing in all the local city and county planning, the environmental groups, the 'I love X species' group, and the general public. They all wanted to play in the game, and that's what you had to do. This is where Gail [Kobetich] became my true hero. I'd go down there to a room full of city developers, county folks and environmental groups in a big conference room at a big table, and all the chairs around the wall were filled. Numerous discussions were going on all at one time, but the one thing that was always guaranteed was that when Gail Kobetich stood up to speak, everyone stopped talking. He was significantly responsible for bringing this approach to Babbitt. Babbitt embraced the prospect of marrying the state law with the HCP process. (White 2020)

This effort, undertaken in late 1993, was early in Babbitt's tenure, but he immediately understood the importance of a state/federal partnership like this, *and* that one had never been done under the ESA. The gnatcatcher had just been listed as a threatened species, which gave the FWS the authority to consider a Section 4(d) rule. These rules begin as blank sheets of paper because each species is different, and the law intended the rules to be tailored to the individual threatened species. The idea was to write a 4(d) rule that mirrored the NCCP, but also stated that *compliance with the NCCP also constituted compliance with the federal ESA*. No 4(d) rule had ever been published to include this much innovation and cooperation with a state. The standards were written to represent the needs of the gnatcatcher as a representative of the coastal sage/scrub ecosystem, while giving the development community clear standards they could plan to meet. This was the most "assurance" the building industry had ever received regarding what they needed to do to offset environmental damages.

Having Babbitt get behind this also involved having him learn to trust that the FWS employees on the ground were committed to finding solutions, not just to regulating.

> When NCCP came in and started to move, the local jurisdictions were looking at it just as Babbitt came in as secretary. Like most new interior secretaries, he didn't have a good view of the FWS. But I'll never forget the time when, after a couple of trips with Babbitt, he said, 'You guys showed me the light,' because what we were doing fit right into his philosophy of planning. Combining that with the state—with Doug Wheeler and Michael Mantell—we moved those processes forward. The state was not always easy to work with and sometimes lacked adult supervision, and staff would not sit down to negotiate in good faith, but we made great strides. In southern California, they had a great staff that really helped move the needle. (White 2020)

In December 1993, Secretary Babbitt approved the Section 4(d) rule, known as the NCCP Agreement, in partnership with Governor Pete Wilson to protect the vanishing sage/scrub habitat for the California gnatcatcher. The rule eased restrictions on developers and gave them the ground rules to follow as they planned their projects. To my knowledge, it is the only Section 4(d) rule ever done to marry the actions of the FWS with a state. This was seen as groundbreaking in the development community and welcomed by construction companies. In the course of my career, I learned that a developer hates nothing more than a surprise that adds costs above and beyond what he has negotiated with his lender. Because the ground rules were known up front, taking care of the sage/scrub in compliance with the NCCP allowed inclusion of those costs in the lending process and eliminated costly delays.

The agreement also gave the State of California more control under the federal ESA than had ever been shared. Once the State approved a project design under the NCCP, no further federal ESA consultation was necessary. In addition, this allowed the establishment of large blocks of coastal sage habitat while allowing development in other areas. This mitigation program followed the template that had been established in the 1980s for conservation of wetland habitats when applying for Section 404 permits. Just as with wetland permits, the applicant was not required to follow the steps of the NCCP/Section 4(d) program, but they would have to follow the previous, longer process if they didn't. It was a real carrot for planned conservation versus patchwork protection under individual permits.

The dedication of FWS employees and their non-federal counterparts in ongoing efforts to find positive solutions to complex issues is part of the most unrecognized value the American public receives for their tax dollar. If an employee misbehaves—and just as with any group of people, the government has a few—that news receives wide circulation. But when hours of unpaid work and dedication result in innovation and compromises that achieve the purposes of the law while allowing otherwise legal activities to occur, very often the response is to accuse the employees of abandoning their environmental responsibilities. The team of FWS employees that worked hard to make the gnatcatcher/NCCP Section 4(d) rule a success received only a special award from those of us who appreciated all their hard work, but little else except the knowledge that they had created positive conservation history.

Two women among the staff in California deserve recognition for going above and beyond the call of duty, but because of the personal nature of their challenges, I will refrain from disclosing their names. On one occasion, I got a call from one of the attorneys representing the Fund for Animals plaintiffs asking how some of the planned plant listings in California were going. I told him that one of our biologists working on the batch was undergoing treatment for breast cancer, and the possibility existed that we might be late on a few of the findings. His response was, "That's your personal problem. I don't care what your employees are going through. Just get the species work done."

I sat for a second while my head was about to explode, then said, "Let me be perfectly clear. You are the most arrogant fucking moron I have ever had the displeasure to speak with over the phone, and you are very fortunate you aren't close enough for me to give you the ass whipping you deserve! Don't ever call this number, or *any* FWS number again to ask about the status of the settlement. Your call will not be taken. If this is unacceptable to you, I'll be happy to call your clients and tell them they now have to receive all information through the U.S. Department of Justice attorneys. Is that clear enough for your piss-ant brain?" I then hung up the phone and told Pat Mitchell, my executive assistant, to ensure that no one ever did anything beyond taking a phone message from him again. The staff employee in question was never made aware of the phone call. She was so dedicated that she often worked despite being ill from treatments. That was more than enough. I never heard from him again.

Wayne White relayed another example.

> One of our employees working on endangered species accompanied me on a field trip to show Deputy Secretary of the Interior David Hayes and one of his staff one of our planning areas. I lined up the trip unaware of the employee's health issue. I flew down and we picked up the two at the airport. We were driving around showing David things when, about three-quarters through the day, I noticed the employee turning pale. When we reached a rest stop where I could talk to her alone, she said 'I just had a miscarriage.' I said, 'What the heck are you doing out here? You need to be home resting!' She replied, 'This isn't the first time. We've got the deputy secretary out here. I can make it through the day. This is more important.' I'll never forget that. (White 2020)

Anyone wishing to disparage the dedication of Fish and Wildlife Service employees can carry their complaint down the hall. My patience is limited.

•••

The Fish and Wildlife Service was about to suffer a painful loss. Mollie Beattie developed brain cancer and had been fighting it for about a year when, on June 27, 1996, cancer won. Mollie was one of those directors we felt honored to serve and more honored to know. The last time I went in to visit her, she was wearing her usual smile and a scarf around her bald scalp. She knew time was short, but wanted all of us to know she felt blessed. I gave her a hug and knew she could see the welling in my eyes. She just hugged me again and told me how much she appreciated me. I left before the tears flowed.

•••

In June 1997, I accepted the deputy regional director position in Atlanta. My going-away party in Portland was highly emotional. I had spent six and a half years with some of the finest people ever to work in the federal government. Together, we had gone through the northwest forest issues, dealt with California water wars, built facilities to bring back endangered species in Hawaii and dealt with the challenge of listing determinations on 314 species, as well as other court-ordered actions. As I looked around the room, I felt tremendous pride in the *team*.

"I wish I could tell you it was fun, but we all know it wasn't. However, I can tell you they have been the most rewarding years of my professional life. We all get in this business to make a difference. There isn't anyone on the planet who could say we failed in that effort. I'm not sure they could have thrown any more historic challenges at us than we have, together, faced over the last six and a half years. The natural resources are better because this team was here, and you did your jobs with professionalism and tenacity. I will never forget you, nor will I ever stop loving you." As I packed to head back east to Atlanta, I hoped that John Turner would be satisfied that I "rode the bull for the full eight seconds."

PART 3

The Southeast and Southwest

CHAPTER 11

The Surprise

I flew to Atlanta in late May to visit with my new boss, Noreen Clough, and the regional directorate team in Region 4. The region covered the ten states of the southeast U.S. and the Caribbean. I had first met Noreen when I was on detail to the D.C. office during the Lake Ophelia days. She was a true "bootstrap" professional whose first job was as a clerk with the U.S. Fish and Wildlife Service (FWS). Through the years she moved her way up through hard work and quality effort, and she had been in Atlanta as the regional director (RD) for several years.

I arrived at the regional office on Century Boulevard in north Atlanta and proceeded to the regional director's suite. The deputy regional director (DRD) and RD shared the space of a reception area where the executive assistants to the RD and DRD sat, as well as a small glass-enclosed meeting room and their two offices. After introductions, Noreen and I sat down in her office to begin our partnership in overseeing the region. She quickly got to one of her most important pieces of information: she had decided to retire at the end of July! I knew that her husband, Dave, had retired due to health conditions, but she had mentioned nothing about her own retirement in our previous conversations. Although knowing about her pending retirement would have made no difference in my decision to move, I certainly had hoped to have an easier transition than to be without an RD in just over a month after my permanent arrival. She relayed that Dave's health was deteriorating, and she wanted to retire to spend what quality time they had left together. Dave loved to travel, and they had purchased an RV and planned to be on the road as long as he could handle it.

We had a meeting with the regional directorate team to discuss my arrival as DRD and to allow Noreen to tell them of her departure. Because the FWS is a small family, I knew nearly the entire team. Sam Hamilton had taken over the position of ARD–Ecological Services; Columbus Brown was ARD–Fisheries; Geoff Haskett was ARD–Refuges; Judy Pulliam was ARD–Administration; Monty Halcomb was ARD–Law Enforcement; Bob Cooke was ARD–Migratory Birds and Federal Assistance; and Vicki Boatwright was ARD–External Affairs. It was a solid team, and I wasn't worried about disruptions following Noreen's departure. The visit was productive, and we all began preparation for the transition.

Jamie Rappaport Clark was confirmed on July 31 as director of the FWS, and she felt it would be best if she assigned someone other than me to be acting RD. I had just arrived and was an obvious candidate for the position. But Jamie was also new and apparently had other thoughts about Region 4. She assigned my longtime friend, Marvin Moriarty, deputy regional director in Minneapolis, to be the acting RD. I had known Marvin for nearly twenty years and held him in the highest regard. I suspected Jamie wanted to see him in the position before deciding on a permanent replacement. The position was advertised and, against my previous decision to never apply for a senior executive service (SES) position again, I applied because no move would be involved, I was qualified to enter the SES ranks, and had nothing to lose. Marvin had always been a joy to work with and that continued in his new role as acting RD.

Jamie had built a strong relationship with Sam Hamilton in their workings over the years. Sam was a highly capable leader and was doing a great job as ARD–ES. I had known him almost my whole career, as we both entered the FWS in 1978, he in Daphne, Alabama, and I in Vicksburg. When Jamie notified me that Sam had been selected, however, I felt I had been kicked in the stomach once again. I had no right to assume I would get the job, but I let my hopes get the better of me. One day Sam

Hamilton reported to me as an ARD; the next, I reported to him as the DRD. I took a long weekend off, as had become my habit after receiving notice of promotion rejection, and repeated the soul-searching meditation process I used to clear my head and bring me back into a peaceful acceptance that I was blessed to have the DRD position. I didn't know what was in store, but accepted that I wasn't in charge. When I returned to work on Monday, Sam asked me to come into his office. His first words to me would set the tone for our working relationship.

"I know this was a blow to you after all your efforts and accomplishments. I just want you to know how much I respect you and how much I will need you going forward. I give you my word that I will treat you with dignity, respect and as a true partner in running this region. But I will have to lean on you to help me with a lot of issues I haven't had to face, but you have."

"I appreciate those words more than you know," I replied. "I accepted the job here as DRD with the full intentions of doing whatever I could to help make Noreen successful. You have my full commitment that I will do that for you to the best of my abilities, and you will never have to worry about your back. I'll have it." From that point forward, Sam and I were a true team. He kept his word, and I kept mine. Together, we did all we could to make Region 4 the best in the FWS.

The first major issue we faced together as the new Region 4 team was at one of the nation's landmark national wildlife refuges (NWR). Okefenokee NWR encompasses over 400,000 acres of forested wetlands (aka swamplands) in southeast Georgia, with headquarters in Folkston. It includes Charlton, Ware and Clinch Counties in Georgia, and Baker County in Florida.

Native Americans inhabited Okefenokee Swamp as early as 2500 BC. Peoples of the Deptford Culture, the Swift Creek Culture and the Weeden Island Culture occupied sites within the Okefenokee. The last tribe to seek sanctuary in the swamp was the Seminoles. Troops led by General Charles R. Floyd during the Second Seminole War, 1838–1842, ended the age of the Native Americans in the Okefenokee.

The Suwannee Canal Company purchased the 238,120 acres (963 km^2) of the Okefenokee Swamp from the State of Georgia in 1891 to drain the swamp for rice, sugar cane, and cotton plantations. When this failed, the company began industrial wetland logging as a source of income. Captain Henry Jackson and his crews spent three years digging the Suwannee Canal 11.5 miles (18.5 km) into the swamp. Economic recessions led to the company's bankruptcy and eventual sale to Charles Hebard in 1901. Logging operations, focusing on the cypress, began in 1909 after a railroad was constructed on the northwest area of the swamp. More than 431 million board feet of timber were removed from the Okefenokee by 1927, when logging operations ceased. (USFWS 2006)

Other attempts to drain or pursue economic activities in the swamp proved fruitless and, in 1937, President Franklin Roosevelt signed an executive order establishing Okefenokee as "a refuge and breeding ground for migratory birds and other wildlife." In 1974, to further ensure the protection of this unique ecosystem, the interior sections of the NWR were included as a National Wilderness Area. In 1986, Okefenokee was designated a wetland of international significance by the Ramsar Wetlands Convention. Okefenokee is predominantly bottomland hardwood wetlands with a highly significant proportion of decaying organic material in the soils due to the high groundwater table, which retards decomposition of the leaf litter deposited by the deciduous forest. This condition makes the area extremely important to fish and wildlife, but also harbors the unusual potential for subsurface fires to burn for months, or even years. As the fire leaps to the surface in one area and is brought under control, the subsurface embers can slowly migrate to an entirely different area miles away and resurface. The hydrologic regime acted in a similar manner, with some parts of the refuge serving as groundwater recharge, and other areas as groundwater discharge, but all interconnected. The highly entwined surface and subsurface system proved to be the centerpiece argument that occurred in late July and early August of 1997 with E.I. DuPont.

DuPont had purchased lands that border the refuge with the intention of mining titanium for use in their paints and other products. History had already proven that attempts to dig drainage ditches in the swamp only resulted in immediate movement of water to fill the ditches, but not leave the property. The FWS was convinced that there was no possible engineering technique that could be economically employed in a mining operation to keep pollution produced from mining from entering into and contaminating the refuge. DuPont was accustomed to opposition from the public for its mining operations and had scheduled a public meeting on August 5 to begin its efforts to convince the public that Okefenokee would not be harmed.

The *Savannah Morning News* published an article on Monday, August 4, titled "DuPont opening talks on Okefenokee mining," which announced that DuPont had called for "collaborative meetings" to discuss how to mine the area's titanium safely. We had decided that the FWS would not participate, as we could find no possible way that mining could be done without significant harm to the refuge. We put out a statement that included a quote from me announcing that the FWS did not believe a compromise was possible in regard to mining titanium near the national wildlife refuge, and that no representatives from the FWS would be attending the meeting. I explained, "What this means is that we are being honest with the public and with DuPont. We cannot participate in a process where people have the idea that compromise is a possible outcome. Compromise is not possible for us." I was also given permission to speak for Secretary Babbitt and stated "Secretary of the Interior Bruce Babbitt believes there is no way DuPont can mine next to the refuge and in parts of the swamp without harming it."

A short time after the meeting, Babbitt came down for a visit with us at the refuge and, with the press present, made the bold statement that he would "veto" the project if DuPont insisted on moving forward. This was incredible! While we loved what he had to say and the tenacity with which he delivered the message, we knew that the secretary of the interior had no such authority to veto a project outside lands under Interior's control, and certainly no authority to deny a 404 permit that might be issued by the Corps. But he was the politician I had come to know through my western issues and, as we had seen time and again, the one who is most bold in an uncertain situation often carries the day. DuPont had committed to abide by whatever decision came out of the collaborative process in which the FWS had refused to participate, and Babbitt's strong persona as well as his position in the cabinet steered enough in the group to demand that DuPont abandon plans to mine.

Once again, Bruce Babbitt had demonstrated his skills as a politician and his will to help do the right thing, even if it created controversy for the administration. The fact that President Clinton had already been elected for his second term, and the people of the area were opposed to the increase of thousands of trucks moving around the clock, mitigated any political damage. Skippy Reeves, refuge manager at Okefenokee, and all his staff were one group of happy FWS employees.

• • •

January 1998 brought a major management evaluation effort to the FWS. The geographic/programmatic ARD (GARD/PARD) split we had been under since Mollie Beattie's appointment in 1994 was receiving considerable resistance from within the agency. While the overarching premise that natural resources should be managed on a landscape basis still enjoyed great support, *how* to make that approach effective and efficient was still an unanswered question. The confusion between the responsibilities of the ARD to be a programmatic ARD on the one hand and a geographic team leader on the other had left many employees wondering where priorities rested. Each program had explicit guidance on how it was to operate, and the ARDs were mostly familiar with their programs, yet they held other responsibilities in their assigned geographic areas.

Tensions were constantly rising and Jamie, as well as her directorate, knew they had to find a solution. The FWS asked The Ohio State University, through the Ohio Cooperative Fish and Wildlife Research Unit, to perform an assessment of the values and drawbacks of the GARD/PARD system. On March 6, Sam Hamilton delivered a written message to the Region 4 employees:

> At 12:00 noon EST today, the Director released a memorandum and a copy of The Ohio State University (OSU) Report on Ecosystem Management. This Report and its findings were the subject of an intense, weeklong meeting of the directorate in South Carolina to address concerns of employees and to assess our progress to date on the ecosystem approach to management in the Fish and Wildlife Service . . .
> **We are not returning to Programmatic Management.** We are, however, addressing the concerns raised about the visibility and support for the Programs. There will be three additional Assistant Regional Directors in each Region that are clearly responsible for Program support and advocacy. There will also be three Assistant Regional Directors that are Geographic ARDs and will have line authority to all field stations in their Area . . . The Program ARD will have responsibility for consolidating budget requests and making a single recommendation to the Regional Director, overseeing policy issues, and being a visible advocate for the Program. The GARDs will oversee the day-to-day operations of the field stations, work

closely with the Ecosystem Teams, and represent the Regional Director on issues in their respective Areas. All ARDs will report to the Deputy Regional Director and me.

When Sam returned from the directorate meeting and relayed the decision to me, my immediate response was "Sam, we have just received instructions from the department and administration to *reduce* the number of GS-15s in all agencies, and we are now going to *increase* the number of 15s by *twenty-one*!" Sam replied, "You wouldn't believe how tense the meeting was. That point was brought up more than once but, in the end, we decided it was the right way to go. Jamie said she could handle questions from above about the additional 15s." As I had promised from our meeting shortly after he was named as the RD, I went to work to support him. A decision had been made, and the time for discussion had passed.

• • •

Steve Thompson was an unknown to me when Sam asked if I thought he would be a good addition to our team. I had met Steve, but really knew little about him. After some research, I discovered that Steve had been one of the main team members, along with Rob Shallenberger and Rick Coleman, who negotiated with Congress on the National Wildlife Refuge Improvement Act. The refuge system was seen by many as the "backbone of the Fish and Wildlife Service" because of its land holdings and regular interface with the public. The system operated under the authority of a myriad of laws, but none provided the resource protections that the FWS believed were needed. On both Bureau of Land Management (BLM) and Forest Service (FS) lands, laws required multiple uses of the resources, from timber harvest to mining. The FWS wanted desperately to have a law that directed "These lands are for wildlife."

During the negotiations, there was significant pushback from members of Congress who believed the term "refuge" was taken too literally and that the ability of people to enjoy lands they owned as citizens was being denied. They argued that many in the public viewed the emblematic blue goose sign to just mean "NO!" After months of give and take, the final agreement was that national wildlife refuge lands would be managed for "wildlife first," then other "appropriate uses." On October 9, 1997, with Steve Thompson standing behind him, President Clinton signed the National Wildlife Refuge Improvement Act (PL 105-57), which amended the National Wildlife Refuge System Administration Act of 1966.

The only system of Federal lands devoted specifically to wildlife, the National Wildlife Refuge System is a network of diverse and strategically located habitats. Over 39 million people visit units of the National Wildlife Refuge System each year to enjoy a wide range of wildlife related recreational opportunities. The passage of this Act gave guidance to the Secretary of the Interior for the overall management of the Refuge System. The Act's main components include:

- a strong and singular wildlife conservation Mission for the Refuge System;
- a requirement that the Secretary of the Interior maintain the biological integrity, diversity and environmental health of the Refuge System;
- a new process for determining compatible uses on Refuges;
- a recognition that wildlife-dependent recreational uses involving hunting, fishing, wildlife observation and photography, and environmental education and interpretation, when determined to be compatible, are legitimate and appropriate uses of the Refuge System;
- that these compatible wildlife-dependent recreational uses are

the priority general public uses of the Refuge System, and
- a requirement for preparing a comprehensive conservation plan for each refuge. (USFWS 2020)

It was no small accomplishment either to require that the health of the wildlife resources guide all refuge decisions or to have the "big six" priority uses identified in law. The FWS now had "organic" legislation making it clear that any use that would harm wildlife was not acceptable under the law. In addition, any management decision made would have to be proposed in the comprehensive conservation plan (CCP), which would guide the management of each refuge for fifteen years. Any modification to those plans is required to go through a full public review process. Refuge managers had been given the stated purpose(s) of each refuge and would develop plans to deliver on such purpose(s), and those plans would have the weight of regulation by virtue of the full public review process. In addition, environmental statements under the National Environmental Policy Act (NEPA) would accompany each CCP. The National Wildlife Refuge System became unique in its driving purpose on U.S. public lands and waters. The significance of this cannot be overstated.

Sam, who knew Steve from his time in D.C., invited Steve to come visit us. Thompson was from Nevada but had strong roots in California. We teased him about being a "surfer boy" and told him the southeast had far better oceans and sandy beaches than California. Geoff Haskett was the ARD–Refuges when I arrived, but he had since accepted the position of DRD for Region 2 in Albuquerque. We showed Steve beautiful photos of the Caribbean and told him we'd really like him to come to Atlanta and be the GARD for the east coast and Caribbean. After he arrived, I asked him to come to my office, where I explained what we really needed.

"Steve, I know we talked to you about the Caribbean and beautiful blue seas with sandy beaches. But our need for strong leadership is in the Lower Mississippi Valley [LMV]. Sam and I will keep our word and let you have the other area, but we're asking you to help us by taking over the LMV." He gave me a Steve Thompson grin. "I see. You lure me down here in this sweltering heat by showing me beautiful pictures of beaches, then when I get here you want me to oversee the muddy, ugly Mississippi River?" He paused, shook his head and gave me another Steve Thompson grin. "If that's where you believe I can do the most good for you, Sam, and the region, of course I will."

That was vintage Steve. A keen mind and an even stronger dedication to the team. We had a project leaders meeting not long after our discussion, at which Sam released the names of some new Region 4 leaders and announced that Steve would be the GARD for the LMV Area. As soon as we broke for the day, the "Mississippi Mafia" grabbed Steve and asked him to spend some time with them. They went to the bar, where someone pulled out a chair and sat it in the middle of the group. Steve recounted it to me this way.

> They put me in that chair, and it wasn't very comfortable by the way, and said they had some questions. I said 'OK, you've got three questions.' Karen Kilpatrick from the Natchitoches Fish Hatchery, trying to be nice, said 'Would you like a beer'? I said 'Yes, thanks, and that's the first question. Two to go.' They asked me about my ties to California and let me know they weren't sure a western guy like me could fit in the LMV culture. I gave them some background and then said 'OK, I've got a question for you.
>
> 'I just visited Tensas Refuge in north Louisiana the other day, and as I was driving in I saw this hock [the way Steve would say "hawk"] fly down and pick up a piglet and fly away! I've never seen anything like that before! Do you know what kind of hock it was?' One of the leaders of the group was George Chandler, a seasoned refuge manager and highly accomplished raptor biologist. He started peppering me with questions about feathers

on the shins, bands on the primary feathers, size and other things. I kept saying, 'No, that wasn't it.' Finally it got quiet and I said, 'You know, I've heard about them but have never seen one. Could this be a *ham hock*?' The group erupted and said, 'He got you good, George! OK, Steve, you're officially in!'

Steve was a natural leader who could fit in with anyone, anywhere. We hit a home run bringing him to Atlanta. Sam, Steve and I gradually became so close, Steve described us as "the three amigos." They were both like brothers to me. Sam was constantly concerned about his health because his father, an Air Force officer, had passed away in his late forties from a heart attack. Sam often brought in a lunch of fruit and salad, and was careful to find ways of working out when he was in town. Steve was a lifelong swimmer, and convinced Sam to join his swim club with the promise that he would accompany Sam and teach him techniques to use in the pool for a good workout. Sam was one of those you could literally see turning red when he was upset or embarrassed. I said "I don't play poker but, if I did, I'd want you at the table!" Sam couldn't hide his emotions, which made him all the more human to us.

Under the new structure, we had to find three new ARDs to bring into the mix. We finished out the team with Dave Heffernan as the ARD–Refuges, Mitch King from my old Vicksburg days as a GARD, Cindy Dohner as Acting PARD–ES, and Linda Kelsey as the PARD–Fisheries (Columbus Brown had taken a new position in Washington, D.C.). The team was coming together with new talent and big dedication to the resource.

• • •

One afternoon in the summer of 1998, I got a call from Rick Lemon at the National Conservation Training Center (NCTC). Rick had surpassed all expectations in planning and building the NCTC just outside Shepherdstown, West Virginia, on a parcel of land owned by a wonderful widow who wanted to make sure that the land upon which she had spent her life would remain relatively wild and have a positive benefit. In 1996, the doors opened for business at that one-of-a-kind facility. Nowhere else could one actually have a training course created specifically to meet the needs of a particular job or skill type.

Rick had overseen the formulation of a world-class curriculum on a fantastic campus, one that would eventually train students from over fifty countries, nearly all federal and state wildlife agencies, and many in the private sector. His most brilliant decision may well have been to keep the teaching staff at NCTC small and nimble, and bring in experts in the subject areas to teach a given class. Most classes last less than a week, but some are career development programs that are extended. Just as the FWS Wildlife Forensics Laboratory in Ashland, Oregon, had gained the reputation of the "Scotland Yard of Wildlife," NCTC would become known as the "Oxford of Natural Resource Conservation."

The group of deputies was seen as an extension of the directorate, and Rick wanted to know if I would be willing to be the head of the newly formed FWS Heritage Committee. The function of the group would be to preserve as much FWS history as possible and engage FWS retirees in a manner to keep them actively involved in the FWS family. I said, "Rick, I really don't know that much about the history of the FWS, so I don't know how I can help." In his typical straightforward, but smooth, manner, he replied, "I know. I'm not asking you because of your history expertise. We need someone that the directorate will listen to for funding and allowing active employees to participate with the retirees. The directorate will listen to you, and frankly, I want you because of your name recognition, and you're a deputy."

Oh well, so much for ego sensitivity! I laughed and accepted the request based on his honesty, and it proved to be one of the best decisions in my career. Helping to create the Heritage Committee, bring retirees together with active duty employees, and establish the FWS

Retirees Association brought me more humility about what those who came before me had done than anything else I could have experienced. It also opened the door for me to finally become friends with one of my true heroes in conservation, Lynn Greenwalt. Lynn regularly called me his "young friend," and the love I developed for Lynn and his wonderful wife, Judy, still grows today. To keep the Heritage Committee tied to the directorate, Rick succeeded in getting the director to officially appoint me as chair of the committee on September 23, 1998.

This new role also allowed me to spend time at NCTC with Rick and his staff, and to see a new type of dedication to conservation. Having begun my career in a "sink or swim" environment, it was nothing short of spellbinding to see people who dedicated their lives to conservation education in every aspect of that term. They got up each morning and went home each evening thinking of ways to make NCTC and the training mission even better. Conservation education was finally more than a slogan in the FWS; it was a significant part of the mission. But to ensure that the Heritage Committee and its efforts to bring retired employees back in the fold would succeed, we needed at least two or three retirees who were bored enough to want to take this on.

Mark Madison was the new FWS Historian at NCTC and an amazing asset. I called in my old friends Jerry Grover from Portland; Denny Holland, whom I had met when he was the assistant area manager for refuges in Jackson, and Arden Trandahl from South Dakota. Jerry and Denny, with their wonderful wives Judy and Kathy, respectively, and Arden started pulling in other retirees they had worked with over the years. As I had admitted from the beginning, I wasn't the historian, but I loved the people who had cut the trail for me to follow. I was honored just being a part of their team.

To bring the historical knowledge of the FWS together, we set our first Retiree Reunion at NCTC and garnered an attendance of thirteen people, including spouses. We established our goal for the next year at Sunday breakfast: each person was responsible for bringing one other person to the next reunion. The next year we had nearly thirty, and by the fourth or fifth year we registered over two hundred retirees at the Spearfish, South Dakota, reunion. In response to requests from retirees in different parts of the country, we decided to have the reunions in different locations each year, but still have it at NCTC every fourth year to bring it "home." It was a pure joy to see those old faces light up as the retirees spotted old friends, had a beverage and started telling lies. This group, more than any other associated with the FWS, made me comprehend how fortunate I was to be part of the U.S. Fish and Wildlife Service family. I have never forgotten that humbling fact.

CHAPTER 12

The Shell Game and the Everglades

Freshwater bivalves are part of the group of mollusks that live in streams and rivers, as opposed to their saltwater cousins. These shellfish are often harvested for table fare but are also critically important in the aquatic food chain. In 1991, Special Agent Robert Lumadue of the U.S. Fish and Wildlife Service (FWS) and state officers from Michigan and Ohio wildlife agencies arrested some "musselers," fishermen who harvest freshwater mussels for commercial use, for violating harvest regulations. Freshwater mussels constitute one of the most endangered groups of aquatic species on the planet, with thirty species extinct and another seventy species listed as threatened or endangered out of a total of three hundred known species in the 1990s. Commercial musseling is legal in several states, but the species and size are strictly regulated. Special Agent Lumadue said "We knew about illegal musseling for any number of years, but the investigation really started coming to a head in 1991 to 1994." The investigation to which Lumadue was referring was one that would culminate in a joint federal/state law enforcement effort involving Michigan, Ohio, Kentucky, Tennessee, West Virginia, Alabama and Louisiana.

The historical role of FWS special agents began in 1900 with the passage of the Lacey Act, which for the first time made it a federal offense to violate a state wildlife law and transport illegally taken fish or wildlife across state boundaries to avoid prosecution. In 1918, the Migratory Bird Treaty Act gave federal wildlife officers their first group of species under primary jurisdiction of the FWS, and for decades thereafter FWS law enforcement was focused on waterfowl and duck hunting. Affectionately known as "Duck Cops," these officers loved their role in enforcing migratory bird hunting laws and believed each duck or goose was "theirs." But things started to change after the passage of the Endangered Species Act in 1973. Special agents had a new role in helping stem illegal trade in threatened and endangered species worldwide.

In press releases regarding illicit trade in endangered species, the FWS stated:

> NOTE TO PUBLIC: Recent studies indicate that more than $100 billion per year is generated in the United States economy directly from activities related to our public fish and wildlife resources. Unfortunately, analysis of worldwide criminal activities conducted by Interpol and published in the November 1994 *Time* magazine story 'Animal Genocide, Mob Style' also reveals that the international illegal trade in wildlife trafficking is the second-largest form of black-market commerce in the world, behind drugs and ahead of illegal arms. The public can help stop wildlife law violations by reporting suspicious activities to State or Federal wildlife officers and by refusing to purchase products made from protected species. (USFWS 1998)

This shift to elevate endangered species priorities equal to those of waterfowl enforcement didn't always sit well with Duck Cops, who loved the game of catching poachers in the act. Books have been written about the exploits of game wardens, both state and federal, and how they often became friends with the offenders in the game of "Catch me if you can." But waterfowl slaughters that resulted in train cars full of ducks and geese being loaded and sent to restaurants in Chicago, New York and other large cities were a thing of the past. Other species were in dire need of protection, and special agents took their long-established skills at stealth and masquerade and transitioned into the dark underworld of illicit wildlife trade. The transition proved to be smooth due to the similarities in techniques, with one exception. Dealing with high-dollar crimes meant dealing with highly dangerous criminals who would think nothing of killing an agent discovered undercover in their midst. The stakes were much higher, and so were the dangers.

In making the case against the multi-state mussel ring, state and federal agents worked together using some of the old techniques. Special Agent Lumadue and his team set up a multi-day surveillance to watch the suspected illegal mussel operation. Each night the musselers waited until after dark to go upriver to collect the mussels. They returned a few hours before dawn and, instead of loading the mussels in the truck, dumped the mussels overboard in less than ten feet of water, where the mussels would stay alive and well until the musselers reached their targeted catch quantity. Then all the mussels were loaded in the truck at once, and the musselers were gone before daylight. The agents followed the truck until it crossed the state border into Indiana and made the arrests under the Lacey Act.

That set off an investigation that lasted until 1998. Numerous arrests in multiple states were made as intelligence slowly began to fill in the details on a large, illegal mussel-shell ring. The company ultimately charged with purchase of the illegally harvested mussel shells was Japanese-owned Tennessee Shell, of Camden, Tennessee. Shells are highly valued in the Japanese pearl culture industry. American mussels have been harvested since the 1950s to be ground into pea-size beads that are then implanted in oysters. The oyster's response to the irritation is to coat the bead with nacre, a hard, iridescent substance that's commonly known as mother-of-pearl, beginning the process that results in the cultured pearl's beautiful finish. Tennessee Shell Company was a subsidiary of Kogen Trading Company of Tokyo, and the largest buying and exporting shell company in the United States. With significant help from the office of the U.S. attorney, Tennessee Shell pled guilty to purchasing illegal products and agreed to pay a $1 million fine, the largest ever secured for an illegal wildlife trade offense.

It is the U.S. attorney's office, not the FWS, that brings a case to court for prosecution; thus, the plaintiff was the United States of America. Attorneys in the Department of the Interior have the title of "solicitor," generally meaning to act on behalf of or give legal advice to their clients. The U.S. attorney general (AG) is the chief lawyer of the United States, and the U.S. attorneys who work under the AG are assigned the task of deciding which cases are taken to court, which are settled and which are dropped. The role of the FWS agent is to bring the evidence to the U.S. attorney for consideration. This distinction is significant. Not even the secretary of the interior can force the attorney general to bring litigation for either civil or criminal action. The U.S. attorney in Memphis was significantly involved in bringing this case. She had to be convinced of the evidence and that it was worth taking to court. Given the history of wildlife cases and their treatment as "minor" by many courts, her decision to prosecute was historic.

Vicki Boatwright, our assistant regional director (ARD) for external affairs, worked with Monty Halcomb, ARD for law enforcement, to put things together for a joint news conference with the U.S. attorney in Memphis. Vicki advised me that she was getting resistance from her counterpart at the U.S. attorney's office about having a joint press conference. This was an extremely big case and a phenomenal win for both wildlife officers and the U.S. attorney. I called Veronica Coleman, U.S. attorney for the Western District of Tennessee, to see if we could resolve whatever issue was standing in the way. I introduced myself as the deputy regional director and offered her my sincere congratulations on a highly significant conviction, then asked if there were any issues I could help with on our end regarding a joint press conference. I started the conversation with what Vicki had relayed to me.

"I am told by our public affairs officer that your press officer thinks it best that you have a separate news conference from ours, and I'd like to confirm if that's the case."

"That's a lie!" Ms. Coleman replied. I was so stunned by the statement that I went silent for a couple of seconds to gather my composure and keep my temper under control. Then, in a calm voice, I said, "I think we need to clear up a couple of things. First, I am the deputy regional director of the U.S. Fish and Wildlife Service. I work with numerous U.S. attorneys across ten states and the Caribbean. You are not important enough for me to lie to. I could certainly be mistaken, but I do not lie, not for you, not for my mother, not for anyone. Now Ms. Coleman, with that clearly understood, I'll ask again if you would prefer to have your own news conference with just the Department of Justice personnel who worked on this case, or would you prefer to have a joint conference with our officers and me there to show the team approach to solving this crime?" Now it was her turn to go silent. "We would love to have a joint news conference on the banks of the Mississippi River, if you agree." We set the date of July 24, 1998, for the conference.

I had hired Debbie Doty Vess to be my executive assistant, and couldn't have made a better decision. Talented and efficient, Debbie looked after me like I was her big brother and made sure everything I needed was lying on my desk or booked for travel. She set up my trip to Memphis as all the others, but when I arrived, expecting to be met by Dave Cartwright, our special agent in Memphis, who was key in the investigation, or West Tennessee Special Agent Zack Green, or Resident Agent in Charge for Tennessee Mike Elkins, I was instead met by Ms. Coleman, who said she wanted to personally pick me up to get to know me and be clear about how much she appreciated our help. Gary Meyers, longtime friend and director of the Tennessee Wildlife Resources Agency, joined us for the announcement, as did several officers from other states. Ms. Coleman made a strong and elegant statement about the tragedy of this case for wildlife, and the importance of bringing wildlife criminals to justice. The FWS news release stated, in part:

> Ms. Coleman stated 'What this case boils down to is the plundering of America's wildlife, for profit.' Acting Regional Director

Hall said 'While freshwater mussels are not cuddly creatures with eyelashes, they are hugely important in the biological scheme of things. They are the proverbial canaries in the coal mine, warning us of danger by detecting and filtering out pollutants and toxic chemicals in the water that may affect human health. They are also a food source for other animals and an anchor for plants on the riverbed. But they are being wiped out as a result of human activities, and, in this case, because of greed.' (USFWS 1998)

I specifically recognized FWS Special Agents Dave Cartwright, Carl Wilson, Emerson Gorham and Andy Pierce for their professionalism and dedication. The fines were directed, with Ms. Coleman's help, to the National Fish and Wildlife Foundation. All conservation officers in the U.S. work long and unusual hours and spend many cold and wet nights away from their families, with spouses wondering if they will make it home for breakfast. There is no greater trust that one human being can bestow upon another than to give him or her a lethal weapon and the shield of the law to use that weapon to harm another human being. This is a heavy burden, and a much higher standard of behavior is required for that position than for others. Throughout my career, I found it was the rare exception when one of our FWS officers betrayed that trust.

Whitney Tilt was there to represent the National Fish and Wildlife Foundation (NFWF) and to assure the public that the fine would support grants to further protect, manage and restore mussel populations. A million-dollar fine doesn't sound like much in comparison to billions from oil spills, but at that time it was the largest in history for intentional criminal harm to fish and wildlife resources. The federal/state teamwork in making the case, and the tenacity of U.S. Attorney Veronica Coleman and her staff, once again proved what good people can do when they come together not caring who gets the credit. Justice was served.

• • •

Everglades (Courtesy of NPS)

The Everglades of south Florida are one of America's treasures, but one that has undergone significant physical, chemical and biological stresses due to human encroachment. The Kissimmee River feeds into Lake Okeechobee just to the southwest of Port St. Lucie. Named the Everglades after the Indian word meaning "River of Grass," there is a continual sheet flow across south Florida from the northeast portion above Delray Beach to the south and west into Florida Bay. The plants in the Everglades evolved with low levels of nutrients; thus when phosphorous was introduced in large quantities through the use of fertilizer in the production of sugar cane, it created significant changes to the plant ecosystem. The introduction of phosphorous, more than any other factor, forced the shift from traditional conservation of the Everglades to one of holistic restoration.

The FWS's main focus in the Everglades is Loxahatchee National Wildlife Refuge, an "overlay" refuge in one of the South Florida Water Management District's (SFWMD) Water Control Areas (WCA). While the FWS does not own the land, a fifty-year agreement through the

Migratory Bird Treaty Act with the SFWMD allowed the FWS full management authority over the refuge. The National Park Service (NPS) is equally focused on Everglades National Park. In the late 1980s, the U.S. Department of Justice, on behalf of the EPA, sued the SFWMD and the Florida Department of Environmental Regulation (FDER) over failure to protect the refuge and park from the onslaught of phosphorous from the Everglades Agricultural Area (EAA), an expanse of land greater than 450,000 acres in which sugar cane is farmed. The significant amounts of fertilizer needed to augment the low nutrient level in the soils of the EAA elevated the natural background level of phosphorous of 10 parts per billion (ppb) or less to concentrations as high as 150 ppb throughout the refuge and into the park. The fragile ecosystem was under chemical assault. The state of Florida, under the leadership of Governor Jeb Bush, reached an agreement with the federal government on reducing the massive loads of phosphorous carried in EAA drainage water.

On February 24, 1992, Judge William Hoeveler of the U.S. District Court, Southern District of Florida, approved the consent decree drafted by the parties to the suit, and addressed the objections of the intervenors to the lawsuit. He stated, in part:

> A review of the terms of the Agreement reveals an ambitious strategy to restore and preserve the Everglades ecosystem. In broad outline, the Agreement establishes interim and long-term phosphorous concentration limits for the Park and Refuge and delineates specific remedial programs designed to achieve these limits. The remedial programs consist of stormwater treatment areas ("STAs") and a regulatory permitting program aimed at agricultural discharges from the Everglades Agricultural Area ("EAA"). The STAs, to be constructed by the District on 35,000 acres of land in the EAA, are large water filtration marshes designed to process and remove nutrients from agricultural runoff destined for the Park and Refuge. The STAs will thus act as

a "buffer zone" between the agricultural area and the Park and Refuge, receiving stormwater directly from agricultural drainage canals and purifying the water before it enters the Park and Refuge.

The regulatory program complements and lessens the work of the STAs by seeking to reduce the level of phosphorous in agricultural runoff entering the STAs. Pursuant to this program, the District or DER will regulate the water quality of agricultural discharges through a permitting scheme by which permit applicants will be required to comply with designated phosphorous load allocations and adopt best management practices aimed at reducing the levels of phosphorous in agricultural discharge. The combination of the STAs and the regulatory program are expected to achieve an 80% long-term reduction in phosphorous loads from the EAA. (Hoeveler 1992, p8)

After addressing all objections from the intervenors, Judge Hoeveler concluded:

I have difficulty understanding the amount of time, effort, and litigation spawned by an understandable effort to seek the truth and, if the truth requires, take the steps necessary to save a precious resource. The time has come, indeed, has passed, when the admitted problems facing the Everglades must be addressed. And yet the solutions must be the product of a meaningful search for the scientific truth. The original parties to this litigation conclude that they have found the answers or, at least, are aimed in the right direction. The Cities and Farm Interests wish to participate in the finality of these conclusions and so they shall. Lest there be any doubt from what has been said before in the Order, it is the Court's hope and expectation that the administrative process in which defendant-intervenors will be involved will be totally uninhibited by this Order and the Agreement to which it makes reference. (Hoeveler 1992, p68)

While the refuge was certainly part of the agreement, many question whether the federal government would have sued had not the high-profile Everglades National Park also been impacted. Arthur R. Marshall Loxahatchee National Wildlife Refuge is one of the first areas to receive water directly from the EAA as it moves down into the Everglades. Created in 1951, the agreement was up for renewal in 2001, and there were still significant questions regarding liability to be answered before the FWS would be able to renew the lease. Jay Slack was the FWS lead on the Everglades and provided assistance wherever he could to Refuge Manager Burkett Neeley and his successor, Marc Museus, in addressing means to implement an aggressive program for restoration. The FWS obviously believed it had no responsibility to expend limited dollars on an issue it had no role in creating. But FDER and SFWMD were looking for all sources of funding they could possibly tap. Time was drawing near for agreements to be made.

Governor Bush eventually worked with the federal government and the Florida legislature to broker a $7.8 billion program, with costs divided equally between the state and feds, to tackle the problems facing the Everglades. While the consent decree and the restoration funding agreement made significant strides in addressing the chemical problem, there remained other physical and biological challenges.

Anglo settlement in cities like Miami brought loss of native habitat and a demand for freshwater that did not historically flow to the southeast. Further, with human settlement came biological disturbances through the introduction of non-native species into this sensitive River of Grass.

Water in south Florida once flowed freely from the Kissimmee River to Lake Okeechobee and southward over low-lying lands to the estuaries of Biscayne Bay, the Ten Thousand Islands, and Florida Bay. This shallow, slow-moving sheet of water covered almost 11,000 square miles, creating a mosaic of ponds, sloughs, sawgrass marshes, hardwood hammock, and forested uplands. For thousands of years this intricate system evolved into a finely balanced ecosystem that formed the biological infrastructure for the southern half of the state.

However, to early colonial settlers and developers the Everglades were potential farmland and communities. By the early 1900s, the drainage process to transform wetland to land ready to be developed was under way. The results would be severely damaging to the ecosystem and the species it supported. With the support of many early conservationists, scientists, and other advocates, Everglades National Park was established in 1947 to conserve the natural landscape and prevent further degradation of its land, plants, and animals. Although the captivation of the Everglades has mostly stemmed from its unique ecosystem, an alluring human story of the Everglades is deeply interwoven with its endless marshes, dense mangroves, towering palms, alligator holes, and tropical fauna. Various groups and people navigated through and wrestled with the watery landscape to make it home, and even to exploit its natural wonder at times. (NPS 2020)

The history of indigenous people in Florida is long and dotted with war, separation and regrouping into new tribes.

Along with the Seminoles to the north, the Miccosukee Tribe called the Everglades home.

The Tribe has a proud history, which predates Columbus. The Miccosukee Indians were originally part of the Creek Nation, and then migrated to Florida before it became part of the United States. During the Indian Wars of the 1800s, most of the

Miccosukee were removed to the West, but about 100, mostly Mikasuki-speaking Creeks, never surrendered and hid out in the Everglades. Present Tribal members now number over 600 and are direct descendants of those who eluded capture.

To survive in this new environment, the Miccosukee adapted to living in small groups in temporary "hammock style" camps spread throughout the Everglades' vast river of grass. In this fashion, they stayed to themselves for about 100 years, resisting efforts to become assimilated. Then, after the Tamiami Trail highway was built in 1928, the Tribe began to accept New World concepts.

To ensure that the federal government would formally recognize the Miccosukee Tribe, Buffalo Tiger, an esteemed member of the Tribe, led a group to Cuba in 1959, where they asked Fidel Castro for, and were granted, international recognition as a sovereign country within the United States. Following this, on January 11, 1962, the U.S. Secretary of the Interior approved the Miccosukee Constitution and the Tribe was officially recognized as the Miccosukee Tribe of Indians of Florida. This legally established the Miccosukee's tribal existence and their sovereign, domestic dependent nation status with the United States Government. (Miccosukee Home Page 2020)

When I arrived in Atlanta and became engaged in Everglade discussions, it was ironic that one of the first things we discussed was the shifting of 800,000 acre-feet of water that historically flowed southwest to Florida Bay but was now being diverted to provide water for Miami. I had just left arguments about 800,000 acre-feet of water in the Central Valley Project Improvement Act (CVPIA), and now we were discussing how to restore that same amount to the Everglades. The extensive karst limestone aquifer provided potential to supply the water from underground sources, but a significant obstacle to returning historical surface flows was the 8.5 Square Mile Area, a piece of land in the Everglades just outside the levee-protected areas in Dade County.

The 8.5 Square Mile Area sits on the outer edge of Shark River Slough, just west of the levee that protects Miami. In the late 1940s, flooding and pressures to develop succeeded in pushing the Corps of Engineers to propose a system of canals and levees under the Central and Southern Florida Flood Control Project. The marshes found in the River of Grass were seen as "wastelands" that had significant development potential if flood protection could be assured. At the same time, conservation interests were successful in creation of the Everglades National Park. The Corps project would provide flood protection for everything south of the Tamiami Trail down to the park, which spurred a frenzy of development projects within the 8.5 Square Mile Area. The higher ground would be relatively safe from storms.

But questions about the project's effects began to emerge. Environmentalists voiced concerns about the possible contamination of the Florida aquifer and potential damage to the park as a result of reduced water inflow. By the 1970s, the Corps had enlarged an existing levee and installed a pump station to evacuate water from areas considered to be "protected." This left those inhabitants in the 8.5 Square Mile Area with little to no flood protection. By 1981, Dade County passed zoning ordinances that restricted development to one house per 40 acres west of the levee, but this was considered insufficient by park and restoration advocates. By 1989, the Corps and the conservation community agreed on a new plan to restore the Everglades flows and return the water to as much of its historical footprint as possible. This meant returning water into the 8.5 Square Mile Area and flooding ground that had been developed.

In 1998, the SFWMD decided that all efforts to find compromise between existing development and residents of the 8.5 Square Mile Area had failed. The SFWMD board voted to buy out existing willing sellers and exercise eminent domain on those who would not agree to sell. A fair price would be offered, but SFWMD was determined to move forward with the Corps in restoring as much of the historical Everglades sheet flow as possible.

Jay Slack described the situation that existed in south Florida at the end of the 1990s and beginning of the new century. The issues of human encroachment and changes to the system required new ways of looking at problems.

> The process and approach put together by the Corps was a clear driver and a brilliant strategy. They realized that the Everglades was a pretty sexy issue, and the public was watching. The Corps realized it was a vehicle to provide water supply and flood protection, but decided to approach it in a different way. Water supply and flood protection were normal for the Corps, but they were now doing it in a manner that was focused on environmental restoration. They were fulfilling their long-term mandates while making the world a better place. This was new to the Corps, but the Everglades was different. It had it all. The Everglades provided something for everyone.
>
> Water supply was all about the quality, quantity and, most important, the timing of water delivery. South Florida has a wet and dry season, not four seasons. It is feast or famine with water. There needed to be a good management system of storage and conveyance capable of holding water or moving it out because the natural water footprint had been changed by development. The challenge was to return to as natural a form of water management as possible.
>
> The 8.5 Square Mile Area was a great example of the problem. The drainage of the swamp in the 1950s and '60s allowed people to develop on the high ground, but from an FWS perspective, that's where the most sensitive species (rare plants, Cape Sable seaside sparrow, Florida panther) lived. When the drainage occurred, the species made use of the low ground that

was made available. But when efforts to return natural flows to the Everglades began to reflood the lower lands, those species were pushed back up to the high ground, which was now condominiums and concrete. It was the largest single problem for the FWS in Everglades restoration. (Slack 2020)

New and innovative ways of working as an interagency team were required. In addition to the massive introduction of phosphorous into the system and the physical alterations to accommodate Miami and other development interests, the Everglades became a dumping ground for "exotic pets" that people bought and later realized they no longer wanted to care for or could no longer handle because the animals had become too large to control. Instead of taking them to a zoo or humanely euthanizing the animals, "pet owners" released them into the uninhabited marshes of the Everglades and went home feeling good about themselves. But what they had done was inject a species into a delicate system for which there was no natural predator. The most famous example is the introduction of the Burmese python, a snake that can reach twenty to thirty feet in length and swallow an entire deer whole after crushing its body through constriction. The culmination of these three stresses formed the comprehensive challenge that the FWS, NPS, Corps and State of Florida had been battling for decades.

My longtime friend and mentor Steve Forsythe was the state supervisor for Ecological Services (ES) in Florida by the time I arrived in 1997, and Dave Hankla was the new Jacksonville field supervisor. We never worried about things being under control with Steve, Dave and Jay in the state. The FWS team was complete. Another great addition to the interagency team was from the Corps of Engineers. Brigadier General Rick Capka was the division commander for the Corps' South Atlantic Division and the polar opposite of the Corps commanders we had dealt with early in our careers. Regional Director Sam Hamilton, Rick and I worked closely together and built a high level of trust.

We were able to talk through every issue where there may have been differences in mission or direction. There were times when agency policy got in the way, but that was the exception rather than the rule. Rick was the epitome of the newer, politically astute Corps of Engineers and he ensured that his district commanders understood how important it was to work with the FWS, the state and local partners. The Corps had not completely changed in its view that they were there for navigation and flood control, but Rick Capka and others like him in the new Corps were making their leadership known; a very welcomed change. As a result, Jay had the same relationship with the district engineer in Jacksonville.

The Corps began to realize how much support there was for Everglades restoration. People from all over the world were interested in this natural treasure, and the Corps was now in a position to be seen as the instrument of restoration. It was a sea change for them. The Corps came to us and said 'We've got 69 species down there listed under the Endangered Species Act, and we'd like to recover those species. How do we do that as we go about restoring the Everglades?' The decision was to write the mother of all recovery plans, with all listed species in south Florida affected by Everglades restoration included. This would be the cookbook, both for recovering the species, and also replumbing south Florida in an environmentally friendly way. It was a huge effort that provided a cookbook, but also a menu of options.

The Corps, however, was uncomfortable with this because it didn't give step-by-step decisions, but instead provided a road map with choices along the way. This became a point of friction because the Corps wanted a plan that said 'Do A, then B, then C, and when you get to X, you're finished.' The scientists were happier with the adaptive management approach with feedback loops and opportunities for course correction, but the Corps wanted to be able to say they were following the steps and it would be done. One of the most important outcomes of the Everglades effort was the landscape conservation view. The other game changer was the coming together of the team. The Corps, FWS, NPS and SFWMD created the Agency Head Roundtable, which was very informal, but we all talked a lot. That turned into trust, especially between the district engineer for the Corps and me. Once we started working together, all the other problems started becoming manageable. We were in it together. (Slack 2020).

• • •

Being in the office much more also allowed me to gather my thoughts on significant issues the FWS was facing and, as a "Deputies Group" member, put them on paper for consideration by my fellow deputies and the directorate. The Fisheries program was receiving less and less attention as budgets got tighter and priorities started shifting toward endangered species. After all my experience with the Endangered Species Act (ESA) out west, I was concerned that the tools to keep species from *becoming* endangered were being relegated to an afterthought of the high-profile ESA. Sam and I were also in regular communication with the state wildlife directors, who were becoming increasingly frustrated with the "cold shoulder" they were getting from the director and leadership in D.C.

Cathy Short was the assistant director for Fisheries and, given my experience as the deputy for Fisheries, she asked for some advice on moving the program forward in the face of new and evolving FWS priorities. In working the landscape approach to conservation, each region had established "ecosystem teams" that included our state and private partners. I took advantage of the opportunity to encourage more true partnerships and, on April 28, 1999, sent Cathy a note. The major emphasis of my advice was to embrace the fact that it is only by working with other conservation entities that success can be achieved.

I think we failed in past policies by not making the philosophy one of working with our partners for *their interests* part of the fabric of all our operations . . . It is in the definitions that we either are partners to our partners or we're staff to whomever is asking the question inside the beltway . . . In my opinion, the most effective avenue to getting in control of our destiny . . . is through the Ecosystem Teams.

But if we do this, we will lose our funding because some of the work isn't on the high-priority trust species, right? I don't think so. I would argue that ignoring our responsibilities as partners and abandoning 'state species' sure hasn't served us very well to get increased budgets in the past, even by giving away/closing hatcheries . . . I submit that if we are working with our partners, private industry (and I don't just mean the fishing industry), and the general concerned public the way we should and will be through our Ecosystem Teams, we will be able to gain the confidence of all those that really matter, the American people.

• • •

President Theodore Roosevelt was a conservation hero to me and to countless others. His foresight and wisdom about wise use, and preservation when necessary, guided the development of the North American Model of Wildlife Conservation and the way conservation is done in the United States. Assistant Regional Director Steve Thompson had met the great-grandson of President Roosevelt, Theodore Roosevelt IV, and discovered he was as down to earth as his great-grandfather was said to have been. Steve, in his winning way, convinced "TR-4" to come to the southeast and revisit the steps President Roosevelt had taken on the famous 1902 journey that culminated with the creation of the "Teddy bear." We all thought it was a fantastic idea and would bring attention to the partnership with the states that our region had worked so hard to develop.

The young Roosevelt was now fifty-six and eager to do whatever he could to keep his legendary great-grandfather in the minds of the public.

The trip would certainly include a stop at Onward, Mississippi, where according to the story, the president's hosts wanted him to be sure to kill a black bear.

> After three days of hunting, other members of the party had spotted bears, but not Roosevelt. Now what? The President's bear hunt would be a failure!
>
> The next day, the hunt guides tracked down an old black bear that the dogs had trailed quite a distance and attacked. The guides tied the bear to a willow tree and called for the President. Here was a bear for him to shoot!
>
> But Roosevelt took one look at the old bear and refused to shoot it. He felt doing so would be unsportsmanlike. However, since it was injured and suffering, Roosevelt ordered that the bear be put down to end its pain. (Theodore Roosevelt Association 2021)

Thus, the legend and the merchandising of "Teddy's bear" were born.

Sam, Steve and Ray Aycock were the primary hosts for TR-4's tour, and the regional office was abuzz for weeks before the August visit. This was an unbelievable opportunity to talk about the changes that had occurred in the Mississippi Delta from 1902 until 1999. Old reports like *The Yazoo Basin: An Environmental Overview* that I had written, recent scientific articles about the heavy pesticide load in the streams of the lower delta near Vicksburg, the loss of bottomland hardwoods, and the strides made to restore lost habitats were pulled together as talking points for Sam and TR-4 at every opportunity. Ted was more than happy to help with an environmental message he strongly endorsed. But before the official trip, Sam and Steve wanted to take him fishing, and Ted needed a fishing license. Steve relayed the story to me about their stop at a Walmart in one of the Delta towns on their way.

> Sam and I took Ted into the store and went to the back where sporting goods and licenses were sold. Behind the counter was an average-looking guy, long sideburns and a mullet haircut. His nametag said 'Earnest.' Sam explained that his friend needed an out-of-state fishing license. Earnest took the driver's license from Ted, pulled out the license book and started filling in the required information. 'NEW YORK CITY!' Earnest said in a slow and loud voice. 'That's a FANCY place!' He moved on down to the name on the license as I watched Sam's face turn beet red in embarrassment. This was Sam's home state, and he drew Earnest out of all the employees that work for Walmart! 'Let's see, Rooooo-se-velt. That's a FANCY name!' T-H-E-O-D-O-R-E . . . Earnest looked up at Ted, jaw dropped, eyes big, and quickly walked away and into the back of the store, never to be seen again! We had to get another employee to finish the transaction, one who was clearly more respectful, and then we left. For the next hour, Sam explained to Ted that Earnest was really not typical of Mississippi people, but I couldn't resist occasionally saying 'I'm the GARD over here and I think he pretty much is!' Sam could have killed me, but Ted took it in stride and we had a great trip. (Thompson 1998)

CHAPTER 13

The Senior Executive Service and a New President

Nineteen ninety-nine proved to be a tough year for the geographic/programmatic assistant regional director (GARD/PARD) system and working out the kinks in the ecosystem approach to management. We regularly discussed how to make the landscape ecosystem approach to conservation work the best it could, and how to include partners in the process. The states and non-governmental organizations participated on the ecosystem teams, but it was hit-or-miss across the country as to the true inclusivity of the non-federal partners. I again decided to write my thoughts about management, this time about "Making It Flow the Way It Should," across all programs and all regions.

The cover memo from me, through Sam Hamilton (which meant he supported it) to the director, deputy director and deputy regional and assistant directors of the U.S. Fish and Wildlife Service (FWS) stated in part:

> I have had the privilege of being actively involved in all the developmental stages of the Ecosystem Approach to management; from preparing Marv Plenert for the first directorate meeting on this subject with then Director Mollie Beattie, to moving into geographic management as a 'wear two hats' Assistant Regional Director, to my present role supervising GARDs and PARDS and being a cheerleader for all the Ecosystem Teams

in the Region. I realize I am biased, but I believe we have succeeded in making the Ecosystem Teams a real part of our management decision-making, and I believe the system works in the Southeast.

However, I see many missed opportunities to really embrace the Ecosystem Approach to management because we too often talk our talk, but we become very reluctant to walk it.

My ten-page attachment covered most of the issues with the ecosystem approach, budgeting conflicts and accountability in supervisory chain of command. While offering my views on all of these, the most important part to me was in attempting to establish the critical aspect of our state and private partners, which was a continuing challenge within our own ranks.

The real challenge we have is in making it all work. How do we take the Director's priorities, create budget requests that support those priorities, make the Ecosystem Teams realize that their ecosystem priorities are important to the Director, bring in our partners and have Congress understand?. . . The first thing we have to do is go back to the beginning and remember what has been emphasized throughout the evolution of the Ecosystem Approach to management.

From the beginning we have continually stated that the Fish and Wildlife Service (Service) cannot accomplish natural resource conservation alone. In every document we constantly reiterate that the other federal agencies have responsibilities under federal law to care for the natural resources and, therefore, should be in full partnership with the Service in all possible activities. We state the premise that natural resource management off Service lands is the primary responsibility of the state or tribal government where those resources occur and that the

Service is there to support those efforts. Finally, we continually try to educate the public that 70% of all fish and wildlife habitat in the United States occurs on non-public land and, as such, the Service simply cannot make the necessary conservation efforts succeed without the active partnership and participation of the private landowners and special interest groups.

In short, we say we're all in this together and we really need to be in partnerships to succeed. The importance of these premises is relayed to our partners in every way possible . . . except one. When it comes time to talk about what the Ecosystem Approach to management really means, and what it might cost us in power or control, we become very unsteady. In the Director's Priority document we begin to talk about the Ecosystem Approach with a quote from Aldo Leopold:

'A thing is right when it tends to preserve the integrity, stability, and beauty of the biotic community. It is wrong when it tends otherwise.'

All of us truly believe this statement to be completely accurate. So, if we really believe it, why do we abandon it when we start talking budget? . . . We believe, and often Congress drives it back home to us, that we have no authority over non-jurisdictional species until such time as the federal authority overrides all else and we list the species under the ESA. Then we pursue its protection and recovery with zeal. So why do we wait while the species declines and do nothing? . . . How can we accept the premise that all biological components of an ecosystem are critical to the survival of that ecosystem, and the human element that depends upon it, and not place the same value on migratory and non-migratory species? When gizzard shad are lost from the river system, striped bass must find another source of food.

When largemouth bass are eliminated by overfishing, environmental contaminants, or disease, then eagles must find another fish base for food in wintering areas of the southeast. When members of the public are lost as Service supporters because we wouldn't support their State's fisheries priorities, they are lost as supporters of endangered species as well. . . .

We have all understood from elementary school through graduate school that ecosystems are chains only as strong as the weakest link. I believe that also fits the definition of a real partnership. The Service has to be a strong supporter of state, tribal and private industry concerns if we can ever hope to have them be strong in the chain that supports 'our issues.' I believe to think otherwise is naïve at best, arrogant at worst. Partnerships are agreements between two or more entities to support each other in a common interest . . . But the Team partnerships face substantial hurdles when the priorities for budgeting raised from the Teams get lost in the federal definition of 'trust issues.' *I implore all of us to remember that a concern of our partners may not fit the federal definition of a trust issue, but it most certainly is an issue of trust.* We will have fully achieved our partnership goals when all partners involved for the good of the resource have extreme difficulty identifying whom an employee on the ground represents . . .

Mark Twain once wrote that 'When I was 18, I thought my father was the dumbest man on earth. When I was 21, I was amazed to see how much he had learned in three years.' We all grow and learn. The Service is no different. Many of us that once espoused the premise that it was our authority and we didn't need anyone else's approval have since learned that none of us has a corner on the knowledge market. We need our partners, their ideas, their experience, and their wisdom. Hopefully, we can provide a little of these as well. But we can't accomplish any of the tasks we have dedicated our professional lives to if we don't do it together. When we do it together, Congress will begin hearing from their constituents (States, Tribes/private business/private interest groups) about how much sense it makes to provide the Service the appropriations [adequate funds to support joint federal/state efforts] to be a supporting member of the local communities." (Hall 1999)

Just as in the Everglades, when the agencies and public come together, the single most important ingredient in the quest for success is trust between the participants. That must first begin with mutual respect.

• • •

After I had become the chair of the deputies group, Director Jamie Clark asked us to perform a detailed evaluation of the GARD/PARD system of management to address the criticisms that had been rumbling throughout the ranks about this "conflicting and cumbersome" management scheme. Roundtable interviews were performed in detail at each regional office and in Washington to ensure that all employees had an opportunity to voice their opinion. The deputies formed teams to carry out the regional/Washington reviews, with each deputy recused from discussions conducted with their own reports and subordinates. I was on the team with my good friends Mamie Parker and Marvin Moriarty. Because we were constantly on the road and staying in different hotels, Mamie suggested we call ourselves the "Road Dogs." As close as we were, going through this review together made us even closer. I have tremendous respect for both Mamie and Marvin, and each eventually achieved the well-deserved position of regional director.

It was the most comprehensive management evaluation I witnessed in my career, and it resulted in a report to the director and directorate in March that spanned well over a hundred pages. The results were not surprising. Just as with the old programmatic management system, in which the associate directors (later renamed assistant directors) controlled the budgets and the regional directors had to argue with their peers to get monies for their priorities, the programmatic assistant regional directors (PARD) had come to be seen as the ones with the money, and the geographic assistant regional directors were believed to be required to "appeal their case" to the PARD in order to get funding placed where they believed it should go. We found this to be true in some areas and untrue in others. But the broad perception among the rank-and-file employees was that this tension was real, and it affected their daily lives.

We therefore recommended that the system be abandoned. The most dramatic lesson I learned from the GARD/PARD experiment is that *if you don't have the right people in the right positions working as a team*, no *organizational structure will work. If you have the right people in the right positions working as a team*, any *organizational structure will work.* It all boils down to ensuring that the team members have respect for each other, and each person is pulling his or her weight. When egos get involved, there must be a stern hand from above to demand respect and teamwork. That means having the right people in the right positions as leaders of the teams. The directorate accepted our recommendation, and in 2001 the FWS returned to a single ARD responsible for each program with line authority over that program. That left us in a position of having to find places for all the "extra" GS-15 ARDs that had been created. But that was our problem as regional and program leaders. A clear line of authority had been reinstated to the field operations for both issues and funding. The field teams, as always, continued to get the job done on the ground regardless of structure.

• • •

George Walker Bush won the 2000 election by the narrowest of margins. Ultimately decided by the U.S. Supreme Court, the Florida electoral college votes would go to Bush. Not long after the election, Sam called me into his office for a phone call with Director Clark. I was informed that I would be promoted to the rank of senior executive service (SES) as a deputy regional director (DRD), along with DRD Rowan Gould. To say I was shocked would be an understatement. After all the years of effort and disappointments, I would finally become a member of the senior executive service. A realization I had to face, however, was the requirement that a member of the SES accept any assignment given, to any location requested, and to arrive on the job within sixty days. I had reached the point of wanting to end my career in Atlanta, but also remained a dedicated member of the team. With gratitude, I accepted the offer.

Governor Bush was sworn in as president and Dick Cheney as vice president of the United States on January 20, 2001. By this time Steve Thompson had left the Atlanta Region to become the manager of the California/Nevada Operations Office in Sacramento, a quasi-region that encompassed my old GARD areas of California and Klamath, with Nevada included. Issues hadn't changed much. There was some peace in the valley over the Bay-Delta Accord in the Central Valley, but the jeopardy opinion that had been delivered in Klamath the year before had blown up a lot of the progress that had been made. Steve knew he had work to do to rebuild trust with the people of that valley, and I offered as much advice as I could to help him get started. He was the perfect person for the job.

In January, the president nominated and the Senate confirmed Gale Norton to be the forty-eighth secretary of the interior. Norton had served in the department when James Watt was secretary and was, unfortunately, dubbed as his clone by many in the press and those in general opposition to the president. She brought in an agenda of what she called the "four C's": consultation, communication, and cooperation, all in the service of conservation. Each time I met with Secretary Norton I found her to be kind, extremely intelligent, a focused listener and adamant that our positions be based on science. In July, the president announced his nominations of Craig Manson to be assistant secretary of the interior for Fish, Wildlife and Parks and Steve Williams to be director of the FWS. Manson was a former judge in Sacramento County and had served as general counsel for the California Department of Fish and Game. Williams was the secretary of the Kansas Department of Wildlife and Parks, and had served as deputy executive director of the Pennsylvania Game Commission, as well as the assistant director for wildlife in Massachusetts. It appeared to us that these were solid selections, but it would take another six months before both were in place due to squabbling on Capitol Hill during the confirmation process.

The real test for the Bush administration, and one that would supersede all others for the remainder of his presidency, occurred in September of that year. Sam and I were having a meeting with Mike Brennan, who had been the special assistant to John Turner and was now a consultant, about some work his clients wanted to perform that might involve our review. He was there to make sure they were doing things correctly and mitigating, if required, at the proper level. One of our executive assistants entered the glass-walled meeting room attached to Sam's and my offices to tell us that a plane had crashed into the World Trade Center in New York City. We were concerned, but assumed it was a small plane that had difficulties and couldn't avoid the town. In a few minutes, she came back in and said a second plane had crashed into the second of the twin tower complex. We knew this was no longer some unfortunate accident.

A TV was pulled into the office and we watched a nightmare in living color. We were in shock. We watched in horror as some people jumped tens of stories out of the tower to avoid an incinerator death. A numbness took over everyone watching. The announcer stated that all flights in the air were ordered down immediately and all airports were being closed after landings were accomplished. Then the announcement came that a third plane had crashed into the Pentagon and a fourth into fields in Pennsylvania, apparently headed to Washington, D.C. We learned later that Rich Guadagno, manager of the Humboldt Bay National Wildlife Refuge, was killed on Flight 93—the one that crashed in Pennsylvania. Rich had just completed his law enforcement training at the Federal Law Enforcement Training Centers in Glynco, Georgia, and was returning home to California. His new credentials and badge were found hanging in a tree by an FBI agent searching the crash site for wreckage and evidence. We had no doubt that Rich would have been one of the active members of the passenger group that charged the cockpit and forced the crash landing short of the assumed target: the White House.

After silently praying for those in the line of devastation and trying to come out of shock, anger set in. Who were the cowardly bastards that would use innocent people as bombs to make their statement? They were Islamic zealots who believed that anyone other than Muslims had no right to be living. Worse, they thought Allah (God) would *reward* them for such despicable acts. Over man's existence on earth, religion has been a means to answer questions for which we had no answers. It has brought peace and kindness, hope and inspiration. There is no doubt religion has served a valuable purpose in the lives of ordinary people. But, it has also been the excuse for various groups of human beings to perform horrendous acts against their fellow human beings in an effort to eliminate different beliefs and prove that their religion was the only correct one. To prove one religion is the "right one," millions of lives have been lost. This is, unfortunately, not limited to the Muslim religion, as was the case here, but has been repeated over thousands of years by all religions.

There are significant similarities between religious zeal and racial, ethnic and gender bigotry. Both are manifestations of insecurity in one's own beliefs, in one's own abilities, and a lack of comfort in being who we are as individuals. Apparently, insecurity can only be satisfied through elimination of those who think differently. These Muslims had, on their own, declared war on America because we represent freedom of thought . . . and religion. I was reminded why I have never committed to a single religion. I remain open to different ways of viewing life and disdain condemnation of one religion by another. The Creator of the universe has the answers, not someone standing in a pulpit.

With the grounding of all flights, Mike was stuck in Atlanta and I insisted that he stay at our home until he could find a way to get back to Wyoming. People everywhere were opening their doors, some to strangers from other countries, because of the unity in disgust that these cowardly acts evoked. More than three thousand people lost their lives that day, and a new president had to kick into a higher gear. America was at war with terrorist groups, and President Bush told Congress and the world that any country that harbored these terrorists would be treated the same as the terrorists. It would be a new kind of war, one that was not nation against nation, but rather good against evil. The die was cast.

In President Bush's memoirs *Decision Points*, he goes into great, emotional detail about the aftermath of these despicable acts, the cowards who perpetrated them, and America's unified response. Tears filled my eyes as I was reminded why America is so loved by those in pursuit of peace and happiness, and so hated by those who have achieved nothing in their lives except to spew hatred in order to give themselves a false sense of superiority. I believe with all my heart in the Creator of the universe and an impending judgment. I pray to the God of love and kindness that the souls taken through those acts of hatred on 9/11 are allowed to witness the expulsion from heaven of all those who perpetrated them. I leave forgiveness to God. I shall forever hold on to my anger and memories of that day lest time erodes the repugnancy.

• • •

On December 7 we were having a regional directorate retreat at the community clubhouse in Sam's neighborhood when Sam walked up to me and said "Marshall wants you to call him at 2 o'clock." I responded that of course I would and asked if he knew what it was about. He was coy, but said he wasn't sure. At the appointed time, I stepped out of our meetings and called Deputy Director Marshall Jones. When I got him on the phone, he said, "Dale, I've got an assignment I need you to do. I want you to go to Albuquerque and be the acting regional director."

"Marshall, you've got Nancy Kaufman there as regional director. Is she doing something else for you? How long will you need me there?"

"I can't say on the first question, but it will either be for several months or permanently."

I had known Nancy for most of my career and considered her my friend. We didn't always agree on methods and approaches to conservation issues, but that didn't mean I didn't like and respect her. Pearl Harbor Day in 2001 marked another turning point in my career. I was SES and understood that my only honorable option if I didn't want to move again was to resign, and quitting was not in my makeup. I told Marshall I would certainly go to Albuquerque if that was where he and the FWS needed me. When I returned to the meeting, Sam threw a Southwest Region 2 T-shirt at me and said "Congratulations!"

That evening I called Nancy to tell her about my phone call and to assure her I had nothing to do with this change in leadership. She was emotional about the turn of events but told me she was glad that I was the one who was coming to take her place. That made me feel better, but it is always painful to see friends in distress. It was not the way I wanted it to unfold, but the next phase of my life was about to begin.

CHAPTER 14

The Rio Grande and Missouri Rivers

Even though it was December, Deputy Director Marshall Jones felt it important that I make a trip to Albuquerque quickly to assure everyone in the region that there would be a smooth transition in leadership. I flew out on Sunday, December 16, 2001, and reported for duty on the 17th. I met with Geoff Haskett, deputy regional director and former member of the Atlanta team, to get a feel for the emotions and anxiety of the employees. Because I had served as a field supervisor in the region, I was known to a significant number of employees and, while they were concerned for Nancy, Geoff let me know everyone was comfortable with me as the new regional director (RD) for however long it lasted. At 9 a.m. I met with the regional directorate, all of whom I also knew, and assured them that I would do all I could to catch up on their issues and support them in any way I could. I spent the next two days getting briefings and walking around the building saying hello to my new teammates, and then on Wednesday, December 19, flew back to Atlanta to spend the Christmas holidays with my family.

I returned to Albuquerque on January 2, 2002, for "several months or permanently," as Marshall had put it, caught a cab to the office, picked up a Durango from our law enforcement folks and headed south to Las Cruces for the Western Association of Fish and Wildlife Agencies meeting. The Western is a sectional group of the national Association of Fish and Wildlife Agencies (AFWA) and afforded me the opportunity to immediately get to know my state partners in the region. Region 2 encompasses only four states, but a lot of geography. New Mexico,

Arizona, Texas and Oklahoma would be my main focus for the foreseeable future, and I wanted to quickly demonstrate my desire to work in true partnership with these important allies. Larry Bell, director of New Mexico Game and Fish, was the host for the meeting. I spent the next three days getting to know Larry, Duane Shroufe of Arizona, Bob Cook (an old friend who had become executive director of the Texas Parks and Wildlife Department), and Greg Duffy of Oklahoma. I considered these the most important partners I could have in the management of fish and wildlife. The states are the frontline managers and have far more capability than the FWS in any given state to address an issue. The timing was perfect to build these critical relationships.

I returned to Albuquerque and settled into my new temporary home at the Residence Inn on the foothills of the Sandia Mountains. When I got up the next morning and drove down the hill into Albuquerque, I was struck by how wide open the landscape appeared. Coming from Atlanta, where there were trees everywhere to block the view, I felt as if I were in a fishbowl and could be seen "forever." It was intimidating, but after a couple of months my perspective changed. On a beautiful morning in March, I drove to work as the sun was shining across the city and on toward the desert. I remember thinking with much pleasure, "You can see forever." I laughed to myself as I recalled a different meaning to that phrase only a couple of months earlier. Albuquerque sits at an elevation of about 5,000 feet, just below the mile-high status. I was unprepared for the pleasant climate because I had the preconceived notion that Albuquerque was in the desert, hot and dry. While the relative humidity is extremely low, there are four distinct seasons and all of them, except for the dust storms of the spring upwelling from the desert below, are magnificent.

Pete Domenici and Jeff Bingaman were the two U.S. Senators for New Mexico and were clear with me that the Middle Rio Grande (MRG), which flowed past Albuquerque, and its most famous resident, the silvery minnow, were at the top of their list of important issues. I

Silvery Minnow (Courtesy of USFWS)

was back into the water challenges of the West and the endangered and threatened species that drove much of the water allocation discussions. The Bureau of Reclamation (BOR) regional office was in Arizona, and Bob Johnson was the regional director. I knew Bob but hadn't worked a great deal with him. That changed quickly with the Rio Grande and the Lower Colorado Rivers.

The BOR had an area office in Albuquerque, similar to the one we worked with in the Klamath Basin, that oversaw the Rio Grande operations and was the main face of the BOR on the river. Dr. Joy Nicholopoulos was the FWS Ecological Services supervisor for New Mexico and a highly capable leader. Egos were left at the door. She was always upbeat and brought that leadership style into every issue. Two thousand two was looking to be a drought year based on winter snowpack in the mountains. To people who live in arid climates with precipitation each year measured at twenty inches or less, the snowpack is critical. Nature evolved to have the snow start to melt in late spring and gradually flow through the summer. The fish in the rivers also adapted to this cycle by evolving their spawning strategy to take advantage of both the melting snow and the explosion of aquatic plant and insect life that emerges as food for the young, much as it does during flooding in bottomland hardwood wetlands.

Arid fish species nearly all spawn in the streams or newly inundated feather edges where the water slows. The silvery minnow (*Hybognathus amarus*) evolved to take advantage of this cycle and lives only one to two years; thus, they make great use of a good water year and "survive" poor years. This 3.5-inch fish was historically very abundant and served as forage food for resident fish and wading birds. But when Europeans expanded their settlement into New Mexico, the demands on a limited water supply increased. Hydrogeologists quickly learned that although the aquifer beneath Albuquerque was once advertised as being the size of a Great Lake, the recharge of the aquifer was far slower than the increased withdrawals. Soon, restrictions were placed on groundwater withdrawals, and the state engineer assumed responsibility to permit new wells. But no one was focusing on the silvery minnow.

The Rio Grande is one of two major rivers in New Mexico, with the Pecos conveying drainage from the eastern part of the state and joining the Rio Grande in Mexico just above the Amistad Dam. The Rio Grande begins in southern Colorado and flows to the Gulf, with its lower reach in Texas constituting the border with Mexico. The total length of the river is approximately 1,900 miles with a watershed that covers approximately 180,000 square miles, but the rainfall in the basin averages less than twenty inches per year. Commercial navigation is impossible due to the shallowness and periodic drying of portions of the river. Because of heavy withdrawals from the river for human use along the entire length of the Rio Grande, due to urban growth and restrictions on groundwater withdrawals, freshwater flows reaching the Gulf of Mexico are less than a quarter of pre-settlement quantities. In a highly populated area that's defined as a desert due to its low average rainfall, stresses on the natural resources are inevitable.

The silvery minnow was listed as endangered by the FWS in 1994 due to the significant decline in its habitat and range. Historically a

Middle Rio Grande River (Courtesy of USACE)

prominent resident of the entire MRG, which is defined as beginning just below the San Luis Valley, loss of aquatic habitat through water management and withdrawals reduced the available area to less than 10 percent of the minnow's historical range. As Joy explained the facts of 2002 that were beginning to develop, I was reminded of the Klamath Basin and the emergency actions we took to sandbag and capture the fish before harm ensued. But no such opportunity existed on the MRG.

The BOR had several "re-regulating" dams along the Rio Grande whose purpose was to capture and control flows on the river, thus managing whatever acre-feet they could for water deliveries and Endangered Species Act (ESA) compliance. As the spring moved into the summer, water conditions did not improve. The BOR reinitiated ESA consultation with the FWS because they realized they might not be able to meet the parameters of the 2001 programmatic opinion. As Joy and her staff worked on the new consultation, a sinking feeling started to develop in the pit of my stomach. An added complication came into play with the triggering of the New Mexico/Texas Rio Grande Compact agreement, which outlined actions to ensure that Texas received their fair share of river flows from New Mexico below Elephant Butte Reservoir.

Between the drought and the Compact requirements, little water remained in Heron Reservoir just above Albuquerque to provide for the needs of the silvery minnow. The BOR's decision-making ability was quickly disappearing. If in a biological opinion under the ESA it is determined that the action proposed by the agency is likely to cause jeopardy to the species, the FWS must make every effort to identify a reasonable and prudent alternative (RPA) to the agency's action that accomplishes some portion of the objective; is not cost prohibitive; and *is within the authority of the action agency*. The BOR was proposing to release all remaining water still under its control to assist the minnow in the Albuquerque Reach of the MRG. If they did that, and the drought continued, there would be no water available in the spring for the critical spawning necessary to keep a species going that only had, at most, two opportunities to spawn in its lifetime. Our biologists believed there was no avoiding a jeopardy determination.

If the water were held in the reservoir for the spring spawning event, they would have to call jeopardy on the immediate needs of the fish during the drought. The FWS found itself in a position of jeopardy if the minor amount of water (still under BORs control) were released at the end of summer, and jeopardy if it were retained in the reservoir. The finding of the opinion stated this, as well as the fact that there was no reasonable and prudent alternative available. I had no experience with this type of situation. No one did. Normally with jeopardy opinions, the action agency is simply directed to either abandon the proposal or cease ongoing activities to avoid jeopardy. That was not an option here. The FWS directed the BOR to leave the water in Heron Reservoir (thus taking no action). The team of biologists that worked on the MRG and managed the minnows would monitor the situation daily and give further directions if the drought continued. I signed the opinion, and Joy delivered it to Ken Maxey of the BOR.

Environmental groups represented by Letty Belin and Laird Lucas sued the BOR and FWS to require that the water in Heron Reservoir be released immediately to benefit the fishes in the Albuquerque Reach. They also demanded that the BOR deny delivery of contract water that could be used to benefit the fish. This lawsuit, in my opinion, helped bring the true conflict to light. The real issue was simply too much demand for water by people and too little water resources to satisfy both people and nature. The silvery minnow was the messenger, not the villain. There were those who wanted to shoot the messenger, but the message remained accurate, nonetheless.

On September 18, 2002, the federal court hearing was convened by Judge James A. Parker on the matter of *Rio Grande Silvery Minnow, et al. vs John W. Keys, III, et al.* John Keys was the commissioner of the BOR and a wonderful individual. Like those of the FWS, however, his hands were tied. He had conflicting responsibilities that had to be reconciled. The witness list was short, so we knew it wouldn't be just a few questions and sit down. The first witness was Ken Maxey, representing the Bureau of Reclamation. I had learned long ago that a witness should never enter a discussion of fact unless s/he observed the fact or it is in one's area of expertise. Maxey was there to testify on the facts of the BOR authority and activities, as well as any other guiding principles that might influence the action of the BOR. Unfortunately, he strayed considerably and offered opinions outside his expertise. This led to substantial cross-examination.

The other two witnesses were to be me, followed by Joy. Our contributions were planned to be about the silvery minnow needs and how the ESA instructed they be addressed. Mr. Lucas did nearly all of the questioning regarding this complicated issue of jeopardy with no RPA, and had apparently not taken time to look at my biographical information prior to the trial. He began by asking, "You're a wildlife biologist, so you don't have any real expertise in fisheries, is that correct?" "No Sir, that's not correct," I replied. "I have a master of science degree in fisheries biology with an emphasis in the early life history of fish. That entails the spawning, larval and juvenile stages of fishes."

From that point forward, his questions led right into my educational training, so I spent as much time answering questions about the biology of the silvery minnow as I did on the ESA. At one point, I took the opportunity to educate a very attentive judge by telling him "Water is not habitat. It is simply a medium in which habitat can be created. Indeed, it can be harmful to aquatic species if it destroys the essential life requisites so important to fish growth and development, instead of providing the medium for them to be created." I wanted the court to understand that pushing significant amounts of water downstream could actually damage the eggs and larvae by blowing them out of the habitat they so desperately needed. The judge was taking that in, and I believe he understood.

The plaintiffs had retained scientific experts who simply recommended that substantially more water be sent down the river. I wanted to make sure that the needs of the fish were out there front and center. The silvery minnow female will broadcast between 2,500 and 3,000 eggs that, once fertilized, normally hatch within twenty-four hours to take full advantage of the short window of good water conditions. Larval growth is also accelerated and can be completed in as little as three days. For this to occur, however, spawning takes place in the shallow water edges that have recently been inundated by the snowmelt, in areas where the velocity of the current is less than one-half cubic foot per second, or very slow. While they are an extremely compacted example of the floodplain, these "feather edges" perform many of the same functions. This allows the eggs to stay in the protected vegetated shallows and the larvae to hatch and begin to feed, and then move into the stronger current as juveniles much more in control of their swimming ability. When higher-velocity water is injected into this dynamic, eggs and larvae are literally blown out of the desired habitat and are either eaten or die when they are no longer in the proximity of algal blooms and invertebrate swarms so necessary for their survival.

In response to a question regarding how many larval fishes are believed to die in the capturing and relocation to safer areas of the stream, I responded "Those numbers of 50 percent mortality are less than commonly occurs in nature. The silvery minnow is a broadcast spawner and has a fecundity—number of eggs produced—of between 2,500 and 3,000. The ultimate objective of the spawning and recruitment process is to replace their spawning parents with one male and one female to successfully reproduce and keep the species going. Obviously, in a species that is in trouble, we would like to see better recruitment than that. But six instead of two stands the chance to triple the population if accomplished across the board. It is not uncommon for 90 percent to die when the yolk is absorbed if no external food is available."

The last line of questioning was on the "jeopardy, no matter what we do" problem. When asked why I wouldn't want the BOR to release water now for the fish, I responded "Because for now, the fish in the Albuquerque Reach are being monitored by competent staff from the FWS, BOR, state and City of Albuquerque. I would rather not play the card that might be our last if the drought continues, and not have any cards to play to continue the spawning and recruitment so important to survival and recovery of a species that only lives one to two years. I believe, and the FWS believes, that the prudent thing to do is monitor day by day and do what is proven to be necessary when, and only when, that proof is before us." As we ended the trial, Judge Parker took the unusual step of asking me a question as I was sitting in the audience. "Mr. Hall. Have you ever faced this type situation before, or do you know of it ever occurring before?" I responded "No, Your Honor. I have not and do not know of it ever occurring."

With that, the trial ended without calling Joy to the stand. Both sides believed they had tortured me enough, and gave Joy a reprieve. Ironically, as I was testifying, I could see the rain hitting the courtroom windows and hear the thunder.

Judge Parker ruled to require that the water be released from Heron Reservoir for the fish. He admitted that the options were few. He fully expected that there would be an appeal, but the rains provided the relief necessary. While Judge Parker was deciding on the case, rain brought enough water for the BOR to meet the 2001 opinion requirements. Everyone, especially Judge Parker, had dodged the bullet of setting precedent for "jeopardy, no matter what we do." However, the other ruling in his opinion—that the BOR had the authority to take water from cities and farms to comply with the ESA, even in other tributary streams—remained a significant question to be heard by the Tenth Circuit Court of Appeals.

In January 2003, the Tenth Circuit heard arguments from environmentalists and water "contractors" about the authorities and obligations of the Bureau of Reclamation to reduce contract water deliveries to provide for the conservation of the silvery minnow. Mayor Martin Chavez and the City of Albuquerque were among the municipal contractors, with the Middle Rio Grande Conservancy District (MRGCD) representing the agricultural irrigation contractors. Governor Bill Richardson and the State of New Mexico were also intervenors. In his ruling, Judge Parker found that the BOR had the obligation to reduce deliveries to both the municipalities and irrigation districts, if necessary, to provide for the needs of a listed species, even to include water from another river. At issue was water from the San Juan–Chama Project in northern New Mexico and a tributary to the Rio Grande.

Historically, only water within the Rio Grande system had been considered fair game for non-contract uses. Judge Parker found that the ESA took precedent over negotiated contracts by the federal government. Water is a natural resource that cannot be owned by individuals, but is instead held in trust for all citizens. Water contracts evolved in the western U.S. to be viewed by the holder as a firm right, even to be passed along in wills. Judge Parker had turned that upside down. Even though releasing water from Heron had been resolved by fall rains, the finding of ESA requirements remained and, if upheld by the circuit court, would apply to New Mexico, Colorado, Kansas, Oklahoma, Utah and Wyoming. There was much at stake in this appeals court hearing.

Both the BOR and the Army Corps of Engineers realized they needed a longer-term solution to managing the Rio Grande for contractors and endangered species. The decision was made to develop a ten-year plan and produce a programmatic biological opinion, much like the one done for the Northwest Forest Plan. While the Tenth Circuit was considering the appeal, a formal request for consultation was received by the FWS on February 9, with the BOR taking the lead on behalf of the Corps and the non-federal agencies: the MRGCD and State of New Mexico. The City of Albuquerque, though not a participant, offered any help in the form of measures to assure success. Mayor Marty Chavez was all in for finding a long-term solution.

Dr. Joy Nicholopoulos had been the field supervisor in Albuquerque since the late 1990s. She later said,

> When I walked in the door and Nancy Kaufman was the RD, she very much wanted to take a hard line on the Rio Grande.

Her reason was the various personalities, previous field supervisors and the way the BOR and Corps had been treating the FWS. Lead FWS biologist for MRG issues Jeff Whitney was trying to get the two groups together, and they came to be known as the 'Green Group and the White Group.' The Green Group was the environmentalists, and the White Group was government agencies, Interstate Stream Commission and the state engineer's office. This eventually evolved into the ESA Working Group, which caught the attention of Senators Domenici and Bingaman, who started putting their support behind this collaborative effort. (Nicholopoulos 2020)

It was clear that the "team" of disparate stakeholders had to come together or there would be constant litigation with no one ever really winning. Joy and her staff took advantage of the ESA Working Group and brought everyone in to sit at the table with the official consulting parties. Building an environmental program to work with the water delivery requirements held the long-term solution, but it wasn't easy.

Renne Lohoefener [ES Texas state administrator] had warned me about the warring parties and that I would be in court, so I needed to understand the different concerns. Through these negotiations, it became clear to the non-federal parties that splitting the federal agencies was not going to work, so they all agreed to come to the same table, and work out how they would work together. (Nicholopoulos 2020)

The programmatic biological opinion came together quickly because of all the work prior to the *Silvery Minnow v John Keys* hearing. I brought some experience from the northwest forests, California Bay-Delta Accord and the Everglades, so I assisted in every way I could to help get a strong opinion over the finish line in short order.

You sat with us in my conference room and helped write the opinion. Then we called Senators Domenici and Bingaman to ask for their help in having all the parties give it a chance. We had welcomed everyone's input, even though it was our responsibility. But that's when we came up with the term 'Parties to the Consultation' so all the activities weren't on the BOR or the Corps. The BOR took it on and became responsible actors and put their heart into it. We wrote into the opinion that this group would do this, the state will do that, MRGCD is responsible for certain things. It wasn't all on the BOR and Corps. That really solidified the ESA Working Group. We really broke new ground! At our highest point, the group received $11 million for conservation on the MRG. (Nicholopoulos 2020)

Once again, progress started occurring when people stopped fighting long enough to sit down and listen to other points of view. A simple show of respect leads to friendship, then friendship leads to trust. On March 17, 2003, I signed the *Programmatic Biological and Conference Opinions On the Effects of Actions Associated with the Programmatic Biological Assessment of Bureau of Reclamation's Water and River Maintenance Operations, Army Corps of Engineers' Flood Control Operation, and Related Non-Federal Actions on the Middle Rio Grande, New Mexico*, in effect upon signing until February 28, 2013, unless modified by future reinitiation of consultation.

• • •

As the summer months started unfolding, it continued to be dry and foretold the probability of more conflict as we entered the late summer and fall in the absence of rain. Senator Domenici began talking about having a "fix to the minnow problem" even before the Tenth Circuit released its opinion that Judge Parker was correct, and the ESA water was to be accommodated *before* contract water. Thankfully, the issue wasn't about our opinion, but about Judge Parker's. In upholding the District Court's findings, the Circuit Court had expanded the lower court opinion to apply in six states instead of just New Mexico. The political realities were heating up, and both Bingaman and Domenici were pushing for serious actions. Senator Bingaman publicly asked Governor Richardson to request the God Squad. To put that in context, that's a Democratic senator asking a Democratic governor to request the God Squad from a Republican secretary of the interior! There would almost certainly be congressional action of some kind due to the magnet pulling in five other western states with their own water issues, but the God Squad was not the right tool.

Headlines of "Domenici Says Ruling 'Favors Fish Over People'" and "Domenici Tries to Stop Minnow Plan" were ever-present as everyone from Mayor Chavez to the State of New Mexico condemned the Tenth Circuit Opinion. Senator Domenici immediately went to work with Senator Bingaman and New Mexico Congressman Steve Pearce to craft changes to the ESA, or at least protect the human interests of the MRG. Senator Bingaman at first opposed some of the changes to the law that Domenici was proposing but, after discussion and compromise, they agreed on specific language to protect the minnow while also protecting contract water deliveries. It turned out that our programmatic biological opinion, crafted with the help of the ESA Working Group, provided the protections that everyone except radical environmental groups, like Forest Guardians and the Center for Biological Diversity, believed were necessary. It provided for the minnow and irrigators without having to plan on water from the San Juan–Chama basin.

I accompanied Senator Domenici, Joy, Mayor Chavez, the BOR and others on an extensive tour of the Rio Grande from Albuquerque south so Domenici could understand all the complex issues we had taken on and tried to resolve. After the trip, I received a nice note thanking me for all our efforts. Senators Domenici and Bingaman had fully bought into our collaborative work with all the partners along the river and were determined to use it as an example of how the federal government should work with local citizens. The hard work of Joy, Jeff Whitney and many others to build partnerships was paying off. Following the Tenth Circuit opinion, work began in earnest to craft legislative language in the 2004 Appropriations Bill that would put a protective shield around our March 2003 opinion. Support from partners like the MRGCD helped push it along. In a letter to Congressman Tom Udall, MRGCD Chief Engineer Subhas Shah wrote,

> The current Biological Opinion recognizes these important facts and implements rational solutions for keeping this stretch of the river wet. The MRGCD has participated in making the intent of the Biological Opinion a reality. The collective effort of MRGCD and many other entities has avoided direct confrontations between irrigators and the United States, and has likewise allowed the City of Albuquerque to go forward with their development of a surface water diversion project for its San Juan–Chama water . . . For this reason, I respectfully urge you to take the following actions:
>
> 1. Contact the Secretary of the Interior to stand behind the positions of the United States Fish and Wildlife Service in their March 17, 2003 biological opinion and in their agreements with the Middle Rio Grande Conservancy District. (Shah 2003)

On July 16, 2003, the Senate Energy and Water Development Appropriations Subcommittee approved language to bar the use of San Juan–Chama Project water to protect the silvery minnow. Senator Pete Domenici also included language that would put into law the March

2003 biological opinion, designed to "ensure the survival of the silvery minnow." Concurrent with the Senate Subcommittee beginning their process, the House was approving a bill with similar language to shield the FWS from litigation on the opinion. The full Senate approved language offered by both Senators Domenici and Bingaman for what the press dubbed the "Minnow Measure" on September 16, 2003. The full appropriations bill was sent to President George W. Bush for his signature on November 20.

> Section 208(b) Complying with the reasonable and prudent alternatives and the incidental take limits defined in the Biological Opinion released by the United States Fish and Wildlife Service dated March 17, 2003 combined with efforts carried pursuant to Public Law 106-377, Public Law 107-66, and Public Law 108-7** [a 108th Congress Joint Resolution to pass the budget] fully meet all requirements of the Endangered Species Act (16 U.S.C. 1531 et seq) for the conservation of the Rio Grande Silvery Minnow (Hybognathus amarus) and the Southwestern Willow Flycatcher (Empidonax trailii extimus) on the Middle Rio Grande in New Mexico.
>
> (c) This section applies only to those Federal agency and non-Federal actions addressed in the March 17, 2003 Biological Opinion.
>
> (d) Subsection (b) will remain in effect for 2 years following the implementation of this Act. (U.S. Congress FY 2004 Energy and Water Development Appropriations Act)

Section 209 formally established the Endangered Species Collaborative Program—the new identity of the ESA Working Group—and funds were appropriated to support its activities. *For the first and only time in history*, an ESA biological opinion developed as an administrative action by the executive branch was embraced by the legislative branch and made into law. The opinion, and legal protection against litigation, was in force for two years or until such time under the law that reinitiation of consultation was triggered. It also entrusted the management of the river to a team that truly represented the people who lived and depended on it.

As we sat in Albuquerque getting the news that this had happened, I called Joy to congratulate her on an achievement of a lifetime. To my knowledge, she is the only field supervisor in history to have a biological opinion made into law. I have no doubt whatsoever that this occurred because of her leadership in pulling people together, being willing to listen and, if an idea made biological sense, to include it in the opinion regardless of the originator. Respect, trust and believing in the team equals good governance. The only real power any of us has is that which we share.

• • •

Dr. Steven A. Williams is a highly intelligent, highly qualified biologist with a résumé of overseeing fish and wildlife management activities in state agencies. His easygoing demeanor and sense of humor sometimes led to the perception that he was just a good old boy. That trap was sprung on more than one person. After a several-month delay due to arguments between Senator Trent Lott and the administration over the migratory bird hunting season, Steve was confirmed as director of the FWS on January 29, 2002. Games like this are often played through a Senate confirmation process to extract an agreement on a topic that has nothing to do with the qualifications of the nominee.

Steve immediately connected with many of us, but it was clear he didn't intend to spend a lot of time on the ESA. "I told them if they wanted an endangered species director, I was not the person for the job," he said. "I wanted as little to do with the ESA as possible." The priority most important to him, which was repairing the significantly damaged relationship between the FWS and the state fish and wildlife agencies, was certainly needed. The eight years of the Clinton administration's disregard for the state agencies had not boded well. Steve and I were never at odds on a strategy or issue.

I was in my office in Albuquerque in mid-October 2003 when I was told Steve was on the line. He got right to the point and, almost apologetically, said "I need you to do something for me." "Sure, if I can," I responded. "What do you need?"

"Craig Manson wants you and Robyn Thorson to head a team to look at the ESA needs on the Missouri River with a fresh set of eyes."

"Why do you need me? The Missouri isn't in my region, and Ralph Morgenweck in Denver has always handled that along with Region 3."

"Judge Manson wants a fresh set of eyes looking at the data and figuring out what needs to be done."

"I see. Is this a request, or are you giving me the assignment?" "I'm afraid you don't have a choice on this one," Steve replied. "You and Robyn Thorson will lead the team."

"OK. Two questions. I will not sign an opinion I do not believe is scientifically and legally correct. Is there a preconceived outcome expected? Second, do Robyn and I have the authority to choose our own team from across the country?"

"I have absolute assurance that your directive is to follow the science wherever it leads. I give you my word you won't be asked to do anything but that. And yes, you have my approval to select whomever you and Robyn believe are the best to look at the interior least tern, piping plover and pallid sturgeon."

I accepted the assignment even though I was not comfortable taking the place of a sitting regional director on an issue that was his responsibility, but also understood that Craig and Steve were the assistant secretary and director, and had the right to bring in anyone they wanted on any given issue. I also knew this would not sit well with Ralph Morgenweck. Steve said he would let Ralph know of this decision and asked me to call the director's office and let him know if we needed anything. I called Robyn and we began making plans. We were given a deadline of

December 15 to complete the consultation. By the time the team was assembled, the deadline would be only forty-five days away. The first order of business was to immediately select the team and plan our first gathering with the Corps. Robyn worked on a schedule and found that the earliest we could get together with the Corps was on November 12 and 13 in Minneapolis.

The Missouri River is the longest river in the United States, spanning more than 2,300 miles. Its headwaters originate at Bower's Spring, Montana, and its mouth is at the confluence of the Mississippi River near St. Louis. The watershed is estimated at more than 500,000 square miles, and drains parts of ten states and two Canadian provinces. Indigenous nomadic peoples are estimated to have been using the river for more than 12,000 years as they traversed the Great Plains. Fur trade began in the early 1800s as trappers explored the new lands and others searched for a pathway to the Pacific Ocean. Steamboat traffic was the primary source of commerce until completion of the transcontinental railroad provided a faster and more economical means for movement of goods and people.

The Yellowstone River is considered the largest tributary by volume of the Missouri, with the Platte as the next largest. Elevation changes from over 14,000 feet at Mount Lincoln in Colorado to less than 500 feet at its mouth. The lower portion of the river becomes flat and has less than a ten-foot change in elevation per mile. Dams were constructed over the years to manage the river for flood control, irrigation and navigation. The Big Muddy, as the Missouri is also called, earned that name by its tremendous sediment (silt) loads. Prior to human intervention, the river carried as much as 290 million metric tons of silt each year. After construction of dams and levees, that number dropped to less than 25 million metric tons.

Like the Mississippi, the Missouri River basin suffered significantly from the flood of 1927, reduced transportation of goods and materials during the Great Depression, and the long drought that turned the southwestern Great Plains into the Dust Bowl. The New Deal under President

Roosevelt put more than 50,000 people to work building Fort Peck Dam in Montana. In the 1950s, construction began on five mainstem dams: Garrison, Oahe, Big Bend, Fort Randall and Gavins Point. These reservoirs capture significant amounts of sediment each year, destructive to the purposes of the dams and depriving the river of sediment for shoreline habitat building. Together they are estimated to be able to store 74.1 million acre-feet of water, significantly exceeding the annual average flow of the river. The longest tributary, and second by volume, is the Platte River, which merges with the Missouri at Omaha. After entering the Mississippi, the Missouri accounts for an estimated 45 percent of that river's flows in any given year.

The people along this massive river generate a myriad of needs and desired uses. Conflict has been a characteristic of this basin almost from the beginning. The Indian Wars and efforts to remove Native Americans from their traditional lands were followed by conflicts in managing the river for flood control and navigation. In 1929, the Missouri River Navigation Commission estimated the amount of goods shipped on the river annually at 13.6 million metric tons. However, that number had been reduced to just over 600,000 metric tons around 2000, and that was in the lower river, primarily carrying gravel and sand. The controversy over navigation as a legitimate use of the river, to the exclusion of other uses, was well under way.

The Flood Control Act of 1944 established federal authorities and operational rules of engagement on the Missouri between the Corps and the BOR. Historically, the Corps' mission is to provide for flood control and navigation, whereas the BOR mission is to manage and deliver water for irrigation and municipal water supply. The Missouri traverses the dividing line in the middle of the continent, so a plan had to be developed regarding federal responsibilities on the river. Lewis A. Pick was the director of the Missouri River office of the Corps, and William G. Sloan was the director of the Billings, Montana, office of the BOR. Both were on-the-ground managers and were tasked with developing a plan to divide responsibilities along the river. The final agreement, implemented in the 1944 Act, in general terms gave the Corps authority over navigation and flood control on the mainstem and the BOR authority for irrigation and water management on the Yellowstone and Platte. The Yellowstone would prove to be a significant recovery opportunity in the biological opinion.

> The employee with the BOR was an assistant regional director, not a commissioner. These were people who had their Bureau's interests at heart and came up with the plan. Part of it was that part of the country crosses the 100th meridian, which generally marks the place where, if you are east of that point, you don't need to irrigate for agriculture. If you are west of the 100th meridian, you generally do need to irrigate for agriculture. It is not exact, but in general it is true. Reclamation's job was mostly to provide water for irrigation of agriculture. The Corps had the navigation side and flood control as their primary missions. In the big picture it was a political turf battle between two big agencies, but in reality it turned out to be a pretty good partnership. (Patterson 2020).

By July 2003 things were heating up on the Missouri River. Federal District Court Judge Gladys Kessler found the Corps of Engineers in contempt of court for refusing to follow the 2000 biological opinion and lower the summer flows of the Missouri for endangered birds. The Corps maintained that they needed to keep the levels high to support barge traffic. Judge Kessler ordered the secretary of the army and the Corps to pay $500,000 per day for each day the Corps refused to comply. She sent the message that tougher penalties could follow if the Corps didn't get in line. My old friend from Klamath and California water issues, Roger Patterson, had retired from the BOR in 1999 to become director of the Nebraska Department of Natural Resources (DNR). By the time I got involved, Roger had been embroiled in the issue for quite some time.

> It was really fueled by this ongoing Upper Basin versus Lower Basin tussle due to the drought in the '90s, which really accentuated the problem, particularly for the folks in the Upper Basin. They watched Garrison and other dams being drawn down to try to float barges downstream, and there weren't any barges! It started getting pretty political and forced higher-ups to say 'Yes, we need to take a look at that.' The Corps went through a process of updating the Master Manual for the operation of the river and rebalancing to the degree consistent with federal law. They looked at what they could do to manage the system in different conditions, especially after going through the drought. That triggered the need for a consultation under the ESA because it was an action of a federal agency that required compliance with the Act. The ESA became the second level of controversy behind the upper versus lower basin states, and the low number of barges that actually floated the Missouri (estimated at less than a dozen per year). In that part of the geography, there were really different levels of experience with the ESA. We knew about the ESA in Nebraska for years because we had been working on the Platte River for the listed species there. In Missouri, the ESA was an unknown, and seen as unimportant.
>
> When the FWS started getting involved in the analysis, they came up with things that cut both ways and impacted folks both upstream and downstream. Things like pulse flows were not viewed in their interest; not helpful to their concerns. The upper basin was seeing water go out of Gavins Point and saying 'What's the deal?' And the lower basin states were saying 'You're just jumping the river up and down.' That's when the focus started shifting over to the ESA. We in Nebraska were

trying to help the FWS. Larry Cieslik, operations manager with the Corps in Omaha, understood the arguments but also knew the Corps had to navigate through the ESA. Senator Kit Bond was making big speeches that he would 'kill this ESA stuff, it was a bunch of baloney,' that he would 'talk to the president and get this mess straightened out.' The decision that came out of the administration was 'we are going to bring in a new team to deal with the ESA.' The response from Missouri was 'See, we got it. Our needs are going to be met. They're bringing in a new team. This is good.' The new team was you and Robyn.

It surprised a lot of people when you picked some people who had been working on this for a long time to be part of the team, which was really smart, but some people's view was that anyone who worked on this in the past are gone. Then you picked some select people, and they were the right ones to work on this. (Patterson 2020).

I had worked on several high-profile endangered species issues and knew where to find the seasoned field and regional biologists who would be up to this task. Not only did we want people who were experts in the ESA, but also experts whose credentials in fish and avian biology were well established. The consultation would involve four species: pallid sturgeon (*Scaphirhynchus albus*), the interior least tern (*Sterna antillarum*), Northern Great Plains population of the piping plover (*Charadrius melodus*) and the American bald eagle (*Haliaeetus leucocephalus*). The finding of no jeopardy for the bald eagle had previously been determined but would have to be reconfirmed under the amended proposal.

Robyn and I decided it was critical to have some on the team from both Region 6 and Region 3 because the implementation of the opinion for the coming years would return to those regions, which meant that having buy-in of the findings was paramount to long-term success. In short, it was critical that they own the opinion. The following all-star team was "drafted" by Robyn and me, with some as willing participants and others who were less pleased. But each one was a professional and accepted the assignment with a dedication to make the biological opinion "rock solid."

> Joyce Collins, ES project leader in Marion, Illinois; Philip Delphey, endangered species coordinator in Twin Cities, MN; Mark Dryer, fisheries project leader in Ashland, WI; Mary Henry, ES ARD in Denver, CO; Lynn Lewis, ES program supervisor in Twin Cities, MN; Renne Lohoefener, ES Texas state administrator in Austin, TX; Joy Nicholopoulos, ES project leader in Albuquerque, NM; Michael Olson, Missouri River coordinator in Bismarck, ND; Charles Scott, ES project leader in Columbia, MO; Michael Thabault, consultation biologist in the Endangered Species Program, Washington, DC; Noreen Walsh, ES deputy ARD in Atlanta, GA; Teresa (Nichols) Woods, special assistant for ecosystems in Twin Cities, MN; and Charles Wooley, ES ARD in Twin Cities, MN. Robyn Thorson and I were the team leaders and would sign the final opinion.

This team was intentionally made up of people who understood the importance of the assignment and had the superior teamwork skills necessary for accomplishing the task. Each was not only scientifically qualified, but had experience working on dynamic teams. Also, there was clear expertise in sturgeons, terns and plovers. We also had the commitment from the U.S. Geological Survey that two of their scientists, Drs. Robert Jacobson and David Galat, would be available to provide technical assistance, but as research scientists would not be deciding team members. We were ready to meet with the Corps in Minneapolis. Prior to that meeting, we assembled the team in the Twin Cities Regional Office at Ft. Snelling to make sure everyone had the chance to ask questions, and we could set the "ground rules" for team operations.

The trepidation some felt when we "asked" them to be on the team was because of the relationship between President Bush and Missouri Senator Kit Bond. During his campaign for president in 2000, candidate Bush met with a group of Corps of Engineers supporters that Kit Bond had assembled who opposed a return to the natural system of a spring rise on the Missouri River. The spring rise performed the same function it did for the Red River in the Avoyelles case: it triggered spawning of fish and the explosion of life so essential to river health. Farmers and barge operators opposed a spring rise and were able to secure a promise from candidate Bush that, if he were elected president, he would oppose any spring rise on the river. Team members who had previously worked on the Missouri were aware of this promise and, understandably, worried that they would be told what the opinion must conclude.

As we sat in the conference room, Robyn and I at the head of the table, we assured the team that neither of us would sign an opinion that did not fully represent their analyses and findings. Further, we relayed the message the director had given us—that our only charge was to follow the science and go wherever it leads. Judge Manson was adamant that his

Pallid Sturgeon (Courtesy of USFWS)

only objective was to have a "fresh set of eyes" go through the existing, and any new, data. We appointed Charlie Wooley as the sturgeon team lead and Mary Henry as the bird team lead. Charlie was from Region 3 and Mary was in Region 6; the perfect combination for follow-up work with the Corps in the coming years. Robyn relayed how the assignment unfolded for her:

> In February or early March, I knew I would be going to the Midwest Region as regional director, but I was still in D.C. as the assistant director for external affairs. I was told I had to go to NCTC [National Conservation Training Center] for a meeting with the Corps to talk about the Missouri River biological assessment situation. The meeting was managed by General [David] Fastabend, the division commander in Portland. He got a Magic Marker in his hand and worked the discussion with the FWS. I had never seen a general get that engaged in a discussion before. I met Mike Olson and Charlie Scott there, both of whom were the stalwarts of the river and had participated in the 2000 biological opinion. That's how it started for me. I was just hoping Ralph would own this thing and I wouldn't have to deal with it!
>
> I started in the Midwest Region in April and as the summer progressed there was more rumbling about the Missouri River, but I thought that was something Ralph did in Denver. Occasionally, I would be briefed by the ES team because we had the state of Missouri, but historically it had really been managed out of Region 6. There was an agreement with the Corps and, on September 29, Judge Manson sent a memo to the FWS saying 'Here is the schedule for formal consultation on the Missouri River.' There was some back and forth in October about their BA [biological assessment] and other issues, but Judge Manson directed the Service to initiate consultation on the Corps' action. On about October 10, I got told I would be working with you

on this opinion. Judge Manson said 'I know it has been looked at twenty times, but I want it looked at for the twenty-first time with a fresh set of eyes.'

Our task was to build the strongest team possible with the people who had both extensive experience working the ESA and were fresh eyes. We got Joy Nicholopoulos, Noreen Walsh, Teresa Woods and others who had varying but significant expertise and experience. They needed to have an open mind and the ability to focus on this for the next forty-five days. One of the things I remember most distinctly was us assuring the team that no one was telling them how this opinion would come out. We just wanted them to look at it anew and follow the science. (Thorson 2020)

Various members of the team later told me their thoughts about that effort.

Noreen Walsh: From the beginning, I felt the teams [fish and birds] were given free rein to do the analyses that they thought were appropriate and come back with conclusions and recommendations that each of the species teams felt were appropriate, well-founded and underpinned with sound science, no matter what the ultimate answer might be. There was no backdrop of 'make sure you don't bring us a jeopardy opinion.' That was liberating for all the folks to know that we could follow where the science took us. (Walsh 2020)

Charles Wooley: I was the ARD-ES in Minneapolis working for Robyn in 2003 when we did this. I knew this was coming and was hoping I'd get an opportunity. What impressed me was the character of the people you and Robyn selected, the very good technical and scientific understanding each of us brought to this issue, as well as the aspect that we knew, as career employees, that there was going to be a little give-and-take with folks in the assistant secretary's office and the army. You, Robyn, Judge Manson and Steve Williams assured us that we could follow the science and that our integrity was not going to be impacted. I know we had some head-butting with the Assistant Secretary of the Army John Paul Woodley, and that was interesting, to deal with the pushback, but I always felt we had a tremendous amount of credibility. The skill set you and Robyn put together concerning the science, but also the ability to articulate what we thought, was pretty impressive. (Wooley 2020)

Joy Nicholopoulos: It was a god-awful mess until the team got involved! It was taken away from one region, and the team took over. There was another regional director who was not too happy that you and Robyn had taken over and created a new team, and he let it be known to everyone. His Region 6 person on the team, Mary Henry, had her work cut out for her. She had to call Ralph every day to let him know what happened that day, did anyone say anything about him, etc. He put her in a terrible, terrible spot. I learned about that after the fact, but it was truly sad. We got an immense amount of work done in a very short period of time, and the way that you and Robyn led the team, going from one location to another, made a real difference. The team jelled and bonded. Everyone gave 120 percent. I remember one night I was so tired I just curled up in the conference room at the Drury because we had sole access to it. I slept for two or three hours in my clothes, got up and went home, took a shower and came back for another day. We didn't mind working because it was fun and rewarding. We felt we were doing something really important. We were treated so well, and everyone listened to our opinions.

It was a defining period in my growth as a biologist and,

frankly, as a leader watching you and Robyn lead the team and how it worked. All those personalities working together, working as hard as we worked, it was good experience and a bright spot in my career. (Nicholopoulos 2020)

• • •

On November 4, 2003, Corps Brigadier General William Grisoli, the new division engineer, formally transmitted the Corps' biological assessment (BA) to Director Steve Williams. Normally, the BA would be sent to the regional director in charge of the FWS for the consultation but, because of the uniqueness of this one, it was transmitted to the director. The biological assessment is done by the action agency and is required to explain the proposed action and the possible effects on listed species that may occur. The agency can recommend a finding that the action "May affect, but is not likely to adversely affect" which, if agreed to by the FWS, would end the consultation process. Generally, this only occurs when there is no "take" of listed species expected. In this case, which involved river operations and reinitiation of an existing opinion, the Corps complied with the ESA and provided a twenty-seven-page BA with five appendices totaling eighty-nine pages of in-depth discussions of data and proposed alternatives.

When we gathered at Ft. Snelling to begin the formal consultation, we invited the Corps to provide presentations on their activities on the river, how the system worked and the challenges they faced. We recognized that it couldn't just be the "FWS Team" that came together; we needed to treat the Corps professionals with respect and convey our belief that success occurred when they were able to carry out their congressionally mandated responsibilities and we were able to say they were in compliance with the ESA. We were as anxious to find a "government" solution as the Corps professionals were. More than once during our discussions, I recalled Judge Scott telling Fred Disheroon that there was only one government, and to bring him the "government position." If we failed to find a long-term solution that satisfied the legislative mandates of navigation and flood control, as well as the ESA, there would simply be yet another team asked to do what we were unable to do. No one involved wanted that outcome.

Larry Cieslik, Karen Durham-Aguilera and others from the Corps gave presentations and led discussions that helped solidify the data as they understood them to be, as well as possible means to accommodate the needs of the listed species. The Fish Team probed the data on the sturgeon and Corps efforts to augment the population through stocking, as well as why the Corps believed they could not achieve the spring rise that had been called for in the 2000 opinion. One revelation occurred when talking about the Yellowstone River. Just upstream from the confluence of the Yellowstone and Missouri, there is a weir at Intake, Montana, designed by the BOR to hold back enough water to provide irrigation for farmers in that area. The weir, however, blocked over one hundred miles of pristine historical habitat for the pallid sturgeon coming upstream in the Missouri, an opportunity that might provide significant relief for the Corps on the mainstem.

Casey Kruse with the Omaha District led the discussions about the birds. The Corps understood that the migrating sandbars that moved with the annual floods created the necessary habitat for the piping plover and interior least tern, both shorebirds that used these sandbars and islands as nesting habitat. Casey had been engaged in extensive monitoring of nests and mortality, and was able to provide data that proved very useful in helping the bird team understand the complexities of this "mobile" habitat, which would be in one place one year and another place the next.

Throughout the process, the relationships between FWS biologists and Corps engineers grew, and we could see the foundation for potential future trust in the making. But there was a lot at stake, and the politics that had historically tried to divide federal agencies was real and becoming more intense along the river. If we were going to succeed, we couldn't allow them to divide and pit us against each other. The Corps proposed a Missouri River Recovery Implementation Committee (MRRIC), which we quickly dubbed "Mr. Ric," which would be composed of stakeholders all along the river who would discuss possible means of adaptive management of the system to respond to changing conditions. We agreed this was a positive move. When people are not given the facts of a situation, they will automatically create their own assumptions, which will almost always be negative. Creating a means whereby everyone gets the same information and hears the same discussions is critical to extending the teamwork to include the public. A significant requirement, however, is that information never be withheld. Once trust is lost, it is nearly impossible to regain.

> One of the things I learned through this process was how the team isn't just our internal team, but the Corps' as well. In implementation, I made a deal. I will never send you a letter you haven't seen in advance. And I held true to it.
>
> I went to dinner with the Corps professionals every time we had meetings, whether at our offices or theirs. Building that trust factor was significant. And it was true with the landowners in the basin. After the opinion, Kit Bond told me I needed to go visit with the farmers who were impacted, so I did. I rode the tractor with them, and I listened. We have to always remember to talk *to* members of the public, not *at* them. (Thorson 2020)

After the two days in Minneapolis, we decided we needed a home base, but one that was "neutral" to the issue. We chose Albuquerque and reserved a significant block of rooms at the Drury Inn. The inn's main conference room, which we set aside for the teams' use, soon became known as the "Pit." The teams had a lot of work to do and only about three weeks to conclude it. The clock was ticking.

• • •

My experience implementing the ESA was both an asset and a liability. Robyn had been chosen to help lead the team because she was regional director in Minneapolis, and the Missouri River flowed through her region. She also had the benefit of being a great leader, but *not* one who had a lot of experience in overseeing ESA consultations. We had chosen well for the team and the team leaders, so I decided it would be better if I spent most of my days at my office taking care of Southwest Region issues, and then going by the hotel for three or four hours after work to help in any way I could. I realized that if I spent extensive time with the team analyzing data, the team would then have to explain that I did not interfere or try to push them in any direction. Robyn, however, being a new regional director with limited ESA experience, had the ability to stay with the team, listen to the discussions and the nuances of the ESA and how the consultation process works, and contribute to the team in ways I was convinced she could help. It was *because* she was not an expert in the ESA that she could ask the commonsense questions that would help the team members see how the public might view their answers.

> We knew we had a lot of information, but we let the Corps know we wanted to be able to ask questions in real time. We were constantly asking 'is there more we can uncover?' and try to do as thorough a job as possible. I was trying to learn the operations of the Missouri River while at the same time I didn't have a lot of expertise in Section 7. I watched the way you formed the team, gave the team their instructions and latitude, asked questions and then stepped back and let others ask their questions. You were never driving this anywhere.
>
> In the hotel in Albuquerque, I was a sponge! I spent hours with Mike Thabault and Charlie Wooley and the rest of the

sturgeon team. I used the external affairs person's way of thinking to show them that 'You say X and then you say Z, but where is the Y? You didn't show your work on Y.' I constantly challenged them to 'show their work,' so anyone challenging how they got to a decision would see the entire thought process.

For me it was critical thinking. We worked hard at showing why the management of flows were so important. I was never going to be a biologist, but where explanations got hung up is where I spent most of my time. To their credit, they were exceptionally kind to a person with so little ESA expertise. (Thorson 2020)

In my mind, Robyn's leadership in guiding the team was far more critical than mine. I always cared deeply for Robyn as a friend, but I gained so much respect for her, her passion about the natural resources and her love for the dedicated employees she was honored to lead, just by watching her win over every member of the team.

We finished the biological opinion on time and asked Judge Manson and Steve Williams to come to Albuquerque to receive a briefing on the findings and conclusions. The team found "no jeopardy" for the Northern Great Plains piping plover and the interior least tern, but found "jeopardy" for the pallid sturgeon. After in-depth briefings of both Assistant Secretary Manson and Director Williams (done separately due to schedule conflicts), each thanked the team for an outstanding effort and kept his word. No effort was made to have any part of the opinion changed, even though it found the Missouri River should be managed to provide a small pulse of water in late winter to mimic the lowland plains melt, and another much larger rise in late spring to mimic the mountain snowmelt. The opinion spanned almost three hundred pages and covered every issue that had been raised in the past as well as any known present challenge.

This all-star team had done the impossible: provided an opinion on a 2,300+ mile river, multiple dams, two main tributaries and very little barge traffic in just over thirty days from our first meeting in Minneapolis. Robyn and I signed the opinion on December 16, 2003, and transmitted it to the Corps. We signed and transmitted copies to Craig Manson and Steve Williams on December 17. With their agreement, their first opportunity to read the entire opinion was *after* it had been transmitted to General William Grisoli, commander of the Northwest Division of the Corps. The opinion analyzed the river section by section and found that the proposed operation of the river would jeopardize the survival and recovery of the pallid sturgeon, and provided an RPA in order to remedy the threats.

Section 7(a)(1) of the ESA directs all federal agencies to do whatever they can within their authorities to assist in the conservation of listed species. In all biological opinions, following the discussion of jeopardy or no jeopardy and RPAs if appropriate, the FWS provides recommendations to the agency to reduce take. These are nonbinding reasonable and prudent measures. The FWS believed, as did the Corps, that a significant opportunity to reestablish pallid sturgeon on the Yellowstone River existed if the weir at Intake, Montana, were removed and an inflatable barrier put in its place. The barrier would be similar to a gigantic inner tube that could be inflated to serve as a weir when the BOR needed to provide irrigation water to their contractors in the area, then deflated during the spring when the sturgeon attempted to move up the Yellowstone and take advantage of 100 miles of pristine stream habitat.

Later in the spring of 2004 I got a call from the White House Office of Management and Budget examiners for the Corps and the BOR to discuss why the recommendation to remove the weir was so important and worth the expense. At the conclusion of the conversation, they agreed it was important but couldn't decide if it was the Corps' responsibility or the BOR's to pay. Each of these examiners wanted to push for the expense to be absorbed by the "other" agency, so as to limit impact on "their" agency's appropriations. The BOR operated it, but the Corps would receive the benefits from a new population of sturgeon in the Yellowstone. To my knowledge, it was never funded. My message to every administration: it's not too late, but time is running out on the Missouri River sturgeon. Find a way to fund it now!

On December 19, I had taken "use or lose" annual leave for Christmas and was sitting at home when my cell phone rang. It was Deputy Secretary Steve Griles, Craig Manson, Steve Williams, special counsel to the secretary of the interior Ann Klee, J.P. Woodley and General Grisoli. Deputy Secretary Griles asked me if I had been aware during the writing of the opinion that requiring the spring rise would cause the flap gates in the levee to close and block drainage from the protected side of the levee. That would cause flooding on farmlands that the levee was built to protect. The flap gate is a structure that only allows water to flow in one direction. These gates were constructed to allow water to flow from the protected side of the levee to the river, but be pushed closed if water from the river was high enough to flow through the structure onto lands on the protected side.

"No Sir. I was not aware of that."

"Oh, you weren't?" Steve Griles said this in a way that portended hope we might change our opinion based on interior flooding.

"No Sir, but it doesn't make any difference. We consulted with the Corps of Engineers. The flood control portion of their project was to build levees to keep the Missouri River water from flooding adjacent lands. That has allowed a considerable increase in tillable lands that historically would have been flooded as the Missouri overtopped its banks in the spring. Their project accomplishes that, and nothing in our opinion allows Missouri River water over or through the levee system. What happens on the protected side of the levee is not an action of the Corps. Therefore, we could not legally consider it." There was a short silence. Griles said "OK, if that's the answer, that's the answer. The opinion stands as is. Does anyone have any questions?" There were no questions.

Throughout the entire process, I was amazed at the integrity that was shown by our chain of command in the department, our director and the entire Corps team. I worked with many political appointees in my career, but none held their word as firmly as Steve Griles, Craig Manson and Steve Williams on the Missouri River Section 7 consultation. We had a wonderful Christmas, a birthday party for Emily and a New Year's celebration. I had to testify before Congress a couple of times in February regarding the opinion, but it generally was accepted. We were, of course, sued. The district court found in our favor, and on August 16, 2005, the Eighth Circuit Court of Appeals upheld the district court's finding that our opinion and the Corps' amended Master Plan were valid.

The 2003 opinion guided the operation of the river for listed species for nearly a decade, a long lifespan for a complicated system. The Corps got busy working with the FWS in a partnership that had not existed before. Robyn, Steve Williams and I gave all team members a cash award for the team effort, but there was little else in the form of thanks for these outstanding professionals who gave everything that was asked to get the job done. To implement the opinion, the Corps' FY 2004 and 2005 budget brought nearly $110 million to the lower Missouri River for ecosystem restoration, driven by the requirements of the ESA biological opinion and the government working together as a team.

> When I was [many years later] being deposed for a claims court case on the Missouri, the attorneys for the plaintiffs kept putting memo after memo in front of me from FWS employees that were scathing and just wanted to stick it to the Corps. But I believe our relationship with the Corps on the Missouri River [after the opinion] was the best of any division or district in the Corps across the country because we worked so closely together to implement the opinion. (Thabault 2020)

CHAPTER 15

The Lower Colorado River Multi-species Conservation Plan

The Colorado River, which is one of the largest rivers in the southwest, passes through seven U.S. and two Mexican states along its 1,400-mile stretch. The Colorado is known for offering a scenic pathway, with Grand Canyon National Park the most highly recognized destination along the route, but the river is also critical in providing water for more than 40 million people.

In the early 1900s, the seven basin states of Wyoming, Colorado, Utah, Nevada, New Mexico, Arizona and California realized they needed to come together with a plan that ensured that each state received a fair share of the river's bounty and also recognized the right of Mexico for its fair share. The Colorado River Interstate Compact, which was agreed to in 1922, accordingly divided up the estimated 16 million acre-feet of flows per year. Unfortunately, the period preceding the agreement was among the wettest periods ever recorded, and the river has failed to provide more than approximately 13.5 million acre-feet during any year since. This over-allocation of water creates a situation that harbors chronic fighting between the states over what is a "fair share."

The 1922 Compact divided the river into an upper and lower basin, with each half receiving 7.5 million acre-feet per year. The upper basin was composed of Wyoming, Colorado, New Mexico, and Utah, while the lower basin included Nevada, Arizona and California. In addition, 1.5 million acre-feet were allotted to Mexico, which was ratified as a

Floating the Lower Colorado River (Courtesy of USGS)

treaty in 1944. Conflicts between the states escalated over time due to the river's inability to deliver the promises of men. As communities continued to appear and grow, more water was needed to satisfy a thirsty population and the agriculture to feed it. One story has Arizona so upset with California's effort to build a dam and divert water that Arizona called out the National Guard to stop this atrocity. It was eventually settled in court, but the distrust between the states was not.

By 2004 a drought was entering its third year and the lower basin needed to figure out how it was going to deal with diminishing water supplies for growing populations. Bennett Raley, a lawyer and rancher from Colorado, was the assistant secretary of the interior for water and science (ASWS), and as such had the responsibility to bring people together to find solutions for water management. He set up a several-day rafting trip beginning just below Lake Powell at the top of the Grand Canyon and invited members of the press, the three top state officials responsible for water, Regional Director Bob Johnson, Steve Thompson and me. I did the first half of the trip, camping overnight on the sandbars, and Steve replaced me halfway down the river for the lower part and discussions with California. Bennett was clever in getting the state officials literally in the same boat and forcing them to discuss how they could work together with the secretary to manage water during a prolonged drought. Obviously, we also had fun. After the trip was completed, I received an email from Bennett regarding my brother from another mother, Steve. The email was sent to the deputy secretary, department solicitor, Craig Manson, Steve Williams, Ann Klee and me.

> Mr. Thompson joined our trip at Phantom Ranch. Notwithstanding the fact that we were in a desert environment at midday and on dry land, he was wearing a set of waterproof camouflage clothing that was obviously designed for dark green dense woodland environments. He looked like a waddling duck blind with an Elmer Fudd hat. At his second camp we all had a wide range of options for the night. Our river guides relayed a radio weather report that predicted rain that evening. There were dark clouds in the sky. Some chose tents. Others, including the ASWS, chose to take advantage of natural rock overhangs.
>
> Mr. Thompson chose to sleep under the stars, and also chose to sleep in a comfortable natural drainage way. It was so obvious that even the press knew enough to avoid it. As Mr. Thompson reported to me the next morning, he awoke later in the night when it rained on his face. Instead of rethinking his decision to sleep in an arroyo in a rainstorm, he bravely covered his head with his raincoat. He then felt his feet being submerged in water. Remaining comfortable with his decision, he did not move. He next felt the water at the knee level. This was not a source of concern to the intrepid RD from Malibu, and he remained in a prone position.
>
> Mr. Thompson reported that he became concerned when the water progressed to his waist (still lying down). Acting quickly on this new information, he abandoned his sleeping spot

and huddled next to a rock wall for over an hour. This time was spent trying to wring the water out of his sleeping bag. He then laid his sleeping bag out (he did not tell me if he returned to his original spot or selected a new one). As he crawled into his bag, he realized that his sleeping bag was still wet, so he put his camo rain suit on and crawled back into the bag. Rumors that he wore his life jacket to bed are unconfirmed. Other members of our party were perplexed to see Mr. Thompson sitting on a rock in full raingear at 5 a.m. On successive nights Mr. Thompson took a cot from another trip participant and balanced it on the highest rocks at the camp site. He was also observed attempting to steal a dry sleeping bag from another trip participant (me).

Mr. Thompson threatened to leave a severed condor head on my pillow if I reported this incident. (Raley 2004)

I cannot verify the accuracy of this email, but must admit I used it on occasion to jab Steve. All I had to say was "Want to borrow a dry sleeping bag?"

The trip, however, had a serious subject. Lake Powell was sitting at 42 percent of capacity, the lowest since it was being filled in 1970. In some spots on the lake, areas were exposed that were normally a hundred feet under water. Lake Mead, which supplies nearly all the water to Las Vegas, was at 59 percent of capacity and was expected to be in the same condition as Powell within four years if the drought continued. The situation was dire. In addition, there were listed species all along the Lower Colorado River that had to be accommodated. Sid Wilson, general manager of the Central Arizona Project, was there representing Arizona. Pat Mulroy was manager of the Southern Nevada Water Authority and Dennis Underwood was former Commissioner of the Bureau of Reclamation and current head of the Metropolitan Water District (MWD) in California. Jennifer Pitt, an environmental specialist with Environmental Defense Fund, was also on the trip. I took advantage of the captive audience to become friends with all participants. My experience clearly showed that when people work together, issues can be solved. The issue I was trying to solve, working with Bob Johnson, was the Section 7 consultation for operations of the Lower Colorado River and, equally important, the non-federal partners' need for a Section 10 permit for their Multi-Species Conservation Plan (MSCP).

The plan had been in the works for nearly ten years, and frustration was palpable. Part of the issue was the sheer number of partners; the other was the large number of species to be considered. There were at least a half-dozen water entities that had obligations or responsibilities on the river. The tribes were also legitimate partners at the table and had hatchery capability for listed fish they could provide. There were at least twenty-seven listed species or species of concern that needed to be addressed. Finally, the simple fact of everyone having their own legal teams to fight everyone else kept agreement just out of arm's reach.

Dennis Underwood had been the commissioner of BOR when John Turner was director of the US Fish and Wildlife Service (FWS). The two were friends and insisted that our two bureaus work together. Bob Johnson was a close partner from the BOR, so we stole time with Dennis Underwood to explore how MWD could help bring the non-federal partners together. I also visited with Sid and Pat, both of whom were eager to find a solution, but the FWS would have to agree to a plan that would meet Section 10 requirements. The more we talked, the more I realized that legal disagreements between our attorneys, prompted by their best intentions to protect their clients, had almost brought negotiations to a halt. As I departed the trip and Steve arrived, I encouraged all three to focus on what they really needed, not what was wanted. I left with their promise, and I committed to get us together to solve the problem soon.

The Department of the Interior (DOI) solicitor in Albuquerque was Justin Tate, a good attorney who was tough as nails, to protect our interests. A lot of the concern was around the commitment for funding from all the parties, with some not being willing to commit until they saw the

BOR commit. Bob Johnson was willing. Bennett Raley was willing. And, after discussions with Secretary Gale Norton, the DOI was willing. But we had to get the non-federal parties to commit. In July, I set up a phone call with the decision-makers of the three states and any of their subcontractors they deemed critical to the deal. I demanded that no attorneys be on the call. "If there is an attorney on the call, I will say thank you and hang up. It's time for decisions, and we need to make them. That will require compromise, but I believe we can get it done." Pat, Dennis and Sid all agreed. They had two or three other irrigation districts on the call, but no attorneys. I began the discussion:

"Good afternoon, everyone. Thank you all for honoring my request. I need to ask, are there any attorneys on the call?"

"Yes, sir," came one reply. "But I am not on the call as an attorney. I have full authority to make the decision for my district."

"Good. I can't hold your education against you. Let's get started."

Dennis had sent me a personal note just prior to the phone meeting, which was held on July 19, with some inside information about solving the issue. I was pleased to see that the non-federal parties had already met in June to narrow down the decision points. Some entities to the agreement wanted to go with an interim agreement for only ten years, rather than the fifty-year permit that had been discussed for the past ten years. Most of those suggesting a short-term permit while issues could be resolved were in Arizona or were subcontractors to the major players. Dennis alerted me that California and Nevada wanted to stay with the fifty-year permit because of the significant investment in money and time that had already been made.

The Metropolitan Water District, Southern Nevada Water Authority and the Colorado River Commission of Nevada had agreed on a side deal under which they would stand behind the non-federal costs, which could be as high as $400 million over the fifty-year life. BOR and Secretary Norton had agreed to commit to the federal share. Under the Colorado River Compact, the secretary of the interior is the "Water Master" and has authority to invoke restrictions or make allowances for solutions to water allocation issues. In return, the FWS would issue a Section 10 permit to the non-federal parties that agreed, with those not agreeing receiving coverage from the primary participants under their permit.

In a discussion that took about an hour, we agreed to all the terms of the permit, which committed $625 million to conservation of listed and non-listed species and created 8,100 acres of riparian and backwater habitat for at least thirty-one listed and candidate species. There would be a thirty-five-member steering committee with five representatives each from the Department of the Interior, State of Arizona, State of California, State of Nevada, Indian tribes, environmental organizations and other public or private entities.

Dennis and Pat agreed to the commitments from their states, but Sid disagreed. However, because of the commitments from California and Nevada, we reached agreement, and Arizona later joined the permit. If I had any doubts that we could not have reached agreement with our attorneys in the meeting, they were removed when Justin Tate objected and said he would not surname the permit as legally correct. He did not believe there were enough firm commitments that the permit holders would satisfy the conditions of the permit. "Justin, I respect you and appreciate that you are looking out for the secretary and FWS. But this is a management decision that requires trust. I have that trust in my partners with the BOR and the states."

I sent Steve Williams and Craig Manson a memo alerting them that I had to decline accepting Justin's recommendations and intended to issue the permit. After a phone call with the two of them to explain my reasons for the decision, as well as our authority to withdraw the permit at any time conditions were not met, they concurred and instructed me to do what I thought was best to solve this long-standing issue. Secretary Gale Norton signed the agreement on September 14, 2004. Lesley Fitzpatrick in our Phoenix field office had worked on this arduous assignment from day one. I called Lesley with the news that her hard work had culminated in the largest commitment of funding in the history of the Endangered Species Act, and told her how proud I was of her dedication and professionalism. Another FWS unsung heroine.

Trust and partnership were the essential ingredients. First, we listened to each other and realized we had a common set of goals. That became trust, and trust led to agreement. The river and its species would have the help $625 million would bring.

• • •

In early 2005, Steve Williams announced that he was leaving the U.S. Fish and Wildlife Service (FWS) to take the position as CEO of the Wildlife Management Institute. He left on March 16 after serving as a solid leader who mended significant rifts between the FWS and our state partners. During the years that had passed since the position of director had been elevated during the Nixon administration to a presidential appointment confirmed by the Senate (PAS), no employee who had spent their entire career in the FWS had been nominated to be the director. Jamie Rappaport Clark was made director under President Bill Clinton, but she had come to the FWS later in her career. The normal course of business was for someone from the Department of the Interior to ask a career senior executive service regional director or assistant director if they would be willing to have their name submitted to the White House for consideration as director. We knew they did this to show they "looked inside, looked outside, and went outside" to nominate a state director or other non-FWS biologist. The 1974 amendments to Section 3 of the Fish and Wildlife Act of 1956 (16 U.S.C. 742b) stated, in part:

> There is established within the Department of the Interior the United States Fish and Wildlife Service. The functions of the United States Fish and Wildlife Service shall be administered under the supervision of the Director, who shall be subject

to the supervision of the Assistant Secretary for Fish and Wildlife. The Director of the United States Fish and Wildlife Service shall be appointed by the President, by and with the advice and consent of the Senate. No individual may be appointed as the Director unless he is, by reason of scientific education and experience, knowledgeable in the principles of fisheries and wildlife management.

The amendments established the director position as one that was appointed by the president and confirmed by the Senate, and changed the name of the Bureau of Sport Fisheries and Wildlife to the Fish and Wildlife Service. Ronald Reagan is said to have attempted to nominate a veterinarian to be director, but was told the person didn't qualify due to no "fish and wildlife management" experience. The career employees knew the game and just smiled and winked as someone in the directorate got the request to put his or her name in consideration.

When Steve left in March, we had no idea how long President George W. Bush and Secretary Norton would take to find a replacement. When I got a call from David P. Smith asking me if I would be willing to have my name submitted for consideration as the director, I was honored but dismissed it as the beginning of the "game," and I was the one who would be proof "We looked inside." In April, I received a call from Brian Waidmann, Secretary Norton's chief of staff, telling me the secretary would like me to come in for an interview. Before Steve Williams was nominated, they had called Sam Hamilton to see if his name could be used, but they didn't ask him to come in for an interview. I thought maybe they wanted to make it look better this time before they announced the outside candidate they wanted, so I flew into D.C. to meet with the secretary.

Secretary Norton could not have been more gracious or kind as we talked conservation philosophy, regulation versus voluntary partnerships, and the situations in which each was the right choice. I firmly believed, and still do, that regulation is the tool of last resort to keep the playing field level for all participants and to go after those who would undermine the progress made by the people who were willing to work together. All the laws and regulations at the disposal of the director of the FWS are valuable in precluding significant harm or destruction of habitat, but none gives the director the authority to order so much as one acre of habitat be *improved for the species.*

The Clean Water Act does not prohibit loss of wetlands; it simply requires that a permit be obtained. The Endangered Species Act does not prohibit the take of species as long as a Section 7 take authorization or Section 10 permit is obtained. Critical habitat may be diminished, but not to the point of adverse modification or destruction. The true answer to an *increase* in habitat—the loss of habitat being the largest single threat to fish and wildlife today—is *voluntary* partnerships with landowners who are willing to improve habitat on their lands. Secretary Norton agreed with my views and thanked me for my time and leadership of the Southwest Region.

On May 4 I received a call from Brian Waidmann saying that the White House wanted to interview me for the position of director. "What! I didn't realize you all were actually considering me for the position. I haven't even discussed this with my wife because I didn't think it was real!" Brian laughed. "Well, I suggest you talk to her. You need to fly into D.C. for an interview next week." I immediately hung up and called Sarah. She knew why I had gone to D.C. to visit with the secretary, but I had told her not to give it any thought because of the way things had been done.

I honestly did not want the job. I knew from my years in the FWS that it was thankless. Everyone took a bite of your ass with every decision you made, and you were considered "political" regardless of the years of fish and wildlife conservation on your résumé. Emily was going to start eleventh grade in four months, and I had promised not to move her after she started tenth grade. In addition, there would be no increase in pay, and our expenses would jump significantly. Finally, the position of regional director was a coveted position in the FWS, and I was loving it!

I went home and sat down with Sarah. "You know, the confirmation process takes months and, if I were nominated, I probably wouldn't be confirmed until well into Emily's school year. We've promised her that we wouldn't move her after she started the tenth grade. I would have to go into D.C. alone for up to two years." I was looking for her to tell me this was too much to ask and give me the excuse to politely remove my name from consideration. She looked at me and calmly said "We can make that work." Really! I'm the one who would be without my wife or my child in her last years of high school, but "We can make it work"?

"You have told me the Service is being hit with big budget cuts," Sarah said. "You also said it takes someone coming in from the outside at least a year to get their feet on the ground and understand the issues. You already know the issues because you worked them. The Service needs you, and we can figure out how to see each other as often as possible." I stared blankly ahead, knowing she was right. The FY 2006 budget was well under discussion, and things were looking bad. I accepted that I might be asked to do something for my family. Not the one I shared my home with, but the one that shared my professional life. When Emily got home, I told her I was being considered for the director's position. She immediately said "I won't have to move, will I?" I told her no but, if I was selected, we would be apart. She just smiled and said "Oh, OK then." So much for being broken up about our living apart!

I flew into Washington on Tuesday evening, May 10, under the guise of meetings on the Hill. I was told to continue keeping everything strictly confidential, as this process was highly secretive. They didn't want anything leaking to the press. On Wednesday morning I met with Ed Moy of the president's staff for vetting personnel appointments. We met off-site at a location on 18th Street that could not have looked less like a venue for a White House interview. We talked for over an hour about my views of the president and his approach to conservation. I was a strong supporter of partnerships, especially with the state fish and wildlife agencies, which fit very well with the president's views. Near the end of the interview, I could tell that Moy, who would later take over responsibility for running the Denver Mint, seemed to be struggling with how to ask a question.

"You know that a lot of people coming into the administration have questions about career employees and where their loyalties lie," he began. I smiled and interrupted him.

"I understand. I have been a career employee for twenty-seven years and have served under both Democratic and Republican presidents. I see my obligation to uphold the laws and Constitution of the United States as non-negotiable. I also believe in innovative use of those laws and partnerships to find solutions to resource conflicts. I fully support the president's view that the federal government should work closely with the states and other partners in delivering conservation to the American people. Whether I am the regional director in Albuquerque or the director in Washington, D.C., I will do all I can to approach my job with that philosophy. That's the best answer I can give."

He smiled and thanked me for my service to the country and my dedication to conservation. We ended the interview, and I went to the airport to await my flight back home. I didn't think anything more about it until Friday afternoon when I got home from work. FedEx had delivered what looked to be about a six-inch stack of documents for me to fill out. The package was from the White House Office of Special Counsel. As I began going through the forms, I realized they wanted to know everything about me, from my bank accounts to my hemorrhoids. I spent all Friday evening mumbling to myself at the dining room table, Sarah and Emily having wisely decided that at this point, distance was probably a good idea. Sarah is meticulous in her record-keeping, so all the information requested was in one of the boxes at my feet. It was around midnight before I finally finished the forms and could get to bed. When I got up Saturday morning I went through them again to make sure they were correct, then took them to the FedEx office and sent them back using the label that had been provided by the White House.

On Monday, I called Brian Waidmann's office to tell him I had returned the forms to the White House, so he'd know in case they called him asking about them. My call went through to his deputy, Doug Domenech, who was also the White House liaison. When I told Doug about the forms, the line got quiet. "Doug, are you still there?" I asked. "Yes," he replied. "Uh, thank you for letting us know." I thought it was odd, but assumed I had interrupted him in the middle of something. Within an hour, Brian called me and said "We didn't know about the forms because the selected nominee is the only one who is asked to fill them out, and the White House had not told us the president had decided to nominate you. Apparently, as soon as you finished your interview with Ed Moy last week, he went to the president and said 'We've found your next director of the Fish and Wildlife Service.' The president liked what he heard and gave the nod. So, my friend, get ready for an in-depth background check and the bumpy ride through the confirmation process. Congratulations!"

The background investigation began almost immediately, with seemingly everyone but my barber getting interviewed about my drinking habits, any drug use, any undocumented domestic help, gambling and just about anything else one can think of. I was told I could tell no one but my immediate family, and they had to be sworn to secrecy. On July 15, 2005, the president announced his intent to nominate me to be the director of the United States Fish and Wildlife Service. Because Congress traditionally takes the month of August off to go home and connect with their constituents, my confirmation hearing was scheduled for September.

I knew that Senator Jim Inhofe of Oklahoma was pushing to have me be the next director. He liked my views on private land partnerships, and I had testified in a field hearing on his bill to make the Partners for Fish and Wildlife Program a permanent line item in the budget. Pete Domenici and Jeff Bingaman were also letting the White House know they supported me, even though they had not informed me. I found out about Inhofe's support when he announced in the well of the Senate that I should be the next director. Senators have a way of advancing their opinions. I greatly appreciated these, and other friends, joining Secretary Norton in recommending me to the president.

Deputy Director Matt Hogan sent out a memo to all employees on July 15 letting the FWS troops know. The Fish and Wildlife Service is a true family, and I was deluged with emails and cards congratulating me and assuring me they would have my back. And, throughout my tenure, they did. Terry Davies was assigned to shepherd me around the Hill to have meetings with each member of the Senate Environment and Public Works Committee, chaired by Senator Inhofe.

The most uncomfortable meeting I had was with Missouri Senator Kit Bond. As Terry and I sat in his office, the senator just looked at me and shook his head. "I know you're his man. But you're the one who did it to us on the Missouri River." The opinion was less than two years old, and the Eighth Circuit had released its concurring opinion during the August recess just three weeks earlier. "My ethics required that I support the science," I said. He nodded his head. "I understand. I just don't like it." In the end, he supported my nomination both in committee and in the full Senate.

At the other end of the scale, my meeting with Virginia Senator John Warner went much better. I handed him my résumé and said "I know your time is valuable, sir. If you'd like, I'll summarize my career experiences for you." "No thanks," he replied. "I'd like to read it." We sat there as he went through my career positions and the places I had worked. "Well, you've done every other job in the Fish and Wildlife Service, I guess you should do this one, too. It's also the job I always wanted."

• • •

The week preceding August 29 was frantic all along the Gulf Coast, but especially in New Orleans. Hurricane Katrina gained strength as it moved through the Caribbean and was expected to make landfall smack on top of New Orleans as a Category 5. In August 1969, the fall after I left Keesler Air Force Base and went to the Philippines, Hurricane Camille made landfall as only one of four Category 5 storms to reach the U.S. coastline. Katrina followed nearly the same path as Hurricane Camille and was a Category 5 storm in the Gulf, but weakened a bit to a Category 3 by the time it made landfall. Nevertheless, Katrina left more damage and destruction than Camille had. The antebellum homes in Biloxi and Gulfport remained on their foundations during Camille, while Katrina left nothing *but* the foundations. Photos of Biloxi showed a single guitar sign in front of what was formerly a casino. The sign, by coincidence, was made by a sign-builder in Sarah's hometown of Bunkie, Louisiana.

The reason Katrina brought such damage was the loss of wetlands off the Louisiana coast that had occurred between 1969 and 2005. Louisiana coastal wetland loss was estimated at an average of 40 square miles per year, representing the equivalent of approximately 1,440 square miles of wetlands lost between the two storms. Marshes and wetlands slow the wind velocity as it approaches and reduces the storm surge. The U.S. Geological Survey has estimated that for every 2.7 miles a hurricane travels over emergent marsh, the storm surge is reduced by one foot. While not exact, that number serves to illustrate the importance of conserving, protecting and rebuilding coastal wetlands. All along the Louisiana coast, it is the wetlands that protect the levees, and the levees that protect the people. Because of the significant loss of coastal wetlands that had occurred since Camille, the levee on Lake Pontchartrain ruptured, and the city of New Orleans was flooded.

Our eldest daughter Erin had received her degree in psychology from LSU, and then had gone to nursing school at Our Lady of the Lake in Baton Rouge. I was sitting in Albuquerque during the August congressional recess nervously watching news of the storm headed toward my "Big Girl," who was still my big girl but also had become a nurse.

She recently recalled her harrowing experience during Katrina in a conversation with me:

> I was a newly graduated nurse working at Baptist Memorial Hospital in New Orleans in the Emergency Room. I was just starting on my own without having to shadow a nurse. You were assigned to either Hurricane Team A or Hurricane Team B. Team A came to the hospital as the hurricane was approaching and remained through the storm. Team B came in after the hurricane had passed and relieved Team A. I was assigned to Team B, but I was single, and a lady with kids was on Team A, and word was coming in that this storm was a bad one. She was very concerned for her family, so I switched with her and she took my spot on Team B.
>
> I had never gone through a hurricane, but my roommate advised me to fill the bathtub with fresh water, get food for several days, and bring a couple days' worth to work. We went in on Sunday, the twenty-eighth, and they put us up in rooms in the hospital after our shift so we could rest. There was a breezeway connecting two wings of the hospital that I could see out my window, and I watched as the storm was coming in. We lost power at some point and all the clocks stopped at the same time. After the eye passed over us and the storm had moved on, we were told we could go check on our homes and pets, but to come right back. Several of us went in one car, and on the way back we received a phone call to hurry. The levee had broken and the town was flooding. By the time we got back on the afternoon of the twenty-ninth, water was coming up on the hospital. We eventually had about eighteen feet of water that didn't drain or couldn't be pumped.
>
> Our goal prior to the storm was to discharge as many patients as possible. We told people who couldn't be discharged that they could have one or two family members stay with them, but that

was on other floors, not in the ER. EMS services stopped at some point due to flooding, so we didn't have any new patients. When the generators kicked on, they only provided power to "red" outlets, dedicated to life support system equipment. I was able to get an email out telling people I was worried about my cats, what was happening, and we didn't know what was going on with the flooding. Later, I got responses from people all over the world saying they were praying for me. It was heartwarming. I remember going up to the Life Care Unit, which included hospice end of life patients and others not expected to make it. They had no power and no ventilator capability. They were all lying on the floor with nurses trying to fan them with pieces of cardboard. They would reach their hands out as I walked by saying 'Help me, please help me.' It was the most awful feeling knowing there was nothing I could do to make them more comfortable. I remember on one occasion I was caring for a lady, and the person next to her on a gurney had died. I gently covered up the deceased body and tried to shield the harsh truth. The hospital morgue was full and we had to put bodies in the chapel. The rumor was going around that drug dealers wanted to loot the pharmacy. A lot of the male nurses had brought their guns to the hospital and slept on top of the parking structure, prepared to shoot at people who tried to come looting. The part of town where Baptist sits was well known for drug dealing. That's just the way it was. The hospital administrators had apparently told FEMA the hospital was empty, so no one was coming to get us. (Hegedus 2020)

My phone rang on Thursday evening, and Erin was on the other end. "Dad, we are passing around the only phone that is working, so I have to be quick. If there is anything you can do to help get us out of here, now is the time. The staff has started doing IVs with saline solution to stay alive. There is no water and we don't know when or if anyone is bringing any." I shot up like a bolt and said "Hang in there! I love you and will be working on getting someone there as soon as we hang up." I immediately called Sam Hamilton in Atlanta and let him know the situation. He called Flip Siragusa, our special agent in Lafayette, Louisiana, and gave him the all-clear to go in for Erin and the others trapped in the hospital. We never got the straight truth, but heard that the hospital stopped sending helicopters to evacuate the patients and staff after taking on gunfire by looters. They allegedly told FEMA everyone was out.

Flip's cousin was a state trooper (this is Louisiana, after all) and he immediately activated a team. Louisiana Wildlife and Fisheries had been ordered to stay out, so Flip asked our friends at Texas Parks and Wildlife (TPWD), who were on their way to New Orleans, if they would help. By the next morning, September 1, there was a caravan of state troopers and conservation law enforcement officers headed for New Orleans and Baptist Memorial Hospital. Flip told me later that when they arrived, martial law had just been declared and they were told by FEMA that they couldn't go in. Flip and the other officers calmly told them they were going in and to have a good day. No one tried to stop them. By that afternoon, I was anxiously sitting in my office when my cell phone rang. "Dad, there's a Louisiana state trooper here who says I'm to tell you I'm in custody." Choking back tears, I asked her to thank the team for me. There was a parade of boats to evacuate the hospital, and each one had officers armed to the teeth with fully automatic weapons. The cowards who were constantly shooting to frighten people away so they could loot seemed to lose their bravado once they saw those officers.

> Someone came to me and said there were police officers in boats at the loading dock and they were asking for me. I went down, and a state trooper asked if I was Erin Hall. I said 'Yes.' He said 'We're here to get you out.' We got everyone out of the hospital and on boats. Once we made it to dry land, I was in a truck with

the Texas Parks and Wildlife officers and one of them said 'Darling, I don't know your dad, but he's one of us and that makes you family. It's like I was going in to get my own daughter.'

I had always taught my children that they were in a much larger family and, if they ever had car trouble or needed help, to call the local office of the FWS. I don't know which officer it was, but I am eternally in his debt for helping my child learn firsthand what teams and family are all about. Louisiana State Troopers David Bryant, Bruce Robinson, Ryan Zimmerman and Steve Volante led the way with their jurisdiction and dedication. Ryan Zimmerman took Erin into "custody." Along with FWS Special Agent Flip Siragusa, TPWD officers Major Butch Shoop and Captain William (W.J.) Rawls and Game Wardens Heath Bragg, David Chavez, Chuck Cotton, Gary Hobbs, Luett McMahen, Mike Morse, Ellis Powell, Brent Whitus, Marvin Wills and Phillip Wood helped evacuate the hospital. Once out and clear, Erin came to Albuquerque for a little R&R. It wasn't long, though, until she told us "I know they need me, so I'm going back." She drove back to New Orleans to do whatever she could in the recovery. The pride I felt in our conservation family, and how this young woman handled a horrifying situation, is beyond any words I can write.

• • •

On September 22, 2005, I had my confirmation hearing with the Senate Environment and Public Works Committee. Part of the long-established ritual of confirmation is to have a senator from the nominee's home state introduce the person to the committee. Senator Domenici made it clear that he expected to introduce me because I was living in New Mexico. Senator Inhofe also made some very cordial comments endorsing my nomination. It went very smoothly, and the questions asked were nothing out of the ordinary. The committee followed up with additional questions in writing, which we answered and submitted back within a week. On October 6, the committee voted unanimously in favor of forwarding my nomination to the full Senate for their approval.

We were having a regional directorate retreat at assistant regional director David Yazzie's house on October 7 when Terry Davies called my cell phone. "Good afternoon, Mr. Director." "Not yet," I said. "I have to be confirmed before you can call me that." "Yes sir. Good afternoon, Mr. Director. The Senate just unanimously confirmed you by voice vote to be the director of the Fish and Wildlife Service. The secretary asked me to relay her congratulations and that you are to fly to D.C. on Monday!" "Wait a minute!" I exclaimed. "It's taking at least six months to get anyone confirmed. I'm not ready to move yet!" Terry laughed. "Too bad. See you next week. Congratulations!" I had been unanimously confirmed within twenty-four hours of it reaching the full Senate. I was in shock.

I hung up, informed the regional directorate team, and then called Sarah. I turned to Geoff Haskett and congratulated him on being the new acting regional director, thanked the team that had allowed me to ride on their shoulders, and headed home to pack for my first week as director of the U.S. Fish and Wildlife Service. I was sworn in by Secretary Norton on Tuesday, the day after I arrived in D.C. I stayed a couple of weeks to find an apartment in Alexandria, Virginia, then went home to get my vehicle and make the move to Washington without my family. This time, however, it would be for nearly two years.

PART 4

The Director

CHAPTER 16

The MacDonald Investigation

I needed to get my feet on the ground and establish whatever normal routine I could accomplish in this new, and frightening, circumstance. No matter how much one thinks he knows about the job of the director, one only knows the surface. As regional director, I understood that I had substantial power to help resolve issues, make decisions and assist people in their daily work. Nothing I had done, however, prepared me for the onslaught of the schedule that began on day one. I showed up at work every morning at 7. Meetings began at 7:30 and were scheduled for every half hour throughout the day, usually ending around 6 p.m. The issues were far less troublesome than they might have been because I had worked on or been involved in briefings about nearly every issue we faced. I had a sound understanding of what our dedicated employees dealt with, but Steve Williams characterized it well when he said "Every issue that reaches my desk is one no one else could solve."

Secretary of the Interior Gale Norton had been unfairly branded by association with former Secretary James Watt and was continually criticized by the environmental community for things she had not even done. In reality she was a joy to work with, and I appreciated her strong desire to have all the facts and assist in any way she could. One of the first issues I had as the director proved to be a powerful illustration of her commitment to do the right thing. Dr. Chris Servheen was the FWS grizzly bear expert and had worked his entire career to bring the animal out of the need for Endangered Species Act (ESA) protection. The states, non-governmental organizations (NGOs) and private landowners had

Gale Norton, Sarah Hall and author at Swearing-In (Courtesy of USDOI)

worked diligently for over three decades to bring populations back to health and had achieved significant success. Chris and his team believed it was appropriate to remove the Greater Yellowstone population of grizzlies from the list of threatened and endangered species.

At my first briefing with Secretary Norton, which occurred on October 29, 2005, I was amazed to learn that she had read every word of the Recovery Plan, all of Chris's memos and justification for de-listing, and yet still had concerns about the health of the bear population. "Are the green groups seeing something we are missing?" she asked. We explained that they had not, and that it was normal for some radical groups to simply not like seeing species removed from the list. To see the ESA work for recovery meant they couldn't use the species to stop or hinder other activities they didn't like. It was only after my November 15 briefing with the secretary, and my firm endorsement of the action, that she agreed. That was the Gale Norton the public did not see.

The traditional process of becoming a presidential appointee is to have the immediate swearing-in with just the secretary or a duly designated representative of the federal government, and then prepare for a formal swearing-in ceremony at a later date, which was when family and friends could be in attendance. We scheduled my formal swearing-in for November 3 at 3:30 p.m. in the secretary's office. By coincidence, it was also my fifty-sixth birthday. Just prior to the ceremony there would be a reception in the Department of the Interior (DOI) penthouse for employees and, immediately following the private ceremony, a full reception in the same penthouse, which is on top of the main Interior Building, where FWS partners and guests could get to meet the "new guy."

I was surrounded by family and friends. Sarah held the Bible as Secretary Norton administered the oath of office where I, once again, swore to uphold the laws and protect and defend the Constitution of the United States of America. I had done it upon joining the Air Force and again when becoming a civilian employee of the government. We invited our close relatives, but Sarah's sister Fernell and her husband Richard were the only brothers or sisters that could come. Erin brought a friend from the hospital. Adam brought Jim McGill, his friend and neighbor from Georgia, and Emily was there, as well as our dear friends Lynn and Judy Greenwalt. We had become close to Lynn and Judy over the years, and I still hold them both in my heart.

I wanted Lynn there to signify the reconnection with the dedicated career employees of the FWS. 2005 marked the first time in thirty years that an employee who had spent an entire career with the FWS was sworn in as director. I knew I was being watched and was aware that my performance, good or bad, would influence future decisions about director candidates from within the agency. Our longtime friends from Vicksburg, Mississippi, Mitch and Carla King, were also there with us. We had watched our children grow up and stayed close over the years. It was a rare day that Sarah and I could be together with all our children, family and friends, and it would be a long journey before we were living together again.

There were also the people who kept me going and let me know they always had my back. Marshall Jones was my deputy director and a man I deeply respected. He had spent most of his career in Washington, D.C., but was a rare exception to the rule. Most biologists who find a nest and permanently attach to Washington lose sight of the field and often become more political than I believe is appropriate. As career employees, we have an obligation to be fair and open to helping everyone, regardless of the political party they support. Unfortunately, the "D.C. marsh gas," as Bill Martin called it, seems to creep into the thought process, too often causing potentially good employees to become stale and believe they have the right to reinterpret laws to say what they think they should have said. They also tend to lose that all-important connection with the work of the field, our true mission. When that happens, a bureaucrat is born—one who doesn't look for solutions, but rather embraces power. Marshall was able to maintain his professional integrity and was never lured into playing with laws or becoming an advocate for issues. I knew I would depend on him a great deal.

Matt Hogan was the political deputy who had been appointed by the secretary at the request of Steve Williams, and I made sure he knew I wanted him to stay. Margaret Hopkins was special counsel to the director.

Gale Norton, Hall Family and the Greenwalts (Courtesy of USDOI)

She was a bright young woman in her late twenties with more experience than one would expect for her age. Margaret was pensive, knowledgeable and ready to find solutions. I knew she would be an important part of the team the first time I visited with her. The other special assistant I brought in from the field was Jerome Ford. Jerome was Tensas River National Wildlife Refuge manager, and I had come to see his talent when I was in Atlanta. I knew he had a lot to offer and wanted him to bring the field view into our decision-making. Like most good field people, however, he wanted to stay in the field. I called him when I was nominated and told him to pack his bags, that he had too much to offer at the national level to stay where he was. He begged me for another year in the field, after which he would be there. I agreed. He wasn't at my swearing-in, but he kept his word and came in less than a year later.

Ken Stansell was the assistant director for international affairs and a solid leader. Marshall privately shared his plans with me at the beginning of 2006, telling me that he would retire the following December. We agreed that there should be some overlap with his replacement, and I coerced Ken Stansell into agreeing to accept the position and help with continuity of command.

> I was loving doing international work and was happy as a gopher in soft dirt when you asked me to be your deputy. It was a hard decision. I thought I might be able to bring some organizational skills to the job, but it scared the shit out of me! We had 9,000 employees with a $2.2 billion budget counting grants, and twenty-two people a lot smarter than I was reporting directly to me. It was hard to wrap my head around. (Stansell 2020)

There are three deputy directors in the FWS; two are career and one is appointed by the secretary. The director has the authority to select the two career deputy directors, and I took advantage of that to bring in Rowan Gould as my second deputy when Marshall retired. Marshall had an exemplary career and held the FWS ship together in the first year of the George W. Bush administration as well as the time between Steve's departure and my arrival, holding down both his position as deputy and the role of acting director. The country and the FWS owe Marshall Jones a debt of gratitude. With Marshall's departure, Ken and Rowan became the two highest-ranking career employees in the FWS, while Matt Hogan performed as if he had been with the FWS his entire career. This would be the close team that helped me survive my tenure as director, along with Steve Thompson, Sam Hamilton, Robyn Thorson, Mamie Parker, Benny Perez, Beth Stevens and a host of others. I remain amazed by the strength, diversity and versatility of our directorate team.

The ESA had grown to be the primary driver of issues in the FWS and in the assistant secretary's corridor. I knew Julie MacDonald only superficially as she dug around in our issues in the southwest and tried to distort scientific facts. Julie was one of the deputy assistant secretaries for Fish, Wildlife and Parks, and worked directly for Craig Manson. Secretary Norton had appointed her to this position at Craig's request. She was from California and seemed to truly hate the FWS employees, and believed they abused the power of the ESA with her former clients, some of which were powerful water entities.

Julie was a rather petite woman who apparently had anger issues, but was adept at keeping higher-ups from seeing that side of her personality. I was perplexed that, as an engineer, she had convinced herself that she knew more about the biology of these species than our biologists did. Since she wasn't actually an expert, her ploy was to demand thousands of pages of information in an effort to harass the biologists while challenging every conclusion in hopes an argument might stick. As regional director I could only push back so far, and directed our staff to document her inappropriate intrusions. But as director, it was a different story. Director Steve Williams had always said he wasn't the ESA director, and everyone should just "Give her enough rope and she'll hang herself." But that wasn't my makeup. I had just spent the previous ten years personally engaged in trying to make the ESA work the way it was intended. To have a non-biologist kidnap and sabotage sincere efforts by dedicated employees was something I simply couldn't let stand.

I had been on the job for less than two months when Judge Craig Manson announced his resignation as assistant secretary, effective December 31, 2005. I liked Craig and believed him to be a good man, but he had health issues, and the job brought a great deal of stress his body didn't need. He spent four years in the position and deserved to move on, but I was uncertain about the waters I would have to navigate over the coming months as a new assistant secretary nomination went through the process. David P. Smith was the principal deputy assistant secretary and assumed the role as acting assistant secretary. I enjoyed working with David, but was not convinced that Julie would respect her boundaries in the absence of a Senate-confirmed assistant secretary. I suspected it would come to me, and it did. Julie started asking for meeting after meeting and copies of all comments submitted, and made other attempts to challenge what the field, especially California, was doing in the ESA.

She had become a regular problem for Steve Thompson, as if he didn't already have enough on his plate. Steve and I had worked closely as friends and professional partners, so I asked him to document Julie's escapades, only to find out he already had a running diary and stack of emails with quotes from Julie. Apparently, she wasn't as cunning as I had given her credit for and actually put in writing some very damaging information that Steve had copied and retained in files. I had to constantly remind her that it was my job to oversee the science, not hers. There were two reasons for this. First, the director of the FWS is the pinnacle of scientific discussion from the field. By virtue of law, s/he is required to have the credentials and experience to do so. It was my responsibility to push back on scientific issues, and I did. Scientists appreciate honest pushback to make sure the decisions match the data at hand. What we do not appreciate is arguing for a preconceived notion. This also means the director is the first step in building the policy position of the department on FWS issues. Julie's role was completely policy, not science. Her unqualified challenges of science were significantly out of order.

Second, I was a presidential appointee confirmed by the Senate (PAS) and she was not. That, in the realm of decision-making in government, is critical. Of all the political appointments made by any given administration—and there are five to six thousand—only about 1,100 require nomination by the president and confirmation by the Senate. Further, fully half of those are ambassadors. That leaves only about 550 people in any administration who have the *authority* to make a decision or change policy. In the Department of the Interior, which has 70,000 employees and nearly 100 political appointees, only about 15 are PAS, possess direct line authority, and have the ability to make binding decisions. Julie was appointed by the secretary, not the president, and she was not confirmed by the Senate. What made her behavior even worse was that she was a rare exception among all the good Schedule C appointees in the department who truly wanted to help get the job done right. Not only was she out of line with me; she was an embarrassment to other political appointees who carried out their responsibilities with ethics and integrity. Her lack of professionalism amplified after Craig resigned.

> On the one hand, there is the concern for scientific integrity. For me, it is and always was the most important responsibility. But the challenge is what constitutes scientific integrity versus appropriate oversight in the generation of scientific documents. Are they clear? Are they well documented? Are the summary statements backed up in fact with scientific evidence? Are the right sources cited for particular claims? Any administration wants the proper documentation to back up a particular decision. That is an appropriate role for any leadership in an organization, but there needs to be clarity between what ultimately constitutes that appropriate quality control oversight versus that which really amounts to interference or changing of the scientific

record. It was a concern because Julie was vigorous within her role with the FWS and assistant secretary's office. She was very vigorous in seeking original documentation and in questioning methodologies to the extent that it triggered an IG [inspector general] investigation. (Scarlett 2020)

• • •

Secretary Norton had weekly face-to-face meetings with all nine of her "Bureau Directors," as we were officially called, in addition to her meetings with the assistant secretaries. Gale was a genuine person who wanted to know the truth and how to solve issues. My meetings were scheduled for Tuesday at 2:00 p.m. if we were both in town. I was in my regular Tuesday meeting with Gale on Valentine's Day of 2006 when my executive assistant, Pat Kennedy, walked unannounced into the secretary's office with a look of panic on her face. She stopped just inside the door and said "Dale, your mother has been in an automobile accident and is seriously injured." I froze, and Gale had a look of sheer fright. She immediately said "Dale, get out of here and go to your mother. Let us know if there is anything we can do."

I went downstairs to my office in a daze, and I don't think I came out of it until the middle of the night. It got dark early in February, and by the time I called Sarah and got out of the building, it was dusk and starting to drizzle rain. I had to snap out of it as I was walking across the street because I almost stepped out against the light in front of a speeding car. Sarah and Emily caught a flight from Albuquerque and Erin flew from New Orleans to Knoxville, Tennessee, about an hour south of Corbin, Kentucky. Adam drove from Atlanta and met Erin's flight. I got home, threw clothes in a bag, including the suit I hoped I wouldn't need, and started driving west on I-66 toward Front Royal. It was a long drive to Corbin, but I had to get there. I didn't make it to Front Royal before my cell phone rang. It was Sarah.

"If you're driving, you need to pull off to the shoulder," she said.

"She's dead, isn't she?"

"Yes," Sarah replied. "I'm so sorry." I took a deep breath. "I'll be OK. I'll see you and the kids soon. I've reserved two rooms at the Fairfield Inn at the Corbin exit off I-75. Just ask the desk clerk to call me. I love you all. Please travel safe."

When I got to Corbin in the middle of the night, my brother, Larry, was already there. The hospital had called him first, and he had driven the four hours from Middletown, Ohio, and arrived just before she died. Larry and Judy Smithers, from my high school class, had eloped just after graduation and had gone to live in Ohio. Judy had succumbed to cancer just one year earlier, on Valentine's Day 2005. It was beyond imagination that these two wonderful ladies had died on the same date just one year apart.

When I found out how the accident occurred, I had to sit down and control myself.

Her husband, Roy, was not supposed to be driving because of his poor eyesight, but insisted on doing so when they went into Corbin to pick up some things that day. Before Momma could get her seatbelt fastened in the parking lot of the drugstore, he pulled out of the parking lot in front of a young girl who was doing nothing wrong. She broadsided the truck on Roy's side, but Momma was thrown into the steering column. She was, for all practical purposes, killed immediately. At least there was that blessing. She had vital signs, but no hope of making it. I had no idea when I got my birthday card and note from Momma saying she would not be able to come to my official swearing-in that it would be the last.

We received over 150 cards, notes and flowers, including one from President Bush and the First Lady. It seemed the whole family in conservation was mourning her loss. The hand that was guiding me was intent that I be reminded of pain and disappointment, but was also making sure I knew that both He and some wonderful people were with me. I felt the pain of being knocked down and having to get up again, as I had so many times before.

...

Over the next two months things only got worse with Julie. Craig Manson left at the end of the year and Julie refused to acknowledge that David was the acting assistant secretary (A/S) and her supervisor. After Momma was killed, it began to weigh on me that I was living alone in an apartment off Van Dorn Street in Alexandria and would be separated from Sarah and Emily for at least another year and a half, and I was starting to rethink my decision to serve as the director. Before long, I found out that Secretary Norton had been more impacted by my mother's death than I knew. She resigned from her position as secretary on March 31 and, in a phone call with several of us in the department, said with tears in her voice, "Dale, you know why I feel I must go back to Colorado and be near my mother." "I do, Gale," I replied. "You're making the right decision. God bless you."

I spent the weekend of April 8 as I did all others when I was not traveling. I did laundry, cleaned my little one-bedroom apartment, did a little shopping and read documents. By Sunday evening I was already dreading going to work because I knew it would be just another day of seeing what Julie had gotten into. What surprised me the most was the way Lynn Scarlett believed Julie really was an ESA expert. Lynn was the deputy secretary and one of those people we all admire. She finds the good in everyone and trusts them to a fault. Unfortunately, Julie took advantage of that as often as she could. I tried to tell Lynn and Brian Waidmann that Julie was going to be an embarrassment to the department, but they thought it was just a personality conflict. When I got home that Monday evening at around 7 after another eleven-hour day of dealing with Julie and a nonstop schedule, I opened a beer and sat in the dark. I needed a sounding board to help guide me through this. The only person I believed could give me that advice was my old friend Lynn Greenwalt. I gave him a call.

I explained all the turmoil between the A/S corridor and my office and my belief that I had to handle things that way to protect the field troops. I told him I didn't think I could do this much longer and was contemplating resigning. I had more than thirty years in government with my military time, and was over fifty-five. I was fully eligible. There was no mistaking his response. In his unique way of pronouncing every word, he said "Don't you even contemplate that possibility. The troops would never forgive you for abandoning them. They need you." I knew my old friend and mentor was right, but I had to figure out how I was going to deal with it.

After our talk, I went to bed and stared at the ceiling until around 2 a.m., when I settled on my plan of action. The alarm went off at 4:45 and I took a wake-up shower and got dressed. The first bus from the apartment complex to the Van Dorn Metro Station left at 5:20 a.m., and I was on it. I had chosen to receive the mass transit subsidy the government offered to reduce automobile traffic in D.C. You should have seen the face of the administrative employee who brought me my parking pass for the basement of the Interior Building when I declined it. I could have either a parking pass or the subsidy, but not both. I chose the subsidy and blew the minds of half the employees in D.C., because a parking pass in the building where you work is one of the most coveted possessions one could have. But I preferred the peace and anonymity of the Metro. The ride home was a welcomed respite from back-to-back meetings all day.

It was around 47 degrees and was expected to be a day without rain and a high of 72. There was a slight breeze as I arrived at my office around six, and I knew I had less than an hour to get the job done before early-arriving employees appeared. I sat at my computer on the morning of April 11, 2006, and wrote an anonymous complaint to the inspector general (IG) about Julie MacDonald and her illegal and unethical intrusions into the ESA matters of the department. Earl Devaney was the IG and a straight shooter, and someone who would welcome the opportunity to investigate a problem like this.

I elaborated on the way she bullied career employees and insulted them on a regular basis; how she treated them with disrespect and harassed the professional staff. In addition, using information Steve Thompson had provided me from his file on Julie, I outlined how she had inappropriately changed science and the findings of the career professionals. I even encouraged the inspector general to interview former Director Steve Williams and current Director Dale Hall to verify these allegations. I placed the letter in a blue envelope, the type used for intra-departmental communications, walked up the stairs and slid it under the office door of the IG. The blue envelope would be a clear indication it came from an employee. I just kept walking and got a cup of coffee from the snack shop.

My internal constitution demanded that I publicly take the issue on and make a formal complaint to both the inspector general and to Congress. But my desire to retain the ability to be effective for the FWS and our employees persuaded me to report these wrongdoings anonymously. If the political structure of the department knew that I was the one who had written the letter, I would have had no ability to get anything done from that moment on. There is an unwritten rule among political appointees that one bites one's tongue and "lets it go," even if it is wrong. I was political, but also firmly believed what I told Ed Moy in my interview about what was non-negotiable. This was new territory for me. I had employees who needed relief that I could only give if I had help. Julie MacDonald had real issues, but she was not unintelligent. She had apparently convinced everyone in the department, except me, that she was a true expert on the ESA. I uncovered no real experience she had in actually working the tough issues, but she had her constituency in California and enough in the department to keep her afloat.

Within a week following the complaint, I sent an official memorandum to Acting Assistant Secretary for Fish, Wildlife and Parks David

P. Smith prohibiting Julie MacDonald from calling or communicating with career FWS employees in any manner. As a secretarial appointee, she had no line authority over FWS staff at any level. I instructed that "recommended edits to documents or any questions" should be placed in writing and directed to my attention. I made it clear that I welcomed discussions with the assistant secretary's office, but I would make the decision on what was formally elevated from the FWS for review. David could overrule my decision, but Julie could not. Dirk Kempthorne, senator from Idaho, had been nominated to replace Gale as the secretary of the interior, and I anxiously waited to see if he would make any staff changes in the department.

• • •

Dirk Kempthorne was confirmed as the forty-ninth secretary of the interior on May 26, 2006. In a fashion similar to my own confirmation, the Senate did it by voice vote and he was sworn in the same day. Secretary Kempthorne was much like Gale Norton in his sincerity and gracious smile. He was clearly relaxed in a position of leadership, having been mayor of Boise, a U.S. senator, and most recently a two-term governor of Idaho. I met the new secretary when he was awaiting confirmation and came to visit me in my office. He asked about the issues we were facing and the ones I thought should be his immediate focus after confirmation. My first impression of Dirk was then reinforced on his first official day in office. Brian Waidmann had asked all political appointees to greet the new secretary on the steps of the main Interior Building adjacent to C Street upon his arrival. There were dozens of us standing there when he got out of the car, and I was blown away as he went from person to person remembering each of our names. The only other politician I had ever met who had that ability was Bill Clinton. For a politician, no asset can exceed remembering people's names. For that and many other reasons I genuinely liked Dirk, and that has never changed.

In November, Lynn Scarlett was confirmed as deputy secretary of the interior to replace Steve Griles, and we swiftly became close friends. Lynn was the reason I was so shocked at my rapid confirmation. She had been nominated to replace Griles months before I was named, so I assumed it would take at least six months to complete my confirmation process. Her prior position was as assistant secretary of the interior for policy, management and budget. She also served as acting secretary between the departure of Gale and the arrival of Dirk. I believe that of all the people in the building, Lynn was the most devastated by the visit from Inspector General Devaney to brief her on the initiation of the Julie MacDonald investigation. Lynn had placed the same trust and belief in Julie that she had given everyone, but Julie had betrayed it. Dirk Kempthorne quickly learned he could not have had a better deputy secretary.

> Lynn Scarlett deserves a whole section in a book about her dedication to doing the right thing. We had a bushel of issues just in the FWS, and Lynn was always there for us. I wasn't quite on the same page with her Libertarian politics, but she never inserted political views into natural resource issues. She was the real deal. (Stansell 2020)

By the time I retired in 2009, I had the same sentiments about and respect for Lynn Scarlett.

CHAPTER 17

Arctic Refuge and the Polar Bear

In December 2005, Rosa Meehan from the Alaska Regional Office came into D.C. to brief Marshall Jones, Renne Lohoefener and me on a petition to list the polar bear as an endangered species due to climate change. Renne had become the assistant director for endangered species not long after working with me on the Missouri River opinion. My first comment after she began her presentation was "Couldn't you have brought me a controversial one?" She laughed and became a bit more at ease. She knew me from my assignment in Alaska and my work with the spotted owl and other species, which gave her comfort that I was a friendly audience. "I don't really think we will have the data to support a proposed listing of the bear due to climate change," she said, "but I also don't think it would be appropriate to ignore the fact that we should do the evaluation." I agreed. The numbers of polar bears circumpolar were holding relatively steady at around 27,000, but the physical health of individuals was starting to show signs of poor nutrition and smaller body size, and there also were signs of a weakening population. Threatened status was created to allow early intervention to preclude the potential of the species becoming in danger of extinction in the foreseeable future. For the polar bear, that would be about three generations of their species, or approximately mid twenty-first century.

"I understand the pressures and risks involved in beginning this analysis, but that's what we do," I said. "I want at least quarterly updates on the evaluation so I can alert the secretary as soon as possible if we're looking at a proposal to list." Rosa thanked me and headed back to Alaska for Christmas. I asked Renne to stay on top of it because this would be a worldwide issue if we determined it was justified. This vicious man-killer was seen by the public as a cuddly, charismatic megafauna on soft drink cans, and it would quickly become the poster child for climate change. President George W. Bush was quoted in the press as saying "It's now recognized that the surface of the earth is warmer, and that an increase in greenhouse gases caused by humans is contributing to the problem." Many in the White House, including Vice President Cheney, did not agree with supporting the Kyoto Treaty or any form of admission that the earth is warming. As a scientist, I knew that thermometers around the world had not been tampered with to create a hoax, so for me it was straightforward. How long would the trend continue (in other words, was it just weather shifts or truly a change in the climate)? The potential cumulative causes of the warming were open for debate, but not the fact that warming was occurring.

As the summer of 2006 arrived it was becoming apparent that the data were illustrating that the ice in the Arctic was melting at an alarming rate, especially in the summer months. This is of critical importance when looking at the life requisites of polar bears. Unlike their land cousins, polar bears have broad, cushion-like pads on their feet to grip and be able to pursue their primary food source, ringed seals, on large platforms of floating ice. Seals feed on fish and other marine life that are abundant over the continental shelf around the circumference of the north pole. The issue that might tie global warming to the polar bear was the diminishing amount of drift ice over the continental shelf during the summer feeding and cub-rearing months. Also at question was the permanent ice in the Arctic Ocean that does not melt each year and is the "anchor" from which seasonal ice forms and expands. It was a tedious analysis, bringing in scientific expertise in hydrogeology, climatology and other non-traditional Endangered Species Act (ESA) evaluations. David Allen, the regional director (RD) in Portland, Oregon, announced his retirement in August 2006. I asked Renne Lohoefener to take Dave's place as

Polar Bear (Courtesy of USFWS)

RD, and asked Bryan Arroyo to become the new assistant director (AD) for endangered species. I had known Bryan for many years, including as ARD for endangered species in Albuquerque, and had tremendous respect for his ability to remain calm and search for solutions to difficult issues. He stepped in just in time to see the polar bear review start to take shape.

By September we realized that the science was leading to a decision to propose listing. Dr. Mark Myers had taken over as the director of the U.S. Geological Survey after the retirement of Chip Groat. Mark was from Alaska, and many believed that the administration was counting on Mark to challenge any science that might lead to a listing. The state of Alaska and Governor Sarah Palin were most certainly opposed, as I heard on several phone calls from the state seeking information on various subjects associated with the evaluation. Governor Palin never came across as the "lipstick on a bulldog" candidate she morphed into as Senator John McCain's running mate. She usually remained silent and let her staff tell us how ludicrous listing the polar bear would be. But Mark Myers proved to be a disappointment to those who thought he would help cover up science, and was a godsend to me. Between Mark and Lynn Scarlett, I had cover to keep the White House gnomes at bay and do the analyses called for by law.

When I briefed Lynn on the evaluation I told her that we likely would be recommending the bear be proposed for listing as a threatened species, and asked her to set up a briefing with Department of the Interior (DOI) Secretary Dirk Kempthorne. The secretary hadn't continued the weekly briefings that former secretary Gale Norton had done with bureau directors, so we had to go through the chain to get on the calendar. Brian Waidmann, as chief of staff to Kempthorne, was the gatekeeper who decided who made it to the secretary's calendar. Lynn secured a time and date before the end of September for a polar bear briefing for the secretary, but an opportunity arose from the Office of Insular Affairs for Kempthorne to go to our most western Pacific trust territory of Palau. My meeting with the secretary was unceremoniously canceled. We were not able to get back on his schedule until November to fill him in on the issue. I was out of town at that time, so Ken Stansell and Bryan gave the briefing to the secretary without me.

Dr. Steve Amstrup from the U.S. Geological Survey (USGS) had become a member of our scientific team with Mark's support, and the data he and his agency were gathering clearly pointed to the need to list. Significant reduction in summer ice had left the continental shelf almost devoid of drift ice, and therefore devoid of platforms from which the bears could hunt ringed seals as they "hauled out" on the ice during summer. Bears were constantly being observed on land and near villages. Without the ability to hunt for valuable seal meat and fat to store for the winter, bear nutrition continued to decline. The data indicated that polar bears would be in danger of extinction by mid-century, with only the Canadian archipelago expected to provide adequate ice for summer feeding. The problem remained, however, that there was really nothing within our authorities that we had not already exercised to assist in polar bear reproduction and survival. ESA could not regulate ice to not melt, nor control pollution emanating from any number of sources, including India or China.

> When USGS got involved in the science, it started coming together that there may be a case for climate change. The department started paying attention and trying to direct USGS to do something different. Mark Myers had just come on board as USGS director. I never will forget the meeting with Kempthorne at which Bryan and I explained to the secretary that we were going to list and there was no way around listing. He had an interesting reaction. He became fairly professional about what was going to happen, but he had the understanding that it was his responsibility, and this was what the science was telling us. (Stansell 2020)

That Christmas was one of the most agonizing of my life. I believed I had done all I could to alert the secretary that this was coming, but photo ops with Pacific Islanders took priority. As a result, Secretary Kempthorne, Brian Waidmann and others acted as if this was some sort of big surprise. While in Sarah's hometown of Bunkie, Louisiana, I spent four hours on Christmas Eve on a conference call with political appointees who seemed to think policy could change science. Waidmann finally insisted that I return to D.C. to be with the secretary as we alerted the White House and prepared to roll out the proposal to list as threatened. I blew up. "Fine! I'll be on a plane the day after Christmas. And when I get there, you and I are going to have a come to Jesus meeting about whether it's more important to have the secretary's picture with a sea turtle or do our damned jobs and carry out the ESA!" There was silence on the phone from everyone.

As promised, I flew back to D.C., where Kempthorne and I called Jim Connaughton, chair of the president's Council on Environmental Quality, to let him know we believed we had no choice but to list based on the science. We heard a very calm voice on the other end. "I've been expecting you to tell me that. I'm not surprised. I'll let the president know." While I do not believe Jim Connaughton ever gave Dirk Kempthorne any pressure to not list, there was no shortage of others in the White House who had no accountability for the decision, but sure knew the right one. My respect for Dirk grew, even as he thought I had let him down with no early warning. That was for Brian Waidmann and Lynn Scarlett to tell him, not me. The proposal to list as threatened went out on December 27, 2006. The U.S. Fish and Wildlife Service (FWS) had one year by law to receive comments, consider them, write responses and prepare a final decision. As expected, lines were immediately drawn in Congress, and around the world, by those who thought a polar bear listing would bring control of all emissions of greenhouse gases and those who thought it would destroy the U.S. economy. The polar bear fun was just beginning.

> The context of this issue was that this would be the first time, should the species be listed under the ESA, where the primary threat was climate change. In the case for the bear, the loss of habitat as a result of melting sea ice was the issue. It was an ice obligate species . . . The initial draft came back recommending to list as threatened but, as we reviewed the initial documentation, we realized there were still a lot of unanswered questions and knowledge gaps that weakened the science presentation such that, were we sued, we would be readily vulnerable. (Scarlett 2020)

• • •

Dirk Kempthorne had spent the summer getting his feet on the ground and prioritizing the issues he needed to address during his time as secretary. The Republican Congress was looking at the Alaska National Interest Lands Conservation Act (ANILCA) Section 1002 language that reserved their right to decide on opening portions of the Arctic National Wildlife Refuge for oil and gas exploration and development. We had discussed the topic when Kempthorne first arrived, and I gave him my interpretation that the decision belonged to Congress. I also advised him that the Hatch Act was in play, and we could not use career employees to advance a political position. I was unsure of any latitude I had as a presidential appointment confirmed by the Senate (PAS) to advise Congress other than giving the position of the administration, but warned our employees to remember that the issue was pending before Congress and they were prohibited from publicly taking a position. They could, however, provide science and information when it was requested.

The Hatch Act works both ways. It protects employees from being used as political pawns in partisan issues, but also prohibits voluntary intervention when the involvement could be interpreted as being partisan or representing the agency. Not only was oil and gas development in the Arctic National Wildlife Refuge a legal issue; it was also highly charged with emotion. FWS employees are not short on opinions, and I was concerned about the potential for someone to make a mistake, violate the law and give an opinion to the press. Such an act would be deemed an attempt to sway Congress based on their opinion as an FWS employee, not their opinion as a private citizen. Knowledge gained through special access of government employment is considered proprietary unless used in taking an administration action. The last thing I wanted was to have to tell an employee I couldn't protect them because they broke the law. If an employee wants to be an advocate for legislation, they should seek employment in the legislative branch or in the private sector. Our oath in the executive branch is to carry out our responsibilities, while staying within existing law.

The secretary decided to go to the North Slope of Alaska and see the oil and gas activities, as well as visit the 1002 area. The opportunity arose in September when Henri Bisson, a friend in the Bureau of Land Management (BLM) that I had worked with in California, was made deputy director and was overseeing the evaluation of the National Petroleum Reserve in Alaska (NPR-A).

> The National Petroleum Reserve in Alaska is a 23-million-acre area on Alaska's North Slope. In 1923, mindful of the land's conceivable petroleum value, President Harding set aside this area as an emergency oil supply for the U.S. Navy. In 1976, in accordance with the Naval Petroleum Reserves Production Act, administration of the reserve was transferred to the Department of the Interior's Bureau of Land Management . . . The NPR-A includes approximately 23 million of the bureau's 25 million acres of federal mineral estate nationwide and is an important resource for meeting America's energy needs . . . Oil and gas leasing in the NPR-A is authorized under the Naval Petroleum Reserves Act of 1976 (42 U.S.C. 6501 et seq), as amended including the Department of the Interior Appropriations Act of 1981 (94 Stat. 2964) . . . The BLM holds annual oil and gas lease sales for the NPR-A. (BLM 2020)

All lease sales ultimately approved through the bidding process require the secretary's signature. BLM announced in January 2006 that they would make available up to 500,000 acres for bid in the NPR-A, and particularly around Teshekpuk Lake, the largest lake in the Arctic and a significant molting area for geese. Geese shed and regrow their flight feathers each year and during the process are unable to fly. An estimated 46,000 caribou are also known to use the area for migration and calving. The FWS had concerns about oil and gas development around the lake, particularly during the summer molting period.

A trip was scheduled for Henri Bisson, the secretary and me to visit the ongoing facilities at Prudhoe Bay and Deadhorse, fly over Teshekpuk Lake and travel to Kaktovik, the only village on the North Slope inside the Arctic Refuge boundary. I flew to Anchorage on August 28 to attend a "Listening Session," which was an opportunity for the public to give advice on natural resource issues, and then to visit with the regional office staff. On Wednesday, the secretary, Henri and I flew to Deadhorse Camp at Prudhoe Bay. The oil and gas industry had prepared for the secretary to receive a full day of briefings and site visits, focusing on how energy operations were carried out in this tender, yet hostile part of the country.

During one of the briefings, a slide came on the screen that caught my attention. "Please stop there for a minute." We were looking at a high-center polygon with a well head in the center. But instead of seeing a depressed, damaged polygon from the board roads that were used in 1986, there were no signs at all of harm to a very fragile tundra. I said, "Mr. Secretary, I want to point out the well head on top of a high-center polygon. When I worked here in 1986, there would have been significant damage to the tundra from the exploration activities." I asked our energy company hosts "How did you do that without building a road?" They responded, "When you were here in 1986, we built roads with boards and then removed them. Even though they distributed the weight, they still left impressions that will take nearly a century to erase. Today, we use ice to build roads. We only operate in the winter, and we spray water to create layers of ice. When it is thick enough to use as a road without compressing the tundra, we do our work. We are gone by the time the ice melts and there are no signs, except for the well head, that we drove heavy equipment on the polygons. In addition, we monitor the well heads remotely and visit the site only in winter unless there is a significant problem. If so, we helicopter in and do the work without the need for heavy equipment."

I was surprised. I made sure the secretary understood the significance of the new methods. On my first visit to Alaska, I was amazed to learn that the tundra supported species of willow (*Salix* spp.) common throughout the Lower 48 but, due to the harsh environment, only grew to a height of two to three inches in that state. Those small willow plants would be far less likely to be harmed in the production of oil and gas with these new techniques. It wasn't a guarantee, but was light years ahead of where energy development had been just two decades earlier. "Is this the method that would be used in the NPR-A and in the Arctic National Wildlife Refuge, if development was approved by Congress?" I asked. The reply was unhesitating. "Yes, Sir. This is the way business is done now." After getting the VIP tour (the secretary was the VIP; Henri and I were able to join the tours), we headed to Kaktovik by chartered airplane. We made a flyover of Teshekpuk Lake on the way and discussed the importance of the lake to waterfowl and wildlife, while Henri provided figures for potential oil and gas production. After the rather lengthy discussion, both Henri and I recommended that the area around Teshekpuk be reduced or even eliminated from the current bidding process. Secretary Kempthorne agreed. As it turned out, a federal judge came to the same conclusion just a few weeks later.

Kaktovik is the only village in the 19-million-acre refuge and has fewer than three hundred inhabitants, nearly all of Inupiat descent. The village rests about 120 miles east of Deadhorse and approximately 90 miles west of the Canadian border. The village elders were more than gracious in welcoming us to their community. We heard about their history and culture, their love of the land and waters, and their need to hunt and fish for survival. Until one has visited an aboriginal community like this, it is difficult to understand that they don't just love nature; they *depend on nature* for life. However, they were also in need of more modern necessities and knew that a balance needed to be found between tradition and twenty-first-century commerce.

The elders explained their needs for more diverse economic opportunities, but also their fears about the potential oil and gas development. It was a dilemma I had heard from Native American tribal elders in the Lower 48. They felt they were entrusted with the history and culture of their people, but the young generation saw the outside world through the Internet, TV and movies. They were concerned about the cultural changes that could take place, yet understood the economic potential of

Dirk Kempthorne (left) and author in Alaska (Courtesy of USDOI)

energy development. We visited the school and talked with the students. Even for a polished politician like Dirk, it was difficult to get the kids to open up and talk with us. To them, we were just "outsiders," and they had been taught to be wary of outsiders. We heard about the more frequent visits of polar bears in the summer as the sea mammal had to search for food on land, and the extra efforts made to protect the children. After a walk through the village, we boarded the twin-engine charter and returned to Deadhorse.

• • •

The challenges facing the director of the Fish and Wildlife Service meant that the majority of my time was spent trying to find solutions to long-standing issues, fighting the political "fire of the day" and working with good people to try to chart a course for the future. "Fun" is not a word I would use to describe the experience, but "rewarding" certainly captures the emotion. Heidi Marquez Smith, David P. Smith's wife and special assistant to the president, had significant influence in the White House social calendar. A woman obviously talented and savvy in the political arena, she was as beautiful on the outside as she was a person. She knew I was separated from my family and had a relatively isolated private life in D.C., so she made sure I got invitations to attend official White House gatherings much more frequently than others at my "political" level.

I was greatly appreciative of this wonderful gesture, but going alone to events at the White House didn't appeal to me any more than attending the Forest Summit with President Clinton had. It just wasn't my cup of tea, but I have never forgotten her kindness in trying to look after me. I did attend a small dinner with the president when he invited Jean-Michel Cousteau to show his film "Ocean Adventures" in the White House movie theater, which seated just over forty people. His father, Jacques Cousteau, is credited as the inventor of the self-contained underwater breathing apparatus (SCUBA), and is an icon in the world of sea exploration and conservation. Dr. Cousteau, like his father, was charming and had the innate gift of drawing one into the subject as if you were there, scuba diving on the reefs. It wasn't until Sarah joined me that I attended another White House function.

But there were two "duties" of the director that I truly loved doing. The first was being a board member with the National Fish and Wildlife Foundation (NFWF), which was created in 1984 to make it possible for FWS and the National Marine Fisheries Service (NMFS) to secure private gifts. NFWF was established by Congress as a quasi-governmental entity; a hybrid that allowed federal budgets in the agencies to include funds for NFWF to manage and leverage for conservation, as well as providing status under the IRS as a not-for-profit foundation. NFWF is expected to raise philanthropic dollars to match the federal funds appropriated, and all monies are directed to conservation and conservation education. By law, the director of the FWS sits as a voting member of the board, as does the director of NMFS. Jeff Trandahl is executive director of NFWF and one of the most talented people in the conservation community.

I first met Jeff through his father, Arden Trandahl, manager of the Spearfish National Fish Hatchery (Arden led the effort to change the name to the D.C. Booth National Historic Fish Hatchery) when I was the deputy in Fisheries. Jeff was just beginning his career as a staff person for Democratic Senator Tom Daschle of South Dakota. He quickly impressed everyone in Congress with his talents and ability to work with staff across the aisle, and eventually became chief clerk of the U.S. House of Representatives, serving as Speaker Dennis Hastert's (R) chief of staff. From there he accepted the position of executive director of NFWF, and it proved to be a historic action. Jeff methodically began growing NFWF into the largest conservation grant-giving organization in America. Working with Jeff, Chairman Paul Tudor Jones, the board and staff at NFWF was a true pleasure, and I looked forward to every meeting. Even though they were the titans of industry, the board members came together with no politics in mind, just conservation. My time serving on the board of NFWF opened the door and allowed me to see just how dedicated to conservation and philanthropy those in finance and industry can be. It was a real awakening.

The other function I loved as director was my involvement in the National Duck Stamp Contest and presiding over the "first day of sale" of the new stamps. The Migratory Bird Division staff came to me in the fall of 2005 and asked if I would be open to having the Duck Stamp contest held out in the regions instead of at the main Department of the Interior (DOI) Building in D.C. In my ignorance I asked, "Do we always have it here?" "Yes," came the reply. "It's so the secretary can just ride the elevator down to the auditorium and announce the winner." I was taken aback that a stamp lobbied for, paid for and supported by the hunters and stamp collectors was held in D.C. at the convenience of the secretary, while the heroes it belonged to had to travel to D.C. for the contest. It should be *their* contest, and the artists should be able to show their works to the people who actually support them! If the secretary believed it important enough to announce the winner, s/he could travel to be with the conservationists to which it belonged.

Ducks Unlimited and Arts Memphis had requested to hold the contest in Memphis at the Memphis Brooks Museum of Art. I quickly agreed, and the wheels started turning to have the first contest held outside D.C. in the fall of 2006. I saw firsthand that the hunters and philatelists were not alone in their dedication to wetlands and waterfowl. The passion I observed in the artists was both a revelation and awe-inspiring. The contest has been held away from D.C. ever since. Jay Norwood "Ding" Darling championed creation of the stamp and, with it, the tradition that the director of the FWS (which was called the U.S. Biological Survey under Darling's tenure as its director) had the honor of purchasing the first stamp each year, followed by the postmaster general. The first day of sale usually occurs at the beginning of June, and it too was held in D.C. at either the DOI Building or the headquarters office of the Postal Service in Washington, D.C. The staff once again came to me and said that Johnny Morris, the founder of Bass Pro Shops, asked if we would hold the first day of sale at his Baltimore store. He offered to stream the broadcast live to all Bass Pro Shops and challenge them to compete for highest number of stamps sold. I immediately agreed.

I had talked to Johnny Morris on the phone but had never met him in person. I knew of him because of his beginnings on the Bassmaster fishing circuit, but didn't know how deeply he loved conservation. We convened at the Baltimore store, where his staff had gone all out to place a stage in the middle of the hunting section, with TV monitors all over the store. Johnny was gracious in every way, and I presented him with an award for his conservation stewardship. Little did I know that our meeting would begin a deep friendship that would last for life. As time went on it became clear that Johnny Morris was the real deal, an icon in fish and wildlife conservation. The tradition of holding the first day of sale, in conjunction with Ducks Unlimited, at a Bass Pro Shop somewhere across the nation was born and continues today.

• • •

December 2006 was a month to be remembered. The proposed listing of the polar bear as a threatened species due to melting summer ice and the release of the Department of the Interior Inspector General's Report on Julie MacDonald brought intense visibility to DOI. Released by the Office of the Inspector General on December 1, the *Investigative Report On Allegations Against Julie MacDonald, Deputy Assistant Secretary, Fish, Wildlife and Parks*, was a scathing indictment of Julie's inappropriate behavior and activities in violation of federal regulations.

Through interviewing various sources, including FWS employees and senior officials, and reviewing pertinent documents and e-mails, we confirmed that MacDonald has been heavily involved with editing, commenting on, and reshaping Endangered Species Program's scientific reports from the field. MacDonald admitted that her degree is in civil engineering and that she has no formal educational background in natural sciences, such as biology.

The report went on to state, in part:

On April 11, 2006, the OIG received an anonymous complaint from an employee of the FWS alleging unethical and illegal activities by MacDonald. The complainant stated that MacDonald had persistently harassed, bullied, and insulted FWS employees to change documents and 'ignore good science' related to the Endangered Species Program . . . When we interviewed the former Director of the FWS Endangered Species Program he stated that many of the scientific reports his office has issued have been edited extensively by MacDonald, who has no background in biology, and cited the Sage Grouse Risk Analysis as an example. He explained that many other officials in MacDonald's position have made changes to reports to reflect their political philosophy, but MacDonald regularly bypassed managers to speak directly with field staff, often intimidating and bullying them into producing documents that had the desired effect she and the former Assistant Secretary wanted. (OIG Report 2006)

The role of the assistant secretary's office is to review the documents for policy accuracy after they have been reviewed by the director's office for biological strength, and the solicitor's office for legal compliance. Julie decided, unilaterally or with the support of Assistant Secretary Judge Craig Manson, that she had the authority to do all three. The report also stated that "the former Ecological Services director stated that overall, MacDonald did not want to accept petitions to list species as endangered, and she did not want to designate critical habitats. He said the overall effect was to minimize the Endangered Species Act as much as possible or ensnare it in court litigation, which happened often." The report contained statements made by several other career employees of the FWS:

The Assistant Director for External Affairs described MacDonald as 'an angry woman' who had been abusive to her and had become a liability to FWS. She stated that MacDonald had demoralized the FWS program with her interference in endangered species studies—often reaching 'way down the line' to have reports reflect what she wanted.

When the Inspector General (IG) interviewed Steve Thompson and his staff at the California/Nevada Operations Office (CNO), they got several damning statements.

The CNO Manager was aware of DOI/FWS headquarters personnel who wanted to file a hostile work environment complaint against MacDonald. He said his employees at CNO were definitely stressed, pushed, and yelled at by MacDonald. The CNO Manager stated he would interject at any point when he felt MacDonald had clearly stepped out of her authority and was demeaning to his staff, even to the point of halting conference calls. . . .

The Portland Assistant Regional Solicitor sent the attorney in the Solicitor's Office at MIB (Main Interior Building) an e-mail with the subject 'and the Red Queen was talking backwards,' after the conference call (on bull trout). The Portland Assistant Regional Solicitor wrote, 'Re: today's call. I'm still reeling from my little taste of it, but its [sic] Alice in Wonderland every day for you, isn't it?' The Assistant Regional Solicitor opined that MacDonald was disrespectful, rude, and unprofessional, and said 'never in over 20 years of government service' had he seen a political appointee behave like she did. (OIG Report 2006)

When they interviewed Craig Manson, he told them "he had complete confidence in MacDonald's abilities, first as his special assistant and then as deputy (assistant) secretary . . . He stated he was personally involved in these issues as they were matters of importance to him." Julie also told the IG that Judge Manson was "very involved regarding endangered species and critical habitat determinations." Violation of federal regulations were found to have occurred on several occasions. It was proven, and Julie later concurred, that she had shared internal, not for public review documents with private western water interests. The draft documents and information she shared were found to have been ineligible for release, even under the Freedom of Information Act, because they were under internal deliberation. In conclusion, the IG Report stated:

Title 5 of the Code of Federal Regulations (C.F.R.), Chapter XVI, Subpart G, Standards of Ethical Conduct for Employees of the Executive Branch Sec 2635.703 Use of Non-public Information states:

(a) *Prohibition*. An employee shall not . . . allow the improper use of nonpublic information to further his own private interest or that of another, whether through advice or recommendations, or by knowing unauthorized disclosure.

(b) *Definition of nonpublic information*. . . . Is information that the employee gains by reason of Federal employment and that he knows or reasonably should know has not been made available to the general public.

An Associate General Counsel of the OIG's Office of General Counsel reviewed the details of our investigation and advised that the C.F.R. had been violated under 5 C.F.R. Sec 2635.101 Basic Obligation of Public Service because of the appearance of preferential treatment and 5 C.F.R. Sec 2635.703 Standards of Conduct, Use of Nonpublic Information. (OIG Report 2006)

We decided that even though the IG's report didn't say it was per se interference with scientific integrity, nonetheless for full transparency and comfort, we thought it prudent to have you go through various decisions that had been made under Julie's review to determine whether any of them really should be reviewed . . . To my mind, it's important not only to do things from the standpoint of scientific integrity right, but also to have really strong approaches to personal dynamics and collaboration, listening and trust building. Good decision-making is as much about trust building as it is about scientific integrity and scientific details . . . I told political appointees who came into the department to remember that there are 70,000 employees in the Department of the Interior. Let's say they have an average of ten years of experience. That's 700,000 years of experience to draw from. I, from day one, have zero experience. The ability to do well hinges on tapping the ability of the many. (Scarlett 2020)

Government employees are no different from any others when it comes to rumors and gossip. The word of the OIG report spread like wildfire throughout the department, and in little time was well known on Capitol Hill. Chairman Nick Rahall of the House Committee on Natural Resources officially requested a copy of the OIG report, and IG Earl Devaney transmitted it to the chairman on March 23, 2007. Julie was still on board in the department, but even those who were aligned with her philosophies started to distance themselves. The only thing Brian Waidmann feared more than Earl Devaney, and a possible OIG investigation, was a congressional investigation. Julie A. MacDonald resigned from the Department of the Interior on May 1, 2007, just over a month after transmittal of the report to the House Committee.

I had already requested that the regions provide any species packages they believed Julie had inappropriately changed or that they believed they had been harassed into changing. Lynn Scarlett and I discussed the situation with a new awareness from Lynn, and we were committed to having packages withdrawn that had been unduly influenced. I asked our endangered species staff in D.C. to collate the input. I had conversations with each RD and Steve Thompson (who was not an RD at the time; we made California and Nevada a separate region at a later date) and allowed them to tell me which packages they would like returned for reconsideration. On July 12, 2007, I sent a memo to Lynn outlining my instructions to the regions and their response.

Before I relay the results of the review, I'd like to outline what was requested and how the review ensued. The roles and responsibilities of the assistant secretary's office include review of documents to ensure conformance with established policy, and the authority to examine current policies and execute changes to those policies based on legal interpretations. The gathering and analysis of any science used is the responsibility of the director of the FWS, working through the career scientists in the bureau. A clear line of separation of duties is imperative if we are to maintain scientific credibility and the trust of the American people . . . It was agreed by all that the list below represents a comprehensive review and the final recommendations of ESA actions that should be re-evaluated. (Hall 2007)

The species identified were the *Arroyo toad Critical Habitat; California red-legged frog Critical Habitat; 12 species of Hawaiian picture-wing flies Critical Habitat; White-tailed prairie dog 90-day finding; Lynx Critical Habitat; Preble's meadow jumping mouse 12-month finding/proposed delisting; Preble's meadow jumping mouse Critical Habitat;* and *Southwest willow flycatcher Critical Habitat*. Lynn was now my full partner in "fixing" this issue of scientific trust and responded, in part:

I appreciate the diligence and thoroughness of you and your staff in all FWS regions as you undertook this evaluation . . . Please extend my thanks to the FWS employees for their professionalism in completing this assignment. (Scarlett 2007)

On November 7, Oregon Senator Ron Wyden requested that the OIG investigate eighteen endangered species actions he believed had been unduly impacted by Julie MacDonald, which was followed by a request from House Committee Chairman Nick Rahall to examine a couple of other listing actions. The OIG undertook the investigation focusing on Julie MacDonald and released a report in December 2008 titled *The Endangered Species Act and the Conflict between Science and Policy*. IG Devaney stated in the cover memo to Secretary Kempthorne,

> Our findings from this investigation are much the same, although we found that the nature and extent of MacDonald's influence varied dramatically from one decision to another. (Devaney 2008)

The Julie MacDonald intrusion into the ethical world of science is a lesson I hope will not soon be forgotten. Political appointees play a critical role in the process of making government work. Whether they are presidential appointees confirmed by the Senate, or Schedule C appointees by the DOI secretary, all can prove to be valuable partners with career employees who have made the Department of the Interior their career home. When team roles are clearly understood and respect is given, trust and teamwork follow, and the process is magical to watch. It is conversely the most painful to endure when respect is absent. No respect, no trust, no teamwork, no success. The final effort resulted in the issue being addressed and the team coming together for good government. Through pain we hope will emerge wisdom.

CHAPTER 18

Drafting Endangered Species Act Regulations and Opposing the Navy Outlying Landing Field

Secretary of the Interior Dirk Kempthorne was feeling the heat of the decision to propose listing of the polar bear and Julie MacDonald's interference with science as well as other issues related to the Endangered Species Act (ESA). Although we didn't have weekly meetings, we often met in his office on particular issues or after work for a relaxed discussion of challenges facing the Department of the Interior (DOI). Ann Klee and Lynn Scarlett were regulars in those after-hours meetings, and they were two people I came to respect. Ann could come across as uncaring to some, but that was her way of distancing herself from the emotional aspects of an issue. I support approaching issues unemotionally. My love of the resource and the emotions that came along with it is why I got into this field. But emotions need to be removed from business decisions. The only good decision I ever made based on emotion was marrying Sarah. All the others didn't turn out so well. Ann was analytical, quick to cut through the BS and always in search of a solution. Lynn was a deep thinker and was fully committed to doing the right thing under the law, and for the resource.

One evening in late January 2007, we were in the secretary's office when Dirk asked if I thought the ESA should be changed or updated. "Of course," I replied. "It expired in 1993!" The look on his face was priceless. He had been a senator, yet apparently had no idea that during the entire time he had been in office, the ESA was being authorized annually through the appropriations process.

"Why hasn't it been reauthorized?" he asked.

"Because both sides are afraid of the outcome. Those who want it weaker are afraid it will end up stronger, and those who want it stronger are afraid it will end up weaker. It's a fear of the sausage-making process."

"How do our employees view the Act?"

"They are very frustrated. In the nearly twenty years since the last reauthorization, highly significant activities and court cases have occurred, including the spotted owl, silvery minnow, Missouri River and grizzly bear. We have learned a lot, and they know what does and doesn't really contribute to their ability to care for species. They also know how other federal and state agencies could help."

"So how do we get that done? Can you get the career employees to help suggest how the law could work more efficiently?"

"Changing the law is out of our realm of authority. But changing regulations is squarely in our wheelhouse. I would be happy to establish an effort with our *career leaders* to propose changes to the regulations, but only under two conditions. First, you have to commit that no political appointee, except me, will even attempt to sit in on or edit the changes proposed by the career professionals. Second, you have to commit to me that you will support those changes as the employees write them and allow no political edits. Our strongest voices will be from the career employees defending their own recommendations. If you or anyone in OMB [Office of Management and Budget] alters their recommendations, I will not direct them to remain silent or support the modified proposal. I know those are big asks, but will you commit to them?" Dirk looked at Lynn and Ann for advice.

Ann said "If Dale can get the career employees to eliminate things that are a pain in the rear for the public, yet don't help the species, that would be a significant improvement." Lynn was excited to include the career employees and understood that was how long-term change occurs.

"All right. You have my commitment to those conditions, and we'll get started trying to get some 'policy time' with POTUS,'" Kempthorne replied. "It won't do any good if the president doesn't let OMB know he wants this to happen."

Setting up meetings with the president of the United States is not an easy task, even for members of his own cabinet. Lynn Scarlett worked with the White House to get on his calendar, and the time was set for February 20 at 2:05 p.m. We met in one of the large meeting rooms to accommodate the people the president wanted there for policy reasons. Secretary Kempthorne, Deputy Secretary Scarlett and I were the three from the Department of the Interior. With President George W. Bush were Vice President Dick Cheney, Council on Environmental Quality (CEQ) Chair Jim Connaughton, Karl Rove, and Rob Portman from OMB. There were several other staff from OMB and the White House as well.

The secretary sat at the conference table with the president; Lynn and I had assigned seats just behind Dirk but facing the president and others on his team. After explaining that the ESA had undergone significant clarification through the courts over the years and that he believed there was a path forward in making the law more workable, Secretary Kempthorne said "Dale Hall, our director of the Fish and Wildlife Service and also a former career employee, believes he can pull together leaders of the FWS from across the country to update and significantly improve regulations for both the public and the species." Karl Rove immediately locked eyes with me as if to say *I'm not buying this. Will career employees really help make the law work better?* I slowly nodded my head yes in a nonverbal response. He continued to stare for a few more seconds, then looked back at President Bush.

The president asked those at the table what they thought. One of them said "It's never too late to do the right thing." President Bush looked at Dirk, Lynn and me and said "OK. I'm sure no one else is going to fight you to do this. Go ahead and give it a shot." The timing was good in that we had nearly two years before the end of his second term, which allowed adequate time for discussing, proposing and finalizing if we kept to a hard schedule. I already knew who the team should be. As a former assistant regional director of Ecological Services (ES), I knew where the hard discussions took place and where the tough pushback had to occur to ensure that a biologically accurate and legally correct decision was made. I pulled in ES assistant regional directors (ARDs) from around the regions for this one. This was less about science and more about how to make a program work, both for the public we serve and for the biologists whose plates are overflowing with needless requirements that didn't benefit the species.

There was some hesitation from the ARDs because they had experience with Julie MacDonald and her previous effort to rewrite the regulations, hand them to staff and attempt to browbeat them into agreement. That approach didn't work very well.

> There was ESA Regulations effort one, in which I was involved and was driven by Julie MacDonald. We found that whatever she wrote, we just could not deal with as an organization legally or fundamentally. From an implementation standpoint, we thought it was so much out to lunch that we just couldn't handle it.
>
> Phase two was formed by you pulling in the ARDs and some headquarters staff to basically develop an agency-derived revision to the regs. I considered the ESA regs piece to be one of the most important things I ever worked on. My philosophy when I was coming up through the ranks was 'Could I do better from the position I was going to than the position I'm in?' Everybody thinks the field supervisor is the best job in the world. You have your piece of ground that is your responsibility. I would maintain that the ARD is the best because you have your feet in two worlds: you get to hire the rank-and-file field people who are

going to implement your program consistent with your vision, and you have your other foot in the national policy arena to help develop policy consistent with your vision. I saw the regs effort as a key component to improve how we can implement the ESA both at a national policy level and the field. I thought it was a great opportunity. (Thabault 2020)

David Bernhardt was the solicitor for the Department of the Interior, which entails being the secretary's advisory attorney and making all legal determinations under laws DOI is charged to administer. The ESA was certainly one of those, and I came to know David very well. He grew up in Rifle, Colorado, and loved the outdoors. While the secretary was gregarious and loved being the politician, David was quiet, low key and always open to hearing your view, especially if different from his own. He loved the law and believed it was alive and open to evolution in interpretation, but not subject to change by the executive branch. He saw his job as helping the Department of the Interior stay within the law, but allow as much latitude and innovation as possible. My respect for him grew, as did our friendship, through the numerous discussions of lawsuits that were constantly pending against the DOI, FWS and me. At one point I asked, "How many lawsuits do I have against me?" David smiled and said "On any given day, you have between fifty and sixty." "Do they think I'm doing too much, or too little?" "About half think you are out of control and abusing the law," he replied. "The other half thinks you are milquetoast and aren't doing anything." "Well," I concluded, "we must be striking a pretty good balance if both sides hate me!"

• • •

As a political appointee, I seemed to have lost all credit for the years I spent working for both Democratic and Republican administrations as a career employee. To those who just like to criticize anyone they see as being part of the "administration," I was obviously a political lap dog. It was like "Yesterday I couldn't spell political and now I are one!" An FWS employee once stopped me in the hallway and suggested I Google myself. "You'll get a real kick out of the discussion about you under SOS Forests." That evening, I Googled myself and clicked on the suggested string of comments. I started laughing out loud as I read them. I had already developed a thick skin relative to comments about me and had adopted the philosophy I had seen somewhere else that said: "Your comments can only upset me if I respect you." Since I didn't respect anyone who would sit at a computer and try to elevate themselves by denigrating others, I decided to print these particular ones as keepsakes.

Fire H. Dale Hall, May 14, 2007

The Director of the US Fish and Wildlife Service, H. Dale Hall, is a monumental screw-up who should be fired immediately with extreme prejudice. Then he should be kicked clean out of the USA with heartfelt alacrity and fresh relish.

Maybe Europe wants him, but we don't. Read all about H. Dale (here), if you want to. You can smell the commie-fascist stench even through the fawning propaganda. Northern spotted owls, Klamath 'Ecoregion,' Hawaiian birds, more than 300 new species placed under the protection of the Endangered Species Act; H. Dale has had his hand in some of the most egregious acts of violence and fraud science against America and Americans in history. Bunch him, dumpsterize him, fire H. Dale Hall to the Moon. Whatever, get him the hell away from the reins of power, and do it today. H. Dale Hall is toxic bad news, and America is sick of him." (Posted May 14, 2007, under Enemies of Forests, The Wild Life).

The responses followed:

Once again, you've nailed it. This guy Hall is a national disgrace. Nothing but a Bush flunkie who does the dirty work of industry. We need someone in there who actually protects endangered species! Keep up the good fight.

You missed the nail. H. Dale is a tool of the eco-Fascists. They took over under slick Willy and Dubya hasn't had the guts to root them out.

I guess I must have been both a Bush flunkie and a Slick Willy leftover! This is why social media has the reputation it has; it earned it the old-fashioned way. I simply recall Theodore Roosevelt's "Man in the Arena"—it's not the critic who counts—and keep going. But you've gotta laugh at stupidity sometimes. Everyone is ignorant about different things. Ignorance is simply not knowing. Stupidity, however, is not caring to know and being comfortable with ignorance. Ignorance can be remedied by factual information. Stupidity has no cure.

• • •

The Team of ARDs and their counterparts from the National Marine Fisheries Service (NMFS) assembled in the FWS building on Fairfax Avenue across the river in Arlington, Virginia, and began their work. Dirk kept his word and denied access to anyone who was a political appointee. Michael Bogert, a special assistant to the secretary and someone I held in high regard, asked if he could sit in on the discussions "to learn." I agreed but admonished him to not engage in the discussions other than to ask for clarification so he could follow the logic. I asked the team members to let me know if they perceived any attempt to influence their decisions. Throughout the process I got nothing but compliments from the team on Michael's behavior. At the end of the process, the team had walked through the ESA regulations, section by section, and proposed changes wherever their experience indicated there could be improvements. They looked at ways other federal and state agencies could play a more proactive role under their own and ESA authorities. The end draft contained seventy-one pages of the most experienced recommendations the ESA had ever seen. Jointly, there were hundreds of years of experience behind these proposed changes. I was extremely proud of the team and the way the NMFS and FWS came together to make the act more uniform between them. It was time to give briefings.

The first one occurred with Secretary Kempthorne, Deputy Secretary Scarlett, and several others in the department. Both Julie and David P. had left by the time these were completed, and Matt Hogan was acting assistant secretary while Coloradan Lyle Laverty was going through the confirmation process. To a person, the political structure of the DOI had nothing but compliments for the depth of thought and the innovative ideas contained in the draft. I surnamed the package with the understanding that the secretary would forward the draft proposed regulation changes to the Office of Management and Budget in the White House for their strenuous review.

Done properly, the review by OMB should question the economic impacts of the proposal, the benefits in efficiency, and the progress toward obtaining both the law's intent as well as the goals of the administration. Regulations take on the force of law once implemented, and the courts rely on regulatory language to a significant degree in judging legal challenges. As a courtesy, we next set up a meeting with the House Natural Resources staff to brief them on the draft. While the Congress has no role to play in promulgating regulations, good government demands that the legislative branch be aware of, and given the opportunity to provide input to, the regulations implementing laws they have passed.

We arrived at our meeting at the Ford House Office Building just southwest of the more prominent Cannon, Longworth and Rayburn House Office Buildings. When we walked into the room, I noticed that only the House majority staff were present. As we waited for the others to arrive, the chief of staff for the House Committee on Natural Resources said "We can get started if you'd like." "Where are the minority staff?" I asked. "I'm afraid you'll have to brief them separately," she replied. "Only the majority staff know about this meeting." I exploded. "Do I understand you correctly that professional adults, both working for the same committee, cannot sit in the same room and hear a briefing from the executive branch?" The committee's chief of staff was obviously embarrassed by the way their lack of professionalism had been called out. "I'm sorry, that's just the way things are working now," she said. "Very well," I replied. "We will brief you, and then the minority staff. But for the record, all future invitations to be briefed by anyone on my staff will go to the chair and ranking minority member of the committee from my office. They will not be sent to you with the expectation that professionalism will occur, nor the belief that you will share that invitation with all committee staff. I have worked with many of you for well over a decade. I am sorely disappointed."

I turned over the briefing to the team and let them handle it in whatever way they had chosen. It was their briefing. I simply endorsed their proposals. We later briefed the minority staff, and then the environmental community. In every case, I opened the meeting by explaining the assignment I had given the team and their autonomy to get the job done as they saw fit. I was not disappointed. These career professionals were proud of the proposals they were making and fiercely defended them against questions of political interference or their ability to achieve efficiency and the purposes of the Act.

After all the work the team did, and the commitment by the secretary that their work would be supported, the draft rules were never officially transmitted to the White House from the department. We were never able to confirm the source, but were certain that someone in the White House didn't think they went far enough to satisfy an agenda and told the secretary not to move them until they were made more draconian. Our career team was proud of the document they had produced.

If one actually understood the ESA, it would have been clear how substantial the proposed changes were to the public. On January 2, 2009, my last official act as director was to clarify for the record that our career employee–driven draft never officially left the Department of the Interior. I wrote a memo to Assistant Secretary Laverty to clarify our position and to protect the work that Secretary Kempthorne had supported.

> I am aware that Secretary Dirk Kempthorne has requested you to forward the draft Endangered Species Act (ESA) regulation changes proposed by our employees . . . The commitment I secured from Secretary Kempthorne prior to my agreement to be involved in proposed regulatory changes included his word that he would not propose any ESA regulation changes that did not have the support of the career team I assembled. (Hall 2009)

My concern at the time was fear of mischief within the ranks of departing "invisibles" in the White House who might make changes on their way out the door while claiming it had been done by the career employees.

> I now officially withhold the proposed regulations drafted by our employees as 'INTERNAL AND DRAFT WITHIN AND ONLY FOR THE FISH AND WILDLIFE SERVICE,' and not ready for movement toward higher level review . . . Movement forward of this draft at this time DOES NOT constitute the proposed position of the U.S. Fish and Wildlife Service. (Hall 2009)

The tremendous effort by the expert FWS staff did, however, finally get recognized and partially adopted by Secretary David Bernhardt under the administration of Donald J. Trump. Having been there through the effort under Secretary Kempthorne, and his knowledge of the significance of the recommendations from the career employees, Bernhardt pushed several aspects of the proposed regulation changes, along with some of his own views, over the finish line.

> Round one was a complete 'cluster' and we co-opted on that one [the MacDonald effort]. Round two [under Kempthorne] went really well, but I was supremely disappointed that things didn't get adopted then. But in round three [under Bernhardt], especially in Section 7 modifications, they adopted almost 90 percent of what we did in round two. You don't always get everything you want, but I think that's a pretty good track record! We had a great team. The ARD cohort at that time, and it lasted for several years afterward, I think it was the best ARD team of any program in the Service. We didn't bitch about money, we didn't quibble over interpretations. We had vigorous conversations for sure, but at the end of the day we were of like mind on how Ecological Services was viewed at the administration level, within the Service and otherwise. The ESA regs piece was a means for me to make a difference for all programs within the Service.
>
> When we were doing round three under the Trump administration, David Bernhardt was there at NCTC [National Conservation Training Center] and we talked about the ESA one and two efforts, Cal-Fed/Bay-Delta and all the stuff we had been involved in together. He was there, and you could make a case to him based on the law. He gave us, even in round three, by-and-large free rein to write what we needed to write. He had a couple of things that he wanted to do, and he told us what they were so we could take them under consideration, mostly in relation to Section 10. That felt good. If you could make a legal argument with science, he would acknowledge you were right and would go with your view. But if you came in emotional, you could count on being hosed.

When (Secretary Ryan) Zinke came in at the beginning of the Trump administration, there was a clear disdain for career people. Everybody made decisions in the absence of any advice because they didn't want to take any advice. They thought they had all the answers. For example, Zinke made this crazy sage grouse decision after we had put in five years of sitting down and working with all the disparate parties. At the agreement signing ceremony, a Republican governor got up with Sally Jewell, Democratic secretary of the interior, and praised what we had done. And Zinke just blew it all up.

I was always given a lot of free rein to find solutions, and it isn't always about getting everything we want. If you lose the war, you don't get to come back for another day. Trying to coach staff and our senior managers in the field was a real challenge for a lot of years. It takes time and energy that people have to be willing to expend. A lot of times it's easier just to follow the rule book. It's a lot harder to work in a true partnership and get to yes. It may be much easier to say no, but that's seldom the right answer. (Thabault 2020)

• • •

My time in the Air Force's "military intelligence" let me see some of the illogical things that can be dreamed up by those who could use a small dose of common sense. When I arrived as director in 2005, I was informed about the Navy's attempt to capture the Darwin Award for audacity. They had begun the planning process in late 2001 and, in September 2003, released the decision to locate and construct, for use by Super Hornet Aircraft Squadrons at Naval Air Station Oceana in Virginia and Marine Corps Air Station Cherry Point in North Carolina, an outlying landing field (OLF) somewhere between the two stations. An OLF is a landing strip onshore where Navy pilots can practice touch-and-go landings to simulate aircraft carrier landings. The Navy proposed a site in North Carolina comprising 23,000 acres in Washington County and 7,000 acres in Beaufort County. The opposition to this site began immediately from local residents, but also involved the FWS because Pocosin Lakes National Wildlife Refuge (NWR) was within a quarter-mile of designated "Site C." Pocosin Lakes is well known for its wintering populations of 20,000 tundra swans and nearly 50,000 snow geese.

The Southern Environmental Law Center (SELC) filed suit on behalf of several environmental organizations in January 2004, challenging the adequacy of the National Environmental Policy Act (NEPA) documentation and the lack of full disclosure of the impacts to birds and other wildlife species of over *31,000 field carrier landing practices each year.* Having dealt with airports around the country throughout my career to avoid bird/aircraft strikes, I almost laughed out loud at the prospect of constant aircraft within a quarter-mile of a large population of *very large* birds. A tundra swan (*Cygnus columbianus*) has an average size of four to five feet in length, a wingspan of up to seven feet and a weight of up to twenty-one pounds! Snow geese (*Anser caerulescens*) are smaller, but still formidable at over seven pounds, approximately thirty-one inches in length and a wingspan of up to sixty-five inches. These are not birds a pilot would like to encounter while operating a jet aircraft!

In February the SELC filed for a preliminary injunction against the Navy, and the court agreed by stating that the plaintiffs had presented compelling evidence that the construction of the OLF at Site C would irreparably harm numerous swans and snow geese through destruction of their habitats. The court also cited the increased noise and the mandatory displacement of approximately one hundred families in Washington and Beaufort Counties. The Navy conducted a bird/wildlife aircraft strike hazard analysis and determined that it was at an acceptable level, *given the actions planned to remove and deter the birds from the area.*

It was first we will plant a type of grass that the geese won't like. Then it was we'll have dogs or something to chase them away. Then it was, if worse comes to worse, we'll put poison out to deter the wildlife from coming to this area. It was a sequence something along those lines and something along the line of preposterous! (Scarlett 2020)

The court didn't accept the findings at face value and noted that the Navy would endure no irreparable harm because they had not even purchased land at that point. In March 2005, a permanent injunction was issued pending rectification of inadequate NEPA documentation. The Navy responded by announcing they would prepare a supplemental environmental impact statement (EIS) and asked the FWS to be a cooperating agency. A cooperating agency bears no responsibility for the adequacy of the full disclosure document, but agrees to provide significant information and analyses to the "action agency"—in this case, the Navy.

All this had occurred prior to my arrival, and I was quite ignorant of a substantial amount of the information when Regional Director Sam Hamilton called to ask for my help. Sam didn't believe the Navy was acting in good faith to perform a proper analysis of alternatives and, further, they had already decided on Site C and were just working on justification. He explained the substantial impacts that would come to the Pocosin NWR and the species that would be harmed, including the red wolf (*Canis lupus rufus*), an endangered species the FWS was attempting to recover through active management in the area.

On March 2, 2007, Sam (via phone) and I briefed Lynn Scarlett in her office on the OLF and our significant concerns. We walked Lynn through the horrendous job the Navy had done as it attempted to dismiss all the devastating impacts that would occur. Pocosin Lakes is a national wildlife refuge, and the director is responsible for ensuring its protection. Sam was well respected throughout the DOI as a true field general, and Lynn was amazed at what she was being told. I let her know that I fully supported the FWS comments that had been provided, but also planned to attend the public hearing and deliver them myself. Sam believed that the Navy would continue to steamroll the public unless I showed up to get their attention.

> I had no knowledge of the OLF until I was deputy secretary because it wasn't in my area as assistant secretary . . . You and Sam came and presented all this information about the refuge, the swans and snow geese and how absurd this particular alternative was. You also said 'Here are the four other sites, and we'll help them find one that works.' You showed me that it was reasonable to work on one of the other alternatives, which would only add five minutes or less of flying time over the preferred alternative . . . From a public sentiment standpoint, the public was opposed to the preferred site, while there was far less opposition to some of the other alternatives.
>
> We decided that we would take a stand here. We're going to send Dale, as the director, to this meeting. Not that Sam couldn't handle it, but we wanted Dale to go make a statement on our position with a list of points of concern. The points were so clear and important that Senator [Elizabeth] Dole, who to that point had not spoken out, wrote a letter to the Navy asking that all the points presented at the meeting be addressed. Of course, it was impossible to answer the points by way of the Navy's preferred alternative. We focused on the science. We focused on the mission. We focused on the law. We used leadership to highlight the evidence to draw attention in a way that was able to build political support. (Scarlett 2020)

I set up a meeting on March 15 with Deputy Assistant Secretary (DAS) of the Navy for Environment Phil Grone to give him a heads-up about what I intended to do. Sam came into D.C. and accompanied me to the 5:30 p.m. meeting at the Pentagon. DAS Grone was cordial, but told me he was assured by Judge Craig Manson throughout the process that the FWS would not object to the landing field at Site C. I responded, "*If* Judge Manson made that statement, it was inappropriate. The Migratory Bird Treaty Act has no 'incidental take' authority and is a 'strict liability' law. The only legal option available to our Special Agents is to make an arrest and let the court decide if a felony has occurred or if it will allow a settlement in the form of fines. It's not up to the executive branch to decide it's OK. Except for certain identified activities such as Tribal religious ceremonies, bird damage to private property and the migratory bird hunting seasons, there is no authorization for intentional *or* unintentional take of migratory birds. The bar for establishing a construction project as a matter of national security, especially one with so many alternatives, would be near insurmountable. In addition, I can't see a time the FWS would support killing or significantly disrupting the migration and wintering of the largest population of Tundra Swans in the United States. To my knowledge, Steve Williams gave no concurrence and neither do I."

For all government activities, I always worked under the premise that "If it isn't written, it isn't said." Judge Manson had never written to the Navy, or provided an internal memorandum that we could find, that confirmed Mr. Grone's assertion. I informed Grone that I was going to North Carolina to personally deliver the formal comments and asked for this meeting to provide the courtesy of informing him in advance. He inquired why the director of the FWS would be going instead of having Regional Director Hamilton deliver the comments. "I want it to be clear that the full weight of the FWS is in opposition to this alternative." Sam and I left. The Navy got busy trying to get Lynn or the secretary to order me to stay in D.C. so the comments wouldn't draw as much attention. But they underestimated the way we did business. Because Lynn had been fully briefed on the absurdity of the proposal, she told them I was simply doing my job.

On March 19 I visited our staff at the NWR and let them know we had their backs on this contentious issue. I wanted them to know that the deputy secretary was standing behind them as well. Too many field people don't know when someone at Lynn's level is standing up for them. Sam and I worked hard to have the troops know they were fortunate to have Lynn and Dirk. It was neither my role nor that of the FWS to argue about aviation safety, but we certainly supported the local community, which didn't want to have their farms condemned or hear an average of *eighty-five touch-and-go landings every day*!

We arrived at the Matamuskeet Elementary School in Swan Quarter, North Carolina, at around 6:30 that evening for the public hearing. It began at 7 with the Navy's explanation of the project, how it had been under study since 2001, and why the Navy believed Site C was the best alternative. Since the FWS was a cooperator in the EIS and an important voice in the discussion, I was recognized to make my remarks.

My comments focused on the loss of foraging habitat for waterfowl, the effects of aircraft noise on wildlife and the visitors to the refuge, and the negative impacts to the red wolf and our ability to manage a refuge that already belonged to the people. I emphasized that the FWS was committed to helping the Navy find a functional location between the two bases in which to build an outlying landing field, but that the Washington and Beaufort Counties option was not it. Following the hearing, I was interviewed by the local radio station and asked, "The Navy biologist and planners say good people can disagree on the impacts of a project. What is your response?" "If we were trying to determine the best way to use a fleet in a battle plan or how to build a seaworthy ship, I would defer to the Navy," I replied. "But the people of the United States entrusted the Fish and Wildlife Service with the responsibility to properly care for migratory birds, and the question of impacts to those species belongs to us."

Following the meeting and my comments, local newspapers picked up on the fact that I was a Bush appointee opposing the Navy's preferred alternative and trying to protect the refuge. One article recalled how some environmentalists had opposed my nomination, saying I would be bad for fish and wildlife. The people of the local communities in Washington and Beaufort Counties, however, voiced their opinion that I was, indeed, up to the job of protecting our natural resources. Just as with articles that said I should be systematically dumped, I kept a copy and just went on to the next issue. If one is going to accept a position in the eye of the public, one must learn to have a prosthetic gluteus maximus and wear asbestos underwear. The complimentary articles are few and far between. A keen awareness that I would be sued for whatever position I took on behalf of the FWS led me to settle into the comfortable mode of doing what I believed to be the right thing. If I'm going to have to defend my decision in court, I'd rather defend our team's interpretation of the law, and how the science meets that law, than what we might have done to try to please one side or the other. I still believe that is the best path for any leader. Ethics and integrity can forge a mighty sword for justice.

Public pressure was mounting against the Navy. In an area of the country where the military was prized in the community for the economic support it provided, this was new territory. In early April, a convoy of farm tractors circled the nearby state Agricultural Research and Extension Center, where the Navy was holding a public hearing on the OLF, to fight the possibility that their farmland would be taken for the project. Throughout the public hearing process, there was overwhelming opposition to building the OLF at Site C, and opponents were starting to get traction with elected officials. Senator Elizabeth Dole (R-NC) sent a lengthy list of questions to the Navy following the hearings and specifically asked the Navy to address my comments. On April 5, Senator Dole wrote to Navy Secretary Donald C. Winter.

> I continue to be deeply concerned about the Navy's proposed outlying landing field in northeast North Carolina. In recent weeks, I have stressed the importance of the ongoing formal public comment period and the valuable opportunity it provides

not only for interested North Carolinians to express their views to the Navy—but also for the Navy to fully appreciate residents' legitimate concerns.

As part of this process, I am enclosing my questions regarding the Navy's proposed OLF. I ask that you provide written responses to these questions as soon as possible before the end of the comment period. (Dole 2007)

Enclosed with the letter were eleven lengthy questions addressing the concerns her constituents had been raising throughout the process. Question number 4 addressed my comments at the hearing in Swan Quarter.

At a March 19 public hearing on the proposed OLF, U.S. Fish and Wildlife Service Director Dale Hall stated that the agency 'continue(s) to have many concerns regarding the potential effects of locating an OLF in close proximity to a National Wildlife Refuge.' . . . Please respond to each of the specific concerns raised by Director Hall in his statement about an OLF in Washington and Beaufort Counties. (Dole 2007)

This letter and the eleven questions loomed as an ominous indication of Senator Dole's views on Site C. For a senator to weigh in on a military project in her state, one that would no doubt create a significant number of jobs, sent a clear message to the Navy that they should look elsewhere. Governor Mike Easley, Senator Richard Burr and eight North Carolina members of Congress opposed Site C, as did the state agencies of Agriculture and Fish and Wildlife. The Navy began searching in earnest for a site for the OLF that would bring fewer environmental and social impacts. Within two weeks, Senator Dole had made up her mind. In a letter to Secretary Winter on April 19, she provided her conclusion.

> I appreciate the extensive discussions that we and our staffs have had over the last several weeks regarding the Navy's proposal for an outlying landing field in North Carolina. As I have conveyed to you, the Navy's proposal to build an OLF in Washington County is simply not feasible . . . In the best interest of both North Carolinians and the service, the Navy must withdraw its recommendation for an OLF in Washington County. (Dole 2007)

Rear Admiral David Anderson of Fleet Forces Command, however, made the bold statement at a meeting the following August that "If all of this work comes back and it fails, we're going after Washington County." Perhaps he was challenging the commitment of elected officials. Perhaps he was sending a trial balloon to tell Congress to answer the question. Or perhaps he was just egotistical enough to think he could force what he wanted on the public. I don't know the answer to the question. But Congress heard him loud and clear and decided to send a message of their own.

The 2008 Defense Spending Bill was passed out of the House of Representatives on December 13, 2007, with clear language that eliminated the Navy's authority to expend monies on the Site C alternative. If the Navy is specifically prohibited from spending monies studying an alternative, that alternative is dead. In January 2008, the Navy officially abandoned its plans to build an OLF in Washington and Beaufort Counties, North Carolina. The National Audubon Society, one of the environmental groups represented by the SELC, hailed the decision: "This is a victory for the hundred thousand birds that winter there and for the farmers that live there. It is a victory for the people of North Carolina and the political leaders who represent them. And it is also a victory for the Navy and its pilots, which deserve the safest training possible, without the threat of catastrophic collisions with large birds." (Severance 2008)

∙ ∙ ∙

Our difference with the Navy over the OLF was an isolated incident. President Bush made it clear that he wanted all of his political appointee team working together, and he didn't want partisan politics to stop a good idea from hatching. In formal gatherings, President Bush always told us "I don't care if it's a Republican idea, a Democratic idea or an Independent idea. If it's a good idea, I expect you to try to make it work!" That was doubly true for working between agencies in the administration. I was blessed to have two old friends as partners in running agencies the FWS worked with on a regular basis. Bob Johnson, former regional director of the Bureau of Reclamation (BOR) in the southwest, was made commissioner of the BOR. In addition, our partner on the Everglades restoration, Brigadier General Rick Capka, was nominated and became the administrator of the Federal Highway Administration (FHWA) in 2006. I talked with each of them on a regular basis, and we did our best to ensure that there were no significant issues between the FWS and either the FHWA or the BOR. No relationships exist between agencies. They exist between people who trust and respect each other and are willing to listen and work together. With Rick and Bob, we had that in spades.

Another ally I got to know was Army Major General Don Riley. I had asked for a meeting with General Carl Strock, Chief of Engineers, to discuss ways the Corps and FWS could better work together on common issues. When I arrived at the meeting, I was escorted to General Strock's office and greeted with a handshake that included his military coin and a smile from the person who bestowed both—someone who long ago saw his first rodeo. One doesn't make it to be a lieutenant general without having significant skills and leadership competence gained through experience. Carl Strock had both. He introduced me to Major General Don Riley, the Corps director of civil works. In that position, "General Riley managed the Army's Civil Works Program as the Nation's primary planner, designer, builder, and operator of flood control, navigation, environmental restoration, and multiple-purpose water resource projects." (ASCEnews 2009) In addition, he had been the commander of the Mississippi Valley Division of the Corps. I locked on to Don Riley and knew he would have the keys to real discussions on how to make water resource projects accomplish their congressional intent and still be environmentally acceptable. My meeting with General Strock was good, but meeting Don and starting that friendship was incredible. In 2008, Don was made deputy chief of engineers. We had many discussions about the mistakes the Corps made in the past and his commitment to support those who, like Rick Capka, were trying to do it right this time. Even though we have all retired from public service, I still deeply value Bob, Rick and Don's friendships.

CHAPTER 19

Finishing the Polar Bear and Killing the Feral Hog

A public hearing on the proposal to list the polar bear as required by the Endangered Species Act (ESA) was scheduled for March 5, 2007, from 6 to 9 p.m. in the Yates Auditorium, Department of the Interior (DOI) Building in Washington, D.C. As expected, the public had aligned on two sides of the issue: those who believed listing was the key to unlocking ESA regulation of global warming and those who claimed it was ridiculous to list a species as threatened when the population numbers were hovering around 27,000 circumpolar. For both sides, the main issue was focused more on global warming than on the species. U.S. Geological Survey (USGS) Director Mark Myers and I were in Secretary of the Interior Dirk Kempthorne's office talking with him about the bear and were taken aback when the secretary asked "Do polar bears kill people?" Mark and I looked at each other in disbelief and said "Of course! Every year! Man is definitely on their menu." As the secretary stared at the image of a polar bear on the Coca-Cola can he was holding, he shook his head and said "I want that bear's PR firm."

The politician in him had a hard time understanding how an animal that regularly attacked people could be seen as harmless and docile by the public. I reminded the secretary that Alexander Douglas, president of Coca-Cola for North America, had written to him in February saying "On behalf of the Coca-Cola Company, I am writing to encourage you to list the polar bear as a threatened species under the Endangered Species Act. Polar bears have been an icon of Coca-Cola marketing for more than 80 years." Kempthorne looked at us with amazement and said "No matter what I do here, I'm going to make half of the people mad at me." As an elected official, he'd had some latitude in choosing his battles. As secretary, they landed on his desk for a decision. I responded, "Welcome to our world. No matter what decision we make on any issue, half of the people are going to hate us."

Under the ESA and the Convention on International Trade in Endangered Species of Wild Fauna and Flora (CITES), we were proposing the bear to be listed "domestically" rather than "internationally." The United States keeps two lists and works them differently. For domestic species—those that are found naturally in the U.S.—the ESA is followed throughout their stay on the list. For international species, the FWS operates under the mandates of the ESA to carry out treaties and agreements with other nations to protect foreign species, as identified through resolutions passed by CITES, within U.S. jurisdictions.

CITES was created by a resolution adopted in 1963 by the International Union for the Conservation of Nature (IUCN) in Nairobi, Kenya, to ensure that international trade in specimens of wild animals and plants does not threaten their survival:

> Annually, international wildlife trade is estimated to be worth billions of dollars and to include hundreds of millions of plant and animal specimens. The trade is diverse, ranging from live animals and plants to a vast array of wildlife products derived from them, including food products, exotic leather goods, wooden musical instruments, timber, tourist curios and medicines . . . Because the trade in wild animals and plants crosses borders between countries, the effort to regulate it requires international cooperation to safeguard certain species from overexploitation . . .

CITES is an international agreement to which States [countries] and regional economic Integration organizations adhere voluntarily. States that have agreed to be bound by the Convention ('joined CITES') are known as Parties. Although CITES is legally binding on the Parties—in other words they have to implement the Convention—it does not take the place of national laws. Rather it provides a framework to be respected by each Party, which has to adopt its own domestic legislation to ensure that CITES is implemented at the national level. (CITES.org 2020)

The Convention holds a "Conference of the Parties" every two to three years to formally vote on additions, deletions or changes to the restrictions. The United States, as a significant party to the Convention, complies with CITES through the Endangered Species Act where the U.S. Fish and Wildlife Service (FWS) works with Customs and Border Patrol at ports of entry into the United States. When dealing with international species, the U.S., acting through the FWS, agrees to only allow import of CITES-regulated animals, plants or products when they are accompanied by proper permits from the country of origin. Without the commitment of the U.S. through the ESA, the FWS would have no legal authority to regulate lions, elephants, tigers or any other species not native to the U.S. Because of the agreement, however, the world works as a team to conserve and protect species in peril. The importance of FWS relationships with its counterparts in other countries cannot be overstated.

The polar bear (*Ursus maritimus*) occurs all around the north pole. Any effort to keep the polar bear from declining would require the assistance and participation from all countries bordering the arctic circle that have bear populations: Canada, Greenland, Norway, Russia and the United States. These five countries were original signatories to a landmark agreement in 1973 for the Conservation of Polar Bears. That agreement was encouraged by the International Union of Concerned Naturalists Polar Bear Specialist Group. It called for the member nations to coordinate research efforts, share information, cooperate on the management of migrating polar bear populations and continue to consult with one another for the purpose of providing increased protection for the world's populations of polar bears.

We used our authorities under the agreement to call for a meeting of the "polar bear range states" to discuss ongoing evaluations associated with our proposed listing, share information, and strengthen our knowledge of habitat trends around the arctic circle. Included in the U.S. delegation was the FWS, USGS, the Department of State, the Alaska Nanuuq Commission and the State of Alaska. We left the invitation open to the other range states to include in their delegation whomever they thought appropriate, but encouraged scientific as well as aboriginal representation for cultural knowledge. I was the head of the U.S. delegation and strongly believed that I should remain at the National Conservation Training Center (NCTC) for the entire conference, including meals and social gatherings. In diplomacy, it is extremely important to understand other cultures and norms. It would have been interpreted as rude for me to depart to do "other business" when I was considered the host. That created a problem when Brian Waidmann called to ask me to come back to D.C., a two-hour drive each way, to be with Secretary Kempthorne at the Lincoln Memorial to announce the removal of the American bald eagle from the list of threatened and endangered species.

This was a big moment for the ESA. There could hardly be a more significant emblem of both our country and the success of the ESA than to announce that the bald eagle had been recovered in the lower forty-eight states. When I told Brian I didn't think it would be proper for me to leave the meetings, he asked "What if we sent a helicopter?" "Brian, I really appreciate that the secretary wants me there. But I'm happy to have him be the face of this great success story. My place is here with the guests of the United States." Once again, with the best of intentions, Brian had not seen the dramatic split between a photo op and the historic work of the Department of the Interior. I wasn't going to have another Palau misstep.

The range states did a marvelous job of including precisely the right balance of scientists and cultural representatives. If the bear ended up listed in the U.S., the range states would have to adopt measures to regulate the harvest and movement of bears or bear parts. Aboriginal hunting of polar bears for subsistence is allowed in every country, even under CITES. In addition to the ESA, the U.S. Marine Mammal Protection Act (MMPA) protects polar bears, yet also allows for native harvest for subsistence. Details would have to be worked out to allow, for instance, a U.S. hunter to legally hunt a polar bear in Canada and bring it back to the United States. Regulated hunting of bears, it was agreed, was not a threat to the bear populations and should not receive further restrictions under the agreement following listing.

The MMPA, however, became a thorn in the side of the United States when trying to bring common sense to the discussion. Under the MMPA, if a U.S. marine mammal is listed under the ESA, it is automatically considered a "depleted population" and, therefore, prohibited from harvest outside subsistence approvals. This became a rallying point for anti-hunters after the species was listed. Even though importation was clearly allowed under the final ESA listing rule, anti-hunting groups were successful in blocking the importation of polar bears or their products by using the MMPA.

What the anti-hunters refused to accept was the fact that each Canadian bear hunted had Marine Mammal Commission approval to be killed by First Nations people. The bears were going to die regardless of who pulled the trigger. The real penalty of blocking imports was to the native people who wanted to sell the hunts to have a revenue stream in isolated communities. The U.S. hunters were not willing to spend tens of thousands of dollars if they couldn't bring the physical manifestation of their lifetime memory home. Those hunters also paid into a bear conservation fund in addition to fees paid to their First Nations permit holder. Both were lost in an effort that didn't save a single bear. The conference was a tremendous success and all delegates, including those representing historical culture, praised the openness and professionalism everyone brought to the table.

• • •

Lyle Laverty was the sitting director of Colorado State Parks when nominated by President George W. Bush to replace Craig Manson as assistant secretary for Fish, Wildlife and Parks. Lyle was a competent leader and brought a smile and calm persona to the job. Confirmed by unanimous consent the evening of October 29, 2007, Lyle became a friend and positive force in a corridor that had been significantly tainted by Julie MacDonald. Lyle was around 5 feet 10 inches, 180 pounds, and had earned his battlefield commissions. Prior to becoming the director of parks in Colorado, he was a career employee with the U.S. Forest Service from 1972 until he accepted the parks position in 2001. Along the way, he was the regional forester of the Rocky Mountain region and was well aware of my involvement in the northwest forest issues. He cared about the resource and made it clear that there would be no interference from his office in the science of either the FWS or National Park Service (NPS). He brought in Dr. Jim Mosher to take over the responsibilities of Julie MacDonald's former position as deputy assistant secretary. Mosher was a competent professional who rounded out the team we desperately needed. From the first day, Lyle, Jim and our FWS team worked well together.

As 2007 approached its end, so did the one-year period following the proposal to list the bear. It was time to make a decision.

• • •

Just before the Christmas break, the Alaska Regional Office submitted the three-hundred-page draft listing package for our review. Bryan Arroyo and Margaret Hopkins would normally review a package, then Ken Stansell or Rowan Gould, and then me. This one, however, would have to be reviewed by all at the same time, coming together to compare notes and questions. Technically, the final decision was due on December 27, 2007, but that obviously didn't happen. There were several hundred thousand comments, and I gave the instruction to our D.C. staff to let Anchorage have all the time allowed and I would take the heat for it being late. No one in the department, including the secretary, was concerned about it being late because they wanted to delay the decision as long as possible.

Randall Luthi, one my former political deputy directors, was appointed to head the Minerals Management Service and was scheduled to testify before Chairman Ed Markey and the House Select Committee on Energy Independence and Global Warming. Both Dr. Steve Amstrup and I were requested to testify with Randall to discuss the status of global warming and what impacts might occur to polar bears and other arctic creatures as a result of the proposed lease sales in the Chukchi Sea. Steve did a great job of explaining what we knew of various fuels and laying the science foundation that natural gas was substantially less harmful than oil, coal or gas in producing greenhouse gases. This was in support of taking as many measures as possible to reduce the amount of oil and coal used as sources of energy and the harmful greenhouse gases they produce. His testimony encouraged a move to natural gas as an intermediate step in the shift to renewable energy. I testified that we had worked with Director Luthi to push the drilling off the continental shelf and restrict timing to winter exploration, when bears were in hibernation.

At one point, Chairman Markey asked, "Director Hall, in your opinion, when should we begin to address global warming?"

"Yesterday, Mr. Chairman. The president has acknowledged that the earth is warming, man is playing a significant role in causation, and we should be taking reasonable steps to reduce our impact."

"Thank you, Director, for being so candid and straightforward. It is refreshing."

I was surprised by his comment because, on numerous occasions, President Bush had stated his acceptance that we need to address global warming. I appreciate that there were those in the White House who wished he hadn't made that acknowledgment, but I was there representing the president's administration. The problem, however, rests not in the truth that global warming is real, but in the fear of the actions that might be taken to arrest the warming. Most people I met, including those who want to argue about the "probable limited lifespan," find it hard to argue with thermometers. It is true that no one knows the entire cocktail of influences that has created this significant trend. Is this a short-term weather cycle or a true climate change? The answer is far less complicated than the question. The impacts are real. Sea surface rise is real. Increased ferocity of storms is real. The economic impacts are real. And, the solution is attainable, but only with a steadfast plan among *all* nations. The ice melting that was impacting America's polar bears very likely resulted from emissions in India, China or elsewhere around the globe. This phenomenon presents the world with the most significant opportunity to abandon squabbles among nations and become a people of the earth. At best, it would take thirty to fifty years to reverse the current trend. But that journey should begin yesterday.

On January 30, Chairwoman Barbara Boxer called a hearing of the Senate Environment and Public Works Committee to find out why there had not been a decision made on the polar bear proposal. I went over to testify.

"Director Hall. Our staff has been told that the listing package and recommendation from Alaska was received in your office in December," Senator Boxer said. "I want to know who is holding up the decision!"

"I am," I replied. Her eyes widened in disbelief. She expected me to make some excuse, cover for the secretary and leave a trail of blood she could follow to give me a sound lecture. Instead, I answered with no equivocation that I was indeed the one holding up the decision.

"I gave the field all of the time allotted under the law because of the extreme amount of work they had to do to properly document the administrative record, review and answer comments, and write their recommendation to me. The region does not make the decision. That will be made by the secretary based on my recommendation. I will release the document to the secretary and for other department review after, and only after, I have read the entire document, asked all questions I want answered and am satisfied with the finding I move forward. I say that because, whatever the final decision, I am confident I will be sitting here once again at your request explaining that decision. As such, it will be one I understand and endorse."

She didn't know what to say. Finally, she said, "Well, let the record show you are late with the determination!"

When it was time for Senator Joe Lieberman to speak, he said, "Director Hall. This committee has a great deal of respect for you as a scientist and for your leadership. Do you believe the science on global warming is good science?" He was referring to the attacks Senator Jim Inhofe, minority ranking member of the committee, had been making against the science of the International Panel on Climate Change. I knew several people who were on the panel and held them in high regard. This was simply one of those issues on which I deeply disagreed with my Oklahoma friend and had to stand by my ethics and principles. Senator Lieberman was a savvy politician and wanted it in the record.

"Yes sir. I do believe it is good science." Lieberman knew when he asked the question that it had tendrils attached to the polar bear decision. He later sent me a note thanking me for my honest approach to science. I only hoped my role in the final process would deserve his support.

Secretary Kempthorne implemented a schedule of holding a polar bear meeting twice a week with Lynn Scarlett, Brian Waidmann, Mark

Myers, David Bernhardt, Lyle Laverty, Steve Allred (assistant secretary for Land and Minerals), Jim Caswell (BLM director), Henri Bisson (BLM deputy director), Drue Pearce (special assistant to the secretary for Alaska issues) and me. The secretary normally had a list of questions (challenges) about the science and definitions of law that had been thrown at him by the White House. Dr. Steve Amstrup had been given free rein by Director Myers to work with our FWS team for the six months preceding the polar bear decision, analyzing the science and explaining hydrogeology and climatology to our biologists. Steve was a phenomenal scientist and a crutch under my arm every time I had to face Congress or the public. I was a wetlands and fisheries biologist who had learned a lot about other species, but I was no physical scientist. Steve was also a biologist, but was given full access to the physical scientists in USGS. This comprehensive study of all science available to inform the polar bear decision was a secretarial priority, and everyone pulled their weight. Between Steve and Mark, they helped me understand significant phenomena like the arctic gyre, albedo effect and anchor ice. Steve and his team of USGS scientists produced nine reports during 2007 to help explain what was happening to the ice and to the polar bears that depended on it.

The most significant challenges we had to overcome were the unusual dynamics creating the threats to the polar bear. The FWS was well versed in how to tackle analyses in animal behavior, physiology and population dynamics, but was totally unequipped to deal with the non-biological pieces of the puzzle. Mark Myers and his team at USGS were critical to the effort.

> This was particularly complex science because it involved not only understanding bear biology, but it also required trying to peer into the future on sea ice, sea ice trajectories, that implicated global circulation models, of which there were at least twenty done by atmospheric chemists and science teams running models that were very, very complex . . . trying to project outward the

trajectory of warming and the implications for sea ice. You not only had your typical species biology that you needed to look at—available forage, hunting impacts, disease. But you also had to look at global dynamics and implications to the ESA.

Working with USGS and FWS, we asked 'What are the knowledge gaps?' and, 'In a 9-month period, whether and how we could close those knowledge gaps.' It is not feasible to go out and say 'We need ten more years to evaluate sea ice, or atmospheric trends, or the response of bears in the Beaufort Sea and Hudson Bay, where there were reductions in reproduction trends and bodily health.'

They came up with a set of science questions, including approaches to getting a better line of sight on sea ice melting, that would provide better credibility in court. We had some knowledge about bear responses in two locations, Beaufort Sea and Hudson Bay, but that was only two of the nineteen known populations . . . We had enough information on bears and how they behave to know that they couldn't just readily adapt to deep sea or land habitat, but very little [information] on the ice and climate.

We gave clear instructions to USGS to go do the studies to answer the questions: 'We will put up a blind wall and give you the freedom to do the science without any interference from the department. At the end of nine months, come back and show us what you found.' (Scarlett 2020)

The melting of the arctic ice cap is a gradual and complicated series of events. The arctic gyre is a term for the wind and sea currents that circle the polar cap and push drift ice until it comes together to form very thick, multi-year ice that doesn't melt in the summer, and provides the anchor for new ice to form at the onslaught of winter. The Beaufort Gyre along the Alaska coastline became increasingly weaker with the warming atmosphere and the initiation of the albedo effect. Albedo is the measure of the reflectivity of a surface, and it is critical in keeping polar ice frozen. The albedo effect is the measure of how much of the sun's energy is *reflected back into space* rather than absorbed by the ocean. Overall, this has a cooling effect because the energy (warmth) is bounced away rather than absorbed, thus keeping the seawater cooler.

Cooler seawater helps keep ice from melting, which also helps reflect the heat of the sun. This principle is used throughout the world in buildings where internal temperature is important. By putting reflective surfaces on the exterior, "heat" will be bounced away rather than absorbed. That cycle describes an arctic system in balance. The opposite is true when ice melts and the energy from the sun is absorbed by the sea and elevates water temperatures. This not only leads to the loss of summer ice to a greater extent and for longer periods, but also begins to melt the permanent ice so important to the cycle. Combining the albedo effect with the reduction of the arctic gyre equates to elimination of essential habitat for polar bear summer platform feeding and rearing of cubs. The time frame for finding answers was unbelievably short and the challenges unprecedented.

> USGS worked with the scientific community, including scientists from NASA and academia, to do Bayesian Modeling and take an ensemble of sea ice models and *backcast* all of them to see how predictive they would have been using data at points in the past, in order to see how accurate they might be for looking forward. The ones that gave the best results were then used to do an ensemble to get a robust, composite sense within a range of what they were showing us about sea ice trends going forward for a certain period of years. (Scarlett 2020)

Steve Amstrup, Mark Myers and the entire USGS team deserve tremendous credit for poring over computer model after model and collaborating with other scientists outside the government to nail down the accuracy we needed to support any decision. The evidence was clear. By mid twenty-first century, the only drift ice in summer would likely be in the Canadian Archipelago. The early signs were already prevalent in smaller polar bear body size and weaker condition. It was happening.

The meetings of the "polar bear group" had become so exhausting that we all dreaded them. I have no idea how much pressure the secretary was getting to simply tell us to change the rule and declare listing not warranted, but it had to be significant. Mark and I were on the other end, constantly reiterating the science that supported listing the bear. More than once, I told the group that listing would not do anything for the polar bear because the ESA couldn't regulate climate, but that did not relieve us of the scientific and legal responsibility to answer whether the bear *qualified* under the five-factor analysis. Believe it or not, we actually heard from "the invisibles" in the White House that listing the bear would cause the stock market to crash! I couldn't believe how ridiculous it was getting.

Secretary Kempthorne related to me how the White House invisibles were making his life very stressful.

> When I got to the Department of the Interior I inherited a very controversial issue: whether or not the polar bear should be placed on the endangered species list. For approximately a year, I would be asked to come to the White House and meet with the president's advisors in the Roosevelt Room. It was never with the president. I would see the president during the week on a variety of issues, but not for this. It was only with the advisors, and at times there would be eight or ten of them.
>
> Usually, when the cabinet member is asked to come to the White House, it is "principal plus one." In other words, the cabinet member and his or her individual [primary person to see that decisions made at the meeting were carried out] with them. I was never given that courtesy. It was principal only.

> I would go into the Roosevelt Room and they would continually make it clear to me that there is only one decision. This polar bear is not to be listed. They had a variety of political reasons. (Kempthorne 2021)

The oil and gas industry had been extremely responsive and was doing everything we asked to assist the bear. It was all about melting ice and CO_2 molecules that could not be tracked back to their point of origin. Therefore, no proof could be displayed that *"This emission from this source caused this ice to melt."* In a case involving environmental regulation, the U.S. Supreme Court had ruled that the government had the obligation to "connect the dots" in assigning responsibility for environmental harm. We couldn't do that, but it didn't seem to matter to the "sky is falling" section of the White House. This went on until almost mid-February before I finally reached my saturation point. I realized that Dirk was under tremendous pressure, but we had all sworn to uphold the laws and defend the Constitution of the United States. As I was leaving for Minneapolis for meetings with Region 3, I stopped by my doorway, where I had two quotes hanging on the wall. One was Roosevelt's "Man in the Arena" and the other was from another great leader.

> In order to be a leader a man must have followers. And to have followers, a man must have their confidence. Hence the supreme quality for a leader is unquestionably integrity. Without it, no real success is possible, no matter whether it is on a section gang, on a football field, in an army, or in an office. If a man's associates find him guilty of phoniness, if they find that he lacks forthright integrity, he will fail. His teachings and actions must square with each other. The first great need, therefore, is integrity and high purpose. (President Dwight D. Eisenhower)

As I left my office to catch the plane to Minneapolis for meetings with Region 3 on the afternoon of February 12, 2008, it hit me like a ton of bricks that I had dozens of highly dedicated employees being pulled through keyholes because unqualified people, making sure they remained anonymous, didn't like the scientific answers the professionals were giving. Eisenhower's words haunted me all night. They were still on my mind the next morning when I awoke and went to the Region 3 office in Minneapolis. When the time came for my polar bear meeting, I called in and was put on speaker phone. Lynn, Mark, Lyle, David and the others were gathered in D.C. I documented the call for the record.

> Note: **February 13, 2008**, Polar Bear Meeting with Sec Kempthorne, Lynn Scarlett, Brian Waidmann, David Bernhardt, Lyle Laverty, Steve Allred, Mark Myers, Jim Caswell, Henri Bisson, Drue Pearce.
>
> Today's regularly scheduled meeting took place in the a.m. and I participated by phone from Minneapolis. I started the meeting by explaining the history of the proposed listing, the information exchange at the range states meeting, the 9 USGS reports delivered to the Service in September and the significant strength of the cumulative scientific data. After recounting issues on strength and dependence of General Circulation Models, legal discussion of "foreseeable future" and other topics that had been discussed at previous meetings, I informed the Secretary that I could not and would not surname or sign any decision document that found listing of the polar bear as not warranted. I explained that my professional and scientific integrity would not allow me to support any decision except listing. (Hall 2008)

When I finished, there was silence. David Bernhardt was the first to speak. "I guess that's it. If the director of the Fish and Wildlife Service will only sign a listing package, I guess we're listing." Mark Myers also spoke and said the science was overwhelmingly in support of listing and he didn't see any new information that would change that. I found out after the meeting that Lynn Scarlett also told the secretary privately that she fully supported my position and could not assist in publishing a finding that was not warranted. While my firm stance on listing got the listing off the dime, I want to be clear that there was significant support from prominent members of the group to list based on the science. My note documenting the meeting finished with this:

> After discussion, the Secretary stated that he could not support a decision that was opposed by 'his Fish and Wildlife Service and USGS Directors,' so the decision was to list the species as threatened throughout its range and to support a 4(d) rule identifying activities that had shown not to be a threat to the species. Remaining efforts were to focus on finalizing the document and addressing comments opposed to listing. (Hall 2008)

The 4(d) rule was to emphasize the cooperation the oil and gas industry had shown throughout the process, the lack of any evidence that cultural subsistence or sport hunting of polar bears was in any way causing its decline, and the importance of working with the range states on circumpolar management of the species. On February 22, we advised the secretary that all remaining issues of concern arising from comments had been resolved or addressed, with the possible exceptions of making sure the text throughout reflected the legal issue resolutions and that there was consistency in all sections of the package. It was also agreed that the 4(d) rule was ready to go. In my note to the file on February 22, I wrote,

> Following that meeting, I surnamed as the Service's final decision document the proposed rule to list the polar bear as threatened throughout its range and delivered the rule to Assistant Secretary Lyle Laverty. (Hall 2008)

But I would discover that wasn't the end of the discussion. I later flew to Hawaii to visit with our staff and was preparing to fly back on Friday, May 2, when Lyle called me to let me know the secretary had decided to **not** list the polar bear. Lyle was not pleased with the decision, nor was I, but we both accepted that it was the secretary's decision, by law, to make if he chose to do so. I said "Lyle, I'm sorry for the way it has unfolded, but I have to let you know I cannot assist in, nor allow my staff to assist in, writing a document to go against all the scientific information at our disposal." "I completely understand," he replied. "I'll keep you apprised of how things are moving."

When I returned home on Saturday, I talked with Ken Stansell by phone. I then called the secretary on his cell phone and let him know Lyle had informed me of his decision, that I was disappointed and was sure he understood why I could not participate in preparing the decision document nor in the press roll-out.

> I could only hurt you by being in front of the press and having to say I don't agree with the decision. I have a meeting planned with the Mexican government later this month. If you are firm with the decision not to list, I suggest that you plan the announcement while I'm in Mexico and I can say I'm not available for comment.
>
> Dirk, I want to give you advice friend to friend, not director to secretary. I assume the president or vice president is pushing you to do this. In seven months, you will no longer be secretary of the interior. You came into this office with a solid reputation for truth and integrity. Do you really want to leave it with a decision that can't be supported by science? Please think about it.

On Monday, May 5, I had several discussions with Lyle, David Bernhardt and others regarding the apparent decision. In the afternoon, the attorneys, Lyle and I went to Mark Myers's office in Reston, Virginia, and spent two and a half hours discussing all the science and policy implications. Mark and I informed the group that the science would not support a decision to not list and that whatever reasons the secretary gave would likely not be upheld by the scientific community, our employees or the courts. Everyone understood that this was a difficult charge given to the department attorneys. However, attorneys are obligated to try to support their client. For the department's office of the solicitor and staff, that client is the secretary of the interior. Mark and I wanted the attorneys to know that we knew they were under the gun to come up with a justification, but strongly advised that they find one other than science. Unfortunately, the law says the decision to list or not list "must be based on the best available scientific and commercial data available." This wasn't critical habitat, in which the secretary would have the latitude to remove areas from regulation based on non-scientific information. This was listing.

Lynn Scarlett reflected on the non-biological questions that surfaced during the discussions.

> The law has two phrases that are not defined by science. *Foreseeable future* is not a science term and, at that time, wasn't defined in law. What is the foreseeable future? Is it based on how the FWS has done it in the past and assign a certain number of generations of the species? Why is that relevant? The other is *reasonably certain to occur*. What is that? It isn't defined by law and in science you use a percentage probability kind of metric, but there is nothing in the law or decision-making that clearly defines these terms. When the law demands that a decision be made within a specific time, there is an amount of uncertainty moving into the future. You can never completely close the gaps in definition, but you need to try to shrink them so the decision can be reasonably defended under the law. (Scarlett 2020)

On Friday, May 9, Lyle shared with me a draft of the arguments the attorneys had developed to challenge certain conclusions we had made and asked for my recommendations on how to address their arguments. I visited with Bryan, Ken, Margaret and Jerome Ford to get their input on the two areas of challenge: "foreseeable future" and the status of "ice ecoregions" remaining after 2053. I listened intently and asked questions when I needed to, but let them brainstorm all the possibilities where we could be wrong. That's how real science works. We constantly challenge what we think we know, searching to see if we are incorrect. I made it clear that I was not going to delegate this assignment. I knew where it was going and it had to be the director, the last in the line of science and the first in the line of policy, that gave the answers. I got up on Saturday and went into the office to write my recommendations to Lyle and to meet with him. I provided them in the form of a memorandum to the assistant secretary for Fish, Wildlife and Parks from the director, FWS.

Per our discussion today and your request for my input, the following are my comments on the draft memorandum from the Department of the Interior Solicitor (SOL) regarding legal issues surrounding the listing for the polar bear.

Issue number one: Will the polar bear be in danger of extinction by 2053? The SOL makes the argument that the Service did not expressly do an analysis of whether the bear will be in danger of extinction (definition of endangered) by the end of the 45-year foreseeable future. In justifying his finding, he selected a single model (the Carrying Capacity Model) in exclusion of the entire body of evidence presented by the Service, including the General Circulation Model Ensemble analysis for projected bear habitat (near shore ice) loss, and the Bayesian Network Model findings were acknowledged to result in 'extinct' for two of the four ecoregions at the end of the foreseeable future. In addition, even the Carrying Capacity Model results are cited to the exclusion of a robust bibliography of literature citations that support the Service's conclusions.

The ESA defines the terms 'threatened' and 'endangered' in relatively general terms while leaving application of these terms to the Secretary. However, in applying these terms, Section 4(b) clearly directs that the Secretary make those determinations 'solely on the basis of the best scientific and commercial data available to him.' Note that this does not say it must be based on unquestionable science; only the best available that leads to a likely outcome. The document prepared by the Service is rich with literature citations describing in detail the projections of trends of ice loss and the likely reductions in bear populations at the end of the foreseeable future. Reports tendered by the USGS predict that, by mid-century, 66% of the ice used by the polar bear for requisite life functions will be gone during the essential summer period of feeding, mating, and rearing of young. We have accepted 45 years, or three generations of polar bears, as the foreseeable future **at any given point in time**. Therefore, we have determined that this is the **minimum** observation period within which reasonable projections can be made.

The definition of endangered in the ESA does not include 'in the foreseeable future.' However, it does include the phrase 'in danger of extinction,' not in imminent threat of extinction. If the presumption that a species was in imminent threat of extinction at the end of the foreseeable future were to drive decisions on listing, then the value of threatened status as defined in the Act would be rendered meaningless. I say this because if we were forced to function under a standard that required us to look further into the future than the science can reliably take us, so that a fixed point in time where extinction would occur is required, we could never justify listing any species as threatened. Our scientific ethics would require us to always say 'We don't know.' Since the SOL draft opinion basically makes the case that we didn't perform this analysis and thus, we don't know, his finding has reinforced my interpretation.

Further, using the best available science, we must identify the clearly supported trends in habitat and/or species population numbers. As pointed out in the draft final rule, at the end of the foreseeable future an estimated 66% of the ice used by bears will be gone and between a third and half of the population will be gone.

The discrepancy in temporal impacts is clearly explained in the rule, with acknowledgement that there will likely be a short-term increase in bear numbers in the Archipelago and Convergent ecoregions due to forced migration of bears that can make it to those areas. However, within the foreseeable future **after 2053**, the population is clearly projected to decline to a continually fluctuating downward point of new equilibrium based on available bear territory and food availability.

By this I mean that as bears are 'eliminated' due to competition for ice habitat and food in the Archipelago and Convergent ecoregions, those ecoregions will in turn be continually declining in ice coverage. Therefore, the trend projections indicate equilibrium only during lag phases of ice reduction (ice loss is not projected to occur in a linear fashion, but rather in spurt and lag oscillations). The trend to the end of the century of nearly complete bear habitat ice loss is clearly reliable based on the best available science and results in population reductions that are expected to have populations that are not functionally viable.

Finally, the total reliance on information at our disposal on bear population numbers as the only criterion available renders the information on ice habitat loss excluded from discussion. The Supreme Court has found on two different occasions (Palila and Sweethome II) that habitat is a reasonable surrogate to determine trends in population of a species and impacts that are expected to occur to the populations. The argument that we will still have more than half the estimated polar bear populations remaining at the end of the foreseeable future ignores the remaining science on trends in ice loss. It is important to note that *all* of the models used by the Intergovernmental Panel on Climate Change agreed that the first ice lost would be the ice over the continental shelf important to the polar bear. In addition, observation data for September 2007 resulted in more 'bear' ice loss than that projected in the models. In science, we have the obligation to examine all of the information at our disposal and make conclusions based on the body of evidence. In the opinion of the scientists that wrote the USGS reports, and the vast majority of other published scientists in the field, as well as the 48 peer review scientists for the rule and USGS reports, the body of evidence supports the findings of the Service that the polar bear will be in danger of extinction by the end of the foreseeable future. This is stated several times in the draft final rule, and we believe it is the correct finding.

Issue number two: With two of the four ice habitat ecoregions remaining after the foreseeable future timeframe, how can we say the species will be in danger of extinction by 2053?

In the SOL draft, question is brought to bear on the 'resiliency' component of the three R's (representation, redundancy and resilience). They do not question representation or redundancy. The Service believes it did address all three of these components in the rule, but we admittedly approached the resiliency component from a qualitative, rather than quantitative, standpoint with the exception of bear response to ice loss. The rule reflects available scientific studies that discuss the bear's ability to adapt to food sources on land, potential impacts of encountering oil sheens from spills, ability to hunt in open water and response to loss of onshore denning sites. The only additional work that could be done would be to perform Population Viability Analyses that would result in quantitative display of predictability. However, we did not perform PVAs due to the strength of the qualitative literature and the quantitative data presented by USGS on ice loss. In my opinion, performing one or more PVAs would only result in stronger support to list the species. I hope this helps in formulating your recommendation to the Secretary on this important issue. (Hall 2008)

I was trying to provide Lyle with the most airtight argument I could because I knew he agreed with us. He would have to convince Secretary Kempthorne that listing was the right thing to do. At least that's what I thought.

That evening I got a call from Lyle telling me there would be a meeting in the secretary's office the next morning at 9 o'clock to discuss the SOL draft, the proposed withdrawal and our comments opposing the reasoning. "Doesn't he know it's Mother's Day? Couldn't this wait until Monday?" I asked. "He knows and apologizes for the poor timing," Lyle replied. "Dale, this is our last shot at getting him to change his mind. I need you there to back up our position." I took a deep breath, reflected on my responsibilities and said "I understand, Lyle. Of course I'll be there." I didn't enjoy telling Sarah that the lunch I had promised to prepare for her would have to turn into dinner, at best. She had seen me go through so much agony over the polar bear and had hoped, as I had, that my involvement had been taken over by the secretary. But if I could possibly sway the secretary to ignore people who would shortly be irrelevant to him, I had to try.

• • •

The "Mother's Day Massacre," as I jokingly refer to it, began when we went into the large conference room next to the secretary's office. David Bernhardt stood up front, where he had written down some legal terms that needed to be discussed. I appreciated David's role, even though I was the meat in the grinder. I knew that no one would be a stronger advocate for our position than David if we could convince Dirk to let him do so. I was also keenly aware of the White House pressure cooker Dirk was in. In our own ways, each of us was feeling the same horrendous pressure to do what we knew was not the right thing to do. After about an hour of going through the challenges that David and his staff had put together on policy/legal terms, Dirk asked, "Would you agree that two well-meaning people can look at an issue and simply disagree on the conclusion?" "I can agree with the premise that reasonable people can disagree," I replied. "But, with all due respect, it wouldn't be two scientists disagreeing over scientific data. I could not tell the public that I respect your different conclusion under the scientific mandates of the ESA." He looked disappointed, but I knew he understood.

The meeting went on with revisit after revisit of the two questions. I was convinced David and Dirk had both been trained by the CIA on how to wear down someone in an interrogation. I was appreciative that no one ever raised their voice, condemned the other's opinion or in any way denigrated the seriousness of the discussion. After about three hours, David was talking about the foreseeable future and the potential for endangered status after 2050. "Dale, I have never asked you this question directly. Do *you* believe the polar bear will be in danger of extinction by 2053?" "Yes, David, I do. I have looked at the data on ice conditions, bear movement, bear health and critical needs of the populations and am convinced that the data are neither wrong nor liberally applied."

David looked at me with near shock and said "I've never heard you say that before now. That certainly makes a difference on how I see this." Secretary Kempthorne concluded the meeting around 1:00 p.m., and we went home to try to salvage as much as possible for our wives on Mother's

Day. As I was leaving, I reminded Dirk that I would be in Mexico starting the next day and would be there for the week. I wanted to make sure I was not available for comment to the press. He clearly knew how I felt. I could only hope he would change his mind.

Secretary Kempthorne called me while I was in Mexico to let me know he had decided to list the bear. I was never more pleased with a decision in my professional career. I also knew he would pay a price with the White House for making it. We both knew this meant he had joined Lyle, Mark and me in telling the president of the United States "No. We can't do that." As a scientist, that is just something we swore to do. Politicians have never been held to the same standard, and it is unarguable that he could have said "not warranted," let the lawsuits be filed and have it overturned in the next administration. He didn't do that.

> Back at the DOI working with outstanding individuals like you, I knew you had come to your final recommendation. I had that recommendation, we had discussed it and I had the material. On one occasion, I asked USGS Director Mark Myers, also part of the DOI, 'What is your recommendation?' He said 'Sir, I don't know.' I said that's a hell of a thing to tell me. He said he had not been asked to do any data. I asked how long he needed and he said three months. I told him he had the three months and to please get to work on it. In the meantime, I kept getting invited back to the White House.
>
> Mark came back with his data and, without exaggeration, it was over three hundred pages, and there were no Cliffs Notes! I spent a few days going through that and sometimes having to go back over the same material to make sure I understood. It was intricate and detailed and I wanted to understand the facts.
>
> I called Josh Bolton, who was an outstanding chief of staff at the White House, and told him it was time for a decision. He said he agreed, and my security detail took me to his office in the

West Wing. I went into his office and Joel Kaplan, his assistant, was there with him. He politely asked Joel to leave so we could talk privately. Josh closed the door and said 'I don't want any witnesses.'

I agreed and said 'Josh, I know the decision you want. You have made it painfully clear for over a year. But I cannot and I will not give it to you. I did not resign as governor of a sovereign state and then pledge to preserve, protect and defend the Constitution of the United States to the best of my ability and to serve the president of the United States, to have a group of advisors tell me "This is the decision you will make." I didn't come here to rubber stamp. However, you have every right to have someone in my position carry out your decisions.'

He said 'Hold on, I don't want another Saturday Night Massacre,' referring to Watergate and Elliot Richardson. He said 'I am absolutely stumped. The only thing I can do is take it to the president tonight, and you must prepare yourself that in the morning in all likelihood you will be fired.' I said 'So be it.' He might have suspected that in my inside coat pocket was my letter of resignation. It was not an acidic letter, but rather one filled with praise and admiration for President George W. Bush, the First Lady Laura Bush, and the honor to serve in his administration. I was ready to resign. I was at peace in my heart. Had I caved in and said OK, knowing that within forty-eight hours I would walk to the podium with national and international media and read the words I did not believe in or agree with, I don't believe I would have ever slept peacefully another night for the rest of my life.

The next morning I got my answer. The president's direct quote was 'I am inclined to agree with my advisors. But what is most important to me is the comfort of my Secretary.' He backed me one hundred percent, even though his advisors were all on the other side of the issue. Two days later I listed the bear as threatened, with no question in my mind.

I commend the President for backing the man he had asked to serve as Secretary of the Interior and putting faith in me. It's interesting to note that after I listed the bear I didn't get a letter from the president of Coca-Cola thanking me. I guess he forgot. (Kempthorne 2021)

The press conference was held in the Interior Building, Yates Auditorium, and the secretary was accompanied by Lyle Laverty and Mark Myers on stage. I was on the phone to answer questions. In the end, the right thing had been done. The secretary had carried out his responsibilities and upheld his oath. The president of the United States had stayed true to the law and his responsibilities. The people of the United States were properly served, and a resource that belongs to them received its recognition under the Endangered Species Act. The ESA may not be able to help the bear overcome melting ice, but the first listing due to global warming was in the record books. No matter how ugly it can get at times, good people make the government work the way it should.

• • •

In the fall of 2007, the Corps of Engineers attempted to resurrect the feral hog project of the Yazoo Basin—the Yazoo Backwater Pumps. Once again, the FWS would have to fight this ridiculous project, which was so devastating to bottomland hardwood wetlands. Sixty-five years after it was first authorized for study in the Flood Control Act of 1941, this damn thing was a monstrosity that just wouldn't die. The second report I helped write in my career with the FWS was on the damage the pumps would bring, and I was more than ready to help Sam Hamilton mount another effort. This time, however, would prove to be different. We had some substantial allies.

In October 2007, the Corps issued the *Yazoo Backwater Area Reformulation Main Report*, which stated:

> The U.S. Army Corps of Engineers, Vicksburg District (Vicksburg District), is reformulating the remaining unconstructed features of the Yazoo Backwater Project Area in the Yazoo Basin, Mississippi. An array of nonstructural, structural, and combination alternatives emphasizing increased urban flood protection, reduced agricultural intensification, and fewer adverse environmental impacts has been evaluated. This report presents the results of studies that evaluate the feasibility of alternatives to address the flooding problems and meet the environmental and economic objectives of the area . . . The recommended plan for the Yazoo Backwater Area consists of a 14,000-cfs [cubic feet per second] pump station with a pump-on operation elevation of 87.0 feet, NGVD [National Geodetic Vertical Datum of 1929], at the Steele Bayou structure; perpetual easements from willing sellers and reforestation/conservation measures on up to 55,600 acres of agricultural land primarily at or below the pump elevation (1 year base condition frequency level at the Steele Bayou structure). (USACE 2007)

Under the 1941 and 1965 Flood Control Acts, it was recognized that the ninety-foot elevation was the lowest level of flood protection that anyone could reasonably expect. But that wasn't good enough for the engineers who worked for the Vicksburg District. Just as we who cared for the wetlands and natural resources of the Yazoo Basin didn't want to see the little remaining bottomland hardwood habitat destroyed on our watch, I believe it became a challenge to each generation of engineers to get the feral hog pump project built and root out all the remaining wetlands. We called it the feral hog because wild hogs are not native to these ecosystems, do significant damage to the habitat through their digging and wallowing, and seem to have a population that cannot be kept under control. One thing the Corps overlooked, however, was the language of the Clean Water Act (CWA) and why Attorney General (AG) Benjamin Civiletti, during the Lake Ophelia deliberations, clearly found that the Environmental Protection Agency (EPA) was the administrator of that law. Whether done by a private individual seeking a Section 404 permit or by a federal agency seeking to "satisfy the requirements of Section 404," the EPA must approve the findings. Under Section 404(c), the EPA has final veto authority over any project, private or public, that will result in the deposition of dredged or fill material in waters of the U.S. The Civiletti decisions made during the Lake Ophelia effort were now unchallenged and proved to be highly significant to the new Pumps study.

As expected, Sam Hamilton and his team in the Southeast Region commented on the plan and alerted the Corps that we reserved the right, and would exercise that right, to elevate the project to the Council on Environmental Quality (CEQ) for resolution of issues. On November 13, Assistant Secretary of the Army for Civil Works John Paul (J.P.) Woodley issued a directive on the Yazoo Backwater Area Pumps that officially extended the time frame in which a federal agency could refer the project to the CEQ for resolution of issues. Two deadlines were set to end the potential for referral, depending on which one came first: one year from the date after the final environmental impact statement has been made available to the EPA and public, or twenty-five days after the EPA completes its review and renders a decision pursuant to 33 U.S.C. Sec 1344(c). The latter was the target upon which environmental organizations and the FWS were focused.

If EPA found the environmental statement inadequate, less than full disclosure, or—and this was critical—too damaging to resources found in Waters of the United States to allow it to go forward, they could veto the project and end the discussion. All efforts were now riveted on getting the EPA to veto the project, not just for the 14,000-cfs pumping plant, but for *any future* project. In the past, pumping capacity as high as 27,000 cfs had been evaluated and could be resurrected again by the Corps. Under the regulations, however, EPA can make a "prior designation" and deny any *future development* if they find that the area is so important it should never be drained or impacted.

The proposed pumping plant would cost the American taxpayers over $200 million *in addition* to all the work that had been done in the 4-million-acre delta. On November 14, 2007, a group of thirteen environmental organizations wrote to EPA Administrator Stephen Johnson asking him to veto the Yazoo Pumps Project.

> As discussed below, it is clear that the Yazoo Pumps would have 'an unacceptable adverse effect on . . . fishery areas (including spawning and breeding areas), wildlife, or recreational areas,' giving EPA the authority—and the responsibility—to veto this project. (American Rivers et al. 2007)

In attacking the economic justification for flood damage reduction, the letter stated:

> An independent economic analysis commissioned by your agency also demonstrates that the Yazoo Pumps are not economically justified. That analysis shows that the Corps overstated the project's agricultural benefits by an incredible $144 million, and that the Yazoo Pumps would produce far less than 14 cents of agricultural benefits for each dollar spent on the project. The project's return is now likely far less as the acknowledged cost of the Yazoo Pumps has increased by $30 million since that analysis was completed, and the final construction costs almost certainly will be much higher . . . At a time when the federal government is poised to spend billions of dollars to attempt to correct the devastating environmental impacts caused by Corps projects to

the Everglades, coastal Louisiana, and the Mississippi River, it is incumbent on this Administration to put a stop to the Corps' plans to spend $211 million to completely alter the hydrology of yet another region of the country. Again, we urge you to veto The Yazoo Pumps project. (American Rivers et al. 2007)

On October 24, Sam flew into D.C. and we met with Lynn on the merits of our arguments and the horrific damage this project would impart. Lynn had learned that the administration was concerned about the project, based mainly on the poor economic return. For a Corps project to meet the economic criteria for consideration, there must be at least a 1:1 ratio of benefits to costs. That can be overturned if there are significant environmental benefits that are "intangible," but not for economic reasons. The current project, based on EPA's independent analysis, was expected to provide much less than a .14:1 for agricultural benefits, the primary purpose of the project.

> There was a lot of political pressure from the Mississippi Senators on the administration on the Yazoo Pumps. The analysis had shown that the project would benefit only a couple of soybean farmers, but would have really adverse impacts on about 250,000 acres of prime bottomland hardwood wetlands, the largest remaining block in the 4-million-acre Yazoo Delta. You and Sam came to me and said 'Here is the science and information, we've got a lot of political pressure, yet here was the analysis that showed how damaging the project would be.' Looking at the balance of interests, I backed you up in terms of what you were trying to do and why it didn't make sense. It was not economically justified, not good for the environment and not good for the public. (Scarlett 2020)

Lynn agreed that this was one of those long-standing project studies that needed to be put to bed. She committed to call Ben Grumbles, assistant administrator for water at EPA, a longtime associate and someone we knew well. We met again on October 30 to solidify our referral to CEQ and continue discussing strategy. Lynn reported that EPA also had serious concerns.

In January, I went to Lynn's office to have an "in-house" call between the CEQ, EPA and J.P. Woodley to determine the course of action the administration would take. J.P. started the call with where the Corps was in its studies and when the advanced documents might be done. Ben Grumbles provided a summary of why EPA in Atlanta was concerned about the project and the potential damage that could be done. David Anderson, who was with CEQ, asked me what I thought about the project.

"I know this project well," I began. "As a GS-9 biologist in Vicksburg, this was only the second project I helped analyze under the Fish and Wildlife Coordination Act. The Yazoo Basin was historically 4 million acres of hill drainage into 4 million acres of pristine bottomland hardwood wetlands. Since the early 1940s, the Corps has systematically moved down the wetland delta providing flood protection and pushing the water like a massive squeegee, allowing wetlands to be cleared for farming while pushing that flood problem down on the poor souls below them. Then the next project did the same, as did the next. The Yazoo Sump area, called that for a reason, contains the last remaining stand of pristine bottomland hardwood wetlands in the Yazoo Delta, and it would be a travesty to say we couldn't allow the last acres to remain for the benefit of fish, wildlife and people. This project is an abomination."

Anderson immediately came back with "Dale, thank you for bringing up what this project would really do. This is not one the White House wants to see happen. It just isn't justified." J.P. Woodley spoke up: "I can just stop it if that's what everyone thinks is best." Ben Grumbles said "Thank you, J.P. That makes everything easier, knowing you will support stopping it, but we think it should be an EPA veto that kills the project." I looked at Lynn with a grin that I know belied *any* attempt at appearing calm. Nearly thirty years before, I had helped Charlie McCabe and Robert Barkley write a report that told the same story, but apparently America wasn't ready to hear it. I thought about Charlie, Robert, Charles Baxter, Steve Forsythe, Curtis James, Ken Quackenbush, Bob Misso and all the other field biologists who put their entire careers into stopping unacceptable projects. I also thought of my brother-by-another-mother Sam Hamilton and his team of equally dedicated biologists, who had held the banner high. Today was a good day for conservation and bottomland hardwood wetlands. It had taken thirty years, but the right decision was under way.

The EPA started preparing their case and sent the message that a veto was under consideration. But to Ben Grumbles and my old friend Deputy Regional Administrator Larry Starfield in EPA's Atlanta Region, a simple veto was too little. Under the ability to prior designate a site as unavailable to receive dredged or fill material, Section 230.80 of the EPA regulations requires a full public review of and comment on the proposed decision. Larry and his shop got busy. On March 19, the EPA published the *Proposed Determination To Prohibit, Restrict, or Deny the Specification, or the Use for Specification, of an Area as a Disposal Site; Yazoo River Basin, Issaquena County, Mississippi* in the Federal Register.

Under Section 404(c) of the CWA, the EPA announced intent to hold a public hearing regarding its proposed determination on April 17 at the Vicksburg Convention Center and Auditorium. Just as with our public hearings on the ESA, the hearing would allow comments to be entered into the official record, but no question-and-answer format. The hearing was to satisfy the Administrative Procedures Act and receive information that might inform the final disposition of the proposal, not to debate it. EPA was in charge, and they had learned well how to handle their authority since the Lake Ophelia days.

The Board of Mississippi Levee Commissioners and others that would benefit financially from the expenditure of federal dollars were predictably opposed to the veto. One must understand the long line of Mississippi congressional leadership that had poured federal taxpayer dollars into the "development" of one of America's largest floodplain wetlands. Landowners in the Mississippi Delta were accustomed to "Ask and ye shall receive" from their members of Congress: Congressman Jamie Whitten, Senators John Stennis, James Eastland, Trent Lott and Thad Cochran. Each had acquired such seniority during their careers that they were able to earmark funds for nearly any project they wanted. To be told "No" was not something they had experienced.

I had first met Ray Aycock early in my career when he was in the Realty Division of the FWS working out of the Jackson Area Office. Ray had transferred from land acquisition into Ecological Services several years earlier and, because Ray was one of our most seasoned professionals, Sam asked him to attend the April 17 hearing and give the statement on behalf of the FWS. Sam forwarded Ray's email description to Lynn and me.

> The hearing room held 500 chairs and the EPA were on a platform above the crowd. It was formal and well run . . . I would guess the room was 2/3 to 3/4 full. Politicians making statements were a Cochran representative that I have never seen and an ex-Senator from the Delta (Neely Cathon) who said she spoke on behalf of the Governor. After that, it was a parade of Supervisors from Issaquena and Sharkey County with a representative or two from adjoining counties. I was the first to speak for an agency and the only one except for Ted Lineger of the Forest Service Lab at Stoneville . . . Our insiders who spoke with some very distraught Corps folks think the project is dead, but I'm waiting for the last shovel to hit the coffin. (Aycock 2008)

That last shovel hit the coffin on August 31, 2008.

EPA signed the final determination prohibiting the discharge of dredged or fill material into wetlands and other Waters of the United States in connection with the construction of the proposed Yazoo Backwater Area Pumps Project (the proposed project). The proposed project is a U.S. Army Corps of Engineers (the Corps) Civil Works project designed to address flooding concerns in a 630,000 acre area situated between the Mississippi and Yazoo Rivers in west-central Mississippi (Yazoo Backwater Area). The primary component of this project is a 14,000 cubic feet per second (cfs) pumping station that would pump surface water out of the Yazoo Backwater Area during high water events on the Mississippi River. Construction and operation of the proposed pumping station would adversely impact at least 67,000 acres of wetlands and other Waters of the United States. EPA has determined that these impacts would result in unacceptable adverse effects on fishery areas and wildlife. EPA continues to support the goal of providing improved flood protection for the residents of the Mississippi Delta; however, it believes that this vital objective can be accomplished consistent with ensuring effective protection for the area's valuable natural resources. (EPA 2008)

The Section 404(c) veto of any project that might be proposed on an identified site has only been used a few times since its passage in 1972. I don't think I ever saw Sam Hamilton more excited about any event than he was about the Yazoo Pumps veto. As citizens of the United States, we are blessed to actually own the natural resources within our borders. The government holds these resources in trust *for the people*. These magnificent resources provide more benefits to all of us than we are capable of knowing. How does one explain the majesty of the mist coming off the water at sunrise as one floats by cypress trees several hundred years old? Or the sound of whistling wings as wood ducks tilt and spin underneath the massive branches? How much is peace of the soul worth? How can it be measured?

I bathe in serenity when I sit by a campfire and watch the dancing flames, or rest under a tall sycamore and hear the riffles of the stream. We are one with our wild kin, whether or not we comprehend it. It is in our DNA. We are creatures of the wetlands, or the mountains or the desert, or the sea. We occupy a separate niche, but we are members of the community of life. If you are ever near Vicksburg, Mississippi, and have the opportunity, I implore you to visit the Yazoo, Theodore Roosevelt, Panther Swamp and Holt Collier National Wildlife Refuges. The tenacity displayed by generations of conservationists ensured that those places would be there for us to absorb into our soul. May the Yazoo Pumps be buried forever in the heap of the misguided.

CHAPTER 20

Lunch with the President

The election to decide the next president of the United States was less than two months away, and President George W. Bush knew that many in his administration would be actively seeking their next means of employment. I received an engraved invitation from Secretary of the Interior Dirk Kempthorne to have lunch with the president as he visited each department and thanked those he had appointed for serving on his team. I have no idea if this is something all presidents do, but George W. Bush made the time to break bread with us and show his appreciation. The luncheon was on September 9 and, in an oddity of events, was held in the same secretarial conference room where the "Mother's Day Massacre" had occurred. Place cards marked where we were to sit, and mine was at the end of the table near to and across from the president. To my immediate left were Mark Myers, Bob Johnson and Lyle Laverty, friends who had become close through the trials of conservation challenges. Secretary Kempthorne sat to the left of President Bush, and David Bernhardt was at Kempthorne's left, directly across from me.

We take things like eating a sandwich with friends for granted, but the president of the United States is not afforded that luxury. Apparently, if he eats outside the White House, he must take his chef to ensure against assassination by poisoning. While we were encouraged to go ahead with our meal, he joked and enjoyed time with people whom he knew had tried their best to serve him with integrity.

We each took a turn to thank him for his support on an issue of our choice. When it came to me, I thanked him for his support to strengthen

Lunch with President George W. Bush (Courtesy of USDOI)

relationships with the states and other potential partners. He immediately reiterated what he had said many times before: "We simply can't get the job of looking after this country's natural resources done without help from the states." I then talked about an issue we were not able to accomplish before his time as president ran out. He joked and said "Dirk, you need to put your polar bear guy on that!" Everyone around the table laughed because they knew that was me. I looked at the president, smiled respectfully, and said "He's on it, Mr. President."

The expression on the president's face immediately changed to one that indicated the wheels were turning and the dots were being connected. He smiled in the realization that I was the director who stood firm in believing the bear should be listed, and then he turned to the others with no sign of concern. After the lunch, he asked each of us to come into Dirk's office and have our photo taken with the Secretary and him. When it was my turn, he shook my hand, looked me directly in the eye and said "Thank you for your service to the country, and for your wonderful service to my administration." I'll never know if he was letting me know he respected the position I had taken, or that the polar bear wasn't one of his priorities. Either way, I walked away still respecting the president who had consistently ordered all of us to do the right thing, regardless of politics.

Many people criticized President Bush for coming across as a yokel from the sticks. Many of those same people ended up being outsmarted by that yokel. What I learned in the half dozen times I was around him was the truth behind the old adage "What you see is what you get." There was no pretense to please the camera. No desire to be smooth; just truthful. No effort to be charismatic; only genuine. I'll take those traits over all the smoke and mirrors that have become the trademark of getting elected as president. Perhaps a few more traits from both Roosevelts, Truman, Eisenhower, Kennedy and both Bushes just might unite our nation and restore America's faith in the White House.

• • •

(l–r) Dirk Kempthorne, author, and President G.W. Bush (Courtesy of USDOI)

I officially retired from the U.S. Fish and Wildlife Service on January 3, 2009, after thirty years and four months. I could have stayed until the inauguration of President-elect Barack Obama, but the FWS had been my home; its employees, my family. I didn't want the next administration coming in and telling me to get out of my house. With military time, I retired with thirty-four years of service to the nation I loved. In retrospect, much of the time was spent fighting battles on issues for which I was condemned by the public I served because I would not rewrite the law to say what they wanted it to say. Some wanted it to say "Stop everything and protect the resource," while others wanted "This is my property, stay out of my business." The law usually said neither. The career employee with the federal or state government is too easily stereotyped as being a "Follow the rules, don't make me think" person when, in truth, few are more open to hearing ideas that would lead to a long-term solution. Part of the problem in the regulatory ranks is creating an atmosphere in which ideas are welcomed. The public is usually acting from a state of fear that their livelihood will be harmed. The executive branch employee did not write the laws, but the legislative branch is all too willing to deny any responsibility for its directives.

Still, there were also times of pure satisfaction when the hard work of the team led to a solution to the problem. In fact, it was always the team that found success, never the individual. Some of us understood that. A few didn't. My wish is that there will come a day when the dedicated *public servant* is appreciated as a human being with a family to support and a country he or she loves, instead of a faceless person with no name who can be easily denigrated for committing their lives in service of others. I know that the people of the Department of the Interior with whom I was privileged to work, and the state employees who were our partners, deserve all the recognition they could possibly attain. I had a blessed career with the federal government; one that was navigated by the hand of my Creator and filled with failures, and some successes, but no defeats. The hand that was compelling me would not let me surrender.

As I began my time as a federal retiree, I promised Sarah I would not accept another full-time position after retiring from the FWS. But, as usual, I was not in charge.

PART 5

The Citizen Conservationist

CHAPTER 21

Ducks Unlimited and Macondo

President Barack Hussein Obama Jr. defeated Senator John McCain to become the forty-fourth president of the United States. On December 17, 2008, President-elect Obama announced his intention to nominate Senator Ken Salazar from Colorado as the next secretary of the interior. Salazar was elected to the Senate in 2005 after serving as the attorney general for Colorado from 1999 to 2005. I had met him, but only in passing. He was concerned about the environment, yet seemed to also understand the middle ground that actually makes things work. Salazar was confirmed and sworn in as the fiftieth secretary of the interior on January 20, 2009.

On May 8, Salazar disappointed many in the environmental community when he announced that he would retain the position we had established regarding greenhouse gases and the Endangered Species Act (ESA). Since it is impossible to determine the exact source of CO_2 that caused the ice to melt off the coast of Alaska, we stood firm that the ESA did not give us the authority to regulate power plant emissions in the United States. Atmospheric greenhouse gases are contributed by literally every country in the world, and no one has the ability to "tag" molecules in order to track their movement and potential affects. Therefore, it is impossible to determine who or what specific activity should be held accountable. In his announcement, the secretary stated "To see the polar bear's habitat melting and an iconic species threatened is an environmental tragedy of the modern age. This administration is fully committed to the protection and recovery of the polar bear."

Another announcement made by Secretary Salazar and the president occurred on June 9 in a news release titled "Secretary Salazar Lauds President's Intent to Nominate Sam Hamilton as Director of the U.S. Fish and Wildlife Service." To say I was elated with the choice of Sam to follow me as director would be the understatement of the century. No one was more qualified than Sam Hamilton to lead the world's preeminent fish and wildlife agency. I was also relieved that they chose a career employee, only the second career U.S Fish and Wildlife Service (FWS) employee to be named director since Lynn Greenwalt, which at least inferred I hadn't screwed things up badly enough to frighten the political ranks away from career candidates.

Steve Thompson called to tell me he had seen the announcement, and we were like schoolkids pleased with the new captain of the football team. I immediately called Sam to congratulate him and let him know he had an army of supporters behind him. He was confirmed on August 1, less than two months after he'd been nominated, and he had an easy transition from regional director to director. He understood that the ESA was an important tool in the conservation of fish and wildlife resources, but didn't believe it was the most important. He highly valued partnerships—especially with the state fish and wildlife agencies—in working to preclude the need to list species, and immediately allayed any fears that the partnerships former director Steve Williams and I had fostered would be diminished.

But none of us is in charge of life and the time we have on earth. Following a meeting of the FWS directorate in Colorado, Sam stayed over the weekend to do some skiing. On February 20, 2010, he suffered a massive heart attack on the slopes and was dead before they could get him off the hill. The shock was monumental, not just for the FWS, but for those of us who were extremely close to Sam. When I heard the news, I wept. I called Steve Thompson to let him know one of the "three amigos" was gone, but got his voice mail. "Steve, call me as soon as you get this message. I have some bad news to give you." Steve called back about three hours later. "I got your message and couldn't get my fingers to punch in your number," he said. "I just knew the bad news had to be about Sam." We recalled how Sam had always worried about his health. His father, who had been an Air Force pilot, had passed away in his late forties. I asked Sam once if there was anything I needed to know about his health. He just answered "The men in my family don't tend to live to a ripe old age. I just want to hedge my bets as much as possible." When we were together in Atlanta, Steve convinced Sam to join the swim club, and they often went together over lunchtime. Sam's death was exceedingly difficult to take, but then, losing a close friend is never easy. At the funeral, Sam was surrounded by Steve, Mitch King, a church full of FWS and state resource agency friends and, of course, Sarah and me. The FWS Honor Guard added a beautiful tribute, and one he would have loved.

After Sam's passing, I was traveling and ended up on the same plane with Secretary Salazar. I knew several of the special agents in his protective detail and asked one if it would be OK to go back and introduce myself. The agent said "Of course, Director. He would like that." Secretary Salazar was traveling as nearly all non-military appointees travel, in coach class. I went back the few rows to where he was seated, introduced myself and we spoke briefly. "If I can ever be of assistance, please don't hesitate to call me." I gave him my card and returned to my seat. It was only a week or two later that he called and asked me for advice on who would be a good choice to replace Sam. I immediately told him there was only one clear choice: Steve Thompson. He thanked me and said he would get back with me.

I called Steve to alert him that he might get a call. He did. Before it was over, he had been asked no less than twice to reconsider his answer of "No." Ken Salazar also called me at least two more times, asking for my help with Steve. When Steve asked for my advice, I said "You are the clear choice to be the next director. But you have given over thirty years in the service of your country and are finally making a comfortable living as a consultant. You would have to take a substantial cut in pay and go back to D.C. However, I'll give you some advice that was given to me once. The troops need you. There isn't a good choice after you. As one whose heart is with the Service, I would love to see you take it. As your friend, I can't encourage you to give up all you have worked for." In the end he declined, and the president and secretary had to look elsewhere.

• • •

In December 2009, I got a call from Dan Sherman, an executive recruiter I had met many years earlier in California. He asked if I would be interested in talking to the Ducks Unlimited (DU) Search Committee about their CEO position. DU is the premier wetlands and waterfowl conservation organization in the world.

The North American Model of Wildlife Conservation is founded on the premise that both the consumptive and non-consumptive users of the resource bear the significant burden for the costs of conservation management, whether on public or private property. While the model specifically recognizes that all wildlife belongs to the people, private landowners have purchased the property, paid annual property taxes and expended their private funds to create wetlands, food plots, reforestation or a myriad of management techniques to benefit deer, waterfowl, turkey or fisheries resources. I have found no lack of obsession to care for the land from any "citizen conservationist"—one who balances harvest of the resources while also providing habitat for hundreds of species—whom I have met. To the contrary, the most common question is "What else can I do?" Unfortunately, the consumptive side of conservation continues to carry the financial burden.

These dedicated stewards of the natural resources who own and care for the land, or fund conservation efforts, are the definition of today's citizen conservationist. S/he is driven by the blend of ensuring that fish, wildlife and their habitats are here for future generations, while enjoying their passion to participate in the predator-prey contest for survival that has evolved over thousands of years and is solidly entrenched in the human DNA. The bonding with nature that takes place through hunting, fishing and outdoor recreation creates a significant foundation for the value system upon which families and nations are bound.

Without the citizen conservationist, there would be no healthy fish or wildlife resources in America today. The federal and state agencies depend significantly on this community of men and women who share their passion and are compelled to be engaged in conservation. When I was director of the FWS, I often spoke to classes at the National Conservation and Training Center (NCTC) about the "sandwich mission" of our agency:

> **Working with others**, to conserve, protect and enhance fish, wildlife, and plants and their habitats **for the continuing benefit of the American people**. (Emphasis added.)

The mission statement of the nation's primary fish and wildlife agency clearly recognizes that our work begins and ends with people. The meat of the mission is the resources for which we care so deeply, but we will only succeed if we work together with partners while recognizing that the beneficiaries are those who are yet to be born. Our price was paid by those who came before us. Our responsibility is to pay the price for those who will follow. Ducks Unlimited is one of the premier examples of the willingness of hunters, landowners and other conservationists to voluntarily find ways to fund and support conservation. After the organization had achieved 12 million acres' worth of conservation and seventy years of volunteer dedication in Canada, Mexico and the United States, the Ducks Unlimited CEO Search Committee had asked me to talk to them about potentially being their next staff leader. I was truly humbled.

I received the basic information in the mail from Dan about DU's budget, their structure of over 450 professional staff and *50,000 volunteers*, and general information about the board of directors and the work the organization was doing in wetlands. As I read and digested the information, deep-seated feelings of energy began to rise in my core; that feeling of challenge and wanting to make a difference. I became acutely aware that if they wanted me, I'd very likely accept. When Dan called after the holidays, I said I would be willing to talk. I flew to Memphis in February for the interview.

Wayne Dierks was the human resources officer for DU and the only professional staff member allowed to know who was being interviewed. At 10 a.m. sharp, Dan walked into the room where I was waiting and said the board was ready. I walked in and was warmly greeted by eight board members, each of whom was on the executive committee of Ducks Unlimited. They immediately made me feel at home, introduced themselves, each in turn, and told me about their backgrounds. John Pope, president; Bruce Lewis, chairman of the board and past president; Bob Hester, treasurer; John Newman, first vice-president and next president; Steve Reynolds, secretary; John Childs, president of Wetlands America Trust (the board of trustees that oversees DU's land and easement holdings, and also provides significant financial support to DU); John Tomke, past president; Jim Hulbert, past president; and George Dunklin, board member and farmer/conservationist. Dan Sherman and Wayne Dierks were also in the room, but the Ducks Unlimited Inc. board was clearly the volunteer leadership of the organization, and equally clear that they were going to run the meeting.

Bruce Lewis, an attorney from Natchez, Mississippi, began by saying "We've seen your very impressive résumé and know you are well qualified, but we'd like you to tell us about you; about what's in your heart." It was immediately clear that they wanted someone whose heart was driven by conservation, not money or position. There were apparently a lot of applicants for the job, all of whom were trying to convince the committee that they were the right person. My love was of the resource, not ego or desire for status that the title of CEO brings. I told them about my history in the lower Mississippi Valley and the efforts to save bottomland hardwood wetlands in the 1970s, when we were losing 300,000 acres per year. I told them of the pain I felt watching the "stinger blades" erase over a hundred years of nature's handiwork in thirty seconds.

Toward the end of the hour-long meeting, Dan asked me to tell them why I had agreed to meet with them when I had turned down requests to talk with other conservation organizations about leadership positions.

"DU is different. Over the course of my career, I have seen the dedication of DU conservationists to roll up your sleeves and fix what's broken. DU is the definition of wetlands conservation by simply going about the work of conserving and restoring wetlands while everyone else argues about their conservation 'agenda.' I couldn't imagine going through the rest of my life knowing I had refused to at least talk with you about conservation of wetlands. I also respect DU because I have observed that you rarely use your resources to bring litigation. That means DU is always welcome at the table as an honest broker, and sometimes mediator, for the resource."

Bob Hester asked me about my leadership style and to give an example of one of my proudest accomplishments.

"Let me start with the latter part of your question. I don't have any accomplishments." Bob's eyes went wide, and I could tell he didn't know how to take that answer. "In my opinion, the only things I ever accomplished were with the help and support of a team of dedicated people. The accomplishment was theirs, not mine. An individual almost never makes things happen. The leader moves people in the right direction so that *they* can accomplish what they didn't believe was possible."

I left the meeting with the friendly thanks of everyone there. Wayne walked me to the door and told me he really appreciated my answers, for what it was worth. I told him it was worth a lot. Over my time at DU, my respect and affection for Wayne Dierks only grew. Conservationists come from all backgrounds. No one gave more to DU and conservation than this human resources officer.

My second and final interview was held in late March. When I landed in Atlanta after that interview for my connection to D.C., I had a phone message from Dan and Wayne asking me to call them. Dan informed me that the search committee had voted unanimously to nominate me to the full executive committee as the next CEO.

On April 14, John Pope called me to say the full executive committee of Ducks Unlimited voted to approve my selection as their next CEO, and officially offered me the job. The wheels would be turning at DU over the next couple of days as they got ready to roll out the announcement. I let Sarah know that I had accepted the position, opened a beer and sat down in my recliner to relax. Sarah said, "I told you you'd take the job and we'd be moving."

• • •

The news release announcing my selection went out on April 16, 2010. Just four days later, the largest natural resource disaster in American history occurred. British Petroleum (BP) was the primary operator of the Deepwater Horizon rig drilling in the Gulf of Mexico approximately fifty miles offshore in the *Macondo Prospect* region. Other companies in partnership with BP included Transocean and Halliburton. On April 20, in the process of drilling a well approximately five thousand feet below the surface, an explosion occurred on the oil rig with 126 people on board. Eleven men were killed, and their remains never found. The rig burned for two days and was spilling 60,000 barrels of oil (42 gallons/barrel) every day. Drilling at five thousand feet was new technology, and shutting off the flow at that depth was unprecedented. Because of the uncharted territory in emergency spill response, oil flowed from the well head for eighty-seven days, spilling 4.9 million barrels of sweet crude that drifted from approximately the Texas-Louisiana border to Florida. During the spill, the federal government ordered all deepwater exploration halted.

John Pope immediately called. "I know you aren't officially on board until May 3, but we need your help in handling this spill." I had worked several spills during my career and knew the process. "The first thing is to tell everyone in DU to do nothing," I said. "That is critical. Any member of DU, or any other non-governmental organization for that matter, that picks up an oiled bird without the express approval from an authorized federal or state agency is in violation of the Migratory Bird Treaty Act. There are three phases of response. First is the emergency response to stop the spill. That is still under way. The second step is to pick up oiled animals and put out booms or other activities directed by the government agencies to clean up as much oil as possible. The final stage is the assessment of damages. We're still in the emergency response phase. I'll call people I know in the FWS and let them know DU staff and volunteers are ready and willing to help, but we *must stand down until we're asked for assistance.*"

John said he understood and would give the order to be ready, but to do nothing until given the word. I knew this would be difficult for DU volunteers, who were always ready to roll up their sleeves and go do work. But that's the way it had to be. At my first DU convention in Grapevine, Texas, just over a month later, I had to tell the one thousand people in attendance that my first action had been to recommend doing nothing. "You can blame me for that order, not the staff or President Pope. I'm sorry, but we have to follow the law. At DU, we don't sky bust when we're hunting, and we don't take actions just for show. When the FWS asks, we'll be there."

The National Convention was held over the Memorial Day weekend, during which I got a call from Jeff Trandahl, executive director of the National Fish and Wildlife Foundation (NFWF) asking if I thought DU could work with NFWF to create habitat in southwest Louisiana away from the mouths of the Mississippi and Atchafalaya Rivers. The projected path of the oil was to remain predominantly offshore until it reached the Mississippi, Alabama and Florida coasts. By then, much of the oil would be "weathered," meaning the highly volatile compounds contained in crude, known as polycyclic aromatic hydrocarbons, would have evaporated and the oil would become less toxic and more like tar. Tar on beaches, while ugly and economically damaging for the summer vacation traffic as well as for those who earn their living in the fishing community, could be cleaned up much more easily than tar that drifts into viable habitat along the Louisiana coast can be.

It was unknown whether a tropical storm would develop during the spill, which would likely push the oil into the coastal brackish and fresh marshes so important to migratory birds. Jeff was asking if we knew how to pull the birds away from marshes that might be impacted by a storm surge. I checked with our biologists and discovered that we had never attempted it, but they believed the birds would move left and right looking for food and cover after they arrived in August. I called Jeff and told him we believed this was a great opportunity to avoid impacts to migratory waterfowl before they occurred, rather than having to address them after damage was done. We decided to quietly pursue the possibility with BP.

The week after the convention, Jeff and I met in New Orleans and traveled south toward the mouth of the Mississippi River to observe the status of the spill and make videos for both of us to use. The DU film team of Clay Baird and Brett Cantrell, Dr. Tom Moorman from our Southern Regional office, Jeff Trandahl and a couple of his staff got in airboats and toured the phragmites marshes at the fringe of the saltwater-brackish water interface. Some oil had begun to come onshore, but not in substantial amounts . . . yet. We filmed footage of Jeff and me picking up oiled plants and also filmed other B-roll suitable for later use, then went back onshore. I thanked our team, told them that I was staying to have dinner with Jeff to talk about DU-NFWF opportunities, and bid them a safe trip home.

I didn't lie. Jeff had used his contacts to set up a meeting with BP representatives at Robert, Louisiana, one of the company's two emergency response locations. The other was in Houma, and I learned that FWS

Deputy Director Rowan Gould was there for the duration of the spill. One of my friends, former Indiana Department of Natural Resources director Glen Salmon, had been hired by the FWS just before my departure and was performing a similar role as Rowan at the Robert location, which is a training facility shared by several of the oil and gas companies and has several classroom-size areas.

We arrived to a somewhat nervous reception from the BP representatives. Jeff had assured them we were not there to criticize or get inside information for negative uses. Glen was there on behalf of the FWS, and representatives of BP were in attendance. After introductions, Jeff explained the reason for our visit and then turned it over to me. I began:

> First, let me tell you that we are not here to judge. There is an ample supply of people, agencies and organizations that are chomping at the bit to do that. You were our friends and partners in conservation before the spill occurred, and you will be our friends and partners in conservation after it is over. And it will eventually be over. We are here to ask you to help us attempt to preclude harm to migratory birds. By the beginning of August, teal, pintail and early migrators will begin to arrive on the Gulf Coast. The normal pathway down the Mississippi Flyway is following the Mississippi River to its mouth, then moving laterally along the coast looking for food and cover.
>
> I cannot tell you that what we are proposing will work. We have never tried it. We would like to create a significant amount of habitat in southwest Louisiana, away from potential points of entry for oil, in an effort to pull the birds away from the mouths of the rivers. If we are successful, it could avoid significant harm to the 9 million or so migratory birds that overwinter in Louisiana. But I want to be completely honest about two things up front.
>
> First, Glen will attest that you will probably get no credit

whatsoever in the Natural Resource Damage Assessment and Restoration Plan that will be produced when the spill is completely contained and damages begin to be calculated. Second, I reiterate that we have not done this before, and I can't tell you with certainty that it will work. We believe it will, but the only thing that is certain in nature is that nothing is certain in nature. We are here to ask you to donate $5 million to NFWF, who in turn will find federal matching monies, and DU will be a major partner in creating the habitat.

Glen confirmed that in the multi-agency damage assessment that would be carried out following the spill, BP would likely not get credit for positive actions taken to prevent harm to birds. The assessment is the legal tool that determines how much the responsible party owes the states and federal government for damages to natural resources that belong to the people. The company representatives asked questions regarding how we would accomplish creating habitat in such a short amount of time. I replied, "This is what we do for a living. We work with partners—in this case it would be the Natural Resources Conservation Service and the private landowners—to put in water-control structures and flood up areas that would normally go dry in the fall." Jeff assured them he could find the matching funds and supported the belief that we could get the habitat created.

A week or so later BP contributed $5 million to NFWF. Jeff worked with Dave White, the chief of the Natural Resources Conservation Service (NRCS), to secure more than $10 million through their conservation programs for work throughout the Lower Mississippi Valley. Kevin Norton, NRCS state conservationist for Louisiana, was completely behind the idea. He was honest in warning that the landowners might not want to sign up for the program, but committed his team in Louisiana to help make it happen. On the first day for landowners to have their properties enrolled, Kevin said "We couldn't believe it! They were lined up all around the building." DU received $3.5 million from NFWF, which we also worked to match, and began putting the habitat on the ground. By mid-August, when the first teal arrived, the partnership we created had put 78,000 acres into waterfowl habitat—78,000 acres in just three months!

When Clay and Brett went to SW Louisiana to video the bird usage, it was amazing. The teal were flying in their usual unpredictable manner and looked like swarms of mosquitoes. Also in the video, cows were calmly standing knee-deep in water as if nothing spectacular had happened. It was the ultimate message that private landowners hold the key to providing conservation for our fish and wildlife treasures, and there does not have to be a tradeoff between making a living farming or ranching and conserving habitat. When the spill was over and the Natural Resource Damage Assessment completed, duck and goose losses were in the hundreds, rather than thousands, out of the 7 million that wintered there. BP justifiably received a solid dose of criticism and fines. But they also deserve recognition for doing what they did not have to do. Negligence was proven during the analysis of the drilling operation, and it had led to the tragic deaths of eleven people and the destruction of significant natural resources. But it is only fair to recognize that the actions that BP took *after* the spill included everything anyone could have expected a company to do.

CHAPTER 22

*Johnny Morris and
Ducks Unlimited Partnerships*

John L. Morris was born on March 19, 1948, in Springfield, Missouri. He grew up loving to fish and hunt in the beautiful Ozark Mountains and wanted more than anything else to be able to fish all the time. His first real opportunity came when a man named Ray Scott created the Bassmaster Tournament series. Ray was a former life insurance salesman, with emphasis on salesman, constantly looking for a new product to push. He lived in Alabama, and I met Ray on an airplane ride from Atlanta to Albuquerque to visit with my family when I was still alone in D.C. Ray told me how he came upon the idea of the bass tournaments.

> A friend of mine in Colorado knew I loved to fish and kept telling me I needed to come visit him so he could take me trout fishing. I finally gave in and drove out there and he put me on this beautiful stream with a couple of his friends and him. One of them caught this little, at least I thought it was little, trout about twelve inches long. He worked it in real slow, letting it run back out then bringing it in, and finally pulled this little net that was clipped to his vest and, real easy-like, got it in the net. They were all smiles. They oohed and aahed about this fish and finally let it go. I thought, 'If a fisherman will get that excited over a twelve-inch trout, what in the world will they do when they

see a ten-pound largemouth bass?' So, I started the Bassmaster Tournament.

Morris wanted to be in the fishing business, but his father owned a liquor store in Springfield, Missouri. When Johnny told his dad what he wanted to do, the response was "We're in the liquor business. That's the business you need to be in." Johnny had entered several of the tournaments and was even more energetic about being in the fishing business. He kept after his father to let him have some space to sell lures and tackle in the liquor store. Finally, his father relented and said "See that little corner back there in the store? You can have that to sell your fishing stuff. When that goes bust, you can start back over here behind the counter." Between Bassmaster Tournaments, Johnny pulled a U-Haul trailer around to people he knew were making lures and fishing equipment and bought them directly to eliminate the distributor. Lure by lure, he started building his business. On the tournament trail, however, were significant obstacles. Equipment was not as safe as it is today, and at our DU National Convention in Portland, Johnny relayed a harrowing experience that made him know the Creator was looking after him.

We were fishing in a tournament when a terrible storm came up. The winds were howling and the waves were like being on the ocean. I was in a small bass boat and was headed for a cove or somewhere I could get shelter from the wind and waves when my boat took on a big wave and started to sink. When the boat went under water, I grabbed hold of the red six-gallon gas tank to stay afloat.

We didn't have life jackets in the boats at that time, so my life depended on that gas tank. I didn't believe I was going to make it and started scratching a good-bye note to my mom and dad on the side of the gas tank with my pocketknife. Nearby, in a cove off the main channel, two guys were waiting out the

Pyramid (Courtesy of Ducks Unlimited)

storm, and one of them saw my tank and thought someone was holding on to it. He told his partner, who said 'We can't go out there! We'll capsize too!' The other man said 'If that was us, I would hope someone would come get me. I think we have to go.' They came out and saved my life. I knew the Good Lord was looking after me to have that man see a gas tank and somehow think someone was holding on. We all had life jackets after that. (Morris 2013)

Johnny went on to prove his father wrong, building a Bass Pro Shops empire that eventually ended up buying Cabela's and becoming the largest outdoor business in the world. When it was announced on April 16, 2010, that I would be the next CEO of Ducks Unlimited, the first person I heard from was Johnny Morris. He was all excited and said "Hey man, you and DU are going to work with us on the Pyramid, right?" I replied "Of course, Johnny! I can't wait to do more things with you and Bass

Pro." Little did I know how much that would entail.

In typical Johnny Morris fashion, he followed that up on April 30 with a handwritten note, one of many I would be privileged to receive from him. One of the things I learned about Johnny is that his note to you will always be the last in the exchange. If you write back thanking him for his note, he will send you another note thanking you for yours. Humility, kindness and integrity form the foundation of who he is as a person. I learned to surrender on trying to be the last to say thank you. By June 15, he had already begun work on the partnership by having a full-page spread in his catalogue about DU, hunting and conservation. At the top it read "Hunter: Another Word for Conservationist" and encouraged everyone to join Ducks Unlimited.

The Pyramid is located in Memphis adjacent to the I-40 bridge crossing over into Arkansas. It was originally built as an event venue for Memphis entertainment, including the Memphis Grizzlies NBA team. When Fred Smith, founder and chairman of FedEx, built the FedEx Forum in downtown Memphis, the Pyramid went empty and the city had a challenge on its hands. The structure had been built as a pyramid in a nod to Memphis's sister city in Egypt, but the shape of the building proved to be a significant obstacle for nearly every type of business that might be able to use approximately 600,000 square feet of space. After the building had been unoccupied for several years, the City of Memphis got Johnny's good friend, TV fishing celebrity Bill Dance, to find out if Johnny would be willing to make the Pyramid a huge Bass Pro Shop.

Johnny had some interest in the possibility, but also had some trouble deciding if he would make or lose money in something that big, even with the City bearing a substantial portion of the costs to retrofit the interior. Then came a day when he and Bill were fishing on the Mississippi River with Johnny's first fishing department employee, Jack Emmitt, for large catfish. Both Johnny and Bill gave me the same account of what happened.

Johnny Morris (right) and author (Courtesy of Bass Pro Shops)

Johnny asked me if he was going to lose his pants or make money if he invested in the Pyramid as a Bass Pro Shop. I said 'I don't know, Johnny. It's like fishing. You don't know if you're going to catch a fish unless you put a line in the water.' Johnny said, 'That's it! If we catch a catfish that weighs over thirty pounds today, I'll build the store. If we don't, I won't. I'll let the Good Lord give me the answer.'

Within an hour, Johnny hooked and landed a thirty-five-pound channel catfish. He picked up his cell phone, called his chief operating officer, Jim Hagel, and said 'Jim, get the process started. We're gonna make the Pyramid a Bass Pro Shop.'

Johnny called to ask if I would like some space in the Pyramid for DU. I assumed he meant a kiosk or something similar to a wall identifying conservation organizations, like he has in nearly all his stores. Few people know how much Johnny Morris gives back to conservation or how much he helps non-governmental organizations like DU. "Of course!" I replied. "Thank you for the opportunity!" Sometime later he called back and said "OK buddy, I got your 8,000 square feet of space. Let us know how you want to use it!" I nearly choked! I pulled Chief Communications Officer Tom Fulgham, Doug Barns (head of our creative design section) and others into my office to get busy figuring out how we would be able to make the best use of 8,000 square feet of prime retail space.

In the end, it was reduced to 4,000 square feet, and we decided to make it a Waterfowling Heritage Center to highlight what the hunter/conservationist has done in America to bring back and manage our waterfowl and wetland resources. He later called and asked if I would like him to put our sign on the entrance side of the building. I assumed he meant a small sign over the entrance doorway or some other modest form of identity. I thanked him and said "Of course, we'd love to have that." The sign that was finally attached to the south (main entrance and exposure to I-40) side of the Pyramid underneath the Bass Pro sign turned out to be over 130 feet across and 30 feet high. That was when I realized that Johnny Morris does *nothing* in a modest way. If it's worth doing, it's worth doing big! Running a business is his means of making a living. Giving back is Johnny Morris's way of life.

Our personal friendship was growing stronger and stronger. I had met his lovely wife, Jeannie, at the duck stamp contest judging on Sanibel Island, Florida, when I was the director of FWS. I had met Johnny at the first day of sale for the duck stamp at his Baltimore store, and meeting Jeannie simply reinforced the goodness of their family. She is an accomplished artist, was a judge in that year's contest, and is a wonderful person. I invited Johnny to speak at the DU National Convention in Portland, Oregon, in 2013. In late May, just before the convention was scheduled to begin, I got a call.

"Hey man, how would you like to have the duck head [DU logo] on Tony Stewart's car at Daytona in July?"

DU NASCAR (Courtesy of Bass Pro Shops)

"Wow! That would be great! Thank you!"

He called back later and said "I'm having one of the race cars brought to Portland so the folks at your convention can see it."

"That's fantastic, Johnny! Thank you!"

"Have your folks check to see how we can drive it onstage in the hotel."

I went to Pattie Kempka and Dana Barton, our event coordinators, and asked them to see what could be done. The hotel was older and undergoing renovation in parts of the building, so getting the car inside was out of the question. We held many of our large gatherings at another building just up the street, and they denied our request to bring it inside. Johnny decided to have the DU duck head on two vehicles in two separate races, one on Tony's car in Daytona and one on Ty Dillon's truck in the Talladega truck race. As a result, the race truck that would be driven by Ty, Richard Childress's grandson, was parked outside the entrance to the building so all could see how the Ducks Unlimited logo would look running around the Talladega track in front of millions of viewers. Instead of displaying the logo at just one race, Johnny had decided that the truck should run at Talladega, and the car at Daytona. That began a seven-year span for DU with NASCAR during my tenure that included Tony Stewart, Martin Truex and Dale Earnhardt, Jr. as drivers, and Bass Pro Shops and Axalta as sponsors. It allowed me to meet many in the NASCAR family, including Richard Childress and his grandsons, Austin and Ty Dillon, as well as Ryan Newman and many other drivers. Richard and Johnny are longtime friends, and Richard is a leader in conservation as well.

The Waterfowling Heritage Center opened on April 29, 2016, and crossed the 1 million visitor number before I left DU in 2019. Between the NASCAR exposure and the Pyramid, Johnny Morris had helped Ducks Unlimited expand our brand to the public beyond our wildest expectations. To think Johnny just chose DU and me to take under his wing would be a mistake. Johnny Morris is *the* citizen conservationist of our time. He is, in my opinion, in the company of Theodore Roosevelt, Gifford Pinchot, J.J. Audubon, Aldo Leopold, "Ding" Darling and Rachel Carson. Each, in their own way, changed America and how conservation is done. In today's conservation world, it is essential that the business community take a leading role. Johnny Morris blazed that trail, and many others have followed.

Johnny took his love of fishing and the outdoors and made it a living passion. According to *Forbes* at the time of this writing, his net worth is in excess of $4 billion. However, the kid inside him is still in cutoff jeans, wading in the riffles and fishing for whatever he can catch. His enthusiasm for nature is unbridled and contagious. No one loves the thrill of catching a fish more than he. Much as Roosevelt loved the hunt, Johnny is today's Teddy Roosevelt and spares no effort to share that love.

Johnny gives back to conservation more than anyone can imagine. DU's contract at the Pyramid is for the life of the Bass Pro Shop and at no cost to DU except maintenance of the educational exhibit we created. In addition, he donated the money to build the exhibit as a world-class education opportunity. When most people think of successful entrepreneurs, they have an image of selfish, uncaring businesspeople. I beg to differ. My experience with Johnny Morris, and many other highly successful people, has proven otherwise. I have come to know and love Johnny as a brother and friend. His wife, Jeannie; son, John Paul; and daughter, Megan, are as humble and kind as he. Johnny is truly one of the gifts the Creator sent to remind me that there is far more good in people than bad, and that successful people worked hard for their wealth and know how important it is to lift others along the way. That is the Johnny Morris I am blessed to call my friend.

• • •

From its inception in 1937, Ducks Unlimited worked to raise money in the United States to do conservation work on Canada's nesting grounds. Jay "Ding" Darling was among the first to understand that management of migratory waterfowl should be driven by science and habitat, not by the traditional European model of raising the birds in captivity and releasing them for the hunt. Through the Migratory Bird Hunting and Conservation Stamp (duck stamp), the U.S. government began investing hunter-derived funds into habitat management in the United States.

It wasn't until the 1980s, however, that the science became evident that migratory birds need habitat throughout their life cycle. I call it the "round-trip ticket." The things we take for granted today had little scientific support in the early decades of the 1900s. Each of the three phases of nesting/fledging, migration, and overwintering needs proper habitat in order to accommodate all the critical life requisites. By the end of the 1980s, DU was well established in the U.S., Canada and Mexico and was busy raising monies to support habitat in each of the three countries. The organization's headquarters were located in Long Grove, Illinois, just outside Chicago, where they found themselves outgrowing their office space with no ability to expand. Peter Coors was president of DU at that time and started making a push for DU to move to Colorado, which was both his home and the home of his beer company. The president of DU wields a great deal of influence, but this would be the largest decision made by DU in decades.

In Memphis, Tennessee, an ardent supporter of DU and leading figure in Memphis commerce had other ideas. William B. Dunavant Jr. was known as "King Cotton" across the south and was a powerful force in Memphis. Billy believed that Memphis was the perfect place to relocate the DU headquarters due to its position on the Mississippi Flyway, its excellent location for travel and, most important, the fact that he wanted DU in Memphis! The county mayor was Bill Morris, former county sheriff and the man who arrested James Earl Ray following the assassination of Martin Luther King Jr. in 1968. Morris is a gifted speaker, and formidable when he sets his mind to a goal. Billy Dunavant asked Bill Morris and Pete Aviotti, a Dunavant employee, to go to the DU board meeting being held in California, where the decision would be made on the new location of Ducks Unlimited's headquarters. Bill Morris and Pete Aviotti relayed the story to me as part of DU's history.

> Billy was headstrong on getting DU to Memphis. As county mayor, I worked with our parks department at Shelby Farms and came up with an offer we didn't think DU could refuse. In return for a one dollar a year lease, DU would help the county analyze opportunities for water management, something we saw as a high skill set in DU. Pete and I flew to California and made the offer to the full board, including the extra incentive Billy Dunavant had offered in a $1 million gift to begin construction of the new building. Pete Coors was pushing hard for his Colorado location, but he had to admit he couldn't match the financial incentives Memphis and Shelby County were offering.

Pete Aviotti and I sat outside the room while the board went into executive session to deliberate the question. We thought it was a bit unfair that Coors got to stay in the room and we had to leave, but he was president and that's how it works. After about an hour, they came out and told us they had voted to relocate to Memphis. We were elated! The doors were opened at the new facility in 1992. (Morris 2018)

Even though Pete Coors was disappointed that the location was not Golden, Colorado, he was a true supporter of DU and realized that Memphis was clearly the better deal. Pete was the youngest person to ever serve as president of Ducks Unlimited and continually worked to support DU and conservation in every way he could. While handling the demands of running one of the largest beer businesses in America, he still maintains his Colorado leadership role on behalf of DU and "the ducks." His willingness to give his time and treasure in support of clean water and conservation are a testament to his dedication. I came to know Pete Coors during my time at DU, and he has my deep respect.

Billy and Tommie Dunavant were among the first people to visit my office and welcome me to Memphis. Billy was the curmudgeon on the outside, but a heart of gold on the inside. Billy's first act with me was to set up a fishing trip with Bill Dance so we could get to know each other. That friendship grew strong as well. Tommie is as sweet and kind as anyone I have ever met. The Dunavants and I became close over the years, and I hunted with Billy every year at his farm in Mississippi until his health finally put an end to those physical excursions. I knew I had made it to the elite group when Billy started calling me a "Dickhead," a term he withheld for only those he truly liked. I owe a great debt of gratitude to both Billy and Tommie for making me feel so much a part of the Memphis family, and conservation owes Billy Dunavant its undying gratitude for his role as citizen conservationist.

...

The presidents of Ducks Unlimited are volunteers who receive no compensation or reimbursement. They usually have over twenty-five years of volunteer work and giving under their belts, then commit to a six-year pathway as first vice president for two years, president for two and chairman of the board for two final years. The average out-of-pocket expenses for a president are around $30,000 per year. The president is expected to attend as many state conventions as possible, at least a few local events, and the normal Ducks Unlimited Inc., DU de México and DU Canada board meetings.

I came on board at the beginning of John Pope's second year as president and did all I could to have him enjoy the remaining time of his two-year term of office. John is a kind and polite man with a true passion for waterfowl and conservation. Losing and replacing the previous CEO took a lot of the pleasure out of the position he had worked so hard to attain, as it did for Bruce Lewis, who had hoped to have a quiet two years as chairman of the board. The volunteer bench at DU is strong, with over 50,000 workers and state chairs across the country. John is from Florida and came up through the ranks there. The board of directors is large by any comparison, with over sixty members, but I encountered no difficulties because everyone understood her or his role and worked properly through the volunteer chain of command. The CEO is the only board member who receives any type of compensation. The president and the CEO run Ducks Unlimited on a daily basis. I averaged speaking to the president two or three times a week.

The first conservation challenge we faced came about when the new Congress convened in January 2011. The Republicans had won back the House of Representatives, and the first budget bill passed by that chamber proposed to zero out many of the federal conservation programs. We immediately came out strong in opposition to the cuts. I wrote an Op-Ed that was published in the *Atlanta Journal-Constitution* and its affiliates condemning the reductions as being done out of ignorance regarding the return on the conservation dollar, and how much is received by the federal government in income taxes generated through outdoor recreation each year. DU put out a news release stating that

> Ducks Unlimited, along with other conservation organizations, is opposing proposed spending cuts in conservation programs released this week by the U.S. House of Representatives Appropriations Committee. The cuts would affect wetlands conservation to the tune of nearly $2 billion, including the loss of $47 million in funding for North American Wetlands Conservation Act grants. The proposed cuts would eliminate all NAWCA funding and also eliminate the match for a total loss of $200 million in habitat work. 'The cuts being proposed could imperil waterfowl populations and the future of the waterfowl hunting tradition in America,' said DU CEO Dale Hall. 'What's being proposed by the House Appropriations Committee will cripple conservation efforts as we know them,' Hall said. 'Elimination of NAWCA, and 81% reduction of acquisition for refuges and seriously reducing many other programs so vital to our mission are things DU strongly opposes.' (DU 2011)

The entire conservation community came together to visit Congress and turn this mistake around. It is not surprising that many in Congress don't understand the amount of private monies that are contributed to conservation each year through purchase of licenses; membership and contributions to conservation organizations; investments in habitat development; and improvements on private lands. The North American Model for Wildlife Conservation is the "greatest story never told," and most hunter and angler conservationists are unaware of their own contributions.

The CEOs of the National Wild Turkey Federation, National Wildlife Federation, Pheasants Forever, the Wildlife Management Institute, National Fish and Wildlife Foundation (NFWF), and I went en masse and succeeded in getting a substantial portion of the former funding levels restored. The ordeal highlighted how poorly the hunting and fishing conservation community educates the public on the values it provides. In general, every federal appropriated dollar is matched by at least two non-federal conservation dollars. It is the best deal for the taxpayer in the appropriation process. Further, nearly all fish and wildlife conservation dollars appropriated by Congress are replenished as income tax in the fishing and hunting industry. If extended to include other outdoor recreation, all outdoor recreation accounts for $1.6 trillion of the economy each year in the United States.

・・・

By April 2011, the BP Deepwater Horizon oil spill had been contained, and the federal government was in the process of determining how the billions of dollars of fines would be used. Many of us were concerned that Congress would see this as a slush fund and simply roll the funds into the general treasury. We believed that because the fines were imposed in response to natural resource damages, the natural resources should be the beneficiary. National Wildlife Federation CEO Larry Schweiger and I held a unique town-hall type of meeting by telephone, much like a broadcast, asking the public to support legislation that ensured that penalties paid by BP under the Clean Water Act and Oil Pollution Act be directed to the Gulf Coast region for habitat restoration. Others joined our cause and supported the RESTORE Act (Resources and Ecosystems Sustainability, Tourist Opportunities, and Revived Economies of the Gulf Coast States Act). The RESTORE Act was signed into law in July 2012 and directed that 80 percent of the money collected go to the Gulf Coast Restoration Trust Fund in the Treasury, with 20 percent going to the Oil Spill Liability Trust Fund, managed by the U.S. Coast Guard. The "pots" of money became complicated, but 80 percent of the total available funding was directed back to the Gulf Coast.

We remained concerned that the federal government, especially Congress, would find a way to raid these funds, as they had the Land and Water Conservation Fund for years. A joint effort among the conservation organizations ensued for an independent group, specifically the National Fish and Wildlife Foundation, to oversee all or a significant portion of the monies intended for conservation. We chose NFWF for two reasons: it was created by Congress as a quasi-governmental foundation yet was still a not-for-profit, and we knew that NFWF and its executive director, Jeff Trandahl, would handle the funds properly. The U.S. Department of Justice agreed that NFWF would receive approximately $2.5 billion to be disbursed as grants for conservation activities along the spill-impacted states of the Gulf of Mexico. That could never have happened without the tremendous reputation of both Jeff and NFWF. Thanks to Jeff's uncanny ability to work both sides of the aisle, the respect he carries with Congress is unmatched. NFWF and the natural resources of America are the beneficiaries of that trust.

• • •

John Newman took over as DU president in Quebec City at the 2011 National Convention. John worked as an executive for an oil and gas exploration company and had been the DU treasurer prior to becoming the first vice president. He invited Rebecca Rimel, CEO of the Pew Charitable Trusts, to be the keynote speaker at the convention. Rebecca is warm and genuine. One is immediately impressed by her not just as a leader, but as a person. We went to dinner one evening with our staffs to discuss the strong relationship that exists between Pew and DU in our work to conserve the Boreal Forests. The Boreal Forests are the largest intact forests remaining in the world, with more than 1.5 billion acres of rich, wet habitat. From the eastern part of Alaska to Newfoundland, the forests are home to a plethora of wildlife and birds.

Of particular interest to DU, the forests provide an average of one-third of all waterfowl that migrate south to the United States. Over the decades, an average of one-third are hatched in the Boreal, one-third in the Canadian Prairies and one-third in the U.S. Prairies. Pew is a significant donor to DU in helping secure massive areas of conservation of the forests through policy dedication. The First Nations and Provincial governments of Canada have significant authority to protect or develop these valuable resources. DU and Pew had decided several years before I arrived that they would try to secure protection for one-half of all the Boreal Forests of North America—750 million acres.

At dinner, Rebecca and I seemed to connect very rapidly through our passion for conservation and willingness to "put it on the line" and set bold goals. During the conversation, she said "Let's double down! We'll put in $4 million per year and DU can put in $2 million and we'll get this done twice as quickly." As a CEO with only one year under my belt, I was not afraid of a challenge but also hadn't really learned all I needed to know about our funding sources to be comfortable. But here was an opportunity to secure $4 million per year for conservation work that was clearly in our wheelhouse. I looked at Dr. Fritz Reid, the person who had cultivated this relationship for several years, and he gave me a big grin. I looked at Rebecca and said "The Double Down is on! Let's get it done." Our new goal was to permanently protect 750 million acres *and* have another 250 million under active management or conservation at any given point in time. To my knowledge, it is the largest challenge in the history of conservation.

We knew that the process would only work if we understood that the impoverished First Nations villages and communities needed to be able to create jobs and have a strong economy. The first question that arose was about tar sands mining. This process uses new and modern techniques to harvest petroleum from sands that historically were uneconomical. Our team asked the First Nations and provinces to work with all their potential industries and identify the areas they would like to develop through timber harvest, mineral extraction or other types of activities. Using this approach, we could also identify the remaining areas that would have less resistance for protection. The prime area for tar sands turned out to be a 1-million-acre block of land in the Northwest Territory. Instead of bringing an air of judgment, our team helped negotiate the permanent set-aside of 3 million acres immediately surrounding that area.

Many gasped at our willingness to support tar sands mining that would "destroy" 1 million acres of pristine habitat. My answer: "How well did we do with ours in the United States? Did we save three out of four acres of habitat in the U.S.?" Had we been able to conserve three-quarters of our natural habitat in the United States as settlement occurred, we would not have the issues we face today in natural resource management. Negotiation is about respecting the needs of the other parties and finding long-term solutions to complicated issues. The First Nations villages in the Northwest Territory are isolated, and many are in dire need of basic necessities. It is easy for us to thump our chests and say those people don't deserve what we have. I respectfully disagree. I'll work for reasonable economic development and take a 75 percent win every time!

Rebecca announced her intended retirement and chose a date just a few months following my planned departure in 2019. Rebecca invited me to a meeting of the Pew Charitable Trusts Board shortly before my retirement to thank them for our partnership and congratulate them on a job well done. When I retired on June 30, 2019, the Pew/DU partnership had stewarded the set-aside and conservation of more than *870 million acres* of Boreal Forest. To my knowledge, no other conservation effort on earth has achieved this level of success, and the effort continues. The goal of *one billion acres* is within reach. In addition, those native communities are properly creating a long-term economy.

CHAPTER 23

Wetlands America Trust and Justice Scalia

Wetlands America Trust (WAT) was created by Ducks Unlimited as a separate 501(c)(3) not-for-profit to recruit powerful conservationists in industry who do not have the luxury of giving their time, but can make significant donations and help connect DU with the corporate world. James Cox Kennedy is an owner of Cox Enterprises, and at the time of his involvement as WAT president was CEO and chairman of the board of Cox. But he wasn't always chairman. He grew up in Hawaii and knew he would work for the family business, but was adamant that he understand how the company actually works. He started off in the mail room of the *Atlanta Journal-Constitution* and, while looking over the advertisements one day, saw an announcement for a Ducks Unlimited Committee meeting. He loved to duck hunt and decided he would find out what DU was all about.

Without telling anyone who he was, this young man signed up to be a DU volunteer at the chapter level and helped carry boxes of merchandise and set up displays for the chapter's fundraising events. Through the years, as he worked as hard as he could to help DU succeed, he became chairman of the Atlanta chapter committee, then area chairman, then district chairman, and finally was asked to join the board of directors. When WAT was being reformulated due to previous legal issues, Kennedy agreed to become its next president. Throughout his life, Jim Kennedy has given more to conservation than anyone could possibly ask. He was compelled to make a difference and help restore habitat across the continent. I consider it an honor to call Jim my friend, and know that he will be doing all he can to support DU and wetlands conservation for as long as he lives. In a conversation that occurred while I was writing this book, Jim said "It gives me great joy to be able to help the dedicated professionals do their work." (Kennedy 2020) Jim Kennedy is another great example of the citizen conservationist.

Wetlands America Trust is composed of approximately thirty trustees and supports only one entity: Ducks Unlimited. There is no staff, and therefore no CEO, but the president oversees a contingent of some of the most influential titans of industry in the United States. After Kennedy stepped down from his time as president, and following John Childs's short tenure in that position, Steve Maritz became president. Steve and his vice-president, Doug Oberhelman, run one of the most phenomenal teams of conservationists one could assemble. While having little time to devote to conservation due to their private company obligations, they provide significant business advice and financial support. I was continually amazed at the shedding of egos and titles when they walked into a WAT board meeting.

One might not see Kennedy, Oberhelman, Dave Grohne, John Dale and the entire team at Wetlands America Trust out working on the restoration of wetlands and grasslands, but their names are written in the blades of grass, the crop of invertebrates hatched in the newly created wetland and on the wings of those regal sojourners. DU, and conservation, are truly blessed to have these citizen conservationists among us.

One of those great leaders is a humble friend named John Thompson. In February 2014, Microsoft announced that Satya Nadella would be their next CEO and, more important to DU and me, John Thompson was named as the next chairman of the board of Microsoft to replace Bill Gates. I met John at my first WAT board meeting and was immediately impressed by his easy persona and genuinely friendly ways. John was previously with IBM and then Symantec, and was asked by Gates to lead the search for a new CEO to replace Steve Ballmer. Gates then asked John to take his place as chairman. John *loves* to hunt birds and often shot mine when we were in the blind together! We joked that I would do the calling for him because he couldn't call, and he would do the shooting for me for an equally accurate reason. For the record, neither of us ever shot over our limits, even in the process of ribbing over my missed attempts.

We became close friends, and I knew throughout my time with DU that John would be there for me. It's just the way he is. His beautiful wife, Sandi, is an attorney who also is dedicated to natural resource conservation. While not a hunter, she is just as compelled as John to make a difference for our natural treasures. My final retirement celebration was graciously hosted by John and Sandi at their beautiful home in Hawaii following the DU National Convention in 2019. John is the epitome of the driven conservationist who cannot stand by and do nothing as valuable wetlands are being lost.

Jim Kennedy, John Thompson, Steve Maritz, Doug Oberhelman, Dave Grohne, Bill D'Alonzo, Dan Ray, Johnny Morris and all the other members of the WAT board deserve tremendous credit for their commitment to Ducks Unlimited, Wetlands America Trust and conservation. These are the equivalent of the air cover in the structure of DU, providing support for the troops on the ground in every aspect of conserving wetlands and waterfowl habitat. All success stories are about the team, and WAT is a critical member of the DU conservation team.

However, nothing actually gets done unless it's on the ground. As I traveled around the country over my nine years with DU, I met hundreds of enthusiastic volunteers and dedicated citizen conservationists. The beauty of conservation is that it is not an activity; it is an American value. It is woven into the fabric of our everyday lives, whether we watch the sun rise while calling ducks or have a cup of coffee watching the beautiful birds at our backyard feeders. In towns across America, mechanics and truck drivers know they are part of something much larger when they belong to Ducks Unlimited, the National Wild Turkey Federation, The Peregrine Fund, Pheasants Forever or any of the other dedicated conservation organizations. This is the citizen conservation army that is

John Thompson (left) and author (Provided by author)

ready to do whatever they can to make the gifts from the Creator better than we found them.

Equally important are the teams composed of people from all walks of life. In Louisiana, I was immediately greeted by Mike Benge, Jay Owen, Matt and Matthew Stuller, Gary Salmon, Luke Laborde, Richard Zuschlag, Paul and Skipper Dickson, Ron and Jackie Bartels, Mike Hruby and a host of volunteers who know how to have fun and make a difference. The "Cajun Navy" is first to respond during a hurricane, and many of those are DU volunteers. Dr. Brian Priddle, a retired OB/gyn who possibly delivered half of Somerset, Kentucky, is an ardent DU leader along with Bruce Jasper, Jeff Adams and my Kentucky DU family. John Bergstrom and his sons Chris and Tim lead the effort with Bruce Deadman and others in Wisconsin. My good friends Pete MacGaffin and Bill D'Alonzo work with Chip Heaps and Charles and Patty Jobes to lead the Chesapeake efforts. Paul Bonderson, Jan Young and Al Montna are front and center in California and the significant issues in the Central Valley. These, and many, many others in between, are the leaders who inspire and recruit the volunteers who make DU possible. From the mechanic to the lawyer, the store clerk to the physician, there is no separation of status when it comes to importance or passion.

I believe that people are compelled to make a difference in any way they can, and the 50,000 volunteers working with the 500 dedicated employees of Ducks Unlimited work as a *team* to hold over 4,000 events every year and raise over $235 million (FY 2019) for conservation, with around 84 percent going directly to the conservation mission every year. People like Bob and Kitty Wilson in Colorado; Mike and Kay Ptachinski, Nels Swensen and Christine Thomas in Wisconsin; Tammi and Ed Kircher and John Kruse in Iowa; Dennis Wooten, along with Dave and Denise Bunning, in Illinois; and Cathy and Steve Christian in Montana. It would be impossible to name all those who deserve historical recognition, but the beauty is that they *don't do it for recognition*. A dedicated staff of people like Amy Batson, Margaret Everson, Tom Fulgham, Wayne Dierks, Earl Grochau, Govan Hornor, Dan Thiel, Torey King, Greg Taras, Kevin Gaschler and all the others bring a dedication to conservation that defines commitment.

In my last seven years at DU, we launched and completed the largest conservation campaign in U.S. history to raise $2 billion and conserve 2 million acres of wetlands and waterfowl habitat. When the final numbers were announced at the 2019 convention in Hawaii, they revealed that $2.3 billion had been raised, and *more than 2 million acres* had been conserved. There was a great celebration, and then it was back to work. The job isn't finished! These traits and dedication to mission are found not only in Ducks Unlimited supporters, but in conservationists across the country who work for and support the National Wild Turkey Federation, Boone and Crockett, Pheasants Forever, Wildlife Management Institute, Rocky Mountain Elk Foundation, The Peregrine Fund, Delta Waterfowl, National Wildlife Federation, National Fish and Wildlife Foundation, Association of Fish and Wildlife Agencies and the dozens of other groups working hard for conservation day in and day out. The North American Model of Wildlife Conservation is alive and well because of the commitment to work together, not as competitors but as partners, for the good of America's natural treasures. I am humbled to have been just a small part of this phenomenal effort.

• • •

Associate Justice of the Supreme Court Antonin Scalia was nominated by President Ronald Reagan on June 24, 1986, and took his seat on the court on September 26, 1986. He replaced Justice William Rehnquist, who had been appointed Chief Justice upon Warren Burger's retirement. Scalia was unanimously approved at age fifty, the youngest justice on the court at that time. I was sitting in my office in the early fall of 2013 when Tom Fulgham came in to discuss possible keynote speakers for the 2014 National Convention in St. Louis. His question was one I certainly hadn't expected: "Do you know anyone in D.C. who has a way to reach Justice Scalia?"

"No. Why do you ask?"

"We have been told that one of his favorite publications is *Ducks Unlimited* magazine, and that he loves to hunt," Tom replied. "How would you feel about a cold call to his office asking if he would be interested in being our keynote speaker next year? Our audience is largely his audience and agrees with his stance on the Second Amendment and other issues." I didn't have any connections who could help me reach the justice, but I was certainly willing to try, especially if he liked our magazine! Tom had the public number for his office. I started there.

I made the cold call to Justice Scalia's office and reached his executive assistant, Angela Frank. Angela was very polite and friendly, and said she would be happy to pass the request along to the justice. She knew he liked hunting and conservation and had the DU magazine in his office, and she believed we might have a better chance than I thought of having him agree. I didn't hear anything more until November 18, when I was driving to Richard Zuschlag's hunting camp in Creole, Louisiana. As I stopped at a desolate stop sign and was looking out over the beautiful marsh, my cell phone rang. "Hi Dale, this is Angela in Justice Scalia's office. He would love to speak at your convention!"

I couldn't believe my ears. An associate justice of the U.S. Supreme Court had accepted our invitation! Angela asked me to send an email "describing your event that takes place next May." In less than two hours I had sent her an email with all the pertinent information about Ducks Unlimited, our conservation mission and the topic I thought he might want to address.

> I understand the justice is an ardent hunter and supporter of the Second Amendment, and I know our more than one thousand attendees would love to hear his views on the current challenges being attempted by the gun control advocates and how that could impact hunting and conservation in the future.
> If he would be willing, our attendees would also be very interested in his personal story of how he became involved in hunting. While DU is a not-for-profit conservation organization, more than 85 percent of our 644,000 members consider themselves hunters and private citizen gun ownership advocates.

We talked back and forth over the next six months, and I was surprised at the openness and friendliness of his office, which nearly always reflects the personality of the leader. Sarah and I drove to St. Louis from Memphis on May 27, 2014, for the opening festivities of the convention that evening. Justice Scalia was scheduled to speak on Saturday, May 31, and we were filled with excitement to have someone of his caliber as our keynote speaker. The DU convention is an effort that would match any TV production. Cameras are placed at different points in the room to give different views on the big screen behind the speaker, and there

Justice Antonin Scalia (right) and author (Provided by author)

is a "green room" backstage for speakers to relax awaiting their turn. Justice Scalia wasn't scheduled until 11:30 a.m. and would close out the business session. At around 8 o'clock I was in the Green Room having a cup of coffee when my phone rang. It was a 202 area code, indicating Washington, D.C.

> Dale? This is Scalia. I'm having trouble with my flight out of D.C. They're having maintenance issues and it might be delayed for quite a while. But I'm not giving up yet! I'm looking at Baltimore to see what they have for St. Louis this morning and I think it might work. I'll get back to you as soon as I know.

My heart sank and at the same time soared. First of all, how could it be that this country boy from the hills of Kentucky would have a Supreme Court justice call his cell phone? It was surreal. Second, it would have been completely understandable for the justice to simply tell me that his plane was delayed due to maintenance and he would have to cancel. But he didn't. Here was a justice of the United States Supreme Court willing to go to another airport so he could keep his commitment and speak at our convention. The good news was that he was in the Eastern time zone and we were in the Central, which might give us the leeway of an extra hour of possible flights early in his morning. He called back and said "Dale, I was able to get it done. My marshal is driving me to Baltimore and we might break a speed limit or two, but should make it. I will arrive in St. Louis in plenty of time before I'm scheduled to speak."

We had arranged to have someone pick him up, but the U.S. Marshal's Office in St. Louis insisted that they pick him up and bring him to the hotel. He called after he landed, and I was waiting for him in the hotel lobby when he arrived. He wasn't staying overnight, so we reserved a private room in the restaurant to let him relax and get a bite to eat. The volunteers were leaving it to me to decide who got to sit and visit. That way they could blame me when other volunteers asked. He did agree to a small reception after he spoke, which allowed others to visit with him as well. But that, too, was limited. I decided on only the past and current presidents of DU and WAT for the meeting in the restaurant.

Bruce Lewis, John Newman, Paul Bonderson, George Dunklin, Steve Maritz, Justice Scalia and I enjoyed a nice break from the hectic activities of the convention, and Justice Scalia could not have been more down to earth. When we got to the subject of hunting, I asked if he had ever hunted in California. "No, but I'd love to!" he replied. Paul Bonderson immediately said "I can make that happen!" Paul and his wonderful wife, Sandi, own a great lodge and rice farm north of Sacramento near Colusa. Paul was highly successful in Silicon Valley and founded Brocade Communications. Paul Bonderson is yet another example of someone who became wealthy, but is driven to give back to the natural resources he cherishes. A big man at well over six feet tall, when he first shook my hand I felt it had been swallowed. I learned quickly that his heart was even bigger than his hands, and count him among the wonderful friends I cherish.

Justice Scalia immediately said "I'd love to. Let's set it up!" Paul looked at me and said, "I'll turn everything over to you to set up the hunt. I don't want to be the one who has to say no to someone who wants to be there." Justice Scalia agreed and we took a few photos, adjourned to the business session of the convention, and then listened to a man with a passion for hunting and guns give an eloquent speech about rights, responsibilities and growing fears from an urbanizing world. In his speech, he said,

> I got started shooting in New York City. I would ride the subway carrying my .22 rifle to go to a school or Scout meeting where I was on the shooting team. If you can believe it, no one ever once asked me why I had a gun on the subway. Times have certainly changed.

I called Justice Scalia after the convention to begin the search for a time on his schedule when he could go to California to hunt. Paul provided his private jet for DU to use so the justice would not have to worry about commercial challenges, and we also invited former Vice President Dick Cheney, a close friend of Justice Scalia's and also an ardent hunter. While serving as director of the U.S. Fish and Wildlife Service with the George W. Bush administration I had been in a meeting with VP Cheney, but had not really met him at that time. It was through Richard Zuschlag that I actually met the vice president. When Cheney was VP, Richard invited him to come hunting at the Creole lodge. They became friends, and Cheney has returned every year since to hunt with Richard.

The vice president and I got to know each other at Richard's lodge right after my phone call with Angela the previous November. I believed it would bring a bit more comfort to the justice if a close friend were along for the California trip, and was doubly honored when VP Cheney accepted the invitation. When I got the justice on the phone, he said "I can make it the last weekend in January 2015." "I'm sorry, Sir, but the hunting season will be closed then," I replied. "Can you do it earlier?"

He laughed and said "I guess you're not in a position to change that anymore," referring to my past role as director, "so we'll have to look at next year [next hunting season]."

We eventually were able to set up the hunt for Friday, October 23, through Tuesday, October 27, 2015. We agreed to pick up Justice Scalia and VP Cheney in Manassas, Virginia, on Friday and fly to Chico, California. Following the hunt on Tuesday, the U.S. marshal would pick up Justice Scalia for a speaking engagement in California and VP Cheney would ride with Jim Kennedy on his plane back to Wyoming. When the day arrived, Paul picked me up in Memphis and we flew on to Manassas to meet our guests. VP Cheney was there when we arrived, and the justice arrived shortly thereafter. They were clearly good friends and happy to see each other. Some ribbing began right away about shooting skills. Cheney is a crack shot and was ribbing the justice that he would help him get his birds!

After everyone was settled in on the plane and we were about halfway across the country, I went up to where the two of them were sitting across from each other and knelt down so we were at eye level. Justice Scalia had headphones on listening to opera while he was reading legal briefs about cases before the court.

"OK, gentlemen," I began. "When we get to the hunting lodge, everyone is going to ask me how they should address you. Should it be Justice and Vice President? What would make you comfortable?"

Justice Scalia took his headphones off and very forcefully said "Nino! Nino! That's my name! Nino!" which brought laughter from everyone in earshot. We assumed he went by Tony or some other shortening of Antonin, but obviously it was Nino. I looked at Cheney, who held up both hands in surrender, smiled broadly, and said "Dick. Just have everyone call me Dick!" Everyone, including Nino, erupted with laughter.

Whatever tenseness there might have been with two such distinguished guests, they wanted no part of it. We landed in Chico, where Paul had several Suburbans there to transport us to Bird Haven Ranch.

We honored their requests for how they wanted to be addressed, so the hunting party consisted of Nino, Dick, Richard Zuschlag, Paul Bonderson, Dave Grohne, Jim Kennedy, John Tomke, Rogers Hoyt, Andrew Lundquist, Dave Hinman (DU supporter and guide), Fritz Reid (DU biologist and guide), Doug Federighi (DU board member and guide) and me. It was an arduous task to herd the cats and get everyone there, but it was a wonderful hunt with tremendous fellowship and fun.

Paul had me make my duck gumbo with andouille and his goose sausage for one of the afternoon meals. I knew Nino was truly comfortable when he acted like he was at home and got up and went back for seconds of my gumbo. Justice Scalia was an ardent Catholic and wanted to attend Mass on Sunday, following the hunt. A woman named Sophia works for Paul and takes care of the lodge and cooking. When Nino asked where he could go to Mass, Sophia told him there weren't any English-speaking Masses at that time of day, but there was a Spanish one she often attended. He quickly agreed, and they went to the Spanish Mass that Sunday. The Creator understands all languages.

On November 24 I got a note from Justice Scalia about the hunt.

> A belated thank-you for the invitation to Bird Haven Ranch. What a wonderful few days—good hunting, good company, and good food. I have expressed my gratitude to Paul, but I am also grateful to you and your fellow members of the board.
>
> Speaking of which, I look forward to seeing all of you in April. We have arranged for a reception at the Court on the 18th, and a board meeting in one of our conference rooms on the 19th.
>
> Best regards, Nino

During the hunt, we had invited Nino and Dick to DU's Washington, D.C., event and the accompanying WAT board meeting, which is held each year in April. The focus is for members of Congress, their staffs and our partners in conservation to simply have a good evening of fun.

Back Row (l–r): Richard Zuschlag, Fritz Reid, Dave Hinman, Paul Bonderson
Middle Row (l–r): Rogers Hoyt, Jim Kennedy, John Tomke, Dave Grohne
Front Row (l–r): VP Dick Cheney, Justice Antonin Scalia, author, Doug Federighi
(Courtesy of Paul Bonderson)

Justice Scalia said he likely couldn't attend, but had invited us to hold a small reception at the Supreme Court Offices, and the WAT meeting the next day in one of their conference rooms. What an opportunity! Once again, I was the heavy on deciding who got to come. I worked with the WAT president and chairman of the DU board on particular invitees they wanted to attend the reception, but most of the remainder were for me to decide, to make someone happy or disappointed. Everything was scheduled for April 18 and 19, and all invitations were proffered. Then tragedy struck.

On Friday, February 13, 2016, one day before the anniversary of my mother's death, the Honorable Justice Antonin Scalia died in his sleep while on a hunting trip in Texas near Marfa. The father of five boys and four girls did not answer his door when his host checked on him. There was no evidence of foul play, and he had a medical history of coronary artery disease, diabetes and other ailments. We were devastated. One reads about high-profile public figures, but seldom do we get to actually know them on a personal level. Nino charmed everyone at our hunt with his candor, kindness and willingness to hear other points of view. Over dinner at Bird Haven, he told us that when President Obama was looking for a replacement for Justice John Paul Stevens, Nino wrote the president a note and asked him to "Send someone over with whom we can have lively debates about the Constitution!" He loved Ruth Bader Ginsburg and even convinced her to go hunting with him. They often went to the opera together. Duck hunters will tell you that sharing a duck blind with someone will result in learning what kind of person they are. We learned that Nino was a wonderful person. With his death, WAT also lost the opportunity to have the reception and meeting at the Supreme Court Building. That was trivial, however, compared to America's loss.

The Supreme Court of the United States is an elite family of intellectual law experts who pride themselves on discovering new understanding with each case before them. When I asked Justice Scalia about the control of video games that teach children guns are to be used to kill people, and the more people that are killed the higher the score, he simply responded "Free speech is sacrosanct and it's a slippery slope I don't see the Supreme Court anxious to pursue." Regardless of their intellectual views, those who believe that any member of the United States Supreme Court hasn't fully earned her or his seat is simply intoxicated with their own ego. By design, the justices were to be isolated from political or public influence. Antonin Scalia was an accomplished jurist, but also a citizen conservationist. I saw his love of natural resources as he, Jim Kennedy and I sat in the duck blind and talked about our surroundings. He loved all of God's creations. I was honored to know him.

CHAPTER 24

California Floodplains and Finishing Up

In 2017, things were heating up again in the Central Valley of California, particularly in the Sacramento–San Joaquin Delta. Concerns about two Endangered Species Act (ESA) listed fish, the delta smelt and the winter run chinook salmon, were driving water decisions that seemed to be without scientific basis. The unsubstantiated belief that salmon and smelt needed more water in the river to survive completely ignored the historical floodplain and how those very species evolved. Most of the natural floodplain has been leveed, and the river is kept from flooding rich farmland that has replaced the native bottomland hardwood wetlands. A lack of scientific evidence that the fish would be harmed by the "warm" water in the rice fields if they were allowed access has resulted in literally starving the fish in the river. The demands to "Take water from the agricultural community" had returned. Our efforts in the Bay-Delta Accord had lasted for nearly two decades, but old agreements fade from memory when water is scarce.

The Sacramento River evolved in much the same manner as the lower Mississippi River. Once the water reached lower elevations it spread out to create a massive floodplain with low topographic relief. Court battles over the years had left the fallback position of the state and federal agencies to send more water down the river rather than have it mimic the historical flooding of adjacent lands, in much the same manner that the lower Mississippi River floodplain worked. Since no one seemed to know what the delta smelt and winter run chinook salmon needed, the answer became "Let's just send more water downstream." In an ironic twist, this could very well be the reason for the increased decline in numbers of both species. These fish evolved in much the same way as those in the lower Mississippi had, and needed the floodplain in which to spawn (in the case of the smelt) or as a nursery for salmon smolt development. My old friends Roger Patterson and Felicia Marcus were both actively engaged in the debate, both with new positions outside the federal government. Roger was working with the Metropolitan Water District, and Felicia was the chair of the California Water Control Board, which establishes flow regimes for the river.

I became involved at the request of Al Montna, Paul Bonderson and several of our volunteers and staff in California. I put a short Power Point presentation together that compared the evolution of the lower Mississippi and lower Sacramento Rivers. The comparison was stark. Both had evolved through active floodplains to provide spawning and rearing habitat as well as a massive amount of invertebrate production to feed the river as the water receded. I gave the presentation to Felicia and her staff in Sacramento, then to other landowners along the river, including rice farmers. Former Secretary of the Interior Bruce Babbitt had become an advisor to Governor Jerry Brown and was also in attendance at the landowner briefing.

I believe there is a clear solution to help care for the fish, and flushing them down the system with more water is not part of the recipe. Prior to construction of the Sacramento River project in the 1940s, unregulated flows down the river varied from a high of around 650,000 cubic feet per second (cfs) during floods to a low of less than 1,000 cfs in late summer during a drought. During the six decades that followed project construction, including the levees, flows varied from a high of 115,000 cfs to a low of 3,970 cfs. Not once since construction of the project have flows been lower than approximately 4,000 cfs, while historically the river saw low flows of below 1,000 cfs. Both species did well throughout the floods and droughts before construction and, if given the opportunity to use the floodplain, stand a high chance of doing well now. But the fight over

"Who has the water?" seems to trump the question of "What do the fish need?"

In order to get our naturalist views of how to solve the problem into the record, I wrote the comments that DU submitted to the California Water Resources Control Board during the open comment period. I titled it *Floodplains: The River's Pantry*. In part, it read:

> Throughout the world, man has settled next to rivers for their water traffic, fish and wildlife productivity and the fertile grounds of the floodplains. Floodplains are among the most productive areas in nature and provide the supply of nutrients and food necessary to keep the river healthy.
>
> In an unmodified floodplain, the ecosystem processes begin with the dropping of leaves in the fall by deciduous trees and shrubs that have evolved to have competitive adaptations that allow them to survive extended periods of saturated soils (anoxic conditions) in their root zones. These adaptations are commonly manifested as aerial or adventitious roots, buttressing with pores in the trunk that allow oxygen uptake in harsh conditions, and the ability to regulate chemical processes to convert harmful byproducts to non-harmful, organic compounds when the root zones are deprived of oxygen. These dominant factors of saturated (hydric) soils, adapted vegetation and hydrology are not only the biological factors that define highly productive wetland habitats; they are also the legal criteria in Clean Water Act Section 404 regulations to determine federal jurisdiction in unmodified habitats due to their importance to society.
>
> The significance of the floodplain adaptations is in the ability to provide the foundation and 'cooking pot' for the food chain necessary to keep adjacent rivers alive and healthy. When the leaves fall to the ground and subsequently become inundated with rising spring flows from spring melts and rainfall, the

soaking action allows the onset of 'leaching' of some of the nutrients, which helps to provide necessary food for phytoplankton that is beginning to emerge due to the warming of the water in the floodplain. The leaves are first colonized by bacteria and fungi. The decomposing detritus is ingested by micro and macro invertebrates, which make use of the bacteria and fungi as food and then discharge the remaining detritus to be re-colonized for further decomposition . . .

As the floodplain vegetation slows the water flow, the first sediments that drop out of the water are the heavier sands, which help to build the natural berms of the river and also delay the outflows as water recedes and slowly re-enters the river. The next sediments to drop out are the silts and clays that are heavy with soil nutrients and recharge the floodplain. The decomposition of the detritus, and the ensuing phytoplankton and zooplankton, creates an explosion of life that includes macro invertebrates so essential to the survival of fish, waterfowl and the entire ecosystem. This overabundance of aquatic food sources serves to feed larval fishes that have emerged from their eggs and developed past the proto, meso and meta larval stages of post-hatching embryonic development. Nature has provided this high concentration of food in order to accommodate the development of mouthparts for larval fishes, which must encounter food or die once the yolk material is completely absorbed. This is known as the 'critical period' in the life of a fish, resulting in life or death depending on the young fish's ability to encounter food.

As the water is held in the floodplain, accompanied by warming of spring, the floodplain holds concentrations of life that are found at no other time in the hydrologic cycle. Young fishes remain in the floodplain as long as possible and either drift or swim into the main river as the floodwaters recede. This huge influx of life is the literal food supply for the river and must sustain the fish and wildlife populations until the cycle can be repeated the following year, or years. However, in order for the river to receive this annual biological injection, the river must have access to the floodplain.

The Sacramento River evolved in the manner described above and benefited from the annual flooding, nutrient (phytoplankton), invertebrate production and ultimate nursery for the fishes that survived in the river. But that cycle does not presently work for the Sacramento River because of the levee and water control structures that keep the rising water from entering the floodplain unaided by man. Instead, the floodplain forests have been cleared and the land planted with rice and other crops capable of withstanding saturated soil conditions.

However, this does not mean that the floodplain can no longer function. Instead, we look to the rice-field stubble to provide the basis for nutrients, fungi and bacteria, micro and macro invertebrates and the ensuing explosion of life that still occurs. It is just not currently allowed to provide nursery habitat for salmon and smelt, nor is it encouraged to feed the river. Instead, we are faced with minimal introduction of food resources so necessary to sustain riverine species during the low water periods of the year. The lack of food creates numerous problems with the health and survival of both the salmon and smelt, with the most prominent one being possible starvation.

We believe this CAN be reversed and, if we desire to have healthy populations of salmon, smelt, and the remainder of Sacramento River ecosystem constituents, MUST be reversed. The fisheries research conducted by California Trout and others at the Knaggs Ranch and Conaway Ranch, as part of the Nigiri Project, has provided the best available science that proves the Sacramento River system evolved to function in this manner. It is imperative that we allow the food produced in the floodplain,

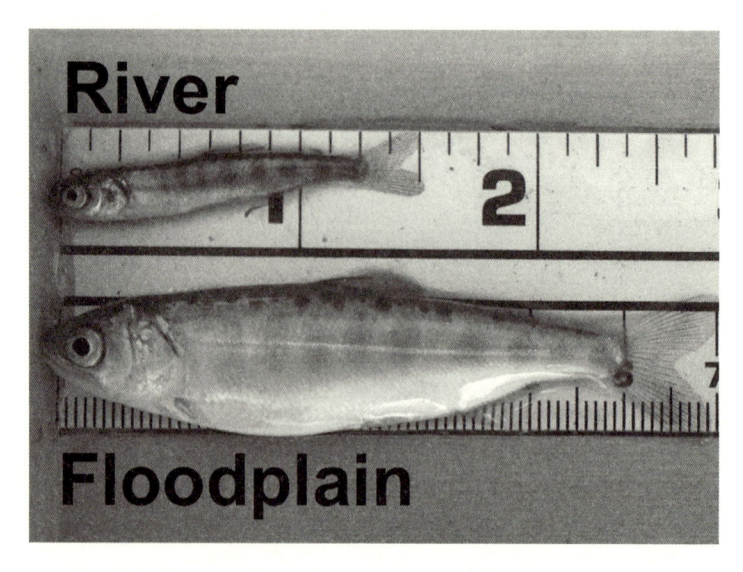

River vs. Floodplain Salmon (Courtesy of Jacob Katz)

along with the healthy growth of fish, to provide much needed biological relief to the sustainability of the River. This can only occur by having water available for the floodplain and encouraged to be used for that purpose.

WATER IS NOT HABITAT

One fact that is abundantly clear is that water alone is not habitat. Water is the catalyst and medium in which aquatic habitat can develop but, without nutrients and the food chain constituents, it can actually be detrimental to the very species it is intended to help. The premise that sending higher flows of water downstream and into the Bay has not yielded positive results over the past decade. [The assumption was that increased instream flows were the key to a healthy river and San Francisco Bay. This comment was meant to reiterate that the increased flows have likely exacerbated the problem rather than mitigating.] Additional flows at the wrong time can actually serve to flush out what minimal food supplies there might be in the river, including larval smelt that likely depend on slow flows and shallow depths in order to encounter food at the critical period. While well-intended, the scientific results of past efforts do not endorse this approach.

The best available science (CalTrout Nigiri Project) dealing with the diminishing populations of both salmon and smelt instead argues to allow the fish to use the floodplain for the nursery nature intended. The demonstrated increase in growth and health of salmon inside the flooded rice fields is clear evidence for more open connections to the river and, conversely, the inability to locate spawning and nursery areas for smelt should well inform that their needs are also in the river's pantry. Before more possibly destructive high flows are sent down the river with the intended purpose of assisting salmon and smelt, applied science dictates that the floodplain be given a chance to work the way it evolved. (Ducks Unlimited 2017)

The research identified is headed by Dr. Jacob Katz of CalTrout and is a cooperative effort by California Trout, UC Davis Center for Watershed Sciences, Cal Marsh and Farm, California Department of Water Resources, California Department of Fish and Wildlife, NOAA SW Fisheries Science Center, Bureau of Reclamation (BOR), state and federal water contractors, and California Water Foundation. (Katz et al. 2017) The name Nigiri is a play on the sushi dish in which salmon is served on rice. In their study, they put smolt chinook salmon in cages in the river and canal adjacent to the levee, and also in the rice fields on the protected side of the levee. After three weeks, invertebrate production in the rice fields surpassed the river by a quantity of *149 times*, the canal by nearly *25 times*, and salmon demonstrated *twice the growth* in rice fields as in the river or canal. These excellent scientists have quantified what we had to discuss in qualitative fashion in the Lake Ophelia case and other

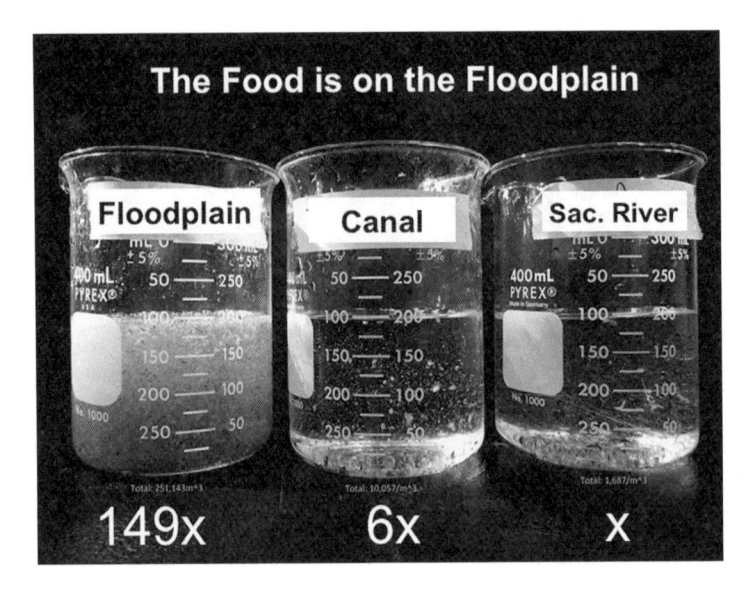

Floodplain Food (Courtesy of Jacob Katz)

floodplain habitat issues across the country. It is ironic that the science I learned in my first significant challenge as a professional helped guide our involvement in one of my last challenges. Science lives on and simply grows with the addition of new data and information.

I have high expectations of my young friend Jacob and his cohorts on the Sacramento River. Their journey is uphill and the obstacles fraught with emotion, but the answer lies with the coalition, the team that has come together seeking the truth. I implore the California environmental community to join this effort and find reasonable ways to manage the river for everyone. Water and global warming will continue to be the most pressing issues of this century. It is time to leave the arguments of the last century behind and look to the future. Only a *team* of all interests can bring a long-term solution to this challenge, and that can only happen when the people who share life in the community come together with a willingness to listen and respect differing views. When asked how much water is needed for a particular use, "More" is an unacceptable answer.

• • •

In 2018, I sat down with Ducks Unlimited President Rogers Hoyt and past president George Dunklin to let them know my plans for retirement. Every year following my arrival, DU met or exceeded the ever-increasing goals we set for ourselves in fundraising and conservation. We had gone from just over $150 million in revenues to over $235 million. In 2010, DU had conserved just over 12 million acres of habitat in North America, and we were on track to surpass 15 million acres by the end of 2019. I decided that nine years was enough for a guy who said he didn't want to work full-time anymore, so Rogers, George and I discussed how we would transition my retirement and finding a new CEO. Rog proved to be as strong of a president as George Dunklin because of his close ties to the earth. Both were rice farmers and both knew how to have dirt under the fingernails. At the same time, both had hearts as big as the Grand Canyon, and their love of conservation was unsurpassed. We met privately so things could be discussed openly and in a relaxed manner. Rog started the conversation.

George Dunklin (right) and author (Courtesy of George Dunklin Jr.)

"First, let's be clear. No one is asking you to leave. We love what DU has been able to accomplish under your leadership, but you have indicated that retirement is getting close. How would you like the retirement and transition to occur?" I thanked them both and said, "I appreciate the professional as well as personal relationship I have with both of you and couldn't be more pleased that you are the ones to have this discussion. I plan to announce my retirement at the 2018 Indianapolis National Convention in about a month. I want to give you and the board plenty of time to have a deliberate search for a new CEO. I will announce there that I will step down at the end of June 2019, following the National Convention in Hawaii. I encourage you to plan how you will conduct the search over the summer and early fall, then begin the process in late fall. If you will allow it, while I do not think it prudent that I be involved in the search and selection, I would like to have at least one month overlap with the new CEO to help in any way I can to prepare her or him to take over."

In Indianapolis, everything went well. I relayed my plans to the board in executive session the day before the business session for the convention. The last part of the convention was devoted to the keynote speaker, and we had secured Fred Smith, founder and CEO of FedEx. However, he didn't want to give a speech. He preferred that I interview him on stage and let him just relax and talk to our volunteers and staff. We loved it. After the interview, we presented Fred with a signed, hand-carved Charles Jobes decoy and he left the stage.

I walked to the center of the stage and let them know that, following the convention in Hawaii the next year, I would be stepping down as CEO. I could hear gasps, which didn't make it any easier. Sarah and I had connected with these people as our conservation family hook, line and sinker. I loved them dearly.

After a pause, I said "However, we still have one year left of the campaign and I make you this promise. I will be at as many of your events and fundraisers as I can for the entire year if you will keep the pedal to the metal and blow our seven-year $2 billion campaign target off the charts! Will you do that?"

The standing ovation answered my question. Rog then walked out on stage and said "I will!" then Paul Bonderson, then George. We wanted to end the convention on a high note, not a sad one, and we did. Sarah and I were asked and agreed to have DU establish the Dale and Sarah Hall Legacy Fund as an extra way people could make donations over our last year. Before we left Indianapolis, $1.1 million had been pledged to that fund.

My final year was everything I hoped it would be. I attended over fifty events, many with Sarah at my side, and saw the energy that an army of citizen conservationists can generate. I refused to allow folks to refer to it as my Victory Tour, but there were still a lot of jokes and ribbing about being a quitter.

In March 2019, Rog and First Vice President Doug Schoenrock walked into my office. I had intentionally asked to be left out of all discussions regarding my replacement. Whoever they selected needed to know it was because s/he connected with the board, not something I did to influence the decision. Rog began the conversation.

"We've made a decision on the new CEO and it's time to involve you. You will be critical in having the DU family welcome him. We selected Adam Putnam, former congressman and former agriculture commissioner of Florida."

I agreed to do whatever I could to help, and believe that I did. Adam arrived in April, and we had the three months to overlap and get him settled in.

• • •

When we finally got to Hawaii, my heart was in my throat. I knew well it was time to retire, and I was ready. But it is never easy to say good-bye to people who have been at your side for nine years while giving their hearts and souls to conservation. When I arrived at DU, I asked Doug Barnes to design a belt buckle with the DU logo that was different from any that could be purchased. I wanted it to be from me to the volunteer who doesn't think anyone is watching, or the employee who works hard every day and thinks no one notices. On the back of the buckle I had engraved "A SPECIAL THANKS FROM DALE HALL, CEO." I had DU order them, then paid back the debt in $500 increments. It was important that the buckles be from me, out of my own pocket. The volunteers expect to receive nothing for their work but the satisfaction of conserving the wonderful gifts of the Creator. It would have meant less if the buckles had been paid for out of DU coffers.

• • •

By the time I reached the stage in Hilo for my final address, I had given 206 Dale Hall belt buckles to very deserving people. I had a rule, which lasted until my farewell, that sitting board members and chief officers were not eligible. This was for the rank-and-file people who seldom got recognition. I wanted them to know the CEO of DU was grateful for their hard work. I broke that at the end, but nearly all went to people you don't read about in *Ducks Unlimited* magazine. One of my deep satisfactions was watching my buckles start to show up on new board members.

The recipients, however, had the last laugh. Jay Owen and several others talked my executive assistant into giving him a list of the recipients I kept on my computer, but nowhere else. He contacted them and they chipped in to have a silver buckle made for me with my tenure of 2010–2019 above the DU duck head. In addition, I had gone alligator hunting with the Louisiana crew during the summer of 2018, and they had boots and a belt made from a gator I helped harvest. Finally, my good friends Charles and Patty Jobes gave Sarah and me a life-size, hand-carved swan decoy. My heart was overflowing with love and gratitude.

Our business session was split between Friday and Saturday mornings to allow people to enjoy Hawaii. I asked that I speak on Friday as the last presenter of the morning so I could say thank you, good-bye and extend my full support for Adam, who for the first time would speak in the normal CEO slot of the business session on Saturday. I struggled with what I would say. At the final board meeting, I had choked up at least twice and had tears flowing as I walked around and hugged the more than sixty members of the board of friends and colleagues. I knew I had to keep it together at the business session, so I decided to give a speech I had been asked to give many times in my career, which answered an important, often-asked question: What is leadership? The more I thought about it, the more sense it made. DU is 50,000 strong in leadership, and 50,000 strong in workers. Everyone is willing to do whatever it takes to have DU succeed. Over the years, I had been interviewed by employees as well as the press regarding my views of leadership. I began to think about it and developed a list of traits I believed I saw in great leaders I respected.

When I got on stage for my last speech as DU CEO, I congratulated them on *their team accomplishment* of nine years in a row of meeting or exceeding every expanding goal, adding "There is a reason for that. Each of you is a leader. There are certain traits that are common among great leaders. Here is my view of those traits, and I believe you have them all:

"**VISION:** Every great leader is driven to accomplish the vision they have, and knows it is real. Theodore Roosevelt spoke of this leadership in the drive to never quit. Failing again and again, but never surrendering. In order to be a leader, one must have followers. People will follow a leader only if it is clear where the leader is taking them. Each follower must know their role and how they fit in the team. I once heard the saying 'If you don't know where you are going, any road will get you there.' People will not follow 'any road.' They want a clear vision of where they are being taken, and why.

"**FAMILY:** We often spend more time with our family at work than we do with our family at home. The great leaders I have witnessed let the people around them know they truly care. The individual is just as important as the mission because, when team members are made to feel unimportant, the team suffers. I saw at DU the immediate response of fellow workers or volunteers when one of our own was suffering. No one ever had to ask. Help was freely given. These relationships come from respect and grow into trust. Trust is the key to team success. The leader sets the tone of family. If it is fake, the followers are quick to recognize it.

"Conversely, the great leaders I have seen give no quarter to anyone on the team who is self-serving and only interested in their personal gains. When a team member undermines the team effort, puts themselves above their peers and believes they should have more power, the cancer must be removed. The remainder of the team is looking to the leader to carry out that responsibility and remove this threat to success. When this happens, the guilty party is wholly responsible for being removed from the family and no longer is worthy of their respect. When the leader removes a team member, it is not to punish. It is to protect the remainder of the team.

"**TEACHER:** A true leader is *always* ready to share information and knowledge. When leaders hold back certain information in order to 'know more than the rest,' the team will surely see it. Meting out information to subordinates is the manifestation of insecurity. The clear role of a leader is to develop subordinates who can take over as leaders and do a *better* job. When the leader is secure in her/himself, they are always open to help instruct or share experience with the team. They *want* subordinates to become better leaders than they. It is a mark of pride.

"**LISTENER:** Great leaders are always the most excited students. Being open to challenges and questions is the hallmark of science, and of leadership. It has been said that 'We have two ears and only one mouth for a reason.' I have learned more from subordinates and employees than I have ever imparted because I have never lost the love of learning. We are all students our entire lives. We become even greater leaders when we understand that we must also be open to new ideas. Great leaders love change because they orchestrate how it will occur. If it is true that the only thing that is constant is change, then listening allows pathways of control rather than reaction.

"**HONESTY:** Great leaders *always* tell the truth. Sharing bad news with the team may well be the highest form of compliment the leader can pay. By telling the truth, leaders understand that the best answer may rest with the lowest-level employee. Churchill's famous 'We will fight' speech may be the clearest form of honest leadership ever given. He told the British people the truth. He gave them his confidence and inspired them to 'Never surrender!' When the team knows they can count on honesty from the leader, the team will be ready for all challenges. Followers are constantly looking for the leader to say one thing today, and another tomorrow. Through honesty is power, and the only power any of us has is that which we share.

"**INTEGRITY:** All great leaders have a moral compass that stays true, no matter what the repercussion. Followers look to their leader in times of stress and challenge to see how they respond to inappropriate requests or orders. Great leaders stand their ground and lead by example, even when the heat gets high. One should never take a leadership position unless he or she is willing to vacate it rather than accept unprofessional behavior or directives. The two worst forms of leaders are those who will tell you whatever you want to hear in order to placate, and those who believe they are the most important part of the team. All teams will eventually migrate in personality to that of the leader. Great leaders have great teams.

"**TRUST:** Accomplished leaders I have witnessed were not afraid to let their employees make mistakes. As long as knowledge or wisdom is gained by the mistake, there is no true failure. That does not mean that the same mistake is expected to be seen repeated. In that case, nothing was learned. Followers need to know that the leader trusts them enough to let them be innovative and take on a task however they see fit. The worst form of supervisor is one who gives the assignment and then stands over the shoulder of the worker telling them how to do it. The leader might as well hand the employee a card that says 'I DON'T TRUST YOU.' Great leaders will either do a task themselves or allow someone else the freedom to accomplish it. Further, great leaders understand, unequivocally, that their success is intricately bound with the success of the team.

"**HUMILITY:** Leadership is an honor that can only be earned. Anyone can be given authority or rank by those above them. Recognition as a leader can only be given by those who would follow. There is a significant difference. Just as my friend Harold Scarlett eventually came to understand, it wasn't about me, but rather the position I was privileged to hold. Supervision is a humble honor that must be earned each day by showing respect to the team. One should never get wrapped around the axle about one's own importance. Leadership is a gift from the followers and is not permanent. ALL great leaders are 'Servant Leaders.'

"**PASSION:** The final, and most important of all traits, is the passion that drives great leaders to never surrender. No matter how many times they are knocked down or criticized, they 'dare greatly.' They are uninterested in the critic, the person who could have, should have, would have. Each and every one had a drive that *compelled* them to reach their goal. For them, there is no option except to continue. Time and again they were told they wouldn't make it, but time and time again they labored on. Followers see the passion for the mission in every great leader, and there is something about that passion that makes one want to follow. They *believe* they will be successful, and surrender is simply not contemplatable."

People in conservation all across this great nation *are leaders*! The drive to make a difference is not negotiable. The citizen conservationist comes in many forms and from many backgrounds. Is it Johnny Morris, who started in the liquor store with a few racks of lures but was compelled to expand his bond with nature? Is it Jim Kennedy, who didn't have to exert extra effort but knew he had to give back to the magnificent resources he was blessed to see? Or John Thompson, an African American child growing up in a white world, whose passion for success removed all color from the conversation? Perhaps Brian Priddle, Jay Owen, Mike Benge, Dennis Wooten, Mike Ptachinski or John Bergstrom because they realize what they have been given and are determined to pass it along to future generations? The answer is yes to all of them and the thousands of other representatives of different jobs and skills. They are all *compelled* to leave a mark that is greater than any individual. They are all citizen conservationists!

Throughout my career, I was able to watch the evolution of conservation move from a position of open trust for our government, to suspicion, and finally to open distrust. Some loss of trust was earned. But I also witnessed issue after issue find resolution when, and only when, people came together with respect and openness to each other's views. Success *always* resulted when teams worked together, not caring who got the credit. Few people I worked alongside during my career were aware of the various issues in which I had been engaged. That is as it should be. None of us will be remembered for the challenges we faced, but rather how we faced them.

As director of the Fish and Wildlife Service, I was once asked by a group of our employees what I thought would be my legacy. "You," I answered. "The only real legacy any of us has is the people we supported, mentored and helped along the way. We won't be remembered for specific issues. We will be remembered by how we performed as a teammate." As I watch the next generation of conservationists assuming their role, with over half of the college DU committees chaired by young ladies, I realize how blessed I have been to see the changes over my forty years. It was a journey that at times felt unbearable. But through the team, there was success. When we gave to each other as well as to the mission, attitudes changed and teams were forged.

There are those who believe America is in trouble, that the challenges today are too great. I respectfully disagree. I have not lived my life with hopes. I have lived with beliefs. When we hope something will happen, we want it to get done but expect someone else to do it. When we *believe,* we take responsibility to make it happen, roll up our sleeves, get to work and never surrender. As I look back on my career with phenomenal people in government service and in the private sector, common threads bind all conservationists: a love for the gifts from our Creator and an inability to stand outside the fire. My time as an active participant in fish and wildlife management is nearing an end, but faith in my conservation family is endless. I have seen the next generation and I *believe* they will be better than we were. There is no shortage of passion. There is no shortage of commitment. They understand listening and working together. They, too, are *compelled* and have my full confidence. The future of our natural world is in good hands. I am humbled and blessed.

REFERENCES

American Rivers, Delta Land Trust, Earthjustice, Environment America, Environmental Defense, Friends of the Earth, Friends of the Sunflower River, Gulf Restoration Network, Mississippi Wildlife Federation, National Audubon Society, National Wildlife Federation, Republicans for Environmental Justice and Sierra Club. November 14, 2007. Letter to EPA Administrator Stephen Johnson RE: Opposition to Yazoo Backwater Pumps Project.

ASCEnews. August 1, 2009. Major General Don T. Riley, Deputy Commanding General, Deputy Chief of Engineers, U.S. Army Corps of Engineers. ASCE.org.

Aycock, Ray. April 18, 2008. Email to FWS Director Sam Hamilton RE: Yazoo Pumps Public Hearing, April 17, 2008 in Vicksburg, Mississippi.

Banks, Sedric E. May 26, 1981. Letter to Assistant Secretary of the Interior Ray Arnett.

Baxter, Charles. February 13, 1979. Letter to EPA Regional Administrator Adlene Harrison, with attached FWS Wetland Determination for the Lake Ophelia Tract.

Bureau of Land Management. 2020. National Petroleum Reserve in Alaska. BLM.gov.

California Department of Fish and Wildlife. 2020. Natural Community Conservation Planning (NCCP). Home Page.

CITES.org. 2020. Convention on International Trade in Endangered Species of Wild Fauna and Flora. Home Page.

Civiletti, Benjamin. September 5, 1979. Letter to Secretary of the Army Clifford Alexander, Jr.

Clark, J.R. and J. Benforado, eds. 1981. *Wetlands of Bottomland Hardwood Forests*. New York: Elsevier.

Clinton, William J. August 25, 1992. Letter to Sigurd Lucassen, William Hubbell, Michael Draper, and Sherry Scott. United Brotherhood of Carpenters and Joiners of America.

Collins, Samuel P. October 5, 1979. Letter to Charles K. Baxter, U.S. Fish and Wildlife Service.

Corn, M. Lynne. October 1989. "Spotted Owls and the Timber Industry." Congressional Research Service.

Cowardin, Lewis M., Virginia Carter, Francis C. Golet and Edward T. LaRoe. December 1979. "Classification of Wetlands and Deepwater Habitats of the United States." U.S. Fish and Wildlife Service, Office of Biological Services.

Devaney, Earl E. December 15, 2008. Memorandum. Report of Investigation: The Endangered Species Act and the Conflict between Science and Policy.

Dole, Elizabeth. April 5, 2007. Letter to Navy Secretary Donald C. Winter on the Proposed Outlying Landing Field.

Douglas, Alexander. February 5, 2008. Letter from President of Coca-Cola North America to Secretary of the Interior Dirk Kempthorne on Proposal to List the Polar Bear as Threatened Under the Endangered Species Act.

Ducks Unlimited, Inc. July 27, 2010. "Interior Secretary Unveils Special Edition Duck Stamp Cachet at Ducks Unlimited National Headquarters." News release.

Ducks Unlimited, Inc. February 14, 2011. "Ducks Unlimited Voices Strong Opposition to Massive Federal Conservation Spending Cuts." News release.

Ducks Unlimited, Inc. March, 2017. Comments to California Water Control Board on Proposed Amendment to the Water Quality Control Plan for the San Francisco Bay/Sacramento-San Joaquin Delta Estuary and Supporting Draft Revised Substitute Environmental Document.

Dwyer, William. December 21, 1994. U.S. District Court, Western District of Washington at Seattle. Order on Motions for Summary Judgement RE 1994 Forest Plan. Seattle Audubon Society et al., v. James Lyons et al. No C92-479WD, C94-758WD, C94-803WD and C94-820WD.

Fund for Animals et al. v. Manuel Lujan et al. December 15, 1991. Listing Settlement Agreement.

Gosselink, James G., Lyndon C. Lee and Thomas A. Muir, Eds. 1990. *Ecological Processes and Cumulative Impacts, as illustrated by Bottomland Hardwood Wetland Ecosystems*. Chelsea, Michigan: Lewis Publishers.

Greenwalt, Lynn A. May 2020. Personal Communication.

Hall, H. Dale. 1985. "Transposing Wetlands Characteristics to Wetlands Values, The 404(b)(1) Analysis." Transactions of the Association of State Wetland Managers, Inc.

Hall, H. Dale. February 14, 1992. Memorandum to Regional Director, Region 1, U.S. Fish and Wildlife Service. Re: Phone Discussion with Director John Turner.

Hall, H. Dale. January 22, 1993. Note to Joel Kaplan on Possible Changes to the Endangered Species Act.

Hall, H. Dale. May 14, 1999. Memorandum to FWS Director, Deputy Director, Deputy Regional and Assistant Directors. Making It Flow the Way It Should.

Hall, H. Dale. July 12, 2007. Memorandum to Deputy Secretary Lynn Scarlett on Review of Documents Under the Endangered Species Act.

Hall, H. Dale. February 13, 2008. Note to the file regarding polar bear meeting and decision.

Hall, H. Dale. February 22, 2008. Note to the file regarding transmittal of polar bear decision to Assistant Secretary Laverty.

Hall, H. Dale. May 10, 2008. Memorandum to Assistant Secretary Lyle Laverty Re: Polar Bear Comments to SOL Draft.

Hall, H. Dale. January 2, 2009. Memorandum to Assistant Secretary Lyle Laverty RE: Request from Secretary's Office for Draft Regulations.

Hall, H. Dale and Stephen W. Forsythe. April 30, 1979. Memorandum to Acting Field Supervisor, ES, Vicksburg, MS, re: Lake Ophelia Sampling.

Hall, H. Dale and Stephen W. Forsythe. May 1, 1979. Memorandum to File re: Lake Ophelia (Lake Long) Hearing.

Hall, H. Dale and Victor W. Lambou, with Panel. 1990. Chapter 15: "The Ecological Significance to Fisheries of Bottomland Hardwood Systems: Values, Detrimental Impacts, and Assessment: The Report of the Fisheries Workgroup." In *Ecological Processes and Cumulative Impacts, as illustrated by Bottomland Hardwood Wetland Ecosystems.* James G. Gosselink, Lyndon C. Lee, and Thomas A. Muir, Eds. Chelsea, Michigan: Lewis Publishers.

Hayden, J. Michael. August 24, 1992. Memorandum from Assistant Secretary of the Interior to Director, U.S. Fish and Wildlife Service. Re: Interim Policy Regarding Enforcement of Prohibition Against Taking for the Northern Spotted Owl.

Hegedus, Erin Paige. 2020. Personal Communication.

Hoeveler, William. February 24, 1992. U.S. District Court Consent Decree. United States v. South Florida Water Management District and Florida Department of Environmental Regulation. Southern District of Florida. No. 88-1886-CIV.

Holmberg, Nevin. February 20, 2020. Personal Communication.

Holthausen, Richard. February 14, 1992. Note to Fred Seavey regarding Don Knowles request.

Houck, Oliver A. 2012. "Rescuing Ophelia: Avoyelles Sportsmen's League and the Bottomland Hardwoods Controversy." *Mississippi Law Journal* Vol. 81, No. 6, 1473–1526.

Johnson, R.R., and J.F. McCormick, Tech Coords. 1979. Strategies for Protection and Management of Floodplain Wetlands and Other Riparian

Ecosystems. U.S. Department of Agriculture, Forest Service, Washington, D.C. General Tech. Rep. WO-12.

Kamensky, John. January 1999. National Partnership for Reinventing Government: A Brief History (formerly the National Performance Review). Home page for National Partnership for Reinventing Government. Govinfo.library.unt.edu

Katz, Jacob V.E., and C. Jeffries, J. L. Conrad, T. R. Sommer, J. Martinez, S. Brumbaugh, et al. 2017. "Floodplain Farm Fields Provide Novel Rearing Habitat for Chinook Salmon." PLoS ONE 12(6): e0177409.

Kempthorne, Dirk. October 1, 2021. Personal Communication.

Kennedy, James Cox. October 18, 2020. Personal Communication.

Knowles, Don. February 4, 1992. Note to Members of the Spotted Owl Recovery Team.

Lujan, Manuel, Jr. April 29, 1992. Report of the Secretary of the Interior to the Endangered Species Committee. Related to the Application by the Bureau of Land Management for Exemption from the Requirements of Section 7(a)(2) of the Endangered Species Act.

Lujan, Manuel, Jr. January 14, 1993. Memorandum to Donald R. Knowles and Marvin L. Plenert. Re: Draft Recovery Plan for the Northern Spotted Owl.

Lujan, Manuel, Jr., John H. Beuter, Ed Cassidy, J. Michael Hayden, David C. O'Neal and John E. Schrote. May 1992. Draft Preservation Plan for the Northern Spotted Owl. U.S. Department of the Interior.

Leopold, Aldo. 1949. *A Sand County Almanac and Sketches Here and There*. New York: Oxford University Press.

McKevitt, James. April 9, 2020. Personal Communication.

Miccosukee Tribe of Indians of Florida. 2020. Internet Home Page.

Morris, Bill. 2018. Personal Communication.

Morris, John L. May 2013. Presentation before the National Convention of Ducks Unlimited, Inc.

Mulder, Barry. February 5, 1992. Note to Dale Hall. Re: Potential Delays in the Spotted Owl Recovery Plan.

National Park Service. 2020. Crater Lake Visitor's Brochure. History and Culture–Crater Lake National Park.

National Park Service. 2020. History of the Everglades. Home Page, Everglades National Park.

Nicholopoulos, Joy. 2020. Personal Communication.

Office of Inspector General, Department of the Interior. December 2006. Investigative Report On Allegations Against Julie MacDonald, Deputy Assistant Secretary, Fish, Wildlife, and Parks.

Oregon Encyclopedia. May 26, 2020. Klamath Basin Project (1906). Home Page/Articles. Oregonencyclopedia.org.

Parenteau, Patrick A. February 21, 1992. Memorandum to Dan Shillito, Office of the Solicitor. Re: U.S. Fish and Wildlife Service Post Hearing Brief and Resignation.

Parenteau, Patrick A. May 13, 2020. Personal Communication.

Patterson, Roger. 2020. Personal Communication.

Plenert, Marvin L. May 27, 1992. Memorandum to Chair, Spotted Owl Recovery Team. Re: Recovery Team Activities and Planning.

Plenert, Marvin, Dean Bibles, Rolland Schmitten and John F. Butruille. 1993. Memorandum Establishing the Interagency Implementation Team for the Northwest Forest Plan.

Raley, Bennett. April 20, 2004. Memorandum titled "Performance Review for USFWS Regional Director Steven Thompson."

Raynor, Peter. May 18, 2020. Personal Communication.

Sanderson, Richard E. EPA Director of Federal Activities. December 27, 1991. Letter to Bureau of Land Management State Director Regarding Possible Violation of the National Environmental Policy Act.

Sansonetti, Thomas L. and Schrote, John H. October 1, 1991. Endangered Species Committee Memorandum on Threshold Determination on Application for Endangered Species Act Exemption.

Scarlett, Lynn. July 13, 2007. Memorandum RE: Review of Documents Under the Endangered Species Act.

Scarlett, Lynn. October 5, 2020. Personal Communication.

Scott, Nauman. June 9, 1979. The Avoyelles Sportsmen's League, Inc. et al. versus Clifford L Alexander et al. Civil Action No. 78-1428, Western District of Louisiana.

Scott, Nauman. March 12, 1981. The Avoyelles Sportsmen's League, Inc. et al. versus Clifford L. Alexander et al. Civil Action No. 78-1428, Western District of Louisiana.

Severance, Nancy. January 22, 2008. Navy Yields to Audubon Opposition to Airfield Near Sensitive Refuge. National Audubon Society Home Page/Take Action. Audubon.org/news/navy-yields.

Shah, Subhas. Chief Engineer, Middle Rio Grande Conservancy District. June 16, 2003. Letter to U.S. Congressman Tom Udall re: U.S. Fish and Wildlife Service Biological Opinion.

Shillito, Daniel G. Undated. Letter to Mr. Patrick Parenteau with Directions to Modify Final FWS Endangered Species Committee Brief.

Shillito, Daniel G. June 4, 1992. Memorandum to Solicitor, Department of the

Interior. Re: Court Decision Upholding Fish and Wildlife Service Regulation Prohibiting Habitat Modification that Kills or Injures Endangered or Threatened Species. Sweet Home Chapter of Communities for a Greater Oregon v Lujan, No. 91-1468.

Slack, Jay. 2020. Personal Communication.

Stansell, Ken. 2020. Personal Communication.

Strahan, Jan. "Regeneration of Riparian Forests of the Central Valley." In *Structure, Status, and Trends in the Condition of California Riparian Systems*. University of California Press E-Books Collection, 1982–2004.

Thabault, Michael. 2020. Personal Communication.

Theodore Roosevelt Association. December 2021. "The Real Teddy Bear Story." Theodoreroosevelt.org.

Thomas, Jack Ward, and Jared Verner. March 1993. "Accommodation Under Socioeconomic Factors Under the Endangered Species Act—More Than Meets The Eye." Presented at the North American Wildlife Conference.

Thomas, Jack Ward, Eric D. Forsman, Joseph B. Lint, E. Charles Meslow, Barry R. Noon and Jared Verner. May 1990. "A Conservation Strategy for the Northern Spotted Owl." Interagency Scientific Committee to Address the Conservation of the Northern Spotted Owl.

Thompson, Steve. 1998. Personal Communication.

Thorson, Robyn. 2020. Personal Communication.

Tripp, James T.B. May 21, 2020. Personal Communication.

Tripp, James T.B. Unpublished. Draft Environmental Defense Fund Memoirs. Quoted with permission.

Turner, John F. May 1991. Memorandum Appointing Mel Schamberger as Head of the Economic Analysis Team for Northern Spotted Owl Critical Habitat Determination.

Turner, John F. 1991. Declaration to the United States District Court, Western District of Washington at Seattle. Northern Spotted Owl et al. v. Manuel Lujan, et al. No. C88-873Z.

U.S. Army Corps of Engineers. October 2007. Syllabus, Yazoo Backwater Area Reformulation.

U.S. Congress. 2004 Energy and Water Development Appropriations Act. Public Law 108-137. H.R. 2754, 108th Congress.

U.S. Court of Appeals, Ninth Circuit, Opinion and Order. March 4, 1992. Lane County Audubon Society et al., v. Cy Jamison et al. Nos 91-36019 and 91-36340. D.C. No. CV-91-06123-REJ (District of Oregon).

U.S. Department of the Army, Waterways Experiment Station. July 1980. Letter from Conrad J. Kirby, Chief, Environmental Resources Division to Gary L.

Hickman, Area Manager, FWS, Jackson, Mississippi.

U.S. Department of the Interior, Fish and Wildlife Service. July 1979. "The Yazoo Basin: An Environmental Overview: A Planning Aid Report."

U.S. Department of the Interior, Office of Hearings and Appeals. November 26, 1991. Order ESA 91-1, Matters for Prehearing Conference. Harvey C. Sweitzer, Administrative Law Judge. Spotted Owl Endangered Species Committee Hearing.

U.S. Departments of Agriculture and the Interior. May 1990. "A Conservation Strategy for the Northern Spotted Owl: Report of the Interagency Scientific Committee to Address the Conservation of the Northern Spotted Owl."

U.S. District Court, Western District of Louisiana. January 31, 1980. Subpoena for Dale Hall to Testify at the Federal District Court. Avoyelles Sportsmen's League et al. v. Clifford Alexander et al. Alexandria, Louisiana.

U.S. Fish and Wildlife Service. May 1981. Letter to Mr. Dave Peters, U.S. Environmental Protection Agency, Dallas, Texas. Re: Tensas Tract FWS Wetland Determination.

U.S. Fish and Wildlife Service. May 1981. Letter to Colonel Samuel P. Collins, Jr. U.S. Army Corps of Engineers, Vicksburg, Mississippi. Re: Permit Response for Tensas Tract.

U.S. Fish and Wildlife Service. June 1982. "Yazoo Area Pump Study, Yazoo Backwater Project, Mississippi: A Fish and Wildlife Coordination Act Report."

U.S. Fish and Wildlife Service. January 15, 1992. 50 CFR Part 17. Endangered and Threatened Wildlife and Plants; Determination of Critical Habitat for the Northern Spotted Owl. Vol. 57, No. 10. 1796–1838.

U.S. Fish and Wildlife Service. May 1992. Memorandum from Deputy Director–Line to Deputy Director–Staff, Regional Directors and Assistant Directors. Re: Testimony Before House Appropriations Subcommittee.

U.S. Fish and Wildlife Service. July 24, 1998. "Japanese-Owned Tennessee Shell Company Pays $1 Million In Restitution for Illegally Buying and Transporting Overseas Thousands of Pounds of Freshwater Mussels, One of the United States' Most Valuable and Least Understood Wildlife Resources. Press Release.

U.S. Fish and Wildlife Service. March 17, 2003. ESA Biological Opinion on the Programmatic Biological Assessment of Bureau of Reclamation's Water and River Maintenance Operations, Army Corps of Engineers' Flood Control Operation, and Related Non-Federal Actions on the Middle Rio Grande, New Mexico. Cons. # 2-22-03-F-0129.

U.S. Fish and Wildlife Service. December 16, 2003. Biological Opinion with the Corps of Engineers on Missouri River Main Stem Reservoir System, Operation and Maintenance of the Bank Stabilization and Navigation Project, and the Operation of Kansas River Reservoir System.

U.S. Fish and Wildlife Service. 2006. Home Page for Okefenokee National Wildlife Refuge.

U.S. Fish and Wildlife Service. 2020. Home Page: National Wildlife Refuge Improvement Act.

U.S. Supreme Court. 1978. Tennessee Valley Authority v. Hill. Docket No. 76-1701. 437 US 153 (1978).

Walters, Alice M., Robert O. Teskey and Thomas M. Hinckley. 1977–1980. Volumes I through VIII. *Impact of Water Level Changes on Woody Riparian and Wetland Communities.* Biological Services Program, U.S. Fish and Wildlife Service. FWS/OBS. Columbia, Missouri.

Walsh, Noreen. 2020. Personal Communication.

White, Wayne. 2020. Personal Communication.

Williams, John. 1975. Personal Communication.

Wooley, Charles. 2020. Personal Communication.

Zielinski, Elaine. April 20, 2020. Personal Communication.

INDEX

aboriginal hunting of polar bears, 436, 437–438
Adams, Jeff, 510
Administrative Procedures Act, 212, 465
Agency Coordination Team under Clinton, 224
Agency Head Roundtable, 302
Alaska
   about, 80–81
   Alaska National Interest Lands Conservation Act (ANILCA), 82, 395–396
   Alaska Native Claims Settlement Act (ANCSA), 81
   Alaska pipeline
      about, 60, 81–82
      Alaska Permanent Fund, 82
      Director Greenwalt and John Dingell, 37–38
      effects on surroundings, 84–85
      FWS involvement during construction, 37, 81–82
      North Slope visits, 60, 84–85, 397–400
      roads built with ice, 85, 398–399
   Alaska Statehood Act, 80–81
   Arctic NWR oil leases, 395–400
   Exxon Valdez tanker aground, 60–61, 101
   Fairbanks visit, Acting Field Supervisor Dale Hall, 83–86
   jurisdictional wetland methodology course, 58–61
   Kaktovik village, 397, 399–400
   Mt. St. Helens on flight to, 59
   National Petroleum Reserve, 397
   natural resources, 81
      arctic polygons, 59–60, 84, 398
      development for people within, 85
      oil and gas development, 84–85, 396, 397
      polar bears as threatened, 392 (*see also* polar bears)
      public "Listening Session," 398–399
      Teshekpuk Lake, 397, 399
      true soil, 59
   wetlands, 59–60
   Pebble Mine opening, 240
   placer mining Section 404 permits, 85–86
   Regional Director Bob Gilmore, 79, 80
albedo effect, 442, 444
Albuquerque, New Mexico
   about, 318
   Acting Regional Director Dale Hall, 316, 317–318
   aquifer recharge slow, 320
   Erin Hall to New Orleans recovery, 371
   Missouri River biological opinion, 347 (*see also* Missouri River ESA needs)
   Rio Grande River, 320–322 (*see also* Rio Grande River)
   San Juan–Chama water, 331
Alexander, Clifford, 14, 32–33
Allen, David, 391
Allen, Frances, 8–9
Allred, Steve, 442, 447–448
American bald eagle, 165, 339, 436–437
Amstrup, Steve, 393, 439, 442, 444
anchor ice, 442, 443–444
Anderson, David (CEQ), 464
Anderson, David (Rear Admiral), 430
Anderson, David R. (FWS), 175
Andrus, Cecil, 33, 114
Anthony, Robert, 138
arctic gyre, 442, 443–444
Arctic NWR lease offerings
   2017 Tax Cuts and Jobs Act, 82–83
   ANILCA Section 1002 language, 82, 395–396
   Hatch Act and career employees, 396
   Kaktovik village, 397, 399–400
   roads built with ice, 398–399
ARD as assistant regional director, 251
Arnett, Ray, 61, 68, 72–73
Arroyo, Bryan
   assistant director for endangered species, 392
   briefing Kempthorne on polar bear, 393, 394
   polar bear draft listing package, 439

548   COMPELLED

polar bear listing legal issues, 451
Arts Memphis, 403
Association of Fish and Wildlife Agencies, 511
Atlanta. *See* Southeast Region of FWS
Audubon, James J., 90
Avioti, Pete, 499, 500
Avoyelles Parish, Louisiana, floodplain clearing
   about, 5
      Lake Ophelia soil types, 44
      Lake Ophelia tract, 14–15, 17, 22, 23
   Avoyelles Sportsman's League lawsuit, 5, 9
      Environmental Defense Fund, 5, 9
      Louisiana Wildlife Federation, 5, 9
   court hearing, 9–14
      Corps declaration of normal activities, 11, 14, 21–22
      CWA authority, 10–14
      trial into two parts, 13–14, 16–17
   court trial one on permits, 16–28
      FWS showing need for permit, 17–19, 23–24
      ruling, 28–32
   court trial two on WOTUS, 46–51
      approval to testify, 45
      fish spawning and nursery areas, 47
      ruling, 51–55
      vegetation in definition of wetlands, 47–51
      wetlands determination, 42–44
   CWA authority per AG Civiletti, 32–33, 461
   EPA meeting, 6, 8–9
   hometown of Sarah Hall, 5, 45
   placer mining reference to, 86
   Waters of the United States, 6–8, 10–14, 26
      court trial, 46–51
      ruling, 51–55
AXALTA and Ducks Unlimited, 497
Aycock, Ray, 304–305, 466

Babbitt, Bruce
   advisor to Governor Jerry Brown, 522
   Assistant Secretary Betsy Rieke named, 253
   biological research functions to USGS, 260
   California gnatcatcher, 261–264
   Chief of Staff Tom Collier, 233, 236
   Endangered Species Committee decision, 185
   habitat conservation plans with state law, 262
   northern spotted owl recovery plan, 219
   Northwest visit, 210, 219–221, 223
   Okefenokee Swamp titanium mining, 275–276
   Orange County Habitat Conservation Plan, 259
   private dinner with, 220
   Secretary of Interior, 208, 219–220, 221, 258
   Supreme Court justice opportunity, 258–259
Baird, Clay, 486, 489
Baird, Spencer Fullerton, 88
Baker, Howard, 12, 112, 113
bald eagle, 165, 339, 436–437
Ballmer, Steve, 508
Banner, Arnold, 10, 43
Barkley, Robert, 3, 62, 465
Barns, Doug, 495, 532
Barry, Cindy, 189, 209
Barry, Don
   Assistant Secretary for FWP, 240
   Deputy Assistant Secretary for FWP, 233
   ESA Section 4(d) for owl, 233–237
   POWDR Bill, 68–74
Bart, Jon
   meetings post–Lujan spotted owl plan divorce, 196–197
   recovery team committee chairman, 136, 137, 138
   draft spotted owl recovery plan, 190–191
   final spotted owl recovery plan, 196–200
Bartels, Leslie Holland, 101
Bartels, Ron and Jackie, 510
Barton, Dana, 496
Bass Pro Shops
   duck stamp first day of sale, 403–404
   founder Johnny Morris, 403, 492, 497
      NASCAR–DU relationship, 495–497
   Pyramid as Bass Pro Shop, 492–494
      Ducks Unlimited space, 492, 493, 494–495, 497–498
Bassmaster Tournament series, 403, 490–491
Batson, Amy, 511
Baxter, Charles, 28, 465
Bay-Delta Accord, 248–250, 256, 257, 312, 521
   collaborative conflict resolution model, 256
Beard, Dan, 253–254
Beattie, Mollie
   Director of FWS, 229
   death, 266
   ESA Section 4(d) rule, 238
   reorganization of FWS, 251, 276–277
   Turner staying until Beattie installed, 234
Behar, David, 252
Belin, Letty, 323–327

Bell, Larry, 318
Benge, Mike, 510, 537
Berg, Melvin, 138
Bergstrom, Chris and Tim, 510
Bergstrom, John, 510, 537
Bernhardt, David
  ESA regulation updates as Secretary, 420–421
  lunch with President George W. Bush, 469–471
  polar bear as threatened
    Kempthorne not listing as threatened, 449, 456
    legal issues surrounding, 456
    meetings with Kempthorne, 442, 447–448, 456
    polar bear extinction, 456
  Solicitor for Department of the Interior, 415
Beuter, John, 138
Bibles, Dean, 166, 167–171
Bingaman, Jeff, 318, 328, 329–333, 365
biological assessments, 345
biological opinion into law, 327–333
Bishop, Mary Ann, 120–128
bison slaughter leading to conservation, 90
Bisson, Henri, 396–399, 442, 447–448
Black, Hugh, 231–232
Black, Ken, 45
Blackburn, Jim, 77
Blanchard, Bruce, 99
BLM. *See* Bureau of Land Management
Boatwright, Vicki, 272, 289
Bogert, Michael, 417–420
Bolton, Josh, 457–458
Bond, Kit
  ESA bunch of baloney, 339
  FWS Director nominee Dale Hall, 366
  George W. Bush relationship, 341
  listening to those impacted, 347
Bonderson, Paul
  California DU volunteer, 510–511
  Central Valley salmon and smelt, 522
  Ducks Unlimited pledge, 531
  hunting with Scalia and Cheney, 515–519
Bonderson, Sandi, 515
Boone and Crockett conservation club, 511
Booth, Tony, 83, 84
BOR. *See* Bureau of Reclamation
Boreal Forests, 504–506
bottomland hardwood wetlands
  Cache River Flood Control Project, 9, 11
  farming on wetlands, 23
    percentage cleared in Yazoo Basin, 42
    rate of being cleared for farming, 27, 45
  fish spawning and nursery areas, 14, 16, 17–19, 24, 47
  court ruling, 31
  forest floor fallen leaves, 22–23, 523–524
  jurisdictional wetland methodology course, 58–61
  Okefenokee Swamp as, 274
  permit needed for clearing, 28–30
    minimal acreage for FWS study, 27
  Sacramento Basin, 241–243
    95 percent developed, 243
  soil erosion and sedimentation, 335–336, 523–525
  vegetation adaptations to saturation, 6–8, 43, 47–51, 52, 523
  Waters of the United States, 6–8, 10–14, 26, 51–55
  Yazoo Backwater Pumps (*see* Yazoo Backwater Pumps project)
  Yazoo Delta cleared for agriculture, 5, 8–14, 23, 25, 26
    fish spawning and nursery areas, 14, 16, 17–19, 24, 47
    percentage cleared, 42
    permit needed for clearing, 28–30, 31
    teaching Jim Tripp, 14–16
    vegetation in definition of wetlands, 47–51
    wetland importance, 30–32
    wetlands as WOTUS, 51–55
    wetlands determination, 42–44
    Yazoo Backwater Pumps project, 62, 464 (*see also* Yazoo Backwater Pumps project)
Boxer, Barbara, 440–441
BP Deepwater Horizon rig, 484–489, 503–504
Bradley, Bill, 246–247
Bragg, Heath, 371
Brennan, Mike
  counterbalance to Don Knowles, 143
  "suggestions" from Don Knowles, 139, 143
  World Trade Center plane crashes, 313–314, 315
British Petroleum (BP) Deepwater Horizon rig, 484–489, 503–504
Brown, Columbus, 272, 282
Brown, J. Cudd, 186–189
Brown, Jerry, 522
Bruce, Charles R., 120–128
Bryan, Fred, xvi
Bryant, David, 371
"buckshot" clay, 44
Bunning, Dave and Denise, 511
Bureau of Commercial Fisheries, 34–35
Bureau of Indian Affairs, 226

550 COMPELLED

Bureau of Land Management (BLM)
   Biological Resources Division in USGS, 260
   Deputy Director Henri Bisson, 396–397, 442
   Director Cy Jamison, 119, 166–167, 168
   National Petroleum Reserve in Alaska, 397
   National Wildlife Refuge Improvement Act, 278–280
   northern spotted owl
      about historic perspective, 121–122, 124
      BLM paying expenses of review, 193, 194
      Clinton-requested SEIS, 225–229, 230–233
      Endangered Species Committee request, 168–171
      environmental impact statements, 117
      evidentiary hearing, 171–180
      Interagency Implementation Team, 225–226
      Interagency Scientific Committee, 116, 119–128
      Jamison strategy, 175, 177–179, 182, 184, 190
      Jamison strategy court ruling, 197–198
      Northwest Forest Plan, 224–229, 230–232
      Oregon and California Railroad Revested (O&C) lands, 132–133, 151, 166
      recovery plan, 198
      supplemental EIS not warranted, 124
      timber sales, 116–117, 132–133, 167–168
   Old Growth Wildlife Research and Development Program, 122
   polar bear meetings with Kempthorne, 442
Bureau of Reclamation (BOR)
   about mission, 336
   Central Valley, California, water
      Central Valley Project Improvement Act, 251–252
      Commissioner Dan Beard, 253–254
      FWS cooperation with, 251–252, 255–256
      Management Study, 244
      Regional Director Roger Patterson, 152, 248
      Water Operations Management Team, 250
   Commissioner Bob Johnson, 431
   Commissioner Dan Beard, 253–254
   Commissioner Dennis Underwood, 357
   FWS cooperation with, 156–157, 251–252, 357
   Klamath Project, 155–156
      critical habitat public education, 163
      lakes drying up, 157–161
   Lower Colorado River multi-species conservation plan, 356–360
   managing water to biological needs, 156–157
   Missouri River, 336–339, 350–351
   Regional Director Bob Johnson, 319
   Rio Grande River
      authority to take water for ESA, 322
      biological opinion into law, 327–333
      re-regulating dams, 322
      tour of river by FWS, 330–331
      water release for minnows, 322–323
      water release lawsuit, 323–327
      water release rulings, 326, 329–330
   water delivery challenges, 152, 156
Bureau of Sport Fisheries and Wildlife, 34, 35, 36, 361. *See also* U.S. Fish and Wildlife Service
Burger, Warren, 111–112, 512
Burr, Richard, 429
Bush, George H. W.
   90-day regulatory moratorium, 190, 191–192
   BLM Director Cy Jamison, 166–167
   Secretary of the Interior Manuel Lujan, 135–136, 137
   sworn in, 95, 135
   leaving office, 207–208
Bush, George W.
   dinner with Jean-Michel Cousteau, 401
   election won, 312
   re-election looming, 469
   ESA regulation updates, 413–415, 419–422
   FWS Director Dale Hall, 361, 365, 427
   Bush noting mother's death, 384
   Bush thanking for service, 470–471
   lunch with the president, 469–471
   retirement, 472
   thanking Bush for partnership support, 469–470
   global warming, 391, 440
   lunch with "polar bear guy," 469–471
   "Minnow Measure" signed, 332
   Missouri Senator Kit Bond, 341
   nominating Lyle Laverty for FWP, 438
   partisan politics banned, 431, 471
   polar bear listing pressure, 445–446, 456
      Kempthorne deciding to list, 457–459

INDEX 551

September 11 (2001), 313–315
Bush, Jeb, 293
Byrd, Robert, 98, 100

Cache River Flood Control Project (Arkansas), 9, 11
Cadillac Desert (Reisner), 220
Cain, Brian, 76
California Department of Fish and Game on ISC, 120–128
California Endangered Species Act, 260–261
California gnatcatcher, 261–264
California water. *See* Central Valley, California
California Water Resources Control Board, 245, 522
CalTrout Nigiri Project, 525–528
Camille, hurricane, 367
Cantrell, Brett, 486, 489
Capka, Rick, 300–301, 431
career employees of FWS
    directors, 360–361, 364, 377, 478
        Dale Hall, 364, 377, 378, 413, 415
        Lynn Greenwalt, 33, 377
        Sam Hamilton, 478
    disdained by Trump administration, 422
    ESA updates, 413, 419–421
    Hatch Act, 396
    honoring through Lynn Greenwalt, 377
    ideas for long-term solutions, 472
Carroll, Phil, 147, 197, 237
Carson, Rachel, 76
Carter, Jimmy
    Alaska National Interest Lands Conservation Act, 82
    Energy and Water Development Act, 115
    senior executive service creation, 71
Cartwright, Dave, 290, 291
Cason, Jim, 179
Caswell, Jim, 442, 447–448
Cathon, Neely, 466
Central Valley, California, water
    about, 241–247
    Assistant Secretary Betsy Rieke, 252–255
    accord between state and federal, 256
    Bay-Delta Accord, 248–250, 256, 257, 312, 521
    California State Water Project (1960), 243
    California Water Coalition, 246
    Central Valley Project (1935), 243
    Central Valley Project Improvement Act (CVPIA, 1992), 246–247
    FWS and BOR cooperating, 251–252
    FWS Section 3406(b)(2) water management, 247, 255–258
    "Club Fed" to Cal-Fed, 248–250, 254
    floodplains, 521–528
    flows inadequate for fish, 244–247
    Bay-Delta Accord, 256
    Geographic ARD Dale Hall, 251
    great flood (1862) raising river beds, 242
    HCP and ESA Section 10 permit, 259
    Natural Community Conservation Planning Act (California), 261
    ESA Section 4(d) rule for gnatcatcher, 262–267
    salmon and smelt driving decisions, 244, 255, 521–528
    San Francisco Estuary Project (1987), 246
    volunteer enthusiasm, 510–511
    water is not habitat, 242
    Water Operations Management Team, 250, 257
    wetlands, 241–242
        loss of, 242–243
CEQ. *See* Council on Environmental Quality
Chandler, George, 281–282
channelization. *See* flood control
Charbonneau, John, 140
Chavez, David, 371
Chavez, Martin, 326, 327, 330–331
Cheney, Dick
    California hunting trip with Scalia, 516–519
    ESA regulation updates, 413–415
    global warming, 391
    sworn in as vice president, 312
Childress, Richard, 496, 497
Childs, John, 482, 508
China visit and Tiananmen Square, 100–101
chinook salmon, 242, 521–528
Christian, Cathy and Steve, 511
Cieslik, Larry, 339, 346
citizen conservationists, 480–481
    Billy Dunavant as, 500
    conservationists funding conservation, 92–95, 480–481, 511–512
    federal dollars matched by two, 503
    fighting Marine Shale Processors, 56–57
    FWS ecosystem team partnerships, 308
    habitat improvement, 144, 362, 480
    habitat percentage in private ownership, 160
    Jim Kennedy as, 507–508, 536
    Johnny Morris as, 403, 497–498, 536
        (*see also* Morris, John L. "Johnny")
    Nino Scalia as, 520
    Pete Coors as, 500
    species are saved by people, 165, 219, 233–234
    volunteer enthusiasm, 509–512

Civil Service Reform Act (1978), 71
Civiletti, Benjamin, 14, 32–33, 461
Civilian Conservation Corps (CCC), 40
Clark, Jamie Rappaport
    Deputy Regional Director Dale Hall, 266
    senior executive service, 312
    FWS Director, 272, 277, 360
        FWS management evaluation, 277–278, 310–311
Clark Air Force Base (Philippines), xiii, 367
clay soils in Lake Ophelia site, 44
Clean Water Act (CWA)
    authority of EPA Administrator, 11–12, 32–33, 461
    Avoyelles Parish floodplain clearing, 5
    authority of Corps versus EPA and FWS, 10–14, 32–33, 52–55
    fish spawning versus land clearing, 19, 31
    permit program authority, 4, 10–14, 28–33
    ruling on navigable waters, 32–33, 53–54
    ruling on normal practice exemptions, 29–30
    ruling on Section 404 jurisdiction, 52–53
    ruling on wetland importance, 30–32
    British Petroleum penalties, 503–504
    Section 404 (*see* Section 404 permits)
    Waters of the United States
        CWA expanding scope of, 6
        navigable waters extent rulings, 32–33, 53–55
        navigable waters use change ruling, 29–30
        navigable waterways of Rivers and Harbors Act, 11–14, 53–54
    wetland loss not prohibited, 362
    wetlands definition, 6–8
    wetlands oversight authority, 11–12, 51–55
Clear Lake, Texas, FWS ES Office
    Galveston Bay Area Navigation Study, 74–79
        environmental contaminants, 76–79
        journalist Harold Scarlett, 74–75, 77, 87–88
    oil and gas in Texas and Louisiana, 83
    Supervisor Dale Hall, 67, 87
        Fairbanks, Alaska, detail, 83–86
climate change, 391, 440
    greenhouse gases, 391, 477
    House Select Committee on Energy Independence and Global Warming, 439–440
    congressional testimony, 439–441
    melting of arctic ice cap, 391, 393, 404, 440, 442–445, 477
    ice ecoregions in future, 451
    polar bears (*see* polar bears)
    USGS sea ice reports, 442–443, 444, 452
Clinton, William Jefferson
    Agency Coordination Team, 224
    disregard for state agencies, 333–334
    election of, 207–208
    Endangered Species Committee decision, 185
    ESA Section 4(d) for owl, 233–237, 238
    owl as political football, 238
    Federal Ecosystem Management Assessment Team, 224
    northern spotted owl recovery plan, 208, 219, 222, 224–225
    northern spotted owl SEIS, 224–229, 230–233
    Forest Summit, 205, 210, 222, 239
    Northwest Forest Plan, 224–229, 230–232
    FWS Director Jamie Rappaport Clark, 360
    impressed with Jack Ward Thomas, 223
    Interior Assistant Secretary Betsy Rieke, 253
    National Wildlife Refuge Improvement Act, 279
    remembering people's names, 388
    second term, 239, 276
    Supreme Court Justice Byron White, 258–259
Clough, Noreen, 271–272
Cochran, Thad, 466
Coleman, Rick, 278
Coleman, Veronica, 289–291
collaboration. *See* partnerships
collaborative conflict resolution model, 256
Collier, Tom
    Chief of Staff to Bruce Babbitt, 233, 236
    ESA Section 4(d) for owl, 235, 236–237
    Pebble Mine, Alaska, 240
Collins, Joyce, 340
Colorado River
    about, 353
    Colorado River Interstate Compact, 353–354, 358–359
    lower basin drought, 354–360
        no drought while camping, 354–356
    multi-species conservation plan, 357, 359–360
    negotiations, 357–359

Colwell, Ina Frances (mother)
  Greatest Generation, vii
  Kentucky childhood, vii, xi
  marriage to Herbert Hall, xi–xii (*see also* Hall, Ina Frances)
  polio in childhood, xi
Colwell, Rubin (mother's father), xi
Combs, Phil, 8, 19
Commerce Clause (U.S. Constitution), 54–55
communication
  Anchorage public "Listening Session," 398–399
  CEQ elevation language, 65, 78
  DuPont Okefenokee public meeting, 275–276
  EPA on Yazoo Backwater Pumps project, 465–466
  ESA critical habitat public education, 162
  ESA listing of polar bears, 433, 459
  ESA regulation briefings to Congress, 418–419
  ESA Section 4(d) rule for owls, 237
  Federal Advisory Committee Act, 137
  listening to those impacted, 347
  Missouri River Recovery Implementation Committee, 347
  mussel shell ring prosecution, 289–291
  nonpublic information for private interest, 407
  northern spotted owl critical habitat, 140, 145–146
    public hearings, 142, 146–151
  northern spotted owl recovery plan, 198–199
  owl "conversation" plan, 195
  placer mining letters, 86
  public education, 74–75
    ESA critical habitat, 162–165
    Klamath suckers and drought, 160, 161–163
    Navy Outlying Landing Field, 427–429
    owl critical habitat, 145–146
    Port of Houston channel project, 74–75, 77–78
comprehensive conservation plans (CCP), 280
conflict of interest as violation, 173
conflict resolution model, 256
Congress
  conservation dollars appropriated are replenished, 503
  CWA amendments veto override, 13
  ESA authorization expiration, 206–207, 411–412
  ESA updates, 418–419

  federal conservation programs cut, 501–502
  House Appropriations Committee Staff visit, 210–219
  House Select Committee on Energy Independence and Global Warming, 439–440
  Inspector General investigation of MacDonald, 409–410
  National Fish and Wildlife Foundation, 401–402
  Navy outlying landing field, 428–430
  refusing Lujan's ESA-avoiding plan, 196
  silvery minnow, 331–332
Connaughton, Jim, 394–395, 413–415
Conrad, Walter, 24, 25, 48–49
conservation groups to support, 511
conservation history. *See* history of conservation
Constitution. *See* U.S. Constitution
Convention on International Trade in Endangered Species of Wild Fauna and Flora (CITES), 434–435
Cook, Bob, 272, 318
Cooper, Brad, xiv
Coors, Peter, 499, 500
Corps of Engineers. *See* U.S. Army Corps of Engineers
Costello, Herbert, 26–27
Cotton, Chuck, 371
Couch, Charlotte, 3
Council of Economic Advisers on God Squad, 112, 114–115
Council on Environmental Quality (CEQ)
  Chair Jim Connaughton, 394–395, 413–415
  Chair Katie McGinty, 228, 230, 237
  Chair Mike DeLann, 182–183
  elevation language, 78
  ESA regulation update, 413–415
  Forest Plan, 228, 230, 237
  God Squad hearing, 182–183
  polar bear listed as threatened, 394–395
  referral to, 65, 78
  Yazoo Backwater Pumps project, 461, 464
Cousteau, Jacques, 401
Cousteau, Jean-Michel, 401
Cowardin, Lewis, 42, 259–260
Crater Lake, Oregon, 152
critical habitat
  decisions marred by Julie MacDonald, 407, 408–410
  designation as law, 109, 134, 143, 163
  ESA critical habitat designation, 107
  FWS process, 109–110, 116, 133–141, 144–146, 151

Klamath suckers, 161–163 (*see also* Klamath sucker critical habitat)
northern spotted owl, 107 (*see also* northern spotted owl)
public education, 161–165
species are saved by people, 165, 219, 233–234 (*see also* citizen conservationists)
tool for recovery, 215–216
Crouse, Mike, 231–232
Cryar, Fernell (Sarah's sister)
making conservation history against pollution, 56–57
swearing-in of FWS Director Dale Hall, 377
Cryar, Richard, 377
Culver, John, 112
Cumberland College, Williamsburg, Kentucky, xiv
CWA. *See* Clean Water Act

Dale, John, 508
D'Alonzo, Bill, 509, 510
Dance, Bill, 493, 500
Darling, Jay Norwood "Ding," 91–92, 403, 498
Darwin Award. *See* Navy outlying landing field
Daschle, Tom, 402
Davies, Terry, 366, 372
Dawson, Mike, 5
D.C. Booth National Historic Fish Hatchery, 402
De la Rosa, Marcos, 75
Deadman, Bruce, 510
Decision Points (G.W. Bush), 315
Declaration of Independence, 89, 186
Deepwater Horizon rig explosion, 484–489, 503–504
DeLann, Mike, 182–183
Delphey, Philip, 340
delta smelt, 521–528
Delta Waterfowl conservation group, 511
Denver FWS Ecological Services Office, 113
Designated Conservation Areas (DCAs), 192–193
Detrich, Phil, 166
Devaney, Earl, 408, 410
Dickson, Paul and Skipper, 510
Dierks, Wayne, 482, 483, 484, 511
Dillon, Austin, 497
Dillon, Ty, 496, 497
Dimick, Frank, 256
Dingell, John, 35–38, 94
Dingell-Johnson Act, 94
Directors, U.S. Fish and Wildlife Service

about process of appointing, 360, 363–366
confirmation, 371–372
swearing-in, 372, 376–377
about scientific discussion, 381–382
career employees, 360–361, 364, 377, 478
Dale Hall, 364, 377, 378, 413, 415
ideas for long-term solutions, 472
Lynn Greenwalt, 33, 377
Sam Hamilton, 478, 479
declined by Steve Thompson, 479–480
Director Bob Jantzen, 70–73, 79
Director Dale Hall
Arctic NWR (*see* Arctic National Wildlife Refuge lease offerings)
confirmation, 371–372
D.C. without family, 363
doing the job, 375–383, 400–401
ESA regulation updates, 411–415, 417–420
ESA regulation updates not per FWS, 420
Executive Assistant Pat Kennedy, 383
Google results, 416–417
Julie MacDonald changing reports (*see* MacDonald, Julie A.)
lawsuits on any given day, 415, 428
legacy, 537
lunch with President George W. Bush, 469–471
meeting with VP Cheney, 516
Navy outlying landing field, 422–432
nomination, 361–366, 387
"polar bear guy," 470 (*see also* polar bears)
retirement, 472–473
"sandwich mission" of FWS, 481
swearing-in, 372, 376–378, 384
team building, 378–380
Yazoo Backwater Pumps project, 459–468
Director Frank Dunkle, 79–80, 95
Director Jamie Rappaport Clark, 272, 277, 360
FWS management evaluation, 277
Director John Turner (*see* Turner, John)
Director Lynn Greenwalt (*see* Greenwalt, Lynn)
Director Mollie Beattie
about, 229
death, 266
ESA Section 4(d) rule, 238
reorganization of FWS, 251, 276–277
Director Sam Hamilton, 478

Director Steve Williams (*see* Williams, Steven A.)
National Duck Stamp Contest, 402–404, 495
NFWF board member, 401–402
presidential appointment confirmed by the Senate, 35–37, 79, 95–96, 360–361
problems no one else could solve, 375
program management to line management, 79
qualifications, 35
U.S. Biological Survey Director Jay N. "Ding" Darling, 91–92, 403
veterinarian nominated by Ronald Reagan, 361
DiRosario, Bill and Kerrie, xiv
Disheroon, Fred, 8–14, 43
Dohner, Cindy, 282
DOI. *See* U.S. Department of the Interior
DOJ. *See* U.S. Department of Justice
Dole, Elizabeth, 428–430
Domenech, Doug, 365
Domenici, Pete
    Middle Rio Grande River, 318, 328
        fix for minnow problem, 329–333
        tour of Rio Grande by FWS, 330–331
        nomination of FWS Director Dale Hall, 365
        confirmation hearing, 371
Douglas, Alexander, 433–434
drought. *See* western drought
Dryer, Mark, 340
DU. *See* Ducks Unlimited
Duck Cops, 287. *See also* special agents of FWS
duck stamps, 92
    first day of sale, 402, 403–404
    habitat management funds, 73, 92, 498
    National Duck Stamp Contest, 402–404, 495
Ducks Unlimited (DU)
    about, 480–482
        conservationists funding conservation, 481, 498, 511–512
        DU fixes what's broken, 483
        BP Deepwater Horizon rig explosion, 484–489
        BP penalties town hall, 503–504
        habitat creation, 485–489
        California floodplains, 521–528
        CEO Adam Putnam, 531, 533
        CEO Dale Hall, 484
            about CEO position, 501
            belt buckle from volunteers, 532
            belt buckles for volunteers, 532
            contacted by Johnny Morris, 492–493
            duck gumbo, 518
            fundraising and habitat conservation, 511–512, 529, 531
            retirement, 506, 509, 529–538
            Search Committee contacting, 480, 481–482
            Search Committee interviews, 482–484
    Congress cutting conservation funding, 501–503
    Dale and Sarah Hall Legacy Fund, 531
    Duck Stamp Contest, 403–404, 495
    formation of, 92–93
    habitat management funds, 92–93, 505, 511
    keynote speaker Antonin Scalia, 512–516
        hunting with Scalia and Cheney, 515–519
    keynote speaker Fred Smith, 530
    keynote speaker Johnny Morris, 495–496
    keynote speaker Rebecca Rimel, 504
        Boreal Forests with Pew Charitable Trusts, 504–506
    Memphis, Tennessee, home, 499–500
    presidents of, 501
        President George Dunklin, 529–530
        President John Newman, 482, 504
        President John Pope, 482, 484–485, 501
        President Peter Coors, 499
        President Rogers Hoyt, 529–530
    promoted by Johnny Morris, 497–498
        DU National Convention, 495–496
        NASCAR relationship, 495–497
        space in the Pyramid, 492, 493, 494–495, 497–498
    volunteers, 481, 482, 501
        leadership of, 533–537
        presidents of DU, 501
        volunteers getting it done, 509–511
    Waterfowling Heritage Center, 492, 495, 497
    Wetlands America Trust, 482, 507, 508–509, 518–519, 520
Duffy, Greg, 318
Dunavant, Tommie, 500
Dunavant, William B., Jr., 499–500
Dunkle, Frank, 79–80, 95
Dunklin, George, ix, 482, 529–530, 531
Dunklin, George, Jr., 529
Dunn, Winfield, 111
DuPont company, 275–276
Durham-Aguilera, Karen, 346
dust bowl, 91–92

556 COMPELLED

Dwyer, Tom, 240
Dwyer, William, 232–233

Earnest, Russ
    Ecological Services in DC, 57
    implicit permission to testify, 45
    Manager of Jackson Area FWS Office, 28, 45, 57, 70
    POWDR Bill, 70–74
Earnhardt, Dale, Jr., 497
Easley, Mike, 429
Eastern Kentucky University graduate school, xv
Eastland, James, 466
Ecosystem Approach to conservation
    assessment of, 277–278
    ESA individual species approach, 109–110, 212
    Federal Ecosystem Management Assessment Team, 224, 230, 231, 237
    FWS Director Mollie Beattie, 229, 251
    habitat (*see* habitat)
    Interior Secretary Babbitt, 220
    memo on Ecosystem Approach opportunities, 306–310
    partnerships with other conservation entities, 302–303, 307–310
    Seattle Audubon lawsuit, 118–119, 232–233
Eden Fisheries, Yazoo City, Mississippi, xvii
EDF. *See* Environmental Defense Fund
education of public, 74–75. *See also* communication
Edwards, Gary, 87, 97, 99
E.I. DuPont company, 275–276
EIS. *See* environmental impact statements
Eisenhower, Dwight D., 81, 446, 447
Elder Realty, Louisiana, floodplain clearing, 5
"the elephant cage," xiv
Elkins, Mike, 290
Elmore, Wayne, 138
Emergency Wetlands Resources Act (1986), 73–74
Emmitt, Jack, 493
Endangered Species Act (ESA; 1973)
    about, 107–110
    prevention as afterthought, 302, 308
    stated intent of, 107–108, 111, 212, 233, 350
    American bald eagle de-listed, 436
    authorization expiration, 206–207
        recommendations for positive change, 211–219
        regulation updates, 411–422
        regulation updates not per FWS, 420
        regulation updates partially adopted, 420–421
    biological opinion into law, 327–333
    BOR authority to take water for ESA, 322
    California gnatcatcher, 261–264
    California's own ESA, 260–261
    Category 1 (C-1) species, 205–206
    critical habitat designation, 107
        FWS process, 109–110, 116, 133–141, 144–146, 151
        Klamath suckers, 161–163 (*see also* Klamath sucker critical habitat)
        northern spotted owl, 107 (*see also* northern spotted owl)
        public education, 161–165
        species are saved by people, 165, 219, 233–234 (*see also* citizen conservationists)
    domestic versus international listings, 434
    economic impacts, 140
        paper presented on, 222
    Endangered Species Committee
        about, 112–113, 171
        about evidentiary hearings, 171–172
        BLM request to convene, 168–171
        decision on owl critical habitat, 184–186
        evidentiary hearing, 171–180
        legal counsel Tom Sansonetti, 169, 172–180, 181–182, 184
        load carried by Barry and Teeter, 189
        post-hearing brief changes, 180–184
        post-hearing report, 184–186
        silvery minnow, 330
        Tellico Dam and Grayrocks Oil Refinery, 113–116, 174
    endangered versus threatened species, 108–109, 199
        determined on basis of best science, 452
        Section 10 permit requiring EIS for taking, 260–261
    "take" defined, 201
    "take" including habitat modification, 200–204
    "taking" an endangered species, 199, 201, 232, 362
    fish impounded by Klamath project, 156
    five factor analysis, 108–109
        economic analysis, 140, 222
    freshwater mussels, 286, 291
    FWS annual listing proposals, 206
        funding appropriations (1993), 214
        species evaluation settlement, 206, 211–212

FWS conferring with FS and BLM, 126, 166
FWS habitat modification lawsuit, 200–204
FWS individual species approach, 109–110, 212
FWS responsibilities under, 162, 211–212, 350
FWS special agents, 287–288
    musselers arrested, 286, 288–289
FWS sued over ESA candidate species, 205–207, 211–212, 240, 264–266
greenhouse gas accountability, 477
grizzly bear, 375–376
habitat conservation plans (*see* habitat conservation plans)
Julie MacDonald changing reports, 404–405 (*see also* MacDonald, Julie A.)
    decisions reviewed, 407, 408–410
Klamath suckers (*see* Klamath sucker critical habitat)
Missouri River wildlife, 339, 341, 346, 349
    pallid sturgeon never funded, 350–351
multi-species conservation plan, 357–360
northern spotted owl (*see* northern spotted owl)
polar bears (*see* polar bears)
reasonable and prudent alternative (RPA) action, 322, 332
recovery teams, 136–139
    critical habitat as tool for recovery, 215–216
    Everglades recovery plan, 301–302
    Lujan plan bypassing ESA, 190–196
    recovery plans, 136–137, 196–197
    recovery plans not law, 137, 196–197
    recovery requiring voluntary actions, 144
    species recovered via regulation, 165
Section 4(d), 199–200
    California gnatcatcher, 262–267
    polar bear listed, 448
    special rule for owl, 233–238
Section 10 permits
    EIS required for taking listed species, 260–261
    habitat conservation plans, 234
    multi-species conservation plan, 357, 359
silvery minnow, 318–323, 324–325
    biological opinion into law, 327–333
    lawsuit over water release, 323–327

snail darter fish, 97, 110–116, 171
state and federal partnerships
    California gnatcatcher, 261–264
    musselers arrested, 286, 288
threatened versus endangered species, 108–109, 199
    determined on basis of best science, 452
    Section 4(d) rule for gnatcatcher, 262–264
    Section 4(d) rule for owl, 233–238
    "take" including habitat modification, 200–204
    threatened species protective regulations, 199–200, 201
whooping crane, 110, 113–116, 171
Energy and Water Development Act (1979), 115
Environmental Contaminants Program (FWS), 76–79
Environmental Defense Fund (EDF)
    Avoyelles Sportsman's League lawsuit, 5, 9
    court hearing, 9–14
    court trial one on permits, 16–28
    court trial one ruling, 28–32
    court trial two on WOTUS, 46–51
    EPA meeting on WOTUS, 6, 8–9
    trial two ruling, 51–56
    wetland science to Jim Tripp, 14–16
    wetlands determination, 42–44
environmental impact statements (EIS)
    about, 118
    ESA Section 10 permit, 260–261
    Navy OLF near Pocosin Lakes NWR, 424–432
    northern spotted owl, 123, 124, 127
        Clinton requesting new, 224–229, 230–233
    timber harvests, 117–118, 175, 178
    Trinity River salmon flows, 244
Environmental Protection Agency (EPA)
    Avoyelles Parish floodplain clearing, 6, 8–14
    CWA authority, 32–33
    EPA included in complaint, 10–11
    Waters of the United States, 6–8, 26, 54–55
    Clean Water Act authority of Administrator, 11–12, 32–33, 461
    CWA authority of Corps versus EPA and FWS, 10–14, 32–33, 52–54
    Department of Justice deciding, 11, 13–14, 32–33
    permit program authority, 4, 10–14, 28–32
    Endangered Species Committee, 112

evidentiary hearing intervenor status, 176
Marine Shale Processors, 56–57
placer mining Section 404 permits, 86
San Francisco Estuary Project, 246
Tellico Dam project, 114
Yazoo Backwater Pumps project, 461–464
  public hearing, 465–466
  veto, 465–468
EPA. *See* Environmental Protection Agency
ESA. *See* Endangered Species Act
Espy, Mike, 220
Estes, Charlie, 98
Everglades, Florida
  about, 292
  DOJ lawsuit over phosphorous, 293–295
  phosphorous and ecosystem, 292
  Everglades Agricultural Area (EAA), 293, 295
  Everglades National Park, 293, 295, 298
  established, 296
  human settlement effects, 295–300
    8.5 Square Mile Area, 297–300
    exotic pets released, 300
    indigenous people, 296–297
  Loxahatchee NWR, 292–293, 295
  restoring water flows, 297–300
    8.5 Square Mile Area, 297–300
  wildlife, 299–300
    exotic pets released, 300
Everson, Margaret, 511
Exxon Valdez tanker aground, 60–61, 101

Farm Fish, Inc., Yazoo City, Mississippi, xvii
Fastabend, General, 342
Faye, John, 138, 219
Federal Advisory Committee Act (FACA), 137
Federal Ecosystem Management Assessment Team (FEMAT), 224, 230, 231, 237
Federal Executive Institute (FEI), 186–189
Federal Highway Administration (FHWA), 431
federal land management without accountability, 118, 178
Federal Lands Policy Management Act (FLPMA), 139
Federal Law Enforcement Training Center (Glynco, Georgia), 97, 314
Federal Water Pollution Control Act (1972)
  Clean Water Act amendments
    authority in Administrator of the EPA, 11–12
    ruling on normal practice exemptions, 29–30
    ruling on wetland importance, 30–32
    Waters of the United States expanded by, 6
The Federalist (Madison, Hamilton, and Jay), 187–188
Federighi, Doug, 519
First Nations of Canada and Boreal Forests, 505
  tar sands mining, 505–506
Fish, Wildlife and Parks (FWP)
  Acting Assistant Secretary David P. Smith, 387–388
  Assistant Secretary Craig Manson, 313, 381, 438 (*see also* Manson, Craig)
  Deputy Assistant Secretary Julie MacDonald, 404–405 (*see also* MacDonald, Julie A.)
  Assistant Secretary Don Barry, 240
  Assistant Secretary George Frampton, 233, 237, 240
  Deputy Assistant Secretary Don Barry, 233
  Assistant Secretary Lyle Laverty (*see* Laverty, Lyle)
  Assistant Secretary Michael Hayden
    enforcement of taking restrictions, 201–204
    post-hearing brief changes, 180–184
    preservation plan for owl, 195
  Assistant Secretary Ray Arnett, 61
Fish and Wildlife Act (1956), 360–361
Fish and Wildlife Coordination Act (FWCA; 1934)
  Corps providing FWS Report on impacts, 3–4, 39
  FWS environmental staff as advisors, 110
  Yazoo Area Pump Study, 61–65
  Yazoo Basin Corps projects evaluation, 39
Fish Car Era of population restoration, 88–89
fish spawning and nursery areas
  arid climate silvery minnow, 319–320, 322, 324–325
  California floodplains, 521–522, 523–524
  Missouri River spring rise, 341, 349
  wetlands
    broadcast spawners, 19, 31
    Central Valley, California, 241–242
    Klamath Basin, 163
    land clearing versus, 19, 31
    larval fish, 18, 23, 524
    Sacramento–San Joaquin River Delta, 241–242
    Yazoo Delta, 14, 16, 17–19, 24, 47
    Yazoo Delta court ruling, 31
Fisheries Academy (Leetown, West Virginia), 97, 98

INDEX   559

new facility, 98, 99–100
Fisheries Program of FWS
    about, 88–89
    Assistant Director Gary Edwards, 87
    China visit and Tiananmen Square, 100–101
    conservation history, 88–95
        conservationists funding conservation, 94
        Fish Car Era of population restoration, 88–89
    D.C. Booth National Historic Fish Hatchery, 402
    Deputy Assistant Director Dale Hall, 87, 97, 105
    divisions of hatcheries and fisheries assistance, 97
    lobbying and budget increase by Bill Maxon, 97–98
    partnerships via ecosystem teams, 302–303, 307–308
    training at Fisheries Academy, 97, 98
    new facility, 98, 99–100
fishing for sport. *See* sport hunting and fishing
Fitzpatrick, Lesley, 359–360
flood control
    about, 39–41
    Cache River Flood Control Project, 9, 11
    central and southern Florida, 298
    Flood Control Acts
        1941 and 1965 Flood Control Acts, 64, 65, 459, 460
        1944 Flood Control Act, 336–337
    flood of 1927
        flood protection philosophy, 39–40
        Missouri River basin, 335
    Missouri River, 351
    Sacramento River flood control projects, 242–243, 521–522
    Yazoo Backwater Pumps project
        about, 41–42, 61–62, 459, 464
        about flood control, 39–41
        CEQ elevation, 65, 461, 464
        Corps reviving project, 63, 459–468
        EPA review, 461–464
        EPA veto, 465–468
        FWS *Environmental Overview* report, 40–41, 62
        FWS *Yazoo Area Pump Study*, 61–65
        soil types, 44
        wetland definition, 42–43
        wetland future development, 41–42
floodplains of California, 521–528
Floodplains: The River's Pantry (H.D. Hall), 523–527
Florida. *See* Everglades, Florida

Floyd, Charles R., 274
Ford, Jerome, 379, 451
"foreseeable future" as term in law, 450, 451, 452–453
Forest Plan (Northwest), 224–229, 230–232, 237–238, 240
Forest Plan Office, 240
Forest Service (FS)
    Babbitt visit to the Northwest, 220
    Chief Jack Ward Thomas, 228, 231
    Klamath FS grazing operation, 163–164
    National Forest Management Act, 117
    National Wildlife Refuge Improvement Act, 278–280
    northern spotted owl
        Clinton-requested SEIS, 225–229, 230–233
        ecosystem health indicator, 129
        environmental impact statement, 117–118
        Interagency Implementation Team, 225–226
        Interagency Scientific Committee, 116, 119–128
        Northwest Forest Plan, 224–229, 230–232, 237–238, 240
        old-growth forest importance, 129–130 (*see also* old-growth forests)
        recovery plan, 178, 198
        supplemental EIS, 123, 124, 127
        timber sales, 116–117
    Old Growth Wildlife Research and Development Program, 122
    oversight by Department of Agriculture, 238
    Regional Guide for Pacific Northwest Region (1984), 122–123
Forest Summit, 205, 210, 220–223, 239
    Federal Ecosystem Management Assessment Team, 224
    information incorporated by Jack Ward Thomas, 223
    Northwest Forest Plan, 224–229, 230–232, 237–238, 240
Forsman, Eric D., 120–128
Forsythe, Steve
    about, 6, 465
    State Supervisor for Ecological Services, Florida, 300
    Vicksburg FWS Ecological Services Office, 3, 4, 5
    Yazoo floodplain forests cleared, 5
    court hearing, 9–14
    EPA involvement, 10–11
    EPA meeting, 6, 8–9

560　COMPELLED

Ophelia tract fish spawning proof,
　　17–19
　trial, 16–17, 19–21, 25, 29, 31, 45
　wetland science to Jim Tripp, 15–16
　wetlands determination defense, 43
Frampton, George, 233, 237, 240
Frank, Angela, 512–513, 516
Frederick, David Charles, 57–59, 133
Frederickson, Leigh, 15–16
freshwater mussels, 286, 291
　commercial musseling, 286
　Japanese pearl culture industry, 288
　musselers arrested, 286, 288
　　news conference, 289–291
　　prosecution, 289
Frugé, Doug, 17
FS. *See* Forest Service
Fulgham, Tom, 495, 511, 512
Fults, Dan, 249, 251, 256
Fund for Animals suit over ESA candidate
　　species, 205–207, 211–212, 240,
　　264–266
FWCA. *See* Fish and Wildlife Coordination
　　Act
FWP. *See* Fish, Wildlife and Parks
FWS. *See* U.S. Fish and Wildlife Service

Galat, David, 340
Galveston Bay Area Navigation Study, 74–79
Garamendi, John, 254–255, 257
Garner, Monty, xiv
Garr, Elizabeth, 225–226
Gaschler, Kevin, 511
Gates, Bill, 508
Gilmore, Bob, 79–80
Ginsburg, Ruth Bader, 259, 520
gleying in soils, 44
global warming, 391, 440
　greenhouse gases, 391, 477
　House Select Committee on Energy
　　Independence and Global
　　Warming, 439–440
　congressional testimony, 439–441
　melting of arctic ice cap, 391, 393, 404,
　　440, 442–445, 477
　ice ecoregions in future, 451
　polar bears (*see* polar bears)
　USGS sea ice reports, 442–443, 444, 452
gnatcatcher, 261–264
God Squad, 112–113, 171
　about evidentiary hearings, 171–172
　BLM request to convene, 168–171
　decision on owl critical habitat,
　　184–186
　evidentiary hearing, 171–180
　post-hearing brief changes, 180–184

　post-hearing report, 184–186
　legal counsel Tom Sansonetti, 169,
　　172–180, 181–182, 184
　load carried by Barry and Teeter, 189
　silvery minnow, 330
　Tellico Dam and Grayrocks Oil Refinery,
　　113–116, 174
Goddard, Ken, 148
gold rushes and mining
　Alaska gold rush, 80
　　placer mining, 85–86
　California gold rush, 242
　　placer mining raising stream beds,
　　　242
Gorham, Emerson, 291
Gorton, Slade, 194–195
Gosselink, Jim, 22
Gould, Gordon I., Jr., 120–128
Gould, Rowan, 312, 379, 380, 439, 487
government training programs. *See* training
Grand Canyon National Park, 353
　Bennett leading camping trip, 354–356
Grant, Mrs. (teacher), xii
Grant, Ulysses S., 88
Graybeal, Nancy, 225–226, 231, 234–235
Grayrocks Oil Refinery, 113–116, 174
Green, Zack, 290
Greenwalt, Judy, 33, 284, 377, 378
Greenwalt, Lynn
　advice on Julie MacDonald, 386
　Congressman John Dingell supporting,
　　35–38
　director nominated by president, 35–36
　Director of FWS, 33–34
　　Alaska pipeline, 37–38
　　career FWS employee, 33, 377
　　Fish and Wildlife Service name restored,
　　　35
　friendship with this hero, 284
　first meeting, 33–34
　swearing-in of Director Hall, 377,
　　378
Gremillion, Lyle, 23, 46
Griles, Steve, 351–352, 389
Grisoli, William, 345, 350, 351
grizzly bear ESA protection, 375–376
Groat, Chip, 392
Grochau, Earl, 511
Grohne, Dave, 508, 509, 518–519
Grone, Phil, 425–426
Grover, Jerry, 284
Grumbles, Ben, 464–465
Guadagno, Rich, 314
Guinee, Roger, 258
Gulf Coast Restoration Trust Fund, 503–504
"gumbo" clay, 44

INDEX 561

Gunderson, A. Grant, 120–128, 177, 231–232
Gutierrez, R. J. "Rocky," 138

habitat
 arctic tundra, 59–60, 84
 barred owl expanding into spotted owl's, 238
 BP penalties paying for, 503–504
 created after BP oil rig explosion, 485–489
 critical habitat (see critical habitat)
 decisions marred by Julie MacDonald, 407, 408–410
 drivers of habitat creation, 59
 duck stamp funds, 73, 92
 Ducks Unlimited funds, 92–93
 flood control mitigation impact report, 40–41
 FWS single species approach to ESA, 110
 Klamath suckers (see Klamath sucker critical habitat)
 Lake Ophelia tract ecosystem, 14, 16, 17–19, 22, 24, 47
 loss of
  endangered species, 212, 214–215
  northern spotted owl, 178
  not prohibited, 144, 232, 362
 "mobile" habitat of migrating sandbars, 346
 National Wildlife Refuge System, 279
 North American Model for Wildlife Conservation, 92–95, 303, 480, 512
 northern spotted owl (see northern spotted owl)
 population trend surrogate legally, 453–454
 preservation incentive, 46
 private ownership percentage, 160, 308
 Sacramento–San Joaquin River Delta, 241–242
 "take" including habitat modification, 200–204
 voluntary actions for improvement, 144, 362
 water is not habitat, 242, 324
  California floodplains, 526–528
 wetlands classification report, 42–43
habitat conservation areas (HCAs)
 50-11-40 rule, 132, 177
  undermining in ESA hearing, 178
 Jamison strategy, 177
 larger blocks than owl habitat areas, 132–133
 Late Successional Reserves, 225
 matrix outside of, 132
habitat conservation plans (HCPs)

ESA Section 4(d) rule for gnatcatcher, 261–264
 multispecies ESA consultations, 258
 northern spotted owl, 125
  enforcing taking restrictions, 203
  ESA Section 4(d) rule for owls, 234
 Orange County, California, 259
Hagel, Jim, 494
Halcomb, Monty, 272, 289
Hall, Adam (son)
 father sworn in, 377, 378
 grandmother's death, 383
 waving goodbye, 105
Hall, Emily (daughter)
 birthday party, 352
 father sworn in, 377, 378
 FWS Director position, 362, 363, 364
 grandmother's death, 383
 not moving to D.C., 363, 385
 waving goodbye, 105
Hall, Erin (daughter)
 12th birthday, 151
 father sworn in, 377, 378
 grandmother's death, 383
 Hurricane Katrina, 367–371
 waving goodbye, 105
Hall, H. Dale
 background
  Air Force career, xiii–xiv, 367, 377, 422
  Appalachian culture, vii, xi
  bottomland hardwood wetlands, 4–6
  Kentucky education, xii, xiii, xiv–xvi
  Limnology Masters degree, xv–xvii, 159, 324
  Loyall along Cumberland River, xii
  parents, xi–xii
 death of father, xiii
 death of mother, 383–385
 employment
  about moving, promotions, and family, 87, 105–106
  D.C. mass transit subsidy, 386
  D.C. without family, 87, 363, 372, 385, 401
  Ducks Unlimited CEO (see Ducks Unlimited)
  Executive Assistant Debbie Doty Vess, 290
  Executive Assistant Pat Kennedy, 383
  Executive Assistant Pat Mitchell, 158, 209, 265
  fish farms, Yazoo City, Mississippi, xvii
  FWS Acting Regional Director, Southwest Region (see

562 COMPELLED

Southwest Region of FWS)
FWS Assistant Regional Director-ES, Portland (*see* Portland Regional FWS Office)
FWS Central Valley, California, water (*see* Central Valley, California, water)
FWS Clear Lake ES Supervisor (*see* Clear Lake, Texas)
FWS Deputy Regional Director (SES), 312, 316
FWS Deputy Regional Director, Southeast Region (*see* Southeast Region of FWS)
FWS Director (*see under* Directors, U.S. Fish and Wildlife Service)
FWS Fairbanks as interim Field Supervisor, 83–86
FWS Fisheries Deputy Assistant Director (*see* Fisheries Program of FWS)
FWS Geographic ARD for California and Klamath, 251
FWS Heritage Committee to preserve history, 283–284
FWS rescue of Erin and others, 367–371
FWS Retirees Association, 283–284
FWS retirement, 472–473
FWS senior executive service, 312, 316
FWS Vicksburg ES Office (*see* Vicksburg, Mississippi)
Google results, 416–417
lunch with President George W. Bush, 469–471
private dinner with Bruce Babbitt, 220
signature on listed species, 206
subpoena to testify, 45
White House dinner with Cousteau, 401
lessons
  collaborative conflict resolution model, 256
  compromises made, 43, 52
  destructive agreement, 118–119
  Emergency Wetlands Resources Act, 73–74
  Federal Register call for comments name, 147
  people working as a team, 311, 537–538
  teamwork and respect, vii–viii, 310, 534 (*see also* leadership; partnerships)
  wise use of resources rather than denying use, 85, 506
marriage to Sarah Reed, xvii, 411
  children, 32, 105, 377, 378
  Dale and Sarah Hall Legacy Fund, 531
  Ducks Unlimited CEO position, 484, 530
  Fairbanks, Alaska, trip, 83–86
  FWS Director position, 362–363, 372
  FWS Director retirement, 473
  FWS Director swearing-in, 376, 377, 378
  move to Portland, Oregon, 105–106
  move to Washington, D.C., 87
  rescue of Erin and others, 367–371
  White House functions, 401
scientist to naturalist
  Alaska wetlands, 61
  bottomland hardwood wetlands, 4–5, 22–23, 523–524
  federal agency cooperation, 156–157, 163–164
  giving information to public, 74–75
Hall, Herbert (father)
  critically wounded in Second World War, xi
  death, xiii
  Greatest Generation, vii
  Harlan County, Kentucky, xi
  marriage to Frances Colwell, xi–xii
  children, xii
Hall, Ina Frances (Colwell; mother)
  death, 383–385
  death of Herbert Hall, xiii
  Greatest Generation, vii
  Kentucky childhood, vii, xi
  marriage to Herbert Hall, xi–xii
  children, xii
  polio in childhood, xi
Hall, Larry
  birth, xii
  death of mother, 384
  marriage to Judy Smithers, 384
Hall, Sarah (Reed; wife)
  Bunkie, Louisiana, hometown, xvi–xvii, 45
  marriage to Dale Hall, xvii
  children, 32, 105, 377, 378
  Dale alone in D.C., 87, 363, 372, 385
  Dale and Sarah Hall Legacy Fund, 531

INDEX 563

Dale in California and Klamath, 251
death of Dale's mother, 383–384
death of Sam Hamilton, 479
Ducks Unlimited CEO position, 484
Ducks Unlimited family, 530
Ducks Unlimited National Convention, 513
Ducks Unlimited retirement, 530–531, 532
Fairbanks, Alaska, trip, 83–86
FWS Director position, 362–363, 364, 372
FWS Director retirement, 473
FWS Director swearing-in, 376, 377, 378
Mother's Day delayed, 455
move to Portland, Oregon, 105
White House functions, 401
Yazoo floodplain site, 5, 45
Hamilton, Alexander, 187–188
Hamilton, Sam
death, 478–479
Erin Hall and others rescued, 370–371
FWS Director, 478, 479
name only, 361
FWS Director Dale Hall team, 380
Southeast Assistant Regional Director, 272
Southeast Ecological Services, 272
Southeast Regional Director, 272–273, 300
adding Steve Thompson to team, 278, 280, 282
Geographic/Programmatic FWS structure, 277–278
Hall Ecosystem Approach to management memo, 306
Navy OLF near Pocosin Lakes NWR, 424–426
promotion of Dale Hall to Regional Director, 315–316
promotion of Dale Hall to senior executive service, 312
Theodore Roosevelt IV visit, 304–305
World Trade Center plane crashes, 313–314
Yazoo Backwater Pumps project, 461–467
Hankla, Dave, 300
Harding, Warren G., 397
Hardy, Joe, 3, 4, 5, 28
"harm" in the definition of "take," 201
Harrison, Adlene, 6, 8–14
Haskett, Geoff, 272, 280, 317, 372
Hastert, Dennis, 402
Hatch, Orrin, 258–259
Hatch Act, 396

Hatfield-Adams Amendment, 127
Hayden, Michael
Assistant Secretary for FWP, 180, 195, 201
enforcement of taking restrictions, 201–204
post-hearing brief changes, 180–184
preservation plan for owl, 195
Hayes, David, 265
Haynes, Richard, 175
Hays, David W., 120–128
HCPs. *See* habitat conservation plans
Heaps, Chip, 510
Hebard, Charles, 274
Heffernan, Dave, 282
Hegedus, Emily (Hall; daughter)
birthday party, 352
father sworn in, 377, 378
FWS Director position, 362, 363, 364
grandmother's death, 383
not moving to D.C., 363, 385
waving goodbye, 105
Heintz, Theodore, Jr., 138
Henry, Mary, 340, 342, 344
Hess, Edwin, xv–xvi
Hester, Bob, 482, 483
Hickman, Gary, 58
Hill, Barbara, 231–232
Hill, Mrs. (teacher), xii
Hinckley, Thomas, 7, 44
Hinman, Dave, 518–519
"Historical Perspective on Northern Spotted Owl Management" (Interagency Scientific Committee; 1990), 120–128
history of conservation
overview, 89–95
citizen conservationists, 480–481
examples of, 497, 500, 505, 507–508
volunteer contributions (*see* volunteers)
conservationists funding conservation, 92–95, 480–481, 498, 511–512
federal dollars matched by two, 503
duck stamps, 92
first day of sale, 402, 403–404
habitat management funds, 73, 92, 498
National Duck Stamp Contest, 402–404
Ducks Unlimited, 480–481
Everglades, 295–297
first federal wildlife management law, 91
Fish Car Era of population restoration, 88–89

564   COMPELLED

FWS careers as callings, 96
    employee dedication, 264–265
FWS special agents, 286–288
    migratory waterfowl slaughter, 91, 287
Missouri River, 335–339
National Conservation Training Center, 282–283
National Fish and Wildlife Foundation, 401
Natural Community Conservation Planning Act (California), 261
    ESA Section 4(d) rule for gnatcatcher, 262–264
North American Model for Wildlife Conservation, 92–95, 480, 512
    conservationist Theodore Roosevelt, 303
    northern spotted owl, 120–128
    Pelican Island National Bird Sanctuary, 89, 90
    public trust in government, 118, 186, 237–238, 259, 537
    right to fish, hunt, and gather food, 89
    Sport Fish Restoration Act, 36, 94
    timber harvesting targets, 116–117
    trust doctrine of public ownership, 68, 70, 82, 89–90
        Seattle Audubon suit settlement, 118–119, 232–233
        treated as if locally owned, 178
    Wildlife Restoration Act, 93
Hobbs, Gary, 371
Hodges, Jimmy, xiv
Hoeveler, William, 293–295
Hogan, Matt, 366, 378, 380, 418
Holland, Denny, 284
Holmberg, Nevin, 67–74
Holt Collier NWR, 468
Holthausen, Richard S. "Holt"
    Forest Plan, 230–231
    spotted owl recovery team, 138, 192–193, 197
Hook, Donal, 49–51
Hopkins, Margaret, 378–379, 439, 451
Hornor, Govan, 511
Horton, Mike, 231–232
House of Representatives. *See* Congress
Houston, David, 245, 248
Houston, Douglas B., 120–128
Houston Post journalist Harold Scarlett, 74–75, 77, 87–88
Houston Ship Channel project, 74–79
Hoyt, Rogers, 518–519, 529–530, 531
Hruby, Mike, 510
Huffman, Terry, 8, 59
Hulbert, Jim, 482

hunting. *See* sport hunting
Huntley Manor (Italy), xiv
Hurricane Camille, 367
Hurricane Katrina, 366–371
Hutton, Patti, 147

Incorvati, Dave, xiv
indigenous hunting of polar bears, 436, 437–438. *See also* Native Americans
Inhofe, Jim, 365–366, 371
Inspector General and Julie MacDonald, 383, 386–387
    congressional requests for investigation, 409–410
    IG reports, 404–408, 410
    integrity in science, 382–383
Interagency Implementation Team (IIT), 225–228, 234
Interagency Scientific Committee (ISC), 116
    FWS Spotted Owl Coordinator, 116, 133
    spotted owl management report (1990), 120–128, 177
        critical habitat designation versus, 143–144
        economic analysis coverage, 222
        management strategy, 130–133
        old-growth forest importance, 129–130
        "Thomas Report," 129, 143
        undermining 50-11-40 rule in hearing, 178
    via interagency agreement, 119–120, 128
interior least tern, 339, 346, 349
international trade in wildlife and CITES, 434–435
interstate wildlife management by Lacey Act, 90–91, 286, 288
Irwin, Larry L., 120–128
ISC. *See* Interagency Scientific Committee
Italy in Air Force tour of duty, xiv

Jackson, Gerry, 221–222
Jackson, Henry, 274
Jacobs, Bob, 226, 227, 230, 231
Jacobsen, Bob, 83, 86
Jacobson, Robert, 340
James, Curtis, 3, 10, 465
Jamison, Cy
    Director of the BLM, 119, 166–167, 168
    forests should be managed as tree farms, 171
    Interagency Scientific Committee, 119–128, 177
    timber sales and northern spotted owl
        BLM paying for review, 193, 194
        Committee decision, 184–186

INDEX   565

evidentiary hearing, 175, 176
God Squad convened, 167–169, 186
Jamison strategy, 175, 177–179, 182, 184, 190
Jamison strategy court ruling, 197–198
Lujan plan bypassing ESA, 190
post-hearing brief changes, 180–184
post-hearing report, 184–186
Jantzen, Bob, 70–73, 79, 87
Jasper, Bruce, 510
Jay, John, 187–188
Jenson, Tom, 247
Jewell, Sally, 196, 422
Jobes, Charles and Patty, 510
    hand-carved decoys, 530, 532
Johnson, Bob
    Colorado River lower basin drought, 354–358
    Commissioner of BOR, 431
    lunch with President George W. Bush, 469–471
    Regional Director BOR, Arizona, 319
Johnson, Edwin, 94
Johnson, Lyndon, 186
Johnson, Norma Holloway, 201
Johnson, Stephen, 462
Jones, Marshall
    Acting Regional Director Dale Hall, 316, 317
    Deputy Director to Director Dale Hall, 378, 379–380
    polar bear listed as endangered, 390
Jones, Paul Tudor, 402

Kaplan, Joel, 210–219, 458
Katrina, hurricane, 366–371
Katz, Jacob, 525–528
Kaufman, Nancy, 316, 317, 327–328
Kelsey, Linda, 282
Keltch, Lynn, xiv
Kempka, Pattie, 496
Kempthorne, Dirk
    Arctic NWR oil leases, 395–400
    ESA regulation updates, 411–413, 417, 418, 420–421
        policy time with POTUS, 413–415
        White House action, 419–422
    lunch with President George W. Bush, 469–471
    polar bear as threatened
        briefings, 393, 394
        Coca-Cola Company, 433–434, 459
        FWS Director will only sign listing package, 447–448
        killer bear PR firm, 433–434
        listing as threatened, 394–395, 445–448, 457–459
        meetings twice a week, 441–442, 445, 447–448
        "Mother's Day Massacre," 455–457, 469
        not listing as threatened, 449–457
        resignation letter ready, 458
        White House action, 445–446, 456, 457–459
    remembering people's names, 388
    Secretary of the Interior, 388
        meetings with, 411
Kennedy, James Cox "Jim"
    citizen conservationist, 507–508, 536
    Ducks Unlimited commitment, 507–508
    flying Dick Cheney to Wyoming, 517
    hunting with Scalia and Cheney, 518–519, 520
    Wetlands America Trust president, 507, 509
Kennedy, Pat, 383
Kent, Jack, 56–57
Kentucky education, xii, xiii, xiv–xvi
Kessler, Gladys, 337
Keys, John, 323
Kilpatrick, Karen, 281
King, Carla, 377
King, Martin Luther, Jr., 499
King, Mitch
    death of Sam Hamilton, 479
    Soil Conservation Service projects, 4
    Southeast Regional Office, 282
    swearing-in of FWS Director Hall, 377
    Vicksburg FWS Ecological Services Office, 3
King, Torey, 511
Kircher, Tammi and Ed, 511
Klamath Basin
    about beauty of, 152–155
    Geographic ARD Dale Hall, 251
    managing grazing to biological needs, 163–164
Klamath Project Act (1964), 162
Klamath sucker critical habitat
    about beauty of Klamath Basin, 152–155
    BOR and FWS cooperating, 157
    BOR managing water to biological needs, 156–157
    drought drying lakes, 157–160
    fish above and below dams, 156
    public education, 160, 161
    FWS sued to designate, 161
    public education, 161–163
    Klamath Basin Ecosystem Office for public contact, 161–163

Klamath Project Operations Plan, 161
Klamath Project to drain water, 155–156
Kuchel's Klamath Project Act, 162
   land leasing for agriculture, 162
Klamath Tribe, 154
Klee, Ann, 351, 355–356, 411
Klinger, David, 147, 197
Knapp, Bill, 101
Knowles, Don
   spotted owl recovery team, 136, 137, 139
      final recovery plan, 208
      Lujan plan bypassing ESA, 190–196
      meetings post–Lujan spotted owl plan divorce, 196–197
      providing win for president, 190–192
      "suggestions" to Turner and Brennan, 139, 143
   team man for Bruce Babbitt, 219
Kobetich, Gail
   hero for people listening to, 262
   Klamath Project drought, 157–158, 159, 161
Kohl, Steve, 100
Kostro, Ed ("Fidel") and Linda, xiv
Kramer, Karla, 133
Kratz, Jacob, 525–528
Kruse, Casey, 346
Kruse, John, 511
Kuchel, Thomas, 162

LaBorde, Cookie, 48–49
LaBorde, Ken "Nookie," 48
Laborde, Luke, 510
Lacey Act (1900), 90–91, 286, 288
Lahay, Harold, 24
Lake Ophelia tract. *See also* Avoyelles Parish
   about, 14–15, 17, 22, 23
   soil types, 44
Lambou, Vic, 24
Land Acquisition Priority System (LAPS), 99
Lane County Audubon Society et al. v. Cy Jamison, et al. (1992), 197–198
Lanich, Steve, 247
LaRoe, Ted, 259–260
Late Successional Reserves (LSRs), 225, 229
Lathrop, Kenneth, 138
Laverty, Lyle
   Assistant Secretary for FWP, 438
   ESA updates memo to, 420
   lunch with President George W. Bush, 469–471
   polar bear as threatened, 448, 459
      meetings with Secretary Kempthorne, 442, 447–448
      proposed rule delivered to, 448
      Secretary not listing as threatened, 449–451, 455
law enforcement
   ARD for Law Enforcement Dave McMullen, 147, 164–165, 204
   ARD for Law Enforcement Monty Halcomb, 272
   Flight 93 death (9/11/2001), 314
   funding for owl cases, 204
   FWS enforcement of taking restrictions, 201–204
   FWS Wildlife Forensics Lab, 148, 283
   Justice Scalia's travels, 515, 517
   Louisiana state troopers saving Erin Hall and others, 370–371
   musselers arrested, 286, 288
      prosecution, 289
   special agents at public hearings, 147–148
      (*see also* special agents of FWS)
   training at Federal Law Enforcement Training Center, 96–97, 314
   voluntary compliance as ultimate objective, 165
laws
   biological opinion into law, 327–333
   career employees advocating for legislation, 396
   compromises made, 43, 52, 99
   conservation history, 89–95
      first federal wildlife management law, 91
      migratory waterfowl slaughter, 91, 287
      Pelican Island National Wildlife Refuge, 89, 90
   critical habitat designation as law, 109, 134, 143, 163
   empowering innovation, 90
   ESA recovery plans not law, 137, 196–197
      (*see also* Endangered Species Act)
   executive branch and personal opinions, 396
   fairness to all under the law, 187
   Fisheries legislation lobbying, 97–98
   interstate wildlife management by Lacey Act, 90–91, 286, 288
   Migratory Bird Treaty Act, 91, 92, 286–287, 426, 485
   Natural Community Conservation Planning Act (California), 261
      ESA Section 4(d) rule for gnatcatcher, 262–264
   negative impact allowed on habitat or species, 144, 232, 362

regulations do not prohibit, they require, 362
right to fish, hunt, and gather food, 89
  2nd Amendment, 188–189
  servants not lords, 160–161
  terms used, 143
    foreseeable future, 450, 451, 452–453
    "harm" in the definition of "take," 201
    reasonably certain to occur, 450
    "take" defined by ESA, 201
  voluntary compliance as ultimate objective, 165, 361–362
  Watt asking for wetlands protection, 68–74
    Emergency Wetlands Resources Act, 73–74
lawsuit by Seattle Audubon, 118–119, 232–233
leadership
  demanding respect and teamwork, viii, 76
  depending on dedication of those below, 239
  Ducks Unlimited style of, 533–537
  effective leader of civilians, 71
  integrity as supreme quality, 446, 447, 535
  "Leadership for a Democratic Society" course, 186–189
  lifting risk off shoulders of subordinates, 159
  memo on Ecosystem Approach opportunities, 306–310
  moving people toward accomplishment, 483
  position and people as priorities, 75–76, 88
  real power is that which we share, 164
  traits of great leaders, 533–537
  Vicksburg trial support, 27–28, 45
Lear, Tom, xiv
legislation. *See* Congress; laws
Lemon, Rick, 99–100, 282–284
Leopold, Aldo, 116, 308
Leshy, John, 254–255, 257
levee construction. *See* flood control
Lewis, Bruce, 482, 501, 515
Lewis, Lynn, 340
Lewis, Steve, 163
Lieberman, Joe, 441
Lineger, Ted, 466
Lint, Joseph B., 120–128, 177–178
LMV (Lower Mississippi Valley), 280–281
Locke, Bob, xiv
logging. *See* timber harvesting
Lohoefener, Renne
  Assistant Director for Endangered Species, 390

Middle Rio Grande biological opinion into law, 328
Missouri River ESA needs, 340
polar bear listed as endangered, 390–391
Regional Director, Portland, 391
Lott, Trent, 333, 466
Louisiana
  Alexandria courtroom of Nauman Scott, 45
  Avoyelles Parish floodplain clearing (*see* Avoyelles Parish)
  Bunkie Christmas conference call, 394
  Bunkie hometown of Sarah Hall, xvi–xvii, 5, 45
  Bunkie marriage of Sarah and Dale Hall, xvii
  Bunkie sign-builder, 367
  citizen conservationists making history, 56–57
  cuisine, 45–46, 518
  Department of Wildlife and Fisheries, 17, 24
  Forestry Commission, 24
  habitat created after BP oil rig explosion, 485–489
  Hurricane Camille, 367
  Hurricane Katrina, 366–371
  Marine Shale Processors company, 56–57
  rescue of Erin Hall and others, 367–371
  volunteer enthusiasm, 510
    Cajun Navy, 510
Louisiana State University (LSU), xvi–xvii, 24, 101
Louisiana Wildlife and Fisheries, 370
Louisiana Wildlife Federation (LWF), 5, 9. *See also* Osborne, Michael
Lower Colorado River MSCP
  about Colorado River, 353
    Colorado River Interstate Compact, 353–354, 358–359
  drought, 354–360
    no drought while camping, 354–356
  multi-species conservation plan, 357, 359–360
  negotiations, 357–359
Lower Mississippi Valley (LMV), 280–281
Loxahatchee NWR as "overlay" refuge, 292–293, 295
Lucas, Laird, 323–327
Lujan, Manuel
  ESA candidate species lawsuit, 205–207
  northern spotted owl recovery team, 136
  final recovery plan, 200, 207–208
  Lujan plan bypassing ESA, 190–196
  meetings post–Lujan spotted owl plan divorce, 196

owl "conversation" plan, 195
"Preservation Plan for the Northern Spotted Owl," 195–196
Northern Spotted Owl v. Lujan, 109–110
Secretary of the Interior, 135–136, 137
timber sales
    evidentiary hearing, 171–172, 176, 177
    God Squad convened, 168–171
    post-hearing brief changes, 180–184
    post-hearing report, 184
Lumadue, Robert, 286, 288
Lundquist, Andrew, 518–519
Luthi, Randall, 439
LWF (Louisiana Wildlife Federation), 5, 9. *See also* Osborne, Michael

MacDonald, Julie A.
    about, 380–381, 382
    after Craig Manson resignation, 381, 382–383, 385
    DOI warned, 385
    driven by policy not science, 382, 404–407
        decisions reviewed, 407, 408–410
        edits to documents monitored, 388
        lingering repercussions, 414, 438
    Inspector General investigation, 383, 386–387, 389
        congressional requests for, 409–410
        IG reports, 404–408, 410
        prohibited from contacting FWS employees, 387–388
    resignation of, 408
MacGaffin, Pete, 510
Madison, James, 187–188
Madison, Mark, ix, 284
Maillet, John, 23
Makalak people, 152–154
Malheur NWR occupation, 196
Manson, Craig
    Assistant Secretary for FWP, 313, 381, 438
    Deputy Assistant Secretary Julie MacDonald, 380, 381, 382–383, 385, 405, 406
    Grand Canyon rafting email, 355–356
    Missouri River ESA needs, 334, 341–343, 344, 349, 350, 351, 352, 359
    Navy OLF near Pocosin Lakes NWR, 426
Mantell, Michael, 263
Marcot, Bruce, 120–128
Marcus, Felicia, 249, 256, 522
Marine Mammal Protection Act (MMPA), 34, 36, 437
Marine Shale Processors company, 56–57
Maritz, Steve, 508, 509

Markey, Ed, 439–440
Marshall, R. C., 42
Martin, Bill
    "D.C. marsh gas," 378
    Deputy Regional Director, Portland, 106
    enforcement of taking regulations, 204
    northern spotted owl recovery plan, 197
    retirement from FWS, 240
Materne, Mike, 23
matrix outside habitat conservation areas, 132
Maxey, Ken, 323–324
Maxon, Bill, 97–98, 100
Mays, Kent, 138
McAninch, Jay, ix
McCabe, Charles, 62, 465
McCain, John, 392, 477
McFarland, Mrs. (teacher), xii
McGill, Jim, 377
McGinty, Katie, 228, 230, 237
McKean, John, 121
McKevitt, Jim, 243–247
McKnight, Sid, 21–22
McMahen, Luett, 371
McMullen, Dave, 147, 164–165, 204
Meehan, Rosa, 390
Memphis home of Ducks Unlimited, 499–500
    Memphis Brooks Museum of Art, 403
    Pyramid as Bass Pro Shop, 492–494
    Ducks Unlimited space, 492, 493, 494–495, 497–498
Mendoza, Carlos, 75
Mesi, Mike, xiv
Meslow, E. Charles, 174
Meyer, Philip A., 175
Meyers, Gary, 290
Michaels, Jim, 166
Microsoft COB John Thompson, 508
Middle Rio Grande (MRG) River
    about, 321–322
    about Rio Grande River, 320
    biological opinion into law, 327–333
    Bureau of Reclamation, 319
    re-regulating dams, 322
    water release by BOR proposed, 322–323
    water release lawsuit, 323–327
    water release rulings, 326, 329–330
    New Mexico/Texas Rio Grande Compact, 322
    silvery minnow, 318–323, 324–325
        fix for minnow problem, 329–333
    tour of Rio Grande by FWS, 330–331
Migratory Bird Conservation Fund, 73
Migratory Bird Hunting and Conservation Stamp, 92, 498. *See also* duck stamps

Migratory Bird Treaty Act (MBTA; 1918), 91, 92, 286–287, 426, 485
no incidental take, 426
migratory waterfowl
Boreal Forests, 505
habitat created after BP oil spill, 486–488
management via science and habitat, 498
protection of, 91, 92, 93
slaughter of, 91, 287
Miller, Gary, 166, 174, 231–232
Miller, George, 246–247
mining
E.I. DuPont in Okefenokee Swamp, 275–276
placer mining
raising stream beds, 242
Section 404 permits, 85–86
tar sands mining, 505–506
Minnich, Don, 70–71, 72
minnow. *See* silvery minnow
Misso, Bob, 57, 465
Missouri Basin Power Project, 114
Missouri River ESA needs
about assignment, 334–335, 339
about Missouri River, 335–339
Corps biological assessment, 345–347
FWS-Corps partnership, 346–347, 351–352
Missouri River Recovery Implementation Committee, 347
ESA wildlife, 339, 341, 346, 349
pallid sturgeon never funded, 350–351
FWS biological opinion, 339–352
Corps implementation, 352
FWS Director Dale Hall, 366
team, 340, 343–345, 348, 349–350, 352
team leader Robyn Thorson, 334–335, 340, 348–349, 352
reasonable and prudent alternative (RPA) action, 322, 332
responsibilities of Corps versus BOR, 336–339, 350–351
Mitchell, Pat, 158, 209, 265
Moellering, John, 8–9, 19
Montna, Al, 510–511, 522
Moorman, Tom, 486
Morgenweck, Ralph, 334, 342, 344
Moriarty, Marvin, 272, 310
Morris, Bill, 499–500
Morris, Jeannie, 495, 498
Morris, John L. "Johnny"
background, 490–492, 493, 536

Bass Pro Shops founder, 403, 492, 497
Bass Pro Shop Pyramid, 492–494
DU space in Pyramid, 492, 493, 494–495, 497–498
Bassmaster Tournament series, 403, 490–491
citizen conservationist, 403, 497–498
contacting DU CEO Dale Hall, 492–493
DU National Convention keynote speaker, 495–496
duck stamp first day of sale, 403–404
NASCAR–DU association, 495–497
Wetlands America Trust board, 509
Morrison, Dick, 77
Morse, Mike, 371
Morton, Rogers, 36
Mosher, Jim, 438
Mount St. Helens, 59
Moy, Ed, 363–364, 365, 387
MSCP (multi-species conservation plan), 357
negotiations, 357–360
Mulder, Barry Stuart
FWS Spotted Owl Coordinator, 116, 133
Clinton-requested new SEIS, 230, 231–232
ESA Section 4(d) for owl, 237
liaison Mel Schamberger, 141
Lujan recovery plan bypassing ESA, 190–191
meetings post–Lujan spotted owl plan divorce, 197
recovery plan and Babbitt, 219
Interagency Scientific Committee, 120–128, 177
Northwest Forest Plan, 230, 231–232
scientific reputation more important than politics, 177
Mulroy, Pat, 356–357, 359
multi-species conservation plan (MSCP), 357
negotiations, 357–360
Murphy, Dennis Daniel, 120–128
Museus, Marc, 295
Muskie, Edmund, 12
mussels, 286, 291
commercial musseling, 286
Japanese pearl culture industry, 288
musselers arrested, 286, 288
news conference, 289–291
prosecution, 289
Myers, Mark
adding Steve Amstrup to polar bear team, 442
lunch with President George W. Bush, 469–471
polar bear listed as threatened, 392–393, 457, 459

570 COMPELLED

polar bear meetings with Kempthorne, 441–442, 445, 447–448, 457
polar bear not listed as threatened, 449–450
polar bears kill people, 433
science overwhelmingly supporting listing, 444–445, 447–448
USGS Director, 392

Nadella, Satya, 508
Nafziger, Richard, 138
NASCAR and Ducks Unlimited, 495–497
National Audubon Society
advisory panel on northern spotted owl, 123–124
Navy outlying landing field, 430
National Conservation Training Center (NCTC), 282–283
ESA regs and David Bernhardt, 421
FWS Historian Mark Madison, 284
Missouri River biological assessment, 342
polar bear range states meeting, 436–437
Retiree Reunions, 284–285
"sandwich mission" of FWS, 481
National Council for Air and Stream Improvement, 124
National Duck Stamp Contest, 402–404
Jeannie Morris, 495
National Environmental Policy Act (NEPA; 1970)
about, 117
California's own NEPA, 261
ESA (Section 10), 217
habitat loss lawsuit, 113–114
lawsuit against Navy OLF, 423–432
lawsuit against Tellico Dam project, 114
NWR Comprehensive Conservation Plans, 280
timber harvests, 117–118, 175, 182, 190, 227
National Fish and Wildlife Foundation (NFWF)
about, 401–402
BP oil spill and creating habitat, 485–489
BP penalty fund oversight, 504
Congress cutting conservation funding, 503
conservation work continues, 511
Executive Director Jeff Trandahl, 402, 485, 504
fines for illegal musseling, 291
FWS Director as board member, 401–402
National Forest Management Act (1976), 118, 121, 138–139, 222, 227
National Marine Fisheries Service (NMFS)
Central Valley Project Improvement Act, 249
challenging to work with, 167, 258
Clinton-requested spotted owl SEIS, 225–226
Director as NFWF board member, 401
Endangered Species Act responsibilities, 211
ESA regulation updates, 417–420
Interagency Implementation Team, 225–226
Northwest Forest Plan, 225–226, 231–232
Regional Director Will Stelle, 240
National Oceanic and Atmospheric Administration (NOAA), 35, 112, 115
threatened species protections, 200
National Park Service (NPS)
Agency Head Roundtable, 302
Everglades National Park, 293
Interagency Implementation Team, 226
Interagency Scientific Committee, 119–128
National Petroleum Reserve in Alaska, 397
National Reclamation Act (1902), 155
National Wetlands Inventory (NWI)
assistance with Avoyelles Parish clearing, 28
"Classification of Wetlands" report, 42–43
member Buck Reed, 6, 7, 28
POWDR Bill, 73
wetlands definition, 6–7
interagency team members, 7
National Wild Turkey Federation, 503, 509, 511
National Wildlife Federation (NWF)
BP penalties town hall, 503–504
Congress cutting conservation funding, 503
conservation work continues, 511
whooping crane lawsuit, 113–115
National Wildlife Refuge Academy (Blair, Nebraska), 96
National Wildlife Refuge Improvement Act (1997), 278–280
comprehensive conservation plans, 280
National Wildlife Refuge System Administration Act amended by, 279
National Wildlife Refuges (NWR)
about National Wildlife Refuge System, 279
Vicksburg, Mississippi, area, 468
Arctic NWR lease offerings, 395–400
"backbone of the Fish and Wildlife Service," 278
Central Valley, California, water, 245–247
comprehensive conservation plans, 280
"gift" of new refuge with no funding, 99

Holt Collier, 468
Humboldt Bay, 314
Klamath Basin leasing for agriculture, 162
Loxahatchee as "overlay" refuge, 292–293, 295
Malheur NWR occupation, 196
National Wildlife Refuge Academy, 96
National Wildlife Refuge Improvement Act, 278–280
Okefenokee, 273–276
Panther Swamp, 468
Pelican Island, 89, 90
Pocosin Lakes, 423–432
Tensas River, 379
Theodore Roosevelt, 468
training in wildlife refuge management, 96
Yazoo, 468
Native Americans
   Alaska
      Kaktovik village, 397, 399–400
      Native Claims Settlement Act, 81
   Crater Lake, 152–154
   Everglades, 296–297
      Miccosukee Tribe of Indians of Florida, 297
   First Nations of Canada and Boreal Forests, 505
      tar sands mining, 505–506
   indigenous hunting of polar bears, 436, 437–438
   Lower Colorado conservation plan, 357, 359
   Missouri River, 335, 336
   Okefenokee, 273–274
   polar bear listing, 436, 437
   Sacramento basin, 241
   starving off land via bison slaughter, 90
   Tennessee Valley Authority reservoir project, 111
Natural Community Conservation Planning Act (NCCP; California; 1991), 261
   ESA Section 4(d) rule for gnatcatcher, 262–264
Natural Resource Damage Assessment of BP oil spill, 488, 489
Natural Resources Conservation Service (NRCS), 488–489
Naval Petroleum Reserves Act (1976), 397
navigable waters extent rulings, 32–33, 53–55
navigable waterways of Rivers and Harbors Act, 11–14, 53–54
Navy outlying landing field (OLF), 422–432
   Navy Secretary Donald C. Winter, 428–430
Nebraska Platte River, 110, 113–116
Neeley, Burkett, 295

negotiations: Why are they upset?, 73–74
NEPA. See National Environmental Policy Act
Nesbit, Roger, 169, 178
New Orleans and Hurricane Katrina, 366–371
Newman, John, 482, 504, 515
Newman, Ryan, 497
NFWF. See National Fish and Wildlife Foundation
Nicholopoulos, Joy
   ES supervisor for New Mexico, 319, 323
   first biological opinion into law, 327–333
   lawsuit over water release, 324, 326
   Missouri River ESA needs, 340, 343
   comment, 344–345
   tour of Rio Grande by FWS, 330–331
Nichols, Teresa (Woods)
   God Squad hearing witness, 174
   Missouri River ESA team, 340, 343
   Oregon spotted owl effort, 166
Nigiri Project, 525–528
Nilke, Jim, 83
Nixon, Richard M.
   Alaska Native Claims Settlement Act, 81
   Clean Water Act amendments, 13
   Commercial Fisheries moved to Commerce, 34–35
   FWS Director Lynn Greenwalt, 33
NMFS. See National Marine Fisheries Service
NOAA. See National Oceanic and Atmospheric Administration
Noon, Barry R., 120–128
North American Model for Wildlife Conservation, 92–95, 480, 512
   conservationist Theodore Roosevelt, 303
northern spotted owl
   about administration political parties, 238–239
   court cases for public decision-making, 118
   critical habitat
      about, 107, 109
      candidate Bill Clinton, 204–205
      commercial thinning, 237–238
      forest versus timber management, 116–118
      FWS Clinton-requested SEIS, 224–229, 230–233
      FWS designation, 141, 145–146, 151–152, 166
      FWS designation as law, 109, 134, 143, 163
      FWS designation concurrent with listing, 107, 109, 139–140
      FWS designation process, 109–110, 116, 133–141, 144–146, 151

FWS designation versus ISC report,
    143–144
  FWS draft jeopardies to BLM,
    167–168, 185
  Habitat Conservation Areas,
    132–133, 177
  HCA 50-11-40 rule, 132, 177,
    178
  HCAs replaced by LSRs, 225, 229
  Jamison strategy, 175, 177–179, 182,
    184, 190
  Jamison strategy court ruling,
    197–198
  public hearings, 142, 146–151
  Seattle Audubon settlement,
    118–119, 232–233
  spotted owl habitat areas (SOHAs),
    123, 126, 127, 132
  taking prohibitions per FWS, 200
  taking restrictions court ruling,
    200–204
economic impacts, 140–141
  economic impact paper presented,
    222
  Lujan's preservation plan, 191–196
  mills closing to avoid retooling, not
    for owl, 150
  public hearings, 142, 146–151
  recovery plan estimating, 151,
    190–196, 197
ecosystem health indicator, 129
Endangered Species Committee
  BLM request to convene, 168–171
  decision on owl critical habitat, 107
  evidentiary hearing, 171–180
  FWS draft jeopardies to BLM,
    167–168, 185
  post-hearing brief changes, 180–184
  post-hearing report, 184–186
endangered species declaration, 124,
    125–126, 133
ISC management report (1990), 119–128
  critical habitat designation versus,
    143–144
  FWS Spotted Owl Coordinator, 116,
    133
  Interagency Scientific Committee,
    116, 119–120, 128
  management strategy, 130–133
  old-growth forest importance,
    129–130
Northern Spotted Owl v. Lujan, 109–110
"owl in a suitcase plan," 228
Portland Assistant Regional Director-ES
  Dale Hall, 107
recovery team, 136–139

FWS recovery plan, 178, 196–204,
    207–208, 219, 222
  Lujan plan bypassing ESA, 190–196
  meetings post–Lujan spotted owl plan
    divorce, 196–197
  public hearings and comment,
    198–199
  recovery plan and God Squad, 178
  recovery plan delayed by Clinton, 208
  recovery plan under Clinton, 219,
    222, 224–225
  recovery requiring voluntary actions,
    144
  threatened species protective regulations,
    199–200
  ESA Section 4(d) rule for owl, 233–238
  Section 4 permits, 199–200
  Section 10 permits, 260
  "take" including habitat modification,
    200–204
Northwest Forest Plan, 224–229, 230–233,
    237–238
Northwest Forest Summit. *See* Forest Summit
Norton, Gale
  FWS Director Dale Hall, 361–362, 366
    swearing in, 372, 376–378
  Secretary of the Interior, 312–313, 358,
    359
    appointing Julie MacDonald, 380
    death of Dale Hall's mother, 383, 385
  working with, 313, 375–376, 383
Norton, Kevin, 488–489
NRCS (Natural Resources Conservation Service), 488–489
NWF. *See* National Wildlife Federation
NWI. *See* National Wetlands Inventory
NWR. *See* national wildlife refuges
Nye, Rudy, 7

Obama, Barack Hussein
  election of, 472, 477
  note from Antonin Scalia, 520
  RESTORE Act, 503–504
Oberhelman, Doug, 508, 509
Office of Biological Services "Classification of
    Wetlands and Deepwater Habitats," 42–43, 259–260
Office of Management and Budget (OMB) and
    ESA updates, 412, 413, 418
Office of the Inspector General (OIG). *See*
    Inspector General and Julie
    MacDonald
Ogden, Peter Skene, 154
Ogden, Wendell, 97, 98
The Ohio State University assessment of FWS,
    277

INDEX   573

OIG. *See* Inspector General and Julie MacDonald
Oil Pollution Act (1990), 101, 503–504
oil rig Deepwater Horizon explosion, 484–489, 503–504
Oil Spill Liability Trust Fund, 504
oil tanker *Exxon Valdez* aground, 60–61, 101
Okefenokee NWR, 273–276
  subsurface fires, 274–275
old-growth forests
  about, 117
  BLM proposal for forest reserves, 179
  importance of, 129–130
  mills closing to avoid retooling, not for owl, 150
  species depending on, 239
  spotted owl as ecosystem indicators, 129
  spotted owl management report (ISC; 1990), 119–128
  spotted owl Northwest Compromise, 127
Old Growth Wildlife Research and Development Program (FS with BLM; 1982), 122
OLF (outlying landing field) for Navy, 422–432
Olson, Michael, 340, 342
OMB (Office of Management and Budget) and ESA updates, 412, 413, 418
one government
  Club Fed, 249
  FWS and BOR, 160, 251, 256
  Judge Nauman Scott, 11, 345–346
O'Neill, Tip, 99
Orange County, California, HCP, 259
Oregon Department of Fish and Wildlife
  Interagency Scientific Committee, 120–128
  Oregon Endangered Species Task Force, 121
  spotted owl as threatened, 125
  spotted owl management plan, 121–122
Oregon State University on ISC, 120–128
Osan, Ed, 253–254
Osborne, Michael
  Avoyelles Sportsman's League lawsuit, 5, 9
  court hearing, 9–14
  subpoena for Dale Hall's testimony, 45
  trial one on permits, 23, 25, 27
  trial two on WOTUS, 45, 46–51
otters and Bureau of Commercial Fisheries, 34–35
outlying landing field (OLF) for Navy, 422–432
Owen, Jay, 510, 532, 537

Pacific Northwest Forest Summit. *See* Forest Summit

Pacific Region FWS Ecological Services. *See* Portland Regional FWS Office
Packwood, Bob, 168, 190, 195
Pagel, Martha, 138
Palermo, Ray, 24
Palin, Sarah, 392
pallid sturgeon, 339, 341, 346, 349
  never funded, 350–351
Panther Swamp NWR, Mississippi, 468
Parenteau, Pat
  FWS lawyer for God Squad, 174–180, 189
  Committee decision, 185
  hearing witnesses, 174–175
  post-hearing brief changes, 180–184
  post-hearing report, 184
  NWF suit on behalf of whooping crane, 113
Parker, Blake, 7, 44
Parker, James A., 323–327, 330
Parker, Mamie, 310, 380
partnerships
  BP and conservation, 487–488
  Ducks Unlimited and Bass Pro Shops, 492–497
  Ducks Unlimited and NASCAR, 495–497
  Ducks Unlimited and National Fish and Wildlife Foundation, 485–489
  Ducks Unlimited and PEW Charitable Trusts, 504–506
  FWS and BOR, 157, 251–252, 255–256, 357
  FWS and Corps, 301, 302, 346–347, 351–352, 431–432
  FWS and Federal Highway Administration, 431
  FWS and international counterparts, 434–435
  FWS and USGS on polar bears, 393–394
  FWS ecosystem team philosophy, 302–303, 307–310
  FWS "sandwich mission," 481
  habitat creation after BP oil spill, 488–489
  Klamath Basin, 160, 164
  one-sided, 422
  Rio Grande silvery minnow, 328–329
  state and federal partnerships
    Bay-Delta Accord, 248–250, 256
    California gnatcatcher, 261–264
    Everglades restoration, 295
    George W. Bush supporting, 469–470
    musselers arrested, 286, 288
    priority of FWS Director Williams, 333–334
    Sam Hamilton supporting, 478

Western Association of Fish and
          Wildlife Agencies meeting, 318
      trust required, 251–252
PAS. *See* presidential appointee confirmed by
      the Senate
Patterson, Roger
    Assistant Secretary of the Interior Betsy
          Rieke, 252–255
    BOR managing water to biological needs,
          156–157
    Klamath Project, 155–156
        Klamath Project Operations Plan,
              161
        lakes drying up, 158–159, 161
        public education, 161
    Metropolitan Water District, 522
    Missouri River
        responsibilities of Corps versus BOR,
              337
        Upper and Lower Basins, 338–339
    Regional Director of BOR, 152, 248
        Bay-Delta Accord, 257
        Central Valley Project Improvement
              Act, 249, 251, 255
        FWS cooperation with, 251–252,
              254, 255–256
        FWS lack of cooperation with,
              254–255, 257
Pearce, Drue, 442, 447–448
Pearce, Steve, 330
Peevy, Walter, 24
Pelican Island NWR, Florida, 89, 90
Peregrine Fund, 509, 511
Perez, Benny, 380
permits
    authority dispute of Corps versus EPA,
          10–14, 28–32
    CWA Section 404 (*see* Section 404
          permits)
    "de minimus" amounts not requiring, 10
    ESA and CITES-regulated wildlife, 435
    ESA and "taking," 217–218
    ESA Section 4
        California gnatcatcher, 262–264
        northern spotted owl, 199–200,
              233–238
    ESA Section 10
        EIS required for taking listed species,
              260–261
        habitat conservation plans, 234
        multi-species conservation plan, 357,
              359
    Klamath FS grazing operation, 163–164
    regulations do not prohibit, they require,
          362

Tellico Dam project, 114
wetlands deposition of material, 10, 16–17
    FWS showing need for permit,
          17–19, 23–24
    ruling on Section 404 jurisdiction,
          52–53
    ruling on Section 404 requirement,
          28–33
    trial centering on need for permit, 10,
          16–17
Peters, David, 8–9, 13
Peterson, Russ, 166, 231–232
PEW Charitable Trusts, 504–506
Pheasants Forever, 503, 509, 511
Pick, Lewis A., 336–337
Pierce, Andy, 291
piping plover, 339, 346, 349
Pipkin, Jim, 224, 227, 228, 230
Pitt, Jennifer, 356–357
Pittman, Key, 93
placer mining Section 404 permits, 85–86
plants. *See* vegetation
Plater, Zygmunt, 111, 113–116
Platte River, Nebraska and Wyoming, 110,
      113–116, 338
    Missouri River tributary, 335, 336
    Platte River Whooping Crane Trust,
          115
Plenert, Marv
    Interagency Implementation Team,
          225–226
    Klamath Basin, 152
        BOR managing water to biological
              needs, 157
    northern spotted owl recovery team leader,
          136, 137, 139
        enforcement of taking regulations,
              204
        ESA Section 4(d) rule, 236, 238
        Lujan plan bypassing ESA, 190–191,
              193–194
        meetings post–Lujan spotted owl plan
              divorce, 196–197
        recovery plan, 139, 199, 208
        timber sales, 168
    Portland Regional Director, 105, 106, 240
    water issues in California, 247, 249, 251
Pocosin Lakes NWR, 423–432
polar bears listed as threatened, 447–448,
      458–459
    about, 390–391, 392
        killer bear PR firm, 433–434
        Obama administration commitment,
              477
    Conservation of Polar Bears international
          agreement, 435–436

INDEX   575

DOI Secretary Kempthorne
   briefings, 393, 394
   Coca-Cola Company, 433–434, 459
   listing as threatened, 394–395,
      445–448, 457–459
   "Mother's Day Massacre," 455–457,
      469
   not listing as threatened, 449–457
   resignation letter ready, 458
   twice-weekly polar bear meetings,
      441–442, 445, 447–448
domestically listed, 434
draft listing package, 439
extinction of polar bears, 456
FWS Director will only sign listing package, 447–448
   memorandum on legal issues,
      451–455
   "polar bear guy," 470
global warming, 391, 446
   congressional testimony, 439–441
   greenhouse gases, 391, 477
   ice ecoregions in future, 451
   melting of arctic ice cap, 391, 393,
      404, 440, 442–445, 477
   USGS sea ice reports, 442–443, 444,
      452
Marine Mammal Protection Act, 437
meeting of polar bear range states, 436
public hearing, 433
village visits more frequent, 393, 400
pollution
   Marine Shale Processors, 56–57
   wetland clearing equipment, 29–30
Pope, John, 482, 484–485, 501
Portland Regional FWS Office
   about Pacific Region Ecological Services,
      106–107
   Assistant Regional Director Dale Hall,
      105–106
   ESA change recommendations,
      211–219
   Executive Assistant Pat Mitchell, 158,
      209, 265
   leaving for Southeast Regional Office,
      266–267
   political facts learned from spotted
      owl, 238–239
   ESA candidate species settlement workload, 206–207, 211–212,
      240, 264–266
   FWS Director Beattie reorganization,
      251
   Interior Secretary Babbitt visit, 210,
      219–221, 223
   Klamath Basin (*see* Klamath Basin)

Mount St. Helens, 59
northern spotted owl (*see* northern spotted
   owl)
Pacific Northwest Forest Summit, 210
Regional Director Renne Lohoefener,
   391–392
timber sales, 116–117
   congressional staffer tour, 210
   ESA Section 4 permits, 233–238
   God Squad and owl, 168–186, 189
      (*see also* northern spotted
      owl)
Portman, Rob, 413–415
Potter, Bob, 246
POWDR Bill (Protect Our Wetlands and Duck
   Resources Act), 66–73
Powell, Ellis, 371
president of the United States
   administration political parties, 238–239,
      415–417
   presidential appointee confirmed by the Senate
      (PAS), 194
   cachet of, 36–37
   how few there are, 382
   director of FWS, 35–37, 79, 95–96,
      360–361
   career employee, 360
   decision-making in government, 382
President's Council on Environmental Quality.
   See Council on Environmental
   Quality
Prevot, Albert
   Avoyelles Parish floodplain clearing, 5, 10
   hiring Herbert Costello, 26
   trial, 20–21, 24, 25
Priddle, Brian, 510, 537
private ownership
   citizen conservationists, 480–481
   endangered species safe harbor agreement,
      259
   FWS ecosystem team partnerships,
      308–310
   habitat created after BP oil rig explosion,
      487–489
   habitat percentage privately owned, 160,
      308
   private land removed from owl critical
      habitat, 145, 146
   special ESA Section 4(d) rule for owl,
      233–234
Protect Our Wetlands and Duck Resources Act
   (POWDR Bill), 66–73
Ptachinski, Mike and Kay, 511, 537
public comment on government rules, 163
public education, 74–75. *See also* communication

576 COMPELLED

public servants
   appreciated, 472
   becoming one, xvii, 3
   career (*see* career employees of FWS)
   training (*see* training)
public trust doctrine, 68, 70, 82, 89–90
   lands treated as if locally owned, 178
   Seattle Audubon suit settlement, 118–119, 232–233
Pulliam Judy, 272
Putnam, Adam, 531, 533
Pyramid as Bass Pro Shop, 492–494
   Ducks Unlimited space, 492, 493, 494–495, 497–498

Quackenbush, Ken, 465
Quayle, Dan, 95
Quinn, Tim, 252

Rahall, Nick, 408
Raley, Bennett, 354–358
Rawls, William J., 371
Ray, Dan, 509
Ray, James Earl, 499
Raynor, Pete
   ESA Section 4(d) for spotted owl, 235–236
   God Squad brief changed, 183–184
   God Squad convened, 169
      FWS represented by Pat Parenteau, 174
Reagan, Ronald
   compromise with Tip O'Neill, 99
   Director of FWS Bob Jantzen, 70–71
   Director of FWS Frank Dunkle, 79–80
   nominating veterinarian as FWS director, 361
   Secretary of Interior James Watt, 61, 66
   Supreme Court Justice Antonin Scalia, 512
reasonable and prudent alternative (RPA) action, 322, 332
red wolf, 424, 427
Reed, Buck
   National Wetlands Inventory center, 6, 7, 28
   wetlands determination defense, 6, 28, 43
   Yazoo Basin hydric soils, 10, 44
Reed, Fernell (Sarah's sister)
   making conservation history against pollution, 56–57
   swearing-in of FWS Director Dale Hall, 377
Reed, Herman
   Louisiana welcome to Dale Hall, xvi–xvii
   Louisiana wetland pride, 57
   Sunday lunch with Jim Tripp, 46
Reed, Nat, 35, 36
Reed, Nell
   Louisiana welcome to Dale Hall, xvi
   Louisiana wetland pride, 57
   Sunday lunch with Jim Tripp, 46
Reed, Sarah
   Bunkie, Louisiana, hometown, xvi–xvii, 5, 45
   marriage to Dale Hall, xvii (*see also* Hall, Sarah)
   Yazoo floodplain site, 5, 45
Reeves, Skippy, 276
Region 4 FWS Office. *See* Southeast Region of FWS
regulations do not prohibit, they require, 362
Rehnquist, William, 512
Reid, Fritz, 505, 519
Reisner, Marc, 220
RESTORE Act (Resources and Ecosystems Sustainability, Tourist Opportunities, and Revived Economies of the Gulf Coast States; 2012), 503–504
Rey, Mark, 151, 238
Reynolds, Richard, 120
Reynolds, Steve, 482
Rhodes, Donald, 8, 26
"Richard Cory" (poem; Robinson), xii
Richardson, Bill, 330
Ridenour, James, 119–128
Rieke, Betsy, 252–255
   Accord between California and federal government, 256
Riley, Don, 431–432
Riley, Tom, 147–148, 165
Rimel, Rebecca, 504–506
Rio Grande River
   about, 320–322
   biological opinion into law, 327–333
   Bureau of Reclamation, 319
      re-regulating dams, 322
      water release by BOR proposed, 322–323
      water release lawsuit, 323–327
      water release lawsuit rulings, 326, 329–330
   New Mexico/Texas Rio Grande Compact, 322
   silvery minnow, 318–323, 324–325
      fix for minnow problem, 329–333
   tour of river by FWS, 330–331
Rivers and Harbors Act (1899), 6, 11, 53–54
"Road Dogs," 310
Robertson, Absalom Willis, 93
Robertson, Dale, 119–128, 228

INDEX 577

Robinson, Bruce, 371
Robinson, Edwin Arlington, xii
Rocky Mountain Elk Foundation, 511
Roosevelt, Franklin
    Darling as head of U.S. Biological Survey, 91–92
    flood control, 39–40
    Fort Peck Dam in Montana, 335–336
    Okefenokee as NWR, 274
    Wildlife Restoration Act, 93
Roosevelt, Theodore
    conservation pioneer, 90, 303
    "Man in the Arena," 417, 446
    National Reclamation Act, 155
    "Teddy bear," 303–304
Roosevelt, Theodore, IV, 303–305
Rove, Karl, 413–415
Ruesink, Bob, 107, 133
Rutzick, Mark, 179
Ryan, Mike, 157, 163

Sacramento River, California
    about, 241–247, 248
    Bay-Delta Accord, 248–250, 256, 257, 312, 521
    Central Valley Project (1935), 243
    Central Valley Project Improvement Act (1992), 246–247
    FWS and BOR cooperating, 247
    FWS Section 3406(b)(2) of the
CVPIA water management, 247, 255–258

    Central Valley water (*see* Central Valley, California, water)
    floodplains, 521–528
    flows inadequate for fish, 244–247
    Bay-Delta Accord, 256
    Sacramento River flood control projects, 242–243, 521–522
    salmon migration via Trinity River, 244
Sadler, Ronald R., 175, 179
Salazar, Ken, 477–478, 479
salmon
    California Trout Nigiri Project, 525–528
    Central Valley, California, 242, 521–528
        river versus floodplain, 525, 527
    Klamath Basin, 155
    migration via Trinity River, 244
    smoltification, 255
Salmon, Gary, 510
Salmon, Glen, 487–488
San Francisco Estuary Project (1987), 246
San Joaquin River. *See* Central Valley, California, water
San Vito dei Normanni Air Station (Italy), xiv

Sanderson, Richard E., 176
Sansonetti, Tom
    BLM requesting Endangered Species Committee, 169
    evidentiary hearing, 172–180, 181–182
    post-hearing report, 184
Scalia, Antonin "Nino"
    California hunting trip with Cheney, 515–519, 520
    death, 519–520
    Ducks Unlimited keynote speaker, 512–516
    "free speech is sacrosanct," 520
    Supreme Court Justice, 512, 520
Scarlett, Harold, 74–75, 77, 87–88, 536
Scarlett, Lynn
    Deputy Secretary of the Interior, 385, 389
    meetings with Secretary Kempthorne, 411
    ESA regulation updates, 411–413, 418
    policy time with POTUS, 413–415
    Julie MacDonald interference, 382–383, 385
    decisions reviewed, 407, 408–410
    inspector general investigation of MacDonald, 389
    Navy OLF near Pocosin Lakes NWR, 424–425
    not ordering Dale Hall to stay in D.C., 426
    polar bear as threatened, 447–448
    meetings with Secretary Kempthorne, 393, 395, 441–442, 447–448
    polar bear not listed as threatened, 450
    science knowledge gaps, 395, 443
    science overwhelmingly supporting listing, 447–448
    USGS sea ice reports, 442–443, 444
    Yazoo Backwater Pumps project, 463–465
Schamberger, Mel, 141, 142, 144–145, 146, 151, 197
Schedule C appointments, 194
Schmitten, Rollie, 249
Schoenrock, Doug, 531
Schrote, John, 169
Schultz, Charles, 114–115
Schweiger, Larry, 503–504
scientific integrity, 382–383
Scott, Charles, 340, 342
Scott, Nauman
    Avoyelles Parish floodplain clearing case appealed, 54–55
    Commerce Clause reach, 54–55

Corps versus EPA authority over
    permit program, 10–14,
    28–32
full trial date and preliminary injunction, 13
hearing, 10–14
one government, one position, 11,
    345–346
temporary restraining order, 5
trial into two parts, 13–14, 16–17
trial one on permits, 16–28
trial one ruling, 28–32
trial two on WOTUS, 46–51
trial two ruling, 51–56
Waters of the United States ruling,
    53–55
    placer mining reference to, 86
Scott, Ray, 490–491
Seattle Audubon suit settlement, 118–119,
    232–233
Seavey, Fred, 192
Section 404 permits
    Corps CWA permit requests, 4
    EPA Permits Branch Chief, 8
    lacking in Avoyelles Parish floodplain
        clearing, 5
    ruling on Section 404 jurisdiction,
        28–33, 52–53
    Vicksburg FWS Office, 4, 5, 39, 58
    EPA approval and veto authority, 461
    federal jurisdiction, 523
    "No Action" letters, 58
    placer mining, 85–86
    Secretary of the Interior powerless to deny,
        276
    Tellico Dam project, 114
    template for California NCCP Agreement,
        264
    wetland plant adaptations, 50, 523
SEIS. See supplemental environmental impact
    statements
Senate. See Congress
senior executive service (SES)
    about, 71, 312
    Assistant Director of Fisheries Gary
        Edwards, 87
    Candidate Development Program,
        186–189
    Deputy Regional Director Dale Hall,
        312, 316
    FWS director appointment process, 360
    Regional Director in Denver Don Minnich, 70–71
September 11 (2001), 313–315
Servheen, Chris, 375–376
SES. See senior executive service

Seward, William, 80
Shah, Subhas, 331
Shake, Bill, 101
Shallenberger, Rob, 278
shellfish harvesting
    commercial musseling, 286
    Japanese pearl culture industry, 288
    musselers arrested, 286, 288
    prosecution, 289
    news conference, 289–291
Sher, Victor, 174–177, 182, 185
Sherman, Dan, 480, 482, 483, 484
Shillito, Daniel, 174, 180–184, 200–201
Shoop, Butch, 371
Short, Cathy, 302
Shroufe, Duane, 318
Silent Spring (Carson), 76
silvery minnow, 318–323, 324–325
    biological opinion into law, 327–333
    lawsuit over water release, 323–327
Siragusa, Flip, 370–371
Slack, Jay, 295, 299–300, 301–302
Sloan, William G., 336–337
smelt in California floodplains, 521–528
Smith, Bo, 18, 59
Smith, Bob, 220
Smith, David P., 361, 381, 385, 387–388
    wife Heidi Marquez Smith, 401
Smith, Dick, 193, 260
Smith, Elaine, 3
Smith, Felix, 68–74, 90
Smith, Fred, 493, 530
Smith, Heidi Marquez, 401
Smith, Mr. (teacher), xii
Smithers, Judy (sister-in-law), 384
snail darter fish, 97, 110–116, 171
snow geese near OLF, 423, 425
Soil Conservation Service (SCS)
    Lake Ophelia tract as wetland, 23, 44
    NWI member Blake Parker, 7
    project work by Mitch King, 4
    Yazoo Basin hydric soils, 10, 44
    Yazoo Basin projects, 4
soils, erosion, and sedimentation
    arctic circle true soil, 59
    arctic polygons, 59–60, 84
    Big Muddy, Missouri River, 335–336
    "Classification of Wetlands" report,
        42–43
    dust bowl, 91–92
    floodplains, 523–525
    forested versus cleared land, 24
    hydric soils, 44, 523
    Okefenokee, 274
Solem, David, 160
Solice, David, 231–232

INDEX

South Florida Water Management District (SFWMD)
  Agency Head Roundtable, 302
  DOJ suing over phosphorous, 293–295
  8.5 Square Mile Area water flows, 298
  Loxahatchee NWR agreement, 292–293, 295
Southeast Region of FWS (Atlanta)
  about, 271–272
  acting Regional Director Marvin Moriarty, 272
  Deputy Regional Director Dale Hall, 266
    Executive Assistant Debbie Doty Vess, 290
  Everglades, Florida
    about, 292
    DOJ lawsuit over phosphorous, 293–295
    8.5 Square Mile Area, 297–300
    Everglades Agricultural Area, 293, 295
    Everglades National Park, 293, 295, 296, 298
    exotic pets released, 300
    human settlement effects, 295–300
    Loxahatchee NWR, 292–293, 295
    restoring water flows, 297–300
    wildlife, 299–300
  Geographic/Programmatic structure of FWS
    changes made by Jamie Clark, 277–278, 311
    reorganization by Mollie Beattie, 251, 276–277
  Lower Mississippi Valley, 280–281
  Okefenokee NWR, 273–276
    titanium mining by E.I. DuPont, 275–276
  Regional Director Noreen Clough, 271–272
  Regional Director Sam Hamilton, 272–273
    FWS Director Sam Hamilton, 478
  Theodore Roosevelt IV visit, 303–305
  Yazoo Backwater Pumps (*see* Yazoo Backwater Pumps project)
Southern Environmental Law Center (SELC)
  suit against OLF, 423–432
Southern Wood Piedmont Company, 57
Southwest Region of FWS (Albuquerque)
  about, 317–318
  Acting Regional Director Dale Hall, 316, 317–318
    confirmation as FWS Director, 365–366, 371–372
    nomination as FWS Director, 361–366
  Acting Regional Director Geoff Haskett, 372
  Lower Colorado River (*see* Lower Colorado River MSCP)
  Missouri River assignment (*see* Missouri River ESA needs)
  Rio Grande River silvery minnow (*see* Rio Grande River)
Spangle, Steve, 133, 166
Spear, Mike
  Agency Coordination Team under Clinton, 224
  directing Buck Reed to assist, 28
  ESA Section 4(d) for spotted owl, 235
  lawsuit over ESA candidate species, 205–207
  POWDR Bill, 67
  Russ Earnest working with, 57
  uncooperative with BOR, 254–255, 257
Spearfish National Fish Hatchery, 402
special agents of FWS
  history of, 286–288
  musselers arrested, 286, 288
    prosecution, 289
  Navy OLF near Pocosin Lakes NWR, 426
  public hearing disruptions, 147–148
  saving Erin Hall in hurricane, 370–371
  Secretary Salazar protective detail, 479
Sport Fish Restoration Act, 36, 94
sport hunting and fishing
  about hunting and fishing, 481
  alligator hunting, 532
  Bass Pro Shops' Johnny Morris (*see* Morris, John L. "Johnny")
  Bassmaster Tournament series, 403, 490–491
  Citizen Conservationists, 480–481
    examples of, 497, 500, 505, 507–508
  conservationists paying for conservation, 92–95, 511–512
    federal dollars matched by two, 503
    not "trophies," 95
  duck hunter James Cox Kennedy, 507, 518, 519
  duck stamps, 92
    first day of sale, 402, 403–404
    habitat management funds, 73
    National Duck Stamp Contest, 402–404, 495
  Ducks Unlimited members, 513 (*see also* Ducks Unlimited)
  fishing trip with Bill Dance, 500
  hunting with Billy Dunavant, 500

580 COMPELLED

hunting with John Thompson, 508–509, 510
hunting with Scalia and Cheney, 515–519, 520
Louisiana cuisine, 46, 518
migratory waterfowl protection, 91
National Wildlife Refuge Improvement Act, 279
North American Model for Wildlife Conservation, 92–95, 480, 512
   conservationist Theodore Roosevelt, 303
polar bear regulated hunting, 437–438
right to fish, hunt, and gather food, 89
   2nd Amendment, 188–189
Sport Fish Restoration Act, 36, 94
Wildlife Restoration Act, 93
Spotted Owl Research, Development, and Application Program (FS with BLM; 1986), 122. *See also* northern spotted owl
Spring Bayou Wildlife Management Area, 24
Sproul, Christine, 138
Stanford University on ISC, 120–128
Stansell, Ken
   FWS deputy director, 379, 380
   polar bear as threatened, 393, 394, 439, 449, 451
   working with Lynn Scarlett, 389
Starfield, Larry, 465
Starkey, Edward, 138
Starnes, Lynn, 97
Starnes, Wayne, 97
state fish and wildlife agencies
   Central Valley, California, water deficiencies, 245
   Clinton's disregard for, 333–334
   conservationists paying for conservation, 92–95
   50-11-40 rule for Habitat Conservation Areas, 132
   FWS ecosystem team partnerships, 302–303, 307–310
   interstate management via Lacey Act, 90–91, 286, 288
   partnerships with federal agencies
      Bay-Delta Accord, 248–250, 256
      California gnatcatcher, 261–264
      George W. Bush supporting, 469–470
      musselers arrested, 286, 288
      priority of FWS Director Williams, 333–334
      Sam Hamilton supporting, 478
      Western Association of Fish and Wildlife Agencies meeting, 318

Stelle, Will, 234, 240
Stennis, John, 466
Stevens, Beth, 380
Stevens, John Paul, 520
Stewart, Tony, 495, 496, 497
Stone, Harlan Fiske, 54
Strachn, Mike, 8, 25–26
Strock, Carl, 431–432
Stroebele, Jerry, 83
Stuller, Matt and Matthew, 510
sturgeon, 339, 341, 346, 349
   never funded, 350–351
supplemental environmental impact statements (SEIS)
   Navy OLF near Pocosin Lakes NWR, 424–432
   northern spotted owl, 123, 124, 127
      Clinton requesting new, 224–229, 230–233
Supreme Court of the United States
   Babbitt opportunity to be justice, 258–259
   environmental harm, 446
   habitat as surrogate to population trends, 453–454
   Justice Antonin Scalia, 512
Suwannee Canal Company, 274
Swan, Ron
   God Squad evidentiary hearing, 174–180, 182
   northern spotted owl critical habitat, 142
   public hearing on critical habitat, 147
swans near OLF, 423, 425, 426
Sweitzer, Harvey C., 171–177
Swensen, Nels, 511

"take" of an endangered species, 199, 201, 232
"take" including habitat modification, 200–204
"take" protections for threatened species, 199–200, 233–237
"taking" restrictions court ruling, 200–204
Tappeiner, John, 138
tar sands mining, 505–506
Taras, Greg, 511
Tate, Justin, 357, 359
Tax Cuts and Jobs Act (2017), 82–83
team. *See* leadership; partnerships
Teeter, Jim, 106, 189, 208–209
Tehan, Mike, 133, 231–232
Tellico Dam project, 110–116, 174, 190
Tennessee Shell Company, 288
Tennessee snail darter fish, 97, 110–116, 171
Tennessee Valley Authority (TVA), 110–116
Teskey, Robert, 7, 44, 50, 51

INDEX 581

Texas Parks and Wildlife Commission (TPWD), 77, 370, 371
Thabault, Michael
   ESA regulation updates, 414–415, 421–422
   Missouri River ESA team, 340, 348, 352
Theodore Roosevelt NWR, 468
Thiel, Dan, 511
Thomas, Christine, 511
Thomas, Jack Ward
   Chief of Forest Service, 228, 231
   drifting from ISC toward Clinton, 222, 227–229, 230–231
      Clinton impressed with, 223
   ESA economic considerations, 222
   Federal Ecosystem Management Assessment Team, 224
   Interagency Scientific Committee, 120–128
      respect for Ward, 129
   ISC report delivered, 120–128
   Northwest Forest Plan, 227–229, 230–231
   "Jack's owl in a suitcase plan," 228
   private dinner with Bruce Babbitt, 220
   witness at God Squad hearing, 175, 178–179
"Thomas Report," 129, 143
   ISC spotted owl report (1990), 120–128
Thompson, John, 508–509, 510, 536–537
Thompson, Sandi, 509
Thompson, Steve
   Colorado River lower basin drought, 354
      wet sleeping bag, 354–356
   escapades of Julie MacDonald, 381
      decisions reviewed, 408–410
      Inspector General report, 387, 405–406
   FWS Director Dale Hall team, 380
   FWS Director Sam Hamilton elation, 478
      death of Sam Hamilton, 478–479
   FWS Directorship declined, 479–480
   getting to know, 278, 280–282
   Lower Mississippi Valley, 280–281
   Manager of California/Nevada Operations, 312
   National Wildlife Refuge Improvement Act, 278–280
   Southeast Regional Office team, 278
   Theodore Roosevelt IV visit, 303–305
      fishing license, 304–305
Thorson, Robyn
   Corps biological assessment, 345–347
      listening to those impacted, 347
   FWS biological opinion, 339–352
      guiding team progress, 348–349
      team, 340, 343–345, 348, 349–350, 352
      team leader, 334–335, 340, 348, 352
   FWS Director Dale Hall team, 380
Threatened and Endangered Species Program (FWS), 107
threatened species per ESA, 108–109, 199
   protective regulations, 199–200, 201
      ESA Section 4(d) rule for gnatcatcher, 262–264
      ESA Section 4(d) rule for owl, 233–238
   "take" including habitat modification, 200–204
Tiananmen Square, China, 100–101
Tilt, Whitney, 291
timber harvesting
   candidate Bill Clinton, 204–205
   commercial thinning, 237–238
   denuded hillsides, 140, 150, 192, 225, 239, 258
   ESA Section 4 permits, 199–200
   ESA Section 4(d) rule for owl, 233–238
   Forest Service Chief Jack Ward Thomas, 228, 231
   forest versus timber management, 116–118
      Clinton requesting new SEIS, 227
      forests managed as tree farms, 171
      "Preservation Plan for the Northern Spotted Owl," 195–196
   mills closing to avoid retooling, not for owl, 150
   90-day regulatory moratorium, 190, 191–192
   northern spotted owl critical habitat
      economic impacts, 140–141
      FWS draft jeopardies to BLM, 167–168, 185
      FWS recovery plan, 198, 222
      God Squad convened, 171–180, 189
      God Squad decision, 184–186
      Jamison strategy, 175, 177–179, 182, 184, 190
      Jamison strategy court ruling, 197–198
      Lujan's preservation plan, 191–196
      Northwest Forest Plan, 224–229, 230–232
      Oregon and California Railroad Revested (O&C) lands, 132–133, 151, 166, 225
      Portland Field Office with FS and BLM, 116, 166–167
      private land eliminated from proposal, 145, 146

582   COMPELLED

Seattle Audubon suit settlement, 118–119, 232–233
Okefenokee Swamp, 274
old-growth forests (*see* old-growth forests)
Yazoo Delta bottomland, 5 (*see also* Yazoo Basin)
Tiner, Ralph, 68–74
titanium mining by DuPont in Okefenokee Swamp, 275–276
Tomke, John, 482, 518–519
training
    Federal Executive Institute, 186–189
    National Conservation Training Center, 282–283
        ESA regulations with David Bernhardt, 421
        FWS Historian Mark Madison, 284
        Missouri River biological assessment, 342
        polar bear range states meeting, 436–437
        Retiree Reunions, 284–285
        "sandwich mission" of FWS, 481
    National Wildlife Refuge Academy, 96
    new Fisheries Academy facility, 98, 99–100
    SES Candidate Development Program, 186–189
    wildlife refuge management, 96
Trandahl, Arden, 284, 402
Trandahl, Jeff, ix, 402, 485–489, 504
trees. *See* bottomland hardwood wetlands; Forest Service; timber harvesting
Tripp, James T. B.
    about, 9
    Avoyelles Sportsman's League lawsuit, 5, 9
    court hearing, 9–14
    cross-examination of Donal Hook, 49–51
    EPA included in complaint, 10–11
    EPA meeting on WOTUS, 9
    larval fish evidence, 23
    learning wetland science, 14–16
    local cuisine, 45–46
    photos entered into evidence, 19–20, 29
    trial one on permits, 16–17, 19–28
    trial one ruling, 28–32
    trial two on WOTUS, 45, 46–51
    trial two ruling, 51–56
    wetlands determination, 42–44
Truex, Martin, 497
Trump, Donald
    ESA regulation update partially adopted, 420–421
    Secretary of the Interior Ryan Zinke, 422
trust
    FWS and Corps in Everglades, 302
    Klamath Basin communities, 157

    Missouri River FWS and Corps, 346–347
    partnerships requiring, 251–252
    public trust in government, 118, 186, 237–238, 259, 537
    reporter's trusted source, 75
    trust doctrine of public ownership, 68, 70, 82, 89–90
        lands treated as if locally owned, 178
        Seattle Audubon suit settlement, 118–119, 232–233
Tuckman, Tom, 234, 240
tundra swans near OLF, 423, 425, 426
Turner, John
    FWS Director, 95–96, 105
        eight seconds on the bull, 105, 267
        staying until Mollie Beattie installed, 234
        working with BOR, 357
    Interagency Scientific Committee, 119–128
    new Fisheries Academy facility, 98, 99
    northern spotted owl critical habitat, 139–140, 151
    economic analysis team, 141
    enforcement of prohibition against taking, 201–204
    Lujan recovery plan bypassing ESA, 193
    Lujan submitting preservation plan, 195
    witness at God Squad hearing, 175, 180
    request for post-hearing brief changes, 180–184
Twain, Mark, 309
Tweten, Randy, 133

Udall, Tom, 331
Underwood, Dennis, 356–357, 358, 359
U.S. Army and Endangered Species Committee, 112
U.S. Army Corps of Engineers (Corps)
    about mission, 336
        newer Corps of Engineers, 301
        Agency Head Roundtable, 302
        agricultural conversion regulatory guidance letter, 55
    Avoyelles Parish floodplain clearing
        Corps Section 404 permit requests, 5, 10–14
        floodplain clearing, 5, 8, 10
        floodplain trial ruling, 28–32
        normal activities declaration by Corps, 11, 14, 21–22
        trial one on permits, 16–28
        trial one ruling, 28–32

INDEX 583

trial two on WOTUS, 46–51
trial two ruling, 51–55
Waters of the United States, 10–14, 26, 46–47, 51–55
Cave Run Reservoir, xv
Clean Water Act
authority of Corps versus EPA and FWS, 9–14, 32–33
permit program authority, 4, 10–14, 28–32
economic criteria for project consideration, 463
elevating to CEQ, 78, 461
Everglades, Florida, 298–302
Fish and Wildlife Coordination Act, 3–4
Galveston Bay Area Navigation Study, 74–79
environmental contaminants, 76–79
Missouri Basin Power Project, 114
Missouri River ESA needs, 334–335, 337–339, 351
biological assessment, 342, 345–347
FWS biological opinion, 350, 352
FWS-Corps partnership, 346–347, 351–352
Missouri River Recovery Implementation Committee, 347
responsibilities of Corps versus BOR, 336–339, 350–351
NWI member Rudy Nye, 7
partnerships with FWS, 301, 302, 346–347, 351–352, 431–432
placer mining Section 404 permits, 85–86
Rio Grande River biological opinion into law, 327–333
Sacramento River Flood Control Project, 242–243
Waterways Experiment Station, 18
wetlands definition, 6–8, 43
court ruling, 51–55
Yazoo Backwater Pumps (*see* Yazoo Backwater Pumps project)
U.S. Biological Survey, 91–92, 260, 403
U.S. Coast Guard, 504
U.S. Constitution
Bill of Rights, 188–189
2nd Amendment, 188–189
Commerce Clause in Avoyelles Parish ruling, 54–55
course by J. Cudd Brown, 186–189
due process and federal land management, 119
Federalist Papers, 187–188
individual rights, 188–189
people not government own natural resources, 89

U.S. Department of Agriculture, 112, 127, 220, 238
U.S. Department of Commerce, 108
U.S. Department of Justice (DOJ)
Avoyelles Parish floodplain clearing, 8–14
CWA authority of Corps versus EPA and FWS, 10–14, 32–33
BLM request for God Squad, 174
ESA candidate species settlement, 206
Everglades lawsuit over phosphorous, 293–295
FWS case prosecution, 289
Marine Shale Processors, 56–57
U.S. Department of the Interior (DOI)
about breadth and reach of, 135–136
power to veto Okefenokee Swamp mining, 276
powerless to deny 404 permit, 276
powerless to force litigation, 289
Arctic NWR lease offerings, 82–83
Assistant Secretary Betsy Rieke, 252–255
Accord between California and federal government, 256 (*see also* Bay-Delta Accord)
biological research folded into USGS, 260
Central Valley Project Improvement Act (1992), 247, 251
Colorado River Interstate Compact Water Master, 358–359
Commissioner of Fisheries and Wildlife, 34, 35, 37
FWS Director appointed by president, 35–37
Deputy Secretary Lynn Scarlett (*see* Scarlett, Lynn)
Duck Stamp Contest, 402 (*see also* duck stamps)
Endangered Species Act five factor analysis, 108–109
Endangered Species Committee, 112, 168
chaired by secretary of the interior, 171
ESA candidate species lawsuit, 205–207
ESA decisions tainted (*see* MacDonald, Julie A.)
ESA determination on basis of best science, 452
ESA recovery team, 136–137
ESA updates, 418, 420–422
FWS Director appointment, 360
FWS Director reception, 377
Klamath Basin land leased for agriculture, 162
Miccosukee Tribe of Indians of Florida, 297

National Wildlife Refuge System
    management, 279
Okefenokee Swamp mining veto power,
    276
PAS, 382 (see also presidential appointee
    confirmed by the Senate)
policy on trial testimony, 45
political appointees, 178, 179, 194, 195,
    236, 382, 410
Secretary Bruce Babbitt (see Babbitt,
    Bruce)
Secretary Cecil Andrus, 33
Secretary Dirk Kempthorne (see
    Kempthorne, Dirk)
Secretary Gale Norton (see Norton, Gale)
Secretary James Watt (see Watt, James G.)
Secretary Ken Salazar, 477–478, 479
Secretary Manuel Lujan (see Lujan,
    Manuel)
Secretary Ryan Zinke, 422
Solicitor David Bernhardt (see Bernhardt,
    David)
Solicitor Don Barry, 68 (see also Barry,
    Don)
U.S. Fish and Wildlife Service (FWS)
    about conservation history, 89–95
        employee dedication, 264–265
        FWS careers as callings, 96, 264–265
        mission statement, 481
    Agency Head Roundtable, 302
    Alaska (see Alaska)
    biological opinion into law, 327–333
    Bureau of Reclamation cooperation with,
        156–157, 251–252, 357
    Central Valley, California, water
        FWS and BOR cooperating,
            251–252, 255–256
        FWS representative Dale Hall, 247
        national wildlife refuge water needs
            study, 245–247
        Section 3406(b)(2) of the CVPIA
            water management, 247,
            255–258
    Clear Lake, Texas, office (see Clear Lake,
        Texas)
    Congressman John Dingell supporting,
        35–38
    CWA authority of Corps versus EPA and
        FWS, 10–14, 32–33
        ruling that permits required, 28–32
        wetland mapping and EPA deferring,
            13
    Directors (see Directors, U.S. Fish and
        Wildlife Service)
    Ecological Services (ES)
        Anchorage, 83

Clean Water Act, 4
Clear Lake Office (see Clear Lake,
    Texas)
endangered species biologists kept
    separate, 107, 110
Field Supervisor Jim McKevitt,
    243–247
Klamath office, 162
offices in D.C., 69
Portland, Oregon, office (see Portland
    Regional FWS Office)
Vicksburg Office (see Vicksburg,
    Mississippi)
Endangered Species Act
    about, 107–110
    California gnatcatcher, 262–264
    critical habitat designation, 107
    critical habitat designation process,
        109–110, 116, 133–141,
        144–146, 151
    economic impacts, 140, 222
    ESA Section 4(d) rule for owl,
        233–238
    five factor analysis, 108–109, 140
    FS and BLM conferred with, 126,
        166
    FWS issues driven by, 380
    God Squad for spotted owl, 168–171
    individual species approach,
        109–110, 212
    lawsuit over ESA candidate species,
        205–207, 211–212, 240,
        264–266
    northern spotted owl critical habitat,
        141, 145–146, 151–152,
        166
    reasonable and prudent alternative
        (RPA) action, 322, 332
    recommendations for changes,
        211–219
    recovery plans, 137
    recovery teams, 136–139
    regulation updates, 417–420
    regulation updates not per FWS,
        420
    responsibilities under, 165, 211–212
    separation of Endangered Species
        offices, 107
    state and federal partnership,
        261–264, 286, 288
    "taking" restriction enforcement,
        201–204
    threatened species protective regula-
        tions, 199–200, 201
Environmental Contaminants Program,
    76–79

executive branch and personal opinions, 396
as family, 272, 285, 366, 371, 472, 479
Fisheries Program (*see* Fisheries Program of FWS)
funding appropriations (1993), 214
Geographic/Programmatic structure
    assessment of, 277, 310–311
    changes made, 277–278, 311
    Ecosystem Approach, 306–310
    reorganization by Mollie Beattie, 251, 276–277
history
    Biological Resources Division in USGS, 260
    Bureau of Sport Fisheries and Wildlife, 34–37, 361
    Director nominated by president, confirmed by Senate, 35–37, 360–361
    Heritage Committee to preserve, 283–284
    name back to Fish and Wildlife Service, 35, 36
    only Bureau in Interior, 35
    Retiree Reunions, 284–285
    Retirees Association, 283–284
    special agents, 286–288
    U.S. Biological Survey, 91–92, 260, 403
    waterfowl focus, 91, 92, 93
international trade regulation via CITES, 434–435
Jackson, Mississippi, Area Office, 5
Land Acquisition Priority System, 99
leadership
    attention to Fisheries and state wildlife, 302
    Directors (*see* Directors, U.S. Fish and Wildlife Service)
    memo on Ecosystem Approach opportunities, 306–310
    optimism over Secretary Babbitt, 219–220
    permit authority at FWS versus Corps, 27–28
    Vicksburg trial support, 27–28
National Conservation Training Center, 282–283
    FWS Historian Mark Madison, 284
    Retiree Reunions, 284–285
National Wetlands Inventory (*see* National Wetlands Inventory)
national wildlife refuges (*see* national wildlife refuges)

northern spotted owl
    Clinton-requested SEIS, 224–229, 230–233
    critical habitat concurrent with listing, 107, 109
    critical habitat designation, 107, 109, 133, 139–140, 151–152, 166
    economic impacts, 140–141, 151, 197
    endangered species declaration, 124, 126, 133
    ESA Section 4(d) rule for owl, 233–238
    forest versus timber management, 116–118
    FS and BLM conferred with, 126, 166
    God Squad convened, 168–171
    HCPs to enforce "taking" restrictions, 203
    Interagency Implementation Team, 225–229
    Interagency Scientific Committee, 116, 119–120, 128
    management report (ISC; 1990), 120–128
    Northwest Forest Plan, 224–229, 230–232
    recovery plan, 196–204
    recovery team, 136–139
    Section 4 rule crafted for, 233–238
    Section 10 permits for habitat conservation plans, 234
    Spotted Owl Coordinator, 116, 133
    threatened species protective regulations, 199–200
Orange County Habitat Conservation Plan, 259
partnerships with Corps, 301, 302, 346–347, 351–352, 431–432
public trust doctrine, 68
    lands treated as if locally owned, 178
senior executive service, 71
special agents
    history of, 286–288
    musselers arrested, 286, 288
    Navy OLF near Pocosin Lakes NWR, 426
    prosecution of case, 289
    public hearing disruptions, 147–148
    saving Erin Hall in hurricane, 370–371
    Secretary Salazar protective detail, 479
training, 96–97

National Conservation Training
Center, 282–283
Vicksburg office (*see* Vicksburg, Mississippi)
Wildlife Forensics Lab, 148, 283
U.S. Fish Commission, 88–89. *See also* Fisheries Program of FWS
U.S. Geological Survey (USGS)
Biological Resources Division, 260
Director Chip Groat, 392
Director Mark Myers, 392, 394
climate change and polar bears, 394
polar bear not listed as threatened, 449–450
hurricane surges reduced by marshes, 367
Missouri River ESA needs, 340
polar bear as threatened, 393, 394
sea ice reports, 442–443, 444, 452
U.S. House of Representatives. *See* Congress
U.S. Senate. *See* Congress
U.S. Supreme Court. *See* Supreme Court of the United States
University of Kentucky, xiii, xiv–xv
Urbom, David, 114
USGS. *See* U.S. Geological Survey

Van der Walker, John, 113
V-blade, 20, 23, 26, 27, 29
vegetation
Boreal Forests, 504–506
Central Valley, California, 241–243
timber (*see* bottomland hardwood wetlands; timber harvesting)
wetlands
adaptations to wetland saturation, 7–8, 43, 47–51, 52, 523
bottomland hardwood fallen leaves, 22–23, 523–524
"Classification of Wetlands" report, 42–43
definition, 6–8, 43, 47–51
fish spawning versus land clearing, 19, 31
ruling that wetlands include vegetation, 30–31
wetlands converted to agriculture, 10–14, 21–22, 23, 25, 26
Verner, Jared, 120–128, 222
Vess, Debbie Doty, 290
Vicksburg, Mississippi, FWS Ecological Services Office
about area covered, 3
about the office, 3–4
personnel changes, 28, 57–58, 67
Clean Water Act
about responsibilities of FWS, 4, 39

Corps Section 404 permit requests, 4, 5, 39, 58
floodplain forests cleared, 5
Fish and Wildlife Coordination Act, cj495
3–4
hiring Dale Hall, xvii, 3
bottomland hardwood wetlands, 4–5
FWCA Report writing and CWA permits, 3–4, 39, 58
Hall to Clear Lake, Texas, 67
Yazoo Backwater Pumps project
about, 41–42, 61–62, 459
about flood control, 39–41
CEQ elevation, 65
Corps reviving project, 63, 459–468
EPA review, 461–464
EPA veto, 465–468
FWS *Environmental Overview* report, 40–41, 62
FWS *Yazoo Area Pump Study*, 61–65
soil types, 44
wetland definition, 42–43
wetland future development, 41–42
Yazoo Delta wetland clearing
about floodplain forests cleared, 5
about Yazoo Delta coverage, 3–4
court hearing, 9–14
court trial two, 46–51
EPA meeting, 6, 8–9
fish spawning and nursery areas, 14, 16, 17–19, 22, 24, 31, 47
FWS leadership support, 27–28
FWS showing need for permit, 17–19, 23–24
jurisdictional wetland methodology course, 58–61
permit required, 28–33
trial one on permits, 16–28
trial one ruling, 28–32
trial two on WOTUS, 45
trial two ruling, 51–56
Waters of the United States, 6–8, 10–14, 26
wetland science to Jim Tripp, 14–16
wetlands determination, 42–44
Volante, Steve, 371
volunteers
Cajun Navy, 510
citizen conservationists, 480–481
Billy Dunavant as, 500
conservationists funding conservation, 92–95, 480–481, 503, 511–512
fighting Marine Shale Processors,

56–57
FWS ecosystem team partnerships, 308
habitat improvement, 144, 362, 480
habitat percentage in private ownership, 160
Jim Kennedy as, 507–508
Johnny Morris as, 403, 497–498 (*see also* Morris, John L. "Johnny")
Nino Scalia as, 512–516
Pete Coors as, 500
Ducks Unlimited, 481, 482, 501, 509
Dale Hall belt buckles, 532
leadership of, 533–537
standing down during BP oil spill, 485
endangered species
illegal trade, 287
recovery requiring volunteers, 144, 362
safe harbor agreement, 259
species are saved by people, 165, 219, 233–234
habitat created after BP oil rig, 487–489
North American Model for Wildlife Conservation, 92–95, 303, 480, 512
special ESA Section 4(d) rule to encourage, 233–234

Waidmann, Brian
bald eagle threatened status removed, 436–437
interview of Hall by Norton, 361
interview of Hall by White House, 362, 365
polar bear as threatened, 395
meetings with Secretary Kempthorne, 393, 394, 441–442, 447–448
Secretary Dirk Kempthorne greeting, 388
Secretary of Interior Chief of Staff, 361, 393
warned about Julie MacDonald, 385
resignation of Julie MacDonald, 408
Walsh, Noreen, 340, 343
Walters, Alice M., 7, 44
Warner, John, 366
Washington Department of Wildlife on ISC, 120–128
water resources
cannot be individually owned, 327
Colorado River (*see* Colorado River)
drought drying lakes, 157–160 (*see also* Klamath sucker critical habitat)
Everglades (*see* Everglades, Florida)
flood control (*see* flood control)
flows inadequate for fish, 244–247 (*see also* Central Valley, California, water)
Interior Secretary Bruce Babbitt, 220
Missouri River (*see* Missouri River ESA needs)
navigable waters extent rulings, 32–33, 53–55
navigable waterways of Rivers and Harbors Act, 11–14, 53–54
Okefenokee NWR, 273–276
E.I. DuPont company, 275–276
subsurface fires, 274–275
Platte River, 110, 113–116
silvery minnow habitat decline, 320–322 (*see also* Rio Grande River)
water is not habitat, 242, 324
California floodplains, 526–528
Waters of the United States (*see* Waters of the United States)
western drought, 107, 152, 156 (*see also* western drought)
wetlands (*see* wetlands)
waterfowl. *See* migratory waterfowl
Waters of the United States (WOTUS)
about history of, 6–8
Judge Scott setting reach and extent, 51–55
navigable waters extent rulings, 32–33, 53–55
navigable waters use change ruling, 29–30
navigable waterways of Rivers and Harbors Act, 11–14, 53–54
authority of Corps versus EPA and FWS, 10–14, 51–55
Avoyelles Parish floodplain clearing, 5
court hearing, 9–14
EPA meeting, 6, 8–9
fish spawning and nursery areas, 47
importance of trial ruling, 42
trial into two parts, 13–14, 16–17
trial two on WOTUS, 32, 46–51
trial two ruling, 51–56
vegetation in definition of wetlands, 47–51
John A. Rapanos case, 56
Solid Waste Agency of Northern Cook County case, 56
wetlands definition, 6–8, 30–31, 42–43, 47–51
Watt, James G.

Central Valley, California, water, 244–245
named Secretary of Interior, 61, 66
Protect Our Wetlands and Duck Resources Act (POWDR Bill), 68–74
Emergency Wetlands Resources Act, 73–74
quotes by, 66–67, 73
Secretary Norton associated with, 312, 375
Weeks, Pete, xiv
Wells, Rich and Linny, xiv
Werner, Fred, 74
Western Association of Fish and Wildlife Agencies (AFWA), 317
western drought
BOR managing water to biological needs, 156–157
Colorado River lower basin, 354–360
Klamath Project lakes drying up, 157–161
about Klamath Basin, 152–155
about Klamath Project draining water, 155–156
fish above and below dams, 156
land leasing for agriculture, 162
managing grazing to biological needs, 163–164
public education, 160, 161
meeting of Pacific Region ES, 107
silvery minnow habitat decline, 320–322
(*see also* Rio Grande River)
water delivery challenges, 152
wetlands
Alaska, 59–60
bottomland hardwood (*see* bottomland hardwood wetlands)
Central Valley, California, 241–242
loss of, 242–243
"Classification of Wetlands and Deepwater Habitats," 42–43, 259–260
conversion to agricultural use, 23, 25, 26
Klamath Project, 155–156
Kuchel's Klamath Project Act, 162
percentage cleared in Yazoo Basin, 42
permit required, 28–33
rate of being cleared for farming, 27, 45
wetland importance, 30–32, 56
Yazoo Backwater Pumps project, 61–62
Yazoo Basin bottomland, 5, 10–14, 21–22, 23, 25, 26
definition
"Classification of Wetlands" report, 42–43
Corps of Engineers, 6–8, 43

protection supported by Congress, 12
ruling on Section 404 jurisdiction, 52–53
vegetation, 6–8, 30–31, 43, 47–51
vegetation included in ruling, 30–31
Waters of the United States delineated, 51–55
duck stamps for conservation, 73, 92, 498
Ducks Unlimited (*see* Ducks Unlimited)
Everglades (*see* Everglades, Florida)
Floodplains: The River's Pantry (H.D. Hall), 523–527
hurricane damage and Louisiana coastal loss, 367
jurisdictional wetland methodology course, 58–61
Louisiana wetland pride, 57
Marine Shale Processors company, 56–57
Okefenokee Swamp, 273–276
permits required, 28–30
CWA oversight authority, 10–14, 32–33
deposition of material into wetlands, 10, 28–32
FWS showing need for permits, 17–19, 23–24
ruling on Section 404 requirement, 28–32
Protect Our Wetlands and Duck Resources Act (POWDR Bill), 66–74
Emergency Wetlands Resources Act, 73–74
Sacramento–San Joaquin River Delta, 241–243
vegetation adapted to, 6–8, 43, 47–51, 52, 523
wetlands include vegetation, 30–31
Waters of the United States (*see* Waters of the United States)
Wetlands America Trust, 482, 507, 508–509, 518–519, 520
Yazoo Basin (*see* Yazoo Backwater Pumps project; Yazoo Basin)
Wetlands America Trust (WAT), 482, 507, 508–509, 518–519, 520
Wetlands Loan Act, 73
Weyerhaeuser, George, 146
Whatley, Tom, xiv
Wheeler, Doug, 248–250, 263
White, Byron, 258–259
White, Dave, 488
White, Jim, 258
White, Rollie, 163–164
White, Wayne
California gnatcatcher, 261–264
California water and Bay-Delta Accord,

"Give her enough rope,..." 380
Inspector General investigation, 387
Lower Colorado Section 10 permit, 359
Missouri River biological opinion, 334, 344, 349, 350, 351, 352
Navy OLF site, 426
Wills, Marvin, 371
Wilson, Bob and Kitty, 511
Wilson, Carl, 291
Wilson, Don, 9, 10, 25
Wilson, Pete, 248-250, 263
Wilson, Sid, 356-357, 359
Winter, Donald C., 428-430
Wood, Mary, 182
Wood, Phillip, 371
Woodley, John Paul, 344, 351, 461, 464
Woods, Teresa (Nichols)
 God Squad hearing witness, 174
Missouri River ESA team, 340, 343
Oregon spotted owl effort, 166
Wooley, Charles, 340, 342-343, 348
Wooten, Dennis, 511, 537
World Trade Center crashes (9/11/2001), 313-315
WOTUS. *See* Waters of the United States
Wyden, Ron, 409-410
Wyoming Platte River, 113-116

Yates, Sidney, 76, 174
Yazoo Backwater Pumps project
 about flood control, 39-41
 CEQ elevation, 65, 461, 464
 Corps reviving project, 63, 459-468
 EPA review, 461-464
 EPA veto, 465-468
 FWS *Environmental Overview* report, 40-41, 62
 FWS *Yazoo Area Pump Study*, 61-65
 wetland definition, 42-43
 soil types, 44
 wetland future development, 41-42
Yazoo Basin
 about, 4
 percentage of wetlands cleared, 42
 soil types, 44
 stream miles supportive of fisheries, 40
 wetland water flow, 15
 wildlife refuges to visit, 468
Backwater Pumps (*see* Yazoo Backwater Pumps project)
 bottomland hardwood wetlands cleared, 5
 court hearing, 9-14
 CWA authority of Corps versus EPA

 and FWS, 10-14, 32-33
EPA meeting on WOTUS, 6, 8-9
fish spawning and nursery areas, 47
FWS showing need for permit, 17-19, 23-24
jurisdictional wetland methodology course, 58-61
normal activities declaration by Corps, 11, 14
trial one on permits, 16-28
trial one ruling, 28-32
trial two on WOTUS, 46-51
trial two ruling, 51-56
vegetation in definition of wetlands, 47-51
wetlands determination, 42-44
 homeroom of Sarah Hall, 5, 45
The Yazoo Basin: An Environmental Overview (FWS), 40-41, 62
Yazoo City, Mississippi; fish farms, xvii
Yazoo NWR, 468
Yazzie, David, 372
Young, Jan, 510-511
Young, Jim, 83
Zabel v. Tabb (1975), 12
Zielinski, Elaine
 BLM proposal for forest reserves, 179
 Deputy BLM State Director, 167
 dignitaries visiting Northwest, 221
 ESA Section 4(d) for owl, 234-235
 Forest Service Chief Jack Ward Thomas, 231
 Forest Summit, 221
 FWS draft jeopardies to BLM, 167, 185
 God Squad hearing attorneys, 175
 Interagency Implementation Team, 225-227
 Interagency Scientific Committee formation, 119
 National Marine Fisheries Service challenges, 167
 Northwest Forest Plan, 225-227
Zilly, Judge, 107, 109-110, 139
Zimmerman, Ryan, 371
Zinke, Ryan, 422
Zuschlag, Richard
 Ducks Unlimited volunteer, 510
 hunting camp in Louisiana, 513
 hunting with Dick Cheney, 516
 hunting with Scalia and Cheney, 518-519

INDEX   589

Central Valley Project Improvement Act, 248–250, 256, 257–258
251, 254, 256
Whitelaw, Ed, 175
Whitney, Jeff, 328
Whitten, Jamie, 466
Whitus, Brent, 371
whooping cranes, 110, 113–116, 171
Platte River Whooping Crane Trust, 115
Wilcove, David Samuel, 120–128
Wilderness Society on ISC, 120–128
wildlife
Boreal Forests, 504–506
California gnatcatcher, 261–264
Central Valley, California, 241–242
inadequate flows for fish, 245–247, 256
loss of, 242–243
conservation history, 88–95
citizen conservationists, 480–481
conservationists paying for conservation, 92–95, 503, 511–512
duck stamp creation, 92
Ducks Unlimited formation, 480–481
Fish Car Era of population restoration, 88–89
FWS careers as callings, 96, 264–265
FWS special agents, 286–288
FWS special agents arrest musselers, 286, 288
interstate wildlife management by Lacey Act, 90–91, 286
migratory waterfowl slaughter, 91, 287
National Conservation Training Center, 282–283
Natural Community Conservation Planning Act (California), 261
North American Model for Wildlife Conservation, 92–95, 303, 480, 512
Pelican Island National Wildlife Refuge, 89, 90
public trust in government, 118, 186, 237–238, 259, 537
Sport Fish Restoration Act, 36, 94
Wildlife Restoration Act, 93
Everglades, Florida, 299–300
fish and Klamath project, 155–156
drought drying lakes, 157–160
Fish Car Era of population restoration, 88–89
fish flows in California, 241–242,
243–247, 256
fish spawning (see fish spawning)
grizzly bear ESA protection, 375–376
habitat decisions marred by Julie MacDonald, 407, 408–410
habitat preservation incentive, 46
Navy OLF near Pocosin Lakes NWR, 422–432
northern spotted owl (see northern spotted owl)
otters and Bureau of Commercial Fisheries, 34–35
polar bears (see polar bears)
red wolf, 424, 427
right to fish, hunt, and gather food, 89
2nd Amendment, 188–189
salmon and smelt driving California water decisions, 244, 255, 521–528
silvery minnow, 318–323
state directors' "cold shoulder" from leadership, 302
taking restrictions court ruling, 200–204
Teshekpuk Lake, Alaska, 397, 399
Tennessee snail darter fish, 97, 110–116
threatened versus endangered species, 108–109, 199
ESA Section 4(d) rule for gnatcatcher, 262–264
ESA Section 4(d) rule for owl, 233–238
threatened species protective regulations, 199–200
whooping cranes, 110, 113–116
wildlife management areas purchased by conservationists, 94
wildlife refuges (see national wildlife refuges)
Yazoo Basin streams capable of supporting fishery, 40
Wildlife Management Institute, 360, 511
Congress cutting conservation funding, 503
wildlife refuges. See national wildlife refuges
Wildlife Restoration Act (1937), 93
Sport Fish Restoration Act (1950), 36, 94
Will, Ken, xiv
Williams, John, xv–xvi
Williams, Steven A., 333–334
CEO of Wildlife Management Institute, 360
FWS Director, 313, 333–334, 360, 361, 375
political deputy Matt Hogan, 366, 378
Grand Canyon rafting email, 355–356
Julie MacDonald